August Neander, Mary Cutler Torrey, Joseph Torrey, K. F. Schnieder

General History of the Christian Religion and Church

Index to Neander's General history of the Christian religion and church

August Neander, Mary Cutler Torrey, Joseph Torrey, K. F. Schnieder

General History of the Christian Religion and Church
Index to Neander's General history of the Christian religion and church

ISBN/EAN: 9783337262792

Printed in Europe, USA, Canada, Australia, Japan

Cover: Foto ©Lupo / pixelio.de

More available books at **www.hansebooks.com**

TO

NEANDER'S GENERAL HISTORY

OF THE

CHRISTIAN RELIGION AND CHURCH.

REV. THOMAS CLAYTON.

BOSTON:
HOUGHTON, MIFFLIN AND COMPANY.
The Riverside Press, Cambridge.
1881.

INTRODUCTORY NOTE.

When the present translation of Neander's Church History was revised and published in its new form in 1872, the original indexes, which were found to be quite defective, were carefully corrected and enlarged. The result, however, was even then seen to be insufficient for all the purposes of reference, and at length, through the liberality of the publishers, a single index is now offered to the public, which includes, not only the general contents of the volumes, but also an analytical list of the citations from Christian and Pagan authors found in the notes, as well as the citations from Scripture scattered through the work. This is but the completion of a plan already partly carried out in the first volume, doubtless under the direction of Neander.

The citations are some of them from works, whether published volumes or manuscripts, which are not to be found in this country, and it is believed that the means of introduction to the great writers on Theology, and to many of the records of the Christian Church, which these valuable notes afford, are increased by the careful classification of the passages cited, under the names of the authors and their works, and, so far as possible, in the order in which they occur in those works. It has been attempted, with what success the reader must judge, to suggest by a brief hint the subject of many of these citations, and thus the drift and tenor of the writings referred to may often be inferred at a glance. To avoid confusion, this portion of the index has been printed in smaller type than the rest.

The main body of the index contains, perhaps, a third more references than those hitherto published, and these have also been arranged with much care according to the nature of the subject. In some cases they are divided by the Periods to which they belong, into paragraphs; or, where the subject appertains chiefly to some one Period or volume, the plan usually followed has been to give first the topics that would best introduce the subject, and to add the rest in the order of the pages. Under the word Tertullian, for example, the first three references enable the reader to turn at once to those passages which give the most general sketch of his life and character. Then follow all the allusions to him or his writings, as they occur in the course of the work. In most cases, it is thought, the principle of arrangement will be readily perceived.

The number of the volume is not generally given a second time in the same paragraph, unless some other volume has been referred to.

It is, perhaps, impossible that, among so many references, there should not occur here and there a mistake, even after repeated revision and verification, but it is hoped that these will be found to be few in proportion to the whole, and that the result of this new effort to render the work more complete in its appointments may prove a real addition to its practical value.

Most of the abbreviations employed in the ensuing pages will be easily understood. A list of the more common is as follows: —

abp.	archbishop.	f.	folium.
Acta S.	Acta Sanctorum (Bollandists).	H.	Heft.
Acta S. (O. B.).	Acta Sanctorum (Order of Benedict).	l.	liber.
		n.	note.
Bd.	Band.	op.	opus.
bp.	bishop.	p.	page.
c.	chapter.	P.	Pars.
ch.	church.	s.	seite *or* sectio.
conc.	concilium	st.	stück.
ed.	edition, editor.	t.	tomus.
ep.	epistle.	Th.	Theil.

GENERAL INDEX

FOR THE WHOLE WORK.

A.

Aarhus, iii. 289.
Aaron, ii. 456 n.; iii. 514.
Abasgians, spread of Christianity among the, ii. 139.
Abatur, i. 377.
Abbess, iv. 329 n. 2.
Abbo, abbot of Fleury, iii. 368, 370 n. 4, 374, 404 n. 1, 470. Life of, 370 n. 4, 374 n. 4. See Acta S. (O. B.), S. vi. P. i. f. 47.
Abbot, office of, ii. 272. Benedict's rules for, ii. 298, 299, 300. At Constantinople, ii. 535, 536, 541, 575 n. 1. As missionaries, iii. 4, 29, 72-74. Frankish, iii. 154. At Council of Rheims (an. 991), iii. 369. Lay, iii. 416 (414). Absorbed in secular business, iv. 133, 364. Obtain the insignia of the episcopal office, iv. 201, 202. Pomp of, iv. 264. At Metz, iv. 324. Abelard on the, iv. 384. Deposition of, v. 17. At Constance, v. 103.
Abdas, bp. of Susa, ii. 133.
Abderlhaman II., Arabian caliph, iii. 338, 340-342.
Abel, with the Cainites, i. 448 With Pelagius, ii. 671, 672. With the Bogomiles, iv. 554.
Abel-Rémusat.

Mélanges Asiatiques, t. i. p. 36, iii. 89 n. 6. In the Mémoires de l'Académie des Inscriptions, t. vi. an. 1822, p. 413, iv. 48 n. 1; p. 393, iv. 51 n. 2.

Abelard, representative of the dialectic tendency, iv. 371. Life and doctrine, 373-401. Introductio in theologiam, 374, 385 n. 4, 451-454. Theologia Christiana, 383-385 and n. 4, 393 and n. 1, 394, 454. Comm. on Romans, 385, 386, 394, 503 n. 1. Scito te ipsum (Ethics), 385 n. 4, 386, 393 n. 1, 394, 493. Sic et non, 390-392, 394. Sentences, 385 n. 4, 393 n. 1, 452 and n. 7. Confession, 398, 399. On the Supreme Good (Dialogue), 391. Apologia, 399, 495. Inscription on his tomb, 400 n. 2. Hugo, 407. Bernard, 386, 393-399, 408, 409, 503, 504. Walter of St. Victor, 410. Richard of St. Victor, 413. Abelard compared with Lull, 64. On the wretched situation of the Jews, 72 n 1. Arnold of Brescia, 147, 148, 151. Hypocritical monks, 243. Norbert, 246 and n. 1. Roscelin, 247 n. 4, 356 n. 2. On the miracles of his time, 246 n. 1, 256 n. 3, 257. Doctrine of transubstantiation, 337. Against the abuse of the mass, 346. Indulgences, 350, 351. Moral standing of the ancient philosophers, 359 n. 1, 383, 384. On faith, 374-378. On love to God, 383-386, 390, 407. Intention in actions, 387-390, 528. Omnipresence of God, 450-452. Omnipotence of God, 453-457, 494. Doctrine of the Trinity, 458-460, 462, 465. Conception of miracles, 467-469. Anthropology, 493-495. Original sin, 494. Sinlessness of Jesus, 495, 496. Doctrine of atonement, 501-505. Usefulness of doubt, 538 n. 1 (392). Peter of Bruis, 595 n. 1.

Citations from his writings:—
Apology, iv. 455 n. 5.
Comm. in Rom. On love to God, iv. 385, 386. L. i. f. 493, on faith, 376 n. 2; ff. 513, 554, his "Theology," 385 n. 4; ff. 522, 652, good intention, 387 n. 2, 389 n.; ff. 538, 539, sinlessness of Christ, 496 n. 3; f. 622, et seq., disinterested love, 386 nn. 1, 2. L. ii. f. 549, redemption, 502 n. 2; f. 552, 501 nn.; f. 503, atonement, 503 n. 3; ff. 586, 591, 595, 597, original sin, punishment, 494 nu.; f. 588, the first sin, 594 n. 5. On redemption, 501 nu., 502 nn. 1, 2.
Confession, 399, 399.
De Joanne Baptista. Worldly monks, iv. 243 n. 3; f. 954, id. 244 n. 1; f. 967, miracles, 246 n. 1; miraculous cures, 256 n. 3, 257.
Dialectics (Cousin, Ouvrages inédits d'Abelard), f 205, Plato, iv. 378 n. 3; f. 228, himself, 373 n. 2; f. 471, Roscelin, 356 n. 2.
Dialog. inter philos. Jud. et Christianum (ed. Rheinwald), f. 11, the Jews, iv. 72 n. 1; f. 67, division of the virtues, 524 n. 1; f. 95, seqq., omnipresence of God, 451 n. 1; f. 115, intention, 388 n. 1. Authenticity of the Dialogue, 309 nn. 2, 3.
Epistles, f. 334, Roscelin, iv. 360 n. 1. Ep. 21, Robert of Arbrissel, 247 n. 4. Ep. to Heloise, 397 nn. 1, 2.
Ethics. See Scito te ipsum.
Exposit. in Hexaëmeron, ff. 1369, 1372, creation, iv. 467 nn. 1-3; f. 1378, id. 468 nn. 1, 2; miracles, 468 n. 3.

Hist. calamitatum, iv. 373 n. 3, 374 nn. 1-3, 382 n. 2.
Introductio in theologiam. Pref. iv. 374 n. 3. L. i. f. 985, Trinity, 459 n. 1; f. 1064, ancient philosophers, 379 nn. 1, 2. L. ii. ff. 1067, 1068, 379 n. 3; f. 1061, on faith, 374 n. 4; ff. 1059-1062, id. 375 nn.; f. 1053, 376 n. 3; ff. 1047, 1053, 1061, on faith and knowledge, 377 nn.; f. 1054, 378 nn. 1, 2; f. 1061. 374 n. 4, 381 n. 4; f. 1061, doctrine of the Trinity, 381 n. 4; f. 1073, id. 462 n. 5; f. 1081, id. 460 n. 1; f. 1085, id. 459 n. 2; f. 1086, id. 459 n. 3; f. 1095, id. 460 n. 4; f. 1084. love, 502 n. 3; opp. f. 1066, Peter of Bruis, 595 n. 1. L. iii. f. 1109, omnipotence, 453 nn. 5-7, 454 nn. 1-4; opp. f. 1111, will of God, 456 n. 1; f. 1126, omnipresence of God, 451 nn. 2-8, 452 nn. 1-3; f. 1133, nature and the supernatural, 468 nn. 4-6.
Lectures, ed. Rheinwald. See Rheinwald.
Scito te ipsum, c. 12, f. 652, intention, iv. 389 n., 390 n. 1; c. 18, sale of the mass, 346 n. 3; intention, 387 n. 3, 388 n. 1; c. 26, indulgences, 351 nn. 1-4, 390 n. 2. See Pez. t. iii.
Sentences, c. 2, faith, iv. 375 n. 4, 376 n. 1; c. 19, f. 50, omnipresence of God, 452 nn. 4, 5; c. 20, omnipotence, 455 n. 3; c. 23, atonement, 502 nn. 5, 7, 503 n. 1; c. 24, person of Christ, 496 n. 2; c. 25, 496 n. 4.
Sic et non. prolog., on judging, iv. 391; inspiration, 391 nn. 2, 3, 392 and n. 1; doubt, 392 n. 3, 538 n. 1.
Theologia Christiana, l. i. f. 1166, love, iv. 502 n. 3. L. ii. f. 1074, the supernatural, 467 n. 6; ff. 1210, 1215, 1240, philosophy, 383 nn. 2, 3. 384 nn. 1, 2, 385 nn. 1, 2. L. iii. f. 1250, faith and knowledge, 385 n. 3; f. 1133, the supernatural, 467 n. 5. L. iv. f. 1308, love, 502 n. 4; f. 1315, transubstantiation, 337 n. 3; f. 1317, the Trinity, 460 n. 2; f. 1340, id. 459 nn. 4, 5, 460 n. 2; f. 1357, omnipotence of God, 454 n. 5, 455 n. 1; f. 1358, 455 n. 2. See Martene et Durand.

Abgarus, iii. 201, 240, 241. See Agbarus, Uchomo, and Bar Manu.
Ability, see Freedom, Force, Will. And inability, iv. 516, 517.
Ablutions, with the Essenes, i. 49.
Abomination of desolation, Janow on the, v. 196. Militz on, v. 178. Huss, v. 311, 364.
Abraham, Arabic prince, ii. 145.
Abraham, converted Jew, iii. 213 n. 2.
Abraham of Edessa, presbyter, ii. 615 n. 3.
Abraham, the patriarch, ii. 244, 313, 642 n. 4 (in art. ii. 324); iii. 114; iv. 375, 396, 544. With the Catharists, 575.
Abraham. See Welenowitz.
'Αβράξας, i. 401.
Absalom, bp. of Roeskilde, iv. 31, 32.
Absentees, iv. 201, 207; v. 9, 86, 101, 160.
Absolute, the, in Plato, i. 26. In Neo-Platonism, i. 26, 27, 391, 417, 418, 589. In Judaism, i. 57. With Celsus, i. 163. With Origen, i. 551, 587, 588. With Sabellius, i. 595. With Julian, ii. 50. In the system of John Scotus, iii. 461-465. With Anselm, iv. 441-443. In De Causis, iv. 445 and n. 3. Absolute perfection, i. 400. Absolute religion, i. 382; iv. 618. Absolute causality, ii. 412 n. 2, 419 n. 5. Absolute predestination, ii. 712. Absolute truth, iv. 381.
Absolution, i. 219-221. In the schism of Felicissimus, i. 226-231, 234, 235. In the schism of Novatian, i. 239-244. In Montanism, i. 522, 523. In connection with penance, i. 647; ii. 188, 213, 246; iii. 137-140. Ratherius on, iii. 441. By the pope, iii. 359, 452, 453. Purchased, iii. 5 n. 2 (see Indulgences). Theological doctrine of, iv. 347-350. Gregory VII. on, iv. 91. John of Salisbury on, iv. 194, 195. With the Schoolmen, iv. 349. Papal, iv. 103, 114, 116, 172, 222, 348; v. 30, 43, 98, 99. General, iv. 348, 349. With the Waldenses, iv. 614. Of Michael Paleologus, iv. 543, 544. Occam on, v. 39. Gerson, v. 81, 98, 99. Wicklif, v. 164, 171. Conrad, v. 189. Huss, v. 277, 280, 281, 283, 291. From oath of allegiance, v. 15, 30. Of Huss, v. 366.
Absolutism, papal, iv. 98, 99, 120, 140, 172, 174, 194, 536; v. 2, 8, 13. Attacked, iv. 174, 175, 185-187. See Henry IV., Frederic I., Frederic II., Philip the Fair, Ægidius, John of Paris, Gerson. Defended, v. 14, 19, 63, 108, 291. In Germany, v. 23, 24. See Interdict. In Switzerland, v. 128. Events leading to its overthrow, v. 47, 48, 78. Wicklif on, v. 146. Huss, v. 363. At Oxford, v. 147. University of Prague, v. 254. See Papacy, Popes.
Abstinence, i. 274, 278; iv. 524. See Asceticism.
Abstinents, i. 274, 458.
Abulfeda.
T. v. f. 145, 146, Frederic II. and Mohammedanism, iv. 181 n. 3.
Abulpharagius, ii. 611.
On Mani, i. 486 n. 2. (In Assemann. B. O. T. 2, f. 291), on Barsumas, ii. 611 n. 1; on Bar Sudaili, ii. 615 n. 1.
Abundius, bp. of Como, iv. 575. Life of, 575 n. 1.
Abyss, i. 373 n. 1. See Bythos.
Abyssinia, diffusion of Christianity in, i. 83; ii. 143-145. Christian empire in, iii. 90.
Acacius, bp. of Amida, ii. 136.
Acacius, bp. of Beræa, ii. 521.
Acacius, bp. of Cæsarea, ii. 450 and n. 1, 454.
Acacius, bp. of Melitene, ii. 528, 555 n. 3.
Acacius, patriarch of Constantinople, ii. 586-588, 592.
Academy at Athens, ii. 106 n. 2.
Academy of Sciences.
Berlin, monthly report, October, 1848, Ehrenberg on the Monas prodigiosa, v. 237 n. 2.
Accident and subject, iv. 335, 336, 447. In relation to justification, iv. 512; v. 171. Accidentia sine subjecto, v. 152-156, 243 n. 1, 337. See Transubstantiation.

GENERAL INDEX. 3

Acco (St. Jean d'Acre, Ptolemais), iv. 60.
Accommodation, i. 597 n. 5. To paganism, i. 70. Theory of, in Gnosticism, i. 388, 470. Of Origen, i. 549, 550. Yves on, iv. 136, 137. Bogomiles, iv. 559. To degrees of culture, iv. 264. See Fraus pia, Paganism, Ritual.
Accusations against Christians, i. 92, 112, 128. Against Jews and heretics, iv. 72, 73, 586. See Unnatural crimes.
Accusers of Christians, i. 97, 116, 118.
Achaian League, i. 206.
Achamoth, i. 389 n. 2, 420.
Ἀχειροποίητα, iii. 201.
Achmed Ibn Foszlani, iii. 315 n. 2.
Achrida (Achris), monastery at, iii. 315 n. 1; bp. of, 580, 584.
Acolytes, i. 201.
Acta Cenomanensium.
  (Henry of Cluny), iv. 590 n. 1, 601 n. 3, 602 n. 1, 603 n. 1. See Mabillon Analect. t. iii.
Acta Collationis Constantinopolitanæ, an. 533, iii. 170 n. 1.
Acta cum Felice Manichæo.
  T. i. c. 9 (Augustini opp. ed. Bened. t. 8), i. 487 n. 3.
Acta episcoporum Leodiensium. See Martene et Durand, Col. ampliss. t. iv.
Acta facientes, i. 132.
Acta Felicis, ed. Ruinart, i. 151 n. 1.
Acta Felicitatis. See Acta Perpetuæ.
Acta Martyrii Justini (Coll. of Symeon Metaphrastes), i. 270 n. 1, 671 u. 3.
Acta Martyrum.
  Greek, i. 118 n. 2. Ed. Ruinart, i. 122 n. 3. Scillitanorum, i. 122 n. 3. Copticæ (ed. Georgi, Romæ, 1793), præf. f. 109, i. 149 n. 1. Assemani, Persiam martyrs, ii. 125 n. 6, 126 nn. 1-4, 129 n. 2, 130 n. 1, 132 r., 134 n. See Stephanus Enodius Asseman.
Acta Maximi, iii. 185 n. 1, 192 n. 1. See Maximus.
Acta Perpetuæ et Felicitatis, præf. i. 122 n. 3, 516 n. 2, 3, 518 n. 4.
Acta Pilati, ii. 5.
Acta proconsularii, i. 152 n. (143 n.)
Acta Procopii, i. 303 n. 3.
Acta Sanctorum (Bollandists).
  Jan. 1, § 19, Abbot Wilhelm, iii. 403 n. 2; f. 61, Wm. of Dijon, iii. 410 n. 3. Jan. 2, § 8, Adelard of Corbie, iii. 449 n. 3. Jan. 17, Society of St. Anthony, iv. 267 n. 1. T. i. f. 370, Simeon Stylites, ii. 293 n. 2. T. i. f. 483, Severinus, iii. 28 n. 2 (25 n. 4, 26, 27, nn.). T. i. f. 629, William of Bourges, iv. 213 n. 2; f. 634, the same, iv. 336 n. 2. T. i. f. 746, Benedictus Biscopius, iii. 118 n. T. ii. § 61, f. 510, Johannes Eleemosyn., iii. 99 n. 2. T. ii. f. 795, lives of pious country people, iv. 295 n. 2.
  Feb. 3, Ansohar, iii. 587 n. 3. Feb. 12, c. 9, Benedict of Aniane, iii. 414 n. Feb. 25, c. 4, § 23, Robert of Arbrissel, iv. 247 nn. 2, 3. Feb. 26, Porphyry, bp. of Gaza, i. 103 n. 1. Feb. 27, John of Gorze, c. 1, § 4, iii. 445 n. 2; § 120, f. 712, iii. 336 n. 2; § 122 f. 713, iii. 345 n. 2. T. i. f. 543, Rabanus Maurus, iii. 446 n. 1. T. i. f. 538, Nicolaus, iii. 542 n. 2. T. iii. f. 577, Tarasius, iii. 225 n. 1.
  March 5, Gervin of Centulum, iii. 420 n. 3. Mar. 6, Fridolin, iii. 37 n. 3. Mar. 7, t. i., Thomas Aquinas, iv. 317 n. 8, 122 n. Mar.

9, f. 19, Cyril and Methodius, iii. 315 n. 1; § 2, 316 u. 3. Mar. 11, c. 2, t. ii., Eulogius, iii. 340 n. 2. Mar. 13, Nicephorus, iii. 583 n. 1, 585 n. 1. T. iii. c. 2, f. 183, Ambrose of Siena, iv. 295 n. 6.
  April 3, app. t. i. f. 23, Nicetas, iii. 535 n. 1. f. 28, §§ 28, 29, iii. 218 nn. 1, 2. Apr. 6, app. § 22, Eutychius, ii. 607 n. 1. Apr. 8, Berthold of Calabria, iv. 296 n. 2. Apr. 14 (t. ii. f. 223), Bernard of Tiron, iv. 312 n. 5; f. 229, iv. 237 n. 1; f. 234 (c. 6, § 51), iv. 97 n. 8; f. 249, iv. 308 n. 2. Apr. 19, Leo IX., iii. 381 n. 2; f. 26, Thrudpert, iii. 37 n. 5. T. i. f. 629, William Roskild, iv. 206 n. 5; f. 678, Aybert, iv. 238 n. 4; f. 760 (c. 2, § 10), Walter of St. Martin, iv. 97 n. 8; app. f. 47, § 8, life of the monk Plato, iii. 100 n. 1; f. 49, § 17, iii. 223 n. 3; § 18, 224 n. 1; § 23, 100 n. 2; § 24, f. 50, 230 n. 1. T. ii. (Apr. 23), life of Adalbert of Prague, ff. 179 and 181, iii. 322 nn. 2, 3 (iv. 42 n. 1); c. 6, § 16, f. 192, iii. 333 n. 1; § 22, f. 195, iii. 332 n. 4, 333 n. 1 (t. iii. c. 6, f. 189, ancient life of A., iv. 41 n. 6). T. iii. app. f. 467, letter from the Gothic churches, ii. 155 n. 2. T. ii., Abundius of Como, ii. 575 n. 1. T. iii. f. 227, Ægidius of Assisi, iv. 312 n. 1; t. iii. c. 2, § 18, f. 691, Peter of Verona, iv. 585 n. 1.
  May 4, c. 4, Godehard of Hildesheim, iii. 408 n. 3, 446 n. 1. May 11, Majolus, iii. 418 nn. 1, 2. May 14, f. 65 (t. iii. app.), letter of Ammon, ii. 454 n. 2. May 18, c. 1, Eric, iv. 45 n. 1. May 19 (t. iv.), Alcuin, iii. 155 n. 5; Dunstan (t. iv.), iii. 411 n. 6, 450 n. 6. May 25 (t. vi.), Gregory VII., iii. 381 n. 2. May 29, Abbot Joachim, iv. 221 n. 2. T. ii. f. 324, 325, Peter of Moustier en Tarnantaise, iv. 214 n. 1. T. iii. f. 634, Ubald, iv. 296 n. 2: app. § 77, Acton, ii. 271 n. 4. T. iv. f. 422, Celestin V., iv. 193 n. 3; Celestin's autobiography, 193 n. 1. T. vi. f. 82, Abilhelm, iii. 152 n. 3; f. 721, Bede, iii. 152 n. 5.
  June 5, Boniface, iii. 55 n. 5, 60 n. 1, 49 n. June 10, Bardo, iii. 446 n. 1. June 27, f. 322, Ariald, iii. 389 n. 3. June 31 (t. v. ff. 645 and 661), Raymund Lull, iv. 61 n. 1, 67 n. June, f. 819, Norbert, iv. 246 n.; f. 824, id. 313 n. 1; f. 826, Bernard, iv. 259 n. 3. T. iv., Mother of Eberhard, iv. 295 n. 3. T. v. f. 115, a pious smith, iv. 295 n. 4. T. v. c. 3, f. 232, Anthelm, iv. 168 n. 3.
  July 4, Ulrich, iii. 405 n. 2. T. iv. f. 326, Zoerard and Benedict, iii. 334 n. 2. T. vi. July 28, Raymund Palmaris, iv. 300 n. 1.
  Aug. 12, Clara of Assisi, iv. 276 n. 2. Aug. 25 (t. v.), Louis IX., iv. 302 n. 1. Aug. 27 (t. vi.), Cæsarius of Arles, ii. 709 n. 2, iii. 4 n. 1. T. i. f. 274, Walter of Melrose, iv. 328 n.; f. 549, Dominic, iv. 269 n.
  Sep. 2 (t. i.), Stephen of Hungary, iii. 383 nn. 2, 3, 334 nn. 3, 4. Sep. 6, Magnoald, iii. 37 n. 2. Sep. 17, Hildegard, iv. 217 n. 1. Sep. 26, Nilus, iii. 420 nn. 5, 6, 421-424 nn.
  Oct., t. ii. f. 699, Francis of Assisi, iv. 60 n. 2.

Acta Sanctorum of the order of Benedict, ed. Mabillon.
  Life of Alwin, iii. 155 n. 5.
  S. ii., Amandus, iii. 41 n. 1; Gallus, 36 n. 2; f. 9, Jonas, 29 n. 2; f. 319, Agil, 38 n. 2; f. 425, Salaberga, 38 n. 2; f. 1004, Benedictus Biscopius, 118 n.; f. 1031, Theodore of Canterbury, 25 n. 1.
  S. iii. P. 1, Bede, iii. 152 n. 5.
  S. iv. P. 1, Monastery of Corvey, iii. 273 n. 2; § 30, Benedict of Aniane, 416 n. 1; l. ii. f. 491, Abbot Wala, 352 nn. 1, 3.
  P. ii. f. 135, Radbert, dedication of his book on the Holy Supper, 407 n. 2; f. 481, Life of Rimbert, c 17, 287 n. 4; f. 502, his letter to Egilo, 497 n. 1.
  S. v. l. i. § 8, Odo of Cluny, iii. 417 n. 1; f. 30, Radbod of Utrecht, 405 n. 6; f. 440, § 42, Ulric of Augsburg, 405 n. 2; f. 471, can-

onization of Ulric, 447 n. 3; f. 617, Ethelwold of Winchester, 408 n. 1; f. 817, c. 13, Wolfgang, 332 n. 3.

S. vi. P. i. f. 45, Abbo of Fleury, iii. 404 n. 1; f. 47, § 11, the same, 370 n. 4, 374 n. 4; f. 205, Bernward of Hildesheim, 408 n. 2, 460 n. 6; ff. 206 and 223, 403 n. 1, 405 nn. 3, 4; f. 330, Abbot Wilhelm, 403 n. 2; f. 370, letter of Poppo to Benedict IX., 445 n. 2; f. 371, seq., hermit Simeon, 448 n. 1.

P. ii., Gregory VII., iii. 381 n. 2; f. 283, John Gualbert, 399 n. 1; f. 330, Gervin, 420 n. 3; f. 344, Herluin of Bec, 410 n. 4; f. 346, the same, 445 n. 2; f. 654, Lanfranc, iv. 329 n. 1; f. 732, William of Hirschau, iv. 86 n. 4.

Acta Sanctorum of Surius.
T. v. f. 634, letter of Louis the Pious to Hilduin, iii. 406 un. 4–6; f. (638) 653, et seq., Areopagitica of Hilduin, 466 n. 7, 467 n. 1.

Acta Saturnini, Dativi et aliorum in Africa (Baluz. Misc. t. ii.), i. 152 n. 1.
Acta Tarachi, Probi et Andronici, ii. 5 n. 3.

Acta Thomæ.
Ed. Thilo; cod. apocr. f. 10, i. 499 n. 4; f. 17, i. 492 n. 1.

Activity in the Christian life, iii. 4. *In the last Period*, Oliva on, iv. 624; Janow on, v. 200.
Actors, i. 267.
Acts of the Apostles, v. 268; read publicly, ii. 342.

Citations. Acts 1: 17, i. 196 n. 1; 2: 38, ii. 122; 2: 46, i. 325; 3: 6, v. 14; 3: 13, 14, 15, iii. 161 n. 1; 3: 21, iii. 522; 8: 15, v. 170; 8: 20, iv. 152; 8: 27–40, i. 83; 8: 37, ii. 122; 9: 3–6, iv. 345 n. 3; 10: 38, iii. 161; 10: 46, i. 186 n. 2; 10: 47, v. 222; 12, iv. 122; 12: 8, v. 36; 14: 23, i. 189; 15, i. 159, iii. 77, 557, v. 27; 17: 16–34, ii. 133 n. 3; 17: 23, i. 427; 19, i. 316; 20, v. 31 n. 2; 20: 7, i. 295; 20: 17, i. 192; 20: 17, 28, i. 184; 20: 34, iii. 77; 23: 8, i. 42 n. 1; 23: 9, i. 41 n. 1; 24: 5, i. 349; 27, i. 290; 28: 19–23, v. 32 n. 3.

Acts of the disputation of Mani with Archelaus, i. 485. See Mani.
Adalbero, bp. of Laon, iii. 404 n. 2.
Adalbero, bp. of Metz, iii. 403 n. 1, 405 n. 5, 408 n. 1, 411. Life of, 403 n. 1, 405 n. 5, 411 n. 4.
Adalbero, bp. of Rheims, iii. 368, 373 n. 1, 453 n. 3.
Adalbero, bp. of Würzburg, iv. 107.
Adalbert, abp. of Bremen, iv. 33, 34.
Adalbert (or Albrecht), abp. of Bremen or Hamburg, iii. 307, 326.
Adalbert, abp. of Magdeburg, iii. 325, 329.
Adalbert, abp. of Prague, iii. 322 and n. 2, 332, 333 and nn. 1, 2; iv. 41, 42. Life of, iii. 322 nn. 2, 3, 332 n. 4, 333 n. 1; iv. 41 n. 6, 42 n. 1.
Adalbert, companion of Otto of Bamberg, iv. 17, 25.
Adalbert, margrave of Toscana, iii. 366, 367.
Adaldag, abp. of Hamburg and Bremen, iii. 290, 291.
Adalhard I., abbot of Corbie, iii. 272, 273, 283.

Adalhard II., abbot of Corbie, iii. 273.
Adalward, bp. in Sweden, iii. 293.
Adam, i. 314, 620. With the Ebionites, i. 351. In the Clementines, i. 354, 355, 357 n. 4, 359, 360. With Valentine, i. 425. With Julius Cassianus, i. 458 n. 3. With Mani, i. 496 n. 1, 498, 499. With Origen, i. 627. With Cyprian, i. 647. His condition and relation to the race in the view of Hilary, ii. 618; of Augustin, ii. 659, 667, 668, 685, 704. With the Pelagians, ii. 666, 676. With Julian, ii. 669 n. 3. With Prosper, ii. 698. With Theodore, ii. 715, 716. With Chrysostom, ii. 719, 720. In connection with infant baptism, ii. 726, 727. In the Koran, iii. 86 n. 1. With Macarius, iii. 195. With the Paulicians, iii. 258–260. Nilus, iii. 422. With Gottschalk, iii. 475. R. Maurus, iii. 476. Prudentius, iii. 482. Servatus Lupus, iii. 484. With the sect at Arras and Liege, iii. 597 n. 2. With Abelard, iv. 494, 495. Aquinas, iv. 495. With the Bogomiles, iv. 554. The Catharists, iv. 572, 573 and n. 1, 579. Headship of, v. 14.

Adam, canonical of Bremen.
De situ Daniæ, c. 96, the Normans, iii. 299 n. 3. Hist. eccles. c. 23, Anschar, Ida, iii. 278 n. 2; c. 41–44, Wulfred, 292 n. 1, Christianity in Sweden, 292 n. 2; c. 43, tomb of Olof, 299 n. 2; c. 77, f. 55 (ed. Lindenbruch, 1595), Poppo, 289 n. 1; the Danes, 291 n. 2; c. 94, f. 66, English clergy in Norway, 297 n.; f. 150, Iceland, 304 n. 1, 306 nn. 1, 2; oppression of the Slavonians, 324 n. 2; c. 138, Gottschalk, 326 n. 1; c. 142, Albrecht, 326 n. 2; death of Gottschalk, 326 n. 4; c. 166 and app., Ansverus, 326 n. 5; c. 230, Horigar, 281 n. 2; c. 237 and 239, Sweden, 293 nn.

Adam Kadmon, i. 351, 491 n. 4.
Adaptation, power of, in Christianity, i. 69, 70, 85.
Adas, Addas, letter of Mani to, i. 499 n. 5.
Addula, abbess, iii. 72.
Adelaide, queen of France, iii. 374 and nn. 2, 5.
Adelard of Corbie, iii. 449 n. 3.
Adelbert, Frankish errorist, iii. 56. Opposed to churches dedicated to apostles, 57. Opposed to pilgrimages to Rome, 57. Respect paid to him, 58, 59. A prayer of his, 58. His arrest, 60. Final fate, 63. Life, 59 n. 5.
Adelmann, bp. of Brescia, iii. 502, 505, 506, 523 n. 5, 526 n. 2.
Letter to Berengar, iii. 502 and n. 3, 403 nn. 2, 4, 5, 505 nn. 4, 5, 521 n. 1.

Adelphius, Adelphians, ii. 276, 277 n. 4, 280.
Ademar of Angoulême.
Chronicle, an. 1025, Adeodat, iii. 593 n. 1. Sect at Orleans, 593 nn. 1, 3. See Labbe.

Ademar, bp. of Puy, iv. 125.
Aden, ii. 142.
Adeodat (Dieudonné), priest, iii. 593.
Adeodat, abbot, iii. 596, 597 n. 1.
Adeodatus, pope, iii. 193.

Adiaphora, i. 260, 261; iii. 337; iv. 387, 524, 525. Adiaphorism, iv. 448; v. 305.
Ado (Wursing), iii. 45.
Adolph, duke of Holstein, iv. 35.
Adoptianism, its author, iii. 156-159. Doctrine, 159-163. Opponents, 163-165. Condemnation at Regensburg, 165. At Frankfort-on-the-Main, 165. Alcuin against, 165-168. Whether in Claudius of Turin, 430 and n. 3, 431.
Adoptio, iii. 157 n. 3. See Adoptianism.
Adrian II., pope, iii. 402. See Hadrian II.
Adrian IV., pope, conflict with Frederic I., iv. 161-167. Apology for the Roman ch., 195 n. 2. Letters to Frederic I., 164, 166. To the German bps., 165. Arnold, v. 301.
Adrianople, ii. 454; iii. 307.
Adrotta, pagans at, ii. 105 n. 3.
Adrumetum, bp. of, ii. 605 n. 2. Monks of, ii. 686, 691.
Adscancester (Exeter), iii. 46.
Adultery, the woman taken in, iv. 577; v. 364.
Advent of Christ, expected, iii. 164, 470 n. 2. Oliva on, iv. 622.
Advocati, iii. 101 n. 4.
Advocatus, Donatist martyr, ii. 228 n. 3.
Ædesius, in Abyssinia, ii. 144.
Ædesius, Platonist, ii. 42.
Ægæ, ii. 26.
Ægidius of Assisi, sayings of, iv. 311, 312 and n. 1.
Ægidius of Rome, tract against Boniface VIII., v. 13-15, 16.
Æizanes, Abyssinian prince, ii. 144.
Ælia Capitolina, i. 153, 344.
Ælius Lampridius, i. 103.

Vit. Alex. Sever. c. 24, templa Hadriani, i. 103 n. 3; c. 45, i. 199 n. 2; c. 49, ii. 167 n. 1. Vit. Caracallae, c. 1, i. 119 n. 6. Vit. Commodi, c. 6 et 7, 119 n. 2. Vit. Heliogabali, i. 125 n.

Ælius Spartianus.

Vit. Hadrian. c. 22, i. 102 n. 5. Vit. Sept. Sever. c. 17, law against change of religion, i. 120 n. 4. Vit. Caracallæ, l. vi. c. 6, i. 703 n. 2.

Æmilia, province, ii. 472.
Æmilianus, ii. 67 n. 2.
Æneas, bp. of Paris, iii. 567.
Æneas Silvius.

Letter of Cesarini (opp. ed. Basil. f. 64), v. 128 n. 1. Hist. Bohemica, f. 34, Huss and Jerome, v. 380 n.; c. 35, Jerome of Prague, v. 245 n. 4; c. 35, f. 52, Peter of Dresden, v. 338 n. 2.

Æons, in Gnosticism, i. 373 n. 3, 375, 379, 381, 384, 388, 613; iv. 553. With Valentine, i. 418, 421, 424. With Ptolemæus, i. 437. With Marcus, i. 440, 441. The Ophites, i. 445. Saturnin, i. 456. Tatian, i. 456. In Manicheism, i. 489-491.
Æra Varroniana, i. 689.

Aërius, ii. 379.
Æsculapius, temple of, destroyed, ii. 26, 27. See Esculapius.
Aëtius, Arian, ii. 44, 71 n. 2, 444, 449, 455.
Aëtius, Roman general, ii. 695.
Affections and religion, i. 21, 22. And faith, see Feeling. Affections and knowledge, iv. 411. Relation to the intellect, Bonaventura, iv. 491. Natural affections, efforts to overcome, ii. 266. Mauritius on, iv. 250. See Asceticism.
Africa, diffusion of Christianity in, i. 83. Persecution in, i. 120-124, 136, 146, 147, 148 n. 1, 150 152. See Carthage, Cyprian. Manicheism in, i. 506 n. Schism in, i. 228. Christianity there in the second Period, ii. 143-145. Councils, ii. 171 n. 3. See Councils. Third Period, church there, Mohammedanism, iii. 84-90. An African prefect, 143 n. 3. Intercourse with Spain, 158. Power of the emperor in, 181. Dyotheletism, 184. See North Africa, Raymund Lull.
African monks, ii. 686, 691. See Monks, Monotheletic controversy.
Afternach (Epternach), iii. 81.
Agapæ, i. 325, 326; ii. 361, 362. In the Armenian church, iii. 589 n. 1. See Lord's Supper, Tertullian, Clement of Alexandria.
Agape, ii. 771.
Agapetus, bp. of Rome, ii. 183 n., 593, 594.
Agapius, Manichean, ii. 771.
Agatha, convent of St., iii. 423.
Agathias.

De rebus Justiniani, ii. 110 n. 5, 128 n. 4, 139 n. 3. Alemanni, iii. 84 n. 1.

Agatho, bp. of Rome, iii. 193, 194.
Agbar Uchomo, the, 180. See Abgarus.
Age, temper of the, in relation to Gnosticism, i. 370.
Aged, care of the, i. 255; ii. 169.
Ages of the church, Joachim on the, iv. 227-232. Sect of the Holy Ghost, iv. 447, 448. Oliva on the, 621-626. Dolcino on the, 634, 637 n. 1. Of the world, 622.
Aggershuus, Stift, iii 298 n. 2.
Ἁγία χαλκῆ, iii. 213 n 1.
Agil (St. Aile) among the Bavarians, iii. 38. His life, 38 n. 2.
Agnes, empress, mother of Henry IV., iii. 387, 395 n. 2, 396; iv. 103, 104.
Agnoetism, ii. 609; cf Theodore, 496; of Theodoret, 525; of Themistius, 613; of Felix of Urgellis, iii. 163, 168.
Agobard, abp. of Lyons, in the Adoptianist controversy, iii. 168. Contends for the independence of the church, 351; for the dignity of the spiritual order, 412. On desertion of public worship by the nobles; abuse of the right of patronage, 413 nn. 2, 7. Improves the liturgy, 428. Against the too artificial

psalmody, 428. His zeal against the corruption of the clergy, 428. His book concerning images, 428, 429, 435. Against the tempestarios, 429. Against judgments of God, 429, 449. Rebellion of the sons of Louis the Pious, 457. On inspiration, 460.

Citations from his works: —
Adversus legem Gundobadi, iii. 130 n. 4 (429 n. 4). Against the doctrines of Felix, 168 n. 6. Opp. (ed. Baluz. t. ii. f. 60), letter of Greg. iv. 352 n. 3. De privilegio et jure sacerdotii, c. xi. 412 n. 4, 413 n. 2. De dispensat. rerum eccles. c. 15, 413 n. 7. De correctione antiphonarii, 428 xn. 1, 3, 4. On images, 428, 429. Adv. Fredegis, 460 n. 5. Opp. t. ii. f. 149, ep. of Amulo to Gottschalk, 460 n. 3.

Ἀγοήτευτον, i. 34 n. 1.
Agonistici, ii. 227, 263.
Agoust, Bertrand de. See Clement V.
Agrestius, iii. 39 n. 2.
Agrippinus, North African bp., i. 318.
Ἀγροὶ ὑποκείμενοι, ii. 193 n. 2.
Ahito, bp. of Basle, iii. 453.
Ahriman in Parsism, i. 369, 376, 402 and n. 3, 403, 479, 480, 482, 487; ii. 126 n. 1, 127–129; in Manicheism, i. 479–487, 493, 497.
Aidan, bp. of Northumberland, iii. 21. His conduct with respect to the difference of time in celebrating Easter, 23.
Aimoin.
De gestis Francorum, conc. Rheims, l. v. c. 45, iii. 369 n. 1, 371 n. 1. Life of Abbo (Acta S. O. B.), iii. 404 n. 1

Αἰών, Gnostic, ii. 127.
Αἰώνιος ζωή, i. 34 n. 2.
Αἵρεσις, definition of the word, i. 338 n.; ii. 14 n. 2.
Aix (Aquae), Lazarus of, ii. 643. Synod at, iii. 167, 168. Abp. of, letter of Innocent III. to, iv. 640 n. 2. See Councils.
Aix la Chapelle, diet at, iii. 415. Benedictine rule published at, iii. 415, 416; iv. 208. See Councils.
Αἰζανᾶς, ii. 144 n. 2.
Ἀκατονόμαστος, of Basilides, i. 373 n. 1.
Ἀκέφαλοι, ii. 588.
Akoemetes, ii. 277 n. 4.
Ἀκροαταί, i. 305 and n. 2.
Ἀκροώμενοι, ἀκροαταί, ii. 357 and n. 4.
Alanus Magnus (Insulensis), iv. 417. On the Trinity, 461.
Citations from his works: —
Ars Catholicae fidei, iv. 417. Regulae theologicae (417 n. 3), f. 189, 461 n. 3. Anticlaudianus, and Summa de arte praedicandi, 417 n. 1. Contra Waldenses, l. ii. f. 206, iv. 615 n. 1.

Alaric, king of the West Goths, ii. 160.
Alberic, iv. 181 n. 2. See Chronicle of.
Alberic of Citeaux, iv. 252.
Alberic of Ostia, iv. 603.
Alberic, patrician, iii. 367.
Albert I., emperor, v. 22.
Albert, abbot of Stade. See Chronicle of.
Albert, bp. in Greenland, iii. 307.
Albert, bp. of Cracow, v. 373.

Albert, patriarch of Jerusalem, iv. 266.
Albert, scholar of Egbert, in York, iii. 153 and n. 4.
Albert of Strassburg.
Chronicle, Clement VI., v. 41 n. 2. See Ursitis.

Albert. See Albrecht.
Albertus Magnus, sketch of his life, iv. 421. Defends the monastic orders, 286. Withdrawal of the cup, 345. Aquinas, 422. Faith and knowledge, 429. The book De Causis, 445 n. 1. David of Dinanto, 446 n. 1, 447 n. 1. Doctrine of God, 449. Trinity, 463. Miracles, 470, 471, 472. Foreknowledge and predestination, 477. Doctrine of grace, 518.

Citations from his writings: —
Liber secundus de terminatione causarum primiarium, Tr. i., opp. ed. Lugd. t. v. f. 563, iv. 445 n. 1. Summa theol. (P. i. Tr. iv. Q. 20, m. ii.), David of Dinanto, 445 n. 4, 446 n. 1, 447 n. 1. P. ii. Tr. viii. Q. 30, seqq., seminal causes, 471 n. 6. On the miracle, 470 nn., 471 nn. On freewill and fate, 477 nn. On theology, 429 nn. 4, 5.

Albic of Unitzow, abp. of Prague, v. 276, 295, 298.
Albigenses (Albigeois), iv. 270, 570, 616 n. 7, 639–642, 644.
Albin, companion of Otto of Bamberg, iv. 20.
Alboin, priest, ep. 2, contr. Bernold, iv. 100 n. 2.
Albrecht (Albert) of Apeldern, iv. 38.
Albrecht (Albert) the Bear, iv. 21, 32.
Albrich, bp., iii. 79.
Alby, iv. 603, 639 n. 2, 640.
Alcibiades, confessor, i. 275.
Alcuin, abbot, sketch of his life, iii. 153–156. His advice with regard to the conversion of the Saxons, 76. Warnings to Charlemagne, 77, 78. His school at York, Liudger, 79, 80, 154. Advice concerning the mission to the Avares, 82–84. Tithes, 77 and n. 2, 82, 83, 101 n. 2. On employing the clergy in war, 102 n. 3. Opposed to the punishment of death, 103 and n. 1. On right of asylum, 105 n. 1. Secular occupations of priests, 105 n. 5. Spiritual power of the papacy, 121, 350. Tribunals over the pope, 122, 350. Zeal for the predicatorial office, 123–125. Study of the Bible, 124, 125. On pilgrimages, 131. Festival of All Saints, 134, 135 n. 1. Albert, 153 n. 4. Master of the Schola Palatina, 154. Improves the Latin version of the Bible, 155. Master of the school at Tours, 156. His death, 156. Elipandus, 158 n. 1, 164 nn. 1, 2, 166 and n. 5. Beatus, 164 n. 3. His stand against Adoptianism, 160–163 nn., 165–168. Felix, 166–168. His proposal for the refutation of Felix, 167. His part in the composition of the Libri Carolini, 235 and n. 4. Influence, 457, 467.

GENERAL INDEX.

Fredegis, 460. Doctrine of the Holy Spirit, 555. Unleavened bread in the eucharist, 581 n. 1. His biography, 155 n. 5.
Citations from his writings: —
Comm. on John, l. ii. c. iv. f. 500, ed. Frob. iii. 235 n. 4; f. 591, 155 n. 2.
Contra Felicem, iii. 167 n. 3. L. i. ff. 791, 792, 166 n. 4. L. ii. f. 809, 163 n. 2. L. iii. c. 3, 163 n. 4; f. 812, 160 n. 4; f. 816, 160 n. 1; f. 817, 160 n. 3; f. 818, 161 n. 4. L. iv. f. 820, 162 n. 2. L. v. f. 832, 161 nn. 3, 5; ff. 834, 835, 161 n. 1; f. 835, 163 n. 3; f. 837, 161 n. 2. L. vi. ff. 839, 840, 160 n. 5; f. 843, 160 n. 2. L. vii. f. 857, 163 n. 1.
Epigram on Virgilius, iii. 63 n. 4.
Epistles. Ep. 3, to a Scottish abbot, conversion of the Saxons, iii. 76 n. 1. Ep. 3, to an English abp., study of the Bible, 124 n. 2. Ep. 20, to Leo III., on the papal power, 121 n. 3. Ep. 28, to Charlemagne, the Saxons, 77 n. 1; the same, on planting the church among the Avares, 82 nn. 5-7. Epp. 31, 31, on the same subject, 83 nn. 1, 2. Ep. 37, to Magenfrid, on planting the church among the Saxons, 76, 77; the same, on worldly priests, 105 n. 5. Ep. 38, to Charlemagne, on his labors at Tours, 156 n. 1. Ep. 59, to the people of Canterbury, 124 n. 3. Ep. 69, to Charlemagne, on the refutation of Felix, 167 n. 2. Ep. 72, to Arno of Salzburg, on tithes, 77 n. 5, 83 n. 7, 101 n. 2. Ep. 75, ed. Froben., on bread used in the Lord's Supper, 581 n. 1. Ep. 76, to Arno, on the festival of All Saints, 135 n. 1; the same, on the conversion of Felix of Urgellis, 168 nn. 1, 2. Ep. 80, to Charlemagne, treatment of the Saxons, 77 n. 6. Ep. 85, to the same, Felix, and Alcuin's book against Felix, 159 n., 167 n. 4. Ep. 90, to the same, on the death of his wife, 155 n. 1. Ep. 92, to Arno, on planting the church among the Avares, 84 n. 1; the same, deposition of Leo III., and authority of the pope, 103 n. 1, 122 n. 3, 350 n. 4; the same, on the recantation of Adoptianists, 168 n. 3. Ep. 108, to Charlemagne, with a copy of the Bible, 155 n. 3. Ep. 112, secular affairs of clergy, 105 n. 5. Ep. 114, to Arno, on the same, 105 n. 5. Ep. 119, Charlemagne to the monks of St. Martin, 154 n. 3. Ep. 124, to Charlemagne, 154 n. 4; the same, on religious instruction, 124 n. 4; the same, on study of Scriptures, 125 n. 1. Ep. 147, to a nun, pilgrimages, 132 n. 1. Ep. 168, his wish to retire from the world, 155 n. 4. Ep. 175, at the abbey of St. Martin, 156 nn. 3, 4. Ep. 176, to Arno, from St. Martin's, 156 n. 2; the same, on the punishment of death, 103 n. 1. Ep. 193, to Theodulf, on preaching, 124 n. 1. Ep. 195, to Charlemagne, on asylums, 105 n. 1. Ep. 208, to Leutfrit, military service of bishops, 102 n. 3. Ep. 221, Irish missionaries, 29 n. 2. Ep. ad. Felicem, 166 n. 1.
Life of Willibrord, iii. 43 n. 4.
Opp. ed. Froben. t. i. P. ii. ff. 870, 872, letter of Elipandus to Alcuin, iii. 158 n. 1, 164 nn. 1, 2; f. 860, letter to the imperial delegates, 166 n. 5. T. ii. f. 573, letter of Spanish bishops to Charlemagne, 164 n. 3 (165); f. 459, 235 n. 4.
Poem on the holy men of York, iii. 153 n. 4.

Aldhelm, bp., life of, iii. 152 n. 3. See William of Malmsbury.

Alemanni, iii. 8, 27, 34.

Aleth, Bernard's mother, iv. 252.

Alexander II., pope, iii. 395, 396, 398, 399 and n. 4, 406 n. 2, 516; iv. 85 and n. 1, 106.
Ep. 35, simony, iii. 397 n. 1.

Alexander III., pope, iv. 167, 168, 171, 173, 194, 201, 207, 214, 218, 416, 582 n. 4, 608.

Alexander IV., pope, iv. 188, 283, 289, 421, 620.

Alexander V., pope, v. 85-90, 91, 93, 94, 259, 260, 262, 265, 300. Bull against Wicklif, 259.

Alexander, bp. of Alexandria, i. 190 n. 1, 722 n. 6; ii. 255, 409, 410, 414, 418 and n. 1, 419, 423, 424, 428 n. 4.
Cited by Theodoret, M. E. l. i. c. 4, on Lucian, i. 722 n. 6.

Alexander, bp. of Antioch, ii. 465.

Alexander, bp. of Constantinople, ii. 429.

Alexander, bp. of Hierapolis, ii. 524 n. 1, 538 n. 4, 540 n. 1, 544, 546-551.
Citations. Ep. ad Theodoretum, ii. 538 n. 4. Ep. 78, 546 n. 4. Ep. 143, 548 n. 1. Ep. 145, 544 n. 2. Ep. 147, 549 n. 4.

Alexander, bp. of Jerusalem, i. 691, 694 n. 1, 703, 704 n. 3.

Alexander, judge in Syria, ii. 84.

Alexander, monk, ii. 277 n. 4.

Alexander, theologian, iv. 174.

Alexander of Abonotechus, i. 30, 72, 92, 104, 161, 173.

Alexander of Hales, representative of the Scholastic theology, iv. 420. Faith and knowledge, theology, 427, 428. Knowledge of God, 443, 444 n. 1. Trinity, 462, 463. Miracles, 469, 470. Prescience and predestination, 476. Original condition, 488-490, 491. Uncertainty with regard to the state of grace, 513. Grace and freewill, 518, 519.
Summæ, P. i. Q. 96, 488 n. 4. P. ii. Q. 42, iv. 409 n. 2. Q. 30, 471 n. 6. Q. 112, art. 5, f. 633, 514 n. 1.

Alexander of Lycopolis.
Tract against the Manicheans, i. 482 n. 2, 495 n. 2; c. 4, 494 n. 3, 500 n. 3: c. 5, 494 n. 1, 500 n. 3; c. 24, 490 n. 4. Introduction, ii. 767 n. 3. See Combefis.

Alexander Severus, i. 103, 125-127, 155, 199, 292, 682.

Alexander the Great, ii. 73. His mission, i. 49, 50.

Alexandria, influence of Hellenic culture on Judaism there, i. 49-60. Number of Jews in, 50 n. 3. Metropolis, 79, 242. The Evangelist Mark, 83 (ii. 203). Religious syncretism, 102. Persecution of Christians, 130, 132, 135, 154. Ecclesia apostolica, 203 (ii. 196, 197). Passover festival, 299. Catechetical school at, 306, 527, 528. Symbolum, 307. Confession of faith orally communicated, 308. Origin of the disciplina arcani, 308 n. 4. Infant baptism, 314. Baptismal rites, 316, 317. Baptism of heretics, 320, 323. Mildness in judging heretics, 364. Platonism there, 377. Cerinthus in, 396. Basilides, 400. Valentine, 417. Carpocrates, 449. Eclecticism, 449. Doctrine of

Sacraments, 648. Origen's influence, 712; ii. 387. See Clement, Origen, Philo, Didymus, Alexandrian.
Second Period. Persecution at, ii. 6, 67 n. 1, 80, 97, 98. Paganism at, 73, 94, 97, 104. Persecution of pagans, 34, 37, 97, 98. Temples destroyed, 98. Georgius, 37 and n. 2, 79, 80, 144. Athanasius at, 72-74, 144, 205, 206, 423-428, 432-434, 436 and n. 4, 437, 443, 444, 456, 460. Heron, 104. School at, 182, 183 (see Alexandrian). Parabolani, 192. Parish churches at, 194. Patriarchate, 196, 198, 203, 204. Power of the patriarch, 252 n. 1, 582, 583. Meletian schism, 252-255. Anthony at, 268-270. Hilarion, 271. Market at, 167, 272. Heron, monk, 275. Poor at, 288. Seasons of worship, 333. Time of feasts made known, Easter, 338. Epiphany, 346. Christmas at, 346 n. 2. Church music, 355 n. 1. Daily communion, 364. Home communion, 365 n. 4. Insurrections at, 434, 436, 443. Doctrinal tendency, 617. Rhetorians at, 767 and n. 4. Monophysites at, 584, 585-587, 592; iii. 177, 178, 228. Patriarch of, iii. 99, 115. See Alexander, Arius, Athanasius, Dionysius, Monophysites, Pistus, Theophilus, Councils.

Alexandrian church, constitution of, i. 190 n. 1. Metropolitan, 242. See Alexandria.

Alexandrian church teachers, iv. 61, 376, 378. See Alexandrian school.

Alexandrian Gnosis, Jewish, i. 66, 657, 658. Christian, 83 (Gnosticism), 374, 377, 475; ii. 395; iv. 568. Within the church, i. 527 n. 2, 529-557, 692. See Alexandrian philosophy of religion, Alexandrian school.

Alexandrian Judaism, i. 49-67, 366, 398, 403, 508. Relation to the Essenean mysticism, 44, 47. Interpolation, 176. Influence, 458 n. 3, 600. Interpretation of Scripture, 658. See Philo. Influence on the Catharists, iv. 571.

Alexandrian philosophy of religion, i. 49-58, 508. Twofold position, 56, 64. Relation to Christianity, 64-66, 351, 381, 575, 657. To Gnosticism, 380-382, 396.

Alexandrian Platonism, i. 51-54, 56-58, 64. Among the Essenes, 44, 47. Of Philo, 47 n. 1, 48 n. 3. Its poverty, 65.

Alexandrian school, origin and character, i. 440, 519, 527-557, 560, 563, 564, 594, 645. Justin precursor of, 662. Logos doctrine, 586-591. Anthropology, 620-640. Sacraments, 648, 649. Chiliasm, 651-653. Ἀποκατάστασις, 656. The individual teachers, 691-722 (364). *Characteristics in the second Period*, ii. 182, 386, 387. Compared with the Antiochian school, 393, 394. Doctrine of the person of Christ, 501, 502-504. *In the third Period*, relation to the Antiochian school, iii. 156, 163.

Alexandrian synodal letter, apolog. contra Arian, ii. 432 n. 2.

Alexandrian theology, i. 398, 458; iii. 170; iv. 378. See Alexandrian school.

Alexandrian version of the O. T., i. 380 and n. 4, 409, 658; ii. 496 n. 2, 745. Labors of Origen on the, i. 707-710; of Hesychius, i. 722; of Lucian, i. 722 n. 6.

Alexias. See Anna Comnena.

Alexiopolis, iv. 564.

Alexius Comnenus, iv. 559, 560, 564.

Alexius II., Greek emperor, iv. 530.

Alfred the Great, iii. 467, 468; v. 150. Life of, iii. 418 un. 1, 2.
Translation of the Ragulæ pastorales, iii. 468.

Alfrid, iii. 80 n. 2.

Alfrid, Anglo-Saxon king, iii. 24.

Alfrid. See Altfrid.

Alger, of Liege, on transubstantiation, iv. 338 n. 3. See Bibl. patr. Lngd. t. 21.

All Saints, church of, at Constantinople, iv. 550.

All Saints, festival of, iii. 134, 135, 446.

Allegorical interpretation of Homer, ii. 41.

Allegorical interpretation of myths, i. 171; ii. 62.

Allegorical interpretation of Scripture. Among the Pharisees, i. 39, 40. Among the Essenes, 44, 47. Among the Alexandrian Jews, 53-59, 657. Among the Therapeutæ, 61. With the Ebionites, 348 n. 2. In the Clementines, 355. With Julius Cassian, 458 n. 3. With Marcion, 460, 463. The Gnostics, 460, 702. With the Alexandrian school, 527 n. 2, 652, 721, 722. With Origen, 552, 555, 556, 694, 700, 719, 722; ii. 388, 598. Artemonites, i. 582. Methodius, i. 721. With Hieracas, i. 714. Porphyry on, i. 171. *In the second Period*, ii. 219, 388, 389, 392, 393, 598, 712 n. 3. *In the fourth Period*, iv. 77; with the Bogomiles, iv. 553.

Allgemeine Archiv.
Für Geschichtskunde des preussischen Staates, vol. viii. f. 97, Anselm of Havelberg, iv. 536 n. 3. See Ledebur.

Almaric of Bena, iv. 221 n., 417 n. 5, 445-447, 449, 480, 618, 619 n. 3, 620.

Alms, almsgiving, i. 255, 647; ii. 103, 259, 349 n. 1. In connection with the Lord's Supper, ii. 368 n. 1; by Constantine, ii. 26; by Julian, ii. 63; to Donatists by Constans, ii. 228. *In the third and fourth Periods*, iii. 149, 282, 408 n. 2, 414. For suicides, 102 n. 4. As opus operatum, 130, 138, 139, 440, 442. Indulgences obtained by, 138, 452. In honor of Christ, 281, 285. Dangers of, 282 n. 2. Nicholas I. on, 311, 312. Ratherius on, 452. The cup of cold water, 421. *Fifth Period*, iv. 294-296, 318, 325. As opus operatum, 122, 302. At Clairvaux, 254. Fraudulent collections of, 267. Louis IX., 285 n. 4, 300, 301. Innocent III. on, 306. Lull on, 310. For the dead, 597. Waldenses, 616. *Sixth Period*, v. 383. Wicklif on, 141, 142. To monks, 141, 189, 407 (see Mendicant friars). Conrad on, 189. Huss on, 305, 324, 353; for the dead, 324; tithes considered as, 335, 345, 346. See Charity, Poor.

Almshouses, ii. 169, 752.
Almundar, Saracenic sheikh, ii. 143.
Alogi, i. 526, 583, 682.
Alphabet, Armenian, ii. 137. Irish, ii. 149. Gothic, ii. 152. Chilperic adds to the Latin, iii. 91 n. 1. Latin, iii. 281 n. 1. Slavonic, iii. 316, 313, 324, 329 n., 330 n. 1.
Alphanus, abp. of Salerno, poem on Hildebrand, iii. 399 n. 4; iv. 83 n. 1.
Alps, iv. 112, 295. Shelters on the, 214.
Alsace, Christianity in, iii. 37, 38 n. 2. Otfrid in, iii. 425. Friends of God in, v. 42.
Altar, i. 291; ii. 321. As asylum, ii. 176, 178, 755.
Altar of victory at Rome, ii. 92.
Altenberga, church at, iii. 50 n. 2.
Altenburg, iii. 324. See Oldenburg.
Altfrid (or Alfrid), life of Liudger, iii. 45 n. 1, 80 n. 2.
Altmann, bp. of Passau, iv. 111, 112.
Altorf, v. 383 n. 2.
Alubert, iii. 73.
Alvarus Pelagius.
De planctu ecclesiæ, l. ii. f. 172, Dolc.no, iv. 633 n. 2.
Alvarus. See Paulus.
Amalarius of Metz, iii. 428 n. 2.
Amalfi, iii. 583.
Amalric. See Almaric.
Amandus, episc. regionar. in Ghent, iii. 40. Among the Slavonians, 41. Bp. of Utrecht, 41. Vita, 40 n. 1.
Amantius, court chamberlain, ii. 531 n.
Amara, Paulician city, iii. 587.
Amasea, ii. 68, 607 n. 1. See Asterius.
Ambrose, bp. of Milan. His election to the episcopate, ii. 472. Influence over the emperors in their attitude towards paganism, 92-94, 99. Theodosius, 95 n. 4, 99, 214, 215, 604. On divine revelation, 117. Advice to judges, 173. Protects widows and orphans, 176. Right of asylum, 176. Penitents, 213 n. 3. Augustin, 240. Monachism, 294. Jovinian, 312. Sarmatio and Barbatianus, 312. Place of the emperor in the church, 321 n. 6. Dies stationum, iii. 2. Observance of the Sabbath, 334. Christmas festival, 344 n. 3. Church psalmody, 354 and n. 4. Sacramentum apertionis, 359 n. 2. Magical power in the Lord's

Supper, 366 n. 1. Bonosus, 377. Creed of Eusebius of Nicomedia, 417 n. 3. Opposition to Arianism, 472. Anthropology, 618, 622-624, 654. De officiis, 679, 680. De vocatione gentium, 699 n. 3. Letter to Demetrias, 701 n. 1. Infant baptism, condition of children who have died without baptism, 730. Doctrine of the Lord's Supper, 731, 732 n. 5. Priscillianists, 772, 775. Opposition to persecution, 775. Vita, 95 n. 4. Milan, celibacy of clergy, iii. 389, 397 n. 2. Berengar, 506, 516. His example used in the contest between Gregory VII. and Henry IV., iv. 110, 111. With the Catharists, 578 n. 5. Allusion of Huss to, v. 304.
Citations from his writings: —
Apologia David altera, § 71, ii. 622 n. 3.
De Abrahamo, l. ii. § 84 unbaptized infants, ii. 730 n. 3.
De fide, l. iii. c. 7, creed of Eusebius of Nicomedia, ii. 417 n. 3; l. iv. c. 10, § 124, transubstantiation, 732 n. 3; l. v. § 83, predestination, 624 n. 1.
De iis, qui mysteriis init., c. 1, sacramentum apertionis, ii. 359 n. 2; c. 9, transubstantiation, 732 n. 2.
De incarnationis dominic. sacramento, l. i. c. 4, § 23, ii. 732 n. 3.
De institut. virginis, c. 5, § 35, worship of Mary, ii. 377 n. 1.
De interpellat. David, l. iv. § 4, responsibility, ii. 623 n. l.
De officiis. i., 679, 680 and n. 1; l. ii. c. 29, widows and orphans, 176 n. 3.
De paradiso, on Apelles, i. 475.
De pœnitentia, l. ii. c. 10, ii. 213 n. 3.
De sacramentis, l. ii. c. 1, ii. 359 n. 2; transubstantiation, iii. 516.
De Spiritu sancto, l. iii. c. 11, § 79, transubstantiation, ii. 732 n 5
Epistles. Ep. ad Valentinian II., treatment of pagans, ii. 93. Ep. 24, to the same, treatment of heretics, 775 n. 3. Ep. 26, ad Ireneum, the same, 775 n. 4. Ep. 29, ad Theodos., pagans, 95 n. 3. Ep. 40, ad Theodos., and ep. 42, ad sororem, Theodosius, 95 n. 4. Ad Theodos. on the massacre at Thessalonica, 215. Ep. 57, ad Eugen. § 3, Valentinian, ii. 93 n. 3; § 4, Theodosius, treatment of pagans, 99 nn. 3, 4. L. vii. ep. 58 (old editions), ad Studium, on judges who pass sentence of death, 173 n. 4. Ep 63, ed. Bened. t. iii. f. 1110, to the ch. at Vercelli, Sarmatio and Barbatian 1s, 312 nn. 5, 6. Ep. to Siricius, 312. Exposit. Lucæ, i. § 10, and vii. § 27, predestination, ii. 623 nn. 2, 3; vii. f. 234, the fall, iv. 622, n. 4.
Funeral discourse, de olitu fratris Satyri, 366 n. 1.
Funeral discourse, Theodosius, 215 n. 2.
In Ps. 43, § 47, and Ps. 118, § 13, responsibility, ii. 623. n. 2. In Ps. 48, § 9, guilt, 622 n. 5. In Ps. 118, § 14, 623 n. 1; § 48, dies stationum, 333 n. 2.

Ambrose, friend of Origen, i. 163 n. 1, 367 n. 2, 582, 700-702, 707-709.
Ambrose of Siena, iv. 295, 296.
Ambrosian church, iii. 394, 398.
America, Christianity there, iii. 307.
Amida, ii. 136.
Amiens, iii. 272, 420. See Peter of.
Ammianus Marcellinus, ii. 75 n. 3, 168, 343.
L. xv. c. 7, Athanasius ii. 22 n. 1, 437 n. 1, 488 n. 2; c. 13, the Manicheans, Strategius,

16 n. 3, 769 n. 1. L. xix. c. 10, pagan sacrifices at Rome, 35 n. 5; c. 12, laws of Constantius against magic, 34 nn. L. xxi. c. 2, Julian, Epiphany, 45 n. 2, 343 n. 3; c. 16, Constantius' rage for synods, 452 n. 1. L. xxii. c. 11, Georgius, 80 nn. 1, 2; c. 4, property of temples confiscated, 35 n. 1; c. 5, Julian, 72 n. 1; cc. 12, 13, Julian, 81 n. 3, 83 n. 1, 84 n. 1. L. xxiii. c. 1, attempt to rebuild the temple, 69 nn 2, 3; c. 2, Julian, 84 n. 4. L. xxv. c. 4, Julian, 75 n. 2 (epigram on M. Aurelius, i. 107 n. 3). L. xxvii. c. 3, pomp of the bishops, 167 n. 3, 168 n. 2; the schism at Rome, 255 n. 2, 257 n. 2. L. xxx. c. 9, Valentinian, 90 n. 2.

Ammianus, monk, ii. 292.
Ammon, bp., letter of, ii. 424 n. 2.
Ammonius, church teacher, i. 699 n. 1.
Ammonius, monk, ii. 752.
Ammonius Saccas, i. 698, 699.
Amœneburg, iii. 47.
Amoin, life of Abbo of Fleury, iii. 404 n. 1.
Amorion, Athinganians at, iii. 592.
Amphictyonic council, i. 206.
Amphilochius, bp. of Iconium, on images, ii. 327. Holy Spirit, 468.
Ampulla Remensis, iii. 8 n. 4.
Amshaspands, in Parsism, i. 489 n. 5, 490 n. 5.
Amulets, i. 73. Basilidean, i. 401. *In the second Period*, ii. 13, 34, 259, 293, 357, 366. *Third and fourth Periods*, iii. 7, 42, 56, 64, 84, 129, 133, 201, 420, 444, 448. *Fifth Period*, iv. 48, 252 n. 3.
Amulo, abp. of Lyons, ep. to Gottschalk, iii. 490, 491.
Amund, Jacob, Swedish king, iii. 292.
Amus, Egyptian monk (Ammun, ii. 269 n. 2), ii. 290.
Amusements, i. 263-267. Waldenses on, iv. 611. See Games, Theatre.
Anabaptists, i. 318; iv. 595.
'Αναβαθμοὶ Ἰακώβου, i. 352.
'Αναβατικὸν Ἠσαΐου, i 716 n. 2. Anabasis of Isaiah, iv. 572 and n. 1.
Anachorets. See Anchorets, Hermits.
Anaclete, Roman bishop, ep. 1 in Pseud. Isidor. Decret., iii. 347 n. 5, 349 n. 3.
Anaclete II., pope, iv. 144-146.
'Ανάδοχος, iii. 201 n. 2.
Anagni, iii. 562; iv. 173, 183; v. 12, 46.
'Ανάγνωσται, anagnosts, i. 201, 203 and n. 3, 743 n. 1.
Anagrates (Anegrey), iii. 30.
Analecta Græca.
Life of Cyrill (Paris, 1688), ii. 581 n. 1. T. i. f. 415, *et sqq.*, life of Stephen, the image worshipper, χριστὸς ὁ ἀντιφωνήτης, iii. 213 n. 3; violence of the iconoclasts, 217 n. 2: the term " saint," 218 n. 3; paintings destroyed, 219 n. 2; concealed image worshippers, 219 n. 3; measures of Constantine, 220 nn. 2, 4, 221 n. 5, 223 n. 1.
Analogy, argument from, iv. 412, 431, 458.
Anamartesia, ii. 728 and n. 1.
Ananias, martyr, ii. 132.
Ananias and Sapphira, iii. 255 n. 1.
Anastasia, church in Constantinople, ii. 464.

Anastasius, bp. of Rome, ii. 750. Letter to John of Jerusalem, 750 n. 2.
Anastasius, disciple of Maximus, iii. 191.
Anastasius, Greek emperor, ii. 589-591.
Anastasius II., Greek emperor, iii. 196.
Anastasius, patriarch of Antioch, iii. 116 n. 2.
Anastasius, patriarch of Constantinople, iii. 209.
Anastasius, presbyter of Nestorius, ii. 507 and n. 2, 516.
Anastasius.
Life of Johann. Eleemosyn. (trans.), iii. 90 n. 2. Life of Leo III., iii. 122 n. 2. Life of Martin I., 186 n. 1. Præfatio ad concil. Constantinop. iv., the Bulgarians, 310 n. 1. Constantine the Philosopher, 314 n. 5. Photius, 559 n. 3.
'Αναστοιχείωσις, iv. 562.
Anathema, ii. 215; iii. 454, 121, 195, 196, 210, 217, 218, 232, 245 n., 249, 396 n. 3, 433 n. 2, 489, 521, 550, 551, 565, 571, 576; iv. 103, 535, 536, 563 n. 3, 572 n. 1; v. 205, 206.
'Αναθήματα. Simplicius on, ii. 109.
'Ανατολικοί, ii. 521 n. 3.
Anatolius, deacon at Rome, ii. 601.
Anatolius, patriarch of Constantinople, ii. 202, 203, 575-580. Letter to Leo, 580 n.
Ancestral religion, iii. 44.
Anchorets (hermits), i. 59; ii. 271, 282, 284-286, 365; iii. 17, 28, 40, 280, 283, 418, 419, 504, 505; iv. 2, 235, 239, 241-243 n. 1, 251, 264-266.
Ancient authors, study of the, Origen, i. 698, 701. Chrysostom, ii. 718, 754. Jerome, 742, 743. School of Berengar, iii. 527 n. 3. Odo, iv. 358, 359. Anselm, 363. Preservation of, 529, 530. False reverence for the ancients, 359, 378. Abelard, 378, 379, 385 n. 4. Contempt for, 415. See Greek culture, etc.
Ancient literature, decline of, iii. 150, 151, 335.
Ancient philosophy, Albert the Great on, iv. 429. Roger Bacon on, 434.
Ancilla, ii. 49, 61.
Ancyra. See Councils, Basil, Domitian, Marcellus.
Andreas, bp. of Samosata, ii. 545.
Ep. 48, his dream, ii. 544 n. 1. See Theodoret, opp. t. v. f. 706, ed. Hal.
Andreas of Bamberg, on Otto of Bamberg, iv. 2 n. 1, 4 n. 1, 7 n., 26 n. 2.
Andrew, abp. of Lund, iv. 39.
Andrew (Andreas), biographer of Ariald, iii. 389 n. 3, 390 n. 2, 392 nn., 393 nn. 1, 2, 398 n. 3. See Acta S. Junc.
Andrew, king of Hungary, iii. 385.
Andrew of Broda, writings against Huss, v. 183 n. 2. Answer to Huss, v. 258 n. 3.
Andrew Saramita, iv. 638.
Andrew, tailor at Prague, v. 318.
Andrew, the Calybite, iii. 220.

Andronicus, governor of Pentapolis, ii. 177 n. 1, 215.
Andronicus, Greek emperor, iv. 448–551. Hist. of, 549 n. 2.
Anegrey, iii. 30.
Angelarius, disciple of Methodius, iii. 320 n. 2.
Angelo, Cardinal Peter de St., v. 293.
Angelo Corario, cardinal, v. 71. See Gregory XII.
Angelophanies, i. 42, 386 n. 2, 597.
Angels, with the Jews, i. 382. With the Sadducees, 42. With the Essenes, 47. With the Ebionites, 351. The Gnostics, 380–382, 477. With Cerinthus, 396, 397, 399. With Basilides, 405, 409. With Isidore, 406. With Valentine, 424, 432–434. With Heraclion, 435. The Ophites, 444, 445. Saturninus, 455. With Justin, 609 n. 1. With the Euchites, ii. 280. With Faustus of Lerins, 706 n. 2. With Theodore of Mopsuestia, 498, 714, 716, 717. With the Priscillianists, 776. Vision of Constantine, 11. Invocation of, 59. Fall of, 75. Images of, 232. Original condition of with Anselm, iv. 486. Robert Pullein, 486. The Bogomiles, 553, 554. The Catharists, 567, 568, 570, 572, 573. Fallen angels and the elect, 554 n. 2. Angels of the last times, Militz on, v. 179; Janow on, 196, 200. Huss on, 257. Worship of, 408. Ægidius, 15. Angels of the devil, i. 307.
Anger of God, Tertullian on the, i. 563.
Angers, iii. 503, 521. See Eusebius Bruno. Count of, iv. 90, 306.
Angilbert, abbot, iii. 242.
Anglia Sacra, P. i. f. 130, Ethelwold, iii. 469 n. 2.
Anglo-Saxon literature, iii. 468, 469 (17 n. 1, 18 n. 1). Language, 468, 469. Grammar, 469 n. 2. Translation of Genesis, 469 n. 4. Gospel of John, 153 n. 3.
Anglo-Saxons, i. 86. Morality of the, iii. 69. Enter Britain, 10 and n. 4, 11. Their conversion, 11–25. See Augustin, Britain.
Angoulême, iii. 104 n. 1, 593 n. 1.
Anhypostasia, iii. 540.
Ania, iii. 251.
Aniana (Aniane), cloister, iii. 167, 414, 415, 461 n. 1.
Anicetus, bp. of Rome, i. 299, 300, 465, 513 n. 3, 525; iii. 32.
Animal food, abstinence from, iii. 592; iv. 579, 594. Animal life, sparing of, iii. 592 n. 4, 600 n. 2; iv. 579. Animal sacrifices, iii. 589 and n. 1.
Animals, compassion for (Francis), iv. 275. Sacred, with the Persians, ii. 128.
Anjou, count of, iv. 121.
Anna (Hannah), ii. 355.
Anna Comnena.

Alexias, l. i. 13, Greg. VII. and the envoys of Henry IV., iv. 108 n. 1. L. xiv., Alexiopolis, 564 n. 4. L. xv. f. 387, the Bogomiles, 550 n. 4.

Anna, Greek princess, wife of Vladimir, iii. 329.
Anna of England, v. 241 n. 1.
Annales Bertiniani, iii. 356 nn. 1, 4.
Annals. See Einhard, Hermannus, Pantoppedan, Roger of Hoveden, Wittekind, Zonaras.
Annates, v. 52, 125.
Annianus, Pelagian, translates some of Chrysostom's Homilies, ii. 657.
Annihilation, with Marcus Aurelius, i. 105. Of nature, in Buddhism, i. 491. In transubstantiation, Wicklif on, v. 152.
Anniversaries, i. 334; ii. 15.
Annubenus, proconsul, i. 150.
Annunciation, the, with the Catharists, iv. 569, 612 n. 3.
Annunciation day, ii. 569.
Ἄνω and κάτω Χριστός, i. 386, 398, 549. With Origen, 640.
Ἄνω and κάτω σοφία, i. 420, 423 n. 3, 491, 492.
Anointing, in baptism, i. 315, 316 n. 1, 477; ii. 188, 359. In confirmation, i. 316 n. 1; ii. 359, 360, 732, 733. Anointing the sick, i. 119 n. 6; ii. 322; iii. 448, 449; iv. 335. The name Christian, v. 214. See Unction. Anointing, among the Gnostics, i. 477.
Ἀνόμοιως κατ' οὐσίαν, ii. 436 n. 1.
Anschar (Ansgar), monk. His education, iii. 272. His visions and longing after the missionary calling, 274. His labors in Denmark and Sweden, 275–287, 323 n. 3. Sent by Louis the Pious to Pope Gregory IV., 277. His death, 287. His biography, 281. See Rimbert, and Acta S. Feb. Life of Willehad, 81 n. 2, 82 n. 2.
Ansegis, abp. of Sens, iii. 366.
Anselm, abp. of Canterbury. His life and doctrine, iv. 361–371. Becomes archbishop of Canterbury, 364. Relation to Abelard, 373, 379, 401. Ordinances of Gregory VII., 100 n. 3. Concerning monasticism, 237, 238. Directory to the spiritual life, 240. Superstitious veneration of saints, 329. Concomitance, 344 n. 5. Roscelin, 360 nn. 2, 3. On the education of youth, 362, 363. Faith and knowledge, 427. The ontological proof, 440–443, 444 (368 n. 2). Omnipotence of God, 453, 455, 456. Doctrine of the Trinity, 457, 458, 460. Prescience and predestination, 474, 475. Anthropology, 485, 486, 492, 493. Sinlessness of Christ, 495. Atonement, 498–501, 503, 505, 506. Operative faith, 511. Freewill, 474, 475, 485, 515. Doctrine of the Holy Spirit, 536. His biography, see Eadmer.

Citations from his writings: —
Cur Deus homo, l. i. c. 1, iv. 498 nn. 3, 4; c. 12, freedom, 453 n. 2. L. ii. c. 10, holiness of God, 453 n. 1; sinlessness of Christ, 495 n. 4.

De casu diaboli, iv. 486 nn. 3, 4.
De conceptu virgine, iv. 498 n. 2.
De fide trinitat., c. iii., Roscelin, iv. 360 n. 2. Definition of Trinity, 360 n. 3.
De libero arbitrio, iv. 485 n. 3; c. 1, 486 n. 1.
De veritate, iv. 441.
Epistles, l. 1. ep. 41, love, iv. 365 n. 3; ep. 42, occupations, 362 nn. 2, 3; ep. 55, to a young monk, teaching, classical culture, 362 n. 4, 363 n. 3. L. i. ep. 56, objective validity of sacraments, 100 n. 3. L. ii. ep. 71, secular business of abbots, 364 n.; ep. 133, evil thoughts, 240 nn. 1-3. L. iii. ep. 29, monasticism, 237 n. 3; ep. 33, 238 n. 1; ep. 56, Matilda of England, fasting, 365 nn. 5-7, 366 n. 1; ep. 116, monasticism, 237 n 4. L. iv. ep. 10, saint worship, 320 n. 2. To an abbot, training of children, 362 n. 5, 363 nn. 1, 2.
Liber apologeticus, iv. 443.
Monologium, iv. 431; c. 14, light of God, 441 n. 1; c. 66, knowledge of God, 457 n. 1; c. 75, dead faith, 511 nn. 1-4.
On heaven and hell, iv. 364. Nominalism, 369 n. 2. Faith, 369 n. 3, 511. Gilbert's disputat. Judaei cum Christiano, 78 n. 1.
Proslogium, iv. 368, ontological proof, 442 n. 2; c. 4, 441 n. 4; c. 14, 441 n. 3.

Anselm, abp. of Lucca, iii. 393. Chosen pope (Alexander II.), 395.
Against Guibert, t. iii. f. 383, iv. 101 n. 2.

Anselm of Havelberg. Conference with Nechites at Constantinople, iv. 536, 538.
His account of the conference, iv. 536 n. 4, 537 nn., 538 nn. 2-4. Dialogue, f. 171, literary studies under the Comnenes, iv. 530 n. 3; l. iii. c. 11, f. 197, difference between the Eastern and Western churches, ii. 383 n. See D'Achery, t. i.

Anselm of Laon, iv. 373.
Ausfrid, abbot of Nonantula, iii. 553 n. 3.
Ausverus, monk, iii. 326.
Antagonisms in thought, iv. 355, 356 and n. 1, 357, 371, 404.
Antagonistic forces in history, v. 274, 275. Tendencies, iv. 400.
'Αντεγκύκλιον, of Basiliscus, ii. 586.
Antetypes, iii. 238.
Anthelm, bp., life of, iv. 168 n. 3.
Anthimus, bp. of Thyana, ii. 462.
Anthimus, bp. of Trapezund, ii. 592-594.
Anthony, ii. 264-271, 291, 294, 370 n. 1; iii. 420.
Anthony, fire of St., iv. 266. Society of St., iv. 266.
Anthony of Padua, iv. 291.
Anthropogony with the Bogomiles, iv. 554 and n. 1. See Man.
Anthropology, i. 610-630. In the heretical sects, see the particular sects. Second Period. Of the Western church, ii. 616-712, 726 (384, 492). Of the Eastern church, 712-722, 617, 632. Third Period. In the Western church, iii. 554. Of the Paulicians, 258-260. In the scholastic period, iv. 389, 390, 429, 485-495, 519. In the sects, see the particular sects. See Man.
Anthropomorphism in the Alexandrian philosophy of religion. i. 56-58. According to Celsus, 168. In the Christian doctrine concerning God, 364, 560, 561. Second Period, ii. 387, 388. See Anthropomorphites. Third Period, iii. 443.
Anthropomorphites, i. 711, 713; ii. 747, 751-757, 766 and n. 3; iii. 429, 443.
Chiliasts, i. 165.
Anthropopathism, in paganism, i. 372. In Christian sects, 364. In Christianity, 561-563, 586. Jewish, 56-58. In Gnosticism, 373, 383, 391. Of Eunomius, ii. 448 n. 1. Third and fourth Periods, iii. 88, 144. Scotus on, iii. 463, 486. Fifth Period. Abelard, iv. 455. In the doctrine of atonement, iv. 505.
'Ανθρωποτόκος, ii. 510.
Anthusa, mother of Chrysostom, ii. 262, 754.
Anti-Athanasian party, ii. 440.
Antichrist, i. 95, 96, 121, 362; iii. 147, 164, 345, 370; iv. 186, 226, 228, 284, 619, 622, 632; v. 380. Hippolytus on, i. 682. Divination of the antichristian spirit, iv. 216. Waldensian tract on, iv. 605, 606, 615, 616 n. 7. Wicklif on, v. 137, 144, 145, 156, 160, 171-173. Militz's work on, 178-180, 181. Conrad on, 184. Janow on, 196-201, 211, 231, 232, 234. Huss on, 238, 239, 249, 250, 257, 258, 265, 266, 290, 291, 300, 311, 315, 319, 324, 331, 350, 360, 377 n. Antithesis Christi et Antichristi, 243 n. 2 Deceitfulness of, 196-199. Miracles of, 197, 198, 266, 267. Origin of, 198, 199.
'Αντιδικομαριανιταί, ii. 377 n. 2.
Anti-Hildebrandian party, iv. 94 n. 4, 98 and n. 2.
'Αντιμεθίστασις τῶν ὀνομάτων, ii. 489 n. 7, 501. See Communicatio idiomatum.
Anti-Nicene party, ii. 431, 444, 457, 462.
Antinomians. Antinomian Gnostics, i. 263, 384, 385, 393 n. 3, 447-454, 472. Euchites, ii. 280. Manicheans, ii. 769 n. 6. Antinomian tendency, whether among the Thondracians, iii. 588 n. 2. Pantheistic, among the mystics, v. 399, 400.
Antinomies, ii. 475 n. 2.
Antioch, councils at, see Councils. Metropolis, i. 79, 242. Church at, Aurelian, 142. Ecclesia apostolica, 203. Epiphany, 301 n. 2. Exegetical bent, 674. Συνείσακτοι, 659 n. 3. Julia Mammaea at, Origen, 125. Peter and Paul at, 171 n. 1; iv. 424. Paul of Samosata, i. 604. Clement at, 691. Paul of, 695. Second Period. Pagan worship at, ii. 3, 4. Persecution at, 6. Julian at (44), 81-85. Restoration of temples, 67 and n. 2. Chrysostom at, 94, 216 n. 1, 302, 332, 339, 340 n. 1, 343, 344, 352, 365, 719, 754. Flavian's intercession for, 174. Ecclesia apostolica; patriarchate, 196-198, 203. Meletian schism, 457, 458. Stagirius, 273. Insurrection at, Macedonius' intercession, 285. Influence of monks, 286. Images at, 324. Seasons of worship, 333 and n. 9. Dur-

ing the fast, 338 n. 6, 339. Good Friday, 341. Epiphany, 343 n. 2. Christmas at, 345 n. 1. Prayer for catechumens, 358 n. 1. Μακρόστιχος ἔκθεσις, 435 n. Arius at, 404. Arianism at, 449. Old city and new city, 461. Nestorius, 504, 552. Style of preaching at, 506. Famine at, 528. In the Nestorian controversy, 554–556. See John of Antioch. Synods assembled by Theodoret, 565. Monophysites, 612. Jerome at, 742, 744. Patriarchs of, iii. 116 n. 2, 583 r. 1, 584, 585, 587. Church at, v. 31. See Councils (an. 341, an. 345), Aëtius, Alexander of, Eudoxius, Flavian, John of Antioch, Macarius, Meletius, Stagirius.

Antioch in Pisidia, iii. 250.

Antiochian bishops in the Nestorian controversy, ii. 556.

Antiochian church teachers, ii. 572 n. 6.

Antiochian creeds, ii. 434, 436 n. 1. The fourth, ii. 417 n. 3, 440 n.

Antiochian diocese, schism in the, ii. 547.

Antiochian school, origin of the, i. 674, 722. Its importance, ii. 182. Opposition to, 346 n. 2. Interpretation of Scripture and doctrine of inspiration, 389–394, 402, 754. Points in which it differed from the Alexandrian school, 393, 394. Doctrine concerning the person of Christ, 493–502, 542–544, 559, 561, 568. Compared with the Alexandrian school, 502–504. Anthropology, 495 n. 2, 656, 712–722. Doctrine of baptism, 726–728. Doctrine of last things, 737–739.

Antiochian tendencies revived, iii. 156, 163, 458; iv. 507.

'Αντιφωνητής, iii. 213 n. 2.

Antipodes, iii. 63. See Virgilius.

Antiquity, false reverence for, iv. 359, 378. Moral position of, 520, 526, 527. See Aristotle.

Anti-reform party, v. 240 (232).

Antitactes, i. 449.

Antonina, wife of Belisarius, ii. 594.

Antoninus, bp. of Ephesus.

Acts of process against, ii. 170 n. 2.

Antoninus Pius, i. 89, 103, 119 n. 2, 130, 663 and n. 2, 664, 365, 673 n. 2, 675.

Antwerp, church at, iv. 592 n. 2.

Anulinus proconsularis Africæ, ii. 225 n. 4.

Anysius, bp. of Thessalonica, ii. 377 n. 1.

Aosta, iv. 361.

Aotas, ii. 271 n. 4.

'Απάθεια, i. 632; ii. 617 n. 1.

Apelles, Marcionite, i. 463 n. 3, 474–476.

Apennines, iii. 419.

Aphaca, temple at, ii. 26.

'Αφθαρσία, i. 615.

Aphthartodocetism, ii. 608, 609; iii. 261.

Apiarius, presbyter, ii. 208.

Apocalypse, i. 452, 453, 527, 652, 682; iii. 134, 164; iv. 221 n., 223, 616, 617 and

n. 2, 618, 620 n. 3, 635 n. 1, 641; v. 179, 194, 195, 221, 359, 380. See Revelation, Commentaries, Joachim.

Apocatastasis, i. 623 n. 2, 625, 627, 629, 630, 656; ii. 615, 643 n. 2, 738 n. 1; iii. 175. See Eschatology, Restoration.

Apocrisiarii, ii. 517 and n. 2, 587, 596, 605; iii. 117 n. 2, 141 n. 1, 185, 192.

Apocryphal writings. 'Ανάβασις τοῦ 'Ησαΐα, i. 716 n. 2; iv. 572. 'Αναβαθμοί 'Ιακώβου, i. 352. Book of Enoch, i. 535. Ep. of Peter to James, i. 361. Περίοδοι ἀποστόλων, i. 500 and n. 4. Προσευχὴ 'Ιωσήφ, i. 36 n. 3; iv. 568 n. 5. Story of Susannah, i. 709; iii. 77 n. 4. Writings used by Basilides, — Prophecy of Parchor, Revelations of Ham, i. 406 n. 3, 407, 408. See Testament.

Apoc. gospels. Εὐαγγέλιον κατ' Αἰγυπτίους, i. 83, 458 n. 3, 600, 601. Καθ' 'Εβραίους (of the Nazarenes), i. 348 n. 3, 350, 361 n. 3, 411 nn. 1, 2, 458 n. 1, 708; ii. 712 n. 3. Gospel of the Ophites, i. 446. Of Judas, i. 448 n. 4. Apoc. gospels used by Tatian, i. 458. Apoc. gospel used by Dionys. of Alex. i. 712. Used by the Priscillianists, ii. 778. Used by the Bogomiles, iii. 591 n. 1; iv. 558; (of John), iii. 591 nn. 1, 2, 595 nn. 1, 2; iv. 553 nn. 5, 6, 554 n. 1, 556 and n. 3. See Thilo.

Apoc. writings at Rome, ii. 346, 350. Of Hierotheus, ii. 615 n. 1. Records of council near Sinuessa, iii. 372 n. 1. Berengar on apoc. writings, iii. 527. Apocryphal sayings of Christ, i. 712; iii. 591 n. 2; iv. 558.

Apollinaris, father and son, write Bible history in verse, ii. 77, 742.

Apollinaris, bp. of Hierapolis, i. 117, 298 n. 2, 635 n. 5, 677. Chronicon paschale Alexandr., 298 n. 2. Quoted in Euseb., l. v. f. 117, the thundering legion, 117 n. 1.

Apollinaris, bp. of Laodicea under Julian, i. 677 n. 1; ii. 77, 544 and note. Doctrine of the person of Christ, ii. 484–492, 495, 498. Opposed by Theodore of Mopsuestia, 497–502.

Apollinarism, Apollinarists, ii. 544, 557 n. 7, 561, 610, 732 n. 6. See Apollinaris of Laodicea.

Apollo, oracle of, i. 172. Worship of, Constantine, ii. 8, 9. Julian, ii. 82–84. Temples of, 3, 82, 298.

Apollonius of Tyana, i. 26, 30, 125, 173, 174. Life of, i. 174.

Cited by Euseb. Præp. evang. l. iv. c. 13, and Porphyry, De abstinentia carnis, l. ii. § 34, on offerings, i. 26 n. 1. Euseb. H. E. l. v. c. 18, Montanus, i. 513 n. 3. Epistolæ (Philostratus, opp. ed. Olearius, cp. 58, I. 401), i. 31 n. 2.

Apollonius, pagan.

Consultationes Zacchæi Christiani et Apollonii philosophi, l. i. c. 28, ii. 112 nn. 3, 4.

Apollonius, Roman senator, i. 118.
Apollos of Alexandria, i. 83.
Apologetic direction in Paganism, i. 28.
  Apologetic tendency flowing from Platonism, 20.
Apologeticus martyrum, of Eulogius, iii. 343.
Apologia Athanasii ad Constantium, ii. 144 n. 2.
Apologists against heathenism, i. 101, 104 n. 1, 136 n. 1, 174-178, 353, 456, 565, 586, 661-674, 676, 687-689. Thomas Aquinas, iv. 422. Against Greeks and Gnostics, i. 529 (see the individuals, and Tertullian, Apologeticus); ii. 36 n. 5, 111-115. Against Mohammedanism, iii. 88; Felix, iii. 159; Raymund Lull, iv. 61-71, 426, 427; William of Auvergne, 423 n. 4; for the Martyrs, Eulogius, iii. 343. Against the Jews, iv. 77-81; Guibert of Nogent, 325. Peter of Cluny, for the divinity of Christ, 328.
Apophthegm, patr., ii. 270 nn. 1, 2.
Apostacy, motives of, ii. 68. Laws against, 104, 119. Punishment of, iii. 310, 334, 339. See Controversies. Of heavenly souls, iv. 567, 568, 571. Janow on, v. 211. Of Satan, iii. 572.
Apostates, i. 97.
Apostles, their idea of the Christian priesthood, i. 180. Their relation to the communities, 183. Differences of character, 212, 337. Relation to the Holy Spirit, 210, 220, 527 (see Apostolic succession). With the Gnostics, 389, 448. With the Manicheans, 501, 502. With the Montanists, 516, 517. In Hades, 646, 656 n. 1. Julian on the, ii. 56. Images of the, iii. 89 n. 4. Authority of their writings, 372. Gradual education of the, 582 n. 5. With the Paulicians, 264. With the Euchites, 591. Worship of, 598. Abelard on the, iv. 391. Withdrawal from secular affairs, v. 14. Relation to the church, 25, 26, 303, 309, 352. Of Mani, i. 504.
Apostles' creed, i. 306, 307, 660; ii. (Descensus ad inferos) 491 n. 4; v. 96, 323.
Apostoli, v. 362 n. 1.
Apostolic age, i. 179.
Apostolic church, i. 328; iv. 603, 605, 623; v. 96, 144, 235.
Apostolic commentaries, i. 364 n. 2, 585 n. 1.
Apostolic decrees, iii. 166 n. 6, 266, 557, 581, 582 and n. 6; v. 209.
Apostolic Fathers, i. 656-661. See Clement of Rome, Ignatius, Polycarp, Hermas, Barnabas, Aquilas.
Apostolic letters, i. 216, 382.
Apostolic origin of churches, i. 80.
Apostolic power, Peter source of, ii. 200.
Apostolic succession, i. 210, 247, 316, 317; ii. 188, 238, 243, 725.
Apostolical canons, i. 660. Number of, iii. 557; c. 17, eunuchs in the spiritual order, i. 703 n. 4; c. 66, against fasting on the Sabbath and Sunday, ii. 333 n. 8; iii. 557.
Apostolical Christianity, change in, ii. 48.
Apostolical churches, i. 216, 203, 318; ii. 203.
Apostolical community of goods, iv. 208.
Apostolical constitutions, their formation, i. 197, 660. Exorcism, i. 309. On the liturgy, ii. 361 n. 2, 362 n. 3.

L. ii. c. 28, clergy to be distinguished at the agapæ, i. 326 n. 1; c. 59, the Sabbath a day of assembly, ii. 333 n. 8. L. v. c 15, fasting on the Sabbath, ii. 333 n. 8. L. vii. c. 22, unction in baptism, ii. 359 n. 7. L. viii. c. 20, ordination of deaconesses, ii. 190 n. 1; c. 26, exorcists, i. 201 n. 4; c. 31, occupations excluding from baptism, i. 292 n. 4; c. 32, on lay-teaching, i. 197 n. 2; c. 33, slaves to rest on the Sabbath and Sunday, ii. 333 n. 8.

Apostolical society, iv. 598.
Apostolical traditions, i. 314, 319, 660, 682 n. 2.
Apostolical truth, iv. 575.
Apostolicals, iv. 34, 219, 303, 593, 604, 607, 610, 626-638; v. 138.
Apostolici (see Apostolicals), i. 352.
Ἀποτακτικοί, i. 458 n. 2.
Apotheosis, i. 12.
Appeals to Rome, iii. 118, 119 n. 1, 358, 359, 361, 364, 507, 565; iv. 123, 160, 165, 166, 199, 341, 544. Of Abelard, iv. 395-397; v. 12, 125, 136. Limited by Innocent III., iv. 199. To a general council, v. 4, 12, 24, 294. To the king, 157. Of Huss, 260, 262, 271, 294, 346, 361, 362, 368, 369.
Applause, at Antioch, i. 604. At Constantinople, ii. 353, 506, 509, 510, 511 n. 1.
Appointments. See Ecclesiastical, Benefices.
Appropriation of the good, ii. 747.
A priori methods, Hugo on, iv. 401.
Aptungis (ii. 222 n. 2). See Felix of.
Apulia, ii. 652; iii. 580; iv. 458; v. 303.
Aquila, city, iv. 193.
Aquilas, i. 290.
Aquileia, i. 652; ii. 608, 746; iii. 167; iv. 111. Council at, v. 76. Rufinus of, ii. 746.
Aquino, iv. 421.
Aquitaine, iv. 145.
Aquitania, ii. 691; iii. 39.
Arabia, spread of Christianity in, i. 79, 81, 82. Beryll, 593. Controversy in, 710. Christianity there, ii. 78, 140, 141-143, 145. Worship of Mary, 376, 377. See Bostra. Pilgrimages to, 378.
Arabia Felix, ii. 142, 145.
Arabian philosophy, iv. 63, 64, 68, 325, 444, 445 n. 1, 449. Plato, 420.
Arabians, marauding expeditions of, iii. 206 n 3 Religious condition of, in the time of Mohammed, 84-89. In Spain, 118, 335-345, 430. Influence on culture, iv. 420.

Arabic language, iv. 62, 63, 65, 68, 70, 436. Translations from the, 417, 444, 445. Platonists, 420.
Arabic literature, iii. 335, 341. See Arabic language, Philosophy.
Aragon, v. 52, 56, 70, 77, 84.
Aramaic gospel, i. 81.
Aratus, quoted by Paul, i. 17 n. 2.
Arausio. See Orange.
Arbiters, bishops as, ii. 171, 172.
Arbon, castle of, iii. 34, 37.
Arcadius, emperor, ii. 100–106, 132, 177, 256 n. 6, 761.
Arcas, iii. 256 n. 2.
Archbishops, iii. 16, 64, 65.
Archdeacons, ii. 189, 217, 220, 221, 518 n. 3; iii. 108, 583. Duties of, 105. Their great authority, 111, 114 n. 6, 399. Laws in relation to, 111 n. 2. *In the fourth Period*, iv. 169, 2.1–213. Wiclif on, v. 173.
Archelaus of Cascar, i. 401 n. 2, 485.
Disputation of Archelaus and Mani, c. 7, i. 505 n. 3; c. 55, in Fabricius' ed. of the works of Hippolytus, f. 193, i. 401 n. 2.
Archicapellani, iii. 109.
Archimandrite, ii. 272, 535, 569.
Architecture, Zeno on, i. 18 n. 1. See Church buildings.
Archiv der Gesellschaft für ältere Deutsche Geschichtskunde.
Bd. v. s. 83, iii. 388 n. 1.
Archiv für alte und neue Kirchengeschichte.
Bd. ii. 1, iii. 505 n. 5, 509 n. 4; Bd. iv. 2tes St. s. 307, i. 346 n. 1.
Archivarius (χαρτοφύλαξ), iii. 195 n. 2; iv. 545, 546.
Ἄρχων (Archon) in the system of Basilides, i. 405–412, 414.
Archpresbyters, ii. 189; iii. 110.
Arcona, iv. 31.
Ardaschad, synod at, ii. 137.
Ardgar, missionary in Sweden, iii. 280–282.
Ardo, scholar of Benedict, iii. 414 n.
Life of Benedict, Acta Sanctorum, Feb. 12, 414 n., 415 nn.; Ed. Mabillon, S. iv. P. 1, § 30; 416 n. 1.
Arefast, iii. 595, 596.
Ἀρετὴ θεία and πολιτική, ii. 676 n. 5.
Arethusa, in Syria, ii. 70, 80.
Aretino, Leonardo Bruno, of Arezzo, v. 71–76, 100, 378.
Epp. Hamburg, 1724; 1. ii. ep. 3, on the schism, v. 71 n. 1, 72 n. 1; ep. 6, Gregory XII., 73 n. 1; ep. 7, 74 n. 1; ep. 10, 75 n. 1; ep. 13, 76 nn. 1, 2, 77 n. 1; Commentarius, 100 nn. 2, 3. Letter of Poggio to, 878. See Muratori.
Arevurdis, or children of the sun, iii. 587.
Arezzo, iii. 419. See Aretino.
Argæus, Mt., iii. 256 n. 2.
Ἀργαῦται, iii. 256 n. 2.
Argaum, city of the Paulicians, iii. 256, 587.
Argobast, ii. 99.
Argument a majori ad minus, Ægidius on, v. 15.

Ariald, iii. 389 n. 3. Preaches against the corruption in Milan, 390–394, 397. Assassinated at Milan, 398. Life of, by Andrew, see Andrew; by Landulph, see Landulph.
Arian sermons.
Maii, Script. vet. collectio nova, t. iii. 1823, f. 212, ii. 467 n. 3.
Arians. Arian controversy, i. 606 and n. 2, 720; ii. 91 n. 4, 134 n. 2, 224 n. 1, 255, 256, 268, 294, 409–473, 505, 740; iii. 170, 515. Arianism in India, ii. 140 n. 5. Among the Goths, 150 and n. 4, 156, 157. In Cappadocia, 155. Among the German tribes, 706 n. 2. View of the person of Christ, 478, *seq*. Theophilus, 142 n. 2, 144. Gregory Nazianzen, 385. Their activity among the newly converted nations, 472, 473; iii. 4 n. 1, 5 and nn., 39. Longobards, iii. 33, 34. Visigoths, 117. Indulgences, 137 n. 3. Expelled from the Roman empire, 5 1. 2. Arians and Origen, ii. 740.
Ariminum. See Rimini, Councils.
Aristides, discourses of, i. 73 n. 1. Eucom. Romæ, 88 n. 3. Letter to Hadrian, 101. Orat. sacr. 1, 103 n. 4. Apologist, 661.
Aristocracy of knowledge, iv. 385.
Aristocratic spirit of the ancient world, i. 29, 58, 70, 208, 268, 366, 378, 388, 540; ii. 158. In Platonism, i. 29, 34. In Judaism, 58. In Christianity, 366, 388. In Montanism, 524. Aristocratic constitution, 191. Element, 192. See under Priesthood.
Aristocritus, ii. 771.
Aristolaus, tribune, ii. 541, 544, 554, 555 n. 1.
Aristophanes, ii. 37 n. 2, 66 n. 2.
Aristotelian philosophy, study of the, iii. 169.
Aristotle. On mythology, i. 7 n. 1. On slavery, i. 46 n. 1, 267 n. 2, 268 nn. 1, 2. With Basilides, i. 408. With the Carpocratians, i. 449 (292). With the Artemonites, i 581. On moral freedom, i. 611. Among the Monophysites, ii. 613 (614). At Athens and in Armenia, ii. 613 n. 1. With Julian, ii. 62. Augustin, ii. 669. *Influence of*, *in the scholastic period*, iv. 356, 417–420, 429, 449, 450, 461. With Abelard, 392. With Richard of St. Victor, 413. Intellectus agens and possibilis, 434 n. 2. The book, De causis, 445 and nn. 1, 4. Anthropology, 488. In the scholastic doctrine of morals, 518–520, 523, 526, 527; of faith, 511. Nicetas, 537. Catharists, 557. Politics of, v. 26. With Wiclif, v. 165 n. 2, 166. Janow, v. 212. Hess, v. 263, 279.
Citations. Categor. § 7 (ed. Bekker, i. p. 8), doubt, iv. 392 n. 2. De anima, l. iii. c. 5, i. 426 n. 1. Ἐνέργεια, δύναμις, iv. 434 n. 2 Ethica, Eudem. l. iii. c. 3, the ταπεινός, i. 19

n. 1. Ethica magna, l. i. c. 34, woman, i.
281 n. 1; c. 34 (ed. Bekker, p. 1197), knowledge of God, i. 558 n. 5. Ethica Nicomach.
l. iii. c. 7, moral freedom, i. 611 and n. 3;
l. ix. c. 13, slavery, i. 267 n. 2, 268 n. 2; l.
x. c. 7, contemplative life, i. 628 n. 6. Met-
aphys. l. x. c. 8, on mythology, i. 7 n. 1.
Politics. l. i. c. 2, slavery, i. 46 n. 1, 268 n.
1; l. iii. c. 5, aristocratic position, i. 29 n. 3.

Arius, doctrine and history, ii. 254 n.,
403–414, 421–430, 445, 552. Doctrine
of the Holy Spirit, 466. Person of
Christ, 478, 483.

Arius, ad Alexandrinos (ap. Epiphan. hæres.
69, § 7), i. 716 n. 1; the Son of God, ii. 412
n. 2. Ad Eusebium, ii. 404 n. 2. Confession of faith, ii. 422, 428 n. 4.

Arles, bps. of, ii. 206, 207, 296, 643; iii.
13 n. 1, 14. Abp. of, iv. 603; v. 46.
See Cæsarius, Heros, Leontius.

Armagh, iv. 337. Richard, abp. of, v.
134.

Armanno Punzilovo, Catharist, iv. 584 n.
1, 585.

Armenia, persecution in, i. 153; ii. 127–
129. Invasion of, i. 489. Arsaces, ii.
86 n. 3. Founding of the Armenian
church, 136–138. Religious wars, 125
n. 1, 127–129, 135, 137, 138. Alphabet,
translation of Bible, literature, 137.
Meletius in, 457, 551. In the Nestorian
controversy, 556. Monophysites, 612;
iii. 261. Aphthartodocetism, iii. 261.
Paulicians in, 244–256, 261, 266, 587–
589. Fire-worship in, 589 n. 1. Euchites, 590, 591 n. 4. Armenian church,
588, 589 and n. 1. Animal sacrifices,
589 and n. 1. Agapæ, 589 n. 1. Canons, 589 n. 1. Pretended monk from,
iv. 52. Raymund Lull in, iv. 68. Hist.
of, see Moses Choronens., St. Martin.

Arno, abp. of Salzburg, iii. 77 n. 5, 105
n. 5, 122 n. 3, 156 n. 2. Among the
Huns (Avares), 82, 83. Among the
Moravians, 316.

Arnobius, i. 150 n. 1, 687–689.

Disputat. contr. gentes, l. i. c. 13, i. 689 n. 3;
l. i. c. 39, 688 n. 3; l. ii. c. 71, 689 n. 1; l.
iii. c. 7, 150 n. 1; l. iv. c. 36, 689 n. 4. Arno-
bii conflictus cum Serapione (Bibl. patr.
Lugd. t. viii.), 599 n. 3.

Arnobius the younger, ii. 702 n. 2, 706
n. 1 (704, 705).

Commentar. in Ps. 77, ii. 706 n. 2; Ps. 77, f.
280, Ps. 117, Ps. 126, Ps. 147, on predestination, iii. 706 n. 1. In Ps. 117, f. 305, 703 n.
1. In Ps. 146, f. 327. 702 n. 2. Prædestinatus, 702 n. 2. See Bibl. patr. Lugd. t. viii.

Arnold, Catharist bp., iv. 589.

Arnold, Franciscan companion of John
of Monte Corvino, iv. 57.

Arnold Hot, Waldensian, iv. 641.

Arnold of Brescia, iv. 147–152, 147 n. 1,
157, 160–162, 172, 180, 208, 268, 398,
626, 630; v. 138, 301.

Arnulph, abbot of Metz, on miracles, iii.
445 n. 2.

Life of John of Gorze, c. 1, § 4, iii. 445 n. 2.

Arnulph, abp. of Orleans, iii. 369, 370.

Arnulph, abp. of Rheims, iii. 368–375.

Arnulph of Carinthia, duke, iii. 320.

Arnulph, Sen., iii. 389 n. 3, 391 n. 4, 392
n. 3, 394 n. 1. Hildebrand, 393 n. 6.
Roman ambition, 394 n. 1.

Hist. Mediolapense (in Muratori script. hist.
Ital. t. iv.), l. 2, c. 27, the sect at Montfort,
iii. 690 n. 3. L. 3, c. 8, Ariald, iii. 390 n.
1; c. 9, Landulph, 392 n. 3, 393 n. 4; c. 11,
Patarenes, 383 n. 3; c. 12, Milanese clergy,
389 n. 3; c. 13, the Milanese, 395 n. 1.

Arras, sect there, iii. 597. Their doctrines, 597. Synod against them, 598.
Their reappearance, 599. See Gerhard.

Arrian, the stoic, Diatrib. l. iv. c. 7,
Christian intrepidity in view of death,
i. 159.

Arrius Antoninus, proconsul, i. 118.

Ars generalis, Raymund Lull, iv. 63, 65.
See Raymund.

Arsaces, king of Armenia, ii. 86 n. 3.

Arsacios, high priest, letter to, ii. 63 n. 1.

Arsenians, iv. 544, 550, 551.

Arsenius, patriarch of Constantinople, iv.
543, 544, 551.

Arsenoe, nome of, ii. 288 n. 3.

Art, opposition to, i. 291–293, 511, 536,
559; iii. 212–217, 236. Valentine, i.
425, 427. Mani, 488. Hermogenes,
565, 566. Objects of heathen art, ii.
35. Art and religion, 39, 75; iii. 198,
214. Works of, ii. 95 n. 4, 101. Relation of public worship to, ii. 319–331.
Irish, iii. 460 and n. 6. Theodore on,
iii. 540. In Cluniacensian monasteries,
iv. 252, 264. Bernard on, 264. Pagan,
14, 15. See Church buildings, Images,
Pictures.

Artabasdus, usurper, iii. 214.

Artemidorus.

Oneirocrit. l. 4, and l. 5, c. 18, ascetic philosophers, i. 275 n. 2.

Artemis, image of, ii. 66 n. 3.

Artemon, Artemonites, i. 580–582, 593
n., 601.

Artists, i. 262; iii. 201, 308; iv. 480.

Artisans, Christian, i. 70, 78. Comparison of the, iv. 479. Vocation of, v. 214.
In Prague, 288.

Arts, iii. 41, 42. Diffusion of the, 53,
118, 315 n. 1, 408 n. 2, 460; iv. 239,
249. Use of, iv. 377. Deceptive, i. 33.

Arverna (Clermont), iii. 93 nn. 2–4.

Ascelin, Dominican, iv. 49, 50.

Ascelin, monk, iii. 510 nn. 1, 2.

Ascensio Isaiæ (Ethiopic translation), ii.
776 n. 4. See Apocryphal writings.

Ascension, feast of, ii. 342. Of Christ,
733, 734.

Asceticism, of the Pharisees, i. 39. Essenes, 44, 45, 47–49. Jews in Egypt,
59–62, 64. Christian, 64, 159, 273–278,
520, 645. Ebionitic, 352, 353, 357.
Gnostic, 384, 416, 454, 455–458 and
n. 3. In India, 442. Manichean, 503.
Montanistic, 512, 515, 520–522, 525.
Egyptian, 713–715. With Marcion,

462, 472, 473. Origen, 696, 697. Clement on, 632. *In the second Period*, ii. 78, 129, 226, 227, 262-284. Jewish, 270 and n. 4 (263). Jovinian on, 304-307, 309. Arius, Basil, Eunomius, 445. Manichean, 770, 771. Priscillianist, 772, 778. Audians, 766 n. 3, 767. Influence of, 633. Ascetic dress with the Eustathians, 281 n. 1. *Third and fourth Periods.* Among the Irish monks, iii. 20, 21 n. 1, 30, 31. Severinus, 26. Anschar, 287. Odo, 417. Boniface on, 54 n. 1. Gregory on, 149. Benedict of Aniane on, 416. Berengar on, 504. Western, 146. In Italy, 418, 419, 451. In the sects, 266, 592, 600 n. 2, 601, 605. *Fifth Period.* Bernard, iv. 2. Otto, 5. Richmar, 79. Bernard of Clairvaux, 144, 241, 253. Thomas à Becket, 169 n. 3. Celestin V., 193. Hildegard on, 217. Monastic, 238, 241, 263. Cistercians, 263. Robert of Arbrissel, 246. Peter of Cluny, 249, 250. Francis of Assisi, 273-275. Laity, 302. Raymund Lull on, 310. Odo, 358, 359. Anselm, 365, 366. Thomas Aquinas, 524. Among the Catharists, 579-582. Other sects, 559, 593, 594. Dolcino, 633. *Sixth Period.* Militz, v. 174. Tauler on, 284, 385, 407, 408. Ruysbroch, 386. Merswin, 388. See Monasticism, Evangelical poverty.
Aschaffenburg. See Lambert.
Aschbach, Hist. Emp. Sigismund, 1. ii. 32, v. 326 n. 3.
Ascholius, bp. of Thessalonica, ii. 150 n. 3, 152, 155. Ep. to Cappadocia, 150 n. 3, 155; § 2, 155 n. 5.
Asclepiades, pagan philosopher, ii. 83.
Ascusnages, Monophysite, ii. 618.
Ἀσέβεια, i. 97 n. 1.
Ases, national gods of Norway, iii. 298.
Ash Wednesday, v. 4.
Asia, spread of Christianity in, i. 79-83; ii. 125-143; iii. 84-90, 181; iv. 45-59. Emigration from, iii. 307.
Asia Minor, propagation of Christianity from, i. 79, 84, 85, 86, 112, 115. Persecutions in, 103, 118. Cerinthus in, 396. Schools of Platonists in, ii. 39, 42. Patriarchs, 196 n. 3, 203. Relation to Constantinople, 197, 203. Quartodecimanians, 506 n. 3. Bishops of, at the council of Ephesus, 527, 528, 529, 533. In the Monophysite controversy, 586. Paulicians in, iii. 250-256. See Asiatic church.
Asiatic church. Church of Asia Minor, Apostle John and, i. 191, 194 n. 1. Excommunicated by Victor and Stephanus, 214, 215, 299. Passover festival, 297-300, 680. Baptism of heretics, 317, 318, 320. Patripassionists, 469. Anti-Gnostic tendency, 508, 674. Montanism, 509, 524, 525, 583. Monarchianism, 583. Character, 674. Teachers, 674-683.

Askelon, ii. 95.
Ἀσκῆται, i. 521. See Ascetics.
Aspebethos, Saracenic chief and bp., ii. 143.
Assassination of excommunicated persons, iv. 129 and n. 4.
Assemani. See Stephen Euodias.
Assembly, Christian places of, restored by Constantine, ii. 16.
Assembly, at Carthage, excommunicating Cæcilian, ii. 225. At Clarendon, iv. 170. Under Philip the Fair (an. 1303), v. 10-12. At Rome, under Louis IV. (an. 1328), 36. At Vincennes, under Philip (an. 1333), 37. At Vincennes, under Charles V. of France, 48, 49. At Prague (an. 1364), 191.
Assembly of presbyters, i. 192.
Asser, bp. of Sherburn, iii. 468.
Assisi, iv. 276, 311. See Francis of.
Assumption, festival of, iii. 134.
Assurance, iv. 513, 514. Wiclif on, v. 140, 172. Huss, v. 302. See State of grace.
Astacene, iv. 550.
Ἀστατοι, iii. 265.
Asterius, bp. of Amasea, ii. 68, 324, 326, 327, 350 n. 4, 371 n. 3, 406 n. 1, 438, 439 n. 5, 740 n. 2.

Adv. avaritiam (ed. Raben, Antwerp, 1615, f. 43), ii. 68 n. 3. De divite et Lazaro, 324 n. 6. On images, 326. In Phocam, 371 n. 3. Orat. on martyrdom of Euphemia, 327 n. 1.

Astorga (Asturica), i. 200 n. 1; ii. 776 n. 1.
Astrology, i. 103, 262, 442; ii. 34; iv. 55 n.
Astronomy, iii. 156 n. 1; iv. 357.
Astura, iii. 26 n. 2.
Asturica. See Astorga.
Asylum, right of, ii. 176-178; iii. 100, 104. Among pagans, iv. 10, 21.
Aterbius, ii. 746.
Athalstan, English king, iii. 293.
Athanaric, Gothic prince, ii. 151 n. 2, 152, 154, 156.
Athanasian creed, iii. 427. See Athanasius.
Athanasius. Characteristics and history, ii. 72-74, 423-451 n. 1, 456, 460. On Sabellius, i. 595 nn., 597-600 nn., 598, 600. On Paul of Samosata i. 602 n. 6, 603 n. 1. Dionysius of Alexandria and Dionysius of Rome, i. 606-608 nn. Accused of magic, ii. 22 n. 1. Against the use of force in religion, ii. 36. Insincere Christians ii. 37 n. 2. Biography of, ii. 67 n. 1, 72 n. 2, 73 n. 1, 80 n. 2. His fortunes under Julian, ii. 72-74, 78, 79. Frumentius, ii. 144. The Gothic Christians, ii. 150. The power of Christianity among the barbarians, ii. 159. Obtrusion into the priestly office, ii. 170 n. 2. Perio'icutai, ii. 193 n. 6. Filial churches at Rome, ii. 195 n. 1. Deposition, ii. 205, 206, 427, 432.

Penitents, ii. 203 n. 3. Date of ecclesiastical transactions, ii. 220 n. Meletius, ii. 254 n. Exile of Liberius, ii. 256. Anthony, ii. 263-269 nn. Extends the knowledge of Monachism in the West, ii. 294. Consecration of churches, ii. 322. Service on Friday, ii. 333 n. 1. Arius and the Arian controversy, ii. 406 n. 1, 423-456; iii. 170. Council of Nice, ii. 415-420 nn. Death of Arius, ii. 430 and n. 1. Doctrine of the Holy Spirit, ii. 468, 469 n. 2, 471 n. 4. Doctrine of creation, ii. 474. Person of Christ, ii. 483. Against Apollinaris, ii. 491, 492. The Lord's Supper, ii. 733. Origen, ii. 740. Rhetorius, ii. 767 n. 4. Confounded with Methodius, iii. 329 n.

Citations from his writings:—
Adv. Apollinaristas, l. i. § 13, ii. 491 n. 3.
Apolog. ad Constantium, § 3, accusation against Athanas., ii. 436 n. 4; § 17, places for prayer, ii. 322, n. 2; § 31, ep. of Constantius to the Abyssinian princes, ii. 144 n. 2.
Apolog. contr. Arianos, § 6, Athanasius and Arius, ii. 424 n. 1; § 20, presbyters of filial churches at Rome, ii. 195 n. 1; § 58, ep. of Ursacius and Valens, ii. 449 n. 5; § 59, Peter and Meletius, ii. 254 n. 1; ep. of Constantine to Athanas., ii. 425 n.; § 62, Constantine and Athanasius, ii. 426 n. 1; § 74 (ed. Patav. t. i. f. 151, n), περιοδεύειν, ii. 193 n. 6.
Contr. Apollinareum, l. i. § 6, Rhetorius, ii. 767 n. 4; l. 2, § 3, Paul of Samosata, i. 602 n. 6, 603 n. 1.
De decretis synodi Nicenæ, § 3, Eusebius, ii. 419 n. 3, 420 n. 1; § 20, Son of God, ii. 417 n. 3; § 21, Scriptural phrases, ii. 417 n. 2 (see Confession of Arius, 428 n. 4); § 26, subordination, i. 607 n. 1; Tritheism, i. 607 nn. 2, 3. Ἀνατροπή of Dionysius of Rome, i. 606 n. 5, 607 nn. 1-3.
De fuga sua, § 24, ii. 444 n. 1.
De incarnatione verbi, § 51, Goths, ii. 150 n. 2.
De sententia Dionysii, i. 606 n. 3, 608 n. 1; § 14, i. 606 n. 4.
De synodis, § 4, Samosatenian doctrine, i. 602 n. 6; § 43, ὁμοούσιον, i. 606 n. 1.
Ep. ad Afros, council of Nice, ii. 415 n. 1; § 5, the same, ii. 416 nn. 1, 3, 417 n. 3.
Ep. ad episcopos Ægypti et Lybiæ, § 13, conc. Nic. ii. 416 n. 3; § 18, confession of Arius, ii. 428 n. 4; § 19, death of Arius, ii. 430 n. 2.
Ep. ad Ruffinianum, ii. 456 n.
Epp. ad Serapionem, ep. i. § 24, doctrine of the Holy Spirit, ii. 468 n. 1, 469 n. 2; epp. i., iii., iv., the same, ii. 468 n. 2; ep. iv. on John 6: 62, ii. 733 n. 3; ep. de morte Arii, § 2, ii. 428 n. 4.
Hist. Arianor. ad monachos, §§ 20, 21, 50, Constantius, ii. 436 n. 4; § 33, force in religion, ii. 36 n. 2; § 37, Constantius, ii. 431 n. 1; § 57, force in religion, ii. 36 n. 4; § 64, Dioclesian persecution, i. 154 n. 5; § 70, Constantius, ii. 431 n. 1; § 71, Zenobia, i. 603 n. 7; § 78, insincere conversions, ii. 37 n. 2, 170 n. 2; § 81, Friday in Alexandria, ii. 333 n. 1; his flight, 444 n. 1.
Hom. in cœcum, §§ 9 and 12, περιοδεύτης, ii. 193 n. 6.
Life of Anthony, § 1, ii. 264 n. 4; § 2, ii. 265 n. 2; § 3, Egyptian ascetics, i. 713 n. 2, ii. 263 n. 1; § 38, ii. 265 n. 3; § 42, Anthony on spiritual conflicts, ii. 267 n.; § 48, advice of Anthony, ii. 268 n. 1; § 56, the same, ii. 268 n. 2; § 70, his appearance, ii. 268 n. 4; § 73, on books, ii. 269 n. 2; § 81, exhortations of, ii. 269 n. 1; on faith, ii. 269 nn. 3, 4.
Opp. t. i. P. 2, f. 68, Hieracas, i. 716 n. 1.
Orat. i. c. Arianos, § 5, doctrine of Arius, ii. 406 nn. 2, 3, 407 n. 1; § 6, the same, ii. 406 n. 4, 408 nn. 2, 3, 466 n. 2; § 16, the Son of God, ii. 424 n. 3; § 28, paternity of God, ii. 474 n. 2; § 29, the same, ii. 474 n. 3; § 48, doctrine of Arius, ii. 407 n. 2. Orat. ii. § 24, the same, ii. 406 n. 1. Orat. iii. § 26, the same, ii. 407 nn. 2, 4. Orat. iv. § 8, Sabellianism. i. 598 n. 4; § 11, the same, i. 597 nn. 1, 2; § 12, i. 598 n. 5, 600 n. 2; § 13, i. 595 n. 2; § 20, i. 598 n. 2; § 21, i. 598 n. 3; § 22, i. 598 n. 1; § 23, i. 599 n. 4; § 25, i. 595 nn. 3, 4, 597 n. 2, 598 n. 6, 599 n. 1, 600 n. 2.
Tomus ad Antiochen, § 5, council of Sardica, ii. 436 n. 3.

Atheism, Simplicius on, ii. 109. See Ἄθεοι.
Atheists, Eustathius on, iv. 531 and n. 5.
Athenæus.

Deipnosoph. l. i. § 36, the city of Rome, i. 204 n. 3.

Athenagoras. Character and criticism, i. 673. On Christianity, 78, 328 n. 4. Second marriage, 522 n. 4. Logos doctrine, 586 and n. 2. Apology, 665 n. 2, 673. Legat. pro Christianis, f. 37, ed. Colon, 328 n. 4, 522 n. 4.
Athenodorus, brother of Gregory Thaumaturgus, i. 718 n. 2.
Athens, i. 10; iv. 316. Paul at, i. 17 n. 2; ii. 133 n. 3. Seat of literary studies and of Hellenism, ii. 39 and n. 2, 45, 76-78, 104-106, 183. In the fifth century, ii. 106 n. 2. Aristotle at, ii. 613, n. 1.
Ἄθεοι, name applied to Christians, i. 92, 93, 111.
Ἀθεότης, i. 96 n. 3, 97 n. 1.
Athinganians, sect, iii. 269 n. 6, 593.
Atomistic system, i. 713 n. 1.
Atonement, Basilides on, i. 404. Doctrine of, iv. 497-508. Mercy and justice reconciled in the, iv. 506. Vicarious, iv. 505. See Satisfactio, Redemption.
Attacks on Christianity, i. 157-174.
Attalus, martyr, i. 113. Confessor, 276.
Atticus, bp. of Constantinople, ii. 135, 721, 762.
Attigny, iii. 79.
Attila, iii. 26.
Atto, bp. of Vercelli, iii. 469. Labors to improve the ch. constitution; against the corrupt manners of the clergy, 409, 411. Against judgments of God, 450. His writings, 469, 470 n. 1. De pressuris ecclesiasticis, 409 n. 1, 450 n. 3. Ep. ad clericos, 411 and n. 2. Works pub. by Buronti, 470 n. 1. See D'Achery, t. i. 416, 439.
Attractive power of the godlike, i. 402, 426.
Attributes of the divine essence, Origen on, i. 568, 570. Gnostic idea of, 373 and n. 3, 400. Irenæus on, 560. See Doctrine of God.

Ancher, works of John of Oznun, his Latin translation of, iii. 250 n. 1.
Audians. See Audius.
Audientes, Auditores, ii. 357. See Catechumens. Among the Manichaeans, i. 502–504; ii. 771; iii. 245. Catharist, iv. 580.
Auditor sacri palatii, v. 322.
Auditores. See Audientes.
Audius, Audians, ii. 766, 767.
Audoen, life of Eligius, iii. 41 n. 2.
Augsburg, iii. 405, 408, 411, 447. School at, iv. 143 n. 5. Projected assembly at (an. 1077), iv. 112–117. Berthold at, iv. 318.
Augsburg, bp. of, v. 326. See Augsburg.
Augurs, auguries, ii. 34; iii. 42.
Augustin, abbot in Rome, among the Anglo-Saxons, iii. 11–18, 23. Made a bishop, 14. Archbishop, 15. His primacy in the English church, 16. Seeks to form a union with the ancient British church, 16–18. His death, 18. Livin, 43 n. 1.
Augustin, bp. of Aquileia, ii. 652.
Augustin, bp. of Hippo, characteristics and history, ii. 394–402. Last years and death, ii. 694, 695. Monica, ii. 262, 754. Platonism, ii. 122–124. His religious and theological course of development, ii. 238, 239. Compared with Tertullian, i. 509 (C15, C83); ii. 394. And Origen, ii. 394. With Ambrose, ii. 679. Life by Possidius, ii. 168 n. 1. Influence on Western theology, i. 540; ii. 652 (see below). In North Africa, ii. 600. The old world and Christ, i. 77. Proverbial hatred against the Christians, i. 92. Porphyry, i. 171 n. 4. Committing to memory the confession of faith, i. 308 n. 3. Manicheans, i. 487 n. 4, 490 n. 2, 494–505 nn., 505. On Tertullian, i. 685. Victorinus, ii. 77 n. 1. Earthly reward, ii. 87 n. 4. Pagan landlords, destruction of temples, ii. 100, 101 n. 5, 102 nn. Robbery of pagans, ii. 103 n. 4. Secret worship among pagans, ii. 104 n. 2. Apology for Christianity, De civitate Dei, ii. 112–115. The oil press, ii. 112, 260. Self-righteousness among the pagans ii. 115. Miseducation, De catechizandis rudibus, ii. 116. Conversion, from external motives, ii. 118, 119. From superstitious motives, ii. 120. From fear, ii. 120. Proselytism, De fide et operibus, 121, 122. The Goths in Rome, ii. 160. Aurelius, the inheritances of the church, ii. 167, 168. Xenodochia, ii. 169 n. 1. Judicial authority of bishops, ii. 171 n. 3, 172 and n. 1. Intercession with Romulus, ii. 175. To Macedonius on intercessions, ii. 175 n. 5. Protection sought from the bishops, ii. 176 nn. Auxilius and the count, ii. 176 n. 5. Priesthood, De doctrina Christiana, ii. 179, 182. Canonical life, ii. 184. The rock, Peter, or Christ; visible church, ii. 200, 201, 239; v. 304. Œcumenical councils, progressive development of the church, ii. 209, 210. Test of truth, ii. 210, 697. Church discipline, ii. 214. Donatist controversy, ii. 218–223 nn., 225–227 nn., 230 nn. Augustin's participation in it, ii. 232–238. Only through the visible church to Christ, ii. 240, 241. Testimony of Scripture over against miracles, ii. 240. The testimony of Scripture dependent on that of the church, ii. 241; v. 27, 40. Purity of the church, ii. 241. The notion "world," in Scripture, ii. 242. De unitate ecclesiæ, ii. 243 n. 3, 247. Tichonius, ii. 244. Brings into prominence the objectively divine, ii. 245. The thing and not the person, ii. 246. Visible and invisible church, ii. 247. Compelle intrare, ii. 248–252. Paganized Christians, ii. 258 n. 1. Surface and essence of the Christian life, ii. 260. The truly pious exposed to contempt, ii. 260, 261. Anthony, ii. 264 n. 4. Anchorets, ii. 284. Augustin promotes Monachism, De opere monachorum, ii. 294, 295. Jovinian, ii. 312 n. 2 Against Jovinian, De bono conjugali ii. 313. The Christian life a divine service, ii. 315. Manuscripts of the Bible, ii. 316 n. 3. Study of the Bible, ii. 317, 318. Sign of the cross, ii. 323 and n. 4. Images, ii. 324 nn. 2, 5. The bodily beholding of Christ, ii. 327. Image worship, ii. 329. Diversity of religious customs, ii. 325; v. 92. Observance of the Sabbath, ii. 334, 335. Yearly festivals, ii. 337. Fasts, ii. 340 and n. 3. Thursday of the great week, ii. 341 n. 5. Octava infantium ii. 342 n. 2, 359 n. 1. Epiphany, i. 301 n. 2; ii. 343 n. 4, 344 n. 1. Faustus, ii. 347 n. 4. Christmas, ii. 348 n. 1. New Year's festival, ii. 350 n. 4, 351. Apportionments of the Bible read in church, ii. 352 n. 1. Extemporized discourses, ii. 353. Competentes, ii. 358 n. 3, 359 nn. 1, 3. Manus impositio, ii. 360 n. 1. The Missa, ii. 361 nn. 2, 3. Agapæ, ii. 262 n. 1. Liturgy with the Supper, ii. 362 n. 3. Daily or less frequent communion, ii. 364 and n. 5. Sacrifice in the Supper, ii. 366, 368, 369; iii. 135. St. Stephen's day, ii. 369. Miracles of the saints, ii. 370 n. 2. Parentalia, ii. 372. Views of honors paid to saints, ii. 372, 373. The central point of Christianity, ii. 386, 659. The Arian Maximin, ii. 473 n. 1. Doctrine of the Holy Spirit, Trinity, ii. 469, 470, 471 n. 4. Doctrine of the creation, of miracles, ii. 474–477. Augustin's Anthropology and Christology connected, ii. 495 n. 2. Influence

of Ambrose, ii. 622, 623 n. 4. Augustin's development in Anthropology, ii. 624-631. Sermon on the Mount, ii. 635 (114). Augustin and Pelagius, ii. 638. Cœlestius, ii. 639 nn. Augustin in the Pelagian controversy, De gestis Pelagii, ii. 640-643 and notes, 644 nn., 645-652. On the power of the state, and the Christian consciousness, against Julian, ii. 650, 653, 654. Leporius, ii. 655. Augustin's system compared with the Pelagian, ii. 658-684. Original condition, ii. 663, 664, 666, 667; iv. 485. See Anthropology. Freewill, ii. 626, 661, 662, 664, 665, 684, 685. Relation of Creation to the Creator, ii. 665. Sin, the fall, ii. 660-670 (626). Imputation of Adam's sin, ii. 665, 668-670. Ethics, pagan virtue, ii. 679-682. Ethics and doctrine, iii. 148. Grace, ii. 674, 675, 679, 682-687, 691. Redemption, ii. 624, 625, 675. Reconciliation, iv. 497, 505. Justification, ii. 678, 679; iv. 509; v. 302. Election, predestination, ii. 627-631, 684-687, 692, 693. Assurance, v. 172, 302. Præsciti, v. 350. Faith and reason, ii. 674. Semi-Pelagian controversy, ii. 687-694. Continued contest between the Pelagian and Semi-Pelagian parties in Gaul, ii. 695-712. Vincentius, ii. 697 n. 1. Prædestinatus, ii. 705, 706. Theodore of Mopsuestia and Augustin, ii. 712 and n. 3, 713, 717. Marius Mercator, ii. 721 n. 2. Doctrine of the sacraments, ii. 723-727. Chrysostom and Augustin, ii. 718, 726, 727; iii. 485. Baptism, limbus infantium, faith of children, ii. 726, 730, 731. The Lord's Supper, ii. 734, 735; v. 225. Purgatorial fire, ii. 736, 737. The classics, ii. 743. Jerome, ii. 750. Rhetorians, ii. 767 n. 4. Faustus, ii. 770 n. 4, 771 n. 3. Priscillianists, against lax morals, De mendacio, etc., ii. 775, 776 nn. 1, 5, 778 n. 5, 779; iii. 150, 350. *In the third and fourth Periods.* Influence and authority, iii. 60 n. 2, 456, 457, 471, 593. Amulets, iii. 64. Influence on Gregory the Great, iii. 143, 148, 150. Isidore of Seville, iii. 151. Fraus pia, iii. 350. Scotus, iii. 463. Gottschalk, iii. 473, 474, 480. Amulo, iii. 490. Servatus Lupus, iii. 483-485. Sect at Arras, iii. 598. Connection of ethics and doctrine, iii. 148. Relation of reason to faith, iii. 150, 463. To church tradition, iii. 471. Sin, the fall, iii. 474. Doctrine of the church, iii. 598. Grace, iii. 144, 483, 598. In the controversy on predestination, iii. 471-477, 480, 483, 484, 492, 493. On the Lord's Supper, iii. 496-498, 504, 506. In the Eastern and Western churches, iii. 553, 554. *In the fifth Period.* Influence, iv. 356, 368, 387, 420, 427, 457, 474, 492, 493, 495, 509, 515. In the question concerning the Lord's Supper, iv. 337. In the doctrine concerning sin, iv. 492, 493. On Odo, iv. 359. Anselm, iv. 361, 368, 369, 441. On Abelard, iv. 376, 387, 389, 392, 452 n. 7, 493. Hugo a St. Victor, iv. 401, 452 n. 7. Peter Lombard, iv. 409, 505. Roger Bacon, iv. 424, 434. Sect of the Holy Ghost, iv. 448. Thomas Aquinas, iv. 479. Pullein, iv. 516. Bernard, iv. 517. R. St. Victor, iv. 517. Franciscans, iv. 518. The Trinity, iv. 457. Evil subservient to good, iv. 479. Sinlessness of Christ, iv. 495. Principle of Christianity, iv. 510. Treatment of heretics, iv. 639. Catharists and Augustin, iv. 566 n. 2, 578 n. 5. *In the sixth Period.* With Marsilius of Padua, v. 27. Occam, v. 40. Gerson, v. 92. Wicklif, v. 141, 167, 172. Conrad, v. 187, 188. Janow, v. 212, 225. Huss, v. 240, 243 n. 1, 267, 302-304, 312, 343, 350, 353 n. 2, 362. On the Lord's Supper, v. 225.
Citations from his writings :—
Breviculus, collat. c. Donatistis, d. iii., tares and wheat, ii. 242 n. 2; d. iii. c. 13, Mensurius and the proconsul, i. 150 n. 2; (t. ix. opp. ed. Beu. f. 508), fanatical confessors, i. 151 n. 2; d. iii. c. 13, § 25, Mensurius, ii. 218 n. 1; Secundus, ii. 219 n. 1; d. iii. c. 20, § 38, two Donati, ii. 225 n. 4; d. iii. c. 21, § 39, petition of Donatists to Constantine, ii. 227 n. 4; d. iii. c. 27, § 30, assembly at Cirta, ii. 220 n. 1; Donatus of Casæ Nigræ, ii. 221 n. 4; N. 30, f. 296, Petilian on the name Donatist, 226 n. 2; N. 32, f. 296, name Donatist, 226 n. 2.
Collat. cum Maxim. Arian, § 26, Arian appeal to the Bible, ii. 473 n. 1.
Confessiones, ii. 240 n. 1. L. i. c. 20, humility, ii. 398 n. L. vi. § 18, manuscripts of the Bible, ii. 318 n. 8. L. vii. §§ 13, 14, intellectual pride, ii. 123 n. 2. L. viii. c. 2, *et seq.*, A. lays aside the rhetorical office, ii. 77 n. 1. L. x. c. 29, his prayer, ii. 638 nn. 2, 3. L. xiii. c. 11, Trinity in nature, ii. 470 n. 3.
Contra Academicos, l. ii. § 5, Platonic writings, ii. 397 n. 2. L. iii. § 43, ii. 399 n. 1.
C. Adimantum, c. 12, symbolism in the Lord's Supper, ii. 734 n. 1.
C. adversarium leg. et prophetarum, l. ii. c. 9, Lord's Supper, ii. 734 n. 2.
C. Cresconium, l. i. § 4, Cresconius on Augustin, ii. 232 n. 3. L. i. § 16, the same, ii. 233 n. 3. L. i. § 25, on dialectics, ii. 233 n. 4. L. ii. c. 1, § 2; the two Donati, ii. 225 n. 4; name Donatist, 226 n. 3. L. iii. c. 27, § 30, assembly at Cirta, ii. 220 n. 1. L. iv. c. 6, § 7, name Donatist, ii. 226 n. 1; f. 296, N. 30, the same, ii. 226 n. 2.
C. duas epistolas Pelagianorum, l. ii. § 5, Pelagians on the Roman clergy, ii. 651 n. 3. L. iv. § 20, ep. of Julian of Eclanum to Rufus, ii. 652 n. 2.
C. ep. Donati, ii. 201 n. 1.
C. epist. fundamenti, c. 5, claims of Mani, i. 487 n. 4; c. 8, βῆμα, i. 505 n. 5; c. 13, Mani on the Supreme God, i. 490 n. 2.
C. epist. Manichæi, § 6, "ego vero evang. non crederem," etc., ii. 241 n. 1.
C. epist. Parmenian, l. i. c. 1, Aug. on Tichonius, ii. 244 n. 4. L. i. cc. 1, 2, Tichonius on the church, ii. 244 n. 2. L. i. § 16, church and state, ii. 250 n. 3, 251 n. 2. L. ii. c. 13, number of sacraments, ii. 725 n. 4. L. ii. § 31, Donatist inconsistency, ii. 244 n. 3. L. iii. c. 12, *et seq.*, wheat and tares, ii. 242 n. 1. L. iii. c. 13, *et seq.*, the same, ii. 214 n. 2 L. iii. c. 17, ii. 244 n. 2.

C. Faustum Manich. ii. 771 n. 3; elect, i. 503 n. 2. L. 5, c. 1, boasts of the Manicheans, ii 770 n. 4. L. 11, F. on blind faith, i. 502 n. 3. L. 18, the same, i. 502 n. 3; c. 5, Sunday with Manicheans, i. 505 n. 4; βῆμα, 505 n. 5. L. 19, cc. 11, 16, symbols, ii. 724 n. 1. L. 20, Faustus on the Holy Spirit, i 494 n. 1. L. 20, c. 4, F. on participation of Christians in pagan festivals, ii. 347 n. 4, 349 and nn. 2, 3. L. 20, c. 18, sacrifice in the Lord's Supper, ii. 366 n. 6; c. 21, the same, ii. 367 n. ; c. 20, agapæ, ii. 362 n. 1. L. 21, c. 21, honors to martyrs, ii. 372 n. 3. L. 22, c. 73, pictures of Abraham and Isaac, ii. 324 n. 5. L. 26, c. 3, harmony of miracles with nature, i. 477 n. 3. L. 32, F. on the crucifixion, i. 500 n. 3; on the New Testament, i. 502 n. 1.
C. Felicem, l. i. c. 19, baptism with the Manicheans, i. 504 n. 3.
C. Fortunatum, l. i. app., Lord's Supper with Manicheans, i. 505 n. 2.
C. Gaudentium, l. i. § 20, church and state, ii. 250 n.; § 32, circumcellions, ii. 227 n. 1.
C. Julian, Pelag. l. i. § 21, Chrysostom on baptism, ii. 727 n. 2. L. ii. §§ 34, 37, Julian's complaints of oppression, ii. 653 n. 4. L. ii. § 36, a competent tribunal demanded, ii. 653 n. 5. L. iii. c. 1, § 3, edicts against Pelagians, ii. 651 n. 1. L. iii. § 8, Julian on sonship to God, ii. 676 n. 1. L. iv. c. 15, Augustin on grace and freedom, ii. 685 n. 1. L. iv. § 16, on the ethical principle, ii. 682 n. 2. L. iv. § 21, intention, ii. 681 n. 5. L. iv. § 24, Rom. 14: 23, ii. 681 n. 1. L. iv. § 26, virtues of pagans, ii. 580 n. 2. L. iv. § 27, the same, ii. 681 n. 3. L. iv. § 28, Julian on the possibility of a sinless life, ii. 681 n. 7; Augustin on the danger of pride, ii. 683 n. 3. L. iv. § 33, intention, ii. 681 n. 4. L. iv. § 65, Aug. on concupiscence, ii. 668 n. 1. L. v. cc. 1, 2, traducianism, ii. 653 n. 3. L. v. § 4, wisdom of the simple, ii. 605 n. 1. L. v. § 17, on temptation, ii. 667 n. 3. L. v. § 35, on sin as penalty, ii. 669 n. 2. L. vi. § 37, Zosimus, ii. 651 n. 3. L. vi. § 75, Adam and the race, ii. 669 n. 3.
C. Julian, opus imperfectum, l. i., Julian on harmony of reason and revelation, ii. 673 n. 4. L. i. c. 51, J. organ of his party, ii. 653 n. 1. L. i. c. 67, J. on sin as habit, ii. 671 n. 3. L. i. c. 76, freedom as state and faculty confounded by A., ii. 684 n. L. c. 79, J. on morality, ii. 681 n. 2. L. i. c. 94, J. on the love of God, ii. 677 n. 1. L. ii. c. 2, complaints of Julian, ii. 653 n. 6, 654 n. 2. L. ii. c. 14, A. on use of force against heretics, ii. 650 n. L. ii. c. 56, J. origin of sin in the individual, ii. 669 n. 3. L. ii. c. 103, complaints of J., ii. 653 n. 7; reply of A., ii. 654 n. 1. L. ii. c. 116, J. on infant baptism, ii. 729 n. 2. L. ii. c. 165, on justification, ii. 677 n. 3. L. ii. c. 166, on the power of Christ's love, ii. 677 n. 2. L. ii. c. 188, on Christ as teacher, ii. 676 n. 2. L. ii. c. 212, on baptismal grace, ii. 729 n. 3. L. ii. c. 227, on the effect of faith on the life, ii. 678 n. 1. L. iii. § 35, remonstrances of J., ii. 651 n. 2. L. iii. c. 106, J. on insufficiency of reason, cultus Dei, ii. 673 n. 3. L. iii. c. 111, on Theodore, ii. 712 n. 1. L. iii. c. 114, on God's inworking, ii. 675 n. 4. L. iii. c. 117, A. on impossibility of equipendency between good and evil, ii. 661 n. 2. L. iii. c. 149, J. on infant baptism, ii. 729 n. 1. L. iii. c. 172, letter of Mani to the virgin Menoch, i. 498 n. 1. L. iii. c. 174, the same, i. 496 n. 1. L. iii. c. 177, the same, i. 499 nn. 2, 3. L. iii. c. 180, the same, i. 496 n. 3, 499 n. 1. L. iii. c. 187, the same, i. 498 n. 4. L. iv. c. 35, J. on sin as punishment, ii. 669 n. 2. L. iv. c. 38, on concupiscence, ii. 667 n. 2; A. on the same, ii. 668 n. 3. L. iv. c. 50, J. on the humanity of Christ, ii. 655 n. 2. L. v. c. 2, et seq., and l. vi. init., J. on the importance of the points in dispute, ii. 650 n. 2 Ll. v. et vi., citations from Julian on moral freedom, ii. 661 n. 1. L. vi. cc. 1, 2, J. on courage in defense of truth, ii. 653 n. 3. L. vi. c. 10, A. on freedom and necessity, ii. 661 nn. 4, 5.
C. literam Petiliani, l. i. § 8, validity of sacraments, ii. 246 n. 2. L. ii. § 146, Fasir and Axid, ii. 230 n. 3. L. ii. §§ 178, 180, Donatist inconsistency, ii. 248 n. 1. L. ii. § 184, the Donatist baker, ii. 232 n. 1; church and state, ii. 250 n. 1. L. ii. § 202, Marcellinus, bp. of Rome, iii. 372 n. 1. L. ii. c. 92, § 205, laws against the party of Majorinus, ii. 225 n. 2. L. ii. c. 92, § 208, death of Ursacius, ii. 226 n. 4. L. ii. § 210, A. on vocation of kings, ii. 250 n. 4, 251 n. 1. L. ii. § 247, the rock, ii. 297 n. 3. L. iii. § 3, A. on the church, ii. 246 n. 3.
C. partem Donati, ii. 234 n. 4.
De anima et ejus orig. l. i. § 26, continual creative agency of God, ii. 671 n. 1; Vincentius Victor, 671 n. 2.
De baptismo contra Donatistos, l. ii. § 3, Authority of councils, ii. 210 n. 1. L. v. § 31, baptism of heretics, ii. 360 n 1.
De baptisme contra Petil. § 27, innocence of Marcellinus, iii. 372 n. 1.
De bono conjugali, ii. 3E3.
De catechizandis rudibus, ii. 116; c. 5, change of mind effected through instruction, ii. 118 n. 2, motives of converts, ii. 120 n. 2; c. 6, spiritual instruction, ii. 120 n. 1; c. 9, hearing of Scripture, ii. 116 n. 2; c. 12, gradual conversion, ii 122 n.; c. 26, salt in baptism, ii. 359 n. 3; c. 48, worldly Christians, ii. 258 n. 1.
De civitate Dei, ii. 113, 115; Porphyry, i. 171 n. 4. L. i. c. 7, Alaric in Rome, ii. 160 n. 3. L. ii. c. 19, submission to government, ii. 113 n. 4. L. v. c. 25, earthly rewards, ii. 87 n. 4. L. v. c. 31, Varro on images, i. 9 n. 5. L. vi. c. 5, et seq., Varro quoted, i. 7 n. 3. L. x. c. 6, sacrifice in the Supper, ii. 308 n. 4. L. xi. c. 5, antinomies, ii. 475 n. 2. L. xi. c. 12, § 14, limits of knowledge, ii. 475 n. 6 L. xi. c. 24, procession of the Holy Spirit, ii. 471 n. 4. L. xii. c. 15, § 2, temporal and eternal being, ii. 475 n. 1. L. xii. c. 15, § 3, confession of ignorance, ii. 475 nn. 3, 4; growth in knowledge n. 5. L. xii. c. 25, preservative agency of God, ii. 665 n. 1. L xviii. c. 5s, temples destroyed at Carthage, ii 101 n. 5. L. xix. c. 23, the oracle of Apollo, i. 172 n. 2. L. xx. c. 25 and l. xxi. cc. 13, 24, purgatory, ii. 736 n. 3.
De consensu evangelistorum, l. i. § 10, pictures of Paul with Christ and Peter, ii. 324 n. 2.
De correptione et gratia, ii. 686, 690; §§ 27, 28, destiny of unfallen man, ii. 664 n. 2; § 31, necessity of grace, ii. 664 n. 3; § 32, the same, ii. 664 n. 1.
De diversis quæstionibus ad Simplicianum (on Rom. 9), ii. 630. L. . Q. 2, Rom. 9, ii. 650 n. 3; § 5, election, i. 630 n. 4; § 13, the same, ii. 630 n. 5, 631 n.
De diversis quæstionibus octoginta tribus, ii. 628; § 4, conditions of grace, hardening of Pharaoh, ii. 628 nn. , 3; § 5, the same, ii. 628 n. 4, 629 nn. 1, 3. Q. 61, § 4, love the principle of virtue, ii. 682 n. 1.
De doctrina Christiana, . ii. c. 11, translations of the Bible, i. 308 n. 1. L. ii. § 60, appropriation of the good, ii 743 n. 1. L. iii. § 13, the prophets, ii. 725 n. 1. L. iii. § 43, Tichonius on the body of Christ, ii 245 n. 1. L. iii. § 45, ii. 247 n. 3.
De dono perseverantiæ ii. 691, 692; c. 20, turning-point in Augustine's views, ii. 630 n. 2; § 49, Ambrose and the doctrine of grace, ii. 623 n.
De fide c. Manicheos, c. i. (opp. ap. vol. viii. ed. Ben.), cp. fundamenti, i. 490 n. 6.
De fide et operibus, ii. 638 n. 1; § 9, on preparation for baptism, ii. 121.
De Genesi ad literam, l. v. § 40, continued creative agency of God, ii. 476 n. 2. L. vi.

§ 17, creation potential, ii. 476 n. 1. L. vi. § 25, seminal principles, ii. 477 n. 2. L. ix. § 32, the same, ii. 477 n. 1.

De Genesi c. Manich. l. ii. § 39, the serpent, i. 497 n. 3.

De gestis Pelagii, ii. 644 n. 4. Pelag. on the punishment of the wicked, ii. 643 n. 2; § 26, letter of Pelagius to Aug., ii. 640 n. 1; § 54, the consultations at Bethlehem, ii. 643 n. 1; § 57, propositions of Celestius, ii. 644 n. 2; § 61, origin of Pelagianism, ii. 639 n. 1.

De gratia Christi, § 4, Pelagius on freedom, ii. 663 n. 1; § 8, on grace, ii. 675 nn. 1, 2; § 11, on Phil. 2: 13, ii. 675 n. 3; § 14, A. on the Pelagian definition of grace, ii. 675 n. 6; § 21, on the roots of good and evil, ii. 661 n. 3; §§ 30, 32, 33, Pelagius, ep. to Innocent I., ii. 645 n. 3; § 33, Pelagians on freedom and grace, ii. 673 n. 1; § 52, A. on grace and justification, ii. 678 n. 3.

De gratia et libero arbitrio, ii. 686; § 33, coöperating grace, ii. 683 n. 2.

De haeresibus, c. 32, ecclesiastical system of Mani, i. 504 n. 2; h. 70, Priscillianists, commonitorium of Orosius, ii. 776 n. 1; h. 72, Rhetorians, ii. 767 n. 4; h. 82, Jovinian, ii. 312 n. 2; h. 86, Tertullian, i. 685 n. 1.

De libero arbitrio, ii. 625. L. iii. c. 23, intermediate state for unbaptized infants, ii. 730 n. 2.

De mendacio ad Consentium, ii. 779 n. 2.

De moribus eccles. Cath., ii. 240 n. 1, 401 n. 4. L. i. § 31, love the source of knowledge of God, ii. 401 n. 1; § 35, objections of Manicheans, i. 504 n. 3; § 37, knowledge and life, ii. 400 n. 2; § 47, knowledge from love, ii. 400 n. 1; § 66, anchorets, ii. 284 nn. 3, 4; § 75, image worship, i. 329 nn. 3, 4.

De moribus Manichaeorum, ii. 240 n. 1, 401 n. 4, 625; c. 10, et seq., signaculum, i. 503 n. 3.

De natura boni, c. 46, Mani on the formation of man, i. 495 nn. 2, 3.

De natura et gratia, §§ 42, 43, sinlessness of Mary, and others, ii. 672 n. 1; § 44, of Abel, ii. 672 n. 2.

De nuptiis et concupiscentia, l. i. § 2, to Valerius, force in religion, ii. 650 n. 1. L. i. § 17, marriage as a sacrament, ii. 725 n. 6.

De opere monachorum, ii. 295, v. 141; § 36, by hypocrisy among monks, ii. 296 n. 1.

De ordine, ii. 240 n. 1. L. i. § 11, retraction of Platonic expressions, ii. 399 n. 2. L. ii. § 26, order of reason and faith, ii. 401 n. 2.

De peccato originale, c. 2, seq., Celestius, ii. 640 n. 4; c. 5, Celestius on infant baptism, ii. 728 n. 4; cc. 5, 6, 23, Celestius on sin, ii. 648 n. 1; c. 13, Celestius and Pelagius, ii. 639 n. 2; cc. 17, 21, ep. of Pelagius to Innocent I., ii. 645 n. 2; c. 29, A. on Adam and Christ, ii. 386 n. 1, 659 n. 5; c. 29, grace, under the law, ii. 679 n.

De peccatorum meritis et remissione, l. i. § 58, intermediate state, ii. 730 n. 5. L. ii. § 5, relation of reason to God, ii. 663 n. 2. L. ii. § 29, grace unconditional, ii. 495 n. 2. L. ii. § 59, traducianism, ii. 671 n. 2. L. iii. § 3, character of Pelagius, ii. 632 n. 3. L. iii. § 14, relation of men to Adam, ii. 668 n. 5.

De perfectione et justitiae hominis, § 39, on the remains of sin, ii. 683 n. 1.

De praedestinatione sanctorum, ii. 691, 692.

De spiritu et litera, ii. 678 n. 4.

De Trinitate, l. iii. c. 10, §§ 19, 20, symbol of Christ's body, ii. 734 n. 3. L. xiii. c. 10, § 13, atonement, iv. 498 n. 1. L. xiii. c. 11, § 15, the same, iv. 497 n. 1. L. xv. § 27, Holy Spirit, ii. 470 n. 3. L. xv. § 29, procession of the Spirit, ii. 471 n. 4.

De unitate ecclesiae, § 7, conditions of membership, ii. 240 n. 1; § 33 et seq., number of the faithful, ii. 248 n. 3; § 37, Donatists on the predicate Catholic, ii. 244 n. 1; §§ 47, 50, testimony of the word, ii. 240 nn. 5, 6; § 49, Christ and the church, ii. 240 nn. 2, 3; § 74, outward communion, ii. 247 n. 4.

De utilitate credendi, ii. 240 n. 1, 401 n. 4.

De vera religione, ii. 240 n. 1, 401 n. 4, 625, iii. 431; § 13, being of the Holy Spirit, ii. 470 n. 3.

Enchiridion ad Laurentium, § 68, purgatorial fire, ii. 736 nn. 5, 6, 737 n. 1.

Epistolae. Ep. 22, ad Aurelium, § 6, offerings for the dead, ii. 369 n. Ep. 29, ad Alypium, feasts at graves of martyrs, ii. 372 n. 2. Ep. 36, ad Casulanum, on diversity of religious customs, ii. 395 n. 1. Ep. 44 (an. 398), proposition to Fortunius, Donatist, ii. 233 n. 1; § 9, times of the O. T. and N. T. distinguished, ii. 234 n. 3. Ep. 50, massacre at Suffetum, ii. 102 n. 2. Ep. 54, ad Januarium, yearly festivals, ii. 387 n. 2; use of sacraments, ii. 725 n. 1; § 3, diversity of customs in religion, ii. 395 n. 1; § 4, daily communion, ii. 364 n. 5; § 9, Holy Thursday in the N. A. church, ii. 341 n. 5. Ep. 55, ad Januarium, right use of sacraments, ii. 725 n. 1; § 53, octava infantium, ii. 342 n. 2. Ep. 73, § 8, to Jerome, on his quarrel with Rufinus, ii. 750 n. 1. Ep. 76, to the Donatist churches, ii. 234 n. 2. Ep. 78, § 3, a martyr's church at Milan, ii. 370 n. 2. Ep. 88, § 3, party of Majorinus condemned, ii. 225 n. 2. Epp. 90, 91, uproar against the Christians at Calame, ii. 102 n. 2. Ep. 93, ad Vincentium, on compulsion in religion, ii. 251 nn. 2, 3; § 17, conc. Carthag. (an. 404), ii. 235 n. 1. Ep. 98, ad Bonifacium, § 10, infant baptism, ii. 731 n. 1; sacramentum fidei, ii. 734 n. 3. Ep. 101, ad Memorium (father of Julian of Eclanum), ii. 652 n. 6. Ep. 102, to Deogratias, §§ 14, 15, on predestination, ii. 629 n. 3. Ep. 104, the uproar at Calame, ii. 102 n. 2. Ep. 118, use of sacraments, ii. 725 n. 3. Ep. 120, ad Consentium, harmony of faith and reason, ii. 402 n. 1. Ep. 128, proposals to the Donatists, ii. 236 n. 1. Ep. 136, ad Marcellin., evils under Christian princes, ii. 113 nn. 1, 2; mild treatment of circumcellions recommended, ii. 249 n. 2. Ep. 138, ad Marcellin., on evils experienced under Christian princes, ii. 113 n. 3; ancient civic virtues, n. 5; precepts of Christ and the state, ii. 114 n. 1. Ep. 143, § 3, ad Marcellin. disclaiming authority to decide matters of doctrine, ii. 694 n. 2. Ep. 146, ad Pelagium, ii. 640 n. 1. Ep. 152, from Macedonius, on intercessions, ii. 175 n. 5. Ep. 153, to M. on the same, ii. 175 n. 5. Ep. 185, § 24, ad Bonifacium, compulsion in religion, ii. 251 n. 4; § 18, violence of the circumcellions, ii. 230 n. 4; § 21, use of suffering, ii. 249 n. 3; § 25, conc. Carthag. (an. 404), ii. 235 nn. 1, 2. Ep. 186, ad Paulinum, on Pelagius, ii. 632 nn. 2, 3. Ep. 193, reply to Marius Mercator, ii. 721 n. 2. Ep. 194, ad Sixtum, on grace and predetermination, ii. 686 n. 1. Ep. 213, gesta eccles. Augustini, ii. 171 n. 3. Ep. 217, see ep. 252. Ep. 234, from Longinianus, a pagan, on the way to God, ii. 115 n. 5. Ep. 237, ad Ceretium, the Priscillianists, Christ's hymn of thanks, ii. 778 n. 5. Ep. 247, to Romulus, a landlord, ii. 175 n. 3. Ep. 250, asylum, case of Classicianus, ii. 176 n. 5. Ep. 252 (or 217), guardianship of bishops, ii. 176 n. 2. Ep. 268 (or 215), ad plebem, asylum, ii. 176 n. 4. Ep. ad Honorarium, in time of persecution, v. 312.

Explicatio propositi. quarundum, de ep. ad Rom., ii. 627 n. 1; c. 60, gift of the Spirit, ii. 627 nn. 2, 3.

Expositio Galat. c. 3 § 19, sacraments, understanding of the, ii. 725 n. 1.

Gesta ecclesiastica Augustini, ii. 171 n. 3.

Guide to the education of the clergy, ii. 743.

Hypomnesticon, iii. 366 n. 1.

In Evang. Johann. Tr. 8, § 1, miracles, ii. 477 n. 4. Tr. 25, c. 10, sordid motives for receiving Christianity, ii. 118 n. 1. Tr. 26, unworthy communicants, ii. 735 n. 3. Tr. 30, § 4, presence of Christ, ii. 327 n. 5. Tr. 80,

§ 3, symbols in Christianity, ii. 724 n. 1. Tr. 97, § 4, Xenodochia, ii. 169 n. 1. T. 99, §§ 8, 9, procession of the Spirit, ii. 470 n. 1, 2. Tr. 110, § 6, reconciliation with God, iv. 497 n. 2. Tr. 124, § 5, the rock, ii. 210 n. 1. In Psalm. Ps. 10, § 5, "per canos Donati," ii. 225 n. 3. Ps. 25, En. ii. § 13 (l. iv. f. 115), arbitration of bishops, 172 n. 1; En. ii. § 14, self-righteousness of pagans, ii. 115 n. 3. Ps. 31, En. ii. § 2, pagan self-righteousness, ii. 115 n. 2. Ps. 32, S. 2, § 13, sign of the cross, ii. 323 n. 4. Ps. 36, S. i. § 2, Bibles sold publicly, ii. 316 u. 3. Ps. 45, § 7, book of creation, ii. 318 n. 8. Ps. 48, S ii. § 4, dislike of piety, ii. 201 n. 2. Ps. 66, §§ 3, 10, on study of the Word, ii. 318 nn. 5, 6. Ps. 73, § 6, sign of the cross, ii. 323 n. 4. Ps. 80, § 1, the oil press, ii. 260 n. Ps. 90, S. i. § 4, abuse towards pious Christians, ii. 261 n. 1. Ps. 132, § 6, circumcelliones, agonistici, ii. 227 n. 1. Ps. 138, § 1, extempore preaching, ii. 353 n. 6. Ps. 140, § 20, paganism propagated secretly, ii. 104 n. 2.
On the festivals and fasts, ii. 340 n. 3 341 n. 8, 342 n. 2, 343 n. 4, 344 n. 1.
Pelagian confession of faith, ii. 652 nn. 3, 4. Quæst. in Levit. l. iii. Q. 84, sign and substance, ii. 724 n. 2.
Retractationes, ii. 694. L. i. c. 3, Platonic language, ii. 390 n. 2. L. i. c. 21, the rock, Christ, ii. 201 n. 1. L. i. c. 26, De diversis quæst. oct. trib., ii. 628 n. 1. L. ii. c. 5, Contra partem Donati, ii. 234 n. 4. L. ii. c. 22, Jovinian at Rome, ii. 312 n. 2.
Sermons, ii. 350 n. 4, 362 n. 3, on 1 ep. Johann. prolog., Scriptures read in the churches, ii. 352 n. 1. S. i. on Ps. 36, and S. i. on Ps. 90, and S. ii. on Ps. 32, and S. ii. on Ps. 48, see In Psalm. S. 2, § 13, sign of the cross, ii. 328 n. 4. S. 15, § 9, the oil press, ii. 112 n. 5. S. 20, § 1, Christmas, ii. 348 n. 1. S. 24 (t. v. ed. Ben.), against popular excitement against idolatry, ii. 100 n. 2; § 17, 100 n. 4; f. 62, pretexts for persecution of Christians, n. 3. S. 46, § 39 (t. v. ed. Ben. Paris f. 146, D.), Secundus of Numidia and the church at Carthage, ii. 221 n. 5. S. 47, § 17, conversion within the church, ii. 119 n. 1. S. 49, § 8, missa catechumenorum, ii. 361 nn. 2, 3. S. 71, § 18, Holy Spirit, ii. 470 n. 3. S. 94, the church in the house, ii. 315 n. 6. S. 105, § 3, light to be sought from God, ii 317 n. 2. S. 161, § 4, intercessions, ii. 176 r. 1. S. 176, § 2, guardianship of bps. and churches, ii. 176 n. 2. S. 179, § 5, on treatment of pagans, ii. 103 n. 4. S. 202, § 2, Epiphany; Donatists, i. 801 n. 2. S. 212, committing to memory the confession of faith, i. 508 n. 3; symbolum, i. 307 n. 2; § 1, Holy Spirit, ii. 470 n. 3. S. 216, competentes, ii. 258 n. 3. S. 231, Hist. resurrect. read in Easter week, ii. 352 n. 1. S. 232, § 1, appointed reading of the Gospels, ii. 352 n. 1. S. 239, the same, ii. 352 n. 1. S. 285 and 272, inward and outward reception of Christ's body, ii. 735 n. 3. S. 294, § 3. intermediate state, ii. 730 n. 5. S. 302, § 3, sign of the cross, ii. 323 n. 5. S. 356, § 5, Aurelius and the gift, ii. 167 n. 5. S. 358, § 4, proposals to the Donatists, ii. 236 n. 1. S. 368, § 3, intercessions, ii. 176 n. 1. S. 370, § 2, the veil in baptism, ii. 359 n. 1. Sermon, opp. app. t. v. f. 279, § 5, amulets, iii. 443 n. 2.
Works, ed. Ben., ep. of Mani to Patricius, i. 497 n. 1.
Augustin, order of St., Augustinians, v. 13, 183.
Augustin, rule of St., iv. 208, 270.
Augustinian doctrine, philosophy, scheme, spirit, iii. 143, 471–477, 480, 482–485, 492, 493; iv. 251 n. 1, 360, 369, 387, 474, 515, 516, 518; v. 167, 212. See Augustin.

Augustus Cæsar, i. 87, 116.
Aulus Gellius, Noctes Atticæ, l. xii. c. 11, i. 158.
Aurelian, edict of, i. 108. Situation of the Christians under, i. 141, 142, 605.
Aurelius, bp. of Carthage, ii. 167, 295, 651 n. 1. Ep. of, 652 n. 1.
Aurelius, martyr in Spain, iii. 341.
Auricular confession, iii. 139 n. 7; iv. 284. Introduction of, iv. 353. See Confession.
Aurillac, iii. 470 n. 3; iv. 423.
Aurilly. See Gerald of.
Ansonius, on Gratian, ii. 92 n. 2.
Anstie, v. 299.
Australian Antinomianism, i. 385.
Austria, v. 183, 184.
Antarchy, in Stoicism, i. 16.
Autbert, monk, iii. 275, 276.
Authority, belief on, ii. 401; iv. 449. Scotus on, iii. 463. Abelard, iv. 374.
Authority of rulers, iv 109, 131, 132; v. 8, 18, 99, 269, 270. Of the church. See Church.
Auto da fe, iii. 344 n. 4.
Autolycus, i. 674.
Autun (Augustodunum), persecution at, i. 114, 115. Constantine at, ii. 8.
Auvergne, iii. 432 n. 4, 470 n. 3; iv. 125, 249. See William of.
Auxentius, bp. of Dorostorus, life of Ulphilas, 150 n. 4, 151 and notes, 152 nn., 157 and n. 5, 472 n. 1.
Auxentius, bp. of Milan, ii. 471, 472.
Auxentius, grotto of, iii. 220.
Auxerre (Antissiodorensis), iii. 497 n. 1. See Councils, an. 578.
Auxiliaris, præfect. urbis, ii. 207 n. 3.
Auxilius, bp., ii. 176 n. 5.
Auxuma, Anxumites, ii. 144, 145 (444).
Avares (Huns), planting of Christianity among them, iii. 39, 82–84.
Ave Maria, iv. 627.
Averrhoës, iv. 70, 426, 431, 449; v. 263.
Averrhoïsts, iv. 70 n. 1.
Aversa, iii. 470 n. 4. See Guitmund.
Avignon, library at, iv. 637 n. 1. Clement V. in, iv. 70. Clement VII. in, v. 48. The papal court in, v. 21–23, 37, 44–48, 56, 57, 66, 67, 71, 97, 136, 160, 182, 183, 232. Alvarus in, iv. 633 n. 2.
Avilla, ii. 772.
Avitus, bp. of Vienne, his labors among the Burgundians, iii. 4, 5 and nn. 2, 4. On the reconsecration of the churches of heretics, iii. 5 n. 4. Gundobad, iii. 9 n. Judgments of God, iii. 130.
Ep. 1, missa, ii. 361 n. 3. Ep. 28 (opp. Sirmond, ii. f. 44), to Gundobad iii. 39 n. 3. Ep. 41, to Clovis, iii. 6 nn. 1, 2, 8 nn. 2, 5.
Avitus, monk, ii. 291.
Awakenings, religious, iv. 125–127, 154–156, 293, 315, 355. See Reformation.
Axid, ii. 230.
Aybert, iv. 238.
Aymar, reformer of Monachism, iii. 418.

Azades, Persian martyr, ii. 132.
Azymites, iii. 584.

B.

Baal worship in Edessa, i. 80. Relic of, in Carthage, i. 124. Priests of, v. 97.
Baanes, ὁ ῥυπαρός, head of the Paulicians, iii. 250, 266.
Babæus, patriarch of Seleucia, Nestorian, ii. 611.
Babylas, bp. of Antioch, i. 126 n. 6.
Babylas, martyr, ii. 82, 94.
Babylon, i. 79 n. 4. Rome compared to, i. 96; ii. 745. School at Tours, iii. 515 n. 6. Sultan of, iv. 60 n. 2. In the Apocalypse, Joachim on, iv. 222, 223. Oliva, iv. 624, 625. The Apostolicals, iv. 628, 635 n. 1. Arnold Hot, iv. 641. Janow, v. 216. Huss on, v. 360.
Bacchins, ii. 67 n. 2.
Bacchus, worship of, i. 513. Myth of, i. 539. Temple of, ii. 97.
Bachiarius, monk, De fide, Ad Januarium, ii. 775 n. 6.
Bacon. See Roger.
Bactria, i. 80.
Bacurius, Iberian chief, ii. 139 n. 1.
Baden, Hans of, v. 326.
Baggiolini, Christofero.
Dolcino e i Patareni, iv. 629 nn. 2, 3, 633 n. 2.
Bagnarea, iv. 421.
Bailiffs, iii. 101 n. 4.
Bal Cernay.
Chronicle of, iv. 570 n. 4.
Balaam, i. 452, 453 n. 3.
Balbinus.
Epitome hist. rer. Bohem. f. 54, Life of Wenzeslav, iii. 322 n. 1. Ed. life of Militz, v. 180 n. 1, 183 n. 1. (Misc. hist. regni Bohem., Pragae, 1682, decadis i., l. iv. P. ii. tit. 34, f. 44), life of Militz, v. 174 n. 3. Same, f. 35, 175 nn. 1, 2; f. 46, 176 n. 2.
Baldrich, bp. of Dole.
Chronique d'Arras et de Cambray (ed. Par. 1834), l. i. f. 114, Fulbert, iii. 405 n. 1; c. 46, penance for a master, iii. 452 n. 1; c. 47, a "pious fraud," iii. 407 n. 1; c. 88, rudeness of clergy, iii. 410 n. 3. Ed. Le Glay, app. f. 373, signs from heaven, iv. 127 n. 2. Second app. f. 356, etc., sect at Arras and Cambray, iii. 600 n. 1. Hist. Hierosol. (see Bongars). the Crusades, iv. 126 n. 2, 127 nn. 1, 3, 4. Life of Robert of Arbrissel, § 23, iv. 247 n. 2.
Baldwin, nobleman, iii. 453 n. 3.
Balearean islands, iv. 61.
Ballads, German, iv. 188.
Balle, John, v. 158-160.
Ballerini, ed. opp. Ratherii. See Ratherius.
Balthazar Cossa, cardinal, v. 89, 90, 340, 342. See John XXIII.
Baltic Sea, iv. 16, 36.
Baluz.
Miscellany, Cæsarius of Arles, sermons of, ii. 700 n. 2. Ep. of Benedict of Aniane, Scotch dialecticians, iii. 461 n. 1. Servatus Lupus, De tribus quæstionibus; on grace, f. 212, iii.

483 n. 3. T. i. f. 177, Agobard adv. Fredegis, iii. 460 n. 5. T. i. f. 213, Oliva, Comm. on Apocalypse, iv. 620 n. 3. T. i. f. 404, Fredegis' work on τὸ μὴ ὄν, iii. 460 n. 4. T. ii. f. 141, vita Eusebii, ii. 256 nn. 2, 3. T. iv., Hugo of Fleury, De regia potestate et sacerdotali dignitate, iv. 141 n. 2. T. iv. f. 69, life of Stephen of Obaize, iv. 312 n. 2. T. iv. f. 78, the same, l. i. c. 4, iv. 243 n. 1. T. iv. f. 130, the same, iv. 293 n. 2. T. v., the organ, iii. 128 n. 4. T. v. f. 295, Gerhoh. De corrupto ecclesiæ statu (Expos. in Ps. 64), iv. 146 n. 1, 195 n. 1.
Capitular. t. i. f. 143, ordinance of Sigibert on synods, iii. 95 n. 2. T. i. f. 239, of Charlemagne against vagrant penitents, iii. 140 n. 4. T. i. f. 197, of Charlemagne on asylums, iii. 104 n. 3. T. i. f. 423 (cap. an. 805, c. 11), on reception of slaves into monasteries, iii. 101 n. 1. T. i. f. 427, on admission of freemen into the spiritual order, iii. 97 n. 3. T. i. ff. 265, 389, 466, on judgments of God, iii. 130 n. 5. T. i. f. 478, on separation of affairs ecclesiastical from political, iii. 97 n. 1.
Vit. pap. Avign. t. i., two lives of Clement V., v. 23 n. 1. T. i. ed. Par. 1693, f. 240, s vita, Benedict XII., v. 41 n. 1.
Registr. t. i. f. 697, Innocent III. on the imperial election, iv. 176 n. 2; f. 715, ep. of Philip's party to the pope, iv. 177 n. 1.
Edition of Petrus de Marca, De concordia sacerdotii et imperii, ep. of Rabanus Maurus to Louis the Pious, iii. 457 n. 6.

Bamberg, iv. 3, 4, 105 n. 4. School at, iii. 471. See Andreas, Hermann, Otto, Rupert.
Ban, threatened by John XII., iii. 368. Threatened against the French church by Gregory V., iii. 374. Of Nicholas II. against Benedict X., iii. 387.
In the fifth Period. Ban of Innocent III. against the oppressors of the Prussians, iv. 45. Threatened against Henry IV., 105 n. 4. Ban pronounced, 108. Effect, 109-114. Absolution of H. IV., 114-117. Ban renewed, 118. Threatened by Urban II. against Philip I. of France, 122. Pronounced, removed, renewed, 123. By Urban II. against his adversaries, 129. Right and authority of the ban disputed, 109, 110, 131 and n. 2, 132, 610. By legates of Paschalis II. against Henry V., 141. By Innocent III. against the kings of Portugal and Castile, 174 n. 1. Ban and interdict against John of England, 174-176. By Innocent III. against King Otho, 177. Penalty of the ban, 178, 545. Ban against Fred. II., 178. Reconciliation, 179. Anecdote of a priest, 183 n. 3. Ban solemnly renewed, with sentence of deposition, 184. Use of the ban in bestowal of benefices, 200. Ban of Arsenius against Mich. Paleologus, 543. Of Martin V. against the same, 548. Against laymen disputing on the faith, 590. Threatened against Henry of Cluny, iv. 499. Against adherents of the Hohenstaufens, 610. Against heretics and their protectors, 640.
In the sixth Period. By Boniface VIII. against the Colonnas, v. 4. Against princes demanding tribute

from the clergy, 5. Threatened against Philip the Fair, 6. Ban pronounced, 10. John of Paris on the, 18. Defensor pacis, 35. Ban and interdict by John XXII. against Louis the Bavarian (Emp. Louis IV.), 24, 37, 43. By Urban IV. on the army of the king of Naples, 51. Threatened by Benedict XIII. against Charles VI. of France, 77. By the council of Pisa against adherents of Gregory XII. and Benedict XIII., 84. Threatened by Balthazar Cossa, 106. In England, 147. Against the doctrines of Wicklif (by the University of Oxford), 157. Ban and interdict against Huss, 272, 273, 294, 295, 296, 300, 301, 317, 322, 355, 357, 366. Huss on the, 282, 296, 300, 301, 353, 369. Against Ladislaus of Naples, 276. Friends of God against the, 383. Against the processions of the Flagellants, 412.

Bandinus Magister.
Sententiarum libris quatuor, iv. 410 n. 1

Banduri.
Imperium orientale, t. i. f. 115, inscription by Stephen the Iconoclast, iii. 213 n. 4. T. ii., vit. Dalmatius, ii. 535 n. 2. T. ii., animadvers. in Const. Porphyrogen., f. 62, Russian embassy in Constantinople, iii. 329 n. 1.

Bangor, monastery, iii. 10, 17, 29.
Banianes, Banians, i. 82 n. 2; ii. 140.
Banner of St. Peter, iii. 398.
Baptisé, Bernard, Franciscan, v. 113.
Baptism, *in the first Period*, i. 304, 305–323. Preparation for, 305–310. Conditions of, 262, 264, 305. Form of, 310. Formula, 306 n. 4, 310, 317, 321 and n. 3, 322. Symbolum, 305 n. 4. Baptismal vows, 309 (98 nn. 1, 3 221). Rites connected with, 238 n. 2, 315. Sprinkling and immersion, 238 n 2. Forgiveness in, 252, 253. Forgiveness of sins after, 221, 244, 246, 647, 654. Spiritual baptism, 316 n. 3. Opus operatum, 314. Baptism of clinici, 238, 310. Of infants, 311–315, 498, 504. Time in case of infants, 313. Controversies respecting, 317–323 (214 n. 5). Superstitious notions respecting, 252, 646, 647. Baptism with Valentine, 431, 432. With Marcion, 473. With the Marcosians, 476, 477. Vicarious, 478. With Mani, 504. With the Montanists, 522. Baptism and Charismata, 510. And regeneration, 522, 655 (see 221, 244, 246, 252–254). Doctrine of baptism, 644, 646, 647, 655. Baptism in Hades, 646. See Catechumens, Catechists, Symbol, Confirmation, Gnostic worship, Manicheism, Irenæus, Tertullian, Cyprian.
In the second Period. Validity, ii. 224. Time, 31, 341, 342, 360, 361. Administration, 355–361. Formula, 726. Regeneration and, 31. Delay of, 31, 258, 355, 356. Viewed as a magical rite, 48, 258, 259. As an outward form, 104, 120, 121. Motives for, 118, 120. Duties of deaconesses connected with, 192. Violation of vows, 213. Superstitious views of, 258. Sins after, Euchites on, 278. Of the Spirit, 304, 308, 728, 730. On the Great Sabbath, 341, 342. By heretics, 219 n. 2. Doctrine of, 660, 725, 726–731. Views of the Euchites, 278. Of the Pelagians, 727–731. Of Jovinian, 308, 309. Hilary on, 619. In the N. African ch., 650. The Cœlicolæ, Jewish, 768 n. 1. See Infant baptism.
In the third and fourth Periods. Difference in the mode of, iii. 17. Baptism and redemption, 492, 493. Final condition of those who have died without, 44, 61 and n. 2, 144, 476 (314). Baptism of barbarous tribes and rulers, 8, 12, 13 and n. 2, 22, 50, 72, 272, 280, 298, 301, 303, 307, 329, 330, 331. Of children, 331, 597. Compulsory, 40, 51, 76, 78, 307. How viewed by the Icelanders, 301 and n. 1. Magical effects, 280. And the Lord's Supper, 18. Form of renunciation, baptismal vows, 42, 53, 312. In private chapels, 109 n. 1. By heretics, 514. Of the Spirit, 263, 595. By immersion, 301. Deferred, 301. In the sects, 592, 595, 597. Paulicians, 249. Samson, 63 n. 4. Alcuin on, 76, 82. Radbert on, 465. Berengar on, 525. See Infant baptism.
In the fifth Period. Baptism of pagan tribes, iv. 7, 8, 9, 16, 36, 38, 41, 53 (by masses, 8, 9, 16, 38). Of Mongols, 57, 58. Of Jews, by compulsion, 75, 76. By laymen, 99. Preparation for, immersion, 8. Vow, 91. Sins after, 347, 577. Unbaptized children, Abelard on, 494. Of infants, 561, 563, 575, 587 n. 3, 595. Spiritual, 571, 574–577. See Bogomiles. Doctrine of, 335, Superstitious views of, 5. In the sects, 564, 595, 596. Bogomiles, 556, 563. Chrysomalus, 561. Xphon, 563. Catharists, 575, 577, 587 n 3. Instructions of Otto, 334.
In the sixth Period. Liturgical form of, v. 81. Wicklif on, 170. Janow, 214, 215. Relation to the Supper, 226. Of children, 303. Validity of Greek, 373. See Infant baptism, Imposition of hands.

Baptism of Christ, i. 83, 347, 430 n., 431; ii. 343, 506. With Felix of Urgellis, iii. 163. The Cathariats, iv. 574.

Baptismal formula, i. 306 n. 4, 310, 316, 317, 321; ii. 726; iii. 63.

Bar Manu. Abgar of Edessa, i. 80.
Bar Sudaili, ii. 615, 616.
Baradæus, ii. 612 n.
Barbara, head of St., v. 189.
Barbarians, inroads of, ii. 102, 156, 695, 706, 769; iii. 4, 25, 26, 75, 112 and n. 2, 277–279, 286, 288, 293, 307, 323, 385, 404; iv. 34, 38, 40. Influence of Chris-

tianity on, see Missions, Christianity, Baptism (*third and fourth Periods*).
Barbarism, Christianity in contact with, iii. 3, 4, 29, 103, 127, 326, 411. See Christianity, Culture, Missions. Remains of, iii. 107, 200. Revivals of, 323, 325, 326. See Paganism. Of the tenth century, 322, 367, 469. Eleventh century, 456, 470 n. 1. Transitions of feeling in, iv. 100.
Barbarous tribes, Christianity among, i. 70, 84, 85. See Missions.
Barbatianus, monk, ii. 312.
Barcelona, Vigilantius of, ii. 373.
Barcochba, i. 103, 344, 668.
Bardanes. See Philippicus.
Bardas, uncle of Michael III., his treatment of Ignatius, iii. 558–560. Death of, 568.
Bardesanes. Himself and his doctrine, 375 n. 1, 440–442. With Abgar, i. 80. Composer of hymns, 304. Origin of Satan, 377.
Bardewik, iii. 325.
Bardo, abp. of Mentz, life, c. vii. §§ 1, 69, iii. 446 n 1.
Bards, ii. 149.
Barhebræus, ii. 611.
Bari. See Councils, an. 1098.
Barnabas, epistle of, i. 66, 83, 381 n. 1. Sunday, 295. Character and criticism, 657, 658.
Ep. cc. 9, 12, i. 658 nn. 1, 2; c. 15, i. 650 n. 1.
Baronius.
Annales. An. 809, N. 54, protocol of Charlemagne's embassy to Leo III., iii. 555 n. 1. An. 859, N. 61, ep. of Photius to Nicholas I. trans., iii. 561 n. 3. An. 861, N. 34, the same, iii. 565 n. 2; § 47, 559 n. 1. An. 879, N. 7, ep. of John VIII. to Basilius (orig. form), iii. 574 n. 2, 576 n. 2. An. 879, N. 47, Commonitorium of John VIII. to his legates, iii. 574 n. 3. An. 1061, N. 32, poem of Alphanus, iii. 399 n. 4. An. 1155, Acta Vaticana, NN. 1 et 4, ashes of Arnold, iv. 162 n. 1.
Barsumas, abbot. ii. 560, 569, 570.
Barsumas, bp. of Nisibis, Nestorian, ii. 611.
Bartholomew, abbot of Crypta Ferrata, iii. 376 and n. 2, 424. Greek life of (see Petrus Passinus), 376 n. 2.
Bartholomew, apostle, in Arabia, i. 81. In India, i. 82.
Bartholomew, Catharist pope, iv. 590.
Bartimeus, i. 364.
Baruch, Jew, iv. 79.
Basil, bp. of Ancyra, ii. 449, 451, 452.
Basil, bp. of Cæsarea in Cappadocia. His education, ii. 183. In Athens, 39 n. 2, 45. His election to the office of bishop, 186 n. 1. Friend of Gregory Nazianzen, 462, 464. Influenced by Origen, 387. Under Julian, 77. Under Valens, 459–461. The forty soldiers at Sebaste, 19 n. 3. Christianity among the Goths, 150. Sabas, 155, 156. The chief cook, 165 n. 5. The Basilias, 169. Exemption of the clergy, 170 n. 2. Intercession for the Cappadocians, 174. Against the frequent exacting of oaths by officers of government, 175. The right of asylum and the governor, 177 n. 1. Οἰκονόμος, 191 n. 4. Country bishops, 193 nn. 2 and 3. Παροικία, 194 n. 1. Eustathians, 281 n. 1. Monachism, 282 and n. 1, 283 n. 1. Manual labor, and education in the cloisters, 287 n. 1, 288. Rule of, 287 n. 1, 288, 316 n. 5. Promotes Monachism, 293. Epiphany and Christmas, 346 nn. 1, 3. Church psalmody, 354 n. 3. Consecration of the Supper, 363 n. 8. Communion at home, 365 n. 4. Eunomius and, 444 n. 3, 445 and n. 3, 447 n. 4, 449 n. 4. The 3d Sirmian creed, 452. On the condition of the church, 461. Doctrine of the Holy Spirit, 468, 469 n, 2, 471 n. 4. Person of Christ, 483. With Julian of Eclanum, 712 n. 1. Origen, 740, 741. Council of Antioch, an. 269, i. 606 n. 2. Number of the saved, Nilus, iii. 421. Theodore Studita, veracity, iii. 541 n. 5.

Citations from his writings: —
Canonica, i., Dionysius of Alexandria on Montanist baptism, i. 320 n. 6; ep. i. canon 10, ἀγροὶ ὑποκείμενοι, ii. 193 n. 2 ; iii., προσκλαίοντες, ii. 213 n. 3.
Contra Eunomium (opp. ed. Garnier, t. i), l. i. § 3, confession of Eunomius, ii. 444 n. 3 ; f. 619, ii. 447 n. 4.
De Spiritu Sancto, c. 16, activity of the three persons, ii. 469 n. 2; c. 27, prayer at the Lord's Supper, 363 n. 8; exhibition of the elements, 364 n. 1.
Epistles (ep. canon. See Canonica). Ep. 38, argument for the Trinity from God's workings in man, ii. 469 n. 2. Ep. 48, Demophilus, 462 n. Ep. 54, to his chorbishops, ordinations for the sake of exemption, 170 n. 2, 193 n. 3. Ep. 66, διοικήσεις, 194 n. 1. Ep. 74, ad Martinian, intercession for the Cappadocians, 174 n. 1. Ep. 79, ad Eustathium, the officers of Valens, 460 n. 1. Ep. 85, to the governor of Cappadocia, on oaths, 175 n. 4. Ep. 91, ad Valerian, calls on the Western church to assist the Eastern, 461 n. 4. Ep. 93, daily communion, 364 n. 4 ; communion at home, 365 n. 4. Ep. 94, the Basilias, 169 n. 3. Ep. 113, to the presbyters in Tarsus on the disunion of the church, 461 nn. 1–3. Ep. 114, § 1, ad Ascholium, conversion of the Goths, 150 n. 3. Ep. 142, συμμορία, 193 n. 2. Epp. 142 et 143, almshouses, 169 n. 5. Ep. 155, to the Dux Soranus, 155 n. 1. Ep. 164, ad Ascholium, the Gothic martyrs, 155 n. 4; § 2, 155 n. 5. Ep. 165, ad Ascholium (or the Dux Soranus), 155 n. 3. Ep. 188, ἀγροὶ ὑποκείμενοι, 193 n. 2 (baptism of heretics, i. 320 n. 6). Ep. 207, § 2, accused of innovation, ii. 283 n 5. Epp. 210 et 214, § 3, et 235, § 6, Sabellius, i. 596 n. 4. Ep. 215, Damasus, ii. 416 n. 5. Ep. 223, ascetic dress of the Eustathians, 281 n. 1. Ep. 235, see ep. 210. Epp. 237 et 285, οἰκονόμος, 191 n. 4. Ep. 259, § 2, Damasus, 257 n. 1. Ep. 240, three of, 266. Ep. 285, see ep. 237. Ep. 290, συμμορία, 193 n. 2.
Homily, incorrectly ascribed to Basil, opp. t. ii. ed. Garnier, f. 602, § 6, Christmas, ii. 346 n. 1 ; and Epiphany, ii. 346 n. 3.
Φιλοκαλία (Christomathy), ii. 741 n. 1.
Regula fus. vii. 2, 346, Cenobites, ii. 283 n. 1 ; § 15, admission into monastic orders, 288 n. 2.

Basil, bp. of Seleucia, ii. 570 n. 1, 571 n. 2, 578 n. 4.

Basil, deacon, ii. 511 n. 3.
Basilius, ii. 169.
Basilideans, i. 401, 413-417, 447. Feast of Epiphany, 302. See Basilides Gnostics, Pseudo-Basilideans.
Basilides, Egyptian bp., i. 712.
Basilides, Gnostic, i. 373 n. 1, 400-417, 420, 430, 436, 445. See Epiphanius, Clement of Alexandria, Basilideans.
   Citations. Tractatus (ἐξηγητικά) in the disputatione Archelai cum Mani, c. 55, the poor and rich principle, i. 401 n. 3, 402 n. 1. Apud Clementem Alexandr. Stromata, l. iv. f. 508, love, 405 n. 2; f. 509, the ruse, 403 n. 3.
Basilides, Spanish bp., i. 216.
Basiliscus, Christian, ii. 67 n. 2.
Basiliscus, usurper, ii. 166, 585, 586.
Basilius, teacher of the Bogomiles, iii. 591 n. 2; iv. 559, 560.
Basilius II., Greek emperor, iii. 329 n., 580.
Basilius Macedo, Greek emperor, iii. 329 n., 307 n. 4, 314, 327, 329 n., 530, 568 and n. 3, 572 and n. 2, 578. Position taken by him in the controversies between the Greek and Western churches, 568.
Basle, iii. 396, 453; v. 43. Council of, v. 129, 130, 381, 390, 391, 401. Appointment and commencement of the council of Basle, v. 128-133.
Bassora, Solomon of, ii. 738 n. 6.
Baths, public, Chrysostom on, ii. 101.
Batu, Mongolian prince, iv. 51.
Baucalis, church, ii. 409.
Baur, Dr.
   Essay on Apollonius of Tyana (in the Tübinger Zeitschrift), i. 174 n. 3. Geschichte der Dreieinigkeitslehre, iv. 461 n. 4; i. 5-2 n. 3, 591 n. 4, 593 n., 595 n. 1, 596 n. 5, 612 n. 3. On Manicheism (Tübingen, 1831), i. 80 n. 1, 497 n. 2; p. 120, *et seq.*, i. 495 n. 2. Treatise on the Pastoral Epistles, i. 185 n. 2. Work on the Gnosis, i. 394 n. 1, 395 n. 1; p. 446, i. 393 n. 3; p. 481, i. 391 n. 1.
Bavaria, planting and restoration of Christianity in, iii. 26, 27, 38-40, 55. Heretical doctrines taught there, 38, 63. Education, 73, 471. Stu:m, 74. Hungarians in, 405. Berthold in, iv. 318. See Reichersberg.
Bavarians at the Univ. of Prague, v. 247.
Baya, Nicholas de, v. 114.
Bayer.
   Hist. Edessen e nummis illust. l. iii. f. 173, i. 80 n. 1.
Beadles, iii. 101 n. 4.
Beasts, Christians thrown to wild, i. 109.
Beatrice, Margravine, iv. 91.
Beatus, opponent of Adoptianism, i-i. 163, 164.
   Contr. Elipand. l. i. f. 301, iii. 164 n. 6; f. 310, 164 n. 4. See Canisius.
Beausobre.
   On Mani, 1 485 n. 4.
Bec, monastery of, iii. 445 n. 2, 470. See Herluin, Lanfranc. Anselm at, iv. 361, 362, 368.

Beccus, Johannes, iv. 545, 546. Writings, 547 n. 1.
   Discourse i. c. 3, on his deposition, iv. 549 n. 1. Disc. ii. (see Leo Allatius), 547 n. 3.
Becket, Thomas à, iv. 169-172.
Becoming, Platonic idea of, with Origen, i. 569. See Being.
Bede, Venerable. Events of his life, iii. 152, 153, 154, 467 (457). Hist. Aug., iv. 468. Christianity in Britain, i. 85. Augustin's oak, iii. 17 n. 2. Pauli nitidus, iii. 18 n. 2. Laurence, iii. 19 n. 1. Dionysius, iv. 382 n. 3. Report on his life and writings, iii. 152 n. 5. Bible translation, iii. 153 n. 3; v. 150. Benedictus Biscopius, iv. 118 n. 1. See Acta Sanctorum, ed. Ben. and Mabillon.
   Hist. eccles. l. ii. c. 1, Gregory the Great, iii. 11 n. 2; ed. Smith, f. 116, Deynoch, 17 n. 1. L. ii. c. 2 Augustin, Ethelbert, 18 n. 1. L. iii. c 18, Wilfrid, 23 n. 1. L. iii. c. 25, Aidan, 23 n 3. L. iii. c. 26, Scottish missionaries, 23 n. 2. L. iii. c. 27, Egbert, iii. 43 n. 3. L. iii. c. 30, relapse into idolatry, 22 n. 1. L. iv. and v. Theodore of Canterbury, 25 n. 1. L. iv. c. 5, synod of Hertford, 25 n. 2. L. v. cc. 11, 12, Egbert, 43 n. 3. An. 731, Willibrord, 45 n. 2.

Begging, Wm. of St. Amour on, iv. 283.
Bonaventura, 291. Bull of Honorius IV., spiritual societies, 627. Priests, v. 54.
Begging monks. See Mendicant orders.
Beghards (Beghardi), i. 44, 450 n. 2; iv. 286, 292, 303, 626, 628 n. 1, 630, 633 n. 2; v. 143, 179. Beghards and Beguines as names of reproach, v. 182, 213, 216, 221, 233, 288, 292, 386, 387. Mystical Beghards, v. 215, 393, 394, 408.
Beginning of creation, i. 568, 569. See Creation.
Beguines (Beguinae, Beguttae), iv. 286; v. 179 and n. 1, 190, 213, 216, 221, 288 and n. 1, 289, 295. See Beghards.
Beheading of martyrs, i. 119.
Being, four kinds, with Scotus, iii. 464. Being and becoming, Athanasius, ii. 474. Augustin, ii. 475. See Origen's doctrine of Creation, ὄν.
Bela, king of Hungary, iii. 335.
Belæus, pagan judge, ii. 67 n. 2.
Belgard, city in Pomerania, iv. 16.
Belgium, iii. 370; iv. 277.
Believers, among the Catharists, iv. 576, 579, 580.
Belisarius, general, ii. 594.
Belitza, first seat of a bishopric in Moravia, iii. 315 n. 1.
Bellay, Life of Anthelm, iv. 168 n. 3. See Acta S. Junæ.
Bells, iii. 75, 300 n. 1, 391; iv. 183 n. 3. Church, iii. 286, 336.
Bema (βῆμα), ii. 511. Manichean festival, i. 505; iv. 566 n 2.
Bena. See Almaric of.
Benatky, v. 176.

Benedict, priest, companion of Adalbert of Prague, iv. 41.
Benedict, rule of, ii. 283 n. 2, 298–300; iii. 30, 75, 106, 415, 416; iv. 208, 252, 264, 634. See Benedict of Nursia, Benedict of Aniana.
Benedict, singer, iii. 128.
Benedict VI. (VII.), pope, iii. 330 n. 2, 331 and n. 1.
Letter to the German archbishops, the Hungarians (see Mansi concil. t. xix.), 330 n. 2.
Benedict IX. (Theophylact), pope, iii. 375–377, 409 n. 1, 445 n. 2, 448 n. 1.
Benedict X., pope, iii. 387.
Benedict XI., v. 19.
Benedict XII., v. 40, 41.
Benedict XIII., v. 56, 62–77, 84, 105–107, 112, 118 and n. 1, 303.
Benedict Cajetan, cardinal, iv. 193; v. 2. See Boniface VIII.
Life of Celestin V., iv. 193 n. 3. See Acta S. May.
Benedict of Aniana, abbot, reformer of Monachism, iii. 167, 414 n. 1, 414–416, 461 n. 1, 579. His rule, 416. His life, see Acta S. Feb. and Acta S. of Mabillon, S. iv. Letter of, Scotch theology, iii. 461 n. 1. See Baluz, Misc. t. v.
Benedict of Nursia, Benedictines, ii. 296–300; iii. 75. Life of, 298–300 nn. See rule of.
Benedictine monasticism, degeneracy of, iv. 251, 252, 278 n. 2.
Benedictine rule. See Benedict, rule of.
Benedictines, iv. 43, 204, 252 n. 1. See Benedict.
Benedictines of St. Maur. See Hist. lit. de la France.
Benedictio, iv. 196. (Benediction before taking food, etc., i. 286.)
Benedictus, Polish monk, iii. 334 n. 2.
Benedictus Biscopius, abbot, iii. 118 n. 1.
Benedictus Levita, deacon at Mentz, collection of capitularies; the decretals, iii. 350 n. 1.
Benedictus Paulinus, ii. 707 n. 1.
Beneficence, works of, iv. 211, 268. See Benevolence.
Benefices, traffic in, iii. 376, 377, 389, 404; v. 23, 110, 111, 144. See Simony. Secular influence in disposal of, iii. 351, 382, 400–404. See Investiture. Papal influence, iv. 200, 201, 222; v. 9, 86, 96, 202. Plurality, iv. 207. Abuses in the distribution of, iii. 351, 400, 401, 409 and n. 1; v. 9, 86, 87, 97, 117. Reservations of, v. 98, 122. Eagerness for, v. 50, 86, 89, 114, 119.
Beneficium, iv. 164–166.
Benevolence, works of (Essenes, i. 46), 74, 197, 222, 255–259, 262, 267; ii. 5, 26, 63, 136, 168, 169, 191, 192, 706, 709 n. 2, 752, 753 n. 2, 756 (as a means of persuasion, ii. 26, 63, 548; iv. 18, 30); iii. 4 n. 1, 21, 26–28, 41, 45, 93 n. 3, 100, 104 n. 1, 282, 408 n. 1, 415, 418, 422 (pagan, iii. 45, 300); iv. 12, 18, 30,

73, 211, 213, 214, 239 n. 1, 254, 266–268, 271, 294–299, 564; v. 383, 407. Catharist, 583.
Benevolent institutions, ii. 63, 168, 169, 192, 755; iii. 322, 419; iv. 214, 266–268, 294–296, 298, 299.
Benevolent societies, iv. 266–268, 293.
Benignus, disciple of Patrick, ii. 148, 149.
Benignus, monastery, iii. 419.
Benignus, S. Divionensis.
Chron. on Greg. VI., iii. 377 n. 1. See D'Achery, Spicileg.
Benjamin, deacon, ii. 134, 135.
Benno, cardinal.
Invective against Hildebrand, in Orthvini Gratii fasciculus rerum, etc., iii. 380 n. 1, 518 n. 2, 519 n. 1; iv. 85 n. 1.
Benvenuto of Imola, Comm. on Dante, iv. 629 n. 4, 630 n. 2.
Bequests, to the church, ii. 166–168; iv. 577. Catharists, iv. 578. See Gifts, Wills.
Berengar II., Italian king, iii. 367.
Berengar, Pierre, disciple of Abelard, iv. 257, 395, 399 n. 3.
His letters, dialogue, 399 n. 3. Miracles of Bernard, 257 n. 5. Opp. Abelard, f. 326, the Carthusians, 262 n. 2. Defense of Abelard, 395 n. 1; f. 398, 397 n. 2.
Berengar of Tours, his education, mode of teaching, and controversies respecting the Lord's Supper (see Doctrine of the Lord's Supper), iii. 502–521; iv. 335, 337, 355; v. 270. Development of his doctrine, iii. 521–530. His efforts in behalf of science, 470, 471, 503. Character of Leo IX., 379 n., 513. Of Nicholas II., 387 n. 6. Exhortatory discourse, 504. On anthropomorphism, 443 n. 2. Gregory VII. 518–521; iv. 84, 86 n. 4, 92 n. 1, 118. Hildebert, iv. 599.
Citations from his writings:—
De sacra coena, f. 36 and f. 40, on Leo IX., iii. 508 n. 3, and 379 n. 1: f. 36, on his ep. to Lanfranc, 507 n. 2; f. 37, Peswil, 521 n. 2; f. 41, the pope's citation, 507 n. 3; f. 42, Henry I., n. 4; f. 43, burning of his book, n. 5: f. 51, conc. of Tours, 509 n. 4; f. 63, corruption of ch., 382 n. 1; f. 71, Nicholas II., 387 n. 6; f. 83, on tropical expressions, 522 n. 2; ff. 94, 198, glorified body of Christ, 522 n. 6; ff. 99, 145, 179, effect of consecration, 524 nn. 1–3; f. 100, reason and authority, 524 n. 2; f. 110, anthropomorphism, 443 n. 2; consecration, 525 n. 1; f. 144, conversion, 524 n. 4; ff. 148, 157, 165, 236, spiritual communion, 523 nn. 1–4; f. 190, substance and accident, 522 nn. 3, 4; f. 222, 522 n. 5; f. 273, cardinals, 387 n. 7; f. 299, presence of the elements, 521 n. 3.
Exhortatory discourse (see Martene and Durand, Thes. nov. an. t. i.), iii. 504 n. 1.
Letter to Adelmann, ff. 37, 38, sacramentum, res sacramenti, iii. 523 n. 5; ff. 38, 39 (ed. Schmid), Paschasius Radbert, 521 n. 1; f. 42, consecration, 525 n. 1; ff. 44, 45, light, 526 n. 2.
Letter to Ascelin (see Lanfranc's works, vita Lanfranci), iii. 510 nn. 1, 2.
Letter to Lanfranc (see as above), ii. 506 n. 5.
Letter to Richard (see D'Achery, Spic. t. iii.); f. 400, on indemnification for his losses, etc., iii. 508 nn. 1, 2, 510 n. 1. Communion, 526 n. 1.

GENERAL INDEX.   29

Tract against Lanfranc, iii. 509 n. 4, 513: ff. 26, 61, 73, his recantation, 412 n. 2; ff. 28, 59, 61, 62, on his recantation, 514 nn. 3-7; ff. 34, 50, Leo IX., 513 n. 3, 511 n. 2; f. 54, number of his followers, 515 n. 3, f. 27 n. 5: ff. 54, 166, majority, in matters of faith, 515 nn. 1, 2; f. 58, corruption of the church, 514 n. 2; ff. 71, 72, Nicholas II., 514 n. 1, 512 n. 2.

Berengarians, iii. 515, 527.
Bergen, district in Norway, iii. 293 n. 2.
Bergeron.
  Collection of; Report of Wm. de Rubruquis, iv. 52-54 nn.
Bernald, abbot, life of Bernard, iv. 145 n., 254 n. 3, 255 nn. 2, 3.
Bernard, bp., missionary in Pommerania, iv. 2, 3, 5, 6.
Bernard, bp. in Norway, iii. 297 n. 1.
Bernard, Dominican, iv. 643.
Bernard, priest, sectarian, iv. 448.
Bernard of Clairvaux. History and character, iv. 252-264. His mother, 234, 252. As orator, 144 and n., 153-155, 253. The crusades, 153-157. His letters, 254. Protects the Jews, 73-75, 74 n. 1. Innocent II., 144-146. Arnold of Brescia, 148 n. 2, 149 n. 1, 150 and n. Admonitions to Eugene III., 152, 157-160, 185, 194, 195, 197, 199, 201, 202. Legates, 198. Appeals to Rome, 199. Corrupt clergy, 206 n. 1 (v. 102). Boys in ecclesiastical offices, 207 n. 1. Abbess Hildegard, 217. Conversion of the condemned robber, 236. Monasticism, 238, 253, 254 (v. 188). Counsels to monks, iv. 240. On love, 259-262, 386. Calumny, 262. Self-knowledge, 263. Doctrine of the immaculate conception, 331, 332. The denier of transubstantiation, 337. Stages of the religious life, 371, 372. His theory of knowledge, 371-373. Abelard, 386, 393-400, 495, 503. Knowledge of the prophets, 405 n. 1. Gerhoh, 408 n. 1. Robert Pullein, 408. Gilbert de la Porée, 408, 409. Peter Lombard, 409. Intuition, 411 (371). Guigo, 413. The Trinity, 460. Confession of faith, 462, 516. Doctrine of atonement, 503, 504. Justification, 509, 510, 570. Freewill, 516, 517. The Catharists, 568 n. 2, 578 n. 5, 580 n. 1, 586, 593. Henry the Cluniacensian, 598 nn., 601 n. 2, 603, 604. Lives of Bernard, opp. ed. Mabillon, t. ii. l. vii. c. 15, the rescued criminal, 236 n. 3. First life, by William, l. i. c. 2, § 4, vision of Christ, 252 n. 3; c. 8, § 14, early asceticism, 253 n. 2, his appearance, n. 4. Second life, by Bernald, c. iv. § 26, Clairvaux, 254 n. 3, declines bishoprics, 255 n. 2; c. vi. § 38, Wm. of Aquitaine, 145 n. 1. Third life, by Gottfried, c. iv. f. 1119, his eloquence, 153 n. 5, 154 n. 1; f. 1120, ep. of Eugene III. on the crusade, 153 n. 2; l. iv. c. vi. §§ 34, 39, his miracles, 256 n. 4; c. vii. § 22, influence,

254 n. 3; c. v. § 11, over Abelard, 394 n. 3. See Miracles.
  Citations from his writings:—
Apologia ad Gulielmum abbatem, on the Cistercians and Cluniacensians, iv. 253 nn. 5, 6, 254 nn.
De consideratione, four books, admonitions to Eugene III., iv. 158-160, 257; prologue, 157 n. 7. L. ii., failure of the crusade, 157 nn. 3-5. L. iv. c. 4, duty of legates, 198 n. 1. L. v c. 1, § 2, inspiration, 371 nn. 1, 2, 372.
De diligendo Deo, c. 7, iv. 260 n.
De erroribus Abaelardi, v. 503 nn. 1, 2, 4, 504 n. 1.
De gratia et libero arbitrio, iv. 516, 517.
De officio episcoporum, c. viii., boys in the episcopal office, iv. 207 n. 1.
Epistles, to Innocent III., against Abelard, iv. 396 n. 6, 503. Ep. 2, § 1, against the luxury of the clergy, 206 nn. 1, 4. Ep. 7, § 12, on obedience, 255 n. 5. Ep. 21, multiplicity of business, 255 n. 1. Ep. 64, the pilgrim turned monk, 238 n. 2. Ep. 106, to a theologian, theology of the heart, 258 n. 5, 259 n. 1. Ep. 107, § 4, justification, 510 nn. 3-6. Ep. 142, humility, 262 n. 1. Ep. 143, to his monks, service of love, 259 n. 5, 6. Ep. 144, the same, 259 n. 4; § 4, sickness, 253 n. 3. Ep. 173, feast of immaculate conception, 331 nn. 2, 3. Ep. 178, to Innocent II., authority of popes, 256 nn. 1, 2. Ep. 180, § 3, to Innocent II., Arnold of Brescia and Abelard, 148 n. 2. Ep. 195, Arnold of B., 148 n. 2, 149 n. 1, 150 n. Ep. 241, to a nobleman, against heretics, 603 n. 2; Henry of Clany, 601 n. 2, 608 n. 2. Ep. 242, to citizens of Toulouse, 257 nn. 2, 3. Ep. 256, to Eugene III., declines to lead the crusade, 154 nn. 4, 5. Ep. 290, a corrupt legate, 198 n. 1. Ep. 359, monks in the crusade, 154 n. 3. Ep. 362, to R. Pullein, 408 n. 5. Ep. 363, to the German clergy, 153 n. 3; the Jews, 73 n. 6. Ep. 365, to abp. Henry of Metz, the Jews, 74 n. 3. Ep. 386, an abbot to Bernard, on the failure of the crusade, 157 n. 2.
Exhortatio ad milites templi, iv. 258 nn. 2, 3.
Life of abp. Malachias, iv. 337.
Sermones in Cantica Canticor. S. x. § 7, lukewarmness in prayer, iv 241 n. 1. S. xi. f. 1296, on self-accusing thoughts, 240 n. 4; § 7, on atonement, 504 n. 2. S. xv. § 6, Jesus in the Christian life, 261 n. 1. S. xx. § 6, degrees in love to Christ, 261 n. 2; § 7, asceticism, 241 n. 2. S. xxii. § 8, justification, 509 n. 5. S. xxiii. § 14, knowledge of the heart, 259 n. 2; § 15, justification, 509 n. 2. S. xxiv. § 2, slander, 262 n 2. S. xxv. § 9, Christ as example, 504 n. 3. S. xxxiv. § 5, self-knowledge, 263 n. 2. S. xxxvi. § 5, the same, 263 n. 1. S. xlvi. § 8, miracles, 258 n. 1. S. lxiv. § 8, f. 1446, treatment of heretics, 586 n. 5. S. lxv. § 5, spread of Henricians, 603 nn. 3, 5. S. lxvi. § 4, Henricians, 603 n. 4; § 12 (t. 1. f. 1499), the sword against heretics, 586 n. 4.

Bernard of Pisa, iv. 152. See Eugene III.
Bernard of Tiron, iv. 97 n. 8, 236, 237 n. 1, 294, 308, 312. Life of, 97 n. 8, 237 n. 1. On works, 308 n. 2.
Bernard Ydros, iv. 606 and n. 4.
Bernard's mother, iv. 234, 252.
Bernhard, bp. of Citta di Castello, v. 330.
Bernhard Baptisatus (Baptisé), v. 113.
Bernhard Chotek, v. 294.
Berno of Burgundy, reformer of Monachism, iii. 417.
Bernold of Constance, iv. 100 n. 2.
Chronicles. (See Blas. monumenta.) Lent Sy-

nod, an. 1076, iv. 108 n. 1 ; f. 57, authority of princes, 110 n. 3 ; an. 1083, monasticism, 283 n. 1 ; f. 171, misfortunes of crusaders, 127 nn. 1, 7 ; Urban II. in Italy, 128 n. 3 ; an. 1091 (t. ii. f. 148), pious societies of laymen, 363 n. 2 ; au. 1095, assembly at Placenza, 125 n. 1.

Bernreider, Paul, canonical priest, iii. 381 n. 2.

Bernward, bp. of Hildesheim. His life (see Mabillon, Acta S. (O. B.), t. vi. P. i.), f. 205, his employments (see, also, Leibnitz, Script. rer. Bruns. t. i.), iii. 408 n. 2 ; Irish art, 470 n. 6 ; f. 206, defense against the Normans, 405 n. 3 ; § 37, f. 223, obedience to magistrates, 403 n. 1, 405 n. 4. Godchard, 408 n. 3.

Berœa, in Syria, i. 349 ; ii. 86. See Acacius.

Berœa, in Thrace, ii. 443.

Berserkers, iii. 301.

Bertha, queen of Kent, iii. 11.

Bertha, wife of Philip I. of France, iv. 121.

Bertha, wife of Robert of France, iii. 374 and n. 5.

Berthold, abbot, iv. 217 n. 2.

Berthold, Cistercian, bp. of Liefland, iv. 37.

Berthold, Franciscan, preacher of repentance, iv. 279, 600. Sayings from his sermons, edited by King, 318–320. Against indulgences, 351, 352.

Berthold of Calabria, founder of the order of the Carmelites, iv. 266.

Berthold of Constance.
Chronicon, an. 1083, men of rank in the monasteries, iv. 233 n. ; an. 1091, pious societies, 303 n. 2. See Bernold of Constance.

Berthrade, iv. 121, 122.

Bertrand d'Agoust, v. 20. See Clement V.

Bertulph of Carinthia, iv. 96 n. 6.

Beryllus of Bostra, i. 591 n. 4, 593, 594, 597, 710.

Berytus, Beyroot, ii. 95, 433 n. 2. Law school at, 590.

Besançon, diet at, iv. 164.

Besanduk, ii. 741.

Beser, renegade, iii. 203 n. 1.

Besse, le Sieur.
Hist. des ducs, marquis et comte de Narbonne, f. 483, assembly at Toulouse, an. 1167, iv. 690 n. 5.

Bethabo monastery, iii. 89.

Bethlehem, v. 313. Jerome at, ii. 159, 640, 641, 643, 712, 745. Monks of, 644, 747, 748. Epiphanius at, 747, 748.

Bethlehem chapel, v. 236, 256, 259, 260, 263, 265 and n. 1, 271, 288, 289 and n. 3, 293–295, 301, 311–315, 321, 323, 332, 333, 358. Record of foundation, f. 105, 236 n. 2.

Beziers, iv. 639 n. 2.

Bible, copies of the. See Bibles, Manuscripts.

Bible, division into chapters, iv. 616 n. 7.

Bible exposition, Waldenses and, iv. 608, 612.

Bible interpretation, *in the first Period*, Jewish, i. 36. With Pharisees, i. 39, 40, 49. The Sadducees, 40–42. The Essenes, 44, 47, 49. The Scribes, 53, 54. The Alexandrian Jews, Philo, 53–59. The Therapeutæ, 61. Proselytes, 68. Celsus, 165. Porphyry, 171. Charisma, 181. The Ebionites, 348 n. 2. The Clementines, 355. The Gnostics, 387–389. Valentine, 426, 427. Heracleon, 435, 436. Marcion, 460, 463, 473. Manichean, 501, 502. Artemonites, 582. Origen, 544–549, 552–557, 700, 717, 288 (ii. 388, 598). Mystical and mythical tendencies, i. 557 (44 ; ii. 389). Chiliasts and Alexandrians, 652. Hieracas, 714. Methodius, 721. Antiochian, 722.

In the second Period. Influence of councils on, ii. 211. In the Alexandrian and Antiochian schools, 388–394, 402, 754. Augustin, 251, 402, 734. Vigilantius, 375 n. 1. Jerome, 388, 391, 392, 745–747. Bar Sudaili, 616. In the Pelagian controversy, 666. Julian of Eclanum, 673 and n. 4. Chrysostom, 754. Priscillianists, 778.

In the third and fourth Periods, iii. 126, 153 n. 3, 155, 430 n. 3, 431, 456–459, 471. Paulicians, 265. Sect at Montfort, 601. See Commentaries.

In the fifth Period, iv. 98 n. 2, 404, 405. The Jews, 77, 78. Joachim, 220, 230–232. Abelard, 377. Bogomiles, 558, 559. Catharists, 571. H. of Cluny, 601. See Allegorical, Commentaries, Interpretation, Scriptures.

Bible, its importance to Christianity, i. 149.

Bible, Julian on the, ii. 46, 52, 53.

Bible, language of the, iii. 460 ; iv. 415.

Bible meetings, iv. 321.

Bible reading, study, *in the first Period*, i. 307, 308. In the family, 283 n. 1, 286, 693. In public worship, 291, 302, 303. At Alexandria, 528, 532, 533. Origen, 693, 719, 722. Pamphilus, 721. Consulted for oracles, 45 (iii. 129). See Scriptures.

In the second Period, ii. 262, 288, 316–319, 328, 333, 339, 743 n. 1, 773. Victorinus, 77. Ulphilas, 158, 159. Among the Goths, 158, 159. At Antioch, 183. Among the Nestorians, 183 n. 1, 611. Anthony, 265. Heron, 275. Pelagius, 635. Jerome, 712 n. 3, 742. Chrysostom, 718. A means to conversion, 122, 123. In preparation for the clerical office, and in the cloisters, 183. Public reading of the, 123, 137, 158, 213, 264 n. 4, 265, 319, 333, 334, 339, 352, 357, 361.

In the Middle Ages, iii. 21, 52, 54, 55, 60, 61, 73, 124, 125, 126, 150 n. 7, 201, 310, 425–427, 457–459, 471. Consulted

for oracles, 129. Gregory the Great on the, 115. See Scriptures.
In the fifth Period, iv. 98 and n. 2, 204, 279, 314, 358, 415, 422, 425, 561, 563. Interfered with by the study of law, of the Sentences, etc., 204, 415, 425. Jews on the, 77, 78. Abelard, 397. Hugo, 401, 402. Aquinas, 422. Reading of, among the laity, 320–324, 425; forbidden, 320–324. Effect of papal authority, 538. In the sects, 321, 558, 559, 561, 563, 594, 595, 597, 601 and n. 4, 602, 609, 632. Knowledge of, 611. Commentaries on, 426. See Commentaries. Concordance, 426. Division into chapters, 613 n. 7. Source of doctrine, 537, 621. Joachim, 220. Anselm, 368. Hugo a St. Victor, 401, 402, 405, 406. Peter Cantor on wresting the sense, 414, 415. Roger Bacon, 425, 426. Waldenses, 606–614 (321). See Scriptures.
In the sixth Period, v. 61, 149. Clemaugis, 114. Wiklif on the, 150, 151. Militz, 181. Janow, 195. Huss, 240, 336. Anna of England, 241 n. 2. See Scriptures.

Bible revision and emendation, i. 582 and n. 2, 700, 701, 707, 708, 721, 722 and n. 6; ii. 745, 749; iii. 126, 153 n. 3, 155.

Bible translation, i. 303, 708. Coptic, i. 83. The Latin, i. 303; ii. 159, 745, 746; iii. 129, 155, 335, 347; v. 150. Of Symmachus, i. 708. Persian by Miesrob, ii. 137. Indian, ii. 140. Gothic of Ulphilas, ii. 152, 158; iii. 129, 281 n. 1. The Syrian, ii. 137, iv. 52; (of Philoxenus), ii. 589. Jerome's, ii. 712 n. 3, 745, 746. Neglected, iii. 129, 426. Swedish, iii. 281 n. 1. Cyrill's Slavonian, iii. 316, 330. German, iii. 425, 471; iv. 320, 609. Paraphrase of the Gospels, iii. 425; of the Psalms, iii. 471. Elfric, iii. 469 n. 4. Among the sects of the Middle Ages, iii. 600, 603, 604. Tartar, iv. 58. In the sects, iv. 320–324. Provençal, Waldensian, iv. 320, 321, 606–611. English, Trevisa, v. 149. Wiklif, v. 149–151. French, Bohemian, British, German, v. 150, 241 n. 1. Luther's, v. 149, 150.

Bibles, iii. 118, 126, 310, 427 (52). See Manuscripts.

Bibles burned, i. 148–150, 689; iv. 324. Confiscated, ii. 217–220.

Biblical expressions in determinations of doctrine, ii. 417, 450.

Biblical tendency, iv. 33, 593.

Bibliotheca Cisterc.
T. ii. f. 44, German bishops, iv. 214 n. 2. T. iv. f. 239, disputat. anor. adv. Abelard, iv. 399 n. 1.

Bibliotheca Cluniacensis.
Life of Odo, iii. 417 n. 1. Collationes of Odo, 417 n. 2. Præf., Vita S. Geraldi, 444 n. 4.

Bibliotheca eccles., ed. Fabric.
Henry of Ghent ou Simon of Tournay, iv. 418 n. 3; f. 114, Sigebert of Gemblours, De script. eccles., iv. 130 n. 2.

Bibliotheca Græca, Fabricii.
Ed. nov. vol. vii. f. 316, epp. of Mani, to Buddas, i. 486 n. 1; to Adas, 499 n. 5.

Bibliotheca Oriental. See Stephanus Enodius Asseman.

Bibliotheca Palatina, burning of the, iii. 150 n. 7.

Bibliotheca Patrum, Galland.
T. iii. f. 762, Methodius on freewill, i. 422 n. 2. T. iv., ep. of Theonas to Lucianus, i. 143 n. 1. T. vii., Pacianus Barcelonensis, i. 246 n. 2. T. viii. ff. 13, 14, tracts of Marcus, ii. 290 n. 4, 308 n. 1. T. ix., Bachiarius, confession of, ii 775 n. 6. T. ix., Life of Porphyry, bp. of Gaza. ii. 103 n. 1. T. ix. f. 353, Maximus of Turin (H. V. in Kal. Jan.), Christmas, iii. 348 n. 2. T. xii., ep. of Nicetius, iii. 8 n. 1. T. xii., letter of Columban, iii. 29 n. 4. T. xii., sermon of Gallus, iii. 34 n. 1. T. xiii. f. 272, dialogue of John of Damascus, iii. 88 n. 1.

Bibliotheca Patrum, Lugdunensis.
T. vi. f. 50, hermeneutic rules of Tichonius, reg. 1, ii. 244 n. 2. T. viii., Arnobius, Comm. in Ps. 146, ii. 702 n. 2; Gelasius, De duabus nat. in Christo, ii. 733 n. 1. T. ix. f. 701, Leontius, contra Nestorium, etc., fragments of Theodore on the incarnation, ii. 496 nn. 3, 4, 497 n. 1, (col. 1) 500 n. 2; f. 700, and of Diodorus of Tarsus, ii 499 nn. 2, 3, (col. 2) 500 n. 4; f. 703, col. 1, Theodore, ii. 502 n. 1. T. xiv., Claudius of Turin, his vindication, iii. 454 n. 4; his comm. on Galat., iii. 431 n. 1, 432 nn. 1, 2; dedication, iii. 432 n. 4; Jonas of Orleans, De cultu imag. f. 130, apolog. of Theodemir, iii. 438 n. 3; Dungal, Respons. adv. Claud. Taur. f. 204, iii. 431 n. 2. T. xv. f. 169, Christian Druthmar, Comm. in Matt., iii. 458 n. 2. T. xviii. f. 417, Hugo of Langres, De corpore et sanguine Christi, iii. 506 n. 3; f. 437, Durand, the same, iii. 503 n. 3, 509 n. 4; f. 441, Guitmund, De corporis et sanguinis Christi veritate, iii. 470 nn. 4, 5, 503 n. 1; f. 459, Guitmund, De veritate eucharistiæ, iii. 526 n. 5; f. 461, Guitmund, De eucharistiæ sacramento, iii. 528 n. 1; f. 532, letter of Deoduin to Henry I., iii. 509 n. 3; f 835, anonymous author on Berengar, iii. 513 n. 4, 515 n. 5, 516 n. 1, 518 n. 2; ff. 858, 859, dialogues of Desiderius, iii. 375 n. 4, 384 n. 4, 399 n. 1. T. xix. f. 916, Zacharias, comm. of, iv. 337 n. 4. T. xxi., tract of Potho, iv. 331 nn. 4, 5; f. 251, Alger, De sacramento, etc., iv. 338 n. 3. T. xxii., Meditations of Guigo, iv. 413 nn. 5, 6; ep. of Stephen of Tournay, iv. 416 n. 1 T. xxiii. f. 602, Eckert against the Catharists, iv. 506 n. 2. T. xxiv. ff. 1537, 1547, 1558, 1583, Ebrardus contra Catharos, iv. 577 nn. 1, 4, 578 n. 4, 579 n. 1. T. xxv., writings of Celestin V., iv. 193 n. 2. f. 17, ep. of Stephen of Tournay, iv. 418 n. 4; f. 195, Lucas Tudensis adv. Albigenses, t. i., iv. 584 n. 5; f. 266–272, Rainer contr. Waldenses (Catharos), iv. 551 n. 2, 576 nn. 2, 3, 577 nn. 2, 4, 578 n. 5, 579 nn. 2, 4, 5, 580 nn. 2, 3, 581 n. 5; f. 278, Pliichdorf contra Waldenses, v. i., iv. 605 n. 1; f. 348, Robert de Sorbonne, on conscience, iv. 393 n. 6; f. 350, the same, 303 n. 5; f. 447, 476, Humbert de Romanis, De erudit. praedicatorum, iv. 267 n. 2, 583 n. 1.

Bibliotheca Patrum, Parisiensis.
T. xi. ff. 431, 432, Theodore of Abukara, ἐρωτήσεις καὶ ἀποκρίσεις, iii. 88 nn. 1, 3. T. xiii. f. 939, Paladii Lausiaca ii. 271 n. 1. See Combefis.

Bibliotheca Pistoriensis. See Zacharia.

GENERAL INDEX.

Bibliothecæ Patrum, on Christians at the Saracen court in Spain, iii. 335 n. 3.
Bibliothèque Orientale, ed. Herbelot, Mani, i. 486 n. 2.
Bibrach, the doctor of, v. 321, 333.
Bilgard, iii. 602, 603.
Billerbeck, ch. at, iii. 80.
Bingen, iv. 217.
Birka (Biorka), iii. 276, 281, 284, 291.
Birthday festivals, i. 301. Birthdays of martyrs, i. 334 and n. 3, 335; ii. 369.
Bisanthe (Rodosto), iii. 563 n. 4.
Bischofteinitz, Militz at, v. 174.
Bishoprics, foundation of German, iii. 55. In Iceland, iii. 306. Prussian, iv. 45.
Bishops, *in the first Period*, objects of persecution, i. 131, 133, 137. Conduct in persecution, 133, 151. Separated from their communities, 137 (133). Office in the apostolic period, 184–186, 659. Later, 190–195, 235. Election, 199, 200. Organs of the Holy Spirit, 207, 210, 517, 519. Growing power, 207, 594. Confirmation, 316, 317. Pride of, in the large towns, 603. Among the Manicheans, 504.
In the second Period, worldliness of some, ii. 18, 25, 32 n. 2, 186, 763 n. 3, 765, 766. Pompous mode of life, 168, 755. Expenses, 168. Court bishops, 758. Simplicity and piety in other cases, 167–169 (120). Judicial authority, 171. Become involved in worldly business, 171, 172. Intercessions, 173, 176, 187. Courage, 174, 175. Protectors of the weak, 176. Oversight of prisoners, 178. Conditions of ordination, 184. Election of, 185, 186. Transfer of bishops, and journeys to the metropolis, 186–188, 225 n. 4, 465, 593. Special functions, 188. Bishops and presbyters, 696, 748. Relations of bishops, 748, 756. Deposition of, 761. Licinius and the, 18, 19. Julian, 71, 72, 78, 79. Constantine, 18, 25, 32 n. 2.
In the third Period, pious, iii. 4. In the metropolitan system, 64. Not allowed to choose their successors, 67. Nomination of, 92–95, 113 n. 4. Assemblies of, 95–97. Exemption, 102. Protection of the poor, 105. Involved in secular affairs, 105 n. 3, 141 and notes. Judicatory power, 105 n. 4. Sends, 107, 108. Duty of preaching, 107, 123–125; of visitation, 107, 108. Diocesan power, 110, 111. Despotic, 98. Want of culture, 154.
In the fourth Period, election, investiture, military service, iii. 400–406. Power to bind and loose, 363. Spiritual judicature, 406, 407. Union of spiritual and secular power, 408, 409. In the Decretals, 348, 349. To be judged by the pope only, 349, 359, 371, 509. Jurisdictions, 452, 478 (iv. 201). Among the Icelanders, 306 and n. 1.

In the fifth Period, deposition of, iv. 107. Relations to the pope, 107, 200–202. Ignorance of, 102 n. 4. Servility of German, 107. Involved in secular business, 133, 214, 215, 286, 421, 639. In the contest between the popes and the empire, 107, 165. Archdeacons, 211, 212. Administration of the office of, activity, the German bps., episcopi in partibus infidelium, suffraganei, 213–215. Hold capital trials, 214 and n. 2. Worldly minded, 265. Abelard on the, 384, 390. Diminished respect for, 639, 640, 643.
In the sixth Period, independence of, v. 6, 17. Secular affairs of, 28, 202. Originally not distinct from presbyters, 31, 170. Irregular appointment of, 34. Titular, 103. Janow on, 202.
Bishop's staff, iii. 300 n. 1.
Bithynia, Christianity in, i. 97. Persecution in, 147. *Second Period*, ii. 3, 42, 71, 547, 753 n. 2. Stephanus, iii. 220.
Beccus, iv. 550.
Bizya, castle of, iii. 192.
Black Forest, iii. 37; iv. 233.
Black Plague, v. 42, 128, 380, 381, 383, 407, 412.
Black Sea, monks near the, ii. 687, 710 (767).
Blanche, mother of Louis IX., iv. 300.
Blandina, martyr, i. 114.
Blas, S.
Monumenta res Allemanicas illustrantia, t. ii., chron. of Bernold, f. 39, iv. 108 n. 1: f. 120, 233 n.; f. 148, 303 n. 2. See Bernold.
Blastus, letter to, i. 680.
Blemmyans, ii. 552.
Blessedness of the righteous, ii. 677; iv. 432, 491 n. 8; v. 402. See Heaven.
Blessing of the clergy, iii. 102.
Blexem (Pleceateshem), iii. 82.
Blois. See Peter of.
Blood, shedding of, iv. 612, 616.
Bobbio, monastery, iii. 29 n. 3, 34, 470 n. 3.
Bodies of the saints, Charlemagne on the, iii. 238.
Body, the material, with the Antitactes, i. 451. Temple of the Holy Ghost, 654. Hieracas, 714. In paganism, ii. 115. Apollinaris, 487. Augustin, 667. Priscillian, 777. With the Paulicians, iii. 258. Bogomiles, iv. 558. Catharists, 572, 575 (heavenly, 568). Glorified, i. 714; ii. 667; iv. 472. Body of Christ, i. 631–635; ii. 490, 498, 538, 565, 777; iii. 261, 262. See Docetism. In the Lord's Supper, i. 647, 648 n. 1. See Lord's Supper.
Boehman, Jacob, i. 482 n. 1.
Boethius, iv. 418 n. 4 (v. 377). Influence of his writings, 355. De consolat. philosoph., 359. Comm. on De Trinitate, 409 n. 1, 461 n. 5.
Bogomiles, ii. 276 n. 2; iii. 245 n., 254 n. 3, 590, 591 nn. 1, 2, 592 n. 3, 594 n. 3,

601. Doctrine and history, iv. 552-564, 566, 572 n. 1, 573 and n. 1, 574. Initiation, 556.
Bogoris, Bulgarian prince, iii. 308, 309, 315 n. 1.
Bohemia, spread of Christianity in, iii. 321-323. From, 330; iv. 6, 18, 49. Legates in, iv. 89 n. 2. *In the sixth Period*, v. 51, 102, 128, 129, 133, 132, 184, 215, 237. Militz in, 181, 182. Conrad, 184. Bible translation, 150, 241 n. 1. Pilgrimages to Wilsnack, 237. The movements of reform in, 48, 93, 119, 173-380. Bohemians at the Univ. of Prague, 244-247, 252-255, 253, 279, 347. Convocation of (an. 1408), 248. Laity, 236. Bohemians in the senate at Prague, 299. Bohemian knights at Constance, 339, 340, 341, 349, 374. Crusade against, 128-131, 133. See Huss.
Bohmisch-Brod, v. 295, 297.
Boivin, ed. letter of Euseb. Cæsariens, to Constantia on images, ii. 326 n. 4. See Nicephorus Gregoras, vol. ii. f. 795.
Bolak, city of the Mongols, iv. 55.
Boleslav I., duke of Poland, iv. 41, 42 n. 1.
Boleslav III. (Krzivousti), iv. 1, 6, 8, 10-12, 14, 17, 24.
Boleslav the Cruel, of Bohemia, iii. 322; v. 290.
Boleslav the Mild, iii. 322.
Bollandists. See Acta Sanctorum of the.
Bologna, university at, iv. 172, 203, 204, 421, 425. Balthazar Cossa (John XXII.) at, v. 89, 90, 100, 101, 277. Council appointed at, 130. Huss cited to, 271, 272.
Bombay, ii. 141.
Bona, De rebus liturgicis, iv. 343 n. 4.
Bona (Hipporegius) in Algiers, ii. 198.
Bona naturalia et gratuita, iv. 495.
Bonacursus.
De vit. hæreticorum, Pasagians, iv. 590 n. 7. See D'Achery, t. i. f. 212.
Bonaventura, life and character of, iv. 420, 421. Life of Francis of Assisi, iv. 60 n. 2, 273-275. Defense of the monastic orders, 286-289. As censor of the same, 289-291. Circular letter, 289 and n. 4, 290. Special letter, 290 and n. 3. Property of the Franciscans, 291 n. Doctrine of transubstantiation, 339, 340. Faith and knowledge, 428, 429. End of Creation, 466. Original condition, 490, 491. Dispositio sufficiens, 491 n. 6. The incarnation and the original plan of God, 507, 508. Successor of John of Parma, 618 n. 1.
Determinationes circa regulam S. Francisci, opp. t. vii. ed. Lugd. f. 330, iv. 287 n 1; f. 333, 288 n. 1; f. 336, 288 n. 3; f. 338 288 n. 7 and 289 n. 1. Q. 24, iv. 291 n. Ep. ad ministros provinciales et custodes, opp. t. vii., iv. 289 n. 4, 290 n. 2. Life of Francis, 60 n. 2, 271 n. 1, 273-275 nn. See 290 n 3, 340 nn. 2, 3, 428 n. 6, 429 nn. 1-3, 490 nn 3, 4, 491 nn. 1-6.

Bondmen, in spiritual and monastic orders, iii. 97-99, 101, 107. Influence of Christianity on the condition of, 98-101. Employed in spiritual offices, 109. See Slavery.
Bondwomen, iv. 601.
Bongars.
Gesta Dei per Francos. t. i. f. 89, Balderic, Hist. Hierosol., iv. 123 n. 2, 127 n. 1 ; f. 384, Fulcher of Chartres, 126 n. 1; f. 482. Guibert, Hist. Hierosol., 124 n. 2 ; f. 641, Wm. of Tyre, 126 n. 3. T. ii. f. 1149, Francis of Assisi, 60 n. 3. See Jacob of Vitry.
Boni homines, iv. 303, 579 (577 and n. 2).
Boni valeti, iv. 303.
Boniface. See Bruno.
Boniface, father of the German church. His origin and education, iii. 46. First journey to Friesland, 46. In Utrecht and Rome, 47. In Thuringia, 47. In Hessia and Thuringia, 47. In Rome, 47. Confession, ordination, and oath, 48 (iv. 200). Design of his mission, 49. His labors compared with those of the Irish missionaries, 49. Boniface in Thuringia, 50. Character and success of his labors, 51. Care for religious instruction, 52. Preaching and study of Scriptures, 52. Efforts to promote spiritual culture, 53. His opponents, 53. His scruples of conscience in respect to holding intercourse with such, 54. In Rome and Bavaria, 55. Influence with Charlemagne and Pepin, 55. His foundations of bishoprics, and arrangement with regard to synods, 55, 56. His report on Adelbert, 57-59. His conduct towards him, 60. Not a worker of miracles, 60. On Clement, 61, 62. On hindrances to marriage arising from the relation of godparents, 61. Controversy with Virgilius, 63. Plainness of speech towards pope Zacharias, 64. Strives to give a fixed organization to the German church, 64. Appointed to the archiepiscopate without a particular diocese, 65. Quarrel with the bp. of Cologne, 65 n. 4. Labors for the Frieslanders, 65. Deposes Gewillieb of Mentz, 66. Wishes to nominate his successor, 67. Anoints Pepin as king, 69. Solicitude for the Eng. church, 69. Appoints Lull as his successor, letter to Fulrad, 70. Quarrel with Hildegar, bp. of Cologne, 71. In Friesland, his martyrdom there, 72. Boniface and Gregory, 72, 73 and n 2. Election of bps., 95. Synods, 96. Opposition to martial service by the clergy, 102. Against the abuse of the rights of patronage, 110 n. 3. Arch deacons, 111 n. 3. Influence on the relations between the Frankish and Roman churches, 119, 127 (49, 64). On changes in the system of church penance, 137 n. 1. Efforts in promotion of the papacy, 210, 243. Eating of horse-

flesh, 295 n. Celibacy, 410. Anointing of the sick a function of the priesthood, 449 n. 1. Picture of, iv. 43. His life, by Willibald (see Perz Monumenta), c. 1, f. 334, iii. 46 n. 2; § 23, 50 nn. 1, 2, 53 n. 2, 69 n. 1. By the ecclesiastic of Münster, 72 n. 4. By the priest of Utrecht (see Acta S. Boll. June), 60 n., 71 n. 3. By the presbyter of Mayence (see Perz Monumenta), 56 n. 5, 63 n. 1, 66 nn. 1, 2.

Citations from his writings: —
Epistles. Ep. 3, Bugga to Boniface, his dream, iii. 47 n. 1. Ep. 4 (ed. Würdtwein), on reading the Scriptures, 48 n. 2. Ep. 12, to bp. Daniel, 51 n. 1; ascetism, 54 n. 1. Ep. 13, from bp. Daniel, mendacium officiosum, 54 n. 2. Ep. 14, from bp. Daniel, on religious instruction, 52 nn. 1, 2. Ep. 19, to Eadburga, 52 nn. 3, 4. Ep. 24, from Greg. II., treatment of offending clergy, 54 n. 3. Ep. 25, the pall received from Greg. III., 65 n. 3. Ep. 31, to an Eng. abbess, 46 n. 3. Epp. 39, 40, 41; f. 88, law of marriage, 61 n. 1. Ep. 51, to Zacharias, Carloman, synods, 56 n. 1; superstitious practices at Rome, 64 n. 2; concerning his successor, 67 n. 1. Ep. 54, books from Rome, 53 n. 3; his commission from the pope, 69 n. 5. Ep. 55, to Ethelbald, with gifts, 69 n. 7. Ep. 60, from pope Zacharias, reform, superstition, the pallium, 56 n. 2, 64 n. 1, 65 n. 2. Ep. 62, Adelbert, 57 n. 2; Virgilius, 63 n. 3. Ep. 69, books from Rome, 53 n. 3. Ep. 70, from Zacharias (ed. Würdtwein), 65 n. 6, 66 n. 2; f. 113, 67 n. 2. Ep. 71, to an English priest, 69 nn. 3, 4. Ep. 72, to Ethelbald, 69 n. 6. Ep. 73, to Cuthbert, abp. of Canterbury, pilgrimages, 58 n. 1; report of administration, 64 n. 4, 70 n. 1. Ep. 74, Zacharias, 62 n. 4. Ep. 79, monks from Eng., 53 n. 1. Ep. 80, the same, 53 n. 4. Ep. 82, from Zacharias, on his resignation, 68 n. 1; Samson, 63 n. 4. Ep. 83 (ed. Würdtwein), on the metropolitan see at Mayence, 71 n. 2. Ep. 86, to Zacharias, 65 n. 2; Fulda, 68 n. 2; concerning Lull, 69 n. 2. Ep. 90, to Fulrad, naming his successor, 70 n. 2. Ep. 105, to Stephen II., 71 n. 1; Carloman, 66 n. 5. Ep. 114, prayer of Adelbert, 58 n. 2. Epp. ed. Würdtwein, f. 116, cupidity of archdeacons, 111 n. 3; f. 140, abuse of patronage, 110 n. 3; f. 142, ordinances, 53 n. 5; of penance, 137 n. 1; unction, 449 n. 1. Epp. to Zacharias, 53 n. 7, 65 n. 7.

Life of Livin, iii. 43 n. 1.

Boniface, fictitious personage, iv. 42 n. 2.
Boniface (Bonifacius) I., bp. of Rome, ii. 208, 235 nn. 1, 2, 652 n. 2.
Boniface (Bonifacius) II., bp. of Rome, ii. 711.
Boniface IV., pope, iii. 32, 34, 134.
Boniface VIII., pope, iv. 67, 632; v. 1–13, 19, 21, 22, 33, 38, 41, 93. Ep. to Philip the Fair, 6 n. See Bulls.
Boniface IX., v. 51, 52, 89, 252, 276.
Bonifacian plantation, v. 52, 98.
Bonifacius, count in Africa, ii. 694, 695.
Bonnaven, ii. 146.
Bonosus, bp., ii. 377. Whether his doctrines were spread among the Bavarians, iii. 38.
Books, in Ireland, ii. 149; iii. 10, 43, 460 n. 6. Brought from, iii. 152, 300 n. 1. Brought from Eng., ii. 149; iii. 52, 53, 156 n. 1. To Eng., iii. 15, 118, 151, 152. From France, ii. 149; iii. 152. In France, iii. 427. In Germany, iii. 52, 53 and n. 3, 151. In Sweden, iii. 281. In Iceland, iii. 800 n. 1. In Friesland, iii. 79. In Italy, iii. 151. In Rome, iii. 150 nn. 4, 7, 151. From Rome, iii. 53 n. 3, 118, 152. Gothic, ii. 152, 158. Collections of, ii. 149; iii. 10, 151 n. 1, 470 n. 3; iv. 270 (see Libraries). Boniface, iii. 52, 53 and n. 3, 71. Chilperic, iii. 91 n. 1. Cassiodore, 151 n. 1. Alcuin, 156 n. 1. Ethelwold, 408 n. 1. Gerbert, 470 n. 3. Anthony on, ii. 269. Clemangis, v. 61. Reverence paid to, iii. 210. Translation of, iii. 330 (see Translation). Illumination of, iii. 201, 219. Decoration, iv. 4 n. 2. Burned by Iconoclasts, iii. 219 n. 1. Images to be removed from, iii. 219. School-books in the image controversy, iii. 543. French theological books burned, iv. 448. In the Eastern church, iii. 247; iv. 545. Loss of, iv. 529. Transcription of, iv. 265, 301 (see Manuscripts). Books of Wicklif, v. 248. Of Huss, v. 364. Burning of, v. 261–263, 286, 316, 342, 370. See Bibles, Literature.

Bordeaux, abp. of, iii. 94; iv. 583 n. 2; v. 20. Sects, iv. 639 n. 2. See Councils.
Boruchtnarians, iii. 44.
Borziwoi, duke of Bohemia, iii. 321.
Bosco, Peter de, v. 7.
Boσκοl, ii. 293 n. 4.
Boso, bp. of Merseberg, iii. 324.
Boso, count, iii. 358 n. 1.
Bosow, iii. 323 n. 3.
Bostra, in Arabia, ii. 67 n. 2, 71, 78. See Titus of.
Botrus, ii. 222 n. 1.
Boulæus.
  Hist. univers. Parisiens. l. i. ff. 687-730, the University of Paris on the schism, v. 53-55 nn., 56 n. 1; f. 729, letter of Benedict XIII. to the king of France, v. 56 n. 4.
  T. ii. f. 402, Walter a St. Victor, Contra quatuor Galliæ labyrinthos, iv. 410 n. 4; f. 524, society of the Trinitarians, iv. 268 n. 1. T. iii. f. 200, Walter of M. on Abelard, iv. 393 n. 1; f. 374, ep. to Clement IV. on transubstantiation, iv. 340 n. 4; f. 383, Bacon's Opus majus, iv. 425 n. 4; f. 686, Wm. of St. Amour, iv. 289 n. 3. T. iv. f. 237, assembly at Vincennes (an. 1333), v. 37 nn. 2, 3; f. 238, conc. Paris (an. 1406), v. 38 n. 1; f. 463, election of Urban VI., v. 46 n.; f. 470, the same, 45 n.; ff. 576, 578, Henry of Hessia, ep. pacis, v. 48 n., 49 n. 1. T. v. f. 269, letter of Gerson, v. 353 n. 1.

Boulay. See Boulæus.
Bouquet.
  Collectio script. rer. Franc. t. v. f. 621, Charlemagne on learning, iii. 154 n. 1.

Bourges, abp. of, v. 13. See Wm. of.
Bowing the knee, iv. 584, 594.
Boys, in the mines, i. 138. Education of, iii. 72, 73. See Education, Schools. In clerical offices, iii. 375, 409 and n. 1; iv. 186, 198, 200, 207; v. 9, 86.

GENERAL INDEX. 35

Brabant, Christianity in, iii. 43 and n. 2.
Braga, iv. 141. See Councils, an. 561, an. 563.
Brahmaism, i. 44. See Brahminism.
Brahminism, in Gnosticism, i. 370.
Brahmins, i. 442. Of the Manicheans, i. 501 n. 2, 503.
Brancas, cardinal, v. 272, 293.
Brandenburg, iv. 21.
Brazen serpent, the, iii. 211 and n. 2, 241.
Bread, breaking of, i. 325.
Bread, consecrated, distributed to filial churches at Rome, ii. 195. Distinguished from the host, given to children, iv. 342 n. 4.
Bread used in the Lord's Supper, i. 331; iii. 18 and n. 2, 581 n. 1, 581–585; iv. 538, 541; v. 92.
Bregenz (Pregentia), iii. 34.
Breisgau, iii. 37.
Bremen, iii. 296. Bishopric, 81. Archbishopric, united with Hamburg, 279, 290, 326. Patriarchate of the north, 292. Missionary station, 328 n. 2. Abps. of, 81, 292, 293, 307; iv. 33, 35, 643. Connection with Liefland, iv. 36–38. School in, 33. See Adam of.
Brescia. See Gaudentius, Adelmann, Arnold.
Breslau, bp. of, v. 182.
Breteuil, iv. 235.
Brethren of the Free Spirit, iv. 633 n. 2; v. 393, 401, 408.
Brethren of the Sword, iv. 45.
Brevicula historiæ Eutychianistarum, ii. 563 n. 5.
Bribery of the papal legates, iii. 354, 562, 563, 565. Dioscurus, ii. 559. Justinian, ii. 600. At the Roman conc., iii. 580; iv. 196, 198; v. 272 n. 1, 331. Elsewhere, iv. 196. Gregory VII. uninfluenced by, iv. 89, 90, 103. Bonifacc VIII., v. 52. By Mohammedans, iv. 69 and n. 2. By Jews, iv. 73, 74 n. 1. Facundus of Hermiane on, ii. 604.
Brief, papal, in favor of the Jews, iv. 76.
Brigitta of Sweden, v. 44, 222.
Brindisi, crusaders at, iv. 178.
Britain, Christianity introduced into, i. 85, 86. Constantius Chlorus in, i. 154. Constantine in, ii. 8. Church in, ii. 146, 148, 149, 632. (Missions from, see Missions, Missionaries. Means of culture in, see Books.) Seminaries for Christianity and Christian education, iii. 10, 23, 29. Corruption of the earlier Christianity there, 10. Anglo-Saxon heptarchy, 11. Relation of the ancient church there to the new church among the Anglo-Saxons, 16–18. Ritual of the British church, 17. Condition of the church there after Augustin's death, 18–25. Differences betwixt the Britannico-Scottish and the Anglo-Saxon-Frankish (Romish) churches, 23–25. Missionaries, 53, 55. Missions,

29. Freedom of the British church, 49, 53. See Anglo-Saxons, Augustin.
British church, ii. 632. See Britain.
Britons, Bible translation, v. 150.
Brittany, iv. 373, 383.
Brixen, iii. 378.
Broda, Andrew of, v. 258.
Brogny, Jean de, bp. of Ostia, v. 344, 360 n. 2.
Brotherly love, i. 76, 90, 255.
Brothers and Sisters of the Free Spirit, v. 393, 401. See Brethren.
Brown.
Edition works of R. Grosshead, iv. 185 n. 1; ep. 107, 207 n. 5.
Bruges, iii. 277. Monastery at, iv. 326. Meeting with papal nuncios at (an. 1374), v. 137, 140, 161.
Brumalia, ii. 347 n. 4.
Brunehault (Brunehild), iii. 33, 113 n. 1.
Bruno, abp. of Cologne iii. 460 n. 6.
Bruno, bp. of Segni (Astensis), iii. 378 n. 2, 381 n 2.
His life of Leo IX., corruption of the church, iii. 378 n. 2. Leo's acceptance of the papacy, 381 n. 2. Leo's synods of reform (opp. ed. 1651, t. ii. f. 148), 384 n. 4. Military service of Leo (f. 147), 385 n. 2. Miracles reported at the tomb of Leo and his warriors, 386 nn. 4, 5. Simony, 389 n. 2.
Bruno, bp. of Toul (Leo IX.), iii. 378, 381 n. 2. Life by Wibert, 378 n. 5, 381 n. 2. See Leo IX.
Bruno, founder of the Carthusian order, iv. 265.
Bruno (Boniface), missionary to the Prussians, iv. 42, 43.
Bruns.
Ed. canones apost. et concil. i. f. 68, conc. Ancyra, can. 10, marriage of deacons, ii. 180 n. 3; f. 71, conc. Neocæsarea, an. 314, can. 1, of presbyters, 180 n. 2; f. 140, fourth synod of Carthage, can. 1, ordination of bishops, 182 n. 6; ii. f. 9, conc. Elvira, Duumviri, ii. 173 n. 1; f. 108, conc. Arles, can. 7, 173 n. 2.
Brussa, iv. 550.
Brussels, v. 401.
Brute kingdom. Basilices, i. 404, 405, 413. Nature of brutes, ii. 668.
Bruttius, cited by Euseb., i. 96 n. 4.
Buchwald (Buchonia), iii 74.
Buddas, predecessor of Mani, i. 480, 485.
Buddha, Buddhas, i. 450, 480, 481, 483, 503.
Buddhism, i. 44. In Gnosticism, i. 370, 405, 450, 451, 484. Relation to Christianity, i. 482–484. In Manicheism, i. 480–486, 488, 490–493, 495, 496, 500, 501, 503. Asceticism in, ii. 263, 276. Pantheism, iii. 461 n. 2. Among the Mongols, iv. 48, 52. In China, iv. 56.
Bugga, abbess, ep. to Boniface, iii. 47 n. 1.
Bugia, Raymund Lull there, iv. 68, 69 and n. 2, 71 and n. 2.
Bugri, iv. 565.
Building of churches, zeal for, ii. 319,

320, 753 and n. 2. Costly buildings, iv. 280, 290, 291. See Churches.
Bulæus. See Boulæus.
Bulgari, iv. 565.
Bulgaria, spread of Christianity in, iii. 307-314, 315 n., 458 u. 2, 497 n. 1 (iv. 90 n. 6). Customs of the people, 312, 313. Mohammedanism in, 329. Paulicians in, 587. In the contest between Rome and Constantinople, 567, 572, 574, 577, 578, 580. Catharists in, 591 n. 1; iv. 565, 566, 590. Bogomiles from, iv. 552, 553 n. 5.
Bulls, papal, John XV. (an. 973), on saint worship, iii. 447. Forged, iv. 204, 205. (See Innocent III. epp.) Bull of Innocent III. in England, iv. 176. Of Greg. IX. against Frederic II., iv. 179, 182. Bull of Innocent IV., an. 1254, limiting the mendicant orders, iv. 282 and n. 4. Bulls of Alex. IV., in their favor, iv. 283. Of Urban IV., an. 1264, and Clement V., an. 1311, establishing Corpus Christi day, iv. 341. Of Honorius IV., an. 1286, against spiritual societies, iv. 627. Of Nicholas III., an. 1288, iv. 591 n. 2; an. 1297 (Exiit qui seminat), iv. 291. *Sixth Period*. Bulls of Boniface VIII., indulgence, v. 3; against the Colonnas, 4; against Philip the Fair, Clericis laicos, 5, Unam Sanctam, 8, 9, 13, 33, pronouncing the ban, etc., 10, 12, 22. Of John XXII., on the condition of departed saints, 38; against the preaching of mystical doctrines, 395. Bull of Clement VI., an. 1349, Unigenitus, 41. Bull of Gregory IX., suspending the law of papal elections, 45. Of Benedict XIII., 77. Of Gregory XI., against Wicklif, 146-148; against Milítz, 182. Of Urban VI. against Clement VII., 164. Of Alexander V. against the Wicklifite heresy, 259-261, 265, 300. Of John XXIII., 111; against Ladislaus, 276-291, 335. Bulls burnt, 8, 286; edict of Wenceslaus concerning them, 287, 288 n. 2. Janow on the form of the papal bull, 207.
Bulosudes, Hungarian prince, iii. 330.
Burburg, bishopric, iii. 55.
Burda, river, iii. 72.
Burdinus, abp. of Braga, iv. 141. See Gregory VIII.
Burgundians, their conversion and Arianism, iii. 4, 5. Embrace the Nicene doctrine, 5 (9 n.). Columban among them, 30-33. Photinian doctrines among them, 39 and n. 3. Judgment of God, 130.
Burgundy, iii. 417; iv. 252, 254, 283 n. 1, 289, 314 n. 2. Duke of, v. 93.
Burial of the dead, i. 334, 335; ii. 128, 192, 262; iv. 290. As sacrament, ii. 725. Burial places, venal consecration of, v. 43.
Burkhard of Worms, iv. 203.

Burning of the dead, iii. 78.
Butler, Franciscan, v. 151 n. 2.
Bythos (Βύθος), in Gnosticism, i. 373 n. 1, 417, 418, 421, 477 n. 1, 489; ii. 127.
Byzacene (Buzazene), ii. 605 n. 2, 686.
Byzantine church, ii. 204. See Constantinople.
Byzantine court, corrupting influence of the, ii. 45, 164-166, 505; iii. 91. Court worship, iii. 108. Empire, iii. 48 n. 6, 88. Principle of church gov't, 191. Era, 315 n. 2. Insincerity and exaggeration, 235, 583 n. 3. Despotism, 543, 604.
Byzantine emperors, alliances with Mongols, iv. 56. In ecclesiastical affairs, ii. 164-166, 223-229; iii. 175 (see the controversies). Dogmatizing spirit, ii. 603; iv. 533. Honors paid to, iii. 241.
Byzantine historians, iii. 203 n. 1, 250 n. 2, 254 n. 5, 269 n. 6, 327; iv. 530.
Byzantium, ii. 197, 422 n. 4. See Leontius of.

C.

Cabala, i. 375, 440. Cabalists, i. 448 n. 1. Cabalistic theology, ii. 776 n. 4.
Cadalous, bp. of Parma, iii. 396. See Honorius II.
Cæcilian, archdeacon and bp. of Carthage, ii. 217, 218, 221-226, 228 n. 3, 237, 245.
Cæcilius, pagan, on private judgment, i. 11. On brotherly love of Christians, i. 76 n. 4. See Minucius Felix.
Cæcilius of Bilta, on exorcism, i. 310 n. 1.
Cærimoniæ Romanæ, i. 87, 175.
Cæsar, rendering to, iv. 142, 147, 151, 167, 172, 223; v. 36, 39.
Cæsar Augusta. See Saragossa.
Cæsarea in Cappadocia, persecution at, i. 707. Origen at, i. 707. Basil, asylum, ii. 177 n. 1. School at, ii. 183. Election of bishops, ii. 186 n. 1. See Basil, Firmilian, Procopius, Thalassius, Theodore Ascidas.
Cæsarea in Palestine, persecution at, i. 153, 706, 707, 709. Church of, i. 299. Origen at, i. 703-707, 709. School at, i. 721; ii. 183. Library at, i. 721; ii. 745. The fraudulent abp., iv. 127. See Acacius, Eulogius, Theophilus.
Cæsares, irreligiositas in, ii. 112.
Cæsariani, i. 142.
Cæsarius, bp. of Arles, ii. 296, 709 and n. 2; iii. 4. On fasting, ii. 340. Doctrine of grace, ii. 709, 711. Amulets, iii. 448. His life, ii. 709 n. 2. Sermons, ii. 709 n. 2. See Acta S. Aug. 27.
Cæsarius, monk, letter of Chrysostom to, ii. 732 n. 6.
Cæsarius of Heisterbach, Cistercian, iv. 155 n. 5, 235. On bearing the yoke of Christ, iv. 156.
Dialogues, Dist. 1. c. 4, different characters of monks, iv. 234 n. 4; cc. 5, 12, 25, 28, mo-

GENERAL INDEX. 37

tives for embracing the monastic calling, 235 and nn. 2, 3; c. 6, crusades, prudence of Bernard, 155 n. 5; effects of the crusades, 156 n. 3; c. 31, the condemned knight, 236 n. 2. Dist. ii. c. 25, German bps., 214 n. 2. D. iv. f. 65, distribution of alms, 239 n. 1; f. 94, etc., 100, reactions of feeling, 239 n. 2. D. c. 27, fatalism, 305 n. 2. D. v. c. 19, f. 138, Catharists, 585 n. 3, 589 n. 5; c. 20, f. 138, Waldenses, 321 n. 1; c. 21, Catharists, 582 n. 4; c. 22, sect of the Holy Ghost, 448 nn. 1, 3; c. 22, f. 142, Catharists, persecutions of, 590 n. 1. D. ix. c. 15, f. 270, Catharist miracle-workers, 585 n. 3; c. 51, kneeling before the host, 341 n. 3. D. xii. c. 48, Peter Cantor, 414 n. 2.

Cahors, bp. of, iii. 95 n. 2.
Caïanians, i. 476 n. 1.
Cain, i. 448; ii. 705; iv. 75. W th the Bogomiles, iv. 554. The Catharists, 573.
Cainites, i. 448, 476 n. 1, 646.
Caius (of Hippolytus), i. 682.
Caius, presbyter at Rome, on Cerinthus, i. 396 n. 1, 399. Montanism, 632, 690. Ep. of Dionysius of Alexandria to, iii. 184 n. 1.
Cajetan, cardinal Benedict. See Boniface VIII.
Calabria, iii. 206 n. 3, 376, 420; iv. 266. See Joachim.
Calame, ii. 102 n. 2.
Calamities, public, charged on Christians, i. 103, 104, 126, 689; ii. 4, 5, 92; iii. 22 n. 1, 448 n. 1; iv. 26, 100.
Calaris, ii. 257. See Lucifer of.
Calarugna, iv. 268.
Caliphs, iii. 206 n. 3, 207. At Cordova, 339.
Calixtus II., pope, iv. 142 n. 3, 143, 245.
Calixtus III., pope, iv. 68.
Calliana (Calcutta), ii. 141.
Calligraphy, art of, i. 7 3.
Calling of grace, Aug. on, ii. 630, 631. The Christian, Hildebert on, iv. 306, 307. Of princes, Lull, iv. 310 n. 7. To preach, Innocent III. on, iv. 323; Huss on, v. 265, 266, 253.
Callinice, iii. 244, 246.
Callinicum, castle of, ii. 95 n. 4.
Calliopas, exarch, iii. 186 n. 1, 187-189, 192.
Calumny, ii. 1, 442.
Camaldolensians, iii. 419; iv. 204.
Camaldoli, iii. 419.
Cambalu (Pekin), iv. 57-59.
Cambray, Robert of. See Clement VII.
Cambray, sect in, iii. 598, 599. See Arras. Adherents of Henry IV., iv. 129. Bernard in, iv. 256 n. 4. Suffragan bp. of, iv. 326 n. 1. Hungarians threaten, iv. 405. Abp. of, v. 90. See Gerhard, Halitgar, Odo, Wibold
Cambyses, ii. 89.
Cammin, city in Pomerania, iv. 9.
Camp bps., ii. 143.
Campania, v. 12.
Cana, miracle at, ii. 306, 344.
Cancelli. See Chancel.
Cancer Cusanus. See Nicholas of Cusa.

Cancrisantes, the, v. 291.
Candace, i. 83.
Candes, iv. 247.
Candia, v. 84.
Candidian. Comes, ii. 527, 531 n. 3, 532-534, 537, 538.
Candidus, the Valent'nian, i. 589, 703 n. 3, 704 n. 1.
Canisius.
Lectiones antiquæ, ed. Basnage, Antv. 1725, t. i. f. 137, Titus of Bostra against the Manicheans, i 496 n. 1. T. i. f. 332, chronicle of Victor of Tununum, i . 604 n. 3 : f. 608, Leontius Byzant. c. fraudes Apollinarist., ii. 491 n. 1. T. ii. f. 301, Beatus contr. Elipand., iii. 164 nn. 6, 7; f. 310, Lu. 4, 5. T. ii. P. ii. f. 354, Walafrid Strabo, poem of, iii. 472 n. 1. T. iii., Cilean. iii. 37 1 . 6: life of Emmeran, iii. 39 n. 4, 40 n. 2. T. iii. P. i. f. 282, ep. of Michael Cerularius, iii. 581 n. 4. T. iii. P. i. Humbert's defense of the Roman ch., iii. 582 nn. 3-6: f. 285, the same, 581 n. 4; f 325, his report of the mission to Constantinople, 583 n. 3. T. iii. P. ii., Rutbert. iii. 40 n. 2; life of Otto of Bamberg, iv. 2 n. 1, 5 nn. 1, 2, 11 nn. 1, 2, 16 nn. 1, 2, 4, 22 n. 2, 26 nn., 27 n. 1, 30 n. 1 ; Anselm of Lucca contra Guibert, iv. 101 n. 2. T. iii. P. ii. f. 62, Otto on the seven sacraments, iv. 235 n. 2. T. iv. f. 124, life of Elizabeth of Hessia, iv. 302 n. 2.
Canon, de canone Novi Testamenti fragm.
Antiq. Ital. jud. ævi ed. Muratori, t. 3, i. 660 n. 1.
Canon, the, with the Sadducees, i. 41. The Bogomiles, iv. 558.
Canon law, v. 325. See Ecclesiastical law.
Canones apostolici, i. 660, 703 n. 4. Number of, iii. 557. See Bruns.
Canonical age, iv. 207.
Canonical community under Ariald, iii. 393.
Canonical law, iv. 204, 279, 425; v. 33. See Canon law.
Canonical life of the clergy, ii. 184, 295; iii. 106, 107, 409; iv. 148, 205-207, 208 (Didacus, 269).
Canonical priests, iv. 207, 269.
Canonici, iv. 208. Canonicals, v. 202. Of St. Victor, iv. 401.
Canonization of saints, iii. 447; iv. 284. Wicklif on, v. 169.
Canoury, candidates for, iv. 196.
Canons, apostolic. See Canones.
Canons of councils, ii. 209, 212; iii. 143 n. 1. Collection of, ii. 212. See Bruns, ed. Canones ap. et corcil.
Canossa, castle of, iv. 114.
Canterbury, Augustin at, iii. 12. Archbishopric, iii. 16. Primacy, iii. 16, 25. Disputes of the abps. with the Norman princes, iv. 141. Abbot of, iv. 196 n. 2. John Balle at, v. 58, 159. Wicklifites at, v. 363. Canterbury hall, v. 135. Archbishops of, iii. 16, 18, 501 n. 3; iv. 174, 194, 279; v. 146-148, 363. See Anselm, Augustin, Cuthbert, Dunstan, Elfeg, Islep, Odo, Richard, Stephen Langton, Sudbury, Thomas à Becket.
Cantimpre, iv. 277. See Thomas of.

Cantores, ii. 354 nn. 2, 3 (iv. 196).
Canute, son of Henry the converter of the Wends, iv. 32.
Canute the Great, iii. 290, 299. Goes to Rome, 290. Zealous for Christianity, 290, 291.
Capital punishment, iii. 103, 104. See Punishment of death.
Capitula, iii. 107 n. 1. Ruralia, 110.
Capitula of Theodore, iii. 102 n. 4.
Capitularies, collection of, by B. Levita, iii. 350 n. 1.
Capitularies of Charlemagne.
   An. 779, on the treatment of persons sentenced to death who took refuge in asylums, iii. 104.
   An. 789, on forged writings, iii. 59 n. 2; for the Saxons, 78 n. 3; against *ordinationes absolutæ*, 108 n. 3; c. 9, on attendance upon parochial worship, 109 n. 3; on church psalmody, 127 n. 2. Cap. 3, c. 4, against consulting the Scriptures for oracles, 129 n. 7; against vagabond penitents, 140.
   An. 794, against *ordinationes absolutæ*, iii. 108 n. 3; on judgments of God, 130 n. 5; against the worship of new saints, 133.
   An. 796, c. 50, on ecclesiastical language, iii. 128 n. 5.
   An. 801, on the participation of the clergy in the affairs of war, iii. 102; on Sends, 107 n. 5.
   An. 803, on the election of bps., iii. 95 n. 1; on judgments of God, 130 n. 5.
   An. 805, c. 2, against appointing archdeacons from the laity, iii. 111 n. 2; c. 11, on admission of slaves into the monastic order, 101 n. 1; c. 15, on the admission of freemen into the spiritual order, 97 n. 3.
   An. 806, on judgments of God, iii. 130 n. 5.
   An. 811, on external works, iii. 131; c. 4, on the separation of ecclesiastical affairs from political, iii. 97 n. 1.
   An. 814, c. 10, and an. 789, cap. 3, c. 18, against divination and amulets, iii. 129 n. 1. See Baluz.
Cappadocia, i. 117, 126. Provincial synods, i. 207. Stephanus, i. 318. Persecution in, i. 126, 707. Influence of Origen in, i. 706, 716. The three great teachers, i. 716; ii. 387, 459, 462, 501 n. 3; iii. 169. Julian in, ii. 40, 41. Goths and, ii. 149, 150, 155. Basil in, ii. 155, 174, 175, 186 n. 1, 460. Patriarchal relations, ii. 196 n. 3. Prima and Secunda, ii. 174, 547. Paulicians, iii. 256. Bishops of and the Bogomiles, iv. 563.
Cappelletti.
   Italian trans. of Elisæus, Venezia, 1840, ii. 125 nn. 3, 4.
Captives taken in war extend Christianity, ii. 124, 138, 149; iii. 276, 307, 308 (273), 331. Educated as Christians, iii. 41, 273, 308. Ransom of, i. 256; iii. 4 n. 1, 21, 26, 41, 104 n. 1, 138, 300, 308; iv. 12, 18, 30, 268. Freed, iii. 27. Anschar, iii. 277, 286. Rimbert, iii. 287. Martyrs in the crusades, iv. 128.
Capua, iii. 422. Siege of, iv. 364.
Caracalla, i. 119 n. 6, 122, 691, 703 n. 2.
Caracorum, chief city of Kerait, iv. 46, 51, 53.
Carbeas, Paulician, iii. 587.
Carcussone, iv. 590, 639 n. 2. Religious conference at, 641. Inquisition in, 643. Archives of inquisition, 553 n. 5.
Cardag, Nestorian missionary, iii. 89.
Cardinal, cardinals, signification of the title, iii. 387 n. 7. College of cardinals, its origin, iii. 387, 388. Legates, iv. 197. Determination of the choice of popes, iii. 387, 388; iv. 167, 192, 193, v. 44–46, 71, 101, 109. St. Francis and the, iv. 272, 273. Authority of, v. 18, 33. At Avignon, v. 21, 22, 44. Corruption of, v. 47, 50, 58, 101. In the schism, v. 51, 56, 70–73, 75–77, 94, 97, 99, 100, 101. Two parties, v. 87. At Constance, v. 106, 109–112, 118–125, 327, 328, 374. Wicklif, v. 160. Janow, v. 231. Huss on the, v. 257, 309, 364.
Cardinal virtues, iii. 148, 149; iv. 520–522.
Cards of invitation to Ariald's preaching, iii. 391.
Care of the sick, ii. 169, 192; see Sick. Of the poor; see Poor.
Careans, i. 42 n. 3.
Caria, iii. 570 n. 2.
Carinthia, churches in, iii. 316. See Bertulph.
Carloman, iii. 55, 56, 65.
Carlstadt, v. 156.
Carmel, anchorets at, iv. 266.
Carmelites, order of, iv. 266. Carmelite preacher, v. 75.
Carnales, iii. 348.
Carolingian family, iii. 368
Carolingian period, iii. 136, 137, 139, 156, 233, 234, 400, 404, 425, 427, 428, 456, 460, 470. See Charlemagne.
Carolinian books. See Libri Carolini.
Carpathus, iii. 229 n. 3.
Carpini, J. de Plano, journey to Tartary, iv. 48 n. 2, 50.
   His report, iv. 48 n. 2; § xii. f. 270, 51 n. 1.
Carpocrates, Gnostic, i. 399 n. 1, 449–451.
Carpocratians, Carpocratianism, i. 292, 449, 451, 484 n. 3.
Carpzov, iv. 79 n. 1.
Carthage. Christianity there, i. 83, 84. Metropolitan church, i. 242. Persecution under Caracalla, i. 123, 124. Under Decius, i. 132, 133. Under Diocletian, i. 152. Liberality, i. 256. Conduct of the Christians there during the plague, i. 258, 333. Catechists, i. 306. Praxeas at, i. 583. Paganism at, ii. 100. Temples destroyed at, ii. 101 n. 5. Church at, ii. 167, 197. Mensurius, ii. 217–219. In the Donatist schism, ii. 220–238. Assembly at, ii. 223. Conference at (an. 411), with Donatists, ii. 236, 237 (220 n. 1, 222 n. 1, 225 n. 4, 226 n. 2). Monks at, ii. 301. Augustin at, ii. 236, 396. Pelagius and Celestius, ii. 639, 640. Leporius at, ii. 655. See Aurelius, Mensurius, Councils, at the beginning.
Carthusians, iv. 168 n. 3, 262 n. 2, 264, 265 and n. 4. Wickliffite doctrines among the, v. 371 n. 2.

GENERAL INDEX.

Carthwitz, Hungarian bp., biography of Stephen of Hungary, iii. 333 n. 2.
Casæ Nigræ. See Donatus of.
Caspian Sea, ii. 141 and n. 3; iii. 89.
Cassian. See John.
Cassian, Julius, i. 458 n. 3. See Encratites.
Cassino, Monte, monastery, iv. 421.
Cassiodorus, East Gothic statesman, ii. 183 n., 639, 682 n. 4; iii. 151 n. 1.
De institutione div. script., iii. 151 n. 1; præfat. l. 1, ii. 183 n.
Caste, among the Essenes, i. 49. Priests as a, iii. 348, 383.
Castile, iv. 174 n., 268.
Castle priests, iii. 109, 413.
Castor and Pollux, ii. 371.
Castrum Cassinum, ii. 298.
Casuistry, Jewish, i. 39, 49.
Catacombs, Greek monks in, iv. 529. Catharists, 590.
Catalonia, iv. 613.
Cataphrygians, i. 525.
Catechists, catechetical school in Alexandria, i. 306, 527–529, 686 n. 1, 691. Augustin's directions to, ii. 118–120.
Catechumens, i. 305–310, 219, 504; ii. 31 n. 3, 121, 357–359, 361, 472. Classes of, i. 305, 700; ii. 30, 213 and n. 4, 357, 358. Probation, ii. 184. Their part in the divine service, Missa catechumenorum, i. 328, 478; ii. 361 and n. 3. Prayer for the, ii. 357, 358 n. 1. Instruction of, i. 305 n. 1, 306–308, 528, 686 n. 1; ii. 358, 506 n. 3, 584. Baptism for, i. 478. With Marcion, i. 460, 478. In Sweden, iii. 280. In Iceland, iii. 301. Catharist, iv. 580.
Catena (Paulus), ii. 34.
Catena Corderii, on John, fragm. Theodor. Mopsuest. comm. in Johann., ii. 390 n. 4, 738 n. 6; f. 288, ii. 496 n. 4. In Psalmos, f. 166, fragm. Theodor., in Psal. 8, ii. 494 n. 1.
Catena Nicephori, on the Octateuch (Lips. 1770), Theodore on Gen., ii. 127 n. 3; t. i. f. 98, the fall, ii. 715 n. 3. (Lips. 1772), fragments of Apollinaris of Hierapolis, and A. of Laodicea, i. 677 n. 1; t. i. f. 1475, A. of Laodicea on the descensus in inferos, ii. 491 n. 4.
Catenæ, the, i. 677 n. 1; ii. 738 n. 5; iii. 169. See Catena.
Catharists, i. 504; iii. 590, 591 n. 1, 594 n. 3, 595, 602 n. 1; iv. 219, 304, 556 n. 2. History and doctrine, iv. 565–590, 592–594, 603 n. 4, 610, 611 nn. 6, 7, 612 and n. 3, 640. Occupations of, 583 n. 2.
Cathedra (θρόνος), ii. 321.
Cathedra Petri, i. 213, 214, 215, 684 n. 1; ii. 199, 200; iii. 569, 573; v. 78.
Cathedra pontificalis, iii. 352.
Catherine of Siena, v. 44.
Catholic church, its formation, i. 207–217 (199). Division of Felicissimus, i. 222–237. Controversy with the Novatians,

i. 222, 246–248. Its doctrine, i. 506–656. Baptism of heretics, i. 317–320; ii. 219. Trinity, i. 573; conflict with Separatism, ii. 216, 237, 238–247 (see Donatist schism); iii. 166, 371 n. 2; iv. 552 n. 3, 553, 578, 623. Opposition to the, iii. 269 n. 6 (see Paulicians). Definition of, v. 302 (ii. 237, 243). See Church, Church divisions, Church discipline.
Catholic element, i. 461, 478 (199). Antiquity of the, 204 n. 3.
Catholicism, ii. 216. Jewish element in, i. 195, 367 n. 1, 478. Mediæval, iii. 87, 88, 146, 200. See Catholic, Jewish.
Catholicus, iii. 250 n. 1, 589.
Cato, i. 15; iii. 381 n. 1; v. 333, 379. De senectute, c. 2, iii. 483 n. 2.
Caucasus, Mt., ii. 139.
Causæ majores, iii. 359, 370.
Causality, divine, iii. 144.
Cause, first, highest, iv. 478–481. Principalis et instrumentalis, iv. 514 n. 5. Primal, iv. 477. Efficient, iv. 449. Final, iv. 449, 466, 473. Formal, iv. 449. Causæ archetypæ, prototypæ, primordiales, iii. 556 n. 4. Primordial and rational, iv. 470, 471. Rationes causales seminales, iv. 470, 472. Cause and effect, iv. 471, 472, 476, 491. Causes contingent and proximate, iv. 477. Necessary and contingent, iv. 477, 478. Second, iv. 478, 483, 515. Natural, i. 23. Internal and external, in history, v. 240.
Causeum (Chaussey) island, iv. 236.
Causis, Michael de, v. 800.
Caves, iv. 529, 590.
Cedrenus.
Annales. (An. 525), persecution of Manicheans in Persia, ii. 708 n. 2. Irene, iii. 223 n. 2, 224 n. 2. Tarasius, 225 n. 1. Paulicians transplanted, 250 n. 2. Ed. Basil. f. 484, the Russian church, 327 n. 3; f. 524, Olga, 328 n. 3, Hungarian ch. 330 n. 3.
Celada, ii. 657.
Celestial bodies as divine essences, i. 162.
Celestin, bp. of Rome. See Cœlestin.
Celestin II., pope, iv. 151.
Celestin III., pope, iv. 173, 221 n.
Celestin IV., pope, iv. 193.
Celestin V., pope, iv. 67, 193, 632; v. 2, 4, 19. Life of, iv. 163 n. 3.
Celestius, ii. 222 n. 1.
Celibacy, estimation of, i. 277, 280, 659. Abstenients, 274. Pagan, 278. With the Essenes, 43, 45. With the Ebionites, 353. With the Gnostics, 385, 416, 456, 457. With the Montanists, 521, 522. In the epistles of Clement, 659. With Hieracas, 714, 715. Methodius, 721. Chrysostom on, ii. 302, 303. Jovinian, ii. 304–306, 300. Helvidius, ii. 377. Pelagius, ii. 643 n. 2. With the Euchites, ii. 281. Priscillianists, ii. 778. Sect at Arras and Liege, iii. 597. Sects from the East, iii. 592, 600 n. 2. Sect at Montfort, iii. 601. Henry the Clu-

niacensian, iv. 600. See Marriage, Celibacy of the clergy.
Celibacy of the clergy, i. 199; ii. 179-182, 191; iii. 382-384, 388-398, 397 n. 2, 410, 411, 469. Roman law requiring, iii. 53. Irish synods concerning, iii. 53 n. 6. Made valid by Nicholas II., iii. 388. Opposition to, iii. 411 n. 7. In the Greek church, iii. 557. Photius on, iii. 567. Ordinances of Gregory VII., iv. 93-100. Results of, iv. 146 n. 2, 206. Relaxation of laws concerning, iv. 119. Robert of Arbrissel, iv. 246. Henry the Cluniacensian, iv. 598, 601 n. 4. Gerson, v. 81. Huss, v. 249. See Marriage.
Celidonius, bp., ii. 206.
Celle, iv. 39. See Peter de la Celle.
Cellot.
  Hist. Gotheschalci, Par. 1655, appendix, Prudentius, tract on predestination, iii. 482 n. 1: Gerbert, De corpore et sang. Dom., iii. 502 n. 1.
Celsus, on Hellenism, i. 4. On Christianity, 70, 71, 88-90, 107, 108, 570. Reverence to the emperors, 91. Origen against, 127, 710 (see Origen). Christianity and the state, 129. His work against Christianity, 160-170, 173. Representative character of, 163. Sibyllists, 177. Public festivals, 265. Administration of offices and military service, 272. Absence of altars, etc., 289. Catechumens, 305 n. 1. For citations from his Λόγος ἀληθής, see Origen contra Celsum.
Celsus the Epicurean, i. 160 n.
Cemeteries, Christians forbidden to visit the, i. 137, 138. Restored, i. 140. Places of assemblage, i. 334; ii. 3. Images in, ii. 329 n. 2.
Cenobites. See Coenobites.
Central point in Christianity, i. 557; ii. 386.
Centralization, in the work of spreading Christianity among barbarous nations, iii. 15, 49, 50.
Centres of public life, i. 79.
Centulum, monastery at, iii. 420.
Cerdana, iii. 156 n. 5.
Cerdo, i. 465.
Ceremonial law, i. 58. See Pharisees.
Ceremonial rites, religion, service, i. 686; ii. 38, 48; iii. 84, 427; v. 237. Paulicians on, iii. 263. Claudius and Agobard, iii. 457. Sect of the Holy Ghost, iv. 448.
Ceremonies, observance of pagan, ii. 8, 9, 12, 20, 21, 22, 28, 34, 59, 67 n. 2, 74, 81-84. See Pagan.
Ceres, worship of, ii. 376.
Cerinthus, i. 396-400, 410, 412, 652. See Irenæus, Dionysius of Alexandria, Caius, Epiphanius.
Cerretauus, v. 330.
Certroy, anchorets at, iv. 267.
Cesarini. See Juliano.

Ceylon, Christianity in, ii. 141.
Chalcedon, bps. of, ii. 539; iii. 570, 573 n. 2. See Councils, an. 451, Maris.
Chalcis, desert of, ii. 742.
Chaldaic elements in Essenean mysticism, i. 44.
Chaldee, iv. 70, 426. Chaldee documents, ii. 125 n. 6.
Chalons sur Marne, iv. 251, 255; v. 53. Sects at, iii. 603-605. Bp. of, iii. 600 n. 2.
Chalons sur Saone. Death of Abelard at, iv. 400. See Councils, an. 650.
Chamberlains, court, in the Nestorian controv., ii. 541 n. 1. Of the pope, v. 47 n.
Champagne, iv. 251; v. 25, 53. See Theobald.
Chancel, ii. 321 n. 5.
Chancellor, of the Roman church, Hildebrand as, iii. 399. William of Modena, iv. 41. Roland, iv. 164.
Chanting of the symbol, iii. 555.
Chaos, in Gnosticism, i. 375-377, 383, 401. With Hermogenes, i. 567, 617. The Bogomiles, iv. 553. Catharists, iv. 572, 575.
Chapels, of martyrs, ii. 160. Private, iii. 109, 413. On the highways, iii. 133.
Chapter of cathedral, iii. 107 n. 1, 409; iv. 207. Origin of the title, iii. 107 n. 1.
Character, militaris, indelebilis, ii. 724.
Charibert, Frankish king, iii. 94.
Chariot and foot races, i. 264, 265.
Charismata, i. 119 n. 6, 180-183, 186-188, 212, 309, 510, 526, 616, 682; iii. 147, 173, 174, 397 n. 2. See Apostles.
Charity, among the Essenes, i. 45, 46. The Gnostics, i. 384. Works of, ii. 136, 192. See Benevolence. Theodulf on, iii. 131. Among the Icelanders, iii. 306. Bernard on, iv. 257. Wicklif on works of, v. 142. Militz, v. 182. Conrad of Waldhausen, v. 189. Friends of God, v. 383, 403, 404. See Good works.
Charlemagne. Endeavors to convert the Saxons, iii. 66, 76, 78, 81, 272, 273. Assigns to missionaries their spheres of labor, 79-82. Proposes to make Hamburg a metropolitan see, 84. Restores free ecclesiastical elections, 95. His ordinances with regard to general assemblies, 96, 97. Taxation of church property, 101. Payments of tithes made legally binding, 101 n. 2. On the military service of the clergy, 102. Asylums, 104. Judicature of bishops, 105 n. 4. Visitations, 107 n. 5. Founds the Frank empire in Italy, 120. His coronation as emperor, 120, 361. His disposition towards the popes, 120-122. Increases the territorial possessions of the Roman church, 122. Procedure with regard to Leo III., 122. A zealous promoter of preaching, 123-125. Procures the publication of a homilia-

rium, which he accompanies with a preface, 126. Church psalmody, 128. Language of worship, 128. Sortes sanctorum, 129. Judgments of God, 130. On adornment of churches, 131. Against new saints, 133. Synods under, 143. A zealous promoter of learning, 154, 468. Letters of Alcuin to, 155 nn. 1, 3, 156 n. 1. See Alcuin. Felix, 159 n. His proceedings with regard to Adoptianism, 165-167. On image worship, 234-243. Age of, 233, 456, 460. Missions, 271-273, 277, 316. Moravians subjected, 315. Wends, 323. Pseudo-Isidorean decretals, 351. Benedict, 414. Claudius of Turin, 432. Haroun al Raschid, 458 n. 2. Doctrine of the Holy Spirit, 555. An opponent of the second Nicene council, 234-243. Proposed restoration of his gifts bestowed on the churches, iv. 133. See Alcuin, Capitularies, Carolingian, Libri Carolini, Monachi.

Charles II., king of Naples, iv. 193.
Charles IV., emperor, v. 42, 43, 174, 182, 184, 244, 335.
Charles V., emperor, iii. 380 n.
Charles V. of France, v. 48.
Charles VI. of France, v. 52, 77, 91.
Charles de Valois, v. 22.
Charles, duke of Lotharingia, iii. 308.
Charles, king of Provence, iii. 354.
Charles Martel, maj. dom., iii. 45, 47, 50, 54, 55.
Charles of Bohemia, v. 42. See Charles IV., emperor.
Charles of Durazzo, king of Naples, v. 50, 51.
Charles the Bald, of France, iii. 353 n. 1, 354, 356 n. 6, 360, 361, 362, 364, 366, 404 n. 4, 450, 453 n. 1, 467 and n. 4, 481, 482, 500. Promotes the sciences, iv. 461, 485, 497.
Charms, iii. 42, 84, 444. See Amulets.
Χειροψίλαξ, iii. 196 n. 2.
Chartres, theological school at, iii. 470, 502. Bp. of, iii. 290 n. 1, 406, 596. Assembly at, iv. 154. Peter de Rusia, iv. 211. Almaric, iv. 446. See Bernard of Tira, Fulcher, Gottfried, Ivo, Peter de la Celle.
Chartreux (Cartusium), iv. 265.
Chase, clergy addicted to the, iii. 53, 66, 410. The nobles, 459. Forbidden to the clergy, 56, 410.
Chassenueil. siege of, iv. 641 n. 5.
Chastity among the Anglo-Saxons, iii. 69.
Chatelat, iii. 41 n. 3.
Chaussey, iv. 236.
Chazars, inhabitants of the Crimea, iii. 315, 316. Jews, 329, 458 n. 2.
Χειροθεσία, ii. 30 n. 3, 190 n. 2. See Imposition of hands.
Χειροτονίαι, ii. 583 n. 1.
Cheops, ii. 89.
Cherson (Kerssan), iii. 329. T. Ailurus banished to, ii. 585.

Chersonesus, iii. 190, 316.
Cherubim, iii. 204, 237.
Chesena, Michael of, v. 25.
Chess, game of, v. 320
Chiersy. See Councils, an. 858.
Chillet, anonymous writer edited by, iii. 513 n. 3, 515 n. 5, 516 n. 1, 518 n. 2.
Childebert, king of the Franks, his law (an. 554) against idols, iii. 9.
Childeric III., king of the Franks, iii. 68; iv. 111; v. 15.
Children among the early Christians, i. 71, 78, 99 and n. 3, 716. Persecuted, i. 138, 152, 156, 664. Christianity propagated through, i. 119 n. 6, 716. Salvation of, i. 552, 715, 716; ii. 717, 727, 731; iv. 503. Unbaptized, i. 715; ii. 729, 730; iii. 476; iv. 494. Consecration of, i. 311, 312; ii. 261, 262; iv. 13, 233, 234, 252, 297, 298. Conrad on their dedication to monastic orders, v. 187. Christian training of, i. 528; ii. 239, 261, 262 and n. 4, 288, 316, 423, 754; iii. 23; iv. 234, 249, 294, 361. Piety among, i. 99 n. 3; iv. 342, 343. Power of early influences, ii. 7, 8; iii. 288; iv. 234; see Christian training of. School-books of, ii. 5; iii. 543. Instruction of, i. 528; ii. 288, 423; iii. 315 n. 1; iv. 362, 363; Gersou on, v. 82. Singing of, iv. 58. Crusade of, iv. 342 n. 5. Exposing of, in Iceland, iii. 305 and n. 2. Destroyed by heathen mothers in Pomerania, iv. 8. In episcopal offices, iii. 409 and n. 1. Care for orphans, iv. 299. See Boys, Girls Education, Infant baptism, Schools.
Children of God, iii. 535 n. 3.
Chiliasm, i. 365. With the Ebionites, i. 348, 357, 365. Of Cerinthus, i. 399. In Asia Minor, i. 463. In Montanism, i. 513, 515, 523, 527. In the church, nature and history of, i. 650-654, 669, 670. Opposition to, i. 657, 651-654, 676. With Commodian, i. 687. Origen and, i. 711; ii. 388. With Methodius, i. 721. Bar Sudaili, ii. 615, 616.
Chiliasts, i. 78, 165, 357, 513, 669, 711. See Chiliasm.
Chilperic, king of the Franks, tract on the doctrine of the Trinity, iii. 91 n. 1. His complaints of the power of the bishops, 101 n. 3.
China, Mani in, i. 488. Nestorians spread Christianity in, iii. 89, 90. Judgments of God in, iii. 130. Exposing of children, iii. 305 n. 2. Catholic missionaries in, iv. 56-59. See Mongols.
Chivalry, spirit of, iv. 36.
Chlum, John of, v. 243 n. 1, 317 n. 4, 320, 321, 326 n. 3, 327, 328, 332-336, 339, 341-343, 347-349, 356, 358, 364, 367, 368.
Chonæ (Colosse), iv. 530.
Choral dance and music, Therapeutae, i. 61.
Chorals, ii. 83.

Χωρεπίσκοπος (chor-bishops), ii. 193. See Country bishops, Ἐπίσκοπος.
Chorentes, ii. 277.
Choristers, ii. 354.
Cho-roes, king of Persia, ii. 110, 612.
Chosru Parviz, king of the Persians, iii. 84.
Chotek, Bernhard, v. 294.
Chozil, son of Privinna, iii. 317 and n. 2.
Chraumus, iii. 104 n. 2.
Chrestus, i. 94.
Chrism, i. 315; ii. 359, 360 and n. 1; iii. 56 n. 4, 309. In confirmation, ii. 359, 360 n. 1; iii. 496.
Christ, preëxistence of, with Origen, i. 588 (see Logos); with Apollinaris, ii. 489; see Son of God. Divinity of: Pliny, i. 98; Theonas, i. 143; Novatian, i. 690; in the early hymns, i. 304; Julian, ii. 55, 56, 57; Arius, ii. 408; in the Gothic tribes, iii. 5 n. 2 (see ii. 472, 473), 38, 39; Bulgarians, iii. 497 n. 1; defended against Mohammedans, iii. 87, 88, 159; the Swedes, 281, 282, 284, 285, 292, 293; the Danes, 289; defended against doubts derived from the Gospels, iv. 328; see Trinity, Adoptianist controversy. Image of God, i. 561. Divine and human in, 340; with the Ebionites, i. 348, 349; Basilides, i. 410; Valentine, i. 428, 429; two tendencies, ii. 483; Julian of Eclanum, ii. 655. God-man, iv. 78, 506, 534. Humanity of, i. 630-640; ii. 646 n. 1; see Person of, Monotheletism, Dyotheletism. Incarnation of, i. 562, ii. 485, iii. 495 n. 4, iv. 66, 230, 325, 384; Bernard on the, iv. 261, 262; Abelard, iv. 502; Huss, v. 337; in the original plan of the world, iv. 507, 508; see Predestination. Personality, iii. 157 n. 1. Two Christs (ἄνω and κάτω, heavenly and earthly, etc.) in Gnosticism, i. 386, 398, 399, 410, 445, 447, 477, 549. Supernatural conception and birth of, with the Ebionites, i. 347, 348, 357 n. 4, 363; Valentine, i. 429; the Monarchians, i. 577, 580; the Persians, ii. 129; Photinus, ii. 482; Paulicians, 261, 262; Ratramnus, iii. 495 n. 4; sect at Orleans, iii. 594. Infancy, with Bogomiles, iv. 559; see Christmas. Body of, i. 633-635; Valentine on the, i. 430, 431; with Origen, i. 639; Marcellus, ii. 480, 481; Hilary, ii. 483 n. 1; Apollinaris, ii. 490, 491; in Monotheletism, iii. 182 n. 2; see Docetism, Glorified body, Lord's Supper, Σάρξ. Soul of, i. 634, 639; see Apollinaris, Person of Christ. Baptism of: with Ebionites, i. 347, 348, 350, 351; Gnostics, i. 386; Cerinthus, 398; Basilides, 410-412; Valentine, 429, 431; the Ophites, 445; Manicheans, i. 502; Felix, iii. 163; Catharists, iv. 574, 575; Gregory of Nyssa, ii. 733. Temptation, ii. 493, 494, 655, 656; iii. 450; iv. 249, 250; v. 199. Servant form, i. 270, 271, 291, 398, 549, 631; ii. 48, 480; iii. 99, 141, 160, 162. Humility, i. 562; iv. 505, 506. Obedience, i. 641, 642; ii. 656. Uncomeliness, i. 169, 631-633. Poverty, iv. 283; v. 138. Received sinners, iv. 100 n. 2 (i. 166; ii. 48). Refusal of secular power, v. 14, 16, 38, 39. Human weakness, iv. 496. Freedom, i. 638, 639. Development, i. 639; Arius, ii. 407; in the Antiochian school, ii. 493-498; Leporius, ii. 656. Mutability, ii. 407. Immutability, ii. 410 n. 3, 497. Knowledge of, ii. 496, 656. Self-possession of, i. 356. Sinlessness of, i. 410, 413, 637, 638, 643; ii. 498; iii. 261; iv. 495-497. Transfiguration, i. 500, 633, 634. Words of, iii. 268; Parables, i. 388, iv. 558, 589, v. 201. Miracles, ii. 49, 50, 280; iv. 472, 502. At Jerusalem, v. 181, 184, 191, 296, 301 n. 3, 369. In Gethsemane, ii. 490, 491, 498. Sorrow, ii. 491. Sufferings and death, i. 301, 398, 412, 430, 445, 446, 470, 500, 562, 642-644; ii. 46 n. 1, 122, 129; iv. 533, 620; ethical and doctrinal significance of, iv. 499-507; as vicarious, i. 412; as satisfaction, iv. 505, 506; with Julian, ii. 46 n. 1; with Gnostics, i. 398; see Redemption. Descent into Hades, i. 656; ii. 491; iii. 61. Resurrection and ascension of, i. 295, 301, 398; ii. 46 n. 1, 490, 497; iii. 163, 470 n. 2, 500; iv. 384, 574. Appearances after his ascension, ii. 48 n. 1; iv. 345 n. 5. At the right hand of God, iv. 555 nn. 2-4. Glorified body of, i 69; ii. 484 and n. 3, 733; iii. 500, 522, 527; iv. 232; v. 154, 155, 238. Ubiquity, iii. 500; iv. 345. In dreams, ii. 9, 119. In the Eucharist, iii. 267, 496, 500, 521; iv. 345; v. 153, 154. Blood of, v. 237-239. See Lord's Supper. Life, character, work, ii. 306, 307, 638; iv. 495-509. Manicheans on, 502; see Manicheans. Oracles concerning, i. 171, 172. Placed beside the gods of Rome, ii. 7. Letter to Abgarus, see Abgarus. A. Severus, i. 125. Worship of, i. 304; ii. 425. Prayer to, i. 590; iii. 211; v. 306. Prayer through, i. 591. Images of, i. 125, 292, 451; ii. 325-327; iii. 89 n. 4, 199, 204, 205, 208, 211, 213, 215, 217, 232, 240, (Χριστὸς ὁ ἀντιφωνητής, iii. 213 n. 2.) Symbol of the Lamb, iii. 557. Traditional image of, iii. 550 n. 1. Prophetic testimonies to, iv. 574. Christ, as moral teacher, i. 714, 716; iv. 502, 503. As example, i. 311; ii. 676, 677; iv. 365, 500, 503, 504; v. 138, 142, 143, 268, 281. Law of, v. 151, 209, 265, 280, 285, 307, 325. Commands, ii. 637. Mediation of, i. 590, 591; iv. 615; v. 411. Redemption, i. 557; see Redemption. Ransom, iv. 502. As sacrifice, iv. 505. Acceptance in, iv. 509. Power of faith in, i. 73-75, 323, 476, 549. Salvation by, iv. 218; v. 168, 169, 172. God in, i. 573, 574; v. 402.

Prophet, priest, and king, i. 180. Centre of religious knowledge and life, Bernard, iv. 258, 261, 262; Huss, v. 264. See Atonement. Relation to sinners, i. 245; to the kingdom of evil, i. 74, 75, ii. 159; to Christians, i. 136, 152, 194, 257, 334, 335, ii. 489, 675–379, 732, iii. 132, iv. 342, 446, v. 172, 193, 205, 206, 210–212, 229, 402, 403; to Christianity, ii. 447; to the church, i. 183, 194, 323, 324, ii. 211. Headship, i. 209, 210, 304; ii. 122, 240, 283; v. 19, 25, 50, 78, 79, 173, 210, 212, 303–309, 352. Church the body of, i. 183; ii. 424, 367, 734; iv. 225; v. 211, 231, 324 The rock, ii. 200, 201; iii. 166, 334 n. 4; v. 25, 154, 304. Bridegroom, v. 309. Presence in Christian assemblies, i. 289. Spirit of, i. 183; v. 200. Fellowship with, ii. 720; iv. 509, 511; v. 172. Imitation of, i. 295; iii. 586; v. 173, 174, 249, 412. Following, iv. 272, 276, 312; v. 138, 143, 151, 165, 172, 353, 365, 369, 402. Seeking, iv. 307. Relation of Christians to, ii. 304, 308, 367. Communion with, ii. 362. Relation to the Apostles, i. 183; to Judaism, i. 339, 340; to the theocracy, i. 324; to Gnosticism, i. 371 (476); to humanity, i. 268, 311, 338, 411, 543, 549 (Christ and Adam, ii. 386, 676; see Adam); to Antichrist, v. 198–200; to nature and history, i. 3, 386, 389; iv. 471, 621. Threefold manifestation, iv. 621. Test of all things, v. 208. Oppositions reconciled in, i. 325, 339. Christ and Buddha, i. 480. Second coming of, i. 130; ii. 161; iii. 470 n. 2; iv. 621, 622; v. 178, 179, 185, 199, 201, 380. As judge, v. 280. Kingdom of, v. 199. Christ with Lucian, i. 158; with Celsus, 168, 169; Hierocles, 173, 174; in the Clementines, 359, 360; with Ebionites, 347–352; with the Gnostics, 381–383, 386–389; Cerinthus, 398, 399; Basilides, 409–413; Valentine, 420, 423, 428–434; the Ophites, 445–447; Carpocrates, 450; Marcion, 459, 462, 473, 562; Apelles, 476; the Manicheans, 493, 497, 500; Judaizing sects, 305 (see Ebionites); Julian on, ii. 49, 50, 55; Euchites, ii. 280; in Pelagianism, ii. 655–657; Paulicians, iii. 261–264; sect at Montfort, iii. 601; Bogomiles, iv. 554, 555, 559; Wicklif, v. 140–145, 160, 161, 173; Conrad, v. 188, 190; Janow, v. 193, 197, 205–235; Huss, v. 239, 249, 264, 274, 278, 280–286, 296, 303–314, 324, 325, 346, 365, 369–371; Ruysbroech, v. 402, 403; Tauler, v. 410, 411; Suso, v. 411.

Christann of Prachatic, v. 298, 310, 367.

Christian, monk.
Life of Wenzeslav of Bohemia, iii. 322 n. 1.

Christian, the term, v. 214.

Christian character, power of, iii. 4, 6, 21, 26–28. See Christian life.

Christian consciousness, i. 308, 339, 461; ii. 654, 658, 660, 693, 765; iii. 2, 60, 243, 443, 586.

Christian doctrine, festivals, images, morals (see Christian life), symbols, worship. See Doctrine, Festivals, etc.

Christian Druthmar, iii. 458. His comm. on Matt., 458 n. 2.

Christian equality, i. 325.

Christian life, i. 249–288; ii. 258–314; iii. 123–140; iv. 293–354. Unity of the, i. 304. Power of, i. 76, 77. Idea of the, i. 644. Obedience to law, i. 259, 261. Occupations, i. 262, 267. In relation to amusements, i. 263–267; ii. 258. In the family, i. 280 (see Marriage). Festivals in honor of the dead, i. 333. With the Paulicians, iii. 263. Waldenses, iv. 611. Dependence of, on the church, iv. 509 514. See Asceticism, Clement of Alexandria, Monasticism, Tertullian.

Christian love, i. 76, 255–258, 335; friendship, iv. 251.

Christian of Oliva, missionary in Prussia, iv. 43–45.

Christian perfection, iv. 371.

Christian principle, power of the, i. 390.

Christian spirit in the dark ages, iii. 441, 443–445.

Christian training, i. 311, 390.

Christian worship, i. 288–335; ii. 314–379; iii. 123–140; iv. 293–354. See Agapae, Baptism of heretics, Festivals, Images, Prayer, Sacraments, Sign of the cross, Worship.

Christianity. Source and essence, relation to the development of human nature, i. 1–5, 207, 253, 336, 337. Relation to Judaism, 3 (see Judaism). Condition of the world at the time of its appearance, and commencement of its spread, i. 5–68. Self-renovating power, 36, 338. Reconciling power, 50. Renewing power, 77. Diffusion, limitation, persecutions, hindrances, causes and means of progress, 69–79, 138, 143. Its relation to human life, 69, 70; to classes of society, 70, 71, 78, 84, 90, 148, 346; to culture, 85, 129; to the pagan world, 92; to the enigmas of thought, 368. Its propagation in particular districts, 79–86. Persecutions, their causes, 86–93. Opposition to, by force, 93–156; by writings, 157–174. Hadrian on, 102, 103. Apologies, 174–178. In high stations, 120, 128, 139, 142, 148. Religio illicita, 100. Religio licita, 125, 126, 140, 141, 145, 156. Rapid increase, 127, 128, 142. Among barbarians, 129. Diffused through persecutions, 128, 145 (ii. 1, 2). The accidental and essential in, 157. Oracles relating to, 171. Power of adapting itself, 253. Prophetic testimony to, 176, 371 n., 547. Relation to the state and existing institutions, 259-274, 439, 440, 184, 202, 206, 260; to the ignorant, 308. In relation to Gnosticism, 366-372, 379-396; see the particular sects. In the Clementines, 394, 395; see Clementines. Transforming power, 249, 254, 507, 667, 668, 670. Contrasted with paganism, 249, 250, 252, 257, 258. Profession of, 250, 251. Gradual evolution of, 260, 269, 336. Aggressive and assimilating power of, 261, 273, 276. Equalizing power, 268, 390. Unfolded from within, 336. A power in history, 365. Basilides, 407. Marcion on, 459, 464, 466. Mani, 486, 487, 501, 502. Anticipation of, 479. Relation of Parsism to, 482-484. Oppositions in, 339, 340, 506-508, 723 (ii. 382). Supernatural and natural in, 507, 510. Spirit and letter in, 512. Annunciation of facts, 78, 368, 543, 550, 557; ii. 115. Two stages according to Origen, 547-556. Historical, i. 368, 549-551, 557 (ii. 123 n. 1). Central point of, 557; ii. 386. Development of doctrine, 723. See Christian life, etc., Church, Manicheism.

In the second Period. Its divine power, ii. 1, 6, 29, 37, 94, 112, 158, 159, 239. Extension, limitation, persecutions, relation to it of individual Roman emperors, 1-110. Impression made by, 1, 8. Religio licita, 9, 12, 14. Its cause injured by worldly advancement, 33, 35; and violent measures in its favor, 36, 94, 96. Hollow profession of, 37 and n. 2, 38, 96, 112. New life in, 39, 113. At the Byzantine court, see Byzantine. With Julian, 45-59. Corruptions of, 46. Relation to human nature, 53, 58. To Hellenism, 57. Pagan predictions regarding, 102. Influence on paganism, 106. On the state, 113. Polemics, 111-115. Hindrances and helps to conversion, 115-124. Wars, 149. Universality, 116, 159. Missions beyond the Roman empire, 124-160. Softening influence of, 158-160. To be appropriated freely, 162, 165. Spirit of mercy, courage, 173-177. Human and divine elements in, 245. Doctrine and life, 382, 446, 463.

In the third Period. New life introduced into the world by Christianity, iii. 1 (ii. 39). Transforming and refining power of, 2. New development, in its relation to the barbarous tribes of Europe, 1-3. Extension and limitation in Europe, 4-84. In Asia and Africa, 84-90. Means of its spread, 4 and n. 1, 51, 288; see Force. Conditions of its real dissemination, 9. Civilizing influences of, 1, 9, 106; see Monasticism. Conditions of its progress in barbarous nations, 46. Among the higher classes, 6, 12, 38, 46, 50, 72, 74. Widely spread, 123. Corrupted, 253; see Image worship. Influence on Mohammedanism, 85. Judaism mingled with, 244. The world and, 251. Principle of truthfulness in, 267.

In the fourth Period. Extension, iii. 271-335. Limitation, 335-345. Introduced by force, 296-299, 309, 329, 330, 334. Mingled with paganism, 291, 305, 333. Importance of the predicatorial office to, 425. Relation to the old and new culture, 456.

In the fifth Period. Extension and limitation in Europe, iv. 1-45. In Asia, 45-59. Among Mohammedans and Jews, 59-81. Means of spread, 1, 624; commerce, 10, 36, 46; political motives, 8, 10, 14, 17; by captives, 18, see Captives; science, 61; see Missions. Among higher classes, 26, 28, 33. Nominal, 34. Civilizing influences of, 40, 41. Philosophy and, 383-385. Obstacles, national jealousy, 31; war, 33; bad lives, 52, 59. Spirit and forms of manifestation, 231, 232; in humble life, 294-300; in the higher classes, 296. Dissolution of, 216, 230, 231, 619. The absolute religion, 618. Primitive, 623. See Church.

Christians, character of the early, i. 76-78, 91, 92, 97, 98, 105, 254. Absent themselves from festivities, 91, 120. Accusations against them, i. 92, 94, 95, 98 n. 4, 99, 109 n. 2, 128 and n. 5, 327. Order of Claudius, 94. Search made for, 100, 107. Popular hatred excited by public calamities, 92, 103, 104, 119, 126, 136. Conduct under persecution, 109. Increase in numbers in spite of persecution, 127, 128, 137, 138, 142. Strength of convictions, 172 and n. 2. Interpolation of oracles, 172 n. 4. In the palace, 142, 143. Poverty, 303, 346. Valentine, 427.

In the second Period. Important political party, ii. 17. Removed from offices by Licinius, 19. Worldly-minded, 37 and n. 2. Nominal, 103, 106, 112, 258, 260. Pretended, 156, 157. Unobtrusive temper of, 260. Temples of the Holy Spirit, 314.

Christmas festival, i. 301, 362, 682 n. 1; ii. 342, 343, 344-350, 351 n. 2, 360, 509 n. 4, 777; iii. 134; iv. 325; v. 312, 313. Baptisms at, iii. 13 and n. 2. With the Manicheans, i. 505.

Christoforo Baggiolini, Dolcino e i Patareni, notizie storiche, iv. 629 nn. 2, 3, 633 n. 2.

Christology. See Person of Christ, Redemption, Trinity.

Χριστοτόκος, ii. 510.

Chrodegang of Metz. Rule of, on the admission of bondmen into the spiritual order, iii. 98, 101. Founder of the canonical life of the clergy, his rule, 106. On preaching, 123. A zealous promoter of church-psalmody, 128.

Chronica Edessena.
(In Assemani Bibl. orient. t. i. f. 301), i. 291 n. 3.

Chronica Slavorum. See Helmold.

Chronicle of Ademar, Adeodat, iii. 593 nn. 1, 3. See Labbe.

Chronicle of Alberic.
Ff. 315, 317, sentence of Henry of Cluny, iv. 604 n. 2. An. 1233, report to Gregory IX. concerning Conrad of Marburg, iv. 643 n. 3. See Leibnitz.

Chronicle of Albert of Stade.
An. 1248 (ed. Helmstad. 1587, f. 220), heretics at Halle, iv. 610 n. 2.

Chronicle of Albert of Strassburg.
Clement VI., v. 41 n. 2.

Chronicle of Bal Cernay.
(In Du Chesne, Scriptores hist. Franc. t. v. c. 2), Albigenses, doctrine of, concerning Christ, iv. 570 n. 4.

Chronicle of Balderic. See Baldrich.

Chronicle of Glaber Rudolph.
Hist. sui temporis, l. iv. c. 5, proposals for a universal peace, treuge Dei, iii. 407 nn.

Chronicle of Jehoschua Ben Meir, iv. 74 n. 1.

Chronicle of John of Winterthur. See Winterthur.

Chronicle of Parma.
In Muratori, Script. rer. Ital. t. ix. f. 326, Segarelli, iv. 626 n. 4, 629 n. 1.

Chronicle of Peter of Vaux-Sernai.
Dedication, name Albigenses, iv. 640 n. 1.

Chronicle of Puy Lorent.
Chronicon magistri Gulielmi de Podio Laurentii, in Du Chesne, Scriptores hist. Franc. t. v. f. 666, the Waldenses, iv. 611 n. 4; f. 667, the curse of Bernard, 604 n. 1; c. 5, f. 668, the Catharist knight, 577 n. 5; c. 3, Pauperes catholici, 614 nn. 1, 2.

Chronicle of Salimbenus de Adam.
(Extracts in Pegna, in his remarks on the Directorium Inquisitionis of N. Eymer cus, f. 271, ed. Venet. 1595, quoted by Moshcim), Segarelli, iv. 626 nn. 3, 5, 627 n. 1.

Chronicles, Second.
15 : 2, i. 253 ; 34 : 4, ii. 607 n. 1.

Chronicles. See Benignus, Cosmas, Ditmar, Helmold, Joh. de Thrwoez, John Malala, Kantzow, Knighton, Marcellini, Richer, Sigebert, Winterthur, etc., Chronicon.

Chronicles of Prague University, v. 247 nn. 2, 3, 272 n. 1, 294 n. 1. See Palacky.

Chronicon Casinense.
(In Muratori, Script. rer. Ital. t. iv. f. 403), l. ii. c. 89, Victor II., iii. 386 n. 6; cc. 97, 100, Hildebrand and the papal elections, 387 nn. 1, 2.

Chronicon Livonicum.
F. 26, death of Sigfrid, iv. 39 n. 4; f. 34, the prophetical play at Riga, 39 nn. 1, 2; f. 43, Andreas of Lund, 39 n. 3 ; f. 46, the civil law in Lietland, 41 n. 1 ; f. 49, incursion of the Letti, 40 n. 2; f. 56, the converted Letti, 40 n. 4; f. 57, the same, 49 n. 3 ; f. 97, Frederic of Celle, 40 n. 1 ; f. 173, William of Modena, 41 nn. 2, 3.

Chronicon Maxentii or Molleacense.
(Labbe, Bibliotheca Manuscriptorum, t. ii. f. 212), Berengar at the council of Poictiers, iii. 518 n. 1.

Chronicon Monasterii Reicherspergensis.
(Monachii, 1611), f. 2, report of Pilgrim of Passau on the spread of Christianity in Hungary, iii. 331 nn. 1, 2

Chronicon of Hugo de Flavigny.
(Bibl. Ms. c. i. Pars altera, ff. 214 et 215), Berengar at the council of Poictiers, iii. 518 n. 2.

Chronicon Paschale Alexandrinum.
Fragments of Apollinaris of Hierapolis, i. 677 n. 1.

Chronicon Richerii Senonense. See Richer.

Chronicon S. Benigni Divoniensis.
(D'Achery, Spicileg. t. ii. f. 392), John Gratian, iii. 377 n. 1.

Chronique d'Arras et de Cambray. See Baldrich.

Chronology, church, iii. 154, 155.

Chrysanthius, Platonist, ii. 42, 44 n. 1.

Chrysaphius, ii. 566, 575.

Chrysippus, i. 16 nn. 1, 3, 5, 7, 22 n. 1; ii. 62.

Chrysomalos. See Constantine.

Chrysopolis (Scutari), iv. 337 n. 4.

Chrysoretes, court chamberlain, ii. 541 n. 1.

Chrysostom. His life and sufferings, ii. 753-762. Mode of life, 168, 758 ; iii. 560. As a representative of the Antiochian school, ii. 394. On the Marcionites, i. 478 n. 3 ; iii 245. The forty soldiers in Sebaste, ii. 19 n. 3. Persecution of pagans, 91 n. 3. Discourse concerning Babylas, fall of paganism, 94. Duty of the landholders to their tenants, 100, 101. The unclassical language of Holy Scripture, 116. Proselytism, 121. Indian Bible translation, 140. Ξενῶνες, 169 n. 1. Flavian, 175 n. 1. Right of asylum, Eutropius, 177. Priesthood, περὶ ἱεροσύνης, 179, 182. Equal dignity of bps. and presbyters, 188. Deacons, 189 n. 4. Olympias, 191. Church discipline, 214 and n. 1, 216 n. 1. Christianity of custom, 259. Church attendance, 258 n. 2. Amulets, 259 n. 1. Home education, 262. A letter of consolation to Stagirius, 273. Episcopal supervision of the Cenobite institutions, 282 n. 1. Anachorets, 284, 285 nn. Cenobites, 286. Complaint in regard to education, 288. Asceticism, 290. View of monasticism, 301 n. 5, 302, 303. Against false notions of the service of God, 314, 315. Prayer, 315, 316. Reading of the Bible, 317-319. Gifts to churches, 319, 320. The church building, 321, 322. The sign of the cross, 322, 323. Images, 324 n. 4. Image of Christ, 327. Nilus, 328. The festivals, 332. Divine worship on Friday, 333 and notes. Passion for theatrical exhibitions, 336. Passover, 338 n. 1. Fast before Easter, 339 n. 1. Period of the fast at Antioch, 339, 340. Palm Sunday, 341. Holy week, 341 nn. Feast of Epiphany, 342, 343. The water in baptism, 343 n. 2. Christmas festival, 344, 345. New Year's festival, 350 nn. 3, 4, 351. Place of the sermon in divine worship, 352. Apportionments of Scripture in divine worship, 352 n. 1. Vanity of preachers, 353. Extemporaneous sermons, 354 n. 1. Congregational singing, 354 n. 3. Delay of baptism, 356 n. 4. Infant baptism, 357 n. 1. Prayer for catechumens, 358 n. 1. Limitation of the time for baptism, 360 and nn. 3, 4. Church prayers, 361 n. 2. Agapae, 361 n. 4. Liturgy in the Lord's Supper, 362 nn. 3, 5. Consecration of the Supper, 363 nn. 7, 10. Daily or infrequent communion, 364, 365. Sacrifice in the Supper, 366. Prayers for the dead, 367 nn. 2, 3, 4, 368 nn. 1, 3. Intercession of martyrs, 373 and notes. Pilgrimages, 377, 378 and nn. 1, 2. Exegesis, notion of inspiration, 390, 391 n. 5, 392. Cyril, 514 n. 5. With Annianus, 657. With Cassian, 687. With Julian of Eclanum, 712 n. 1. Anthropology, 718–720. Doctrine of the church, 722. Doctrine of baptism, 726, 727. The Lord's Supper, 731, 732 n. 6. Eternity of punishment, 737 and n. 3. Number of the saved, iii. 421. Whether Christ died for all, iii. 485. The oath, v. 250. Miracles, v. 267. With the Bogomiles, iv. 559. Eustathius of Thessalonica compared with, iv. 531. His life by Palladius (opp. ed. Montfauc., t. xiii.), ii. 170 n. 2, 753 n. 2.

Citations from his writings: —

Adv. Judæos, vi. § 7, t. i. f. 661, the temples of God, ii. 314 n. 2; iii. § 4, t. i. f. 611, the passover, ii. 338 n. 1; the fast, 338 n. 6, 339 n. 1.
Argumentum, in ep. ad Philem. t. xi. f. 772, ii. 391 n. 5; f. 773, 392 n. 2.
Contra oppugnatores vitæ monasticæ, ii. 285 n. 2, 301 n. 5.
De sacramentis, l. iv. c. 4, the words of institution in the Eucharist, ii. 363 n. 7.
Ep. to Cæsarius, genuineness, ii. 732 n. 6.
Expos. in Ps. 109, § 6, t. v. f. 259, the cross on the forehead, ii. 323 n. 4; pilgrimages, 378 n. 1. In Ps. 149, t. v. f. 498, the church, 321 n. 7.
Homilies. De cruce et latrone, H. 1, § 1, t. ii. f. 404, place in worship, ii. 316 n. 1. De incomprehensibili, H. 3, § 6, t. i. f. 469, prayers in the church, 321 n. 8, 352 n. 2; for energumens, 361 n. 2. De Lazaro, H. 3, t. i. f. 737, use of the Bible, 318 nn. 1, 4. De pœnitentia, H. 5, § 5, t. ii. f. 315, misuse of the fasts, 340 n. 2. De prodit. Judæ, H. 1, § 6, t. ii. f. 384, words of consecration in the Eucharist, 363 n. 7. De statuis, H. 4, § 6, t. ii. f. 58, modes of observing the fast, 338 n. 6; H. 5, § 1, f. 59, pilgrimages, 378 n. 1; § 7, f. 70, right use of preaching, 315 n. 2, H. 20, intercession of Flavian, 175 n. 1. In Act. Ap., H. 1, §§ 6, 8, seasons for baptism, 360 nn. 3, 4; H. 14, deacons, 189 n. 4; H. 18, § 5 (ed. Montf. t. ix. f. 158), church building, 101 n. 1, 367 n. 4; H. 21, § 4, prayers connected with the Eucharist, 367 n. 2, 368 nn. 1, 3, 373 n. 1; H. 38, fin., pagans under Valens, 91 n. 3; H. 45, § 3, ἔσονες, 169 n. 1. In Annam, H. 1, § 1, t. iv. f. 700, fast at Antioch, 339 n. 3; H. 4, § 6, f. 738, prayer, 316 n. 2; H. 5, f 739, seq., formal religion, 258 n. 3. In baptism, Christi (t. ii. f. 367, ed. Mont.), the same, 258 n. 2; § 2, Epiphany, 343 n. 2. In 1 Cor. H. 3 (ed. Ben. x. 20), Greek of N. T., 116 n. 4; H. 6, § 4, anchorets, 303 n. 2; H. 8, § 4, headship of Christ, 720; H. 12, § 7, superstitious customs in relation to children, 357 n. 1; H. 25 (x. 226), love, 303 n. 4; H. 27, agapæ, 361 n. 4; H. 39 (t. x. ed. Montf. f. 372), restoration, 737 n. 3. In 2 Cor. H. 2, § 5, the prayer for catechumens, 358 n. 1. In diem natal. Christi, § 1, t. ii. f. 355, 345 n. 1. In Ephes. H. 3, § 4, on right participation in the Lord's Supper, 365 n. 2; § 5, administering it, 363 n. 10; H. 7, § 4, anchorets, 303 n. 1; H. 10, § 2, images in churches, 327 n. 6. In Eutrop. (t. iii. f. 386), the church, 321 n. 7. In fest. Epiph. § 2 (Ben. t. ii. f. 369), 342 n. 5; f. 374, impenitent communicants, 214 u. 1. In fest. Philogon. (t. i. f. 492), Christmas, 345 nn. 2, 3. In Genesin, H. 2, § 1 (t. iv. f. 8), the fast at Antioch, 339 n. 2; H. 6, 340 n. 1, § 2 (f. 673), the church in the house, 315 n. 4; H. 29, the Scriptures, 318 nn. 2, 3. In Heb. H. 7, § 4, marriage, 302 n. 1; H. 17, § 3, sacrifice in the Lord's Supper, 366 n. 4; § 4, right participation, 365 n. 1. In Johann. H. 5, § 4, grace, 720; H. 11, § 1 (ed. Montf. t. viii. f. 72), duty of purchasing the Bible, 319 n. 1; H. 18, § 1, deferring of baptism, 356 n. 4; § 3, grace, 720 n. 3; H. 46, § 3, the Eucharist, 731 n. 6; H. 78, § 4 (f. 464), anchorets, 285 n. 1, Cenobites, 286 n. 4. In Matt. H. 1, § 2 (t. vii. f. 5), discrepancies in the gospel narratives, 390 n. 5; H. 7, § 2, pilgrimages, 378 n. 1; H. 11 (f. 158), formal worship, 315 n. 3; H. 27 or 28, § 2, image of Christ, 327 n. 4; H. 32, § 6, miracles by the oil of the sacred lamp of the ch., 322 n. 1; § 7, desecration of the ch., 315 n. 5; H. 39, § 3 (f. 435), keeping the feast, 315 n. 1 (H. 47, treatment of heretics, iii. 255 n. 4); H. 50, § 3, offerings, 320 n. 1; H. 78 or 79, § 4, image of Christ, 327 n. 3; H. 80, § 2, offerings, 320 n. 1; H. 2, exclusion from the sacrament, 214 nn. 1, 3. In Meletium, H. (t. ii. f. 519), figures of Meletius, 324 n. 4. In Pentecost, H. 1, § 1 (t. ii. f. 458), 332 n. 2, Epiphany, 343 n. 1. In Rom. proem. (t. ix. f. 426), evils springing from ignorance of the Bible, 318 n. 7; HH. 7 et 8, justification by faith, 720 n. 2; H. 10, § 3, power of faith, 720 n. 1. Homilia in Seraphim, § 1 (t. vi. f. 138), prophetic vision for all, 392 n. 2. In 1 Thess. H. 8, and 2 Thess. H. 3, restoration, 737 n. 2. In 1 Tim. H. 5, § 3 (t. xi.), communion on Friday at Antioch, 333 n. 5, once a year, 365 n. 2; H. 11, in Tim., equal dignity of bps. and presbyters, 188 n. 3. Homil. Kalend. 350 n. 3. Hom. on Christ's divinity, § 9 (t. i. 571), sign of the cross, its prevalent use, 323 n. 4. Homilies preached at Antioch, confession and penance in the Greek ch., 216 n.; ad. pop. Antiochen. H. 19, § 4 (t. ii. f. 197), the Gospels as amulet, 259 n. 1; during the Great Week, 311 n. 1; Thursday (t. i. f. 386), 341 n. 4; Good Friday, 341 n. 7. Homilies published first by Montfaucon (t. vi. f. 273), § 1, Friday at Constantinople, 333 nn. 6, 7; H. 8 (t. xii.), on missions, 158 n. 2. Homily to neophytes, grace of baptism, 726 n. 6, 727 n. 1. Other homilies, 350 n. 4 (t. iii. f. 248), 354 n. 1, 362 n. 3. See Adv. Judæos. Opp. t. iii. f. 300, against heretics, 767 n. 4; t. x., sermon of Nestorius, ii. 720 n. 4.

In baptism, Christi, t. ii. f. 367, ed. Montf., paganized Christians, ii. 258 n. 2.

GENERAL INDEX. 47

Church, situation of, under the emperors, i. 93-156. Recognized as legal corporation, 140, 142. Apostolic constitution, 179-190. Constitution after the apostolic times, 190-217. Outward unity of the, 207-217 True unity, 304. Visible and invisible, 210, 217, 247, 304, 646. Development through conflict with sin, 217, 218. Novatian on the conception of the church, 243, 246-248. Catholic idea of the, 518. Man, 502-504. In Montanism, 517-519. Outward mediation of the church, 645, 646. See Tertullian, Cyprian.
Second Period. Extension and limitation, ii. 1-160. Constitution. 161-212. Internal organization, 178-212. Secularization of the, 162, 179, see Secularization. Spiritual nature of the, 179. Doctrine of the, 199-212, 232, 237-252. With Jovinian, 311, 312. In the Greek church, 722, 723. Visible and invisible, 199, 201, 238, 233, 311, 722, 723, 736. Outward unity, 199, 216. On earth and in heaven, 246. Body of Christ, 247, 367, see Christ. With Augustin, 238-243, 244, 247. Mediation of the, Gregory of Nyssa on, 447. See Papacy.
Third Period. Extension and limitation, iii. 4-105. Internal organization, 106-122. Doctrine of the church, 111-122. Gifts to the, 9, 130. Visible and invisible, 92. Visitations, 107. Paulicians on the, 259. See Frankish church, Greek church, Roman church.
Fourth Period. Extension and limitation, iii. 271-345. Constitution, 346-399. Internal organization, 408-414. Doctrine of the church, Stephen of Hungary, 334 n. 4; Claudius of Turin, 438 n. 2; Berengar, 515, 526. Independence and sovereignty of the, 348, 349. See Church and state, Greek church, Western church.
Fifth Period. Extension and limitation, iv. 1-81. Constitution, 82-292. Corruption of the church, 82, 93, 187 n. 2, 211, 215, 216, 220, 592, 628, 631, see Church property. Mediation of the, 354, 509, 514. Progressive development of the, 332. Periods of development, see Joachim and Oliva. Dolcino, 635. Authority, 431. The Bogomiles, 559. Spiritualis et carnalis, 636. See Investiture.
Sixth Period. The church constitution, history of, v. 1-133. Corruption of the, 47, 56, 178, 193, 324, 388, -12. The schism, 47. Efforts to restore tranquillity, 49-133. Doctrine of the church, Philip the Fair on the, 5; Gerson, 78, 80, 96, 353; Wicklif, 172; Matthias of Janow, 202; Huss, 258, 298, 299-310, 350 (see Huss, De ecclesia); Jerome, 374. Definitions of the, 26, 172, 296, 298, 302, 353. Unity of the, 19, 63, 78, 82, 92, 120, 172; Janow on this point, 208, 211, 231; Huss, 306-308. Authority, 28. Church visible and invisible, 302, 374. Need of a visible head, 121, 172, 173, 308, 352, 353. Progressive advances of the, 308. Testimony of the, 27, 28, 40. See the following heads.
Church and state, ii. 15, 16, 36, 37, 111, 114, 161-178, 207, 216. Exemptions, 169-171. With the Donatists and Augustin, 223-231, 247-252. Interference of the state in the doctrinal controversies, 382, 383, 413-415, 417 n. 3, 418-423, 425-438, 443, 453-456, 459-462, 464, 518, 525-528, 532, 534-541, 548, 566-569, 572, 578, 580, 585-609, 611, 650, 651, 658, 764. See those controversies, also Chrysostom, life of; Force.
Third Period. Church in relation to the state, iii. 91-105. Considered as a representative of God, 92. Influence of the Frank monarchs in it, growing out of their power of appointing bishops, 92. Laws of the church, influence of the State upon them, 95, 96. Exemption of the church from state burdens, 97. Protects slaves, 98-101. Heerban, 102. Its possessions, see Church property. Influence of the church on the administration of justice, 102-104. Asylums, 104 (see ii. 176-178). Care of prisoners, 105 (see ii. 178). *Fourth Period,* iii. 400-407, 352. *Fifth Period,* 138, 139, see Investiture, Papacy. *Sixth Period,* v. 16-19, 25-29, 78, compare Papacy, 1-133. See State.
Church assemblies. Forbidden, i. 137, 138, 148 and n. 1. Rescript of Licinius, ii. 19. On the Sabbath, ii. 333, 334. Other days, ii. 194. Separate, ii. 281. See Festivals, Sunday.
Church attendance, ii. 258, 259, 315; iii. 108, 109, 413, 426; iv. 302, 316, 317, 325. Bogomiles, 557, 558, 561.
Church benevolent institutions. See Benevolent.
Church books, ii. 358 n. 2.
Church buildings, i. 80, 142, 290-293. Demolished, 148, 155. *Second Period.* Erected, ii. 3, 18, 194 (281), 319-322, 377. Over graves of martyrs, 370; offerings there, 371. Augustin on, 101. Closed or demolished, 19, 79, 84, 95, 100, 131. Rebuilt, 66, 67, 133. Preservation of, 168. Consecration of, 321, 438. See Asylum. *Third Period.* Erection of, iii. 40, 50 and n. 2, 51, 55, 79. Charlemagne on, 131, 239. Dedication to saints, 57, 208. Sacredness of, 239. Adornment of, 130, 131, 217, 232, 235, 236. Gifts to, 130, see Gifts. Destroyed, 79, 84 (78), 202, 278. Reconsecration of, 5 n. 4 (iv. 26). *Fourth Period.* Erection of, iii. 277, 278, 285, 301, 303, 307, 315 n. 1, 322, 470 n. 2. Sacredness, 598. Adornment, 418, 470

n. 2. Gifts, 452. *Fifth Period.* Erection, iv. 5, 16, 17, 22, 32, 34, 58, 293 and n. 1, 295. Indulgences for, 350, 351. Restoration of, 271, 272. Consecration, 17, 22, 29, 352. Destruction, 26, 27, 597. Reverence for, Francis of Assisi, 272, 275 (557, 636). Splendor of, 291, 293. Profanation of, 385. Bernard on the embellishment of, 264. The sects, 557, 577, 597, 636. Purification of, 549. *Sixth Period*, v. 51. Decay of, 123.

Church collections, ii. 63 n. 3.

Church constitution, i. 179-217; ii. 161-212; iii. 91-122, 346-424; iv. 82-292; v. 1-133. See Church, Church and state.

Church discipline, i. 217-221; ii. 209, 213-216, 241; iii. 136-140, 450-455; iv. 347-354.

Church divisions. See Schisms.

Church doctrine. See Church theology.

Church elections, i. 189, 199, 200, 223; ii. 185, 186 and n. 1. Among the Franks, 92-95. Laws against interfering with the freedom of, 94. Restored by Charlemagne, 95. Elsewhere, 95. *Fourth Period*, iii. 400-403. *Fifth Period.* Free, iv. 134, 142, 143. Papal confirmation of, 196, 200. Gregory VII. and, 101 and n. 3. *Sixth Period*, v. 65, 113, 125, 137; Papal, Gerson on, 99, 100. See Election.

Church fathers, i. 656-723. Study of, ii. 122, 183; iii. 157, 178, 180, 202, 461, 473, 503, 588; iv. 358, 401, 597; v. 62, 240. Authority, ii. 740 n. 2; iii. 60, 232, 517, 518; iv. 416, 424, 534, 551, 578 n. 5; v. 291. Appealed to in the controversies: on Adoptianism, iii. 166-168; Monotheletic, iii. 177, 178, 180, 184, 194; on image worship, iii. 202, 203, 230, 232, 533, 551; on ecclesiastical government, iii. 350; on predestination, iii. 493; on transubstantiation, iii. 496, 516-518; by Manuel Comnenus, iv. 534. Dionysian writings and the, iii. 170. Collections from the, iii. 169, 533, 551; iv. 409, 410, 607. Transcriptions of, iv. 301. Abelard on the, iv. 391, 392. Bacon, iv. 424. Wicklif, v. 157. Janow, v. 207. Huss, v. 240, 336. See Church teachers.

Church funds, i. 232, 233. See Church property.

Church government, in Judaizing sects, i. 184. Gregorian principles of, iv. 4. Roger Bacon on, iv. 425. See Church constitution.

Church history, i. 675. See History.

Church hymns. See Hymns, Church music, Psalmody, Bardesanes, Paul of Samosata (i. 304).

Church jurisdiction. See Jurisdiction; also v. 28, 29. See Church and state, Defensor pacis.

Church language, how the Latin came gradually to be regarded as such, iii. 127. Slavonian, iii. 316, 317, 323, 330. See Language.

Church law. See Canonical law, Ecclesiastical law, Church and state, Decretals, Law.

Church legislation, iii. 55, 56. See Councils, Synods, Bulls.

Church liberty, v. 63. See Freedom, Liberty.

Church life, ii. 212. See Christian life.

Church music, i. 304; ii. 354, 355. In the Frankish church, improved by Pepin, iii. 127. Remodeled by Charlemagne, 128, 242. Influence of Gregory the Great on, 142. Agobard of Lyons zealously opposed to it, 428. See Church psalmody, Organs.

Church of Rome. See Roman church. Rebellion against the, v. 15.

Church offices, multiplication of, i. 190, 200, 201; ii. 191. Sought after from worldly motives, ii. 168, 184, 186. Worldly motives in the choice of candidates, ii. 184-186. Filling of them in the *third Period*, iii. 108-110. The Paulicians, 264, 265. *Fourth Period*, iii. 400-404. *Fifth Period*, iv. 200. *Sixth Period*, v. 97. See Benefices, Bishops, Church elections, Investiture, Patronage, Simony.

Church ordinances, mutability of, iv. 344 n. 4.

Church ornaments, iii. 408 n. 1, 418. See Church buildings.

Church penance. See Penance.

Church property, ii. 166-169, 191, 199, 222 n. 3; iii. 101, 102. Restoration of, ii. 16, 18. *Third and fourth Periods.* Insecurity of its landed estates, iii. 101. Taxation of, 101. Oversight of patrons, 110. Used in redemption of captives, 4 n. 1. Confiscated, 55. Ethelbald, 69. Gregory's care of, 113. Inviolate, 348. Investiture, 400-404. Tenure, 402. Defense of, 405, 406. Misused, 412. Inherited, iii 410, 411; iv. 97 n. 8. *Fifth Period.* Squandered, iv. 93 (v. 21, 54, 123). Treaty of Sutri on, 133. Placidus of Nonantula on, 138, 139. Gottfried of Vendome on, 142, 143. Source of corruption, 215, 216, 224, 284. Prediction of its spoliation, 284. *Sixth Period.* Power of the pope over, v. 16, 17. Council of Constance on, 121. Wicklif on, 136, 138, 146, 160, 163, 170, 171. Militz, 178. Huss, 268, 269. See Gifts, Investiture, Property, Secularization, Wealth.

Church psalmody, i. 304; ii. 354, 355. In the Frankish church, improved by Pepin, iii. 127. Remodeled by Charlemagne, iii. 128, 242. Gregory the Great, iii. 142. Agobard, iii. 428. In the sect at Arras, iii. 598. Influence on doctrine, iii. 543 (see Hymns). In China, iv. 58. German, iv. 155. Peter

of Bruis on, iv. 597. See Church music, Hymns.
Church schisms. See Schisms.
Church system, conflicts with the, iv. 390–398. See Church constitution, Ordinances of Hildebrand, Schisms, Sects.
Church teachers, *of the first Period*, their history, i. 656–723. Witnesses of miraculous phenomena, 72, 73. How regarded, 128. See the individuals. *Of the second Period*, ii. 260. Honors to, 369. On slavery, iii. 98. *Of the third Period*, iii. 141. Authority *in the third and fourth Periods*, iii. 169, 170, 180, 352, 430 n. 3, 431 n. 2, 582. Infallibility, 485. *Fifth Period*, study of, iv. 98. Abelard on the, 390–392. Appealed to, 540, 541, 545. Authority denied, 595. *Sixth Period*, Huss on the, v. 323, 339, 353. See Church fathers.
Church theology. See Anthropology, Church teachers, Doctrine, Eschatology, Montanism, Theology.
Church tradition. See Tradition.
Church tribunal, ii. 212.
Church usages, differences in, i. 296–300; ii. 337–339; iii. 15–17, 23–25, 32, 35, 568, 580–585; iv. 92, 538, 541; v. 92.
Church utensils, profaned, ii. 131; iii. 217. Destroyed, ii. 231. Sold to redeem captives, ii. 136, iii. 287; to feed the poor, iii. 408 n. 1, 418; to meet extortions, v. 54. Given as bribes, ii. 229. Stolen, iii. 6 n. 2. In missionary work, iii. 15; iv. 6, 23, 46. Adorned with images, iii. 217, 232. Purified, iv. 549. Communion vessels, iv. 213, 265.
Church visitations. See Visitations.
Churches founded, iii. 40 (46, 48, 53, 68), 72, 78, 80, 81, 279, 280, 298, 316, 322, 326, 330; iv. 9, 16, 21, 32, 36. See Missions, Church buildings, Saints.
Churches, organization of, i. 261; iii. 330.
Chusistan, i. 488.
Cibalia, battle of, ii. 18.
Cibossa, iii. 248.
Cicero.
> De natura deorum, l. iii., Cotta, i. 8. De legibus, 1. 2, c. 8, i. 86, Hortensius (Augustin), ii. 396. De senectute, c. 2, iii. 483 n. 2.

Cilean. See Cyllena.
Cilicia, Christianity in, i. 79. In the controversies respecting baptism, i. 318. Temple at Ægæ, ii. 26, 27. In the Nestorian controversy, synods in Cilicia Secunda, ii. 547, 713. Meletius expelled from, ii. 551. See Tarsus.
Cilicium, iv. 285 n. 4.
Ciutius, Roman, iv. 108.
Circular letters, ii. 215. Of Gothic churches on the death of Sabas, ii. 155 and n. 2. Of Synesius against Andronicus, ii. 215. Of the bps. of Alexandria announcing Easter, ii. 338. Of Alexander, bp. of Alexandria, against Arius, ii. 410. Of Athanasius, ii. 434. Of Basiliscus, ii. 585, 586. Of Zosimus in Pelagian controv., i. 651, 652, 657. Of Charlemagne, iii. 154. Of Sophronius, iii. 179. Of Photius, iii. 327, 567. Of Theodore, iii. 537. Of Innocent III., iv. 44. Of Frederic II., iv. 180. Of Bonaventura, iv. 289. Of Nicephorus Blemmydes, iv. 542. Of Dolcino, iv. 631, 632. Of Nicholas IV. against the Apostolicals, iv. 623.
Circumcellions, ii. 226–231, 235, 249 n. 2, 294.
Circumcision, i. 49, 440, 658, 690 n. 2; iii. 592; iv. 591. Forbidden to Romans, i. 89. Of Christ, festival of, ii. 351; iii. 134; iv. 334.
Cirta, in Numidia, assembly there (A. D. 305), ii. 219. See Petilian.
Cistercian abbots and the mission in Prussia, iv. 43 n. 1, 44. Innocent III., iv. 173 n. 4. Order, iv. 236 n. 2, 251–263, 314. Monasteries, iv. 252–254, 296. Cistercians sent to put down the sects, iv. 269, 640. Monks, iv. 37, 39, 235, 414 n. 2, 417; v. 183 n. 2. Abbots, iv. 252, 254, 324, 398; v. 340. Bernard on the Cistercians and Cluniacensians, iv. 263, 264. See Bibliotheca Cisterciensis.
Citeaux (Cistercium), iv. 251, 252 and n. 1, 253, 398.
Cities, Christianity in, i. 79, 97, 202, 203.
Citta di Castello, v. 390.
City communities, i. 79, 202, 203; ii. 194, 195. City bps., i. 202; ii. 193. Bishoprics of chief cities, ii. 186. See Metropolitan.
Civic virtue, the old, i. 77.
Civil and evangelical law, Defensor pacis on, v. 26, 27. Huss on, v. 325, 326. See Law.
Civil authority, followers of Chrysomalos and, iv. 562. Marsilius of Padua on, v. 28. Wicklif on civil affairs, v. 160, 161.
Civil life, relation of Christians to, i. 270–274.
Civil power, interposition of in church affairs. Julian and Augustin on, ii. 653, 654. See Church and state, Controversies, Byzantine emperors.
Civil trials, iv. 614 n. 7.
Civilization, degeneracy of the ancient, i. 5, 76. Christianity and, ii. 159. Source of modern, iii. 1, 9 (46). See Missions, Monasteries.
Clairvaux, iv. 238, 254. See Bernard.
Clara of Assisi, iv. 276. Life of, 276 n. 2.
Clarendon, assembly at, iv. 170.
Classes of society reached by Christianity, i. 70, 78, 84, 90. See Christianity.
Classicianus, ii. 176 n. 5.
Classics, study of the, i. 75–78, 183, 484, 742–744, 754; iii. 150, 482, 527 n. 3; iv. 359, 362, 363, 374, 415, 530. See Greek literature, Greek philosophy.
Claudianus Mamertus, De statu animæ, ii. 706 n. 2.

Claudiopolis, iii. 205 n. 1, 206.
Claudius, emperor, i. 94.
Claudius Albinus, i. 119.
Claudius Apollinaris, bp. of Hierapolis. See Apollinaris.
Claudius of Turin, his life and doctrine, iii. 429–439, 457. Accused of Arianism and of Adoptianism, 430. His doctrine, 430, 431. His Biblical commentaries, 430–434. Opposed to pilgrimages and to the worship of saints, 433–438. Accused as a heretic, 439. His death, 439. Berengar, 504. The Waldenses, iv. 605, 609.

Citations from his writings:—
Apologeticus against Theodemir (Bibl. Patr. Lugdun. t. xiv.), f. 197, his removal of consecrated gifts from churches, iii. 433 nn. 1, 2; f. 199, Col. i., Paschalis I., iii. 433 n. 3.
Commentaries. Arianism, iii. 430 n. 4. Dedication, his residence at the court of Louis, 432 n. 4; his interruptions, 434 n. 2. On Gal. f. 142, ch. visible and invisible, 438 n. 2; f. 147, Peter and Paul, 437 n. 3; f. 150, on Gal. 3: 6, 432 n. 1; f. 151, significance of Christ's death, 436 n. 3; f. 155, Adoptianism, 431 n. 1; f. 162, Col. ii., sin, 432 n. 2; f. 164, intercession of saints, 437 n. 2. On 4 Kings (see Bibl. Pistoriensis), Theodemir, 434 n. 3. On Leviticus, Augustin, 431. On Romans, preface, grace, 432 n. 3.
Ep. to Theodemir, iii. 434 and n. 3.
Fragments, published by Rudelbach (Havniæ, 1824), f. 44, sufferings of Christ, iii. 436 n. 1.
Vindication, iii. 434 n. 4.

Cleanthes, i. 17 n. 2.
Clemangis, Nicholas de, v. 53–62, 64–70, 77, 84, 88, 91, 93, 114, 116. On the schism (see Baluz), 53–55. De ruina ecclesiæ, 56–60, 62. De studio theologico, 60–62.

Citations from his writings:—
De ruina ecclesiæ, c. 13, v. 58 n. 2; c. 42, 57 n. 2. De schismate (see Boulæus, i.), f. 690, v. 53 nn. 2, 3; f. 693, 54 n. 1; f. 694, 54 nn. 2, 3; f. 695, 55 n. 1. De studio theologico, f. 476, v. 62 nn.
Epistles. Ep. 2, to Benedict XIII., v. 65, 66 and n. 1. Ep. 3, to his friends at Avignon, 66 n. 2. Ep. 13, to Benedict XIII., f. 51, 68 n. 3, 70 n. 2. Ep. 14, Avignon, 67 nn. 1, 3. Ep. 17, f. 63, to the king of France, 69, 70. Ep. 42, Avignon, 67 n. 4; f. 129, bull of Benedict XIII., 77 n. 2. Ep. 73, f. 210, on his times, 68 n. 1. Ep. 77, corrupt morals in France, 68 n. 2. Ep. 102, f. 290, *seq.*, to Nicholas de Baya, on the council of Constance, 114–116. Ep. 112, ad conc. gen., 116–118. Ep. 132, ad Reginaldum, f. 336, the treatment of Benedict XIII., 118 n. 1.
Super mater. conc. gener. opp. 64, 70, v. 88 nn. 2, 3; f. 75, 90 n. 2, 91 n. 1.

Clemens Romanus, i. 79, 85, 184, 189. Genuineness, 196 n. 1. Clementines, 353. Sanctification, 644. Character and criticism of his writings, 658–660. Ep. i. to James in Pseudo-Isidorean decretals, iii. 347 and n. 2.

Citations from his writings:—
Ep. 1. ad. Cor. c. 5, Paul in Spain, i. 85 n. 4; cc. 32, 33, faith and works, 644 n. 4; c. 40, f. 196, priesthood, 659; c. 42, f. 79, bps., 185 n. 1; filling of church offices, 189 n. 1; c. 44, the same, 189 n. 2. See Clementines.

Clement II., pope, iii. 378.

Clement III., pope, iv. 118, 120, 121, 129, 417. See Guibert.
Clement IV., pope, iv. 289, 340, 424, 425 n. 1.
Clement V., pope, iv. 70, 341; v. 7 n. 6, 2–23.
Clement VI., pope, v. 41–43, 51, 183, 232, 412.
Clement VII., v. 47–49, 52, 55–58, 164.
Clement, abp. of Bulgaria, iii. 320 n. 2. His labors in Bulgaria, 315 n. 1. Life of, 315 n. 1, 320 nn. 2, 3.
Clement of Alexandria. Account of his life and writings, i. 691–693, 673 and n. 2. As representative of the Alexandrian school, 528–543; ii. 386. Pistis and Gnosis, 308, 529–543. On persecutions, 119. Idealistic sects, 208. Hypocritical profession of Christianity, 251. Crowning, 260 n. Fraternal kiss, 262, 317. Asceticism, 278–281. Τίς ὁ σωζόμενος πλούσιος, 279. Community of goods, 280. Marriage, 281. Use of wealth, 282. Prayer, 286. The church, not the place, 289. Conduct in and out of church, 290. Uncomeliness of Christ, 291. Images, symbols, 292, 293. Epiphany, 301. 302. Catechumens, 305 n. 1. Searching the Scriptures, 307. Analogies sought in the pagan mysteries, 307 n. 1. Infant baptism, 312 n. 1. Agapæ, 326. Bartimeus, 364 n. 6. Biblical interpretation of the Gnostics, 388. Basilides, 401 n. 3, 402, 405 n. 2, 412. Archon, 410. Isidorus, 415. The cross as a symbol, 419 n. 3. Heracleon, 434. Pseudo-Basilideans, 447 n. 3. Carpocrates, 449 and n. 2. Epiphanes, 451. Nicolaitans, 452, 453. Tatian, 456, 457. Celibacy, 457. Marcion, 473. Prophecy in Montanism, 520. Περὶ προφητείας, 520 n. 2, 610. Montanism, 525. Catechist's office, 528. The Holy Scriptures, 532–534. Defense of science, 533–539. The education of mankind up to Christ, 536–539, 541. Conversion of heathen after death, 537. The true in heresies, 538. The Logos as θεῖος παιδαγωγός, 541. Limits of comprehension, 542. Faith and speculation, 551. Toleration, 551. Parabolical character of Scripture, 553 n. 2. Knowledge of God, 558, 559. Doctrine of the Logos, 586. Doctrine of the Holy Spirit, 610. Anthropology, 620, 622 (ii. 617). Humanity of Christ, 631–633 (ii. 473 n. 1, 608). Baptism of the pious men of the Old Testament in Hades, 646. Purification of the dead, and Christ's descent into Hades, 656 and n. 1. Origen, 694, 698.

Citations from his writings:—
Παιδαγωγός, l. i. c. 1, the Logos, as teacher of mankind, i. 692 n. 2. L. i. c. 6, faith and life, 531 n. 4. L. i. f. 103, milk and honey in baptism, 317 n. 1; f. 118, Christ "the just one," 564 n. 8. L. ii. c. 8, f. 176, his

GENERAL INDEX. 51

conversion, 691 n. 1; c. 12, costly apparel, 282 n. 2; f. 142, agapae, 326 n. 3; f. 194, family worship, 286 n. 5. L. iii. c. 1, uncomeliness of Christ, 282 n. 1; ff. 246 and 247, seal rings, 293 n. 1; f. 247, infant baptism, 312 n. 1; f. 250, the Christian matron, 281 n. 3; f. 255, the Christian calling. 278 n. 1, 279 n. 2; f. 256, fraternal kiss, 317 n. 3; f. 257, external religion, 290 n. 1.
Προτρεπτικός, f. 45, doctrine of God, i. 358 n. 4; f. 69, the serpent, 620 n. 6.
Stromata, l. i. f. 272, hypocritical profession of Christianity, i. 251 n. 2; f. 273 A, faith and knowledge, 530 n. 2; f. 274, his teachers, 691 n. 3; f. 278, defense of philosophy, 534 n. 5, 535 n. 3; f. 282, Greek philosophy preparatory, 537 n. 2; ff. 291, 292, uses of culture, 533 nn. 4, 5; f. 292, works, 541 n. 3; f. 298, unity of truth, 539 nn. 1, 2; f. 304, Prodicians, 452 n. 1; f. 309, weakness of Greek philosophy, 537 n. 5; f. 310, truth in paganism, 536 n. 1; f. 311, false prophets, 520 n. 1; f. 313, on 1 Cor. 1 : 20, 621 n. 2; f. 318, use of philosophy, 534 nn. 1, 2; f. 319, faith without knowledge, 308 n. 2; stages of moral development, 537 n. 5; f. 320, Cassian, 458 n. 3; f. 340, Christmas, 302 n. 1. L. ii. f. 302 A, faith and knowledge, 530 n. 2; f. 363, Basilides on faith, 414 nn. 1, 2, 415 n. 1; f. 364, intuitions of faith, 578 n. 1; f. 365 B, the same, 531 n. 6; f. 371, the same, 414 n. 3; recipiency of faith for the Godlike, 531 n. 1; f. 372, indestructibility of faith, 530 n. 3; f. 373, its relation to the higher life, 530 n. 4; f. 375, Archon, 419 n. 2; Valentine on the creation of man, 425 n. 2; f. 379, baptism in Hades, 646 n. 5; f. 381, scientific faith, 532 n. 4; f. 384, positive character of faith, 531 n. 3; f. 407, symbol of the cross, 419 n. 3; f. 408, Basilides, 402 n. 3; f. 409, Valentine on purity of heart, 432 n. 1; f. 411, Antinomian Gnostics, 388 n. 1; Nicolaitans, 453 n. 1; f. 414, martyrdoms after the death of Commodus, 119 n. 5. L. iii. f. 257 (or 457?), fraternal kiss, 262 nn. 2, 3; f. 427, will and power, 415 n. 5; Christian society, 416 n. 1; f. 431, Marcion, 466 n. 1; f. 436, Nicolaitans, 453 n. 2; f. 438, Prodicians, 452 n. 1; f. 441, Antinomian Gnostics, 451 n. 5; f. 444, the Gnosis, 531 n. 7; f. 446, *et seq.*, abstinence, 278 n. 3; imitation of Christ, 457 nn. 2, 3; f. 448, women as teachers of their own sex, 188 n. 1; f. 449, community of goods, 280 n. 1; f. 451, the psychical Messiah, Valentine on, 429 n. 5; f. 453, innocence of children, 620 n. 1; f. 460 D, Tatian on marriage, 457 n. 4; asceticism, 632 n. 4; f. 465, Tatian, 456 n. 5; Julius Cassian, 458 n. 3; f. 466, the fall, 620 n. 7; f. 469, inherited sin, 620 nn. 1, 3; f. 470, he fall, 620 n. 7; uncomeliness of Christ, 683 n. 1. L. iv. f. 490, unity of knowing and being, 532 n. 1; f. 503, Heracleon, 434 n. 4; f. 506, Basilides on providence, 407 n. 1; B. on sin and suffering, 412 n.; f. 507, on the devil, 408 n. 1; f. 508, ethics of B., 405 n. 2; f. 509 A, Basilides on evil and good, 403 n. 3; f. 500, on providence, 406 n. 1; f. 409 B, Valentine's doctrine, 433 n. 4; f. 509 C et D, the same, 424 n. 1; f. 511, Montanism, 520 n. 2, 690 n. 2; ff. 518, 519, Gnosis, 540 n. 1; f. 528 D, Gnosis and Pistis, 530 n. 2. f. 533, marriage, 280 n. 2; f. 536, sins of ignorance, Basilides, 413 n.; f. 537, Neo-Platonism of Clement, 586 n. 6; f. 539, peace, Basilides on, 400 n. 4. L. v. f. 546, Marcion, 468 n 1; f. 549, purgatory, 654 n. 4; f. 554, philosophy, 535 n. 4; f. 560, human systems of science compared with revelation, 538 n. 6; f. 565, the Logos, 586 n. 5; f. 582, symbolum, 307 n. 1; f. 583 D, Basilides, 407 n. 2; f. 587, power of the Word, 533 n. 3; f. 588, knowledge of God, 558 n. 2; redemption, 620 n. 8; f. 591, the Holy Spirit, 610 n. 2. L. vi. f. 621, Isidore, 402 n. 2; f. 636, *seq.*, preparation for the gos-

pel, 538 nn. 2, 3; f. 638, 639, Christ in Hades, 656 n. 1; f. 641, Isidore on the demon of Socrates, 406 n. 3; on the source of truth in ancient philosophy, 408 n. 2, 409 n. 1: Valentine on the same, 427 n. 2; f. 644, stage of philosophy, 537 n. 3, 538 n. 4; f. 645, Gnosis and Pistis, 540 n. 1; f. 647, Montanism, 520 n. 2; the truth contained in error. 536 n. 1; f. 649, Docetism, 632 n. 1; f. 652, the Gnosticus, 540 n. 2; f. 655, the vulgar fear of the Greek philosophy, 535 n. 1; f. 659, the fear of philosophy, 535 n. 2; f. 659 B, catechetical office, 528 n. 2; f. 660 C, use of culture, 528 n. 4; f. 662, original condition, 620 n. 5; f. 663, πίστις, moved by secondary ends, 541 n. 1; f. 667, freedom, 622 n. 2; f. 669, virtue of the πιστικός, 540 n. 3; f. 672, the grafted olive, 176 n. 1, 538 n. 5; f. 677, heresies, 539 n. 3; f. 677, Scripture parabolical, 553 n. 2; f. 680, Ebionites, 364 n. 6; f. 688, revelation, 538 n. 6; f. 690, uncomeliness of Christ, 633 n. 2; f. 691, meanings of φρόνησις, 541 n. 2; f. 693, Satan not the source of philosophy, 536 n. 2; ff. 694, 695, the human race united in Christ, 537 n. 1. L. vii. f. 700, the Logos ground of existence, 586 n. 5; f. 702, Θεῖος παιδαγωγός, 541 n. 3; f. 708, see f. 700; f. 715 B, the church, 289 n. 3; f. 722 prayer, 286 nn. 1, 2; Prodicians, 452 n. 1; f. 728, prayer, 286 n. 3; f. 730, οἰκονομία, 551 r. 2; f. 732, faith, in the Gnosis, 308 n. 1, 532 n. 2; f. 741, the married life, 281 n. 2; f. 753, sects, 164 n. 4; f. 754, searching the Scriptures, 307 n. 4; f. 755, the same, 307 n. 4; idealistic sects, 208 n.; f. 756, the Gnostic and the Scriptures, 533 n. 2; f. 757, the same, 532 n. 3; f. 759, agape, 326 n. 1; ff. 762, "63, the Gnostic and Scripture, 533 n. 1; f. 764, Glaucias, 417 n. 1.

Θεοδότου ἐπιτομαί (Didascer l. Annot.), f. 794, retribution, with Basilides, i. 404 n. 1; f. 796 D, the Demiurge, i. 411 n. 3; f. 797, creation of man, Valentinian doctrine of, 424 n 3, 425 n. 1. See Theodotus.
Τίς πλούσιος σωζόμενος, c. 11, the rich young man, i. 279 n. 3; c. 21, grace and will, 621 n. 1; c. 42, κλῆρος, 196 n. 1.
Ὑποτυπώσεις, apud Euseb. praep. evang. l. ii. c 2, his conversion through inquiry, i. 691 n 2. Euseb. l. vi. c. 1, 691 n. 5.

Clement, recognitions of, i. 358, 376 n. 3. L. viii. c. 53, i. 359 n. 1.

Clement, the opponent of Boniface, iii. 60. On the authority of the church fathers and of councils, 60. On the marriage of bishops; on the hindrances to marriage as customarily received, 61. On the doctrine of Christ's descent to Hades, 61. On predestination and restoration, 62. Last events of his life, 62, 63.

Clementines, the, i. 353–362. Description of the longing in paganism, 32. Essenes, 48. Ebionitism, and system, 353–362, 394, 395, 399. Sabaeans, 376 n. 3. Seth, 428 n. 3. Simon Magus, 454 n. O. T. criticism, 501 n. 5. The Clementines and Sabellius, 501 n. 1. Purgatorial fire, 654 (ii. 736). On Judaism, 658. Forged under the name of Clemens Romanus. 659. Fire the element of the evil one, ii. 767 n. 1. And darkness, iii. 257. In ecclesiastical law, v. 204.

Citations. II. ii. c. 6, necessity of revelation, i. 354 n. 2; c. 9, the prophet, 354 n. 3; c. 17, the false gospel preceding the true, 362 n. 2; c. 38, criterion of truth and error in the disposition, 358 n. 2. II. iii

c. 19, love of Jesus, 360 n. 1; c. 20, Adam, 354 n. 4, 355 n. 2, 357 n. 4; cc. 22, 23, seqq., false prophets, 257 n. 2; c. 26, discourses of Christ, 355 n. 3; c. 42, fall of Adam denied, 354 n. 4; c. 51, Matt. 5: 17, 359 n. 5. II. viii. c. 5, why revelation was necessary, 355 n. 1; c. 7, Jew and Christian, 360 n. 2; c. 10, law revealed to Adam, 354 n. 6; cc. 11, 12, the prophet, 356 n. 1; cc. 22, 23, Jews misled by false prophecy, 356 n. 3. II. xvi. c. 10, the Scriptures test the man, 358 n. 3; c. 12, 601 n. 1. II. xvii. c. 18, revelation from within, 359 n. 3; c. 19, Peter and Simon Magus, 362 n. 1. H. xviii. c. 13, Matt. 11 : 27, 357 n. 1.

Cleomenes, Patripassian, i. 584 n. 3.
Clergy, special object of persecution, i. 137–139, 149. Clerus, 195. Engage in worldly employments, 197. Receive maintenance, 198. Retire from worldly employments, 198, 199, 604. Election, 199. Allow themselves to be distinguished at the agapæ, 326. Celibacy, 521, 522.

In the second Period. Pagan books, etc., ii. 62 n. 2. Condition of ordination, 64 n. 3. Under Julian, 71, 78–81. Worldly, 78. Persecuted in Persia, 131, 132. Captive, 149. Support of, 168. Exemptions, 169–171. Jurisdiction in the Greek church, 171 n. 3. Celibacy, 179–182. Channels of the Holy Spirit, 179, 181, 182 (see i. 181). Education, 182–184. Election, 184–186. Transfer of, 186, 187. Different grades, 188–194. Worldly-minded, 261, 765, 766 (170). Their place at the Lord's Supper, 321. Ignorant, 744, 745. At Constantinople, 755. Infidelity, 763 n. 3. See Bishops.

Third Period. Deficient in culture, iii. 53, 66, 106, 107, 125–127. Military service, 55, 56, 66, 97, 102. Efforts of Boniface to reform, 56. Hostility of Saxons to the, 79, 81. Recruited from the class of bondmen, 98, 101. Offices in war, 102. Intercessions; care of prisoners, 103–105. Worldly-minded, 105 n. 5, 221. In the Frankish empire, become monastic, 106. Tonsure, 106 n. 1. Dependence on the bishops, 107. Court clergy, 109. Dependence on patrons, 110. Employed in negotiations, 119 (283, 284). Accused of withholding knowledge of Scriptures from laity, 251. With the Paulicians, 264. See Canonical constitution.

Fourth Period. Education of the, iii. 277, 425, 426. Ignorance of the Bulgarian, 315 n. Of the Romish, 370 (378). German clergy in Moravia, 317, 321. Concubinage, 322, 383, 386. Immorality, 382, 383. Military service, 385, 386, 404–406, 450. Corruption and ignorance, 390, 410, 420, 592. Education in the lower grade, 410. Employed in degrading offices, 412, 413. Rebuked, 441. Awakened spirit of inquiry in France, 592. See Ariald, Celibacy, Vagrant clergy.

Fifth Period. Sent on embassies, iv. 4. Involved in secular affairs, 17, 30, 133, 146, 147, 149, 207, 214 (see Investiture). Military, 31. Education of the Nestorian, 45, 46. Roving Nestorian, 46, 48, 52. Gregory VII. on the corruption of the, 93; Robert Grosshead, 207 n. 5, 278; Hildegard on the same, 219, 220; Abbot Joachim on the same, 222–224; Peter Cantor, 588. Popular feeling excited against, 96, 97, 99, 100, 107, 146–150, 151, 161, 248, 565, 599, 601, 604, 610, 611. Hostility between them and the mendicant orders, 97, 277, 278, 280, 285, 287. Criminal, relation to civil tribunals, 170. Frederic II. on the, 180. Amusements, 206, 207 n. 5 (see Hunting). Transitory order according to Joachim, 231. The degeneracy of the clergy favors monasticism, 233, 280, 286, 287. Ignorance, 287. Hostile to Bible reading by the laity, 321. Relation to the sacraments, 343, 346, 447, 514. Ignorance of the Bible, 611. Love of money, see Indulgences, Simony. Censured by Robert of Arbrissel, 248. Attacked by John of Soissons, 325; by Henry of Cluny, 598, 599, 601, 603; Oliva, 625. Regarded with contempt in South France, 639. Among the Bogomiles, 559 and n. 3. Catharists, 590. Other sects, 594, 616. Efforts at reform, see Hildebrandian system, Reform. Compare Celibacy, Marriage, Simony.

Sixth Period. Philip the Fair demands tribute of the, v. 5, 6. Independence of the, 8, 17, 18. Employed in menial offices, 54 (iii. 412, 413). Ignorance of Scripture, 33, 34, 59, 151 n. 2, 195. Corruption, 50, 54, 56, 58, 129, 132, 138, 256–258, 300, 379. Ignorance, 58, 59. Ignorance of church forms, 81. Gerson on the, 86, 87. Hireling, 101. Bernard Baptisé on those assembled at Constance, 113. Contempt of the laity for, 123, 129, 131, 148 n. 1. Deprivation of goods discussed, 132, 136, 161, 163, 170, 269, 274, 335. Amenable to civil law, 136. Popular hatred excited against, 157–159. Sons of, 159. In secular affairs, 161. Power to bind and loose, 146. Devout, 195, 196, 235, 309. Gradations, 202. Pride, 215. Jealousy and contempt towards laity, 193, 194, 217, 219, 221. Two parties among the, 232, 235. Persecuted in Bohemia, 272, 273. Marsilius of Padua on the, 28, 29. Wicklif, 138, 139, 151, 160, 162, 170, 173, 242, see Priests. Janow, 195–197, 202–205, 215, 216, 221. Huss, 248–250, 256, 257; on duties of, 249, 282, 307, 309, 324; on the effect of reproving, 256, 257; on the wealth of the, 268, 269. Jerome of Prague on the, 379.

Clerical offices. See Spiritual.

Clerici conductores conductitii, iv. 206 n. 3.
Clerici regulares, irregulares saeculares, iv. 208.
Clerici vagi, acephali, iii. 412, 413.
Clericis laicos, bull, v. 5.
Clermont (Arverna), iii. 93 n. 2. Assembly at, iv. 125. See Sidonius, Councils.
Clerus, clericoi, i. 195, 196. Clerus evangelicus, v. 248. Clerus Christi et Antichristi, v. 300. See Clergy.
Cleves, iv. 244.
Cliff (Cloveshove). See Councils, an. 747.
Clinici, i. 238 and n. 2, 310.
Clodeswinde, Longobard queen, iii. 3 n. 1.
Clodona (Clouoda, Gollnow?), town in Pommerania, iv. 16.
Cloister life, ii. 271-273.
Cloisters as seminaries for education, ii. 149, 183, 288, 298.
Close associations, law against, i. 120.
Clotaire I., iii 94.
Clotaire II., iii. 41, 94.
Clotilda, wife of Clovis, iii. 6-8.
Cloveshove. See Cliff.
Clovis, king of the Salian Franks, his conversion, ii. 13; iii. 6-8. Its influence, iii. 9. Successors of, iii. 92, 93 n. 2. War against the Visigoths, iii. 129 n. 2.
Club law, iv. 40.
Cluniacensians, iv. 249-252, 263, 264. Art among the, 252.
Cluny, monastery, iii. 417, 418 n. 1, 419. Hildebrand at, 381 n. 2. Controversy between Jews and monks at, iv. 77 n. 2. See Glaber Rudolph, Henry of, Hugo, Peter of, Odo.
Cluny, order of. See Cluniacensians.
Coadjutores, iv. 215.
Coalitions, v. 253.
Cochlaeus.
   Hist. Hussitarum, f. 29, seq., synod of Prague, an. 1418, v. 297 n. 1; f 39, Stephen Paletz, 252 n. 2; f. 42, Andrew of Broda against Huss, 183 n. 2, 258 n. 3; f. 157, 330 n. 1.
Cod. Babenberg. See Eccard.
Cod. Carolin.
   Ed. Cenni, t. i. f. 285, ep. of Stephen I. to Charlemagne, iii. 121 n. 1; f. 288, same, 121 n. 2; f. 352, ep. of Hadrian I. to the same, 122 n. 1; ff. 371, 390 (506), the same, 121 n. 4; ff. 389, 443, 510, 519, the same, 120 n. 1.
Cod. Justinian.
   L. i. tit. iv. ll. 22 et 23, on visitation of prisons, ii. 178.
Cod. Theodos.
   L. ii. tit. 8, 1. 1, on the observance of Sunday, ii. 333 n. 4, 336 n. 2; 1. 2, on the observance of the weeks before and after Easter, ii. 342 n. 3. L. viii. tit. 8, 1. 3, on the observance of Sunday, 336 n. 4. L. ix. tit. 3, 1. 7, duty of bps. in regard to prisoners, 178 n. 4; tit. 16, cc. 1 ct 2, granting religious liberty, 22 nn. 2-4; l. 9, the same, 90 n. 3; tit. 40, l. 16, on intercessions, 175 n. 5; tit. 44, l. 4, on right of asylum, 178 n. 8. L. xii. tit. 1, l. 63, on monasticism, 301 n. 6; l. 112, toleration of temple worship, 97 n. 2. L. xiii. tit. 1, l. 1, on the burial of the dead, 193 n. 1. L. xv. tit. 2, l. 38, granting the power of appointing advocates, 192 n. 1; tit 7, 1.5, forbidding the exhibition of spectacles on Sunday, etc., 336 n. 6. L. xvi. tit. 1, l. 3, on the power of patriarchs, 196 n. 2; tit. 2, l. 2, on exemption of the clergy, 170 n. 1; § 4, on the sacredness of wills, 167 n. 2; l. 6, prohibiting persons of the higher ranks from entering the spiritual order, 170 n. 4; l. 18, religio paganorum, 90 n. 5; ll. 42, 43, on Parabolani, 192 n. 5; tit. 4, 1,2, on conferences in regard to controversial matters, 150 n. 4, 157 n. 3; tit. 5, 1. 65, against heretics, 553 n. 4; tit. 7, against apostates, 104 n. 1, 119 n. 2; tit. 8, l. 9 (an. 393), against the destruction of synagogues, 95 nn. 2, 4; tit. 10, c. 1, on the haruspicia, 23 n. 1; c. 2, against sacrifices, 33 n. 1; c. 3, on the employment of magic, 23 n. 2; ordering the preservation of certain temples, 35 n. 3; l. 12, offering of sacrifice made equal to crimen majestatis, 99 n. 2; l. 16, on the destruction of temples, 101 n. 2; l. 18, the same, 101 n. 4; l. 20, confiscating estates belonging to the temples, 92 n. 3; tit. de Indulgentiis, 341 n. 2.
Codex Canonum, iii. 360.
Codex Can. eccles. African.
   Cc. 6 et 7, limiting duties of presbyters, ii. 188 n. 2. C. 28, on appeals, 208 n. 1; can. 37, milk and honey in baptism, 360 n. 2; can. 39, on the title of the bp. of the first church, 198 n. 1. C. 41, on Thursday of the Great Week, 341 n. 5. C. 42, agapae, 362 n. 2. C. 58, on the destruction of temples in the country, 101 n. 3; can. 61, on the public shows, 336 n. 5. C. 75, can. 10, on advocates, 192 n. 1. C. 92, concerning the Donatists, 234 n. 1. C. 93, the same, 235 n. 2. C. 97, on advocates, 19 n. 1. C. 107, on religious freedom, 102 n. 32.
Codran, iii. 300.
Coelestin. See Celestin.
Coelestin I., op. of Rome, ii. 147 n. 2. In the Nestorian controversy, 515, 519, 520, 521, 525, 531, 535 n. 1, 552, 553 n. 4, 721. The Semi-Pelagians, 695-698, 705, 710 n. 3. His letters to the clergy at Constantinople, and to Cyril, 521 and n. 1. To the Gallic bps., 695, 696, 697 nn. 1, 2. See Celestin.
Coelestius, Pelagian, ii. 639, 640, 644-652, 655, 659, 666, 670, 697 nn. 1, 2, 721. Doctrine of baptism, 728, 729, 730. His letters to his parents, 639 and n. 1.
Coelicolae, ii. 768 n. 1.
Coenobia, Cenobites, ii. 271-273, 282-284, 286-289, 639 n. 1.
Coins, cross on, i. 80. Of Constantine, ii. 8 n. 3, 21, 24 n. 4, 33 n. 4.
Colberg, history of its conversion, iv. 16.
Colchians, ii. 139. See Lazians.
Colchis, iii. 177.
Colebrooke.
   Diss. on the school of Sanchya, Essais sur la philosophie des Hindous, par Colebrooke, traduit par G. Pauthier, Paris, 1833, p. 32, i. 450 n. 2.
Collation of benefices, v. 65. See Benefices.
Collator, Semi-Pelagian, ii. 696 n. 2, 697 n. 3, 698 n. 1.
Collectio originum rerumque Constantinopolit.
   Combefis, f. 162, interview of Nicephorus and Leo, iii. 532 n. 1; f. 171, 535 n. 3.

Collection of Symmicta.
Report of Phocas, iv. 266 n. 1.
College, literary, under the Comnenes, iv. 530.
Collegium illicitum, i. 120.
Collision between paganism and Christianity, i. 70, 75.
Cölln, Dr. von.
On Tertullian, i. 684 n. 2.
Collyridianians, ii. 376 n. 1.
Colmann, bp. of Northumberland, iii. 24.
Cologne, as centre of missionary operations, iii. 65, 66, 71, 275. Archbishopric, iii. 279. Arnold, iv. 57. Persecution of Jews, iv. 74. Crusaders from, iv. 74. Hermann, iv. 79, 81. Witchcraft, iv. 91 n. 1. Bruno, iv. 265. Synod at, iv. 279. Kneeling before the host, iv. 341. Albertus Magnus at, iv. 421, 422. Catharists near, iv. 580 n. 1, 586 n. 7. Sects at, iv. 593, 604. University at, v. 375. Friends of God at, v. 381. Bps. of, ii. 436 n. 4; iii. 65, 71, 79, 80, 275, 354, 356, 396, 460 n. 6; iv. 245, 592 n. 2.
Colonia, iii. 248, 253.
Colonna, the family of, v. 4, 5, 12, 20, 73. Otto of Colonna, 126, 271, 272. See Martin V.
Colosse, church at, i. 351.
Colossians, ep. to the.
1: 15, ii. 439 n. 1: 1: 22, ii. 637 n. 3. 2: 14, ii. 778 n. 1: 2: 15, iii. 175 n. 3; 2: 16, i. 13 n. 4; 2: 21, i. 700. iii. 269 n. 6, 592 and n. 1; 2: 22, i. 700. 3: 9, 10, ii. 121. 4: 15, i. 185, 290 n. 2. Interpretations of, ii. 480.
Colossians, Paulicians, iii. 256 n. 2.
Columba, abbot among the Picts, iii. 10, 24.
Columban, abbot, missionary among the Franks, iii. 29–35. His contests and difficulties, 32. On synods, 32, 95. His contests with Brunehault and Thierri II. of Burgundy, 33. Banishment, 33. At Bregenz, founds Bobbio, 34. Conduct towards the Romish church, 34, 35. His successor, 38. Life of, 33 n. 2.
Ep. to his monks, iii. 33 n. 2. To Boniface IV., 34 n. 2, 35 nn. To the French bps., 32, 95 n. 3. His rule, 30; c. ii., 31 n. 3; c. iii., 31 n. 1. Instructiones variæ, 32; Inst. i., 32 n. 1; Inst. ii. et xi., 31 n. 2.
Comana, Comanum, ii. 356, 761.
Combefis.
Report of the Archivarius of the Constantinopolitan ch., iii. 196 n. 2. Auct. Bibl. patr. Paris (ed. 1672), P. i. f. 113, Methodius on prophecy, i. 358 n. 1; (ed. 1648) P. ii., Alexander of Lycopolis, his tract against the Manicheans, introd., ii. 767 n. 3; Hist. Monothelet., iii. 213 n. 2: life of Nicolaus, iii. 542 n. 2; John of Nice on the Christmas festival, ii. 347 n. 1. See Collectio originum, etc.

Comes orientis, ii. 95 n. 4, 550.
Comfort, spiritual, Ruysbroch on, v. 406. Tauler, v. 408.
Comgall, iii. 10, 29.
Commandments of God, of Christ, ii. 637; iii. 76. Wicklif on the, v. 138, 139, 142; Janow, v. 202–210; Huss, v 321; Ruysbroch, v. 403. See Christ.
Commentaries of the Apostles, i. 364 n. 2, 585 n. 1.
Commentaries on the Bible, i. 714; iii. 169, 457, 458; iv. 411, 426; v. 149.
On Genesis, ii. 127 n. 3, 494 n. 1, 613 n. 3; iv. 314 n. 1, 467 n. 1, 468 n. 1. On Exodus, iv. 338 n. 1. On Lev., iii. 431, 433. On Joshua, iii. 457. On Kings, iii. 150 n. 7, 434 n. 3. On Job, see Gregory I. On Psalms, i. 630 n. 5, 702, ii. 616 (see Ambrose, Arnobius, Augustin, Chrysostom, Hilary, Gerhoh), iv. 83 n. 2, 349 n. 3; Ps. 8, ii. 494 n. 1. On the Song of Solomon, iii. 471, see Bernard. On Isaiah, ii. 142 n. 3, see Joachim. On Jer., ii. 639 n. 1; iv. 135 n. 1, 226, see Joachim. On Lament., i. 702. On the Minor Prophets, ii. 393 n. 5. On Ezekiel, iii. 141 n. 2. On Daniel, i. 682. On Joel, ii. 393 n. 2. On Micah, ii. 393 n. 3. On the New Testament, iii. 431; iv. 220. On the four gospels, ii. 738; iv. 337 nn. 4, 5. On Matt., i. 708 n. 4, 710; ii. 618 n. 1, 619 nn. 2, 7, 620 n. 1, 622 n. 1; iii. 468 and n. 2, 501 nn. 1, 2, 511 n. 1. On Luke, ii. 622 n. 4, 623 nn. 2, 3. On John, i. 702; ii. 738 n. 6; iii. 235 n. 4, 281 n. 1; iv. 337 n. 6. On the epistles of Paul, ii. 605 n. 2, 638; iii. 470. On Romans, ii. 471 n. 1, 716, 717; iii. 482 n. 3; iv 376, 385. On 1 Cor., ii. 737 n. 3. On 1 and 2 Cor., ii. 635 nn., 636 n. 4, 637 n. 2. On Gal., ii. 391 n. 3, 725 n. 1; iii. 481 n. 1, 432 nn. 1, 2, 4. On Ephes., ii. 355 n. 3, 641 On Titus, ii. 188 n. 3, 261 n. 3. On Heb., i. 708. On Rev., ii. 605 n. 2; iv. 221 n., 228, 620 n. 3, see Joachim. Cassian on the study of, ii. 687. See Abelard, Gregory the Great, Jerome, Origen, Homilies of Chrysostom.
On other books. On the Alcibiades of Plato, ii. 105 n. 7. On Boethius de Trinitate, iv. 409 n. 1, 461 n. 5, 462 nn. 1–3. On Dante, iv. 629 n. 4. On De causis, iv. 445 and n. 1, 480. On the Eternal Gospel, iv. 618–620. On Homer, iv. 530. On the sentences, iv. 410, 421, 422, 472. Stephen of Tournay on Commentaries, iv. 416. Bacon on, iv. 425.
Commentationes soc. reg. Gotting. recentiores, t. v., ii. 141 n. 6. See Tychsen.
Commerce, a means of extending Christianity, i. 79; ii. 124, 141, 142, 144; iii. 282 n. 1, 285; iv. 10, 36, 46. See Merchants.
Commodian, character and writings, i. 686, 687. The proselytes, 68 n. 1. The confessors, 228, 229. The Separatist tendency, 237. True martyrdom, 280. Prayer, 288. Speaking in church, 303 n. 4, 329 n. 1.
Citations. Instructiones, i. 68 n. 1. N. 6, 26, 49, 57, 61, 80, i. 687 nn. N. 47, 229 n. 1. N. 48, 220 n. 4. N. 59, 281 n. 5. N. 62, 280 n. 5. N. 66, 237 n. 4. N. 69, 198 n. 3. N. 76, 303 n. 4, 329 n. 1. N. 79, 288 n. 2.
Commodus, emperor, i. 108 n. 3, 117, 119, 665 n. 2, 673, 674.
Common people, the, and the mendicant monks, iv. 276–280. And preachers of repentance, 313. See Clergy.
Commonitorium.
Quomodo sit agendum cum Manichæis (August. ed. Bened. t. 8, app.), i. 504 n. 3.
Communicatio idiomatum (interchange of attributes), with Apollinaris, ii. 489. With Theodore of Mopsuestia, ii. 501. In the Alexandrian school, ii. 502.

With Felix of Urgellis, iii. 159-162. In the Monotheletic controversy, iii. 183. In transubstantiation, iv. 340. See Interchange of predicates.
Communion, administered to the confessors in prison, i. 123, 135. Cyprian on the, i. 138. Tertullian, i. 218, 282. Granted to the lapsed, i. 234, 235. Kiss before, ii. 362. With the marriage ceremony, i. 284. Daily during Pentecost, i. 301. Of infants, i. 333, 648; iii. 496; iv. 341-343, 345; v. 337. Of the sick, iv. 343, 345. In memory of the dead, i. 334, 335. Daily, i. 332, 648 (301); ii. 221 and n. 1, 332, 364, iv. 614 n. 5; v. 213, 217-231. With Christ, i. 647, 648; ii. 362; iii. 498; iv. 224. In the hour of death, ii. 213. Free in the Greek church, ii. 216. Superstitious use of, ii. 259 (iv. 825). The Eustathians, ii. 281. On the dies stationum, Sabbath, and Sunday, ii. 365; iii. 333. In one kind, ii. 365, 366. In warlike expeditions, iii. 102. Spiritual, ii. 362; iii. 498, 499. See Lord's Supper.
Communion of saints iii. 134, 135; v. 324.
Communion with God, iii. 174; iv. 429.
Communities, in the early church, i. 84, 179-186. Irenæus and Cyprian on the freedom of, i. 215, 213.
Community, impulse to, iv. 233 (298, 303).
Community of goods, i. 46, 280, 352; iv. 208, 310, 608, 629 n. 5, 630.
Comnena, Anna. See Anna.
Comnenes, the, iv. 530.
Comnenus, Alexius, iv. 559, 564.
Comnenus, Manuel, iv. 529, 530 n. 1, 533-535, 560, 563, 564.
Comnenus II., John, iv. 536.
Como, iii. 390. See Abundius of.
Competentes, ii. 358, 359, 361 n. 2.
Compiegne, dialectic school at, iv. 356.
Compositiones, iii. 5 n. 2, 52 n. 6, 103, 105, 137, 138.
Compromise, in great historic epochs, v. 274, 275.
Conception, immaculate, iv. 331-333.
Conceptional development of doctrines and the life of faith distinguished, ii. 381, 387.
Conceptions, general, doctrine of with Augustin, ii. 669. Objective, significance of, iv. 355, 356, 360. Reality of, v. 165 n. 2, 343 and n. 2, 375, 376. See Realism, Nominalism.
Concil. œcumen., V.
Theodore on the person of Christ, Collat. iv., ii. 494 n. 3; c. 4, 498 n. 1; c. 5, 498 n. 4; cc. 6, 7, 13, 499 n. 1; c. 8, 501 n. 4; c. 14, 497 n. 2; c. 15, 497 n. 5; c. 19, 494 n. 1; c. 25, 497 n. 4; c. 27, 498 nn. 2, 8; c. 29, 501 n. 1; c. 49, 495 n. 1. Collat. v. ep 180 of Theodoret, 557 n. 7. See Theodoret.

Concilia Galliæ.
T. ii. f. 621, Charlemagne on studies of clergy, iii. 154 n. 1.

Conciuæ, iv. 15 n. 1.
Conclave, iv. 192.
Concomitance, doctrine of, iv. 344, 345.
Concordance, Biblical, iv. 426.
Concordat of Worms, iv. 143. Of Zeno, ii. 588.
Concordiæ vet. et nov. Test. See Joachim.
Concubinage of the clergy, iii. 322; iv. 96, 211; v. 81, 87. See Celibacy, Clergy.
Concupiscence, ii. 668. With the Pelagians, 658, 667, 668. With Augustin, 668.
Confession, i. 219; ii. 213, 216, 282, 370; iii. 58, 102, 137, 139 and nn. 6, 7, 149, 453, 460; iv. 238, 287, 301, 302, 325, 347, 353; v. 194, 207, 222, 276, 305, 306. To the pope, iii. 452. With the Catharists, iv. 577, 587 n. 5, 612. The Mendicants, iv. 279, 280. Law concerning auricular, iv. 353. To God, iii. 139; v. 171.
Confession of faith, i. 306-309 (218); ii. 358; iii. 53, 267. For ecclesiastics, ii. 763. Written, iii. 48 and n. 1. Of Eusebius of Cæsarea, ii. 416, 417. Of Arius, ii. 422, 428. Of Eunomius, ii. 444 n. 3. Of Lucidus at Arles, ii. 707. Of Bacchiarius, ii. 775 n. 6. Of Guibert at Rheims, iii. 271 n. 2. Of Gottschalk, iii. 474 n. 4, 479 and n. 5, 490. Of Berengar, iii. 511-514, 518-521. Of Bernard, iv. 462, 516. Catharist, iv. 588. Pauperes Catholici, iv. 612. Waldensian, iv. 615, 616 n. 7. Of Dolcino, iv. 631. Of Huss, v. 273, 274. See Creeds.
Confessores, iv. 212 nn. 3, 4.
Confessors (martyrs), i. 114. Reverence paid to, i. 159, 200, 228-231; ii. 217, 218, 268, 369. Heracleon on confession, i. 436, 437. Catharist, iv. 582 n. 2. See Meletian schism.
Confirmation, i. 238 n. 2, 316, 318, 321 (see Imposition of hands); ii. 188, 359, 360, 732; iii. 72, 496; iv. 16. Hilary on, ii. 165. Wicklif on, v. 170.
Confiscation of the property of heretics, iv. 640-642.
Congregatio præscitorum, v. 302.
Congregational singing, ii. 354 and n. 3.
Conon, legate, iv. 382.
Conrad, emperor, iii. 385 n. 2.
Conrad, priest, iv. 279.
Conrad I., abp. of Salzburg, iv. 141 n. 1, 143 n. 6.
Conrad III., emperor, iv. 151, 172.
Conrad IV., iv. 610.
Conrad of Marburg, iv. 543, 644.
Conrad of Vechta, abp. of Prague, v. 295, 316, 317.
Conrad of Waldhausen. See Waldhausen.
Conscience, ii. 74, 120. Liberty of, 217. Particular, iv. 84. Law of, v. 208, 209. See Religious freedom.

Consciousness of God, iii. 267. Religious, its dependence on the church in the Middle Ages, iv. 509 (ii. 369). See Christian consciousness, God.
Consecration, Berengar on, iii. 524, 525. Sect at Arras and Cambray, iii. 598. Francis of Assisi, iv. 275. Claudius of Turin on consecrated gifts, iii. 433.
Consent, as a test of truth, Proclus on, ii. 105.
Consentius, letter of Augustin to, ii. 402 n. 1.
Consilia evangelica, i. 39. Germ of the doctrine, i. 277, 645. Its further development, ii. 304, 634, 635, 643 n. 2, 677; iii. 459; iv. 283, 304, 414, 525, 526, 532; v. 213, 216, 249, 282. And præcepta, Janow on, v. 213, 216.
Consistorium imperatoris, ii. 96.
Consistory, v. 10, 194.
Consolamentum, iii. 595, 598, 600 n. 2; iv. 571, 575–578, 580–582, 590, 593. Reconsolatio, iv. 581.
Consolati, iv. 576, 585. See Consolamentum, Perfects.
Constance, bishopric of, iii. 36, 440 n. 4. Bp. of, iv. 150; v. 322, 339, 340 n. 1. Bernard at, iv. 155 n. 5. Banishment of the clergy at, v. 42. Letters missive for the council of, v. 100, 101. Council of Constance, v. 90, 100, 103–128, 129, 132, 133, 271, 316–380. Mode of voting, v. 103, 104. Deposition of John XXIII., v. 103–112. Collegium reformatorium, v. 112. Huss at, v. 244 n. 2, 255, 257, 279, 288 n. 2, 317, 318, 321–371, 390 and n. 1. Jerome of Prague at, v. 254, 372–380. Burgomaster of, v. 326. Adherents of Huss at, v. 357. See Bernold, Otto.
Constance, lake, iii. 34, 35.
Constans, emperor, son of Constantine the Great, ii. 33, 228. Arian controversy and Athanasius, ii. 433–438, 449 n. 5.
Constans II., emperor, his edict, τύπος τῆς πίστεως, iii. 184–192.
Constantia (Salamis), ii. 328, 741. See Councils, an. 401.
Constantia, mother of Frederic II., iv. 176, 226.
Constantia, on the island of Cyprus, ii. 531.
Constantia, queen of France, iii. 395.
Constantia, sister of Constantine, ii. 18, 324, 325, 422.
Constantina, ii. 227.
Constantine, bp. of Nacolia, iii. 203, 205, 206.
Constantine, bp. of Rome, iii. 197.
Constantine (Silvanus), head of the Paulicians, iii. 247, 248, 264.
Constantine, patriarch of Constantinople, iii. 219. Executed, 222.
Constantine, priest in Philippopolis, ἐγχειρίδιον, etc., iii. 587 n. 5.
Constantine, son of Irene, Greek emperor, iii. 233, 536 n. 2. Under the guardianship of Irene, 224, 234.
Constantine Chrysomalos, monk, iv. 560–562. On Christian character, 561 n. 1. On works, 561 nn. 1, 2.
Constantine Copronymus, Greek emperor, iii. 128 n. 4, 214–225, 229, 293, 539. Iconoclast, 214, 218–223, 231, 236, 533 n. 1, 539. Said to have been opposed to the worship of Mary and of the saints, 218 and nn. 2, 4. Enemy of the monks, opposed to relics, to devotionists, 218, 221, 222, 225, 536 n. 1. Opposed to Θεοτόκος, 222. Paulicians, 250 n. 2. Bogomiles, iv. 557. Life of, iii. 218 n. 4. Orat. adv., iii. 221 n. 1.
Constantine Cypharas, monk, iii. 307, 308.
Constantine Monomachus, Greek emperor, iii. 583.
Constantine Pogonatus, Greek emperor, iii. 193, 247, 248.
Constantine Porphyrogenitus, Greek emperor.
Life of Basilius Macedo, Photius, iii. 568 n. 3; c. 4, the Bulgarians, 307 n. 4; c. 44, Photius, 572 n. 2; § 95, 314 n. 4. Continuat., reign of Theophilus, emp., § 13, iii. 547 n. 2; l. ii. c. 3, f. 27, ed. Par., Athinganians, iii. 592 n. 2; l. iv. c. 4, f. 95, Theodora, iii. 549 n. 1; cc. 14 et 15, Bogoris, iii. 308 n. 3; c. 15, 309 n. 2; c. 16, f. 103, Paulicians, iii. 587 n. 1; c. 38, the emp. Michael, iii. 561 n. 1. His work on the ceremonies of the Byzantine court, ed. Niebuhr, vol. i. p. 594, reception of Olga, iii. 328 n. 3; Animadvers. in, iii. 329 n. 1. See Banduri.
Constantine the Great, his course of development, ii. 6–14. Sign of the cross, 9–14, 119. First and second religious edict, in conjunction with Licinius, 14–16, 21 (i. 148). Renewed, 17. Rescript to Sabinus, 17. First war with Licinius, 18. Second, 20, 351 n. 1. Sole ruler, 21. Previous religious position, 21; as sole ruler, 21–33 (v. 322). Prohibition of sacrifices in private dwellings, 21, 22. Toleration of paganism, 22, 23, 25. Flattery of the bps., 25. Destruction of temples, 26, 27. Prohibition of sacrifices, etc., 22, 28. Magical arts, 22, 23 (i. 145 n. 2). On the conversion of pagans at the Nicene council, 29. Baptism and death, 30. Pagan narrative relating to his conversion, 31, 32. Political interest predominant, 43. Proselytism, 64. Restoration of churches, 16, 66. Banishment of Athanasius, 73, 428. In the chain of events, 37. Fortune of, 87 n. 4. Intercedes for Persian Christians, 125. Conversion of the Iberians, 138. Theophilus Indicus, 140 (i. 83). Embassy to Arabia, 142. Conversion of the Abyssinians, 143. Ulphilas, 152 n. 1. His position in relation to the church, 162–164. Grants to the church the right of receiving legacies, 167. Exemption of the clergy, 169, 170. Judicial authority of the

bps., 171. Bps. of the great cities, 186. In the Donatist controversy, 223–228 (i. 155 n. 1). Saint Anthony, 269. Introduces many Christian monuments, 324. Law as to the observance of Friday, 333 n. 4. Concerning the observance of Sunday, 335 n. 4, 336. Easter festival, 337, 338 and n. 3, 767. In the Arian controversy, council of Nice, 409 n. 4, 413–431, 460; (v. 85). The Manicheans, 769. Theonas, i. 143 n. 1. Fire at Nicomedia, i. 153. Arnobius, i. 688. First creates a court clergy, iii. 109 n. 1. Deeds of gift forged in his name, iii. 122. Gregory II. on iii. 212. Embassy to Pepin, iii. 233. Harald Blaatand compared to, iii. 289. Transfer of power to the pope, iii. 349. Primacy of the Roman ch., v. 82. Gift of, v. 7, 19, 39, 42, 50, 304, 305, 335, 345, 350.

Proclamation after his victory over Licinius, ii. 8 n. 1. Letter publishing the decisions of the Nicene council, 3.8 n. 3 (164) Ep. to Alexander and Arius, cited by Euseb. de vit. Constantini, I. ii. c. 69 409 n. 4.

Constantine the philosopher (see Cyrill), iii. 314–316, 317 n. 2 318 and n. 5.
Constantine the younger, ii. 33, 36, 317, 428 n. 3. Arian controversy, 432. Anonymi monod. in, 317 n. 1.
Constantines, family of the, ii. 324, 377.
Constantinople, Constantine at, ii. 24, 30. 422 n. 4, 427, 428. Julian at, 41, 42, 47 n. 4, 79. Obelisk at, 47 n. 4. Chrysostom at, 100, 158, 177, 302, 352, 719, 754–761. Synesius at, 123. Respect to Persian bp., 126. Conference at (an. 388), Ulphilas, 157. Goths at, 158. State assumed by bps. of, 168. Flavian at, 174. School at, 183. Church assembly (an. 381), Gregory's farewell discourse at, 185 n. 1. Number of deacons, 189. Number of clergy, 194. Churches at, 194, 202–204. Patriarchate, 196 n. 3, 197, 198. Claims equality with Rome, 197, 202. Alexander, 277 n. 4. Nilus at, 286. Observance of Friday, 333. Arius at, 422 n. 4, 428–430. Popular discussion of doctrinal questions at, 432 and n. 1, 507. Euseb. us of Nicomedia, bp. at, 433 n. 2. Nicene creed at, 462–464. Gregory Nazianzen at, 465–466. Ulphilas at, 472 n. Nestorius at, 504–539 (547). Primacy of ch. at, 559 n. 2. Party of Dioscurus, 560. Monophysite controversy at, 589–595. Origenistic controversy at, 595, 596. Pelagian controversy, 710, 721 Marius Mercator at, 721. Jerome at, 744. Origenistic monks at, 753, 756, 757. Epiphanius at, 758. See Arthimus, Demophilus, Eudoxius, Eutychius, Macedonius, Mennas. Theodore Studita at, iii. 100. Relation to the Roman church, iii. 113 and n. 2, 115, 557. Gregoria, iii. 145. Ecthesis and Type at, iii. 184–187. Martin I. at, iii. 189,
190. Maximus, iii. 191, 192. Patriarchs of in the Dyotheletic controversy, iii. 193, 196; see that controv. Primacy, iii. 203. Paulicians at, iii. 248, 249, 250 n. 2, 255. Image worship at, iii. 213 n. 3 (see Image controversies) Efforts to convert the Russians, Olga at, Russians at, iii. 327–329. Hungarian princes at, iii. 330. 'Ἐπίσκοπος οἰκουμενικός, iii. 580. See Michael Cerularius, Photius, Sergius. Conquest of, iv. 215. Eustatius at, iv. 531. Conference at (an. 11–6), on questions in dispute between the Roman and Greek churches, iv. 536–538. Latin empire at, iv. 539. Paulicians transplanted to, iv. 564. The patriarch John of, v. 330. See Councils.
Constantius, monk, ii 651.
Constantius, son of Constantine the Great. As emperor, ii. 28 n. 3, 33–40, 42, 44, 45, 70, 71–78, 79, 82, 92, 144 and n. 2, 151, 152 n. 1, 165, 256. In the Arian controversy, 431–456.
Constantius Chlorus, father of Constantine the Great, i. 145, 154; ii. 6, 7.
Constitution. See Caurch constitution. Of Martin V., v. 127, 128.
Constitutiones Apostolicae. See Apostolical constitutions.
Consummation, final. See Restitution.
Contemplation, Platonic, i. 378, 379. Gnostic, i. 381. Philo on, i. 57, 59, 60. Plotinus, i. 393. Carpocrates, i. 450. Prodicians, i. 451. Origen, i. 638. Julian, ii. 50. Maximius on, ii. 173. Anschar, iii. 286. Joachim on, iv. 227–230. Bernard on, v. 240, 241, 372. H. of St. Victor on, iv. 402, 404. Rupert of Deutz, iv. 411–413. Aquinas, iv. 429, 523–525. See Friends of God.
Contemplative life, spirit, tendency, etc., i. 45, 57, 59, 60, 61, 277, 628 n. 6; ii. 445, 492, 502; iii. 169–171; iv. 220, 292, 302, 310, 317 (see Joachim). Wicklif on the, v. 143. United with the practical, v. 393, 400, 403, 409. See Asceticism.
Contention, sowing, iv. 310.
Continents, i. 274, 521. See Ascetics.
Contingency and foreknowledge, iv. 476.
Contributions, ch., i. 198, 255, 256. To crusades, iv. 70, 127, 210. Catharist, benev., iv. 583.
Controversies, i. 224 n. 1; ii. 136, 282 n., 381–384, 712; iv. 359, 371. Settled by imperial authority, ii. 164–166. Positive and negative interests in, ii. 413.
Controversy. Concerning penance, i. 220–248. Between the Donatists and the Catholic party, ii. 238–252. On saint worship, ii. 373–377. Between Aerius and Eustathius, ii. 879. See Jovinian. The Arian, ii. 309–466. Nestorian, ii. 504–583. Monophysite, 583–600. Origenistic, ii. 595–598, 641, 739–765. Of the Three Chapters, ii. 595, 597–608,

764. Pelagian, ii. 639-687. Semi-Pelagian, ii. 687-712. Adoptianist, iii. 156-168. Monotheletic, iii. 175-197. Respecting image worship, iii. 197-243, 532-553. On predestination, iii. 471-494. On transubstantiation, iii. 494-530. With Jews, iv. 77 and n. 2. Philosophical, iv. 359-361 (see Realism, Nominalism). On exclusion of sons of priests from ch. offices, iv. 361. Between the dialectical and the practical church party, iv. 371, 374. Bernard and Abelard, iv. 393-400. Concerning faith and knowledge, iv. 404. Concerning true love to God, iv. 407. Gilbert and Bernard, iv. 408, 409. In the Greek church, under Manuel Comnenus, iv. 533-536. Concerning union of the Greek church with the Latin, iv. 548. Concerning the condition of the saints, v. 37. Between the Greek and Latin churches, iii. 557-586. Concerning the patriarchate of Ignatius and Photius, iii. 557-579. Touching Roman rites in the Greek church, iii. 581-586. Efforts at reunion, iv. 536-548.

Conventicle at Rome, ii. 256. Conventicles, i. 185; iv. 323.

Convents, iii. 55; iv. 584 n. 4. Exeter, Nutescelle, iii. 46. Afternach, iii. 81. Rupert, iv. 127. Fontevraud, iv. 247. Dola, v. 251. Reception to, v. 186. See Monasteries.

Conversio, in the Lord's Supper, iii. 498, 499.

Conversion, different ways of, i. 688, 691; ii. 117-124 (see Monasticism). Two processes, ii. 618. Of masses of people, iii. 51, 428; iv. 17, 26 (see Baptism, Force). True, iii. 476. Imperfect, iv. 1; iii. 9, 18. False, outward, iv. 37, 46, 48. Effect on the mental powers, iv. 62. Lull on the conversion of infidels, iv. 67, 68, 191. Of Jews, iv. 70-72, 74, 78-81. Hermann on, iv. 71, 72. Bernard on, iv. 74. Through preaching, iv. 155, 209-211, 246, 318, 598; v. 175, 176, 182, 185 (see Preaching). Free will in, iv. 515-519 (see Freedom, Grace, Justification).

Copiatæ, ii. 193.

Coptic language, i. 83, 713, 714; ii. 264. New Testament in, i. 83.

Copts, education among the, ii. 264. Monophysitism; Coptic patriarchate, iii. 88 n 4. Abyssinian and Nubian ch., subject to the Coptic patriarchs, iii. 90 Christians in India in connection with the same, iii. 90 n. 2.

Copyists, ii. 184; iii. 264. See Manuscripts.

Corace (Curatinm), iv. 220.

Coracion, i. 652, 653.

Corario, Cardinal Angelo. See Gregory XII.

Corbeil, iv. 373.

Corbie, monastery at, in France, iii. 272-274, 278, 449 n. 3, 458, 494, 495 nn. 1, 4. See Ratramnus.

Corbinian, among the Bavarians, iii. 40.

Corderius. See Catena Corderii.

Cordova, ii. 31; iii. 336 n. 2, 337-340. Hyginus of, ii. 772. See Councils, Hosius.

Corinth, i. 79. Ecclesia apostolica, i. 203. Church at, i. 185. Agapæ, i. 325.

Corinthians.
Ep. 1 to the, i. 187; iii. 434. 1:10, iii. 568; 1:20, i. 621; 1:25, i. 705; 1:27, ii. 205, v. 221. 2:2, ii. 122 (iii. 143); 2:6, i. 388, ii. 248; 2:9, i. 531, 675; 2:12, ii. 471; 2:15, v. 19; 2:14, i. 628. 3:4. ff., v. 324; 3:10, ii. 122; 3:12, ii. 736; 3:13, ii. 637; 3:17, i. 253; 3:21, v. 269. 4:1, iii. 265. 5:4, i. 190; 5:7, i. 297 n. 3; 5:8, ii. 814. 6:11, ii. 48; 6:12, i. 385; 6:15, i. 189; 6:18, iii. 258. 7, i. 680 n. 2, v. 207; 7:2, iii. 383; 7:5, i. 457; 7:9, iv. 94; 7:21, i. 269; 7:25, ii. 643 n. 2; 7. 26, ii. 306; 7:27, iii. 557; 7:39, ii. 306. 8:6, i. 574; 8:8, iii. 579; 8:9, i. 385; 9:9, i. 555; 9:15, 18, iii. 77; 9:22, i. 245; 9:24, i. 253; 9:27, iii. 146. 10:1, ii. 636; 10:4, iv. 576, v. 25 n. 1, 154; 10:33, iii. 483 n. 4, i. 245. 11, iii. 499; 11:4, 5, i. 679; 11:5, i. 182; 11:19, i. 341; 11:28, v. 225. 12, i. 180, iii. 209; 12:26, i. 245; 12:28, iv. 160. 13, iii. 216, iv. 250; 13:10, i. 487; 13:12, iv. 381. 14, iii. 319; 14:19, iv. 214; 14:23-25, i. 327; 14:30, i. 32, iii. 124; 14:34, i. 182. 15, i. 655; 15:10, iii. 145 n. 1; 15:21, ii. 508; 15:28, i. 600, ii. 481, 737 n. 3, 738 n. 2; 15:29, i. 478; 15:46, iv. 492. 16:19, i. 185; 16:19, 20, i. 290 n. 2.
Ep. 2 to the, 3:18, iii. 237. 4:13, ii. 390. 5, i. 546; 5:16, iii. 216, 522; 5:19, iii. 161. 8:19, i. 189. 10:5, iv. 431. 11:3, ii. 637 n. 2. 12:9, iv. 514 n. 4; 12:20, ii. 636. 15:2, i. 253.

Cormac, Irish prince, ii. 148.

Cornelius, bp. of Rome, i. 136, 201, 202, 237-242, 316 n. 3, 690.
Ep. ad Fabium episc. Antiochenum, ap. Euseb. H. E. (l. 6, c. 43) 201 n. 2, 238 n. 2, 690 n. 1.

Cornelius, centurion, i. 273; ii. 46.

Curotic, British chieftain, ii. 149.

Corporeality of the soul, ii. 706 n. 2.

Corpus Christi day, iv. 341.

Correspondence among the churches of the Roman empire, i. 205.

Correzar (Ozilia) island, iv. 39.

Corruption, of revelation, according to the Clementines, i. 355, 358. Propagation of, ii. 735 n. 4 (see Sin). Of manners, ii. 59, 81. Of Christianity, threatening, i. 186, 191. In the church, ii. 111, 112, 119, 636, 739; iv. 82; v. 47, 56, 178, 193, 324, 412 (see Church). Clemangis on, v. 60. Gerson, v. 80, 81. Reactions against, iv. 146-152 (see Reform, Sects). Janow, v. 202-235. In Rome and Italy, iv. 83, 84 (see Rome). Corruption of the papacy, v. 1-3, 11, 21, 33, 34, 43, 48, 202-207. See Avignon, Clergy, Nicholas de Clemangis, Papacy, Rome.

Corsica, ii. 709; iii. 113; iv. 89 n. 2. Roman diocese, ii. 199.

Corvaro, Peter of. See Nicholas V.

Curvey, in Germany, iii. 273, 275, 276, 281 n. 1, 289 n. 1, 323 n. 3.

Cosfeld, church at, iii. 80.
Cosmas, bp. of Majuma, iii. 206 n. 3.
Cosmas, Christian captive, iii. 206 n. 3.
Cosmas, dean of Prague.
Bohemian chronicles of, Baptism of Borziwoi, iii. 321 n. 5. L. ii., Severus, iii. 328 n. 1. App. use of Slavonian, iii. 323 n. 2.
Cosmas, patriarch of Constantinople, iv. 564
Cosmas Indicopleustes, i. 82; ii. 140, 141, 145.
Τοπογραφία Χριστιανική (ed. Montfaucon), in Collectio nova patrum, t. ii., ii. 141 n. 1; f. 178, ii. 141 nn. 2, 5; f. 179, ii. 145 n. 4; f. 194, ii. 346 n. 2.
Cosmic principle, i. 409.
Cosmogonic process, i. 371. See Creation.
Cossa, Balthazar. See John XXIII.
Coteler.
Patres apostolici, ii. 347 n. 1. Monumenta eccles. Græc. t. i., apophthegm. patr. §§ 4, 21, sayings of Anthony, ii. 270 nn. 1, 2. T. ii., Life of Euthymius, ii. 135 n. 4, 143 n. 3, 276 n. 2. Letters of the patriarch Michael to Peter of Antioch on image worship, etc., iii. 583 nn. 1, 2, 584 n. 1; f. 123, Peter of A. on bread in the Lord's Supper, iii. 584 n. 2; f. 155, 585 n. 3. T. lii., Origenistic leaders at Constantinople, ii. 506 n. 1; Timotheus de recept. hæreticorum, ii. 277 n. 3; vita S. Sabæ, ii. 704 n. 3; § 58, λαύραι, κοινόβια, μοναστηρια, ii. 271 n. 4.
Cotta, i. 8.
Coucy, forest of, iv. 245.
Councils and synods. At *Jerusalem*, under the apostles, i 159, 342; iii. 357 At *Carthage*, under Agrippinus, on the baptism of heretics, i. 318. At *Carthage*, under Cyprian, bishops to be chosen with the concurrence of the communities, i. 200 n. 1. Third at *Carthage*, c. 18, church officers required, as a condition of ordination, to have brought their families into the church, ii. 6- n. 3. Fourth at *Carthage*, spurious decisions of the, c. 1, on the examination of candidates for the episcopal office, i. 182 n. 6; c. 12, on the instruction of deaconesses, ii. 191 n. 2. At *Carthage*, under Cyprian, three councils, maintaining the independence of bishops against the claims of the Roman church, i. 215, 216, 217. Synod against Beryll (an. 244), i. 593 n., 594. At *Carthage* (an. 251), under Cyprian, on the treatment of the lapsed, i. 234. At *Carthage* (an. 252), under Cyprian, on the age at which infants should be baptized, i. 313. At *Carthage* (an. 255), two under Cyprian, declaring the baptism of heretics to be invalid, i. 319. At *Carthage* (an. 256), in the time of Cyprian, interrogation of catechumens, i. 308 n. 5; exorcism in baptism, i. 309, 310. At *Antioch* (an. 269), Paul of Samosata deposed, i. 605; the expression ὁμοούσιον condemned, i. 606. Pretended, under Diocletian, near *Sinuessa* (third century), iii. 372 n. 1. At *Iconium* and *Synnada* (third century), two synods, baptism of heretics declared to be valid, i. 318. At *Elvira* (Illibertis) (an. 305), on the probation of catechumens, i. 305; c. 13, on fallen virgins, i. 277 n. 5; c. 18, the clergy forbidden to engage in secular employments, i. 198 n. 3; c. 25, on the recommendatory letters of confessors, i. 229 n. 2; c. 26, concerning fasting on the Sabbath, i. 296 n. 3; c. 29, names of donors to be introduced into the church prayers, ii. 367 n. 4; c. 33, on the deposition of married clergy, i. 277 n. 2, ii. 180 and n. 1; c. 36, against painting the walls of churches with objects of adoration, i. 293, iii. 429; c. 43, on the limitation of Pentecost to one day, i. 301 n. 1; c. 56, on the exclusion of Duumviri from the churches, ii. 173 and n. 1; c. 62, on certain occupations, excluding from baptism, i. 262 n. 4. At *Ancyra* (an. 314), c. 10, on the marriage of deacons, ii. 180; c. 13, on the authority of chor-bishops, ii. 193 n. 4; c. 17, on catechumens, ii. 213 n. 4. At *Neo-Cæsarea* (an. 314), c. 1, on the marriage of presbyters, ii. 180; c. 5, on ἀκροαταί, ii. 357 n. 4; c. 12, on the exclusion of clinici from the priesthood, i. 238 n. 1; c. 15, number of deacons limited to seven, ii. 189 n. 2. At *Arles* (an. 314), c. 1, on the time of Easter, ii. 337; c. 7, concerning the presidents of the provinces, ii. 173; c. 8, on the validity of baptism, ii. 224; canon concerning the validity of ordinatio s, ii. 224; c. 13, on traditores, ii. 224 At *Alexandria* (an. 321), under Alexander, deposition of Arius, ii. 409. First œcumenical at *Nice* (an. 325), assembled by Constantine, ii. 415, v. 85; history, 415-421, 439, 444, 450; Constantine at, ii. 32 n. 1; his exhortation to the bishops, ii. 29; gives a banquet at its close, ii. 32 n. 2; his influence at, ii. 164, 418-422, 767; influence exerted over him, ii. 164 n. 2, 419, 422; influence of Constantia, ii. 422 n. 1; creed adopted, ii. 419 (see Nicene creed); on the persecution under Licinius, ii. 19; on the marriage of clergy, ii. 180, 181; on the ordination of deaconesses, ii. 190; on the Meletian schism, ii. 255 and n. 1; on the observance of Easter, i. 337, 338, 767; can. 2, on the conditions of episcopal ordination, ii. 184; can. 3, against συνείσακται, ii. 182 n. 2; can. 5, on the validity of excommunications, ii. 756; can. 6, on the jurisdiction of metropolitans, ii. 196, 199, 203, 252 n. 1 (appealed to in support of the Roman primacy, ii. 207 n. 2, 208, v. 350; in support of the ecclesiastical laws, iii. 369 and n. 2); canons 11, 12, against various classes of sacrificati, ii. 19 nn. 1, 2; can. 13, on penitents, ii. 213 n. 1; can.

15, against the transfer of bishops, ii. 186; can. 18, concerning deacons, ii. 189 n. 6; can. 19, on the Samosatenean clergy who joined the Catholic church; deaconesses, ii. 190 and n. 2; doctrine concerning the Holy Spirit, ii. 466, iv. 537; Theophilus the Goth at the council, ii. 150; Athanasius at, ii. 415 n. 1, 419 n. 5, 424; Marcellus at, ii. 439; confounded with that of Sardica (an. 347), ii. 206, 207 n. 2, 208; reports of the council, ii. 415 n. 1, 417 n. 3 (see Athanas. de decretis synodi Nicenæ; ep. ad Afros); manuscript records of the council, ii. 208. See Nicene creed. At *Cæsarea* ? (an. 335), against Athanasius, ii. 426, 427. At *Tyre* (an. 335), against Athanasius, ii. 426 n. 3, 427 and n., 432. At *Antioch* (an. 341), against Athanasius, ii. 205, 432, 433; semi-Arian confession drawn up, ii. 434, 436 n. 1; on the deposition of bishops reinstated by secular power, ii. 761; can. 9, on the authority of chor-bishops, ii. 193 n. 4; can. 11, against unauthorized visits of ecclesiastics to the emperor, ii. 187; can. 12, deposition of Athanasius confirmed, ii. 432; can. 20, against the transfer of bishops, ii. 187. At *Antioch* (an. 341 and 345), five semi-Arian creeds drawn up, ii. 434, 436 n. 1. At *Alexandria* (circ. an. 341), against Arius, ii. 409; synod of *Egyptian and Libyan bishops* (an. 341), against Arius, ii. 409. At *Rome* (an. 342), Athanasius recognized as bishop, ii. 434. At *Sardica* (an. 347), to settle disputes between the Eastern and Western churches consequent on the Arian controversy, ii. 435, 436 and n. 4, 440; against visits of bishops to the imperial court, ii. 187; ep. to Julius, ii. 199 n. 2; cc. 3, 4, and 5, conceding supreme jurisdiction to the Roman bishop, ii. 205, 206, 207 n. 2, 208, iii. 364; c. 6, against the appointment of chor-bishops, ii. 193 and n. 5; c. 10, candidates for episcopal ordination required to have passed through the previous grades, ii. 184. At *Philippopolis* (an. 347), sentence of deposition against Athanasius renewed, ii. 435; symbol, ii. 436. At *Tribur*, marriage of priests permitted, iii. 383, 411 n. 7. At *Gangra* (middle of fourth century), against the Eustathians, ii. 281; date, ii. 281 n. 1; on the agapæ, ii. 362; on communion with married priests, ii. 180, 302, iii. 383. First at *Sirmium* (an. 351), against Marcellus and Photinus, ii. 440; creed, ii. 440 n. 1, 451 n. 1. At *Arles* (an. 355), signatures obtained to the condemnation of Athanasius, ii. 440. At *Milan* (an. 355), the same, ii. 440. Second at *Sirmium* (an. 357), Arian creed, ii. 256, 450, 451, 482 nn. (Third Sirmian creed, ii. 451 n. 1.) Sirmian formulas of faith, ii. 220 n. Second at *Ancyra* (an. 358), semi-Arian doctrines promulgated, ii. 451 At *Rimini* (Ariminum) (an. 359), ii. 452; Nicene creed confirmed, ii. 453; semi-Arian creed accepted, ii. 454. At *Seleucia* (an. 359), ii. 452; fourth Antiochian creed maintained, ii. 453; semi-Arian creed accepted, ii. 454. At *Constantinople* (an. 360), creed of Rimini re-confirmed, ii. 454. At *Alexandria* (an. 362), council of bishops returned from banishment, to heal the divisions consequent on the Arian controversy; Meletian schism, ii. 456–458, 468, 491. At *Laodicea* (an. 363). c. 7, baptism of sects, ii. 360 n. 1; c. 11, on the ordination of deaconesses, ii. 190 and n. 3; c. 15, on the church singing, ii. 354 n. 3; c. 16, directing that the Gospels shall be read on the Sabbath, ii. 334 and nn. 1, 2; c. 19, place of the prayer for catechumens in the church service; energumens, ii. 361 n. 2; c. 25, on deacons, ii. 189 n. 6; c. 28, on the agapæ, ii. 362 n. 2; c. 29, on the observance of the Jewish Sabbath, ii. 334 n. 3; of Sunday, 335, 336; c. 48, on unction in baptism, ii. 359 n. 8; cc. 49 and 51, on fasting on the Sabbath, ii. 334 n. 4; c. 57, power of chor-bishops limited, ii. 193 n. 4; against the appointment of chor-bishops, περιοδεύται, ii. 193 nn. 5, 6; c. 59, on the hymns to be used in the church service, ii. 354 n. 4. In *Illyria* (an. 375), the ὁμοούσιον extended to the doctrine of the Holy Spirit, ii. 468. At *Saragossa* (Cæsaraugusta) (an. 380), against the Priscillianists, ii. 772; c. 3, against those who did not partake of the sacrament at church, ii. 366 n. 2. Second ecumenical (œcum. I. at *Constantinople*) (an. 381), to settle disputed questions, and inaugurate Gregory Nazianzen, ii. 464; patriarchs, ii. 196 n. 3; Nicene creed adopted with an addition to the doctrine concerning the Holy Spirit, ii. 466; against the doctrine of Apollinaris, ii. 492; farewell discourse of Gregory Nazianzen, ii. 185 n. 1, 465, 466; c. 3, on the rank of the bishops of Constantinople, ii. 197, 199, 203, iii. 557; c. 7, ποιεῖν χριστιανόν, ii. 357 n. 2. At *Burdegala* (Bordeaux) (an. 384), against the Priscillianists, ii. 773. At *Rome* (an. 390), against Jovinian, ii. 312. At *Milan* (an. 390), against Jovinian, ii. 312. At *Hippo* (an. 393), Parentalia, ii. 372 n. 1; Cod. can. Afr. c. 39, on the title patriarch, ii. 198; c. 41, the Lord's Supper to be received after a meal on Holy Thursday, ii. 341 n. 5; c. 42, on agapæ, ii. 362 n. 2. At *Alexandria* (after an. 399). Several under Theophilus, against Origen's doctrines, ii. 753. First at *Toledo* (an. 400), dogmas against the Priscillianists, ii. 777,

778 n. 4; Dictinnius, ii. 778; c. 14, against those who did not partake of the Lord's Supper at church, ii. 366 n. 2. At *Carthage* (an. 401), c. 12 (Cod. can. Afr.), on defensores, ii. 192 n. 1; c. 61, on the public shows, ii. 336. At *Constantia* (an. 401), under Epiphanius, for the condemnation of Origen, ii. 757. At the *Oak*, near Chalcedon [πρὸς τὴν δρῦν] (an. 403), against Chrysostom, ii. 758, 759. At *Carthage* (an. 403), proposal for a conference with the Donatists, ii. 233. At *Carthage* (an. 404), on penal laws against the Donatists, ii. 235. At *Carthage* (an. 407), c. 3, on defensores, ii. 192 n. 1; c. 28, on appeals, ii. 208. At *Carthage* (an. 412), Cœlestius excommunicated, ii. 640. At *Jerusalem* (an. 415), on Pelagianism, ii. 6–1–643. At *Diospolis* (an. 415), on Pelagius, ii 643–645, 648, 736. At *Carthage* (an. 416), against Pelagius and Cœlestius, ii. 645. At *Milere* (an. 416), against the same, ii. 645. At *Carthage* (an. 417 ?), the same; letter to Zosimus, ii. 203, 649. At *Carthage* (an. 418), on appeals, ii. 208; c. 2, against the doctrine of an intermediate state, ii. 730; canons 4, 5, 6, and six others, against the Pelagian system, ii. 650, 651. At *Carthage* (an. 419), on pretended Nicene canons, ii. 208. In *Cilicia*, against Julian of Eclanum, ii. 713. At *Constantinople* (an. 429), under Nestorius, ii. 511. At *Rome* (an. 430), against Nestorius, ii. 521, 523. At *Alexandria* (au. 430), against Nestorius, ii. 523. Third ecumenical, at *Ephesus* (an. 431), against Nestorius, history, ii. 526–541; sequel, ii. 541–583 (546, 553 n. 4, 560, 564, 568–578, 585, 588, 610); influence of Pulcheria, ii. 164 n. 3; Theodosius II., ii. 164; on the Christmas festival, ii 346 n. 2; actio vi., the Quartodecimanians, ii. 506 n. 3; acts of, ii. 164 n. 4; Pelagius and Cœlestius condemned, ii. 721. At *Ephesus*, under John of Antioch (an. 431), against Cyrill and Memnon, ii. 533, 537, 540. In *Cilicia Secunda* (an. 432 ?), against Cyrill, ii. 547. At *Antioch*, ii. 556, 557. First at *Orange* (Arausiacum) (an. 441), c. 26, against the ordination of deaconesses, ii. 191 n. 1. Under Hilarius of *Arles* (an. 445 ?), Celidonius deposed, ii. 206. At *Constantinople* (an. 448), against Eutyches, ii. 560 nn., 563 n. 2, 563–567. At *Ephesus* (Robber Synod) (an. 449), against Nestorianism; history, ii. 567–573, 574, 576. *Armenian* (an. 450), letter of the bishops in defense of Christianity, ii. 137. At *Nice* (an. 451), ii. 576, 577; transferred to Chalcedon, ii. 577. Fourth ecumenical, at *Chalcedon* (an. 451), against Nestorianism, history, ii. 577–583; sequel, ii. 583–608, 612, 613; Pulcheria at the, ii 519 n. 2; symbol first proposed, ii. 573, 581 n. 1; symbol agreed upon, ii. 580, 581, 585; complaints against Dioscurus, ii. 559 n. 1, 581 (571 and n. 4); Dioscurus deposed, ii. 581; Theodoret at the, ii. 581, 582; cc. 9 et 16, on exarchs, ii. 196 n. 2; c. 25, on the appointment of stewards, ii. 191; last canon but one, on the rank of bishops of Rome and Constantinople, ii. 197, 199, 202, iii. 557. At *Tribur*; see Tribur. *Irish* (an. 456), on wives of the clergy, iii. 53 n. 6. At *Arles* (an. 475), recantation of Lucidus; Faustus commissioned to expound the doctrine of grace, ii. 707. At *Lyons* (an. 475), commission of Faustus, ii. 707. First at *Orleans* (Aurelianense I.) (an. 511), c. 4, on admission to the spiritual order, iii. 97 n. 3; c. 10, on consecration of the churches of heretics, iii. 5 n. 4; c. 30, against oracles taken from the sacred Scriptures, iii. 129. At *Epaona* (an. 517), c. 21, on deaconesses, ii. 191 n. 1; c. 33, against reconsecration of the churches of heretics, iii. 5 n. 4; c. 39, on protection of slaves, iii. 100 n. 8. At *Orange* (Arausio) (an. 529), on the doctrine of grace, ii. 711. At *Valence* (an. 529 ?), confirms the decree of the council of Orange, ii 711. At *Vaison* (Vasense II.) (an. 529), c. 2, on the reading of Scriptures by deacons, ii. 189 n. 1. Second at *Orleans* (an. 533), c. 15, on oblations in behalf of suicides, iii. 102 n. 4; c. 18, on the ordination of deaconesses, ii. 191 n. 1. At *Clermont* (Arvernense) (an. 535), c. 2, on ecclesiastical elections, iii. 93 n. 4; c. 15, on church attendance, iii. 109 n. 3. At *Thiven* (an 536), against the decisions of the council of Chalcedon, ii. 612. At *Constantinople* (an. 536), under Mennas, against the Monophysites, ii. 591 n. 1, 593 nn. 1, 2, 4, 593, 594; name περιοδευτής, ii. 193 n. 6. Third at *Orleans* (an. 538), c. 6, on the interstitia, iii. 93 n. 1. Fourth at *Orleans* (an. 541), cc. 7 et 26, on the abuse of rights of patronage, iii. 110 n. 3. At *Constantinople* (an. 541), under Mennas, ii. 597; fifteen canons against the Origenistic doctrines, ii. 764. At *Constantinople* (an. 547 ?), ii. 602. Fifth at *Orleans* (an. 549), c. 10, on ecclesiastical elections, iii. 93 n. 4; c. 20, on care for prisoners, iii. 105; c. 22, on excommunication of masters who break their word, iii. 100 n. 8. At *Constantinople* (an. 551), against the three articles, ii. 603. Fifth œcumenica (œcum. II. at *Constantinople*) (an. 553 , under Eutychius, against the three articles, ii. 607; condemnation of Didymus and Evagrius, ii. 765; act. 5, see Hardain; c. 12, condemnation of Origen, ii. 764. At *Paris* (an. 557), c. 8, on ecclesiastical

elections, iii. 93, 94. First at *Braga* (an. 561?), c. 12, against the Priscillianists; on church hymns, ii. 354 n. 4. At *Braga* (an. 563), against the Priscillianists, ii. 779. At *Xaintes* (Santones) (an. 564), for the deposition of Emeritus of Xaintes, iii. 94. Second at *Tours* (Turonense) (an. 567), c. 17, the January fasts, ii. 351 n. 3; c. 22, against pagan observances, ii. 372 n. 2. Second at *Lyons* (an. 567), Salonius and Sagittarius deposed, iii. 119 n. 1. Second at *Braga* (an. 572), c. 1, on church visitations, iii. 107. At *Auxerre* (an. 578), c. 4, against superstition, iii. 129 and n. 1; c. 17, on oblations in behalf of suicides, iii. 102 n. 4. Third at *Toledo* (an. 589), addition to the creed, ii. 471; c. 18, on judges attending the assemblies of bishops, iii. 105 n. 2; c. 19, on abuse of patronage, iii. 110 n. 3. At *Wigorn* (an. 601), on differences in the English church, iii. 17 and n. 2. Frank council (an. 602), on diversity in ecclesiastical usages, iii. 32. *Frank* (an. 613), for the spread of Christianity, iii. 38. Fifth at *Paris* (an. 615), c. 1, on free ecclesiastical elections, iii. 94. At *Rheims* (an. 630), c. 19, on archpresbyters from the lay order, iii. 111 n. 2. Fourth at *Toledo* (an. 633), its canons contained in the Isidorean decretals, iii. 347 n. 1; c. 13, on church hymns, ii. 354 n. 4; c. 32, on the care of the bishops for the people, iii. 105; c. 39, on deacons, iii. 111 n. 1; c. 41, on tonsure, iii. 106 n. 1; c. 74, on admission of bondmen to the spiritual order, iii. 98. At *Constantinople*, σύνοδος ἐνδημοῦσα in behalf of the ἔκθεσις, iii. 180. At *Rome*, the Lateran (œcumenical) (an. 648), against Monotheletism, iii 186, 188. At *Chalons sur Saone* (Cabilonense) (an. 650), c. 7, on archdeacons, iii. 111 n. 2; c. 14, on private chapels, iii. 109 n. 2. Ninth at *Toledo* (an. 655), c. 2, on rights of patronage, iii. 110. At *Whitby* (Pharensis) (an. 664), on conformity with Roman usages, iii. 24 n. 1. At *Merida* (Emeritense) (an. 666), c. 5, on episcopal delegates to councils, iii. 111 n. 1. At *Hertford* (an. 673), against conformity with Scottish usages, iii. 25. Sixth œcumenical, œcum. III. at *Constantinople* (Trullan I.) (an. 680), on the opposite views of the Greek and Roman churches, iii. 179 n. 5, 193-196. *Quinisextum* (Trullan II.) at *Constantinople* (an. 691 or 692), decisions of conc. œcum. VI. in regard to Dyotheletism confirmed, iii. 196; Christians forbidden to take part in the Brumalia, ii. 347 n. 4; c. 2, on the number of apostolic canons, iii. 557; c. 13, on the ordination of married persons, iii. 557; c. 16, on deacons, ii. 189 n. 4; c. 31, on the use of private chapels for baptism or the Lord's Supper, iii. 109 n. 1; c. 36, on the rights of the patriarch of Constantinople, iii. 557; c. 48, on the ordination of the wives of bishops as deaconesses, ii. 191 n. 3; c. 55, against fasting on the Sabbath (Saturday) before Easter, iii. 557 n. 4; c. 62, against maskings and comical processions, iv. 334 n. 1; c. 67, on the apostolical decrees, iii. 557 n. 7; c. 73, against laying pavements with the sign of the cross, ii. 323 n. 1; c.74, on agapæ, ii. 362 n. 2; against representations of Christ under the form of a lamb, iii. 557 n. 8. Sixteenth at *Toledo* (an. 693), on the authority of kings, iii. 96; c. 4, on the punishment of those who attempt suicide, iii. 102 n. 4; c. 6, on bread used in the Lord's Supper, iii. 581 n. 1. Seventeenth at *Toledo* (an. 694), on the transaction of affairs of church and state in public assemblies, iii. 97. *German* synod (an. 742), for the suppression of superstitious customs, iii. 56 n. 3. At *Soissons* (an. 744), metropolitans appointed, iii. 65 n. 2. *Several* under Boniface, from an. 744 and onward, for reformation of the clergy, iii. 56. *Frank* council under Boniface (an. 745), deposition of Gewillieb, iii. 66; against the cupidity of archdeacons, iii. 111 n. 3. At *Rome*, against Adalbert, iii. 58 n. 2, 59 nn. 1, 5. At *Cloveshove* (Cliff) (an. 747), for the reformation of the English church, iii. 70; participation in the communion, iii. 136; c. 3, on church visitations and preaching, iii. 107, 123; c. 10, on qualifications of the clergy, iii. 126; cc. 26 and 37, on good works, iii. 138, 139. At *Constantinople* (council of Iconoclasts) (an. 754), against the worship of images, history, iii. 214-219, 227; letter of Eusebius on images, ii. 326 n. 4; Epiphanius cited, ii. 329 n. 2 (see Harduin). At *Gentilly* (Gentiliacum) (an. 767), on images, iii. 234; on the doctrine of the Holy Spirit, iii. 555. Seventh œcumenical (œcum. IV. at *Constantinople*), in favor of image worship (an. 786), iii. 227; opened, iii. 229, 230; disturbances at this time, iii. 229; removed to *Nice* (second at Nice) (an. 787), iii. 230; history, iii. 230-233 (216 n. 3, 219 n. 1, 236, 243, 549); false plenipotentiaries, iii. 228, 575; oath required of bishops, iii. 223 n. 1; imperial sacra, addressed to the council, iii. 229 n.; address of Tarasius, iii. 227 n. 2; actio iv., Leontius on images, ii. 330 n. 1; letters of Leo the Isaurian, iii. 204 n. 1; actio v., deeds of iconoclasts reported, iii. 219 n. 1; Xenayas on images cited, H. E. of John the Schismatic, ii. 331 n. 4; Constantine, bp. of Nacolia, iii. 203 n. 1; actio vi., letter of Eusebius of Cæsarea against images, ii. 326 n. 4;

fragment of Amphilochius of Iconium, ii. 327 n. 2; Epiphanius against images, ii. 329 n. 2; letter of Eusebius to bp. Alexander, on Arius, ii. 412 n. 2; Charlemagne on the council, iii. 234-243; Alcuin on, iii. 235 n. 4; reactions against, iii. 532 and n. 3; Nicephorus, iii. 533 n. 1; its decrees abolished by Theodotus, iii. 540 (see conc. Const. an. 815). See Harduin. At *Forum Julium* (Friuli) (an. 791), on the doctrine of the Holy Spirit, iii. 555. At *Regensburg* (an. 792), against Felix of Urgellis, iii. 165. At *Frankfort-on-the-Main* (an. 794), against Adoptanism, iii. 165; c. 2, against the adoration of images, iii. 243; c. 40, against honors paid to new saints, iii. 133. At *Aix* (an. 799), on Felix of Urgellis, iii. 167. At *Rome* (an. 800), to decide on the matter of Leo III., iii. 122. At *Aix* (an. 809), on the doctrine of the Holy Spirit, iii. 555. Sixth at *Arles* (an. 813), c. 5, on patronage, iii. 110; c. 10, on religious instruction, iii. 125. At *Mentz* (an. 813), on the separation of ecclesiastical affairs from political, iii. 97; preface, on the improvement of the spiritual order, iii. 143 n. 1; c. 23, on private masses, iii. 136; c. 25, on religious instruction, iii. 125; c. 35, on festivals, iii. 133, 134. Second at *Chalons* (an. 813), c. 3, on schools, ii. 126; c. 34, on the divine forgiveness of sins and priestly absolution, iii. 139 n. 6; on right penitence, iii. 139 n. 5; c. 36, on external works, iii. 138, 139; c. 38, on libelli pœnitentiales, iii. 137 n. 2; c. 45, on pilgrimages, iii. 131. Second at *Rheims* (an. 813), on the improvement of the spiritual order, iii. 143 n. 1; c. 15, on the translation of homilies, iii. 127 n. 1. Third at *Tours* (an. 813), c. 3, on the improvement of the spiritual order, iii. 143 n. 1; c. 17, on translation of homilies, iii. 127 n. 1. At *Trusley*, on the ignorance of the clergy, iii. 441. At *Constantinople*, σύνοδος ἐνδημοῦσα, against images, iii. 539. At *Constantinople* (an. 815 ?), against the worship of images, iii. 540. At *Aix* (an. 816), confirmation of the rule of Chrodegang of Metz, iii. 98, 107; c. 119, against the exclusive adoption of bondmen to the spiritual order, iii. 98, 101. At *Aix-la-Chapelle* (an. 817), rule of Benedict, iii. 415; iv. 208. At *Paris* (an. 825), on the use of images, iii. 551 (439 n. 5). At *Mentz* (an. 829), Gottschalk released from his monastic vow, iii. 473. At *Mentz* (an. 847), c. 2, on sermons necessary in order to religious instruction, iii. 425; c. 31, on penance, iii. 451. At *Mentz* (an. 848), against Gottschalk, iii. 477, 478. At *Chiersy* (an. 849), against Gottschalk, iii. 478. At *Pavia* (Ticinum) (Synodus Regiaticina) (an.

850), on the anathematized, iii. 454; c. 8, on priestly unction in the case of the sick, iii. 449; cc. 18, 23, against the clerici acephali, iii. 413. At *Cordova* (an. 852), against fanatics, iii. 342. At *Chiersy* (an. 853), four capitula against the doctrine of Gottschalk, iii. 492; defended by Hinkmar, iii. 493. At *Pavia* (an. 853), on the decline of parochial worship, iii. 412, 413. Third at *Valence* (an. 855), six capitula against the decrees of the synod (an. 853) at *Chiersy*, iii. 492, 493; c. 2, on the relation of predestination to sin, iii. 492 n. 2; c. 5, on perseverance, iii. 492, 493; c. 6, errors of Scotus condemned, iii. 493; c. 7, on the maintenance of the rights of ecclesiastical elections, iii. 400; cc. 11 and 12, against judgments of God, iii. 449; c. 16, on religious instruction, iii. 426. At *Chiersy* (an. 858), c. 10, the Scots, iii. 460 n. 6. At *Langres* (conc. l. Lingonense) (an. 859), on schools, iii. 426. At *Savonnieres* (apud Saponarias) (an. 859), on the founding of schools, iii. 426; on contested points of doctrine, iii. 493. At *Constantinople* (an. 859), against Ignatius, iii. 561, 562; transactions burnt, ii. 561 n. 2. At *Constantinople* (an. 861), against Ignatius, 562-565, 571. At *Aix* (an. 862), on Lothaire's marriage with Waldrade, iii. 354. At *Metz* (an. 863), on the same, iii. 354. At *Rome* (an. 863), decrees of the council of Metz annulled, iii. 355; against Photius, Rhodoald, and Zacharias, iii. 565. At *Soissons* (an. 863), against bp. Rothad, iii. 358. At *Constantinople* (an. 867), under Photius, against Nicholas, iii. 567, 575; false plenipotentiaries, iii. 575. At *Rome* (an. 868), against Photius iii. 569. Eighth œcumenical (œcum. IV. at *Constantinople*) (an. 869), under Ignatius, history, iii. 569-571 (561 nn. 1 and 2); on the iconoclasts, iii. 550, 551; against those who held to two souls in man's nature, iii. 559 n. 3; transactions of the council of Const. (an. 859) burnt; on the patriarchate of Photius and Ignatius, iii. 569-571; pretended plenipotentiaries, iii. 575. At *Donzi* (an. 871), against Hinkmar of Laon, iii. 364. At *Constantinople* (an. 879), on the patriarchate of Photius, history, iii. 576-578; statement of Photius, iii. 572 n. 2, 573 n. 2; delegates from the patriarchs among the Saracens, iii. 575; on the pretensions of the pope to Bulgaria, iii. 577; on the choice of patriarch; on the general adoption of the Nicene creed, iii. 577. At *Rouen* (Redoni) (an. 879), c. 14, on church attendance, iii. 426. At *Soissons* (an. 899), priests advised to supply themselves with Bibles and other religious books; c. 16, on attention to the schools (for boys and girls),

iii. 427. At *Trosley* (an. 909), c. 3, on the decline of monachism, iii. 416; c. 15, negligence of bishops, iii. 441. At *Rome* (an. 963), against pope John XII., iii. 367. At *Rheims* (an. 991), against John XV., iii. 369. At *Muson* (an. 995), against Gerbert, iii. 373 and note. At *Rheims* (an. 996), against Gerbert, iii. 374. At *Seligenstadt* (an. 1020), c. 13, against the abuse of the rights of patronage, iii. 413. At *Seligenstadt* (an. 1022), c. 6, on superstitious use of the Lord's Supper, iii. 450 n. 4; c. 18, on penance, iii. 453. At *Orleans* (an. 1022), against the sects there, iii. 593 n. 2, 596. At *Arras* (an. 1025), against the sects there, iii. 598. At *Bourges* (an. 1031), c. 11, against the marriage of the clergy, iii. 411 n. 3. At *Cambray* (?), against the sects there, iii. 599. At *Limoisin* (concilia Lemovicense II.) (an. 1031), proclamation of the interdict, iii. 454, 455 and note. At *Sutri* (an. 1046), deposition of three popes, iii. 377. At *Rome* (an. 1046), election of Clement II., iii. 377, 378. At *Rome* (an. 1050), against Berengarius, iii. 507. At *Vercelli* (an. 1050), ordinations of simoniacal bishops, iii. 379 n. 1; against Berengarius, iii. 507, 508, 510 n. 1. At *Paris* (?), against Berengarius, iii. 509 and n. 4, 510. At *Mantua* (an. 1052), on the maintenance of the laws of celibacy, iii. 385. At *Tours* (an. 1054), against Berengarius, iii. 509 n. 4, 510, 511, 518. At *Rome* (an. 1059) (Lateran), against Berengarius, iii. 512; on the election of pope by the cardinals, iii. 387, 395 n. 2; ecclesiastics living in wedlock forbidden to hold worship, iii. 388. At *Milan* (an. 1060?), against simony, iii. 393, 394. At *Basle* (an. 1061?), by the Lombardian and imperial party, iii. 396 and n. 1. At *Osborn* (an. 1062), and at *Mantua* (an. 1064), on the recognition of Alexander II. as pope, iii. 395 n. 2, 396 and n. 2. At *Rome* (Fast synod) (an. 1074), ordinances of Gregory VII., iv. 93, 94. At *Erfurt* (an. 1074), on the ordinances of Gregory VII., iv. 95. At *Erfurt*, on the same, celibacy of the clergy, iv. 96. At *Paris* (an. 1074), on the same, iii. 97 n. 8. At *Rome* (Second Fast synod) (an. 1075), against the right of investiture, iv. 101. At *Poictiers* (an. 1076), on transubstantiation, iii. 518. At *Worms* (an. 1076), against Gregory VII., iv. 106-109. At *Rome* (Fast synod) (an. 1076), ban pronounced on Henry IV., iv. 108. At *Mentz* (an. 1080?), against Gregory VII., iii. 118, 119. At *Brixen* (an. 1080?), against Gregory VII., iv. 118. At *Soissons* (an. 1093), against Roscelin, iv. 360. Concilium *Melfitanum*, c. 16, on false penance, iv. 348 n. 2. At *Soissons* (an. 1093), against Roscelin, iv. 360. At *Rheims* (an. 1094), against Yves of Chartres, iv. 123. At *Autun* (an. 1094), ban against Philip I., king of France, iv. 123. At *Placenza* (an. 1095), Urban II. brings forward the crusade, iv. 125. At *Clermont* (an. 1095), ban against Philip pronounced anew, iv. 123; Urban preaches the crusade, iv. 125 (126 n. 1); indulgence of Urban II. to crusaders, iv. 125, 349. At *Bari* (an. 1098), differences between the Roman and Greek churches, iv. 458, 536. At *Rome* (Lateran) (an. 1112), treaty between Paschalis II. and Henry V. declared null, iv. 140, 141. At *Rheims* (an. 1119), Norbert taken under the protection of the pope, iv. 245. At *Soissons* (an. 1121), against Abelard, iv. 382, 383. At *Rome* (Lateran) (an. 1123), Concordat of Worms confirmed, iv. 143. At *Troyes* (an. 1127), rule of the order of Knights Templars, iv. 258. At *Pisa* (an. 1134), Bernard and Innocent II., iv. 146; Henry the Cluniacensian, iv. 603. At *Rome* (Lateran) (an. 1139), under Innocent II., iv. 146; Arnold of Brescia commanded to quit Italy, iv. 150. At *Sens* (an. 1140), Bernard and Abelard, iv. 394-396; letter of the council to the pope, iv. 395 n. 2, 396 and notes; Gilbert de la Porée, iv. 409. At *Constantinople* (an. 1140), condemnation of Chrysomalos, iv. 560. At *Rheims* (an. 1148), Gilbert de la Porée, iv. 409; the Manichean, iv. 587; against Henry the Cluniacensian, iv. 604. At *Constantinople*, several endemic synods against Niphon and his followers, iv. 563. At *Pavia* (an. 1160), Victor IV. recognized as pope, iv. 167, 168 and n. 2. At *Lombez* (Lumbariense) (an. 1165), against the Catharists, iv. 587 n. 5, 588. At *Constantinople*, formula introduced by Manuel Comnenus, iv. 534. At *Constantinople* (an. 1166), endemic synod on the same formula, iv. 534. At *Scutari*, on the oath prescribed to converts from Mohammedanism, iv. 535. At *Rome* (Lateran) (an. 1170), the Waldenses forbidden to preach, iv. 608, 609. At *Rome* (Lateran) (an. 1179), laws against ecclesiastical abuses, iv. 207; c. 1, ordinance relating to papal elections, iv. 169. At *Montpellier* (an. 1208), against the sects, iv. 269. At *Beziers* (conc. Biterrense), against the sects; against abuses in the granting of indulgences, iv. 353. At *Paris* (an. 1210), the Lord's Supper in the school of David of Dinanto, iv. 447 n. 3. At *Paris* (an. 1212), against the abuse of the mass, iv. 346 n. 4. At *Rome* (Lateran IV.) (an. 1215), election of Frederic II. ratified by the pope, iv. 177;

GENERAL INDEX.

against ecclesiastical abuses, iv. 207; Didacus, iv. 269 n.; Dominic obtains the sanction of the po)e, iv. 270 ; ordinance on appointment of teachers of theology, iv. 287; on transubstantiation, iv. 335, v. 153; decision in favor of Peter Lombard, iv. 411; the clergy forbidden to take part in judgments of God, iv. 588 n. 3; c. 3, measures against heretics, iv. 642; c. 7, on appeals, iv. 199; c. 10, on deputies of the bishops, iv. 212, 270; c. 13, against the formation of new spiritual orders, iv. 268, 270, 284; c. 21, the Lord's Supper to be partaken of at least once a year, iv. 346, 353; laws on confession, iv. 353; c. 62, on indulgences, iv. 352 n. 5. At *Rome* (Fast synod) (an. 1227), against Frederic II., iv. 178. At *Cologne*, on the encroachments of the Dominicans iv. 279. At *Toulouse* (an. 1229), establishment of the inquisition, iv. 642; c. 14, against the translation of the Bible, and the reading of such translation by laymen, iv. 324. Projected council to be held at Rome (an. 1241), iv. 182. At *Lyons* (an. 1245), against Frederic II., iv. 183. At *Bordeaux* (an. 1255), c. 5, on communion of children, iv. 342 n. 4. At *Constantinople* (an. 1261 ?), against Arsenius, iv. 543. At *Lyons* (an. 1274), under Gregory X., new crusade projected, crusades discussed, iv. 188-190, 544; regulation with regard to papal elections, iv. 192; death of Bonaventura at the, iv. 421; Albertus Magnus at the, iv. 421; death of Thomas Aquinas on the way to, iv. 423; union consummated between the Greek and Roman churches, iv. 546 (544); c. 23, against communities of "mendicants" existing without papal confirmation, iv. 628. At *Constantinople* (an. 1283 ?), against Beccus, iv. 550. At *Brussa*, Beccus at, iv. 550. At *Wurzburg* (an. 1287), c. 34, against the Apostolicals, iv. 628 n. 1. At *Chichester* (an. 1289), c. 39, against the Apostolica s, iv. 628 n. 1. At *Rome* (an. 1302), v. 8, 10. At *Vienne* (an. 1311), ordinance for the establishment of professorships of the Oriental languages, iv. 70; memory of Boniface VIII. vindicated, v. 22; order of Knights Templars abolished, v. 23; Beghards condemned, v. 215. At *Vincennes* (an. 1333), on the condition of the saints, v. 37, 38; (an. 1378), on the election of Clement VII., v. 48, 49. At *London* (an. 1382), against Wicklif, v. 162, 163. At *Prague* (an. 1389), against the frequent communion of the laity, v. 220, 233; against reform, on image worship, v. 233-235; Matthias of Janow at the, v. 194, 233-235. At Paris (an. 1406), v. 38 n. 1. At *Prague* (an. 1406), against those who taught Wicklifite doctrine, v. 247. At *Aquileia* (an. 1407 ?), under Gregory XII., v. 76. At *Aregon* (an. 1408 ?), under Benedict XIII., v. 77. At *Prague* (an. 1408), diocesan synod on the Wicklifite heresy, v. 252, 260. At *Pisa* (an. 1409), for the reformation of the church, v. 77, 78, 82-88, 104, 107; election of Alexander V., v. 84. Cardinals united in one college, v. 87, 92, 97. Confirmation of the, v. 104. Recognition of the, v. 255 259. Results of, v. 92, 93, 94, 97, 99, 112, 123, 132. At *Rome* (an. 1412), under John XXIII., v. 90, 91. At *Prague* (an. 1413), to investigate the proposals of the Hussite and the church party, v. 295-297. At *Prague* (an. 1414), Huss not allowed to appear, v. 317 (see Huss). At *Constance* (an. 1414), for the reformation of the church, preparation for the, v. 100-102; history of council, v. 103-128; arrival of John XXIII., v. 103; mode of voting, v. 103, 104; flight of John XXIII., v. 106; discourse of Gerson, v. 107; principles proclaimed by the council, v. 109; cardinals at the council, see Cardinals ; John conveyed to Ratolfszell, deposed, v. 111; abdication of Gregory XII., deposition of Benedict XIII., v. 112; discourses of Bernard Baptisé, v. 113; Clemangis on the, v. 114-118; the Germans, see Germans; death of Hallam, v. 121; resolution on the appointment of general councils, v. 124; points settled in regard to reform, v. 125; election of Martin V., v. 126, 271; Poles and Lithuanians, constitution put forth by Martin V., v. 127; Cesarini on the, v. 132; Huss on the, v. 256; trial and martyrdom of Huss, v. 316-371 (255, 257, 290 and n. 1, 299); Jerome of Prague, v. 371-380, 286 n. 1. At *Pavia* (an. 1423), v. 128; transferred to *Siena*, v. 128. At *Siena* (an. 1-24), v. 128, 132. At *Basle* (an. 1431), against the Hussites, v. 128-133; council appointed to meet at Bologna, v. 130. See Synods, Ecumenical councils, also D'Achery, Harduin, Mansi concilia, Codex canonum ecclesiæ Africanæ.

Counsels of men, Janow on, v. 207. Of Christ, v. 216. See Consilia evangelica.
Country bps., i. 79, 202; ii. 169, 193, 194.
Country churches, i. 79, 97, 202.
Country parishes, iii. 125.
Court, influence of the Byzantine, ii. 585, 596; iii. 180, 181, 197, 224. See Byzantine, Papal court, Theodora.
Court priests, iii. 108, 109, 401.
Courtney, bp. of London, v. 148. Of Canterbury, 162.
Cousin, Ouvrages inédits d'Abelard, iv. 356 n. 2, 373 n. 2, 378 n. 3, 390 n. 3, 391 n. 2.

Covetousness, iv. 364; v. 122. Alcuin on, iii. 77.
Cowardice of degenerate civilization, i. 76.
Cracow, v. 373.
Cracowce, v. 316.
Cratinus, archdeacon, iii. 93 n. 3.
Crato, presbyter, iii. 93 n. 3.
Creation, doctrine of, i. 564–570; ii. 473–477; iv. 473–477. Theophilus of Antioch on the, i. 559. Hermogenes, progressive development of, i. 566, 567. Origen on the, i. 568, 569, 571, 588, 621, 622, 638. Theodore of Mopsuestia, ii. 713, 714. Gregory the Great, iii. 144. John Scotus, iii. 464–466, 486, 488. Joachim, iv. 229. Abelard, iv. 378. Thomas Aquinas, iv. 463 and n. 7, 464, 466 (479). Lull, iv. 465, 481, 482. Arius, ii. 405, 406. Priscillianists, ii. 776. Paulicians, iii. 245, 257. Sect at Orleans, iii. 594. Bogomiles, iv. 553, 554. Catharists, iv. 566, 567, 572, 573. Christian and Gnostic views, i. 372, 373, 379, 381, 382, 684 n. 2. Gnostic, i. 375, 377, 380, 387, 388. See Demiurge, Emanation. Views of particular Gnostics, Cerinthus, i. 396. Valentine, i. 420, 422–425. Ptolemæus, i. 437, 438. Marcus, i. 441. Ophites, i. 444. Saturnin, i. 453. Tatian, i. 456. Marcion, i. 467, 468. Doctrine of Mani, i. 489, 491. Ancient view, i. 372. In Parsism, i. 369. In Neo-Platonism, i. 374–376, 380; iv. 445; Julian, ii. 50; Proclus, ii. 105. See ὕλη. Creation from nothing, i. 372, 373, 565, 568; iv. 482. Beginning of, i. 372, 567–569, 588; ii. 405 (446), 474, 475; iv. 465, 466. Act of, ii. 425. Christ in the, i. 584. The six days, iv. 467, 468. Continuous creative energy of God, and the powers implanted in nature, preservation, i. 566, 567; ii. 476, 477; iv. 482. End of, iv. 466, 490. Creation and miracles, i. 470, 570, 571; iv. 469–473; and Providence, iv. 477, 492; and redemption, iv. 507, 508. Creation and generation, ii. 404–408, 410, 411 n., 417 n. 1, 435 and n., 446, 448 (see Trinity). New creation, ii. 617. Creation and nominalism, v. 166. Francis of Assisi and the, iv. 275.
Creationism, i. 626; ii. 670, 671; iv. 568, 573.
Creature, relation of to the creator, i. 568; iv. 508.
Credentes (Catharists), iv. 576, 579, 580.
Credere aliquid et in aliquid, iv. 608.
Credulity, i. 71.
Creed, the, i. 306–309; ii. 49 n. 1, 53, 108, 136, 427. The Apostles', i. 306, 307, 660; ii. 491 n. 4; v. 96, 323. Nicene, ii. 417 n. 3, 418 n. 1, 419–422, 428 n. 4, 157, 238, 441, 453, 454, 564, 568–570, 585 (Arius and the, ii. 428 n. 4). Five Antiochian, ii. 434, 436 n. 1. First Antiochian, ii. 434. Fourth Antiochian, ii. 417 n. 3, 440 n., 453. Of Philippopolis, ii. 436. Council of Sardica on creeds, ii. 436. Sirmian, ii. 256. First Sirmian, ii. 440 n. 1, 451 n. 1. Second Sirmian, ii. 450, 451, 482 nn. Third Sirmian, ii. 451 n. 1. Creed of Nicæ and Rimini, ii. 452–455, 471. Niceno-Constantinopolitan, ii. 466–469, 588. Creed of Nestorius, i. 506 n. 3. Of the Orientals at Ephesus, ii. 538, 542. Creed subscribed by Cyrill, ii. 542, 543. Niceno-Ephesian, ii. 570–572. Of Chalcedon, ii. 579–581, 584, 585. Pelagian, ii. 652. Of the sixth ecum. council, iii. 195, 196. Monotheletic, iii. 196, 203 n. 3. See Confessions.
Cremona, iii. 367 and n. 2; iv. 49, 120, 299.
Cremsia, v. 174.
Crescens, the cynic, i. 93, 671.
Crescentius, Roman usurper, iii. 422.
Cresconius, Donatist, ii. 226 nn. 1, 3, 232, 233.
Creutz, merchant, v. 236.
Creutzer,

Symbolik, Th. i. ss. 312 u. 504; 2te Aufl., the serpent, i. 445 n. Last ed. Th. ii. ss 53 u. 207, incarnations of the Son, i. 499 n. 4.

Crimea, spread of Christianity in the, iii. 315. Martin I. in the, iii. 190. Gazzarei, iv. 565.
Crimen majestatis, i. 91, 96; ii. 34; iii. 187.
Crimes. See Unnatural.
Crispus, son of Constantine the Great, ii. 31, 32 n. 1.
Critical element, tendency, ii. 402; iv. 256 and n. 3, 392, 520, 557, 595.
Criticism, Biblical, i. 387, 388, 460, 473, 652, 682 and n. 2, 700, 707–710. 721; ii. 47, 402, 745; iii. 126, 155, 430 n. 3. Manichean, i. 501, 502. With the Artemonites, i. 581, 582. With the Paulicians, iii. 267–269. See Antiochian school.
Criticism, historical, i. 506 n., 676; iii. 170, 187, 366 and n. 1.
Crosier, iv. 201.
Cross, banner of the, ii. 10, 11; iii. 238; iv. 57, 126, 598; v. 164. See Labarum.
Cross, bearing the, iii. 311, 436; iv. 307. Preaching of the, i. 65.
Cross, sacrament of the, ii. 620, 621.
Cross, sign, symbol of the, i. 145, 293; ii. 75 n. 1, 330; iii. 20 and n. 1, 36, 42, 43, 74, 328, 424 n. 1, 429, 435; iv. 14, 15, 28, 189, 210, 299, 307, 308. On coins, i. 80. In baptism, i. 139 n. 2, 316 n. 1; ii. 359. Catechumens, ii. 357 n. 2; iii. 301. Universal use of the, i. 293; ii. 259, 322, 323. To mark places of assembly, iii. 58. On shields and helmets, iii. 296, 299. With Constantine, ii. 9–14, 20, 21, 23, 24, 33 n. 4, 119. With Julian, ii. 49. With the Paulicians, iii. 249, 262, 263, 268. Hacon,

iii. 295. Olof Tryggweson, iii. 296. Olof the Thick, iii. 299. With the Monammedans, iii. 336 n. 1. With the crusaders, iv. 125–127, 154. Raymund Lull, iv. 308. Koblaikhan, iv. 57. Supernatural effects of the, ii. 13, 20, 21; iv. 256 n. 4, 557, 564. Worship of the, iii. 213, 214, 232, 238, 355, 430, 433, 435, 436. (Compare Image controversy.) Leontius on, ii. 330. Claudius of Turin, iii. 430, 435–437. Jonas of Orleans, iii. 439, 440 n. 1. Wicklif, v. 156. With the sects, iii. 598, 603, 604; iv. 564, 594, 596. The Bogomiles, iv. 557, 560. Appended to the signatures of bishops, iii. (564); 573 n. 2. Images substituted for, iii. 546.

Cross, the, with Valentine, i. 419. With Mani, i. 500. With pagans, ii. 20.
Crucifratres, v. 412.
Crucifix, iii. 296; iv. 300, 308, 325.
Crucifixion, the, with the Gnostics, i. 398, 412, 431, 446, 447, 418. With Mani, i. 500. Marcion, i. 562. Justin, i. 642. Clovis, iii. 8. The Paulicians, iii. 262. Commemorated, ii. 341. Of martyrs, i. 119.
Crusades, first idea of, with Gerbert, iii. 375. In Liefland, iv. 38. In Prussia and Finnland, iv. 45. Spirit of the, iv. 126–128, 205, 233, 293. Occasion intercourse with the Mongols, iv. 47, 51. With the Mohammedans, iv. 59. Between the Greek and Latin church, iv. 536, 538. Plan of Lull, iv. 70, 190–192. As affecting the Jews, iv. 71 n. 3, 72, 76. Design of Silvester II., iv. 104, 123. Gregory VII., iv. 104, 124. Victor III., iv. 124, 349. Urban II., Peter the Hermit, iv. 123–129, 349. Eugene III., Bernard of Clairvaux, iv. 153–157, 256–258 (73, 74). Honorius, iii. 177, 178. Gregory IX., iv. 178. Frederic II., iv. 178, 179. Against Henry IV., iv. 129, 130. Innocent III. against John of England, iv. 175. Against Frederic II., iv. 179. Diminution of enthusiasm; reasons for and against, iv. 188–192. Gerhoh on the, iv. 205. Fulco, iv. 210. Louis IX., iv. 300. Against the Albigenses, iv. 270, 639 n. 2, 641, 642. Of children, iv. 342 n. 5. Indulgences connected with, iv. 348, 349. Crusades and the Greek church, iv. 536, 538, 539. Gregory X., iv. 544. Against the Apostolicals, iv. 633. Against the Stedingers, iv. 644. Pasagium, iv. 591. Money collected for the, iv 127, 210. (The first crusade, iv. 71 n. 3, 123–128, 129, 154, 156, 215; the second, iv. 153–157, 73, 74; the fourth, iv. 59; the fifth, iv. 177–179; the seventh, iv. 188, 300.) Motives for engaging in the, iv. 126, 127, 155, 156. Influence of the, iv. 47, 51, 59, 127, 156. Against the Colonnas, v. 5. Proposed by John XXII. against Louis IV, v.

30, 31. By Urban VI. against Clement VII., v. 164. Against the Bohemians, v. 128–133. Against Ladislaus of Naples, v. 276–288, 291, 335. Huss on the latter, v. 279–285. Militz, v. 179, 180.
Crypta Ferrata, iii. 376 and n. 2.
Ctesiphon, Jerome's letter to, ii. 641 nn. 5, 6.
Cubicularia, iii. 145.
Cubicularii, Christian, i. 142, 143. Of the papal palace, iv. 193.
Cucusus, ii 761.
Culture, among the early Christians, i. 164. Christianity and, i. 4, 83, 339, 510; ii. 52, 53, 75; iii. 1, 23, 92, 305, 425–428, 456, 467–469; iv. 61, 62. Greek, i. 4, 339. Among the nations of the West, i. 5. Its relation to the Roman state religion, i. 6, 7. Jewish and Hellenic, i. 339, 342. Antique culture and religion, their close connection, ii. 39, 52–54, 75 84 n. 6, 85. In Montanism, i. 511, 527. In the Alexandrian school, i. 527, 631. In Egypt, i. 652. Tertullian and, i. 177, 558, 631. Clement, i. 528, 533–539. Origen, i. 624, 629, 711. Of the clergy, ii. 182; iii. 427; v. 113; see Clergy. Among the monks, ii. 560, 561. Hostility to, ii. 742, 743, 767. Chrysostom, ii. 754. Monasteries, sources of, iii. 9, 10, 20, 21, 37, 53, 415. In Eastern monasteries, iv. 529, 532. Extended by missionaries, iii. 21, 23, 29. In the Frankish church, iii. 92, 154–156, 233, 368, 469–471. Effect of pilgrimages on, iii. 118. Hierarchical tendency and, iii. 92, 469. The Roman, iii. 141. Destruction of the ancient, iii. 151, 335. In the West, iii. 150–155. In Spain, iii. 151, 152, 156. In England, iii. 467–469. In Germany, iii. 471. In the Eastern church, iii. 169, 530. Efforts to support, iii. 411. Classical, iii. 482; v. 53. Revival of, iii. 506, 602. Gregory the Great and, iii. 141, 150 and n. 7. In Poland, iv. 3. Among the Nestorian clergy, iv. 46, 52. In China, iv. 56. In the service of missions, iv. 61–71. Arabian, iv. 420. Under the Comnenes, iv. 530. Greek and Latin church, 536, 537. Abelard on, iv. 376, 377. Peter Cantor, iv. 414. Peter of Blois, iv. 515. The Bogomiles, iv. 559. Niphon, iv. 563. Clemangis on, v 54, 58, 60–62. Improvement in, v. 66 67. In Bohemia, v. 245 and n. 5, 262. Friends of God, v. 582. Worldly, i. 629; iv. 324. See Books, Education, Libraries, Schools, Scholasticism, Studies, Theological schools.
Culture of the soil, iii. 29, 30, 53.
Cultus. See Worship.
Cunibert, bp. of Turin, iii. 383; iv. 95.
Cupidity, in the first sin, iv. 507. Of the Eastern monks, iv. 529. Of the Roman court, v. 21, 35. Wicklif on the, v.

137, 138. Papal, v. 122, 276. Of the clergy, see Clergy, Simony.
Curia Romana, iv. 195-197. See Rome.
Curiosi, i. 100 n. 1.
Curland, the conversion of, iv. 38.
Curubis, i. 138.
Cusa, Nicholas of, v. 130.
Cuthbert, abp. of Canterbury, iii. 58 n. 1, 64 n. 4, 70, 153 n. 2.
Cybele, worship of, i. 80, 115, 513; ii. 86, 307.
Cyclades, iii. 209.
Cycles, i. 5, 9, 16, 17.
Cyllena (Cilean), iii. 37, 38, 61.
Cynegius, præfect, prætor, ii. 94, 95 n. 5, 96 n. 5, 97.
Cynicism, iii. 250.
Cynics, i. 9, 92, 93, 158.
Cynoschora, iii. 256, 265.
Cypharas, Constantine, monk, iii. 307.
Cyprian, bp. of Carthage, his life, i. 222, 223 (134-140). Character, i. 223, 224. The persecution under Decius, i. 130, 131 n., 132 nn., 133. His conduct in the persecutions, i. 134-140. Thibaritans, i. 136. His letter to the Christians in the mines, i. 138. His trial, i. 137. Martyrdom, i. 140. Schism of Felicissimus, i. 222-237. Novatian controversy, i. 237-248. The Christian prisoners from Numidia, i. 256. On benevolence, i. 257. The plague in Carthage, i. 258; ii. 192 n. 3. His relation to his presbyters, i. 192. Episcopacy, i. 192-195, 209; ii. 208, 219. De lapsis, i. 198. Clerus, election to church offices, i. 199, 200. Council of the church, i. 200. Officers of country communities, i. 202 n. 1. The Catholic church, i. 209; ii. 219. Outward mediation of the church, i. 209, 210; ii. 219. Primacy of Peter, i. 212. The Roman church, i. 214-217; ii. 208; iv. 100. Church discipline, i. 220. On conversion, i. 249. Libri testimoniorum, i. 227, 253, 685. Theatrical exhibitions, i. 266, 267. Profession of stage players, i. 267. Virgins, i. 277. Subintroductæ, i. 277 n. 5. The Lord's Prayer, i. 287. Silent prayer, i. 288. Symbol in baptism, i. 306 n. 4. Question in baptism, i. 308 n. 5. Sprinkling in baptism, i. 310. Exorcism, i. 310 n. 1. Infant baptism, i. 313 (ii. 729). Anointing in baptism, i. 315. Confirmation, i. 316 n. 3. Baptism of heretics, i. 319-323 (ii. 219). Idea of sacrifice in the Lord's Supper, i. 330 nn. 1, 2, 331. The fourth petition, i. 332. Daily communion, i. 332. Sacramental bread, i. 332 n. 3. On the efficacy of the sacraments, i. 253. Mourning for the dead, i. 333. Communion of children, i. 333 n. 2, 648 n. 4. Veneration of martyrs, i. 334, 335. On inherited sin, i. 620 n. 2. Sins after baptism, i. 647. Lord's Supper, i. 648. Purification after death, i. 654 n. 5. Supplementary remarks on his life and writings, i. 685, 686, 690. Cited by Huss, v. 351. See Carthage, Councils, North African church, Pontius, Tertullian.

Citations from his writings:—
Apologia, the pestilence, i. 136 (n. 1).
De habitu virginum, i. 277 n. 4.
De lapsis, on flight in persecution, i. 134 n. 3. Worldly bps., i. 198. Communion at home (ed. Baluz, f. 189), i. 332 n. 3; in one kind to children, i. 333 n. 2; of infants, i. 648 n. 4.
De mortalitate, the pestilence as a test, i. 258 n. 3. The Christian view of death, i. 334 n. 1.
De opere et eleemosynis, i. 257. Elements of the communion a gift of the community, i. 330 n. 1. Merit of alms, i. 647.
De oratione dominica, *sursum corda*, i. 329 n. 1.
De rebaptismate, objective validity of baptism, i. 322 nn. 3, 4, 323 n. 1. Authorship of this book, i. 322 n. 4.
De spectaculis, i. 265 n. 5, 332 n. 3; c. 29, wresting of the Scriptures, i. 266 n. 3.
De testimoniis, i. 685, 686. L. i. pref., i. 686 n. 1. L. i. et iii. introd., i. 686. L. ii. c. 25, necessity of outward participation in the sacraments, i. 253, 648 n. 5; c. 26, but also of reformation, i. 253 n. 3. L. iii. c. 28, sins after baptism, i. 227 nn. 4, 5; c. 54, inherited sin, i. 620 n. 2.
De unitate ecclesiæ, i. 209, 210.
Epistolæ (ed. Baluz.) Ep. 1, ad Donatum, on eloquence, i. 222 n. 1; his own conversion, i. 249, 250; the gladiatorial show, i. 263 n. 2. Ep. 2, his flight, i. 134 n. 1; treatment of the fallen in the Roman church, i. 231 n. 5. Ep. 3, falsification of church letters, i. 205 n. 1, 226 n. 1. Ep. 4, to his clergy, Christian prudence, i. 134 n. 5. Ep. 5, his relations with his presbyters, i. 192 n. 4; with the community, i. 200 n. 2; Novatus, 224 n. 1. Ep. 6, counsels to the confessors, i. 229, 230. Ep. 7, the persecution, prayer, i. 135 n. 1. Epp. 9 and 11, on denial of the faith, i. 227 n. 6. Ep. 12, restoration of the lapsed, i. 231 n. 1. Ep. 13, the same, i. 200 n. 3, 231 n. 1. Ep. 14, to the Roman church, his flight, i. 134 nn. 2, 3, 226 n. 1; *libelli pacis*, i. 229 n. 2, 231 n. 2. Ep. 18, the persecution, i. 133 n. 1. Ep. 21, Luciani ad Cyprian., the same, i. 133 n. 2. Ep. 22, his treatment of the lapsed, i. 229 n. 3. Ep. 26, the confessors at Rome to Cyprian, i. 139 n. 3, 229 n. 4. Ep. 31, from the Roman clergy, *acta facientes*, i. 132 n. 2; on absolution to the lapsed, i. 239 n. 2. Ep. 33, letter to his flock, i. 199 n. 3. Ep. 38, Felicissimus, i. 233 n. 3. Ep. 40, the persecution, i. 131 n. 1; synods, 207 n. 1; the five presbyters, i. 223 n. 1. Ep. 42, Novatian schism, 241 n. 1. Ep. 49, Novatus, 224 n. 1, 225 n. 1. Ep. 52, ad Antonianum, penance, absolution, 220 n. 3, 231 n. 2, 235 n. 1, 243 n. 3; Novatian, 239 n. 1, 240 nn. 1-8, 244 n. 2, 245 n. 1; Cornelius, 242 n. 2; the libellatici, 244 n. 3; purgatory, 654 n. 5. Ep. 54, the lapsed, 234 n. 3. Ep. 55, ad Cornelium, the edict concerning sacrifice, in the pestilence, 136 n. 2; Petri cathedra, 214 and n. 1; Fortunatus, 225 n. 1; Felicissimus, 233 n. 2; unity of the church, independence of bps., 235 n. 2. Ep. 56, to the Thiberitans, 136 n. 3. Ep. 59, to Fidus, time of infant baptism, 313. Ep. 60, to the Numidian bps., 256 n. 3. Ep. 61, ad Euchratem, actors, 267 n. 1. Ep. 62, ad Pomponium, subintroductæ, 277 n. 5. Ep. 63, wine mingled with water at the Lord's Supper, 332 n. 1. Ep. 66, ad Fornenesium, clergy forbidden to engage in

worldly business, 198 n. 2, 199 n. 1. Ep. 68, to the communities at Lyons and Astorga, choice of bps., 200 n. 1; Basilides, 217; ducenarius procurator, 604 n. 1; unworthy priests, 248 nn. 1, 2. Ep. 69, ad Fapinnum, 236 n. 1. Ep. 70, unction in baptism, 315 n. 2; magical influence of the priestly office, 322 n. 2; baptism of heretics, 323 n. 2. Ep. 71, ad Quintum, baptism of heretics, 318 n. 5, 319 n. 2, 320 n. 1. Ep. 72, ad Stephanum, the same, 316 n. 3, 319 n. 4. Ep. 72, ad Jubajanum, baptism, 316 n. 3. Ep. 73, baptism of heretics, authority of tradition, 320 n. 2, 323 n. 1. Ep. 74 ad Pompeium, the same, 214 n. 6, 216 nn. 1, 2; the Spirit, 322 n. 1. Ep. 75, Firmilliani Cæsariens., the persecution under Maximin, 126 n. 4; exorcists, 201 n. 3; synods, 207 n. 1; the Roman church, 214 n. 6, 216 nn. 3, 4; penance, 220 n. 2; the controversies respecting baptism, 318 n. 2, 320 n. 3, 322 n. 4; consecration of the Supper, 229 n. 2. Ep. 76, ad Magnum, symbolum, 306 n. 4; questions in baptism, 308 n. 5; exorcism in baptism, 310 n. 1; efficacy of priest y acts, 322 n. 2. Ep. 77, to his flock under persecution, 138 n. 1. Ep. 82, ad Successum, rescript of Valerian, 139 n. 2. Ep. 83, last letter to his church, i. 139 n. 3. Ep. ad Demetrianum Christians accused as the cause of the pestilence, 136 n. 1, 258 n. 2.

Cyprus, isle of, ii. 328, 330, 531, 741. Louis IX. at, iv. 51, 300. Raymund Lull in, iv. 68. Cruelties in, iv. 539 and n. 1, 540.

Cyrene, school of, i. 6. Gospel in, i. 83. Synesius, ii. 123, 388, 763.

Cyrenean inscriptions, i. 451 n. 3.

Cyrenius. See Quirinus.

Cyrill, bp. of Alexandria. The Holy Spirit, ii. 471. Person of Christ, 502. Nestorian controversy, 507 and n. 3, 512–557, 558–560, 562, 563 n. 5, 566 n. 3, 568. Anathemas of, 523–525, 541, 542, 588, 471. The Syrian church teachers, 598. Letter of Nestorius to, 511 n. 5. In Persia, 610. His life, 581 n. 1. Dionysian writings, iii. 170.

Citations from his writings: —
Contra Julian. L. i. f. 39, Julian on Christianity, ii. 59 n. 4. L. ii. f. 43, J. on the bad choice of the Christians, 57 n. 3. L. iii. ff. 100, 106, J. on the Apostle Paul, 55 nn. 4, 5. L. iv. f. 143, J. on the relation of God's commands to the nature of things, 58 n. 1; f. 148, J. on the God of the Jews, 54 n. 3. L. v. f. 159, J. on the worship of the Sun, 56 n. 1. L. vi. ed. Spanheim, ff. 191, 194, 213, J.'s opinion of Jesus, 49 n. 3, 50 nn. 1, 2; f. 198, J. on cessation of oracles, haruspicia, 58 n. 5, 59 n. 1; f. 200, Æsculapius, 59 n. 2. L. vii. f. 235, the same, 59 n. 3; f. 238, J. on the relation of Christianity to Judaism and paganism, 57 n. 1; f. 262, cn Photinus, 71 n. 3. L. viii f. 253, J. on the prophet foretold by Moses, 56 n. 3. L. ix. f. 306, J. on the Jews, 54 nn 1, 2; f. 319, laws of the O. T., 55 n. 2. L. x. ff. 327, 333, J. on the deterioration of doctrine; Logos doctrine of John, 56 nn. 4, 5; ff. 351, 354, on the Jewish religion, 54 nn. 4, 5, 6 56 n. 3.
Epistolæ. Ep. to Nestorius, ii. 515. Ep. 4, to Nestorius, 516 n. 2. Ep. 5, to the clergy of Constantinople, 517 n. 2. Ep. 6, to the bp. of Marcianopolis, 507 n. 3; Cyrill reproached for his attack on Nestorius, 514 n. 1. Ep. 7, the same, 514 n. 1. Ep. 8, Anastasius, 517 n. 1. Ep. 98 (Theodoret., app. t. v. ed. Hal.), 542 n. 1. Ep. 166, to Aristolaus, 554 n. 2. Ep. 167, to John of Antioch, 555 n. 1 Ep. 179, to Aristolaus, 554 n. 2, 555 n. 1. Ep. 180, 554 n. 3. Ep. to John of Antioch, 521 n. 2. Ep. to Nestorius, summoning him to recant, 523; to the clergy of Constantinople, 529 n. 2. Ep. to Acacius of Melitene (opp. t. v. P. i.), 543 nn. ; f. 197, 555 nn. 3, 4. Ep. ad Theodosium (f. 854), 551 n. 1. Ep. ad Proclum (f. 200), 566 n. 4.
There is but one Christ, ii. 557.

Cyrill, bp. of Jerusalem, on Mani, i. 484. On conversion, ii. 118. Candidates for baptism, 358 and n. 2, 359 n. 1. Moderate Semi-Arianism, 458. Baptism, 726. Doctrine of the Lord's Supper, 731, 732 nn. 2–4.
Citations. Catechesis. prologue, on conversion, ii. 118 n. 3; § 1, ὀνοματογραφία, 35ʰ n. 2; præf. c. 5, veiling in baptism, 359 n. 1 L. v. § 7, hindrances to Bible reading, 318 n 8. L. xv. § 9, purgatorial fire, 736 n. 3. L xvii. cc. 17, 18, grace in baptism, 726 n. 3; λόγοι μυσταγωγικοί, myst. ii. c. 3, iii. c. 4, the double unction in baptism, 359 nn. 7, 8; myst. iii. c. 3, myst. iv. c. 1, transubstantiation, 732 nn. 2, 4 ; myst. iv., the Lord's Supper, 731 n. 4; myst. v. § 7, intercession for the dead, 368 n. 3. L. v., liturgy connected with the Supper, 362 nn. 3, 4.

Cyrill (Constantine), missionary among the Slavonians, iii. 314–316, 317 n. 2, 329 n., 330 n. 1.

Cyrill of Scythopolis.
Life of Sabas, § 58, ii. 271 n. 4; § 83, 596 n. 1; § 85, 596 n. 2, 597 n. 2; § 86, 597 n. 3; § 89, 764 n. 3.

Cyros, bp. of. See Theodoret.

Cyrus, bp. of Phasis, iii. 176 nn. 1, 2; becomes patriarch of Alexandria, 177. His compact with the Egyptian Monophysites, 177–179.
Ep. to Sergius of Constantinople, iii. 176 n. 2, 177 n. 1.

Cyzicus, ii. 71, 455, 509 ; iii. 203 n. 3.

D

Dacher, court marshal, on the council of Constance, v. 118 and n. 2, 326 n. 3.

D'Achery.
Notes in his edition of Lanfranc, ep. of Berengar to Lanfranc, iii. 506 n. 5; (f. 19, ed. Venet.) ep. of B. to Ascelin, iii. 510 n. 1.
Spicilegia. T. i., report of conference at Constantinople, an. 1146, by Anselm of Havelberg, iv. 536 n. 4, 537 nn., 538 nn. 2–4. — consultationes Zachæi Christiani et Apollonii philosophi (l. i. c. 28, images), ii. 112 n. 3 ; Ratramnus and Paschasius Radbert on the sacrament, iii. 495 n. 4 ; Ratramnus and Æneas of Paris, in defense of the Latin church, iii. 567 n. 4. T. i. f. 171, Anselm. Havelbergens. Dialog., iv. 530 n. 3; f. 197, ii. 383 n. 1; f. 212, Bonacursus, De vit. hereticorum, iv. 590 n. 7; f. 291, Jonas of Orleans, De inst. laicali., iii. 452 nn. 2–5, 459 n. 5; f. 297, ep. of Theonas to Lucianus, i. 143 n. 1; f. 347, Ratherius of Verona, De contemptu canonum, iii. 366 n. 4, 412 n. 2; f. 349, the same, 366 n. 4; f. 350, seq., the same, 411 n. 3; f. 354, the same, iii. 382 n. 3; f. 358, Ratherii, Qualitatis conjectura, iii. 409 n. 1, 441 n. 5; f. 359, the same, iii. 412 n. 1; f 363, Ratherii, Discordia inter ipsum et clericos, ii. 388 n. 1; f. 364, the same, 410 n. 1; f. 371, Ratherii, Synodica ad presbyteros, ii. 411 n. 1; ff. 377, 378, the same, 410 n. 3; § 8, 441

n. 4; f. 381, Ratherii, Itinerarium, iii. 387 n. 7; f. 384, et seq., 442 n. 1; f. 386, 442 n. 3, f. 388, 443 n. 3; f. 400, Ratherii, Sermo II. de ascensione, iii. 444 n. 3; f. 416, et seq., Atto of Vercelli, De pressuris ecclesiasticis, iii. 420 n. 3; f. 423, iii. 409 n. 1; f. 439, Atto, letter to his clergy, iii. 411 n. 2; f. 473, Clemangis, De studio theologico, v. 60 n.; f. 574, rule of Chrodegang, iii. 133 n. 3; f. 604, Gesta Synodi Aurelianens., iii. 593 n. 2, 594 n. 2, 595 n. 5; f. 697, synodal letter of abp. Gerhard I., iii. 598 nn. 2, 3, 599 n. 1.

T. ii. nov. edit., life of Eligius of Noyon, iii. 41 n. 2; f. 97, sermon of Eligius, iii. 448 n. 3; f. 293, Jonas of Orleans, De inst. laicali., iii. 413 n. 8; f. 302, Chronicon S. Benigni Divonienisis, life of Halinardus, iii. 377 nn. 1, 4, 378 n. 4; f. 645, Richerii Chron. Senonense, iv. 285 n. 7; f. 744, Hist. abbots of Laub, iii. 501 n 5; f. 889, Hermann, Hist. abbey of Tournay, iv. 357 n.

T. iii. f. 110, prevalence of vice, v. 412 n.; f. 395 (ed. fol.), Gundobad, iii. 9 n.; f. 400, Berengarii, ep. ad Ricardum, iii. 508 n. 1, 526 n. 1; f. 470, ep. of Ernulph, bp. of Rochester, to Lambert, iv. 344 n. 4; f. 524, Walter a St. Victor on Abelard, iv. 380 n. 3, 381 nn. 1–3, 5, 382 n. 1; f. 525, the same to Abelard, iv. 450 n. 4.

Dagobert, king of the Franks, iii. 40.
D'Ailly, Peter, chancellor of the University of Paris, v. 38 n. 1, 63, 66, 84, 97, 99. Made cardinal, 90. On the necessity of reformation, 90, 101, 102. Letter to Gerson, 94, 97, 99. Letters to John XXIII., 102. At Constance, 103, 105, 108, 118, 257, 299, 340, 343, 345 n. 1, 347, 348, 350–356, 368, 376. In transubstantiation, 245.

Monita de necessitate reformat. ecclesiæ, in Gerson. opp. ii. f. 885, et seq., v. 101 nn. 2–7 102 nn., 299 n. 1; c. 26, 90 n. De difficultate reformationis, ep. ad Gerson. opp. Gerson. t. ii. f. 867, 94 n. 1.

Daily communion, i. 332, 648. See Communion, Lord's Supper.
Dalen, Norwegian province, iii. 298.
Dalmatia, ii. 601, 605, 742; iii. 114. Apostolicals in, iv. 631, 632.
Dalmatius, archimandrite, ii. 535, 536, 541 n. Life of, 535 n. 2.
Damascius, pagan philosopher, ii. 110.
Damascus, i. 81. Sultan of, iv. 60 n. 2. See John of.
Damasius II., pope, iii. 378.
Damasus, bp. of Rome, ii. 92, 181, 187, 206. Schism of, 255–257, 206. Jerome, i. 684 n. 1; ii. 744, 745 and n. 4. Priscillianists, ii. 772.

Ep. 9, ad Ascheolinum, ii. 187 n. 2.

Dambrowska, wife of Mjesco, iii. 330.
Damiani, Peter, bp of Ostia, Gratian, iii. 377. Reformation of the papacy, 379, 380. Concubinage of priests, 382 nn. 2, 3. Celibacy, 383, 384 nn. 1–3. Judgments of God, 384 n. 4. The secular sword in the hands of the pope, 385, 386; and of priests, 405, 406. Benedict X., 387 and n. 3. Reformation, 388. In Florence, 389 n. 1, 398. In Milan, 393, 394. The election of Alexander II., 395 n. 2. Cadalous, 396 n. 2. Alexander II., 396 n. 3, 397. Relations to Hildebrand, 399. The priestly unction as a sacrament, 449. On the number of sacraments, 449 (iv. 334 n. 4). Penance, self scourging, 451. Transubstantiation, 519. Christian spirit of, 605.

Citations from his writings:—
Disceptatio synodalis, iii. 395 n. 2.
Epistles, ep. 1, to Gregory VI., iii. 377 n. 2. L. i. ep. 12, to Alexander II., 396 n. 3; ep. 13, simony, 404 n. 1; ep. 15, to Alexander II., military service of clergy, 406 n. 2; ep. 16, Hildebrand, 399 n. 2. L. iii. ep. 4, to Henry, abp. of Ravenna, 387 nn. 3, 4, 5. L. iv. ep. 9, the pope and the secular sword, 386 nn. 1, 2 (t. i. 56), 405 n. 7. L. v. ep. 8, ad clericos Florentinos, 451 n. 1; ep. 13, to the chaplains of Godfrid, 383 n. 4.
Life of Odilo, iii. 418 n. 3, 419 nn. 1, 3, 4, 6.
Life of Romuald, 419 nn. 1–6, 446 n. 1.
Opuscula. opusc. 5, to Hildebrand, on Ariald, iii. 393 n. 6, 394 nn. Opusc. 6, Liber gratissimus, § 35, 379 n. 1. Opusc. 17, ad Nicolaum II., de cœlibatu sacerdotum (t. iii. opp. f. 188), 382 n. 2, 383 n. 3, 384 n. 3. Opusc. 18 (t. iii.), to Cunibert, contra clericos intemperantes, 383 nn. 2, 6; diss. 1, f. 195, 384 n. 2; diss. 2, c. 2, 388 n. 3, 384 n. 1; diss. 2, f. 206, Cadalous, 396 nn. 1, 2. Opusc. 19, ad Nicolaum II., de abdicatione episcopatus, the judgment of God, 384 n. 4. Opusc. 30, disturbances at Florence, 389 n. 1. Opusc. 43, de laude flagellorum, 451 n. 1. Opusc. 61, ad Penzonem, 418 n. 4.
Sermo 69 (t. ii. f. 180), unction, iii. 439 n. 4.

Damietta in Egypt, siege of, iv. 59, 60.
Dances, mystic, i. 61. Dancing, i. 265.
Danes, iii. 271. Rudeness of manners, iii. 291. In England, iii. 288, 290, 467, 469. In Riga, iv. 39. See Denmark.
Daniel, iii. 35; v. 262, 332, 358, 364.

Dan. 2, v. 35. 4:17, iii. 302. 11:33, v. 290. Comm. on, i. 682.

Daniel, abbot of Schönau, iv. 236 n. 2.
Daniel, bp. of Winchester, iii. 47, 51 n. 1. His advice to Boniface on the subject of religious instruction, 52. Of fellowship with married priests, 54.

Ep. 13, ad Bonifacium, officiosum mendicium, iii. 54 n. 2. Ep. 14, ad Bonifacium, 52 nn. 1, 2.

Dante, on Dolcino, iv. 637. On Boniface VIII., v. 11.

Inferno, c. 28, V. 55, iv. 637 n. 2.

Dantzic (Gedania), Adalbert at, iv. 41.
Danube, Severinus on the, iii. 26, 27. Upper, iii. 37. Amandus, iii. 41.
Daphne, grove of, ii. 82.
D'Argentre.

Collectio judiciorum de novis erroribus (on Peter Waldo), iv. 666 n. 4.

Dark ages, iii. 366–368, 420, 441, 469, 471, 456.
Darkness, with the Audians, ii. 767 n. 1. Paulicians, iii. 248, 257. Kingdom, powers of, iv. 776, 777. See Powers of.
Date, the, in ecclesiastical documents, ii. 220 n.
David, Jew, iv. 445 n. 1.
David, king, i. 265, 357; ii. 215 and n. 1; iii. 197, 450; iv. 624; v. 284, 351.
David, Nestorian bp. of China, iii. 89.

David of Dinanto, iv. 445-448. De tomis, 445 n. 4.
David the Armenian, ii. 613 n. 1.
Days of fasting and penance, i. 274, 294, 296. Pagan observance of days, iii. 42, 312. Days of creation, 6th day, iv. 623.
De causis, iv. 445 and notes, 480.
De La Celle, abbot. See Peter.
De mortibus persecutorum, Diocletian, i. 145. Edict of Constantine, 148 n. 1. C. 36, Maximin, ii. 3 n. 2, 5 n. 2; c. 44, vision of Constantine, 11 and n. 2; c. 48, rescript of Licinius, 14 nn. 1, 2, 16 n. 2.
De promiss. et praedict Dei.
(Opp. Prosp. Aquit.), P. v c. 7, homage paid to image of emperor, ii. 112 n. 4.
De vocatione gentium, ii. 124, 202 n. 1, 691 n. 1, 699-702, 703, 707; iii. 472.
Dea coelestis, ii. 84.
Deaconesses, i. 188, 283; ii. 189-191.
Deacons, i. 123, 135, 139, 188, 195, 196 n. 1, 197, 200, 233 and n. 2, 316, 332; ii. 184, 188, 189, 214 and n. 1, 358 n. 1, 362, 363. Manichean. i. 504. In the North African and Spanish churches, i. 233. Manage the church funds, i. 233 n. 2. Increased power of the, iii 111. Preaching of, iii. 124. In the Roman church, iii. 141. Wicklif on, v. 170, 173.
Dead, mourning for the, i. 333, 334 Festivals in memory of the, i. 334, 335. Burial of the, i. 333-335; ii. 128, 192, 370; iv. 267, 290 and n. 1, 308. Burning of the, iii. 78. Prayers for the, ii. 367, 379. Offerings for the, ii. 368, 369, 379. Sacrifice for the, iii. 135, 130. In the Armenian church, iii. 589. Masses for, iv. 353. Relics of the, ii. 370. Attempts to raise the, iii. 195; iv. 246 n. Condemnation of the writings of the, Pontianus on, ii. 601; Ferrandus on, ii. 602; Eutychius on, i. 607 n.
Dead Sea, i. 43.
Deans, iv. 196. See Decani.
Death, Christian and Stoic views cf, i. 105. Basilides on, i. 403, 405; Valentine, i. 433. With the Manichoans, ii. 769. Bogomiles, iv. 558. As consequence of sin, ii. 617, 667, 670, 715, 716, 719, 720. Christian deaths, iv. 299, 301. See Martyrs. Death-bed repentance, ii. 707 n. 1.
Death, punishment of, iii. 78, 103, 104, 312, 322. For heretics, iii. 604-606. See Punishment.
Debtors, asylum for, ii. 176. Released, iv. 23.
Decalogue, Wicklif on the, v. 139, 140, 142. Janow, 207, 209. Huss, 321, 336.
Decani (Deans), iii. 108; iv. 196.
Decennalia, ii. 69 n. 3.
Decentius, bp., ii. 195 n. 1, 335, 360 n. 1.
Deception, i. 389; iii. 282 n. 8. With the Paulicians, iii. 249, 250, 267. See Dissimulation, Falsehood, Mendacium, Veracity.
Decian persecution, i. 130-136, 139 n. 2, 224 n., 225, 227, 232, 237, 239, 242, 711, 712, 720; ii. 252, 264. See Decius.
Decius Trajan, i. 130-136.
Decoration of churches, iv. 264. Of monasteries, 252, 254. Of the cross, 308. See Art.
Decrees, papal, Gerbert on the validity of, iii. 372. See Decretals.
Decrees of God, i. 622. Secret, of God, iii. 478. Unchangeable, iii. 474.
Decretals, collection of Dionysius Exiguus, ii. 212; § 3, ii. 361 n. 1. Decretal of Siricius to Himerius, ii. 360. Of Innocent to Decentius, ii. 360 n. 1. Pseudo-Isidorean, iii 122 n. 3, 346-351, 360, 364-366. Collection by Raymund à Pennaforte, iv. 205 and n. 3. Decretum, Decretals, v. 204. See Pseudo-Isidorean.
Decretists, iv. 204.
Decretum Gratiani, iv. 204.
Defensor Pacis, v. 25-35.
Defensores, ii. 192; iii. 101 n. 4, 113. In the Roman church, ii. 192 n. 1.
Definition of terms, ii. 584; v. 346.
Degeneration of mankind, Pelagians on the, ii. 671. Theodore, ii. 716. Isidore, ii. 722.
Deism, i. 8, 42, 572, 601; ii. 28, 111 n. 1, 408, 413; iii. 447 n. 1; iv. 444. In the church, iii. 446. Of Frederic II., iv. 181.
Demetrianus, i. 136 n. 1, 258 n. 2.
Demetrias, Pelagius' letter to, ii. 633, 634 nn., 635 nn. 3, 6, 637 nn. 3, 4, 671 n. 3. Another, ii. 701 n. 1.
Demetrius, ambassador, iv. 534.
Demetrius, bp. of Alexandria, i. 81, 197, 696, 698, 702-704, 705 n 4, 712.
Demetrius, deacon at Constantinople, iii. 219 n. 1.
Demetrius, St., iii. 201 n. 2.
Demetrius Chytas, pagan philosopher, ii. 34.
Demetrius the silversmith, i. 92.
Demiurge, the, in Gnosticism, i. 371, 379-385, 388, 389, 391, 392, 394, 396 n. 3, 477, 543. With Basilides, 405 (see Archon). With Valentine, 421-434, 443. Ptolemaeus, 437-439. Heracleon, 441 n. 2. Ophites, 443. Cainites, 448. Antitactes, 451. Tatian, 457. With Marcion, 464, 466-472, 641. Apelles, 475. Florinus, 680 n. 3. With Julian, ii. 54. With the Paulicians, iii. 245, 251 n. 2, 257-263.
Demmin, Pomeranian town, iv. 18, 25.
Demonax of Cyprus, the Cynic, i. 10.
Demoniacal possession, i. 15, 73, 74, 157, 237, 238 n. 2, 265 and n. 1, 659; ii. 285; iii. 301. Nilus on, iii. 421. Element, ii. 115. Spirit, i 356. See Exorcists.
Demoniacs, ii. 370. See Energumens.

Demons, i. 28, 383; iii. 301, 589 n. 2. Plutarch on, i. 28. Faith in, i. 73. In Gnosticism, i. 431 n. 1. In Manicheism, i. 483.
Demophilus, bp. of Constantinople, ii. 462, 464.
Δημοσιεύοντες, in the Decian persecution, i. 132 n. 6.
Dendrites, iv. 529.
Denial of the faith, i. 226. See Apostacy, Lapsi.
Denis, St., iii. 466. See Dionysius.
Denmark, Willibrord in, iii. 45. Spread of Christianity in, iii. 271–280, 285–291. Revivals of paganism, iii. 285, 290. Olof, iii. 297. Canute, ii. 290, 299. Danish kings, iii. 324 n. 2; iv. 36. The nobleman's son and Mizlav, iv. 23. Conquest of Rügen, iv. 31. Henry the Wend in, iv. 32. Witchcraft in, iv. 90, 91. Laity and clergy in, iv. 100. Monasteries, iv. 254. Pilgrims from, v. 237.
Deodnin, bp. of Liege, ep. to Henry I. of France, iii. 509.
Deposition of popes, v. 36, 84, 94, 125, 126. Of John XXIII., v. 111. See Popes.
Descensus Christi ad inferos, i. 471, 654, 656; ii. 491 and n. 4. Common view of this doctrine, views of Clement, iii. 61. Of Probus, iii. 602.
Desert, man's, ii. 689, 690. See Merit.
Desertion, spiritual, v. 406, 410.
Deserts. See Anchorets, Monks, Scetic.
Desiderius, abbot of Monte Cassino (Victor III.), iii. 375 n. 4 (iv. 121). Sylvester III., 376 n. 3. Benedict IX., 375 n. 4, 376 n. 4. Gregory VI., 377 nn. 3, 4. The church at Rome, 378 nn. 1, 3.

Dialog. 3 (Bibl. Patr. Lugdun. t. xviii. f. 853), Benedict IX., 375 n. 4: f. 356, Hildebrand, judgments of God, 384 n. 4, 399 n. 1.

Desiderius, bp. of Vienne, iii. 150.
Desiderius, Catharist, iv. 575 n. 1.
Desiderius, charlatan, iii. 56 n. 5.
Deskereh, castle of, i. 488.
Despair, iv. 239, 305; v. 410.
Despondency, v. 409, 410.
Despotism, effect of, on culture, iii. 169. See Byzantine.
Destruction of the world anticipated, iii. 164 n. 3, 470 and n. 2; v. 93. Catharists on, iv. 575.
Detwig, Hessian prince, iii. 47.
Deuteronomy.

1 : 31, i. 57 n. 2. 4 : 19, i. 587 n. 3. 18, i. 195. 18 : 15, iv. 568. 18 : 18, ii. 56. 22 : 5, i. 267. 23, i. 703 n. 4. 25, iii. 61. 27 : 26, i. 642. 32 : 7, ii. 740 n. 2. 32 : 8, 9, i. 380 n. 4. 32 : 39, iii. 155 n. 1. 32 : 43, i. 409 n. 2.

Dentz. See Rupert.
Development, of Christianity, i. 508–513, 516–519; iv. 621–626; v. 93, 157. Of Theism, Origen, i. 587 n. 3. Moral, Origen, i. 629. Of doctrine, i. 508, 609 n. 1. In Christ, ii. 493. Of spiritual life, ii. 682. Of nations, iv. 528.

Devil, with Basilides, i. 403. John Scotus on the, iii. 487. The Catharists, iv. 567. Wicklif, v. 169. Janow, v. 197. Huss, v. 270. Syrian devil-worship, iv. 558 n. 2. See Pompa diaboli.
Devonshire, iii. 46.
Devotees, ii. 106.
Devotion, seasons of, i. 274.
Dews, in Parsism, ii. 128 n. 4, 129, 137.
Deynoch, abbot of Bangor, iii. 17.
Διαγράμμα, i. 477.
Διάκονος, of Basilides, i. 410 n. 1.
Dialectic tendency in the Greek church, iii. 169, 171. In the fourth Period, iii. 471. In the Irish and Scotch church, 460, 461 n. 1, 463, 470, 471. With Scotus, 463. Berengarius, 526. In the fifth Period, iv. 33, 220, 227, 237, 355–360, 362, 370, 371, 474, 545 n. 2, 623. United with the practical, 400–411. Theology, 210. With Joachim, 220, 227. In the thirteenth century, 416–427, 446. See the individuals. United with the mystical, 419, 421. With the Catharists, 583. See Abelard (iv. 374–377).
Dialectics, with Augustine and the Donatists, ii. 233. Among the Monophysites, ii. 613. In the Greek church, iv. 545 n. 2, 549. See Dialectic.
Dialects, iii. 127.
Dialogus inter philos. Judæum et Christianum, iv. 388 n. 1. See Abelard.
Διατάξεις ἀποστολικαί, i. 660. See Apostolical constitutions.
Dichotomy of Tertullian, i. 635. Of Photius, iii. 559 n. 3. Mystics, iv. 562.
Dictates, pretended, of Gregory VII., iv. 120.
Dictinnius, Libra, ii. 778, 779.
Dicuil, monk from Ireland.

De mensura orbis terræ, f. 29, Thile ultima, iii. 300 n. 1; f. 39, Orcades, iii. 300 n. 3.

Didactic element in the pagan cultus, ii. 62. Eunomius, ii. 447.
Didacus (Diego), bp. of Osma, iv. 269, 641.
Διδάσκαλοι, in the apostolic age, i. 187. Paulician, iii. 264. Didascalia, with Paul, i. 510.
Didymus, church teacher in Alexandria, ii. 182, 270, 386, 468, 706 n. 2, 738, 740 and n. 3, 745 n. 1, 765. De Trinitate, 706 n. 2, 738 n. 1.
Diego. See Didacus.
Diepenbrock.

Suso's life and writings (Regensburg, 1829), p. 249 (2d ed. p. 181), v. 411 n. 3; p. 253 (2d ed. p. 184), n. 4.

Dierolf, Hessian prince, iii. 47.
Dies natales, natalitia martyrum, i. 334 n. 3.
Dies natalis invicti solis, ii. 347; iii. 294.
Dies natalis virtutum domini, ii. 344.
Dies novorum, ii. 342 n. 2.
Dies stationum, i. 296, 520; ii. 332, 333.
Dieteric (Theoderic), bp. of Verdun, iv. 119.

On Gregory VII. (see Marteue et Durand, thes. nov. t. v. f. 217), iv. 84 n. 3, 86 n. 3, 99 n. 6. Divine right of princes, 109 nn. 1, 2. Council at Meutz, 119 and n. 1. Letter from Henry IV., 120 nn. 2, 3.

Digesta, tit. 12, 1. 12, c. 4, § 14, rescript of Severus, i. 120 n. 3. Tit. 14, l. 1, c. 4, *et seq*, rescripts of the emperors against the Christians, i. 126 n. 1.

Dijon, iii. 419, 580; iv. 252.

Δικαιοσύνη, i. 400.

Dillingen, iv. 421.

Dio Cassius, toleration, i. 87. Nerva, i. 97 n. 1.
L. 55, § 23, catalogue of the legions, L 116 n. 2. L. 67, § 14, Domitian and the Christians, 96 nn. 3, 4. L. 71, § 8, the victory of Marcus Aurelius, 116 n. 3. L. 72, § 4, Ma-cia, 118 n. 1.

Dio Chrysostom, i. 86 n. 1. Defense of images of the gods, 27.
Orat. 12 (ed. Reiske. 11. vol. 1. f. 405, et *seq*.), i. 27 n. 2; sources of religion, 86 n. 1.

Diocæsarea, synod at, ii. 491 n. 1.

Diocesan authority of bps. interfered with, iv. 201–203.

Diocesan union, iii. 108–111.

Dioceses, iii. 107, 120. Διοικήσεις, ii. 194 n. 1.

Diocletian, i. 142–155, 291, 688, 689, 720, 722; ii. 410. The Manicheans, i. 144, 506; ii. 768. Synod under, iii. 372 n. 1.
Edictum contra Manich. (Hilarius in epist. sec. ad Timoth. 3, 7), i. 144; edictum e Christian. (Euseb. H. eccl. l. viii. c. 2, viz. Constant. l. ii. c. 32, Lactant. de mort. persecut. c. 10), 148 n. 1.

Diocletian persecution, i. 147–155, 303 n. 3, 689, 720, 722; ii. 1, 3, 5 n. 3, 6, 8, 16, 17, 21, 66, 124, 193 n. 6, 217, 220, 224, 252, 319, 427 n., 768, 769.

Diodorus of Tarsus, Julian on, ii. 77, 78. Exegesis, 389. Person of Christ, 488, 493, 499. Controversy concerning Diodorus, 555. In the Eutychian controversy, 562, 563 n. 3. Influence among the Nestorians, 610. Apocatastasis, 737, 738.
Fragments in Leontius of Byzantium (opp. Bibl. Patr. Lugd. t. ix. f. 700), ii. 499 nn. 2, 3; περὶ οἰκονομίας, ii. 738.

Diodorus Siculus, l. 1, § 25, ii. 47 n. 4.

Diognetus, letter to, description of Christians, i. 69 n. 1. Doctrine of redemption, 642. § 12, sanctification, 644. Character and criticism, 670.

Dionysius, bp. of Alexandria, i. 190 n. 1. Philip the Arabian, 127. On the Decian persecution, 130 n. 2, 132, 135. Valerian, 127, 137 n. 1. In exile, 138. The Novatian controversy, 241, 243. The Christians in the time of the pestilence, 257, 258. Baptism of heretics, 320, 321 n. 3, 323; of Montanists, 320 n. 6. Sixtus II. of Rome, 321. Corinth, 396 n. 1, 399. Sabellius, 399 n. 2. Doctrine of the Trinity, 606–608, 610 (ii. 403, 404, 420). The Chiliasts,

652, 653. Character, i. 712; ii. 411, 420.
Citations. (Apud Euseb. H. eccles.), Euseb. H. E., 5, 5 (epist. ad Stephanum), i. 321 n. 1; 6, 41 (ep. ad Fabium Antiochanum), 130 n. 2; 6, 46 (ad Novatianum), 241 n. 2; 7, 7 (ad Philemonem), 712 n. 1; 7, 8, Novatian, 243 n. 2; 7, 9, baptism of heretics, 308 n. 5, 321 n. 3; 7, 10 Valerian, 137 n. 1; 7, 22, the pestilence at Alexandria, 258 n. 1; 7, 24 (περὶ ἐπαγγελιῶν, 653 nn. Euseb. Præp. evang. l. 14 (περὶ φύσεως), 713 n. 1. Apud Athanasium, de Sententia Dionysii (ἔλεγχος καὶ ἀπολογία, ad Dionysium Rom.), 608 n. 1, ii. 404; § 14 (ep. ad Ammonium et Euphranor.), i. 606 n. 3. Apud Routh, reliquiæ sacræ, vol. ii. (ep. ad Basilidem), i. 712 n. 2.

Dionysius, bp. of Corinth, iii. 467 n. 1; iv. 382 n. 3.

Dionysius, bp. of Paris, founder of the church there, i. 84; iii. 466. Compare Dionysius the Areopagite.

Dionysius, bp. of Rome, controversy with Dionysius of Alexandria, i. 606–608; ii. 404. On the Holy Spirit, i. 610.
Apud Athanasium, de decretis synodi Nicænæ, § 25 (ἀνατροπή), i. 610 n. 3.

Dionysius, Egyptian magician, i. 161.

Dionysius, fable of, with the Manicheans, i. 493.

Dionysius Exiguus, Roman abbot, Decretales, ii. 212; iii. 346, 360. Time of Easter, ii. 338.

Dionysius of Halicarnassus.
Archæol. Rom. l. ii. c. 18, Greek and Roman religions compared, l. 6 n. 1; c. 19, toleration, 88 n. 4; c. 20, on popular faith, 29 n. 1; c. 68, on Theophanies, 12 n. 2; l. iv. c. 62, Sibylline books, 177 n. 3.

Dionysius the Areopagite. Mystico-theurgical tendency of the writings diffused under his name, ii. 388, 615, 723, 725, 740 n. 3. Confounded with Dionysius of Paris, iii. 467, 467 and nn. 1, 3. Influence of these writings, ii. 725; iii. 169, 171, 176, 206 n. 1; iv. 420, 444, 479 n. 4; v. 8. Their genuineness disputed and defended, iii. 170; iv. 382. Their diffusion, iii. 467.
Hierarch 3, the Lord's Supper, ii. 364 n. 1. Ep. ad Caium, iii. 184 n. 1.

Dioscorides, i. 82; ii. 140. See Diu.

Dioscuri, ii. 105 n. 3.

Dioscurus, bp. of Alexandria, ii. 557 n. 7, 559–584, 611.

Dioscurus, bp. of Hermopolis, ii. 752.

Dioscurus, confessor, i. 132.

Diospetes, ii. 49.

Diospolis. See Councils, an. 415.

Diptycha, Δίπτυχα, iii. 193, 196; iv. 544.

Δίφροι, ii. 376.

Disciplina arcani, i. 305 n. 1, 308 n. 4, 327 n. 1.

Discipline, monastic, iii. 30, 31. Anselm on, iv. 362, 363, 366. See Church discipline.

Discussion of matters of faith, Abelard on, iv. 374, 375. Stephen of Tournay, 416. Oliva, 621.

Disease, healed at graves of martyrs, ii. 370. See Miracles.
Dismissal before communion, i. 327–329. See Missa.
Disorders of sixth and seventh centuries, iii. 28 and n 3. Of ninth and tenth, iii. 413. See Dark ages. Sin as disorder, iv. 495.
Dispensations, v. 98, 125.
Disposition. See Intention.
Disputatio Archelai cum Mani.
   C. 7, Opera Hippolyti, ed. Fabricius, f. 193, i. 505 n. 3.
Dissimulation, iii. 54 and n. 2. With the Bogomiles, iv. 557–559. Catharists, iv. 585, 587, 610, 612. Dolcino, iv. 631. See Deception, Veracity.
Distinctions of rank and Christianity, i. 325, 326.
Distinguishing without separating, iii. 261.
Disunion in human nature, i. 73.
Ditmar, bp. of Merseburg.
   Chronica, l. ii., Harald, iii. 289 n. 1; (f. 22, ed. Rehneccii, and t. i. ed. Leibnitz), Boso, 324 n. 1. L. viii., Geisa, 333 n. 1 : ed. Leibnitz, Script. rer. Brunsv. t. i. f. 354, Philagathus, 422 n. 4.
Dittmar, priest, iv. 35, 36.
Divination, pagan, Eusebius on, i. 145 n. 2. Natural power of, i. 616 and n. 3, 618. Julian, ii. 43, 45. Valens, ii. 91. Simplicius, ii. 108. In the New Year's festival, ii. 350. Nicholas I. to the Bulgarians on, iii. 312. Among the Germans, iv. 15 and n. 3.
Divine in man, Platonic idea of the, i. 18. Divine and human in prophets, i. 426.
Divine right of princes, iv. 109, 110, 141, 142, 165.
Divisiones mensuræ, i. 198 n. 1.
Divisions, church, i. 208, 209. See Schism.
במדה, i. 613.
Dnieper, iii. 329.
Dobrowsky.
   Moravian legends on Cyrill and Methodius, Prague, 1826, f. 60, iii. 318 n. 1; f. 71, 316 n. 4; f. 114, 321 n. 5; f. 115, 320 n. 2.
Docetism, antagonism of the church consciousness to, i. 630, 631, 634. Clement, 632. In Gnosticism, 386, 387, 402 n. 3, 429, 447, 448, 456, 458 n. 3, 469–471. Of Mani, 494 n. 1, 499, 505; ii. 511. *In the second Period*, ii. 502, 511, 561. With Priscillian, 777, 778. With Hilarius, 483 n. *Third and fourth Periods*. Image worship and, iii. 204. Among the Monotheletians, 182 and n. 2. Among the Paulicians, 261. Iconoclasts accused of, 540. Among the sect at Orleans, 594. Berengarins accused of, 505 n. 5. *Fifth Period*, iv. 335, 336, 496. Bogomiles, 554, 555, 557. Catharists, 569, 570, 572, 574.
Dochingen (Dockum), iii. 72, 80.
Doctors of theology and law allowed to vote at the council of Constance, v. 103, 104.
Doctrinal element, with Eunomius, ii. 447.
Doctrine, history of Christian, i. 336–656; ii. 380–779; iii. 141–270, 456–606; iv. 355–644; v. 134–412. History of particular doctrines, i. 557–656; ii. 403–779. Beyond the limits of the Roman empire, ii. 609–616. *In the third Period*, in the Latin ch., iii. 141–168, 233–243. In the Greek ch., 169–233. Reaction of the sects, 243–270. *Fourth Period*, in the Western ch., iii. 456–530. In the Greek ch., 530–551. Participation of the Western ch. in the controversies of the Greek ch., 551–553. Relation of Greek and Latin churches to each other, controversies between them, 553–586. Reaction of the sects, 586–606. *Fifth Period*, in the Western ch., iv. 355–528. In the Eastern ch., 528–531. In the sects, 552–644. *Sixth Period*, the reformatory movements in England, v. 134–173. In Bohemia, 173–380. The Friends of God in Germany, 380, 412.
   Expositions of doctrine, i. 174. Instruction in, i. 186–188, 191, 305 n. 1. Innocent I. on purity of, ii. 2–4 and n. 1. Systems of, i. 337. Progressiveness of, ii. 209–212. Permanence of, ii. 211. Forms of, Apollinaris on, ii. 484. Preaching of, ii. 692. Test of, Augustin's, ii. 697. Importance disputed, ii. 767. Corruption in, iv. 605. Uniformity of, iv. 391; v. 93. Errors in doctrine and morals, iv. 384; v. 128. Value of formal conceptions, ii. 584; v. 157. See Gnosticism, Manicheism, Sects.
Doctrine of the Trinity, Mohammed opposed to, iii. 86. Chilperic on the, 91 n. 1. See Trinity.
Dorum. See Dochingen.
Dodo, Franciscan, iv. 278.
Dodwell.
   Dissertat. in Irenæum, Philip of Sida on the life of Athenagoras, i. 673 n. 2.
Δόγμα, ii. 740 n. 2.
Dogmatics, iv. 427.
Dogmatism, ii. 117. Dogmatical tendency, iv. 356, 390, 391. Dogmatic elements in Christianity, iv. 384. Greek emperors, courtiers, ii. 164–166, 603; iv. 533.
Dola, abbot of. See Stephen.
Dola, bp. of, v. 340.
Dolcino, iv. 629–638. Circular letters of, iv. 631, 632.
Domestic missions, v. 144.
Domesticus, iii. 421.
Dominica in albis, ii. 342 n. 2.
Dominicans, iv. 268–270, 279; v. 171, 180, 191, 328. Visit the Mongols, iv. 49, 56, 57. As missionaries, iv. 56, 57. Suffragans, iv. 215. As preachers, iv. 278, 279. Joachim and the, iv. 221 n.

Louis IX., iv. 285 n. 7. Delegates to Constantinople, iv. 540. Attacked by heretics, iv. 610. Inquisitors, iv. 643. Generals of the order, iv. 63, 189, 205, 267, 279, 314, 332, 583. Individual Dominicans, iv. 277, 295, 296, 302 n. 2, 314, 326 and n. 1, 340, 421, 422 585 n. 1, 618 n. 1; v. 13, 19, 127, 381, 382, 383 n. 2, 389, 393, 407, 411. Scholastics, iv. 421, 422. Emendation of the Vulgate, iv. 426. Writers, iv. 618 n. 1. Articles of the order, c. iii. § 63, on property, iv. 270 n. 3. See Mendicants.

Dominick, iv. 268-270, 641; v. 171. Rule of, iv. 634. Life of, iv. 269 n. 1, 270 n. 4.

Donislav, father and son, Pomeranians, iv. 9.

Domitian, i. 96.

Domitian, bp. of Ancyra, ii. 595-597, 598 n., 599. Ep. to Vigilius, ii. 598 n. 1.

Domitian, quæstor, ii. 548. See Theodoret, ep. 106.

Domitius Ulpianus, De officiis proconsulum fragm. digest., t. xiv. l. i. c. 4, seqq., rescripts against the Christians, i. 126 and n. 1.

Domnizo.

Life of Mathilda, l. ii., iv. 112 n. 1.

Domnus, bp. of Rome, iii. 193.

Domnus, patriarch of Antioch, ii. 557 n. 7, 562, 563 n. 3, 572. Letter of vindication, 562, 563 n. 3.

Dona naturalia and superaddita, iv. 522; v. 26.

Donations to churches, ii. 259, 367 and n. 4, iii. 452; and monasteries, iii. 9. See Gifts.

Donatists. Donatist schism, ii. 214, 216-252, 294, 642 n. 2; iii. 372 n. 1; v. 158. Polemics between Donatists and Catholics, ii. 238-252. Sacraments, ii. 245, 246, 724. Acta Saturnini, i. 152 n. At Rome, i. 233 n. 3. Epiphany, i. 301 n. 2; ii. 343.

Donatus, Donatist martyr, ii. 228 n. 3.

Donatus, friend of Cyprian, i. 222.

Donatus, grammarian at Rome, ii. 742.

Donatus of Casæ Nigræ, ii. 221, 224, 225 and n. 4.

Donatus the Great, bp. of Carthage, ii. 225, 228 n. 3, 229, 230, 231.

Donum lachrymarum, iv. 306.

Dorostorus (Silistria), ii. 150 n. 4.

Dorotheus, presbyter in Antioch, i. 722.

Dorovern (Canterbury), iii. 12.

Dorstatum, Dorstede (Wyk te Duerstade), iii. 275, 280, 282, 285 n., 328 n. 2.

Dorylenm, Eusebius of, ii. 563.

Dositheus, i. 454 n. 1.

Doubt, iv. 380, 537. Abelard on, 392. See Skepticism.

Δόξα, i. 29, 540; and ἐπιστήμη, ii. 401.

Dracontius, knight, ii. 80.

Dragomans, i. 303 n. 2.

Dragons, stories of, iii. 207 n.

Drahomira (Dragomir), Bohemian princess, iii. 321 n. 5, 322.

Δραστικὴ ἐνέργεια. See Ἐνέργεια.

Dreams, i. 71, 73, 75, 107, 236, 688; ii. 27, 47 and n. 4, 106, 119, 120, 147, 279; iii. 19, 47, 293, 417, 421; iv. 42, 271, 298, 332, 361. Anschar, iii. 274, 283, 286, 287. Huss, v. 332, 333, 364. Charlemagne, iii. 240. Interpretation of, ii. 45, iv. 113.

Drembitza, iii. 315 n. 1.

Drenthe, ii. 80.

Dresden, v. 338.

Dress, of women, i. 231; v. 176, 185. Of monks, iv. 244, 263, 275. William of St. Amour on, iv. 285, 286. Louis IX., iv. 301. Elizabeth of Hessia, iv. 302. R. de Sorbonne on, v. 303. Ordinances relating to, v. 192, 223.

Drontheim in Norway, iii. 298 n. 2.

Dructeram, abbot, iii. 432 n. 4, 434 n. 2.

Druids, ii. 148.

Drunkenness, iii. 138, 410, 442; iv. 52.

Druthmar, Christian (Grammaticus), iii. 458, 459.

Dryinos, Paulician, iii. 251 n. 1.

Dschingiskhan (Temrdschin), iv. 48, 49.

Dsunovas, Arabic prince, ii. 145.

Du Boulay. See Boulæus.

Du Chesne.

Scriptores hist. Franc. f. 639, Ordericus Vitalis, iv. 92 n. 5. T. ii., Gerbert's epistles, ep. 2, 8, 44, 45, 130 iii. 470 n. 3; f. 816, ep. 113, Balduin, iii. 453 n. 3; f. 824, ep. 152, Adalbero, iii. 373 n. 1; f. 879, ep. 38, to John XV., iii. 373 n. 1. T. iv. f. 53, Glaber Rudolph, iii. 377 n. 1; f. 64, Helgaldi vit. Roberti regis, iii. 450 n. 5; f. 291, Paschalis II., iv. 140 n. 4. T. v. ff. 447 et 451, Life of Louis IX., iv. 285 n. 4; f. 456, the same, iv. 285 n. 5; e. 2, Chronicle of Bal Cernay, iv. 570 n. 4; ff. 667, 668, Chronicle of Puy Lorens, iv. 577 n. 5, 604 n. 1; f. 666, Waldenses, iv. 511 n. 4. T. vi. f. 81, Hist. Aquitanica, iii. 598 n. 3.

Du Pin.

Collection of monumenta vet. ad Donatist. hist pertinantia, f. 138, rescript of Constantine, ii. 227 n. 2; f. 174, ii. 218 n. 1, 219 n. 1; f. 175, assembly at Cirta, 220 n. 1; f. 176, assembly at Carthage, 222 n. 4; f. 189, rescript to Verinus, 227 n. 5; third rescript, 228 n. 1; f. 190, memorial discourse, 228 n. 3; f. 319, Donatus of Casæ Nigræ, 221 n. 4. Gesta. collat. Carthag. f. 184 (ep. of Constantine to the Numidian bps.), 225 n. 1; f. 247, 235 n. 3; f. 243, 237 n. 2; f. 301 et 302, 243 n. 2; f. 312, 245 n. 2; ff. 313 et 314, 242 n. 2, 243 n. 1; f. 313, 247 n. 1; f. 323, 235 n. 4.

Dualism, i. 375. Oriental, i. 15, 276, 478. In Parsism, i. 369, 378, 488, 489. In Gnosticism, i. 370, 374, 375, 378, 379, 393 n. 3, 394, 438, 455 467, 476; iv. 444, 613, 620, 721. Of Basilides, i. 400, 402-405, 407. Of Marcion, i. 458, 464, 465, 467. Apelles, i. 475. In Platonism, i. 375, 378, 379, 393 n. 3. In Buddhism, i. 481, 482. Manichean, i. 481, 488, 489, 500. With the Apologists, i. 565. Augustin, ii. 398. In the sects, iii. 243, 594. Priscillianists, ii. 776. Paulicians, iii. 251, 257-263. Euchites, iii. 590; iv.

552. Catharists, iv. 565-567, 569, 570, 579, 581, 582, 592, 594. Bogomiles, iv.
553. Western sects, iv. 565. Eastern, iv. 592. Among the Mongols, iv. 54.
Duba, Wenzel of, v. 320, 321, 342, 348, 358, 367.
Dubrach, Mac Valubair, ii. 149.
Ducas Vatazes, John, iv. 539.
Duel, iii. 429 n. 4, 449, 450.
Dulcitius, imperial tribune, ii. 238.
Dulcitius, notary, ii. 573.
Düna, river, iv. 36, 37.
Dunaan. See Dsunovas.
Δύναμις, with Basilides, i. 400, 418. With Philo, i. 601 n. 1.
Dungal, against Claudius of Turin, iv. 430 n. 1, 431 n. 1, 439 and nn. 1, 2, 4, 5. Responsa adv. Claud. Bibl. Patr. Lugd. f. 204, 431 n. 2; f. 223, 439 n. 1.
Duns Scotus, v. 245.
Dunstan, abp. of Canterbury, iii. 460 n. 6. Zealously contends against the corruption of the clergy, iii 411. Reforms the clergy in England, iii. 468, 469. Life of, 1. i. c. 8, § 47, 411 n. 6 (see Acta S. May 19).
Duophysites, ii. 581 n. 1, 613. See Monophysite controversies.
Durand de Osca, iv. 612, 613.
Durandus, abbot of Troanne, v. 245.
De corpore et sanguine Domini, Bibl. Patr. Lugd. t. xviii. f. 421, transubstantiation, iii. 529 n. 1; f. 424, 528 n. 2; f. 427, 529 n. 2: f. 437, Berengar, iii. 503 n. 3, 515 n. 4; and conc. Paris., 509 n. 4, 510 and n. 2.

Durham, bp. of, iv. 418 n. 4.
Duty, Aquinas on, iv. 524.
Duumviri, excluded from the church, ii. 173.
Dux Osrhoënæ, ii. 95 n. 5.
Dux Soranus, ii. 154, 155.
Dux Syrianus, ii. 443.
Dyarchy (Arius), ii. 405.
Dyotheletism, iii. 181. Dominant in Rome and Africa, iii. 184-186, 193. Its triumph and establishment as an article of faith, iii. 195-197. See Monotheletic controversy.

E.

Eadbald, king of Kent, idolater, iii. 18. Converted, iii. 19.
Eadburga, abbess, iii. 52.
Eadmer, monk, iv. 366.
Life of Anselm, iv. 362 n. 1, 365 nn. 2, 4, 366 and n. 2, 367 n., 368 nn. 1, 3, 442 n. 1.
Earlier and later stages of development, i. 40.
Earth of light, Mani, i. 490.
Earth worship, Persian, ii. 128.
Earthquake council, v. 162, 163, 346.
Earthquakes, i. 103, 126. At Constantinople, ii. 535, 760; iii. 562 n. 1. In the image controv., iii. 209, 214.
East, paganism in the, ii. 102-110.

East, Roman ch. property in the, iii. 113.
East Frankland (Germany), iv. 153. East Franks, 73.
East Goths, iii. 4 n. 1.
East India, i. 81, 82; ii. 140.
East Roman Empire, ii. 162, 382; iii. 112, 113 n. 1, 117, 119, 307, 327, 586, 587. See Eastern church, Byzantine.
Easter cycle, i. 681 n. 4.
Easter festival, i. 149, 297-300; ii. 174, 175, 272, 339, 341, 342, 351 and n. 2, 352 n. 1, 438; iii. 294; iv. 39, 53, 325. Differences in the time of celebrating, i. 206, 214 n. 2, 297-300, 676, 678, 680; ii. 337, 338, 415, 751, 767; iii. 17, 23, 32. Time made known, ii. 751. Easter Sabbath, ii. 333 n. 8, 334, 341, 342, 360 and n. 2, 361. Easter Sunday, ii. 341, 360 n. 2; communion at, ii. 360 n. 2, 365, iv. 346, 353. Easter with the Manichæans, i. 505. See Passover.
Eastern church, character in the *first Period*, i. 508. Acolytes; exorcists, 201. Country bps., 202. Metropolitan system, 203. Doctrine of the Trinity, 585-610. *Second Period*. Character, ii. 204. Relation to the state, 162, 166, 214. Celibacy, 180, 181. Ordinations, 185. Transfer of clergy, 186, 187. Deaconesses, 191. Schisms, 196 n. 3. Contrasted with the Western, 204, 383, 384, 403, 404, 469, 471. In relation to the Roman church, 204-206, 208. Monachism in the, 263-293, 615. Image worship, 330, 331. Sabbath, 333. Passover, 337, 338. Period after Easter, 342. Christmas, 342-346. Epiphany, 342-346. Song, 354 n. 3. In the great dogmatic controversies, 383-386, 471. Interpretation, 388-394. In the Arian controv., 404-466. In the Meletian schism, 458. Doctrine of the Holy Spirit, 466-471; of the person of Christ, 478-504. Nestorian controv., 504, 609. Anthropology, 616-618, 624, 666, 712-722. Doctrine of redemption, 617, 676, 718, 726. Pelagius, 632, 640-648. Sacraments, 722, 726. Last things, 737-739. *Third Period*. Interstitia, iii. 93. Slavery, 99, 100. Hist. of doctrine, 169-233. *Fourth Period*. Hist. of doctrine, iii. 530-551. Relations and controversies with the Western ch., iii. 553-586. Doctrine of the Holy Spirit, iii. 554-557, 585, 586. *Fifth Period*. Labors of R. Lull, iv. 68. Gregory VII. on the, iv. 86, 104. Worship of the host, iv. 341. Efforts for union with the Western church, iv. 536-551 (104). *Sixth Period*. Gerson on the, v. 86, 92. Clemangis, v. 117. Negotiations with, on the subject of union, v. 130, 133. Jerome of Prague, v. 373, 374.
Ebbo, abp. of Rheims, iii. 271, 272, 277, 278.
Ebbo (Eppo), Wendian priest, iii. 326.

Ebedjesu, Nestorian bp., catalogue of ch. writers. i. 681 and n. 5, 682 ; ii. 553 n. 3. Letter to Maris, iv. 46. See Assemani Bibl. Orient. t. iii. P. i.
Eberhard. See Roland.
Eberhard, abp. of Salzburg, mother of, iv. 295.
Eberhard, count, iv. 92 n. 6.
Eberhard of Friuli, iii. 475.
Eberhard of Schönau, iv. 579.
  Contra Catharos, c. 8, iv. 577 nn. 1, 4 ; c. 16, 579 n. 1; c. 19, 578 n. 4; f. 596, 583 n. 6; c. 25, Waldenses (Sabotiers), 609 n. 2. See Bibl. Patr. Lugd. t. xxiv.
Ebersberg, monastery, iii. 471.
Ebionitarum socii, i. 349.
Ebionites, i. 331 and nn. 2, 3, 344–350, 410, 577. See Ebionitism.
Ebionitic gospel according to the Hebrews, i. 708 n. 2. See Apocryphal.
Ebionitism, i. 344–364. Elements possessing affinity with, 364, 365, 675. In Cerinthus, 396, 398, 399. In Basilides, 410, 417. In relation to Montanism, 512. With Justin, 363, 364, 674. Hegesippus, 675.
Ebnerin, Margaret, v. 383 n. 2.
Eboracum (York), archbishopric, iii. 16, 19.
Ebrard (Everard), of Breteul, count, iv. 235.
Ebert, abbot of Schönau.
  Sermo contra Catharos, f. 602, iv. 566 n. 2, 568 n. 2, 577 n. 1; f. 615, 576 n. 4. See Bibl. Patr. Lugd.
Eccard.
  Scriptores rer. Germ. Cod. Bamberg. t. ii. cp. 142 of Gregory VII., iv. 96 n. 4. Ep. 149 of Gregory VII., iv. 117 n. Ep. 162, f. 732, cp. of Henry of Speier against Gregory VII., iv. 92 n. 6, 99 n. 2, 113 n. 1 ; c. 173, f. 194, Clement III., iv. 129 n. 2.
Ecclesiæ, i. 183. Apostolicæ, i. 203, 204 ; ii. 197.
Ecclesiastes.
  4: 10, ii. 282. 7: 29, iv. 492 n. 3. 9: 4, ii. 32. 19, iv. 396.
Ecclesiastical and civil power, limits of, v. 28, 29, 160-162.
Ecclesiastical appointments. See Ecclesiastical offices.
Ecclesiastical elections. Laity participate in, i. 189, 199 ; ii. 185, 186. Freedom of, iii. 93–95, 400.
Ecclesiastical freedom, iii. 49, 368, 369, 411, 507.
Ecclesiastical hours, v. 207.
Ecclesiastical independence in British church, iii. 16, 17. Frankish, iii. 118, 119, 368, 395, 507, 509 and n. 2 ; v. 92.
Ecclesiastical jurisdiction, v. 18.
Ecclesiastical laws, ii. 335 ; iii. 56, 61, 62, 66, 67, 93–95, 305, 346, 351, 361, 364–366, 368, 369, 372, 375, 387, 388 and n. 1, 411, 507, 562, 564, 570, 574, 577, 604 ; iv. 142, 214, 416, 639 ; v. 47, 86, 136, 380. Old and new, conflict of. iii. 346–398, 507, 509 and n. 2 ; iv. 101, 105, 131, 139, 193, 194, 199, 200, 203, 204, 207, 395 ; v. 47, 48, 63, 78, 97, 123. Collections, study of, writings on, iii. 346–351 ; iv. 193, 203–205. Introduction of, iv. 41, 42. Defensor pacis, v. 28, 29. Gerson on, v. 79–83, 97, 107, 108, 353. Spirit and letter, v. 80, 83, 92, 94, 112. At Constance, v. 112. Janow on, v. 205–210 ; predicts their dissolution, v. 207. Huss, v. 264, 265, 324, 325, 346.
Ecclesiastical legislation, ii. 212 ; iii. 95, 96, 305.
Ecclesiastical monarchy and Byzantine despotism, iv. 528.
Ecclesiastical offices, appointment to, iv. 86, 104, 200, 201, 206, 207, 361 ; v. 9, 33, 34, 37, 41, 47, 50, 54, 55, 58, 65, 86, 87, 97, 117, 119, 122, 123, 125, 144. Laity in, ii. 184–186, 472 ; iii. 93, 94, 409, 410, 559, 574, 577 ; v. 58. Among the Waldenses, iv. 314, 616. See Benefices, Elections, Investiture, Simony, Nepotism.
Ecclesiastical reckoning of time, iv. 3.
Ecclesiastical usages, differences in, iii. 15, 17, 23–25, 32, 564. See Easter.
Eccbolius, rhetorician, i. 41.
Echard.
  T. i. f. 162, Albert the Great, iv. 421 n. 1.
Echo, i. 441 n. 2.
Eckart, Master, v. 393–396. Sermons, v. 394 nn. 1–4.
Eckhel.
  Doct. nummorum vet., ii. 13 n. 1. Vol. iii. f. 64, medal of M. Aurelius, i. 116 n. 5. Vol. viii. f. 75, coins of Constantine, ii. 8 and n. 3 : f. 78, the same, ii. 21 n. 3 ; f. 84, col. 2, f. 88, the same, ii. 24 n. 4 ; f. 122, of Magnentius, ii. 33 n. 4.
Eclanum. See Julian of.
Eclectic philosophy, Eclecticism, i. 20, 34, 125, 127, 155, 170, 355–374. Religious, i. 20, 374, 449, 453 ; ii. 7, 16, 21, 163, 768 n. 1. Mongol, iv. 56.
Eclipse, iv. 37.
Ecstasy, i. 181, 356, 511, 513, 514, 519 and n. 2, 520, 673, 680 ; ii. 390 ; iii. 590.
Ecthesis, the, iii. 180, 184–186.
Ecumenical bishop, opposition of Gregory the Great to the title, iii. 115–117.
Ecumenical councils, ii. 164, 182, 209–212 ; iv. 343 n. 1. Authority. iii. 60, 365, 369, 371 n. 2, 555 ; iv. 195, 332, 621 ; v. 17, 27, 50, 54, 63, 76–78, 104, 109, 119, 207. Constitution of, iii. 575. And papal absolutism, iv. 195. Desire for these at the close of the Middle Ages, v. 4, 12, 33, 49, 50, 53, 54, 94. Authority to convoke, v. 76, 79, 80, 82, 85, 86, 96, 99, 107, 108. Gerson on, v. 79–85, 96–100, 107, 108, 353. Militz, v. 179. Janow, v. 207. Proposed constitution of, v. 53. Gerson's definition of, v. 107. Resolution regarding, at the council of Constance, v. 124, 125. See Councils, an. 325 (Nice) ; an. 381 (Constantinople) ; an. 431 (Ephesus) ; an. 451 (Chalcedon) ; an. 553 (Constantinople) ; an.

681 (Constantinople); an. 787 (Nice); an. 869 (Constantinople); an. 1123 (Lateran); an. 1139 (Lateran); an. 1179 (Lateran); an. 1215 (Lateran); an. 1245 (Lyons); an. 1274 (Lyons); an. 1311 (Vienna); an. 1409 (Pisa); an. 1414 (Constance).

Edda, vol. iii. ed. Copenhag. 1828, p. 141, Illustrations, iii. 301 n. 1.

Edessa, Christianity there, i. 80. Very early a church building there, i. 80, 291 n. 3. Bardesanes in, i. 80, 441. Image of Christ at, ii. 331; iii. 201. School there, ii. 610, 611. Pagan temple at, ii. 95 nn. 4, 5, 97 n. 5. Cloister at, ii. 614. Conquest of, iv. 153. See Abraham of, Bar Sudaili, Jacob, Orestes, Rabulas.

Edicts. Of Antoninus Pius, i. 104. Under Marcus Aurelius, i. 104, 105. Of Aurelian, i. 108. Of Decius, i. 131, 132, 135. Of Valerian, i. 139. Of Gallienus, toleration of the Christians, i. 140, 141; ii. 15. Of Diocletian, renewing the persecution, i. 148; another, i. 154, 155. Of Galerius, toleration, i. 156; ii. 2, 9, 12, 17 n. 1, 220. Of Maximin, i. 155; ii. 4 n. 1, 5 n. 1. Of Constantine and Licinius, ii. 14; another, ii. 14-16, 21. Of Licinius, ii. 19. Of Julian, ordering the rebuilding of the temples, ii. 67 n. 1, 80; recalling the bishops from banishment, ii. 71, 72; against Athanasius, ii. 73; on education, ii. 75; Themistius on, ii. 89. Of Honorius (an. 415), ii. 92 n. 3; excluding pagans from places of trust, ii. 102. Of Theodosius, forbidding religious conferences, ii. 157. Of Constans to the Donatists, ii. 229. Of Julian, in favor of the Donatists, ii. 231. Of Theodosius II., against the Nestorian bps., ii. 548; against Nestorius, ii. 552. Of Justinian, against the three chapters, ii. 599-601, 606 (208); on Aphthartodocetism, ii. 609. Of Honorius (?), against the Pelagians, ii. 651. Of Heraclius, the Ecthesis, iii. 180, 184. Of Constans (an. 648), the type, ii. 184, 185. Of Leo the Isaurian, against images, iii. 209, 210, 212. Of Leo the Armenian, iii. 537. Of Manuel Comnenus, on the oath taken by converts from Mohammedanism, iv. 535. See Laws, Rescripts.

Edification, i. 181.

Education, early, i. 694. Christian, ii. 316, 318, 396. Divine, of man, ii. 679. In the cloisters, ii. 288, 296. Sources of, iii. 3, 9, 10, 21, 23, 30, 51, 73, 305; iv. 31, 45, 58, 209. In England, iii. 468, 469. Among the Mongols, iv. 56, 58. Anselm on, iv. 362, 363. Eustathius, iv. 532. Of girls, ii. 316; iv. 584 and n. 4. Of the clergy, ii. 182-184, 298; iii. 126, 152, 206 n. 3, 277, 425, 457, 593; iv. 3, 31, 45, 102 n. 4, 132 n. 4. See Culture, Missions, Schools.

Edward, prince of England, iv. 188.
Edward III., v. 134, 146, 147.
Edwin, king of Northumberland, his conversion and death, iii. 19, 20.
Effeminate civilization, i. 76.
Egbert, abp. of York, iii. 137, 153.
Egbert, bp. of Münster, iv. 79.
Egbert, monk, iii. 43.
Egilo, abbot of Prüm, iii. 497 n. 1.
Egilo, bp. of Sens, iii. 481 n. 2.
Egino, bp. of Schonen, iii. 293.
Ἐγκρατῖται, i. 458 n. 2.
Ἐγκύκλιον of Basiliscus, ii. 585, 586.

Egypt, i. 34 n. 2, 59, 61, 62; ii. 87, 111 n. Gospel in, i. 83, 153. Persecution in, i. 83, 121, 140, 149 n. 1, 155; ii. 124, 193 n. 6. Magical arts in, i. 33, 161, 162. Church interpreters in, i. 303. Medium of revelation to the Greeks, i. 666. Ascetics in, i. 713. Paganism in, ii. 47 n. 4, 96 n. 5, 97, 98, 105 n. 3, 111 n., 117, 124. Periodentai, ii. 193 n. 6. Meletian schism, ii. 196, 252. Monks in, ii. 263-276, 283, 288, 289, 290, 301, 444. Origen with them, ii. 741. In Origenistic disputes, ii. 750-754. Epiphany and Christmas, ii. 346 n. 2. Egyptian theology, ii. 502, 503, 507, 511 (see Alexandrian school). Cyrill's influence in, ii. 512-514. Nestorius banished to, ii. 552-554. Egyptian party in the Robber Synod, ii. 569; at Chalcedon, ii. 578, 579. Power of the bp. of Alexandria, ii. 582, 582 (512). Monophysite controv. in, ii. 583, 589. Monophysites in, ii. 611; iii. 176-178. Conquered by Chosru-Parviz, iii. 84. Under the Mohammedans, iii. 88 and n. 4, 228. Crusaders, Francis of Assisi in, iv. 59, 60 n. 2. Sultan of, iv. 179. See Origen.

Egyptians, gospel of the, i. 83, 458 n. 3, 600, 601.

Ehemann, Studien der Ev. Geistlichkeit, ii. 111 n. 1.

Ehrenberg, on the *Monas prodigiosa*, v. 237 n. 2.

Eichstadt, iii. 386.

Eigil, abbot, life of Sturm, iii. 75 n. 3.

Εἰκών τοῦ θεοῦ, i. 613, 641 n. 2. See Image of God.

Einhardi annales.

An. 757, introduction of the organ into France, iii. 128 n. 4; an. 786, contest between Roman and Frankish ch. singers, iii. 128 nn. 2, 4; an. 796, Tudun, iii. 82 n. 3.

Einsiedeln, monastery (Notre Dame des Eremites), iii. 332.

Εἰρηνάρχαι, i. 100 n. 1.

Εἰρήνη, i. 400.

Eisenmenger.

T. i. Kap. 8, s. 836, אֲסֵרָה זָרָה, i. 354 n. 5.

Ἐκ δύο φύσεων, ἐν δύο φύσεσι, ii. 581 n. 1.

Ἔκδικος, ii. 192. See Defensores.

Ἔκθεσις τῆς πίστεως, iii. 180 and n. 1, 184-186.

El, iv. 553, 555 and n. 1.
Elbe, iii. 323; iv. 18, 34.
Elbert (Albert), master of the school at York, iii. 153.
Elders, i. 184. See Presbyters.
Eleazar, v. 361, 362.
Elect, the, ii. 685, 687; iii. 145, 462, 474, 478, 482-484, 487, 488; iv. 304, 554 n. 2, 615; v. 140, 172, 201, 212, 237, 284, 302, 324, 354. With the Paulicians, iii. 265. With Oliva, iv. 622, 624 With Basilides, i. 411, 414. With the Manicheans, i. 483, 501 and n. 2, 503-505; ii. 770, 771; iii. 245; iv. 304, 579, 581; v. 212. See Predestination.
Electi, i. 483, 501 and n. 2. See Elect.
Election of grace, Ambrose on, ii. 622, 623. Augustin, ii. 627, 630, 631, 690. Prædestinatus, 704. Fulgentius, 711. Felix, iii. 162; iv. 513. With Basilides, i. 414. See Elect, Predestination.
Elections. See Church elections.
Elections, imperial, the pope and iv. 118, 164, 165, 176, 177; v. 23, 24, 43
Elections, papal, iii. 378, 381 n. 2, 387, 395; iv. 85, 92 and n. 6, 144, 167, 168, 177, 188, 214; v. 19, 20, 45, 46, 71, 112, 118-124. Law of Nicholas II. on, iii. 387. Ordinance relating to, iv. 169. Law to hasten, iv. 192. Law suspended, iv. 192, 193. Clemangis on, v. 117. Constitution of the electoral college, iii. 387, 388; at Constance, v. 126.
Elements, with the Manicheans, i. 491, 505.
Elesbaan, Abyssinian king, ii. 145
Eleusinian mysteries, i. 30.
Eleutheropolis, ii. 741.
Eleutherus, bp. of Rome, i. 85, 524, 525 and n. 1, 583.
Elfeg, abp. of Canterbury, iv. 329
Elfric of Malmesbury, iii. 469. Anglo-Saxon grammar, 469 n. 2. Sermons, etc., 469. Translation of Genesis, preface, 469 n. 4. See Usser.
Elias (Elijah), i. 347; iii. 327; v. 134, 200, 201. Spirit of, 177. See Elijah.
Elias, disciple of St. Francis, iv. 275, 291.
Elias, ecclesiastic, iii. 575.
Eligius (St. Eloy), bp. of Noyon, 41, 42. Life of, iii. 41 n. 2. Sermon, iii. 448 n. 3. See D'Achery, Spicileg. t ii.
Elijah, i. 265; ii. 234, 703; iii. 255; iv. 266. Spirit of, v. 183 n. 3. See Elias.
Elipandus, abp. of Toledo, iii. 156-158, 164 nn. 1, 4, 164-168. His controversy with Migetius, 157 n. 1. Whether author of Adoptianism? 156-158 His conduct in this controversy, 164 His letter to Alcuin, 166. On the Romish church, 166 n. 6.
 Ep. to Migetius, in España Sagrada, t. r. ed. ii. Madrid, 1763, f. 514, iii. 165 n. 6; f. 524, iii. 157 n. 1; ep. to Alcuin (Alcuin, opp. ed. Froben. t. i. P. ii. f. 870), 164 nn. 1, 2; (f. 872), 158 n. 1; ep. to Felix (f. 916), 164 n. 2. See Canisius, España Sagrada.

Elisæus, Armenian 1 p.
 Hist. religious wars in Armenia (Eng. trans. by Newman, Lond. 1830), ii. 125 n. 1; ff. 11, 12, proclamation of Mihr Nerseh, i. 489 n. 1, ii. 127 n. 2; f. 14, the Christian Mobed, ii. 125 nn. 3, 4; f. 20, reply of the Christians, ii. 138 nn. 1, 2; f. 22, edict of the Persian king, ii. 128 n. 2; f. 23, objections to the Christians, ii. 127 n. 1, 128 n. 5; f. 30, Jezdegerdes II. on the persecutions, ii. 129 n. 5. 133 n. 1, 111 n. 3; f. 42, Varanes, ii. 136 n. 2.
Elisha, iv. 266; v. 191.
Elizabeth of Hessia, iv. 302.
Elizabeth of Schönau, iv. 217.
Elohim, i. 409.
Elpidius, rhetorician, ii. 771.
Elster, battle on the, iv. 118.
Elvira. See Councils, an. 305.
Elxai, i. 352 n. 1.
Ely, bp. of, v. 136.
Elymas, i. 72.
Em, a Schelstrate. See Schelstrate.
Emanation, in Gnosticism, i. 372-375, 380. With Basilides, i. 400, 401. Valentine, i. 417, 418. Saturnin., i. 455. Marcion, 467. Hermogenes, i. 566. With Origen, i. 568, 589, 621; ii. 403, 405 n. 2, 474. In the doctrine of the Trinity, i. 592; ii. 403, 405 n. 2, 474; with Arius, ii. 410; with Tertullian, i. 605, 684 n. 2; Hieracas, i. 716. In Parsism, ii. 128. Priscillianists, ii. 776 and n. 4. In the Dionysian writings; Scotus Erigena, iii. 461. The sect at Orleans, iii. 594. Catharists, iv. 565, 569.
Embrun (Ebrodunensis), iii. 119 n. 1.
Emendation of Biblical manuscripts, Origen, i. 700, 707. See Bible revision.
Emerita. See Idacius of.
Emeritus, bp. of Xaintes, iii. 94.
Emeritus, Donatist bp., ii. 242, 243 n. 2.
Ἡμεροβαπτισταί, i. 376 n. 3.
Emesa, in Phœnicia, persecution at, ii. 6. Paulus, ii. 346 n. 2. Eusebius, ii. 389.
Emigrations of tribes, ii. 102.
Emma, wife of Canute the Great, iii. 290.
Emmanuel Comnenus. See Comnenus.
Emmaus, i. 709 n. 1.
Emmeran, in Bavaria, iii. 39, 40. Life of, 39 n. 4, 40 n. 1. See Canisius.
Emmeran, St., abbey of, iii. 324.
Emmerich (Henry), Hungarian prince, iii. 334.
Empedocles, ii. 89 n. 2.
Emperors, reverence paid to the, i. 90, 91; iii. 241. Chiefs of the Roman religion, ii. 91. Tertullian on the conversion of the, i. 272 n. 1. Chrysostom and Ambrose on the relation of the Christian emperors to the church, ii. 214. Admitted within the chancel, ii. 321 n. 6. Emperor of Germany in papal elections, iii. 377, 378, 381, 386, 387, 395, 418; iv. 92 and n. 6, 167, 168, 177; Greek emperors in church affairs, ii. 162-166, 414, 585, 596, 597; iii. 212, 537; iv. 533. (See Byzantine, Edicts, Image contro-

versies, Monophysite controv., Nestorian controv., Origenistic disputes, Pontifex Maximus, Rescript, Three Chapters.) Relation to the pope, iv. 138, 139, 161, 163-167, 176, 177, 184, 185. Synods convoked by, iii. 122, 367; v. 85. See Church and State, Elections, Popes, Frederic I., Frederic II., Henry IV.

Empirical tendency, iv. 356, 401, 493.

Employment of the faculties of sense, ii. 277.

Employments. See Occupations.

Emund, king of Sweden, iii. 292.

Encodric, ecclesiastic, iv. 21.

Encratites, i. 456, 458 nn. 2, 3, 505. See Severinus.

Encyclopedia, with the Greeks, i. 701.

End of creation, iv. 466, 490, 508. Of rational beings, iv. 473, 490, 491, 521. Of man, natural and supernatural, iv. 429, 430, 507, 521. Of theological virtues, iv. 523. See Final cause.

End of the world anticipated, iii. 164 n. 3, 470 and n. 2; v. 93. Theodore, ii. 718. See Eschatology.

Endura, iv. 582.

Ἐνέργεια, iii. 182, 183, 192 (ii. 269 n. 3).

Ἐνέργεια δραστική, ii. 438 and n. 3, 439, 479, 480.

Ἐνέργεια θεανδρική, iii. 176, 180, 183, 184 n. 1, 195.

Energumens, i. 201, 309, 310 n. 1; ii. 213 n. 4, 331. Prayer for, ii. 361 n. 2. See Demoniacal.

Engelhardt.
Kirchengeschichtliche Abhandlungen, on Joachim and the Everlasting Gospel, iv. 220 n. 2, 221 n., 619 nn. 1, 3. S. 27, Ascension of Isaiah, ed., iv. 572 n. 1. See Studien u. Kritiken, J. 1828.

England, spread of Christianity among the Britons, i. 85; ii. 146, 632. Conversion of the Anglo-Saxons, iii. 10-23. Revivals of paganism, iii. 18-20. Differences in ecclesiastical usages, iii. 23-25. Missions among the Germans, iii. 29, 43-84. Influence of Boniface on the English church, iii. 69, 70. Education of youth, iii. 73. Patronage, iii. 95. Relation of the English to the Romish church; pilgrimages to Rome, iii. 118. Theological culture, iii. 152-154, 467-469. Books, iii. 151, 152, 156 n. 1. Danes in; Canute, iii. 288, 290, 299. Missions to Denmark, iii. 290. To Sweden, iii. 291, 392. To Norway, iii. 293, 297. Theological culture in the fourth Period; efforts at reform of monastic and clerical orders, iii. 411, 412, 467-469. Guitmund on the conquest of, iii. 529 n. 3. Mathilda, iv. 90. Reform, iv. 91. Struggle between the secular power and the church; à Becket, iv. 141, 169-172; John, iv. 174-176, 178. Crusades, iv. 188 n. 3. Influence of Fulco, iv. 210, 211. Bernard's monks in, iv. 254. Saints in, iv. 329. The immaculate conception, iv. 331, 332 and n. 2. Communion of the sick, iv. 343. Roscelin in, iv. 361. Anselm, iv. 261, 364. Pilgrims from, v. 51. Movements towards reform in, v. 48, 134-173, 240. Speculative element in; practical bent, v. 93, 135, 240. Feudal relations to the pope, v. 136, 147. Parliament, v. 134, 136, 147, 160, 161. Political and religious disturbances, v. 157-159, 160, 161. English at the council of Constance, v. 103, 106, 107, 118 and n. 2, 121, 125, 126. At the trial of Huss, v. 343-346, 363. See Alcuin, Alfred, Augustin, Bacon, Bede, Grosshead.

English language, iii. 21. Instruction in, iii. 468. See Anglo-Saxon.

Enjoyment, spiritual, Ruysbroch on, v. 405-407. Tauler, v. 408, 410. Sensual, v. 408.

Ennodius.
Life of Epiphanius, ii. 192 n. 2; iii. 28 n. 3. (Sirmond. opp. t. i.)

Enoch, v. 200. Book of, i. 535.

Ἕνωσις (τῶν φύσεων, φυσική), ii. 502, 504, 505, 523, 525, 581 n. 1; κατ᾽ ἀξίαν, εὐδοκίαν, ii. 523; καθ᾽ ὑπόστασιν, ii. 525; ὑδροβαφής, iii. 178 n. 1.

Ἐνθουσιασμός, in the Clementines, i. 356.

Ἐνθρονίστικα, ii. 587.

Enthusiasm, of Christians, i. 76, 105, 106, 109. Awakened by preachers of repentance, iv. 209. Of twelfth century, iv. 246. Francis of Assisi; the mendicants, iv. 271, 272, 277. Lull, iv. 426, 427.

Enthusiasts, ii. 277; iii. 604; v. 158. Sect of, iii. 589, 590, 603. See Euchites.

Entychites, i. 454.

Envoys, fraudulent, iv. 47, 51.

Eoban, bp. of Utrecht, iii. 65, 72, 73.

Epnon. See Councils, an. 517.

Eparchius, monk, iii. 104 n. 1.

Ephesians.
Ep. to the, 1:21, v. 303. 2:15, ii. 740, 743
3:10, i. 382 n. 4, iii. 537; v. 25 n. 1. 4:3, 15, v. 324. 4:4, 5, ii. 636. 4:5, 6, i. 318.
4:6, i. 572. 4:9, i. 471. 4:16, iv. 160. 4: 25, ii. 778. 5:2, iii. 161 n. 1. 5:4, i. 262. 5:5, i. 245. 5:5, 6, ii. 636. 5:16, i. 262. 5:19, ii. 355. 5:21, ii. 283 n. 1. 5:27 ii. 244. 6:1, i. 133 n. 4. 6:14, v. 248. 6:18, ii. 302. 6:19, ii. 543 n. 3.

Ephesus, metropolis, i. 79. Ecclesia apostolica, i. 203. Church at, ii. 197. Maximus, ii. 43, 44 n. 1. Chrysostom at, ii. 755. Bps. of, iii. 214, 255. See Councils, an. 431 and 449.

Ephraem Syrus on Bardesanes, i. 441. The soldiers at Sebaste, ii. 19 n. 3.
The Manicheans (see Wegner de Manich. Indulg. pag. 69, seqq.), i. 503 n. 4. Opera syriace et latine, sermo 1, f. 438, seqq. Marcion, i. 462 n. 1. S. 14, f. 408, D., the same, i. 466 n. 2. S. 102, § 6, ff. 551 et 552, the same, i. 471 n. 2; ff. 553 et 555, Pleroma with Bardesanes, i. 442 n. 1. Adv. Haeres. S. 24 (t. ii. ed. Quirin. f. 493), Audius, ii. 706 n. 4.

Epictetus, i. 159.

GENERAL INDEX. 81

Epicureanism, i. 8, 15, 93, 393, 713 n. 1. Of Celsus, i. 162, 168 n. 1.
Epicurus, Julian on, ii. 62.
Epigonius, Patripassian, i. 584 n. 3.
'Επίνοια, Sabellius on, i. 599.
Epiphanes, Gnostic, i. 449-451.
Epiphanius, archdeacon of Cyrill, letter of (Theodoret, opp. t. v. ep. 173), ii. 518 n. 3, 519 n. 2, 541 n. 1. See Lupus.
Epiphanius, bp. of Constantia. His character, ii. 741. His narrowness, 184. In the Origenistic controversy, 747, 748, 753, 757. In Constantinople, 758.
 On interpreters, i. 303 n. 3. The Ebionites, 331 n. 2, 344, 345, 351-353 n. 2, 358 n. 1. Gnostics, 385. Cerinthus, 398, 399. Valentine, 417 n. 3. Basilides, 400. Bardesanes, 441. Cainites, 448. Saturninus, 455 n. 1. Tatian, 458 n. 1. Marcion, 461 n. 1, 462 n. 1, 463 n. 3, 464. Apelles, 475. Mani, 484. Montanus, 513 n. 3, 515 n. 4. Gospel of John, 526 n. Theodotus, 580 and nn. 2, 3. Sabellius, 598-600. Gospel of the Egyptians, 600, 601 n. 1. Ep. of Clement, 659 n. 2. Apostolic constitutions, 660. Origen, 696 n.
 Πρεσβύτιδες, ii. 190 n. 3. Churches in Alexandria, 194. Meletian controversy, 252 n. 1, 254 n. Euchites, 277 n. 7, 280 n. 2. Eustathians, 281 n. 1. Images, 328, 329 n. 2. Dies Stationum, 333 n. 2. Feast of Epiphany, 346 n. 3. Intercession in the Lord's Supper, 368 n. 1. Opponents of Mary, 377 n. 2. Arius, 404 n. 2, 409 nn. 2, 4, 412 n. 2. Athanasius, 426 n. 2, 427 n. Semi-Arian negotiations, 452 n. 2. Audians, 766 n. 3.

Citations from his writings: —
De mensur. et pond. c. 15, flight of the Christians from Jerusalem, i. 343 n. 3.
Ep. ad Theodosium imperator., images, ii. 329 n. 2.
Expositio fidei Catholicæ, Epiphany, ii. 346 n. 3; prayers for the dead, ii. 368 n 1; c. 21, interpreters, i. 303 n. 3; c. 22, fasting on Wednesday and Friday, ii. 333 n. 2.
Hæres. h. 26, §§ 3, 9, Ophites, i. 446 nn. H. 29 (Arian), parishes in Alexandria, ii. 194 n. 2. H. 30, name Ebionite, the, i. 345 n. 1; Ebionitic view of Jesus, i. 351 n. 1; Elxai, i. 352 n. 1; his sources of information, i. 353 n. 2; § 13, gospel of the Hebrews, i. 348 n. 3; § 15, the prophets, i. 358 n. 1; § 16, communion, with the Ebionites, i. 331 n. 2; § 18, the prophets, i. 358 n. 1; § 25, Paul i. 346 n. 5. H. 33, § 3, Ptolemæus, ep. ad Floram, i. 437 n. 4. H. 44, § 2, Apelles, i. 475 n. 3. H. 48, Montanus, Maximilla, i. 515 nn. 1, 4. H. 51, anti-Montanistic views of John's Gospel, i. 526 n. 1; Photinus on the Logos, ii. 482 n. 2. H. 54, Theodotus, i. 580 n. 3. H. 62, Sabellius, i. 596 n. 2, 597 n. 4; gospel of the Egyptians, i. 601 n. 1. H. 64, Origen, i. 696 n. 1. H. 67, Paul of Samosata, the Logos, i. 602 n. 1; Hieracas, i. 713 n. 4. H. 73, Meletian, ii. 252 n. 1, 254 n. 1; Euchites, and the monkish spirit, ii. 277 n. 7; and pantheistic mysticism, i. 28; Athanasius, ii. 429 n. 2, 427 n. 1. H. 73, Sirmian creed, ii. 452 n. 2; inaugural discourse of Meletius, ii. 457 n. 2.

H. 75, Eustathians, ii. 281 n. 1. H. 79, deaconesses, ii. 190 n. 3.

Epiphanius, bp. of Ticinum, ii. 192 n. 2; iii. 28 n. 3.
Epiphany, i. 301, 682 n. 1; ii. 332, 338, 342-344, 346 and n 1, 751; v. 31. As a time of baptism, ii. 360.
Episcopal system, i. 190-193; ii. 171, 188, 193. Office, ii. 124, see Bishops. Succession, ii. 282, 289. Supervision, ii. 243.
Episcopi, in partibus infidelium, iv. 215.
'Επίσκοπος, i. 184, 190. See Bishops, Church offices.
Episcopos episcoporum, i. 214.
Episcopus œcumenicus, iii. 115, 580.
Episcopus regionarius, iii. 48 n. 3, 300 n. 3.
'Επιστήμη, Clement on, i. 541.
Epistles, apostolic, read in churches, i. 303.
Epistola formata, i. 205 and n. 1, 255, 704 n. 3. Communicatoriæ, i. 205. Clericæ, i. 206.
Epistola fundamenti, i. 487, 489, 490, 498, 501.
Epistolæ.
Ecclesiæ Romanæ ad ecclesiam Carthaginiensem (Cypr. ep. 2), acta facientes, i. 132 n. 3; the lapsi, i. 231 n. 5. Confessorum ad Cypr. (Cypr. ep. 26), penance, i. 229 n. 4. Ecclesiæ Smyrnens. (Euseb. l. iv. c. 15), persecution at Smyrna, i. 109 n. 1; relics of Polycarp, i. 335 n. 1. Ecclesiarum Lugd. et Vienn. (Euseb. l. v. c. 1, *seqq.*), the persecution under Marcus Aurelius, i. 112 n. 1, 276 n. 2. Petri ad Jacobum (præfatio Clementinorum), i. 361. Synodi ad Paulum Samosatenum (Mansi conc. i. f. 1034), i. 603 n. 1.

'Επιστολαί κανονικαί, ii. 252 n. 2.
Epochs, of transition, i. 29, 340; iii. 456. Of new outpouring of the Spirit, iv. 293, 621. In the history of the church, v. 246; Joachim, iv. 227, 617; Oliva, iv. 621. Foreseen, v. 178, 185. In the history of doctrine, iv. 497. Of the Papacy, iii. 112, 353; iv. 82, 173. Of the world, i. 69; v. 274. See Periods.
Epulæ Thyestiæ, i. 93 n. 4.
Equality of men, i. 46, 388; iv. 40. In the church, i. 179-181, 212, 603 n. 5. Of communities, i. 202. In Monachism, i. 287. Christian, iv. 40.
Equanimity, i. 10.
Eraclius, presbyter, ii. 694.
Eremites, and the Lord's Supper, v. 227, 228. See Hermits.
Erfurt, bishopric, iii. 55. School there, iii. 305. See Councils, an. 1074.
Eric, king of Sweden, iv. 45. Life of, iv. 45 n. 1.
Erich, king of Sweden, iii. 284.
Erigena. See John Scotus.
Erimbert, iii. 283, 285.
Erlembald, iii. 390 n. 2. Labors in Milan, iii. 398.
Erlich.

Dissertation: De erroribus Pauli Samosat

6

(Lips., 1745), f. 23, fragment of Paul of Samosata, i. 602 n. 2.

Ermeland, bishopric, iv. 45.

Ermenberga, mother of Anselm, iv. 361.

'Ερμηνευταὶ, i. 303 n. 3.

Ernest, abp. of Prague, v. 174, 186.

Ernulph, bp. of Rochester, on the withdrawal of the cup from the laity, iv. 344 nn. 4, 6.

Error, relation of intellectual and moral, i. 22.

Ertenki Mani, i. 488.

'Ησαΐον ἀναβατικόν (ed. Lawrence, Oxon, 1819), ff. 58, 59, v. 32–36, i. 716 n. 2.

Esau, ii. 622 n. 2, 627.

Eschatology, or doctrine of last things, i. 649–656; ii. 718, 730, 736–739; iii. 135, 136, 470 n. 2. Of Mani, i. 500, 501. Jewish, i. 710. Proclus, ii. 105. Abbot Joachim, iv. 222, 225–232, 617. Franciscans, iv. 291. Sect near Cologne, iv. 594. Oliva, iv. 621–626. Dolcino, iv. 634, 635, 637. Intuition of God, John XXII., v. 37, 38. Suso, v. 388. Compare Antichrist, Apocatastasis, End, Heaven, Intermediate state, Intuition of God, Restoration.

Esculapius, i. 73, 92, 145 n. 3; iii. 132. With Julian, ii. 59. Temple at Ægæ, destroyed, ii. 26, 27; at Athens, ii. 105; at Adrotta, ii. 105 n. 3.

Esnig, Armenian bp., on the doctrine of Marcion, i. 463 n. 3, 467 n. 1, 469; iii. 257 n. 4.

F. 72, i. 466 n. 3; f. 74, 468 n. 2, 470 n. 2; f. 75, 473 n. 2. See Illgens Zeitschrift.

Esoteric and exoteric, i. 41 n. 1, 58, 66, 367, 437, 460, 539; ii. 763; iii. 245, 254 n. 2, 267. Doctrines, Catharist, iv. 567, 579.

España Sagrada. See Florez.

Essence, primal, i. 487, 489, 595; ii. 107, 128. Divine, i. 575, 587, 596; ii. 474. Valentine on, i. 418. Enchites, ii. 280. Of the Son of God, ii. 450. Incomprehensibleness, Arius, Eunomius, ii. 445, 450 n. 1. Unity of, in the Trinity, i. 590. Supreme, Eunomius, ii. 448, 449. Of spirit, i. 612. See ὄν, οὐσία.

Essenes, or Essæans, i. 39, 43–49; ii. 263, 273 n. 2. Relation to the Therapeutæ, i. 61, 62, 64 (compare Ebionites, i. 351, 357, 359, 360, and Gnostic sects, i. 396).

Essex, Christianity there, iii. 16. Suppression of it, iii. 18, 19. Unfavorable circumstances, iii. 22 n. 1.

Esthland, history of the conversion of, iv. 38, 40, 41.

Eternal life, v. 68.

Eternity, i. 373 n. 3. And time, iv. 475, 476, 481.

'Ετεροούσιον, ii. 140 n. 5.

Ethelbald, king of Mercia, iii. 69.

Ethelberga, iii. 19.

Ethelbert, king of Kent, iii. 11, 15–18, 22 n.

Ethelwold, bp. of Winchester, iii. 408 n. 1. Promotes the cause of schools, iii. 469.

Etherich, bp. of Arles, iii. 14.

Etherius of Othma, opponent of Adoptianism, iii. 163.

Ethical tendency, one-sided, ii. 767 and n. 3. Ethical character of Mohammedanism, iii. 85. Ethical principles, Huss, v. 346.

Ethics. Christianity and, i. 612. Among the Essenes, i. 47 n. 2. Gnostic, i. 405, 415, 439, 458 (system of Isidore, i. 415). In the later Platonists, i. 379. Christian, ii. 635. In the Pelagian controv, Augustin, ii. 679–684. Of Augustin and Gregory, iii. 148–150. Of Abelard, iv. 386–390, 399. Scholastic, iv. 474, 488, 490, 519–528. See Doctrine, Moral Systems.

Ethiopia, i. 82. Diffusion of Christianity in, i. 83; ii. 140, 141, 143, 145 n. 1; iii. 90 n. 2. Pestilence in, i. 104. Monophysites in, ii. 611, 612. See Auxuma.

Ethiopic, ii. 776 n. 4.

Εὐαγγέλιον διὰ τεσσάρων, Tatian, i. 458 n. 1.

Εὐαγγέλιον κατ' Αἰγυπτίους, i. 83, 458 n. 3, 600, 601. Apud Epiph h. 62, i. 601 n. 1.

Εὐαγγέλιον καθ' Ἑβραίους, i. 361 n. 3, 458 n. 1, 708.

Eucharist, i. 329 and n. 2. See Lord's Supper.

Euchites, ii. 276–281 (276 n. 2), 614 n. 3, 722 and nn. 1, 2; iii. 589, 590, 598, 601; iv. 286 n. 3. *In the third and fourth Periods*, iii. 245 n., 254 n. 3, 264 n. 1, 269 n. 1, 588 nn. 1, 2, 589–591, 592 n. 3; iv. 552 nn. 2, 3, 553, 558 and n. 2, 566. Their origin, iii. 590. Their Dualistic doctrines, iii. 590, 591. Different parties among them, iii. 590. Church psalmody, iii. 598. Sacraments, iii. 595 nn. 3, 4.

Euchrotia, Priscillianist, ii. 774 n. 3.

Endemonism, i. 542; iv. 407, 408.

Eudo, enthusiast, iv. 604 n. 2.

Eudocia, empress, ii. 518, 566, 575, 583.

Eudoxin, empress, ii. 103, 755–760.

Eudoxius, bp. of Antioch, ii. 449, 459. As bp. of Constantinople, 454, 455, 457.

Euelpistus, i. 270.

Euemerus, i. 6, 21.

Eugenius, emperor, ii. 99.

Eugenius, pope, iii. 192, 193.

Eugenius II., pope, iii. 332 n. 1, 551.

Ep. to Urolf, abp. of Lorch, iii. 332 n. 1. See Mansi.

Eugenius (Eugene) III., pope, iv. 152. Takes refuge in France, Bernard and the second crusade, 152–154 n. 4, 157, 256, 257. Returns to Rome, 157. Admonitions of Bernard, 157–160, 197, 199, 202. Arnold, 160, 161 n. 3. Gerhoh, 195 n. 1, 214. Character, 197

Hildegard, 217. Peter Mauritius, 251. Robert Pullein, 408. Council of Rheims, 409, 587. Anselm of Havelberg, 536. Cluniacensians, 608. Ep. to Wibald, 161 nn. 1, 3 (see Marteue et Durand).

Eugenius IV., pope, v. 128-133.

Eugippius, disciple of Severin, iii. 25 n. 3, 26-28 nn.
 Ep. ad Paschasius, iii. 25 n. 3. Life of Severinus, 26 n. 3, 27 nn., 28 nn. 1, 2. (Acta S. Bolland. Jan.)

Eulogius, bp. of Cæsarea, ii. 643.

Eulogius, patriarch of Alexandria, iii. 13 n. 2, 115.

Eulogius of Cordova, abp. of Toledo, iii. 340-343. Life of, 340 n. 2. (Acta S. Mar.)
 Apologeticus martyrum, iii. 343; f. 313, 337 n. 5 Memoriale sanctorum, 335 n. 3. L. i. f. 242, 339 n. 1; f. 245, 340 n. 1; f. 247, 336 n. 1. L. ii. c. 1, 338 n. 2, 339 n. 2; c. 8, 339 n. 3; c. 10, 341 n. 1; c. 13, 341 n. 2; c. 15, 342 n. 1.

Eumenii, Panegyricus Const., ii. 8 n. 2.

Eunapius, ii. 114. The Goths under Valens, 156.
 Excerpta (see Maii collectio), the Goths, ii. 157 n. 1. Vit. Ædesii, demolition of the Temple of Serapis, 98 n. 2; vol. i. f. 23, Constantine and Sopatros, 22 n. 1, 428 n. 1; f. 43, Alexandria, 97 n. 4. Vit. Maximi, vol. i. f. 49, *et seq.*, Julian, 44 n. 1; f. 58, 88 n. 1. V t. Oribasii, 45 u. 3. Vit. Proæresii, vol. i. f. 92, 76 n. 4.

Eunomius, Eunomians, ii. 444-452, 455, 463, 472. Eunomius on the Holy Spirit, 467. Person of Christ, 478, 484. Against Platonism, 387. Encounter with Agapius, 771. Apologia (Confession), 444 n. 3, 447 n. 4, 449 n. 3. See Basil, Valesius.

Eunuchs, i. 703 n. 4. At the court of Constantine, ii. 431, 437.

Euodiæ, i. 119 n. 6.

Euodius of Uzala, doctrine of Mani, i. 490 and n. 6.
 De fide contra Manichæos, c. 4, i. 501 n. 3; c. 10, "Thesaurus" of Mani, 494 n. 1; c. 11, "epistola fundamenti," 490 n. 6; c. 28, the same, 500 n. 3. (Augustin. opp. ed. Ben. vol. viii. app.)

Euodius, prefect, ii. 774.

Euoptius, bp. of Ptolemais, ii. 530.

Euphemia, martyr, ii. 327 n. 1. Church of St., at Chalcedon, ii. 606. Relics of St., iii. 221.

Euphemites, ii. 768 n. 1.

Euphemius, patriarch of Constantinople, ii. 589.

Euphrates, bp. of Cologne, ii. 436 n. 4.

Euphrates, Gnostic, i. 447.

Euphrates, river, ii. 169, 547.

Euprepius, cloister of, ii. 552.

Europe, spread of Christianity in, i. 84-86; ii. 145-160. *Third Period*, iii. 4-84. *Fourth Period*, 271-345. *Fifth Period*, iv. 1-45.

Eusebius, bp. of Armenia, ii. 135.

Eusebius, bp. of Cæsarea in Cappadocia, ii. 186 n. 1.

Eusebius, bp. of Cæsarea in Palestine. Character, ii. 25, 32 n. 2, 411. Doctrinal system, demonstratio evangelica, 411 and n. 1, 412. Position in respect to Arius and the Arian controversy, 411-422. Council of Nice, 415 n., 416-420. Against Eustathius, 422. At the synod of Tyre, 426, 427 n. Against Marcellus, 439, 740 n. 2. School, 417, 450. Plan of conciliation, 416, 417, 450 n. 1. On the Lord's Supper, 735, 736. On the Abgar Uchomo, i. 80. Demetrius of Alexandria, i. 81. Pantænus, i. 82. Persecution of the Christians in Thebais, i. 83 n. 3. Paul's journey to Spain, i. 85. Bruttius on Domitian, i. 96 n. 4. Hadrian's rescript, i. 101 n. 1. Rescript of M. Aurelius, i. 104 n. 1. Philip the Arabian, i. 126 n. 5. Edict of Gallienus, i. 140 n. 2. Marius, the martyr, i. 140. Aurelian, i. 142 n 2. Pagan divination, i. 145 n. 2. Paganism and Christianity, i. 145 n. 3. Diocletian, i. 146. Edict of Constantine, i. 148 n. 1. Edict of Diocletian, i. 148 n. 1, 149 n. 1. The fire at Nicomedia, i. 153. Constantius Chlorus, i. 155. Fragments of Porphyry, i. 171 n. 4. Church offices, i. 201. Images of Christ, i. 292 n. 2. Polycarp's journey to Rome, i. 299 n. 1. Cerinthus, i 396 n. 1. Bardesanes, i. 441, 442. Προπαρασκευὴ εὐαγγελικῆ, i. 442 (171 n. 4). Tatian, i. 457 n. 4, 458 n. 1. Mani, i. 485 n. 1. Montanus, i. 513 n. 3. Letter of the church of Lyons, i. 524, 525. Alexandrian catechists, i. 527. Origen, i. 528 n. 1, 693 n 2, 697 n. 1, 704 n. 3, 710 n. 2. Beryll of Bostra, i. 593 n. 1, 594. Malchion, i. 605 n. 1. Quadratus, i. 661. Apology of Justin Martyr, i. 663 n 2, 664 n. 1, 665. Ἐλεγχος of J. M., i. 666. Death of Justin, i. 671. Apollinaris, i. 677 n. 1. Florinus, i. 680 n. 3. Hippolytus, i. 681. Tertullian, i. 684. Clement, i. 691, 693 n. 1. Ammonius, i. 699 n. 1. Symmachus, i. 708 n. 2. Julius Africanus, i. 709 n. Immortality of the soul, i. 710 n. 3. Death of Origen, i. 711 n. 3. Dionysius, i. 712 n. 1. Methodius, i. 720. Pamphilus, i. 721, 722 and n. 3. Christian benevolence, ii. 5. Discourse of Constantine, ii. 8 n. 1. Translations in Eusebius, from Latin into Greek, ii. 13 n. 2, 14 nn. 1, 2. Licinius, ii. 20 n. 3. Letter of Constantine, ii. 24. Motives of Constantine, ii. 25. False Christians, ii 30. The banquet at Nice, ii. 32 n. 2. Churches among the Saracens, i. 142. Constantine ἐπίσκοπος, ii. 163 and n. 2, 164 n. 1. Meletian schism, ii. 254 n. Image of Christ, ii. 324-326. Constantine's law respecting the observance of Sunday, ii. 336. Constantine on the observance of the Passover, ii. 337 n. 5. Origen's influence, ii. 387, 388. Alexander, ii. 409 n. 4. Origen's περὶ ἀρχῶν, ii. 740. Marcellus, ii. 740 n. 2. Catalogue of ch. fathers, iii. 170.

Citations from his writings:—
Adversus Hieroclen, i. 174.
Comm. in Isaiam, churches among the Germans, i. 142 n. 3. See Montfaucon.
Contra Marcellum, ii. 439 n. 6. L. i. f. 23, Marcellus against Origen, ii. 740 n. 1. L. ii. c. 2, f. 36, words of Marcellus, ii. 439 r 3; f. 44, Christ the firstborn, ii. 480 nn. 1, 3; f. 45, Logos doctrine of M., ii. 480 n. 2; ff. 48, 49, incarnation, ii. 479 n.; ff. 51-53, Logos doctrine of M., ii. 481 nn. 1-3.
De ecclesiast. theolog., ii. 439 n. 6. L. i. c. 8, Son of God, ii. 411 n.; c. 12, the faith necessary to salvation, ii. 412 n. 1; c. 20 (f. 87, ed. Colon.), doctrine of Marcellus of Ancyra, ii. 439 n. 2. L. iii. c. 4, f. 168, the same, ii. 439 nn. 4, 5; c. 12, the Lord's Supper, ii. 726 n. 2.
De martyribus Palæst. cc. 1, 3, 9, i. 154 nn. 1, 3 4; c. 4, study of Scriptures, school of Pamphilus, i. 721 n. 8; c. 10, the Marcionites, persecution, i. 472 n. 4; c. 11, f. 388, Porphyrius, i. 722 n. 1.
Demonstratio. evangelica, l. i. c. 10, f. 39, the Lord's Supper, ii. 736 n. 1. L. iii. f. 134, oracles concerning Christ, i. 172 nn. 3, 4. L. iv. c. 3, Son of God, ii. 411 n. 1.
Ep. ad Alexandrum, ii. 412 and n. 2.
Ep. ad Constantium, on images, ii. 325, 326.
Ep. ad S. Parœciæ hom. (pastoral letter, in Athanas. op. ed. Ben. t. i. l, f. 189), Council of Nice, ii. 415 n.; § 5, ii. 419 and n. 4; § 7, ii. 420 and n. 1; § 10, ii. 420 and n. 2.
Historia eccles. l. i. c. 7, Julius Africanus, on the genealogies in Matt. and Luke, i. 709 n. 1; c. 10, Pantænus, i. 82 n. 5; c. 10, § 2, Paul in Spain, i. 85 n. 3. L. ii. c. 2, Tertullian at Rome, i. 684 n. 1; c. 13, Justin's apologies, i. 665 n. 5, c. 23, James the apostle, i. 675 n. 1. L. iii. c. 1, Thomas in Parthia, i. 80 n. 3; c. 2, Constantine and the sign of the cross, ii. 13 n. 3; c. 5, flight of Christians from Jerusalem, i. 343 n. 3; cc. 19, 20, Hegesippus on Domitian, i. 96 n. 6; c. 28, parish churches, ii. 194 n. 1; Dionysius on Cerinthus, i. 399 n. 3; c. 37, apolog. of Quadratus, i. 661 n. 3. L. iv. c. 3, the same, i. 661 n. 3; c. 6, church at Ælia Capitolina, i. 344 n. 1; c. 11, i. 665 n. 5; c. 13, Methodius and Origen, i. 720 n. 4; c. 15, letter of the ch. at Smyrna, i. 109 n. 1, 335 n. 1, the Marcionites, 472 n. 4; cc. 16 and 17, apologies of Justin Martyr, i. 665 n. 5; c. 22, Hegesippus, i. 676 n. 1; c. 23, benevolence of the Roman bps., i. 204 n. 2; church letters, i. 205 n. 1; c. 26, rescripts of Hadrian, i. 101 n. 1, 102 n. 2; Melito of Sardis, 104 n. 2, 289 n. 3, 676 n. 5; c. 29, Tatian's harmony, i. 458 n. 1; c. 30, Gregory Thaumaturgus, i. 718 n. 2. L. v. c. 1, letter from the churches at Lyons and Vienna, i. 112 n. 1; c. 3, Alcibiades, i. 276 n. 2; the church at Lyons on Montanism, i. 524 n.; c. 5, edict of M. Aurelius, i. 116 n. 1; legio fulminea, 117 n. 1; ep. of Dionysius Alex., i. 321 n. 1; c. 12, Maximus, i. 721 n. 3; c. 13, Rhodon on Marcion, i. 467 n. 1; on Apelles, 474 n. 7; c. 16, Maximilla, i. 515 n. 3; c. 17, Quadratus, i. 661 n. 3; c. 18, Montanus, i. 513 n. 3; c. 20, Irenæus on Polycarp, i. 677 n. 3; c. 21, the Christians under Commodus, i. 118 n. 2; c. 24, ep. of Polycrates, i. 194 n. 1, 298 n. 2; ep. of Irenæus to Victor, i. 215 n. 1, 300 n. 1, 382 n. 2; c. 26, ep. of Irenæus to Florinus, i. 680 n. 3; c. 27, Maximus, i. 721 n. 3; c. 28, divinity of Christ, i. 575 n. 3; Natalis, i. 680 n. 5; Zephyrinus, i. 581 n.; Artemonites, i. 582 n. 2. L. vi. c. 1, persecution in Thebais, i. 83 n. 3, 691 n. 5; c. 6, Origen and Clement,

i. 528 n. 1, 694 n. 1; c. 7, persecution under Septimius Severus, i. 121 n. 1; c. 8, Origen, i. 691 n. 1; c. 9, Hadrian's rescript, i. 101 n. 2; c. 10, Alexandrian school, i. 527 n. 2; c. 11, Clement of Alex., i. 692 n. 1; c. 13, Clement and Pantænus, i. 691 n. 4; c. 14, Origen, i. 693 n. 2, 694 n. 1; c. 15, Origen and Heraclas, i. 700 n. 3; c. 17, Symmachus, i. 708 n. 2; c. 19, O. in Arabia, i. 81 n. 3; Porphyry on interpretation, i. 171 n. 3; lay preaching, i. 197 n. 2; Ammonius and Origen, i. 699 n 1; troubles in Alexandria, i. 703 n. 2; c. 20, Beryll of Bostra, i. 583 n. 1; c. 27, O. and Firmilian, i. 707 n. 5; c. 28, Maximin, i. 126 n. 3; c. 31, Julius Africanus, i. 709 n. 1; c. 32, O. at Athens, i. 710 n. 2; c. 33, doctrine of Beryll, i. 593 n. 1; c. 36, Origen's excommunication, i. 704 n. 3; c. 37, controversy on the resurrection, i. 710 n. 3; c. 39, Origen in prison, i 711 n. 2; c. 41, Dionysius Alex., ep. to Fabius, i. 130 n. 2, 132 n. 4; c. 43, church offices, ep. of Cornelius of Rome, i. 201 n. 2, 228 n. 2, 316 n. 3, 690 n. 1; c. 46, ep. of Novatian to Dionysius, i. 241 n. 2; reply of D., 243 n. 1; number of deacons, ii. 189 n. 3. L. vii. c. 2, death of Origen, i. 711 n. 3; c. 6, Dionysius Alex. on Sabellius, i. 599 n. 2; c. 7, ep. of Dionys. Alex. to Sixtus II., i. 320 n. 5; to Philemon, i. 712 n. 1; c. 8, Dionysius and Novatian, i. 243 n. 1; c. 9, ep. of Dionysius, catechumens, i. 308 n. 5; D. to Sixtus II., i. 321 n. 2, 323 n. 3; c. 10, D. on Valerian, i. 127 n. 2, 137 n. 1; c. 11, D. on his banishment, i. 138 n. 2; c. 12, Marcionites in persecution, i. 472 n. 4; cc. 13, 15, rescript of Gallienus, i. 140 nn. 2, 3; c. 18, pagan images of Christ, etc., i. 292 n. 2; c. 22, the plague at Alexandria, i. 258 n. 1; c. 24, Coracion, i. 653 n. 1; c. 30, synodal letter on Paul of Samosata, i. 602 n. 4, 603 n. 4, 659 n. 3; c. 32, school of Pamphylus, i. 721 n. 7. L. viii. c. 2, edict of Diocletian, i. 148 n. 1; c. 4, Christian soldiers under Galerius, i. 147 n. 3; c. 13, Egyptian martyrs, ii. 254 n.; c. 14, Maxentius, ii. 9 n. 1. L. ix. c. 1, mandate of Sabinus, ii. 3 n. 1; c. 2, petitions against the Christians, ii. 3 n. 2; c. 3, the statue of Jupiter, ii. 4 n. 2; c. 4, Maximin, ii. 5 n. 2; c. 5, acta Pilati, ii. 5 n. 3; c. 6, end of the Diocletian persecution, ii. 6 n.; martyrdom of Peter of Alexandria, ii. 254 n. 1; c. 7, edict of Maximin, ii. 5 n. 1; c. 8, impression made by acts of benevolence, ii. 5 n. 8; c. 9, statue of Constantine at Rome, ii. 13 n. 2. L. x. c. 5, rescript of Licinius and Constantine, ii. 14 nn. 1, 2; c. 6, Donatists, ii. 223 n. 5.
Præparatio evangelica, l. ii. c. 2, conversion of Clement, i. 691 n. 2. L. iii. c. 7, Porphyry on image worship, i. 27 n. 3. L. iv. c. 2, reality of paganism, i. 145 n. 2; c. 7, Porphyry on revelation, i. 31 n. 7; c. 13, Neoplatonic view of prayer, i. 26 n. 1; cc. 21, 22, of demons, i. 28 n. 4. L. v. c. 1, Æsculapius, i. 145 n. 3. L. vi. c. 10, spread of Christianity, i. 80 n. 4; Bardesanes against the power of the stars, i. 442 n. 2. L. vii. c. 8, Philo's defense of the Jews, i. 43 n. 3.
Vita Constantini, l. i. c. 27, conversion of C., ii. 9 nn. 2–4; c. 28, θεοσημία, ii. 12 n. 2; c. 40, statue of C. at Rome, ii. 13 n. 2. c. 44, council of Nice, ii. 164 n. 1; c. 56, C. and the bishops, i. 18 n. 2. L. ii. c. 5, Licinius, ii. 20 n. 3; c. 6, Christians in the provinces of Licinius, ii. 20 n. 1; c. 9, C. and the cross, ii. 21 n. 1; c. 12, inspiration of C., ii. 25 n. 1; c. 19, festivals, ii. 351 n. 1; c. 32, i. 148 n. 1; cc. 44, 45, ordinance against idol-worship, ii. 28 n. 3; c. 49, proclamation of C. to the people of the East, ii. 8 n. 1; c. 53, persecution extends Christianity, ii. 124 n. 1; c. 55, invocation of C., ii. 24 n. 2; c. 56, proclamation of C., ii. 25 nn. 3, 4; cc. 56 and 60, the same, ii. 26 n. 2; c. 58, the belief in one God, ii. 29 n. 2; cc. 64–72, ep. of C. to Alexander and Arius, ii. 414 n. 1; c. 69, the

same, ii 400 n. 4. L. iii. c. 3, emblem exhibited by C., ii. 24 n. 4; c. 4, troubles in Egypt, ii. 414 n. 4; c. 15, banquet at Nice, ii. 32 n. 2; c. 18, observance of the passover, ii. 337 n. 5; c. 21, C. on conversion, ii. 30 n. 1; c. 47, Helena, ii. 7 n. 2; c. 49, C. and religious objects in art, ii. 324 n. 1; c 54, spoils of the temples, ii. 27 n. 3, 28 n. 2; c. 55, demolition of temples, ii. 26 n. 3; 2. 56, the same, ii. 27 n. 1; c. 57, unbelief, ii. 28 n. 1; c. 58, C.'s gifts for the poor, ii. 25 n. 4; c. 60, bishops of the large cities, ii. 186 n. 2. L. iv. c. 9, C. and Sapor 11., ii. 125 n. 5; c. 17, court clergy, private chapels, ii. 109 n. 1; cc. 18, 19, form of prayer required of pagans, ii. 29 n. 1; cc. 19–20, military exercise on Sunday forbidden, ii. 336 n. 3; c. 23, pagan worship forbidden, ii. 28 n. 3; c. 24, C. episcopos, ii. 163 n. 2; cc. 41, 42, accusations against Athanasius, ii. 426 n. 3; c. 48, C. and the bishops, ii. 25 n. 2; c. 54, hypocrisy, ii. 30 n. 2; c. 62, baptism of C., ii. 30 n. 4, 31 nn. 2, 3; app., orat. Const., ii. 8 n. 1.

Eusebius, bp. of Dorylæum, ii. 563, 564, 566 n. 1, 571, 572.

Eusebius, bp. of Emisa, ii. 389.

Eusebius, bp. of Nicomedia, baptizes Constantine, ii. 30. In the Arian controversy, 404 n. 2, 406 n. 1, 410, 415 n. 1, 417 n. 3, 421, 422. Ambition, 433 n. 2.

Eusebius, bp. of Vercelli, ii. 184, 294, 441, 456.

Lib. de Synodis, § 91, Nicene creed, ii. 441 n. 1; Opus. hist. fragment, 1, § 3, his confession of the Nicene creed, ii. 441 n. 2. Lib. 1, ad Constantium. ii. 441 nn. 3, 4.

Eusebius, Christian in Antioch, ii. 84.
Eusebius, court chamberlain, ii. 431.
Eusebius, Egyptian monk, ii. 752.
Eusebius, monk in Syria, ii. 292.
Eusebius, Platonist, ii. 42.
Eusebius, presbyter in Rome, ii. 256 and nn. 2, 3. Life of, 257 nn. 2, 3.
Eusebius Bruno of Angers, iii. 508, 509, 511 and n. 1, 516 and n. 2, 516–518. Ep. to Berengar, iii. 516 and n. 2, 517.
Eustasius, abbot of Luxeuil, among the Bavarians, iii. 38. Among the Warnskians, i. 38 n. 2. Life of, 38 n. 2, 39 n. 1.
Eustathius, abp. of Thessalonica, iv. 529–533, 535.

Comm. on Homer, iv. 530. Discourse to a Stylite, xi. § 7, f. 62, iv. 533 n. 1; f. 186, 532 n. 4; xxii. § 66, f. 193, 532 n. 2. Ep. xix. ad Thessalonicenses, iv. 531 n. 2. Free thinkers, iv. 531 n. 4. Fast sermon. xi. f. 66, iv. 531 n. 5. On the monastic life (o p. ed. Tafel), iv. 529 nn., 530 n. 2, 532 n. 3 Orat. II. in Ps. 48, § 14, f. 10, iv. 532 n 1, 533 n. 4; f. 11, iv. 533 nn. 2, 3. Monodia ch, iv. 531 n. 1.

Eustathius, bp. of Antioch, Eustathians, ii. 389, 416 n. 4, 417 n. 3, 422, 457, 458, 465.

Cited by Theodoret, H. E. i 7, on the council of Nice, ii. 416 n. 4, 417 n. 3.

Eustathius, bp. of Sebaste, Eustathians, ii. 276, 277 n. 3, 280, 281, 379.
Eustachium, letter to, ii. 744.
Eustratius, life of Eutychius, ii. 607 n., 609 n. 1.

Euthymius, monk, ii. 143. Life of, 135 n. 4, 143 n. 3, 276 n. 2.
Euthymius, monk, life of Cyrill, ii. 581 n. 1.
Euthymius, Origenistic monk, ii. 752.
Euthymius Zigabenus, iv. 530. The Bogomiles, iii. 591 n. 2; iv. 558.
Panoplia, iv. 552–558 nn.; c. 23, "Bog milni," iv. 552 n 2. Tract against the Bogomiles, iv. 559 nn. 2, 3. See Gieseler, Tolle.

Eutropius, imperial favorite, ii. 177, 754, 755.
Eutyches, abbot, Eutychians, ii. 541 n., 560 and nn., 561, 563 n. 2, 563–569, 573, 574 n. 1, 575, 580, 582, 589; iii. 34 n. 2.
Eutyches, missionary among the Goths, ii. 150, 155, 156 and n. 1.
Eutychian controversy, ii. 560–583, 589. Entychianism, ii. 588; iii. 179, 215.
Eutychius, patriarch of Alexandria, on the constitution of the Alexandrian church, i. 190 n.
Eutychius, patriarch of Constantinople (καθολικος,, ii. 607 and n., 609 and nn. 1, 3. Life of, ii. 607 n., 609 n. 1.
Euzago, ii. 390.
Eva, i. 498.
Evagrius, church historian, Nestorius, ii. 554 n. 1. Creed of Chalcedon, 581 n. 1.

H. E. i. 7, ep. of Nestorius to the prefect of Thebais, ii. 553 nn. 1, 3; i. 21. φροντιστηρια, 271 n. 4; iii. cc. 5, 9, Acacius, 586 n. 2; c. 14, Zeno's Henoticon, 588 n. 2; iv. c. 2, Amantius and Justin, 591 n. ; c. 27, image of Christ at Edessa, 331 n. 3; c. 38, 596 n. 3; Theodore Ascidas, 598 n.

Evagrius, deacon, ii. 752, 765.
Evangelical counsels, v. 239. See Consilia evangelica.
Evangelical law, the, v. 26, 27.
Evangelical perfection iv. 262, 290; v. 16, 25, 33, 215, 216.
Evangelical poverty, iv. 268, 272, 276, 283, 291, 303, 593, 594, 605, 607, 608, 616, 617, 620, 624, 626; v. 7, 14, 16, 33, 132, 404. Wicklif on, v. 138, 141, 151, 161, 170. Militz on, v. 174. Huss on, v. 268, 269.
Evangelists, the, i. 661 and n. 2; iv. 4, 578 n. 5. See the individuals, Bible.
Evangelium ad Hebræos.

Apud Epiph. h. 30, § 13, and Justin. Dial. c. Tryph. f. 315, i. 348 n. 3; apud Hieron. de vir. illust. c. 3 and in Mcham. 1. 2, c. 7 (t. 6, f. 520), i. 350 nn. 2, 3; apud Orig. in Joann. t. 2, § 6, i. 350 n. 3. See Gospel.

Evangelium æternum, iv. 618. Processus in, 618 n. 1. Introductorius in, 618, 619 n. 1, 620. See Everlasting gospel.
Eve, i. 498; ii. 485; iii. 597 n. 2; iv. 554, 555 n. 1, 573.
Everlasting gospel, the, iv. 618–620; v. 150. See Joachim.
Everstein castle, iv. 33.
Everwin of Steinfeld, letter to Bernard, Catharists near Cologne, iv. 580 nn. 1, 4, 593 and n. 1.
Evidences, iii. 147.

Evil, necessity of, according to the Stoics, i. 16, 106, 611. In Platonism, i. 378. Origen on, i. 630; others. ii. 718, 738; iv. 479, 486, 508. Origin of, in Platonism, Celsus on, i. 163, 168, 611. In Gnosticism, i. 370, 372-375, 392, 401-403, 420-422, 438 n. 4, 566. In Parsism, i. 489, see Individual Gnostics. Christian view, i. 611. Hermogenes, i. 566, 617, 618. Tertullian on, i. 615. Clement, i. 620. Origen, i. 621, 623. Augustin, ii. 397, 625, 638, 661, 662, 666-668, 685. Pelagius, ii. 638, 666-668. Theodore, ii. 715, 718. Gregory on, iii. 144. John Scotus, iii. 461, 465, 466. Gottschalk, iii. 474-476. Rabanus Maurus, iii. 476, 477. Euchites, iii. 590, 591. Scholastics, iv. 474, 475, 477-480. Wicklif on, v. 167, 168. Destruction of, ii. 718, 737 and n. 3 (see Restoration). Occasion of good, ii. 715, 738. God's knowledge of, iv. 575, 576. Limitation of, iv. 576. Negative nature of, iv. 475, 479. Necessity of, iv. 479. Subservient to good, iv. 479, 480, 504, 508. Kingdom of, i. 309. Principle of, iv. 553, 561, 566, 572 (see Demiurge). With the Catharists, iv. 567, 569, 570, 572. Evil and good, ii. 715. With the Gnostics, i. 402, 403, 489. Manicheans, i. 480. See Anthropology, Dualism, Sin, Ὕλη.

Evil spirits, i. 74, 309. With Gnostics, i. 456, 475. Bogomiles on, iv. 557. Catharists, iv. 569, 574, 575. Conflict with, iv. 273; v. 400, 405. Miracles of, v. 239. See Demoniacs.

Evil thoughts, control of, iv. 240. See Monks, temptations of.

Evodius. See Euodius.

Evolution, Neo-Platonic doctrine of, i. 25, 27. Of the conception, i. 391. Of truth, i. 588. Cosmical, with Plotinus, i. 392. Basilides, i. 400, 405. Julian, ii. 50. Marcellus, ii. 439. The Paulicians, iii. 260. Scotus, iii. 461, 466, 488. De Causis, iv. 445. Of ideas, iv. 445. In sin, iv. 517. Of the idea in time, iv. 475, 482. Of doctrine, ii. 749; iii. 536, 537. In justification, iv. 509. Kingdom of God, iv. 617, 621, 622. Good and evil principles, iv. 622.

Exarchs, ii. 196.

Excerptores, ii. 184, 192.

Excitements of the religious consciousness, i. 186.

Excommunication, i. 218; ii. 213-216, 241, 756; iii. 454; iv. 129 n. 4, 132, 219; v. 81. Papal, iii. 373; iv. 102-106, 108-111, 176, 178; v. 18, 146. Gerbert on, iii. 373, 374. Gerson, v. 81. Wicklif on, v. 146, 161. Of Origen, i. 703 and n. 5. Of Huss, v. 272, 294. See Ban.

Exegesis, of Marcion, i. 473. Of Origen, i. 552-557. Hippolytus, i. 682. At Antioch, i. 722. Of the Alexandrian and Antiochian schools, ii. 388-394. See Catenæ, Interpretation.

Exemptions, ii. 169-171; iii. 97, 101, 102. Granted by the pope, iv. 201-203; v. 86.

Exeter (Adscaucester), English convent at, iii. 46.

Exhortations, i. 303. Of Hildegard, iv. 217.

Exile of Christians, i. 133, 135-139. Of Nestorius, ii. 552-554. Of Chrysostom, ii. 761.

Exodus.
10: 27, i. 613 n. 2, 629 n. 3. 28, i. 705 n. 4. 33: 18, i. 558. 34: 20, i. 554. See Commentaries.

Exorcism, exorcists, i. 73, 74, 157, 201, 238, 303 n. 3, 359; ii. 359; iii. 421, 422 n. 2. At baptism, i. 309; ii. 359; with the Gnostics, i. 477 n. 5. Heathen and Christian, i. 73.

Exorcistæ, i. 201.

Ἐξωθούμενοι, ii. 357 n. 4.

Experience and knowledge, iv. 258, 259, 369, 370, 371, 372.

Expiations, ii. 115.

Expositions of Scripture, ii. 734; iii. 52. Of Genesis, ii. 713; iv. 314 n. 1. See Bible exposition, Homilies.

External influences and inward causes, i. 370. External forms, i. 208, 219, 220 332; iii. 351. Religion, ii. 258, 259. Observances, Tauler on, v. 408.

Externalization of religion, iv. 304, 305, 306, 338, 387, 510, 514 n. 5. Opposition to, iv. 575, 577, 578, 596, 636; v. 138, 308. Friends of God on, v. 383, 401, 404, 407, 408. Externalization of the conception of the church in the Theocracy, ii. 178, 179.

Extortions, in behalf of the crusades, iv. 188 and n. 3, 189. Of officials, iv. 212, 213. By the Roman court, iv. 178, 182, 222, 280; v. 21, 52-54, 58, 87, 89, 97. In Germany, v. 101. Council of Constance on, v. 113. Wicklif, v 137.

Extremists, ii. 703.

Ezekiel.
9: 4, ii. 241. 13: 18, iv. 243. 14: 14, iii. 437 18; 20, v. 283. 33, iv. 347. 33: 11, ii. 135, iii. 481.

F.

Fabian, bp. of Rome, his martyrdom, i. 133, 241. Ordination of clinici, i. 238 and n. 2. Origen, i. 702, 704 n. 3.

Fabius Marius Victorinus, ii. 76.

Fabius, bp. of Antioch, i. 130 n. 2, 238 n. 2, 243.

Fabricius.
Edition of Hippolytus, i. 683; vol. 1., engraving of the statue of Hippolytus, 681 n. 4; Christian Druthmar, iii. 458 n. 2; f. 193, Disput. Archelaus and Mani, i. 401 n. 2. See Bibl. eccles., Hermas, Mani.

Facundus of Hermiane, ii. 211, 215, 602–604.
Contr. Mocian. (Sirmond), ii. 600 n. 5; f. 592, D, 602 n. 4; f. 593, C., 603, n. 1; f. 593, E., 595 n. 1; f. 594, A. D., 602 nn. 2, 3; f. 595, 603 n. 6. Pro defensione trium capitulorum, 603 nn. 1, 3. L. iii. c. 4, Theodore, 497 n. 5. L. iv. f. 379 (Sirmond. opp. t. ii. f. 376, ed. Venet 1728), Julian's letter to Photinus, 71 n. 2; f. 389, 78 n. 1; c. 3, 601 n. 2; c. 4, 593 n. 1, 600 nn. 1, 2, 604 n. 1; c. 8, 602 n. 1. L. v. c. 5 (Sir. ii. 407), authority of councils, 211 n. 4. L. viii. f. 460, bps. at Antioch to Proclus, 556 n. 5; c. 3, to Theodosius, 557 n. 1, the Sacra., 557 n. 2; c. 7, f. 483, councils, 211 n. 5. L. xii. c. 4, dogmatism of the emperors, 603 n. 4; c. 5, f. 584, D., his words to Justinian, 215 n. 3, 604 n. 2.

Fairies, tales of, iii. 207 n.

Faith, definitions of, ii. 269 ; i. 414 and n. 3; iii. 174; iv. 432. Foundation of, iii. 2. In Jesus Christ, i. 1, 545–552, 644. Place of faith in Christianity, i. 194, 215, 308, 322. Faith and authority, i. 366, 367, 389, 543, 645 ; ii. 239, 241, 249, 629 ; iv. 392. And miracles, ii. 375; v. 238. And will, iii. 76; v. 201. And conviction, iv. 586. Gift of grace, ii. 630, 689, 711. Cyprian on, i. 210. Clement, i. 308. Simplicius on, ii. 108, 109. Louis IX., iv. 300. Two kinds in Gnosticism, i. 432, 529. Jewish notion of, i. 460, 645. Marcion's, i. 460. Faith and knowledge, ii. 387, 395, 627, 628 ; iii. 174 ; iv. 64. In the Alexandrian school, i. 529–557, 305 n. 1. Origen, i. 544–546, 550. In Gnosticism, i. 366, 367, 450. With Basilides, i. 413–415. In the Clementines, i. 394, 395. With Anthony, ii. 269. Apollinaris, ii. 484, 485. Maximus, iii. 174. John Scotus, iii. 462, 463. Anselm, iv. 367, 369–371. Bernard, iv. 371–373. Abelard, iv. 373–380, 385, 392, 399. Bernard and Abelard, iv. 396, 397. Walter à St. Victor, iv. 381, 382. Hugo à St. Victor, iv. 402–407. Peter of Blois, iv. 415. Alexander of Hales, Bonaventura, Albert the Great, T. Aquinas, Wm. of Paris, R. Bacon, R. Lull, iv. 427–429, 432–435. F. and reason, i. 502; iii. 150, 173; iv. 360, 399, 409, 415, 417, 440. F. and intuition, i. 541. F. and opinion, i. 530, 540 ; iv. 372, 397, 403, 512. F. and light of nature, v. 166. Relation of feelings and knowledge to F., iv. 367, 404–408, 427–429, 432–435. Fides praecedit intellectum, ii. 402 ; iv. 367, 369–371, 379, 435. F. and theology, iv. 519. F. in conflict with skepticism, iv. 324–328.

Christian system of, ii. 659. Proper objects of, i. 1, 545–552, 644 ; iii. 2; iv. 376. Unity of life in (Jovinian), ii. 304 (Ratramnus), iii. 568.

Faith and works, ii. 290 n. 4, 304, 638, 678 ; iii. 83, 442, 459 ; iv. 579 ; v. 212. And morals, ii. 120, 121, 122 ; iii. 148. And love, iv. 44. A virtue, iv. 432, 433, 522. Meritum fidei, v. 238. Dead faith, iii. 442, 459 ; iv. 302, 327, 434, 511, 615.

Faith and salvation, i. 210, 646 ; ii. 638 ; iv. 379, 510, 511. Waldenses on, iv. 615. Faith and life, ii. 678 ; iii. 173, 174. And sacraments, i. 646 ; ii. 120, 636 ; iii. 76, 484. The baptized child, ii. 731. As opus operatum, ii. 636. Justifying, iv. 511. Informis and formata, iv. 304, 511, 512, 519 ; v. 68, 199, 215. False and true, potential and actual, iv. 440. Power of faith, iii. 147. In the pagan world, iv. 379. Of angels, iv. 486.

Fakirs, ii. 291.

Faldera (Wippendorf, Neumünster), a village of the Wends, iv. 34.

Falkenberg, John of, v. 127.

Fall, the, i. 354, 392, 402 n. 3, 445, 456 ; iv. 485, 493–495. Marcion, i. 468. See Sin, Original state.

False prophets, among the Jews, i. 38.

Falsehood, in the ancient world, i. 58, 388. With the Gnostics, i. 388. Gregory on, iii. 150 and n. 2. Isidore, iii. 152 and n. 1. The Paulicians, iii. 266, 267. Christianity and, iii. 267. Nicholas I. on, iii. 357. In the Greek church, iii. 531 ; iv. 530. Theodore Studita, iii. 541 n. 5, 542. Berthold on, iv. 320. The Waldenses, iv. 615. See Dissimulation, Fraus pia, Mendacium, Veracity.

Family, Christianity and the, i. 280. Woman and the, i. 182. Children, i. 257, 311. Images in the, i. 292. Family feuds in Italy, iii. 366. See Marriage, Woman.

Famine, i. 136 ; iii. 308 ; iv. 239.

Fanaticism, Christianity regarded as, i. 173, 175. Heathen, i. 30, 71, 72, 79, 101, 112 ; ii. 2, 6, 8, 70, 72, 81, 97. Christian, i. 109, 143 ; ii. 217, 223, 226, 227, 231, 238, 253. Gnostic, i. 446, 475 (391). Montanistic, i. 510, 513. Monkish, ii. 273, 289, 291–293. Popular, iv. 154, 243, 328 ; v. 380. From religious anxiety, iv. 305, 514. Nilus, iii. 420. Francis, iv. 271. In Spain, iii. 339. In France, iii. 374. Against heretics, iii. 604, 605 ; iv. 643. Against the Jews, iv. 72, 73. Leaders of, v. 158. Fanatical bent among the "Friends of God," v. 398–401. See Circumcelliones, Donatist schism, Meletian schism, Persecution in Spain.

Fåreyinga-Saga (ed. 1833), ff. 321, 322, Faroe Isles, iii. 307 n.

Faroe Islands, spread of Christianity in the, iii. 306, 307.

Fasir, ii. 230.

Fast synods. See Lent synods.

Fasting, Fasts, with the Therapeutæ, i. 61. In Christianity, i. 117, 219, 256, 274, 278, 281, 282, 520, 521, 523, 526 ; ii. 338–340 ; iv. 295, 305, 365, 366 ; v. 81, 207, 266, 305. Substituted for pagan festivals, ii. 351. On the Sabbath and Sunday, see Sabbath, Sunday. On Friday, i. 300; ii. 333; iii. 294; and Thursday, i. 295, and Wednesday, i. 296; ii. 379. Weekly and annual, i. 295. Quadragesimal fast, i. 300; ii. 338–340, 379. In the preparation for baptism, ii. 360 n 3. For the dead, v. 324. By proxy, iii. 139. On particular occasions, i. 256; iii. 284, 355, 519; iv. 28, 85; v. 43, 116. In the newly converted nations, iii. 78, 281, 294, 311; iv. 17. In honor of Christ, iii. 281, 285. Estimates of, i. 278, 300; ii. 291; iii. 440; iv. 91, 262, 306; v. 171, 386. The Montanists, i. 280, 294, 684 n. 2. Ptolemæus on, i. 440. The Euchites, ii. 278. Jovinian, ii. 304–307, 309. Aërius, ii. 379. The Paulicians, iii. 266. Gerhard, iii. 407. Ratherius, iii. 441, 442. Lull, iv. 308, 310. Aquinas, iv. 524. Francis of Assisi, iv. 273. In the sects, iv. 593, 616. Friends of God, v. 284–386. In the Greek church, iii. 557, 567, 581. See Friday.

Fasting and prayer, days of, i. 117 and n. 3, 274, 296. Fasting and alms, i. 256, 274, 278, 281; iii. 281, 285, 442.

Fatalism, i. 106, 441, 442; ii. 684, 704, 719; iv. 305. In Mohammedanism, iii. 85.

Fate, i. 16; iv. 476, 477. Fatality, i. 5.

Father, the, iii. 554; iv. 227–229. In Gnosticism, i. 380. Janow on, v. 208. See Trinity.

Fathers. See Church fathers.

Faucense (Füssen), iii. 37.

Faulfisch, Nicholas of, v. 243, 245 n. 4.

Fauriel.
 Collection des documents inédits sur l'histoire de France; War against the Albigenses, in verse, iv. 639 n. 2, 611 nn. 3–5.

Fausta, wife of Constantine the Great, ii. 31.

Faustinus, Donatist bp. of Hippo, ii. 232.

Faustinus, presbyter, petition of, ii. 256 n. 6.

Faustus, bp. of Rhegium, character and controversy, ii. 296, 702 n. 2, 706–708, 710, 711; iii. 4. Corporeality of the soul, ii. 706 n. 2.
 Ep. ad Leontium, ii. 706 n. 3; De gratia Dei et lib. arbitr., ii. 707 n. 2, 708 nn. 1–3.

Faustus, the Manichean, i. 494 n. 1, 500 n. 3, 501, 502, 503 n. 2; ii. 347 n. 4, 349, 397, 770 n. 4, 771. Fragments, ii. 771 n. 3. See Augustin c. Faustum.

Faviana (Vienna?), iii. 26 n. 2.

Fear, in religion, i. 58. As a motive, ii. 299; iv. 235, 510; v. 383.

Feasts. See Festivals.

Febrnationes, ii. 372 n. 2.

Feeling, religious, iv. 256, 298, 305, 324, 514; v. 387, 392. Predominance of, in the Middle Ages, iv. 324. Repose in, v. 405, 409. Opposed to understanding, iv. 371. Relation to knowledge, iv. 385.

And faith, iv. 403, 404, 429. See Faith. Ruysbroch on, v. 405. Tauler, v. 409–411. Suso, v. 411.

Felicissimus, i. 222, 225, 233–235, 687. See Church schisms.

Felicitas the martyr, i. 123, 124.

Felix, African bp., i. 151.

Felix, bp. of Aptungis, ii. 222, 224, 237.

Felix, bp. of Rome, ii. 256.

Felix III., bp. of Rome. Letters to Acacius and Zeno, ii. 586 n. 3.

Felix, bp. of Urgellis, iii. 156. Probable author of Adoptianism, 158. Whether urged on by the writings of Theodore of Mopsuestin? 158. His defence of Christianity against Mohammedanism, 159. Contends against the confounding together of the predicates of the two natures in Christ, 159. In what sense is Christ called Son of God, and God? 159. Idea of adoption, 160. His appeal to Scripture, 160, 161. Whence, according to him, the ἀντιμεθίστασις τῶν ὀνομάτων? 161 n. 2. Opposed to calling Mary the mother of God; on baptism, 163. Agnoëtism, 163, 168. Character of Felix, 165. He recants at Regensburg and Rome, 165. His defence of himself against Alcuin, 166. His view of the church, 166. Felix in Aix la Chapelle, 167. Placed under the oversight of the archbishop of Lyons, 168. His death and posthumous writing, 168. Influence on Claudius of Turin, 430. His work against Alcuin, 167. Fragments in Alcuin, 167 n. 3. See Adoptianism, Alcuin, espec. A. contra Felicem.

Felix, Numidian bp., i. 150.

Felix de Valois, iv. 267.

Felix the Manichean, i. 504 n. 3. See Augustin, c. Felicem.

Fellowship, Christian, i. 179, 180, 182, 201, 219, 289, 390, 414; ii. 362, 367; iii. 98. Basilides on, i. 414, 416. With Christ, iv. 342, 511. With God, iv. 521.

Feria, i. 296 n. 3.

Fermentarians, iii. 584.

Ferrara, iv. 585.

Ferrieres, monastery, iii. 154, 404 n. 4, 459.

Ferula, ii. 213.

Festival of infants, ii. 347.

Festivals, Jewish, i. 294, 297; iv. 76. See Sabbath, Passover.
 Heathen, i. 91, 301 n. 1; ii. 258, 347, 349, 350; iii. 294; iv. 8, 17, 52. (See Pagan.) Opposition to, i. 301 n. 1; ii. 350, 351. Replaced by Christian, i. 720; ii. 347–351; iii. 15, 294.
 Christian, i. 293–302, 334, 335, 720; ii. 331–352; iii. 133, 134; iv. 52. In the Gentile churches, i. 297. Of Martyrs, i. 334, 335; ii. 155, 328, 351, 352, 369. On the consecration of churches, iii. 15, 134; iv. 22, 23. In the newly converted nations, iii. 315 n. 1, 311.

Observance of, i. 230; ii. 194, 258, 328; iii. 123, 125, 126, 311, 426, 447; iv. 278, 297, 300, 317, 384; v. 224. Chrysostom on, ii. 314, 315, 332. Nicholas I. on, iii. 311. Abuse of, iv. 354, 384. Wicklif on festivals, v. 168, 161. See Lord's Supper.
    Particular festivals, Octava infantium, ii. 341, 342 and n. 2. Ascension, ii. 342. Dies natalis virtutum Domini, ii. 344. New Year's festival; circumcision of Christ, ii. 351; iii. 134; iv. 334; v. 81. St. Stephen's day, ii. 369. Dies natalis Apost. Petri et Pauli, ii. 369; iii. 134. Anniversary of ordination of Roman bp., iii. 113. Presentation of Christ, in the Greek church; Fest. purificationis Mariæ in the Western church, iii. 133, 134. Assumptio Mariæ, iii. 134. Feast of St. Michael, iii. 134. John the Baptist, iii. 134; iv. 68. Natales Andreæ, Remigii, et Martini, iii. 134. All Saints, iii. 134. Olof the thick, iii. 299. Festival of orthodoxy in the Greek church, iii. 549. Immaculate Conception, iv. 331-333. Trinity, iv. 334. Corpus Christi, iv. 341. Innocents, v. 81. See Christmas, Easter, Epiphany, Pentecost.
    Manichean, i. 505. Mohammedan, iv. 52.

Festum fatuorum, follorum, hypodiaconorum, iv. 334; v. 81.

Fetahil, i. 377, 383 n. 1.

Feudal tenure, transferred to the property of the church, iii. 401, 402.

Fideles, ii. 360 n. 1.

Fidus, North African bp., i. 313.

Fifty, sacredness of the number, v. 41.

Fig tree, the barren, v. 152, 153 n. 1.

Filial churches, ii. 194, 195.

Filius major, minor (Catharist), iv. 580.

Fines, iii. 78, 103, 137, 138.

Finni Johannæi.
    Hist. Eccles. Island (t. 1. Hafniæ, 1772) f. 42 note b, sign of the cross, iii. 301 n. 2; f. 68, infanticide, iii. 305 n. 2.

Finns, history of the conversion of, iv. 45.

Fire, ordeal by, iii. 130, 399, 480, 519; iv. 60 n. 2.

Fire, with the Manicheans, i. 500, 501. Euchites, ii. 280. Audians, ii. 767 n. 1. Paulicians, iii. 257. Catharists, iv. 567. Fiery Spirit, i. 501.

Fire-worship, temple, ii. 128, 133 and n. 3; iii. 589 n. 1.

Firmilian of Cæsarea, exorcists, i. 201 n. 3. Against Stephanus of Rome, 216. Church discipline, 220. Symbol, in baptism, 306 n. 4. Baptism of heretics, 320. Advantages of common deliberation, 320. Formula of baptism, 322 n. 4. Consecration of the Lord's Supper, 329 n. 2. Origen, 707.
    Epistola ad Cypr. (Cypr. ep 75), persecutions under Maximin, i. 126 n. 4; exorcists, 201

n. 3; Symbols, 207 n. 1, 220 n. 2, 320 n. 1; Stephanus, the Roman ch., 216 n. 3, 318 n. 4; formula of baptism, 322 n. 4.

First fruits, ii. 107.

Fishing, iii. 30, 34, 35, 36.

Flagellants, v. 412.

Flanders, iv. 245, 343, 380 n. 1, 593; v. 412. See Robert of.

Flattery, v. 75.

Flavian, bp. of Antioch, ii. 174, 175, 280, 465, 754.

Flavian, patriarch of Antioch, ii. 589, 590.

Flavian, patriarch of Constantinople, ii. 562 n. 3, 564-576, 578 n. 4, 579 n. 3, 580.

Flavius Marcellinus, imperial tribuno, ii. 236, 237.

Flavius Vopiscus.
    Saturninus cf. c. 8, i. 102 n. 6. Vita Aureliani, c. 20, 142 n. 1.

Flensburg, ii. 289 n. 2.

Flesh, the, in Christ (Marcellus), ii. 480, 481. See σάρξ. And Spirit (conflict of), ii. 688; iv. 389, 390. Mortification of, iv. 510. Abstinence from, iii. 78.

Fleury, monastery, iii. 268; iv. 141. See Abbo of.

Flodoard.
    History of Rheims, l. iii. c. 29, Hinkmar on image worship, iii. 440 r. 6.

Flora, enthusiast, martyr, iii. 339, 340.

Flora, letter of Ptolemæus to, i. 437 and n. 5, 438 and *Note* on p. 725.

Florbert, abbot, iii. 43 n. 2.

Florence, controversies between clergy and laity, iii. 389 n. 1, 398, 399. Bishops of, iii. 387; iv. 198; v. 111. See Martin, Zabarella.

Florentine province, iii. 419.

Florentines, v. 111.

Florentius, officer of state, ii. 565.

Florentius, priest, ii. 298.

Florentius Pupianus, confessor, letter of Cyprian to, i. 224 n., 236, 237.

Florez.
    España Sagrada of, t. v. (ed. ii. Madrid, 1763), i. 524, ep. of Elipand. to Migetius, iii. 157 n. 1, 166 n. 6. T. xi. (ed. iii. Madrid, 1772), Indiculus Luminosus, see Paulus Alvarus and Samson, abbot of Cordova.

Florinus, false teacher, i. 677, 680.

Floris, monastery, iv. 220.

Florus, police officer, ii. 219.

Florus of Lyons, deacon, iii. 489, 490.
    Against Scotus Erigena, iii. 489, 490; ff. 591, 642, 671, on the divine foreknowledge, 489 nn. 4-6; f. 629, grace in the state of innocence, 490 n. 1; f. 718, on the temper requisite in the study of scripture, 490 n. 2.

Folmar, provost of Traufenstein, on the withdrawal of the cup, iv. 345.

Fondi, v. 46.

Fontaines, iv. 252.

Fontenay, iii. 30.

Fontevraud (Fons Ebraldi), convent of nuns at, iv. 247.

Forbidden fruit, the, ii. 667, 715; iii. 85, 259; iv. 573.
Force, use of, in matters of religion, ii. 234, 235, 247–252; iii. 202, 256; iv. 191, 639, 640. In spreading Christianity, iii. 13 and n. 1, 296–299, 309, 310, 322–324, 330, 334, 335; iv. 1, 11, 12, 14, 31 n. 2, 36, 38, 39. Athanasius on, ii. 36. Nicholas I. on, iii. 309, 310. Lull on, iv. 191. See Augustin, Donatist Schism, Christianity, Church and State, Crusades, Persecutions.
Foreign elements in Christianity, iii. 2. See Judaism, Paganism.
Foreknowledge, in God, Origen on, i. 630. Arius, ii. 448. Theodore of Mopsuestia, ii. 495. Hilary, ii. 622. Ambrose, ii. 624. Augustin, ii. 629. Prosper, ii. 698. Praedestinatus, ii. 704. Gregory the Great, iii. 144. Gottschalk, iii. 474, 475. Maurus, iii. 476. Prudentius, iii. 482. Servatus Lupus, iii. 484. Scotus, iii. 486. Florus, iii. 489. Hinkmar, iii. 492 Schoolmen on, iv. 474–485, 515. Huss, v. 337. See Predestination.
Foreordination, iii. 474, 482, 486, 487, 492. See Predestination.
Forged writings, i. 176, 177; ii. 329 n. 2; iii. 59 and n. 2, 372 n. 1, 411 n. 7. Deeds of Constantine, iii. 122. See Apocryphal, Decretals, Dionysius the Areopagite, Interpolated writings.
Forgiveness, human, ii. 174, 178; iii. 442; iv. 348, 526. Forgiving spirit in martyrs, i. 114. By the priest, iv. 347. By the pope, v. 30, 99. Huss on, v. 283, 284. See Absolution, Asylum, Indulgences.
Forgiveness of sin, divine, foundation of the kingdom of God, i. 324. And repentance, i. 62 n. 2; iii. 442. Presupposes guilt, i. 561. Forgiveness and works, iv. 348. Order of, in the operations of grace, iv. 513. Freedom of, iv. 273, 593. In baptism, i. 316, 647; ii. 726, 728, 729. And absolution, distinguished, iii. 139; iv. 347. And indulgences, iv. 349, 350. In connection with crusades, iv. 126, 130, 132, 153. Basilides on, i. 413. The Montanists, i. 522. Julian, ii. 48. Pelagians on, ii. 677, 678. Waldenses, iv. 615, 616. Erroneous views of, ii. 120. Huss, v. 283, 284. See Baptism, delay of, Justification, Redemption.
Form and matter, in the Scriptures, i. 54.
Formalism. See External, Pharisees, Rites.
Forms, i. 49; ii. 117, 352 n. 1; iii. 2, 169, 351, 459; iv. 231, 232. Of doctrine, iii. 84. Bernard on manifoldness of, iv. 263. Peter of Cluny, iv. 264.
Formula of baptism, i. 306 n. 4, 310, 317, 321 and n. 3, 322; ii. 726. See Baptism, validity of.
Formularies, doctrinal, iii. 493.

Formulas, dogmatic, ii. 259.
Fortification, art of, iv. 37.
Fortitude, iv. 521, 524.
Fortress at Yxküll, iv. 36; and Holm, iv. 37–39.
Fortunatianus, i. 152.
Fortunatius, bp. of Carthage, i. 225 n. 1, 235.
Fortune, temple of, ii. 65.
Fortune-tellers, iii. 449; v. 61.
Fortunius, Donatist bp., ii. 233, 234.
Forum, statue of Constantine in the, ii. 13. Forums, 101.
Forum Julium. See Friuli.
Fosites-land. See Helgoland.
Fossores, ii. 193.
Founders of churches, their influence, iii 109, 110.
Fountain, sacred, iii. 45.
Frähn, Essay of; the Chazars, iii. 315 n. 2.
France, Franks (Gaul). Spread of Christianity thither, i. 84. Constantine in, ii. 8. Julian in, ii. 45, 343. Patrick in, ii. 141. Books, ii. 149 (iii. 152, 156 n. 1, 427; iv. 447, 448). Deaconesses, ii. 191. Monasteries in South France, ii. 147 n. 1, 296, 353. Intercourse with Eastern church, ii. 296, 343; iii. 580. Epiphany, ii. 343. Semi-Pelagianism in, ii. 687, 696, 706 n. 1, 711, 712.

In the third and fourth Periods. Progress of Christianity in, iii. 4–9, 29–34, 37, 38, 40–43. Caesarius, 4 n. 1. Reconsecration of churches, 5 n. 4. Conversion of the Salian Franks, 6–9. Renovation of the church among them, 9, 29–33. Influence of the Franks in spreading the Gospel, 23, 24, 25, 28, 29, 38–42. Monasticism in, 30, 106, 415–420; iv. 237. Education, 30, 73, 152, 154–156. Influence of Boniface, 55, 56, 64, 65, 119 Synods, 56. Impostors, 56 n. 5. Church and state, 91–96. Clergy, 106, 107. Sends, 107. Private chapels, 109. Metropolitan constitution, 111. Love of freedom, 111, 118, 368, 507, 509 (iv. 203), see Sixth Period. Relation of the Frankish church to the pope, 118–122, 242, 352–375, 507, 509 and n. 2 (v. 5. Bible, iii. 126, 426, 427; iv. 320; v. 150). Church Psalmody, 127. Liturgical language, 128. Adoptianist controversy, 165–168. Image worship, 199, 200. 233–243, 428, 429, 551–553, 584 n. 1. Participation in the image controversies, 234–243, 551–553. Harold in, 275. Privileges, 361. Culture, 368, 432, 456, 468, 470, 471. Reformation of clergy, 384 and n. 4. Appointment of bps., 401. Trengae Dei, 407. Reformation of monasticism, 415, 416. Patron saint of, 466, 467. Influence of Berengar in, 515. Chanting the Symbol, 555. Doctrine of the Holy Spirit in, 555. Sects in, 594–600, 603.

In the Fifth Period. Jews in, iv. 75, 76. French bps. and Gregory VII., 92 n. 6. Ordinances of Gregory VII. in, 94, 97 n. 8. Gregory VII. on the condition of, 102. Bps. and Paschalis II., 140 n. 2. Popes in, 144, 145, 152, 153, 157, 168 and n. 2, 183, 197, 203, 220 (v. 57, 58, 232.) Otto of Freisingen, 148 n. 2. Arnold, 147, 148 n. 2, 150. Bernard's influence in, 153, 254, 256. A Becket, 170. Pragmatic sanction, 203. Dialectics in, 237. Norbert, 245. Dominic, 269. Students from, 357, 373. Anselm, 361. Appeals to Rome, 395, 396. Catharists in, 577 n. 5, 583 n. 2, 584, 586, 587 and n. 5, 590. Other sects, 257, 594–626, 639–643. See Fulco.
In the Sixth Period. Colonnas in, v. 5. Spirit of freedom, 5, 21, 48, 63, 77, 92. Friends of God in, 42, 392, 401. Morals, 57, 68. Benedict XIII. 62–70, 77, 118 n. 1. French church, 63, 92, 217. The French at Constance, 103, 106, 107, 118, 119, 126. Flagellants, 412. See Avignon, Boniface VIII., Gallic church, Gaul, Paris.
Francesco Pegna, on the Directorium Inquisitionis, extracts from Chronic. of S. de Adam, on Segarelli, iv. 626 nn. 3, 5, 627 n. 1.
Franche Comté, iii. 30.
Francis of Assisi, history and character, iv. 270–276, 296, 311. Sympathy with nature, i. 484 n 2; iv. 275. Among the Mohammedans, iv. 59, 60 and n. 2. Rule of, 290. Oliva, iv. 620, 621. Dolcino, iv. 634. Festival of, iv. 63. Life, see Bonaventura; Life by Celano, iv. 60 n. 2. Opuscula, ed. Wadding, iv. 275 nn. Wicklif on, v. 171. See Franciscans, Jacob of Vitry.
Francis Zabarellis. See Zabarella.
Franciscan convent, prison of Huss, v. 342, 375. Monastery in London, v. 162.
Franciscans, iv. 49, 57, 73, 229, 268, 311, 420, 424 ; v. 37, 84, 138, 150, 184, 188, 191. Among the Mongols, iv. 50–59. Among the Mohammedans, iv. 59, 60, 65. Suffragans, iv. 215. Orders of, iv. 276, 292. Generals, iv. 291 420, 241. Stricter and milder party, iv. 291, 617 ; v. 24, 36. Scholastics, iv. 420. Heretical, pantheistic tendency ; abbot Joachim, iv. 221 and note, 275, 617–626. Doctrine of grace, iv. 518. Delegates to Constantinople, iv. 540. Attacked, iv. 610. Assemblies of, iv. 620, 621. And Gregory XII., v. 74, 75. Individual, iv. 318, 608; v. 25, 84, 113. See Wadding.
Franciscus de Roye.

De vita Berengarii, f. 48, iii. 516 n. 4.

Frangipani, iv. 128.
Frankfort-on-the-Main. See Councils, an. 794.

Frankish empire, iii. 28, 29, 44, 50 n. 1, 64, 278, 315, 323, 3–9, 351, 456. Opposition of Saxons, iii. 76, 78, 79. Slavonians, iii. 84. Relation to the church, iii. 92. Gregory the Great, iii. 113 n. 1. See Emperors, France.
Frascati (Tusculum), iii. 423, 424 n. 1.
Fraternal kiss. See Kiss.
Fratricelli, iv. 637 n. 1.
Fratres adscripti or conscripti, iv. 238. Fratres domus Sanctæ trinitatis, 268. Fratres mendicantes; minores; ordinis tertii; poenitentes, 276.
Fraudulent collections of alms, iv. 267, 628 n. 1. Fraudulent envoys to general councils, iii. 228, 575; iv. 47, 51.
Fraus pia, ii. 280, 597, 778, 779 ; iii. 54 and n. 2, 150 and n. 2, 266, 267 (309, 310, 311), 350, 407 r. 1, 519, 541 n. 5; iv. 127, 350, 631 ; v. 96.
Fredegis, abbot, τὸ μὴ ὄν, iii. 460. See Baluz.
Frederic, abbot of Monte Cassino (Stephen IX.), iii. 387.
Frederic I., abp. of Cologne, iv. 244, 245, 592 n. 2.
Frederic, burgrave of Nuremberg, v. 342, 351.
Frederic, cardinal, iii. 583.
Frederic I., emperor, iv. 172, 276. Arnold of Brescia, 147 n. 2, 148 n. 1, 161. Contest with the popes, 161–169, 171–173, 203, 214, 220, 582 n. 4. History of, 74 n. 2.
Frederic II., emperor, iv. 422. Contest with the popes, 49, 172, 176–185, 226 and n. 3, 590, 610. Accusations against, 179–182, 325, 418 n. 4. Dante, v. 11. Legend concerning, v. 44.

Ep. 1, to Gregory IX., iv. 183 n. 1. Ep. 2, circular to the princes, 184 nn. 3, 4. Ep. 14, to the cardinals, 183 n. 2. L. i. ep. 20, de Vineis, 177 n. 2. Ep. to king of England (an. 1228), 178 nn. 1–3.

Frederic of Austria, Duke, v. 24, 102, 106, 107, 111.
Frederic of Celle, Cistercian, iv. 39.
Free inquiry and church tradition, iv. 355, 424.
Free Spirit. See Brethren of the.
Free thinking, iv. 531.
Free will. See Freedom, Will.
Freedmen, i. 139.
Freedom, intellectual, iii. 502, 503.
Freedom, moral, doctrine of, i. 324, 611, 614, 618. In the North African church, 614–620. In the Alexandrian school, 620–626, 630. Gnostics on, 373, 374 ; Basilides, 404 ; Bardesanes, 442 ; Hermogenes, 566. Plutarch and Aristotle, 612.
In the second Period. Proclus, ii. 106. Arius, 404, 406–408, 438 n. 4. Apollinaris, 485, 492. Athanasius, 492. Theodore, 494, 714, 718. In the Eastern church, 617. Chrysostom, 719, 720. Consciousness of, 617. In the Western

church, 617; Hilary, 621; Ambrose, 622, 623. In the Pelagian controversy, 661-671, 674, 675, 678, 683-686; Augustin's earlier views of, 626-629; later, 662-668, 678, 683-686 (iii. 472); Pelagius, 638, 645, 646, 669; Jerome, 641; North African church, 650. Relation of grace to, 673, 674, 678, 683-686. In the Semi-Pelagian controversy, 689, 690, 700, 701, 707, 708; Cassian on, 689, 690.

Third and fourth Periods. In the conflict with Mohammedanism, iii. 88. Gregory the Great on, 144, 145. Servatus Lupus, 483, 484. John Scotus, 485, 487, 488. Hinkmar, 492. In the Eastern church, 554. Paulicians, 260, 261.

In the fourth Period. Gregory IX., iv. 76. The Scholastics, iv. 485-487, 515-519. The Catharists, 568, 569. Bernard on formal and material, 516.

Sixth Period. Wicklif on, v. 167, 172. See Predestination.

Freedom, political, i. 46, 268-270; iv. 31, 149, 150, 168, 175. See Bondmen, Liberty, Slavery.

Freedom, religious, in relation to the State, i. 86, 175, 259; in the West, ii. 102; iv. 141, 223, 528. Under Constantius, ii. 441, 442. In relation to external observances; to the hierarchy, i. 280, 512, 521; iii. 49, 118; iv. 195, 203, 208, 231, 289 (see France). Bernard on, iv. 255, 259. Dolcino, iv. 635. Struggles for, v. 1. Philip the Fair on, v. 5. In Italy, v. 24. Conrad on, v. 187. In Prague, v. 265, 266. See Church and State, Emperors, Force, Papacy, Persecutions.

Freher.

Scriptores rerum Bohemicarum, f. 19, Privinna, iii. 316. Methodius, 317 nn. 2, 3.

Freiburg, iv. 421.
Freienwalde, iv. 43.
Freisingen, bishopric, iii. 40, 55. See Otto of.
Fretela, Goth, ii. 159.
Freyr, sun-god in Norway, iii. 294, 302.
Friday, observance of, i. 296, 298, 300, 684 n. 2; ii. 178, 332, 333, 335. 337 and n. 1, 341, 365, 379; iii. 294, 407. Good Friday, i. 300, 337 and n. 1, 341; ii. 341, 352 n. 1, 379; iv. 329.
Frideburg, pious widow, iii. 282.
Fridolin, monk, iii. 37. Life of, 37 n. 3.
Friedland, fortress, iv. 39.
Friedrich, bp., iii. 300.
Friends of God, iv. 552; v. 42, 222 n. 1, 360, 380-412. See Schmidt, Prof.
Frieslanders, planting of Christianity among the, iii. 40, 41, 43-47, 65, 67, 71, 73, 79, 81. Schools, iii. 73. Missionary from, iii. 289. Dodo, iv. 278. Disturbances, iv. 643.
Fritigern, Gothic leader, ii. 156.

Fritzlar, iii. 51, 55. Monastery, iii. 74.
Friuli, iii. 475, 555.
Frobenius (Frobein), Alcuin, iii. 77 n. 6, 155 n. 5.
Frollent, bp. of Senlis, ep. to Berengar, iii. 508 n. 1.
Frundation, iii. 302 note.
Frudegard, monk, iii. 496 and n. 6.
Frugality, iv. 294.
Frumentius, Abyssinian bishop, i. 83; ii. 144.
Fulbert, bp. of Cambray, iii. 405.
Fulbert, bp. of Chartres, iii. 290 n. 1, 470, 597 n. 1. Military service of bishops, 406. His efforts to promote science, 470, 502, 503. Sacraments, 396.

Ep. 1, ad Adeodat, iii. 597 n. 1. Ep. 97, ad Canut., 290 n. 1. Ep., duties of bps., 406 n. 3, 408 n. 1. See Martene et Durand, Thes. Nov. t. i.

Fulcher of Chartres, iv. 126 n. 1. The Crusaders, 129 n. 1.
Fulco, bp. of Amiens, iii. 420.
Fulco, bp. of Toulouse, iv. 270.
Fulco, preacher, iv. 209, 210, 600.
Fulda, monastery, iii. 68 and n. 2, 70, 71, 155, 459, 472, 473, 602. Founded by Sturm, 74, 75. Privileges, 75. In danger from the Saxons. 76. Rabanus Maurus, school at, 457.
Fulgentius (surname of Gottschalk), iii. 474.
Fulgentius, bp. of Ruspe, ii. 709, 711; iii. 5 n. 2, 474.
Fulgentius Ferrandus, ii. 601, 602. "Christian Rules of Life," 601 n. 1.
Fulrad, Frankish court chaplain, iii. 70 and n. 2.
Fundamental doctrines of faith, i. 572; iii. 2, 164, 244.
Funds of monasteries, iii. 414.
Funerals. See Burial.
Fünfkirchen, iii. 334 n. 2.
Füssen, monastery at (Faucense monasterium), iii. 37.

G.

G. of Bergamo, on the Pasagians, iv. 590 n. 7. See Muratori.
Gabriel, the archangel, iii. 134 n. 1.
Gaeta, monastery of Nilus near, iii. 423.
Gain, love of, among the clergy, ii. 766. At Rome, v. 122. See Simony.
Gaiuk, Khan of the Mongols, iv. 51.
Gaius of Corinth, i. 289.
Galano, Clemente.

Conciliat. eccles. Armen. cum. Romana (Rom. 1661), P. ii. f. 405, iii. 589 n. 1.

Galatia, i. 318; ii. 71, 86, 438; iii. 229 n. 3, 251. Julian's letter to the high priest of, ii. 63-65. See Ancyra.
Galatians, ep. to the.

1: 8, iii. 209, 371, v. 27, 28. 1: 10, i. 262. 1: 12, iv. 405. 1: 17, i. 81. 2: 1. 171 n. 1, 319 342, 361 n. 2; ii. 779; iii. 269; iv. 132. 2:

20, ii 392. 3 : 6, iii. 432 n. 1. 3 : E, iii. 262.
3 : 19, i. 382. 3 : 27, i. 138, 256, 321 : iii.
99. 3 : 28, i. 268, 342 iii. 99, 545. 4 : 1. 204,
548. 4 : 4, i. 3, 77 ; ii. 487. 5 : 2, iii. 48.
5 : 12, ii. 301. 5 : 17, ii. 487. 5 : 9, 20, i
499 ; ii. 250. 6 : 2, 5, iii. 437 n. 2. 6 : 6, i.
478 n. 2. 6 : 15, iii. 109.

Galen, physician, i. 164 n. 1, 172 n. 2.

De differentia pulsuum, l. 2, c. 4, i. 164 n. 1.
L 3, c. 3 (ed. Charter, t. viii. f. 68, l. 172 n. 2.

Galerius, Caius Maximianus, Cæsar, i. 144–156; ii. 1, 2, 8, 9, 12, 17 n. 1, 220. Edict of toleration, i. 144 n. 2, 156 n. 1.

Γαλιλαῖοι, of Hegesippus, i. 376 n. 3.

Galileans, epithet applied to Christians, i. 100 n. 4, 159, 502 n. 4.

Galland. See Bibliotheca patrum.

Gallic church, ii. 148 ; iii. 127 ; iv. 395 ; v. 21, 92. See France.

Gallienus, Cæsar, i. 137, 140, 154, 257, 291, 687; ii. 15, 167 n. 1. See Edicts.

Gallus, bp. of Arverna, iii. 93 nn. 2, 3. Life of, 93 n. 2.

Gallus, brother of Julian, ii. 40, 44 and nn. 45, 82. Letter to Julian, 44 nn.

Gallus, Cæsar, i. 136, 258, 711 n. 3.

Gallus, Irish missionary, in Bregenz, iii. 34. Founds St. Gall, 35, 36. Dies in the castle of Arbon, 37. Sermon of, 36 n. 1. Life of, 29 n. 1, 36 n. 2. L. 2, c. 34, penance for homicide, 140 n. 3. See Acta S. (O. B.), S. ii. Pertz.

Gamaliel, i. 40 ; ii. 346 v. 218.

Gambling, iv. 235 n. 2.

Games, i. 472 ; iii. 410 n. 3 ; v. 321. See Sports.

Gangra, ii. 180, 281, 302, 362 ; iii. 383. See Councils, middle of 4th century.

Gap (Vapigensis), iii. 111 n. 1.

Garlands, i. 91.

Garnier, on Eusebius of Doryleum, ii. 563 n. 5.

Garz, iv. 16 n. 1.

Gaston, founder of society of St. Anthony, iv. 266.

Gâtinois, iii. 459.

Gaudentius, bp. of Brescia, ii. 19 n. 3, 91, 353 n. 5.

Serm. 13 (in vet. Brix. episcoporum, opp. Brixæ, 1738, f. 319), ii. 91 n. 2.

Gaudentius, comes, ii. 101 n. 5.

Gaudentius, companion of Adalbert of Prague, iv. 41, 42.

Gaudentius, Donatist bp. of Thamurgade, ii. 238, 243 n. 2, 248.

Gaul, Christianity in, i. 84. Persecution, i. 84, 112–115, 154, 155. Pestilence in, i. 104. Montanism, i 524. Constantine in, ii. 8–10, 223. Julian, ii. 45. Patrick in, ii. 147 and n. 1. Gallia Narbonnensis, ii. 206. Monachis n, ii. 294. Benedictines, ii. 500. Arian controversy, ii. 441. Semi-Pelagianism, ii. 687, 690, 691, 692, 695, 696, 702, 706 and n. 1. Ithacius in, ii. 772. German tribes Christianized there, iii. 1–10. Church customs in, iii. 15. Property

of Roman church in, iii. 113. Relation to Roman church, iii. 118. See France, Gallic church.

Gaunilo, Anselm's opponent, iv. 442, 443. Liber pro insipiente, 442 n. 3.

Ganzbert (Simon), bishop, iii. 277, 280, 281, 283.

Gaza, ii. 95, 103 and n. 1, 271.

Gazzari, Gazzarei, iv. 565.

Gebhard, abp. of Salzburg, iv. 96.

Ep. to Hermann of Metz, defence of Greg. VII., iv. 105 n. 4, 109 n. 3.

Gebhard, bp. of Eichstadt (Victor II.), iii. 386, 387.

Gebuin, bp. of Chalons, iii. 604.

Gedonia, iv. 41 n. 5.

Gegnaesius, head of the Paulicians, iii. 249, 267.

Geiger,

Was hat Mahomed aus dem Judenthum aufgenommen ? S. 100, iii. 86 n. 1.

Geilane, wife of duke Gozbert, iii. 38.

Geisa, Hungarian prince, iii. 331, 333 and nn. 1, 2.

Geiserich, Vandal king, ii. 473.

Geismar, demolition of the oak there, iii. 51.

Gelasius, bp. of Rome, ii. 658, 699 n. 3, 733.

De duobus naturis in Christo (see Bibl. patr., Lugd., t. viii.), ii. 733 n. 1.

Gelasius II., pope, iv. 141, 245.

Geldbussen, iii. 5 n. 2.

Gemblours. See Sigebert.

Gemel-ed-din, Mohammedan scholar, iv. 181 n. 3.

Gemmulus, deacon, iii. 62 n. 3.

Gems, Basilidean, i. 40.

Genealogies of Jesus, i. 709 n.

General assemblies in the Frankish kingdom, iii. 95.

General conceptions. See Conceptions.

General councils. See Ecumenical.

Generals of mendicant orders, iv. 280. See Franciscans, Dominicans.

Generid, pagan general, ii. 102 n. 5.

Genesis, book of, ii. 666; iii. 427; iv. 493. On the creation, i. 672.

Gen. 1 : 3, i. 457. 1 : 26, i. 444 n. 2. 1 : 27, i. 614. See Image of God. 2 and 3 : i. 54 n. 2. 2 : 7, i. 444 n. 3. 2 : 21, 22, i. 56 n. 1. 2 : 24, i. 281 ; ii. 306. 3 : 7, ii. 127 n. 3. 3 : 21, i. 425 n. 3. 11 : i. 51 n. 3. 12 : 3, ii. 393. 14 : 14, i. 658. 17, i. 658. 19, ii. 310. 19 : 9, iii. 347 n. 5. 19 : 26, ii. 310. 31 : 13, i. 397. 33 : 13, ii. 299. 41 : 26, v. 154. 49 : 11, i. 670 n. 1. See Abelard, Expos. in Hexaem. Augustin de Gen. Commentaries, Expositions.

Genesius,

Hist. regg. ed. Lachmann, l. i. p. 26, Leo the Armenian, iii. 532 n. 4. L. iii. p. 71, Theodore, iii. 547 n. 3. L. iv p. 99, life of Iguatius, iii. 558 n.

Genii, i. 377 ; ii. 127. Genius, redeeming, i. 412, 413.

Gennadius, bp. of Lower Hermopolis, ii. 587.

Gennadius, presbyter. Semi-Pelagian, ii. 657; iv. 477. Cœlestius, ii. 639 n. 1. Augustin, ii. 708, 709.

Bachiarius (c. 24), ii. 775 n. 6. De eccles. dogm. c. 21, ii. 708 n. 4. De script. eccles., i. 322 n. 4; c. 15, Commodian, i. 686 n. 3. De viris illust., c. 28, ii. 748 n.; c. 38, ii. 709 n. 1; c. 44, ii. 639 n. 1. De v. Julian Eclan., c. 45, ii. 653 n. 1; c. 59, ii. 655 n. 3.

Genoa, iv. 255; v. 77. Lull at, iv. 65, 69, 70. Genoese fleet, iv. 182, 183. Abp. of, v. 4, 119. Urban VI. at, v. 51. Genoese, v. 73.

Gentianus, v. 110.

Gentile Christians, i. 297, 299, 349. In relation to the Ebionites, 362, 363. In the Clementines, i. 359.

Gentiliacum. See Councils, an. 767.

Genuflectentes, ii. 357.

George, Tartar prince, iv. 58, 59.

George Pachymeres.

Hist. Mich. Paleologi, l. iv. c. 25, iv. 544 n. 1; c. 28, iv. 544 n. 2. L. v. c. 8, title of cardinal, iii. 387 n. 7; c. 12, iv. 545 n. 1; f. 381 n. 2. L. vi. c. 14, iv. 548 nn. (549 n. 1); c. 31, 533 n. 7. Hist. Androniei, l. i. f. 27, iv. 549 n. 2; f. 34, 550 n.; f. 60, 551 nn.

Georgia, Christianity in, ii. 138.

Georgius, bp. of Alexandria, ii. 37 and n. 2, 79, 80, 144, 444.

Georgius, bp. of Laodicea, ii. 451, 452.

Georgius, bp. of Pisidia, iii. 229 n. 3.

Georgius, patriarch of Constantinople, advocates Dyotheletism, iii. 194, 195 n. 2.

Gerald, Count of Aurilly, iii. 444, 445. Life of, 444 n 4. See Odo.

Gerald, papal legate, iii. 516 n. 2, 518.

Gerald of Bordeaux, iv. 583 n. 2.

Gerbert, master of the cathedral school at Rheims, iii. 368, 470. His early life, abbot of Bobbio, 470 n. 2. Abp. of Rheims, 371. The council at Rheims, 369 and n. 1. Stands forth against John XIV., 371–374. Deposed, 374. Otho, iii. 374, 375. Abp. of Ravenna, 374. Pope, 375. Influence, 470. Efforts to promote science, 368, 470 and n. 3. Writings, 501, 502 n. 1. Confession of faith, 371 n. 2. Letters, ed. Du Chesne, 473 n. 3. See Silvester II., Lord's Supper.

Ep. ad Constantinum abbatum, iii. 371 nn. 3, 4. Ep. to Adelaide of France, 374 nn. 2, 3, 5. Ep. to Saguin, 371 nn. 4, 5. Ep. 10, f. 330, interdict, 451 n. 3. Ep. 38, to John XV., 373 n. 1. Ep. 113, pilgrimages to Rome, 153 n. 3. Ep. 152, 373 n. 1. De corpore et Sanguine Domini, 502 n. 1. See Cellot, Du Chesne; Harduin, t. vi.; Mausi Concil.; t. xix.; Pez, t. i.

Gerhard I., abp. of Arras and Cambray, iii. 404 n. 2, 407, 598 n. 2.

Ep. to Adalbero of Laon, iii. 404 n. 2.

Gerhard II., abp. of Arras and Cambray, iii. 599.

Gerhard, bp. of Angouleme, iv. 145.

Gerhard, bp. of Florence (Nicholas II.), iii. 387.

Gerhard, Franciscan, Introductorius in evang. etern., iv. 618, 619.

Gerhard. See Segarelli.

Gerhoh (Geroch), abbot of Reichersberg, iv. 143 n. 5. Wresting of the Scriptures, 98 n. 2. The Crusades, 155, 156. Death of Arnold, 162. Revived religious spirit, 205. Reformation of the clergy, 208. Secular avocations of bps., 214, 215. On love to God, 407, 408. Science and theology, 410.

Citations: —

Arnold of Brescia, iv. 162 n. 2. Comm. in Ps. (see Pez. t. v.), iv. 83 n. 2, 208 n. 1. Ps. x. f. 157, ordinance of Greg. VII. addressed to the laity, iv. 94 n. 2. Ps. 29, f. 630, the ban, 110 n. 1. Ps. 39, f. 792, Bernard; the crusades, 153 n. 4, 155 nn. 2, 3; f. 793, free church elections, 101 n. 3; the crusades, 156 n. 2; f. 794, 86 n. 3; capture of Edessa, 153 n. 1; German sacred song, 155 n. 4, 313 n. 2; revived religious spirit, 205 n. 4. In Ps. f. 895, love to God, 407 n. 5, 408 nn. 1–3. Ps. 64, f. 1181 (see Baluz), 83 n. 2, 195 n. 1; troubles at Rome, 157 n. 6; f. 1182, 151 n. 1; f. 1183, papal sovereignty, 83 n. 2. Ps. 67, f. 1352, canonical rule, 208 n. 4; f. 1353, n. 2. Ps. 72, f. 1479, worldly science in theology, 410 n. 3; f. 2089, his own contests, 208 n. 1. Ps. 133, assembly at Pavia, 168 n. 1.

De aedificio Dei (see Pez), the mingling of spiritual and secular concerns, iv. 183 nn. 1, 3, 214 n. 3. De corr. statu eccles. (expos. Ps. 64) (see Baluz, t. v.), 83 n. 2, 195 n. 1; f. 205, castigatory preachers, 146 n. 1. De gloria et honore fil. hom., c. 13. Folmar, 345 n. 3. De investigat. antichristi (see Gretser), 148 n. 3, 149 n. 2, 162 n. 2. Dialog. de differentia clerici sæc. et reg. (see Pez.), 206 n. 3. Ep. to Alex. III., 215 n. 2. Essay on the confusion between Babylon and Jerusalem, 195 n. 1. Syntagma, de statu eccles. (see Gretser, t. vi.), c. 21, f. 251, Henry V. and Paschalis II., 134 n. 1; c. 22, f. 257, 140 n. 2, 141 n. 1: c. 24, f. 258, 147 n. 1, 163 n. 2; f. 259, 138 n. 3. Letter to Alex. III. (see Pez.), 215 n. 2. On Gregory VII., 100 n. 3. Wresting of the Scriptures, 98 n. 3.

German and English theology, ii. 383 n.

German church, its origin, i. 84; iii. 25 (1, 2), Progress, ii. 146; iii. 25–84, 271; iv. 1–45. Arianism, ii. 472, 706 n. 2. Relation to the Roman, iii. 49. To the Moravian, iii. 316–321. To the Greek, iii. 320. Scriptural tendency, ii. 159, 160; iii. 471. Church psalmody, iii. 242. Culture and its sources, ii. 151, 152; iii. 457, 468, 471. Character of bps., iii. 370, 378, 408; iv. 214, 215, 421. Reformation of clergy, iii. 384; v. 129, 132, 133. Crusades, iv. 153–155. Joachim, iv. 220, 223. Monasticism, iv. 233. Norbert, iv. 245. Immaculate conception, iv. 331. Worship of the host, iv. 341. See Germans, Germany.

German empire, iii. 310, 316, 317, 331. Invasion of Schleswig, iii. 288. See Emperors, Frankish empire.

German knights, iv. 45, 164; v. 127.

German language, iv. 155, 313. See Language, and Sacred Song.

German national bards, iv. 180, 188.

German tribes, Christianity and the, ii. 124, 472, 706 n. 2; iii. 2, 3, 4.
Germanic races, judgment of God, iii. 130.
Germans, attempt to spread the Gospel by force, iv. 38, 41. Bernard's letter to the, iv. 73. Letter of Gregory VII. to the, iv. 114 n. 3, 116 n. 4. Right of electing emperor, iv. 177. At the council of Constance, v. 103, 106, 107, 118 and n. 2, 119-126. Their protest, v. 121-124. Church tendency, v. 235. At the University of Prague, v. 235, 244, 246, 247, 251, 252-255, 258, 274, 347. Emigration of the Germans from Prague, v. 253, 274, 347. Germans in Prague, v. 294, 299. Hostile to Huss, v. 301, 320. Sense of religious need, v. 381 See German Church, Germany.
Germanus, bp. of Adrianople, and patriarch of Constantinople, iv. 543.
Germanus, patriarch of Constantinople, friend of images, iii. 203 and n. 2. Advocates Monotheletism, iii. 203 n. 3. His reasons in favor of image worship, iii. 204, 205. His transactions with Constantine of Naeolia, iii. 205, 206. Resigns his office, iii. 209.

'Ἀντατοδοτικὸς, vindication of Gregory of Nyssa (See Phot. cod. 233), ii. 738 n. 4; iii. 203 n. 2. Discourses in praise of the Virgin, iii. 203 n. 2. Letter to Thomas of Claudiopolis (see Harduin, v. ff. 258, 259), iii. 205 nn., 206 and n. 1.

Germanus, patriarch of Constantinople, letters to Gregory IX. and the cardinals, iv. 539 and n. 2, 540. See Matthew of Paris.
Germany, diffusion of Christianity in. (See German church, German tribes.) Rude state of society, iii. 63 n. 1, 64, 70. Northern Germany, iii. 75, 271. Revival of intellectual life, iii. 471. Otto in, iv. 4. Sacred oaks, iv. 15. Sacred horses, iv. 15 n. 3. Jews in, iv. 73-76. Witchcraft, iv. 91 n. 1. Ordinances of Gregory VII. in, iv. 94. Commotions in, iv. 94, 117. Crusades preached in, iv. 153-155. Papal absolutism, in, iv. 165, 176; v. 23, 24. Papal legates in, iv. 166. Joachim, iv. 220, 223. Norbert in, iv. 245. Bernard's monks in, iv. 254. Students from, iv. 357, 373. Heretics in, iii. 602; iv. 582, 609, 628 n. 1, 643. Inquisition in, iv. 643. Reactions in, v. 42, 43. Friends of God in, v. 42, 380-412. Pilgrims from, v. 51. Cesarini in, v. 129. Tendencies to reform, v. 129, 133, 192, 320, 322, 380. Journey of Huss through, v. 320, 321. Flagellants, v. 412. See German church, Germans, etc., Reformation.
Germs of future development, iii. 84, 470 (530); iv. 228; v. 1. Theological, iv. 376, 497.
Germs of life, in Gnosticism, i. 401, 409, 413, 420, 421, 426, 427, 433, 441, 492. Spiritual seed, i. 444, 445, 455. With the Paulicians, iii. 258, 266, 267. See Seminal principles.
Germs of reformation, v. 202, 240 (302, 318).
Geroch. See Gerhoh.
Γεροκομεία, ii. 169.
Gerold, bp. of Mentz, iii. 66.
Gerontius, prefect of Egypt, ii. 73.
Gerovit, war-god of the Pommeranians, iv. 21.
Gerson, chancellor of the university of Paris, v. 53, 63. His principles of reform, 78-83, 84. His discourse before the council of Pisa, 85-87, 119. On union with the Greek church, 86, 92, 374. Before the king of France, 91-93. "De modis uniendi," 94-100. Discourse before the council of Constance, 107, 108. Right of appeal from the pope, 127, 128. On the troubles in Bohemia, 316, 352, 353 n. 1. Huss and, 345, 352, 353. Jerome of Prague, Wicklif, 372, 375, 376. Feeling in religion, 405.

Citations:—
Acta in conc. Const. circa damnat. Joann. Parvi (opp. ed. Du Pin, 1706), v. 330 n. 5. De difficultate reformationis, 94 n. 1. De modis uniendi, 94 n. 2, 95-99 nn., 100 n. 1. De unitate eccles., 82 n. 2. Ep. to Conrad of Vechta. (see Boulaeus), 353 n. 1. Opp. t. ii. f. 901, D'Ailly ou Huss " de ecclesia," 299 n. Orat. coram conc. Const. (see V. d. Hardt), 107 n. 2, 108 n. 1. Propositiones (opp. ed. Du Pin. Antw. 1706 t. ii. ff. 112, 113), 79 nn., 80. Quatuor considerationes, p. 119 A., 83 n. 1. Rememoratio, f. 109, 82 n. 1. Sermo coram Alexandro, etc. (f. 131). 85 n. 2, 85-87. Sermo coram rege (opp. t. ii.), 92 nn., 93 nn. Tractatus, quomodo et an liceat a summo pontifice appellare, etc. (opp. t. ii. f. 303), 127 n. On feeling in religion, 405 n. 2.

Gervin, abbot of Centulum, iii. 419. Life of, 420 nn. 2, 3.
Gesenius.

In the Jenaischen Literatur Zeitung, J. 1817, Nos. 48-51, on the Liber Adami, i. 376 n. 2.

Gesta de nomine Acacii. (See Sirmond), ii. 563 n. 5.
Gesta Dei per Francos. See Bougars.
Gesta ecclesiastica, ii. 185, 192.
Gesta ecclesiastica Augustini, ii. 171 n. 3.
Gesta Trevirorum (ed. Wyttenbach et Mueller, vol. 1, p. 164, 1836), ep. of Henry IV. to Dieteric of Verdun, iv. 120 nn. 2, 3. (Ed. Augustæ Trevirorum, 1836, vol. 1, c. 104, p. 319) Waldenses, iv. 609 n. 5. (c. 104, 105) Conrad of Marburg, iv. 643 n. 2.
Geta, i. 124.
Geusa, king of Hungary, iv. 88 and n. 2.
Gheerbald, bp. of Liege, pastoral letter of, iii. 125 n. 2.
Ghent (Gandavum), iii. 40, 43 n 2; iv 418 n. 3.
Ghibellines, v. 3, 4, 11, 24, 36, 412.

Ghosts, fear of, iii. 408 n. 3.
Gibbon, on Constantine, ii. 7 and n. 1.
Gideon, iv. 39.
Gieseler.
  On the edict of Aurelian, i. 108 n. 3. Slaves as informers, i. 118 n. 2. Irenæus on the Roman church, i. 204 n. 3. Alcuin and the Libri Carolini, iii. 235 n. 4. Essay on the Paulicians, iii. 244 n. 3, 246 n. 1, 256 nn. 2, 4, 263 n. 4, 264 n. 6, 266 n. 1, 269 n. 4. The council of Paris, iii. 509 n. 4. Heretics in Sardinia, 693 n. 2. Sententiæ Abælardi, iv. 393 n. 1. Panoplia of Euthymius, c. 23, iv. 552 nn. 2, 3; pp. 7, 33, 35, iv. 553 nn. 2, 3. Kirchengeschichte, Bd. ii. s. 187, Law of Papal elections, iii. 388 n. 1. s. 436 (2d ed.) festum follorum, etc., iv. 334 n. 3. On the Ebionites (see Archiv. für Kirchengeschichte, Bd. iv.), i. 346 n. 1. See Studien u. Kritiken.
Gift of teaching, i. 186, 187, 188.
Gift of tears, iv. 306, 533.
Gift of tongues, i. 186 n. 2; iii. 147.
Gifts of grace, ii. 630, 682; iii. 147, 173; iv. 511. See Charismata, Grace, Prophecy, Seven Spiritual, iv. 522.
Gifts to churches, etc., ii. 109, 319, 320, 367 and n. 4; iii. 9, 101, 433, 452; iv. 45, 122, 300, 302. Memorial, ii. 368. To the Roman church, iii. 120, 122. To monasteries, iv. 264, 265, 300, 302, 529. See Mendicants, Presents.
Gilbert, abbot of Westminster (Gislebert), iv. 78. Disputat. Judæi cum Christiano, 78 n. 1.
Gilbert de la Porée (bp. of Poictiers), ii. 614; iv. 408, 409, 410, 461, 462.
  Comm. on Boethius de Trinitate, iv. 409 n. 1, 461 n. 5, 462 nn. 1-3.
Gildas, presbyter, De excidio Britanniæ, the Anglo-Saxons, iii. 10 n. 4, 11 n. 1. On asceticism, 21 n. 1.
Girls, schools for, iii. 427 n. 2.
Gisela, wife of Stephen of Hungary, iii. 333 n. 2, 334.
Gislemar, monk, iii. 276.
Gissur, iii. 302-305.
Glaber Rudolph.
  History of his times (see Du Chesne). Benedict IX., iii. 375 n. 4. Gregory VI., 377 n. 1. L. ii c. 12, Hilgard, 602 n. 3; Paganism in Sardinia, 663 n. 2. L. iii. c. 4, zeal for church building, 470 n. 3; c. 8, sect at Orleans, 593 n. 2, 594 and n. 1, 595 n. 5, 596 n. L. iv. c. 1, Wm of Dijon and John XIX., 580 n. 1; c. 2, sect in Montfort, 6 0 n. 3; c. 3, pretended relics, 446 n. 1; c. 5, proposals for universal peace, 407 nn. 1, 2; truces of God, n. 3; boy bishops, 409 n. 1; c. 6, pilgrimages to Jerusalem, 470 n. 2.
Gladiatorial contests, i. 30, 263.
Gladiators, i. 10.
Glaucias, i. 417 n. 1.
Glory of God as motive, ii. 682; v. 392, 404.
Glossa ordinaria, iii. 458.
Gluttony, iii. 138, 442.
Gnesen, archbishopric, iii. 330; iv. 6. Abp. of, and Prussian missions, iv. 43 n. 1, 43-45. Bull of Greg. XI., v. 182.
Gnomes of Sextus, i. 697 n 2; ii. 288.

Γνωσίμαχοι, ii. 767.
Gnosis, i. 181, 208, 305 n. 1, 308. Ante-Christian, i. 447. Ebionite, i. 352. Of the Gnostics, i. 366-396. Jewish, i. 476; Alexandrian, i. 66, 83. Christian, 305 n 1, 352, 528-557. With Paul, i. 510. Clement, i. 530-544, 692. Origen, i. 543-557, 622, 643, 701. With Augustin, ii. 395. See Faith, Knowledge.
Gnostic elements in Priscillianism, ii. 776 and n. 4. Maximus, iii. 173. In Paulicianism, iii. 244-248, 251-263, 266, 267, 268, 269 n. 6. 270, 588 n. 2. In the Sect at Orleans, iii. 594. Bogomiles, iv. 553, 556. Catharists, iv. 565, 567, 568. In the Koran, iii. 86 n. 1.
Gnostic systems. See Gnosticism.
Gnosticism, general character of, i. 365-374. Speculative element in, 368-377. Practical spirit, 377-380, 385, 386. Alexandrian and Syrian, 374-378. Classification of Gnostic systems, 379-387, 394-396. Interpretation and secret doctrines, 387-389. Position towards the church, 389, 390. Particular sects attaching themselves to Judaism, 396-442. Anti-Jewish, 394, 395, 442-476, 556; iii. 245. Opposition to, i. 340, 361, 390-394, 670, 674, 676; ii. 380, 408; iv. 593. Attitude of science within the church toward, i. 506-509, 564, 565. 620. Gnosticism and Parsism, i. 369, 374, 376, 378; ii. 128 (see Parsism). And Protestantism, i. 367 n. 1. And Christianity, i. 363, 366-368, 379, 381-391, 411, 478, 506-509. And Manicheism, i. 478, 506 n. 1; iii. 244. And Montanism, i. 509, 511, 526. And the Alexandrian school, i. 529, 530. And Chiliasm, i. 651, 654. Doctrine of Redemption (see Redemption). Of Resurrection, i. 655. Ethics of, i. 631 (384-386) (see Antinomian). Hades, i. 653, 654. Porphyry and, i. 170. Hermogenes and, i. 564-566. Origen, i. 588, 589, 591, 622, 627, 695, 700, 703 n. 3, 704, 706. Clement, i. 622. Florinus, i. 680 n. 3. Tertullian, i. 684 n. 2. Jerome, ii. 391. Theodore, ii. 713. See Person of Christ.
Γνωστικοί, i. 381. See Gnostics.
Gnostics, i. 78, 103, 203, 263, 317, 351, 353, 355, 364, 365-478, 514, 529, 645; ii. 276 n. 2, 392, 768; v. 399. Christmas with the, i. 302. Baptism, i. 323; iv. 556.
Goar, hermit, iii. 28.
Gobarus, Stephen (in Photius, cod. 235), i. 675; iv. 390.
Gobat, S., Journal in Abyssinia, i. 83 n. 6.
Gobelinus, Persona.
  (Cosmodrom, in Meibom. rer. germ., t. i.), f. 339-341, v. 109 n. 2, 110 n. 1, 111 n. 3, 126 n. 2.
God, doctrine concerning, 557-610; ii. 403-473; iii. 461-466, 486, 488, 489;

iv. 440-466. Idea of God in Deism, i. 8. Strabo on the, i. 9. In Stoicism, i. 10, 16. In Platonism, i. 18, 25. Neo Platonism, i. 22, 23, 25-27. In Judaism, i. 9, 22, 35. Sadducees, i. 42. In the Alexandrian philosophy of religion, i. 57. Christian idea, i. 137, 291. Doctrine of Celsus, i. 163. Gnostic, i. 372, 373, 379-384. (Basilides, 405-407, 409-411. Valentine, 418, 419. Marcion, 462, 464. 466-472, 562. The Supreme, see Supreme Essence. Personality of, 406, 571. Hidden, 400, 423) With Mani, i. 489-491. Unworthy ideas of, i. 463. Constantine's invocation, ii. 23. Views of Julian, ii. 57, 58. Mohammed, iii. 85. The Paulicians, iii. 257-261. Pantheistic views of, v. 392-396. Ruysbroch, v. 396, 398, 403. Tauler, v. 410, 411. See Clement, Tertullian, Origen, Theophilus of Antioch, Marcion, Irenæus, Novatian, Alexandrian School.

God as an object of knowledge, i. 25, 78, 400, 558, 559; ii. 117; iii. 461-464; iv. 20, 66, 69, 312, 402-404, 411-413, 435-438, 443, 514. Universal consciousness of God, i. 177, 178, 537-550; ii. 654; iii. 267, 304 n. 1; iv. 443. The Ontological proof, iv. 368 and n. 2, 440-442. The unknown, i. 106; iv. 20. Self-manifestation, i. 57; iii. 461, 462, 464. Attributes of God, i. 560; iii. 464, 489; iv. 450-457. Spiritual nature of, i. 560 (676). Incomprehensibility, i. 558; ii. 445-447; iii. 461-464, 486, 488; iv. 438. Different senses of the name God, iv. 462. First cause, ii. 448; iv. 449, 466, 478, 480, 481 (see Creation). Continuous agency, i. 568, 569; i. 665. Omnipresence, i. 558; iv. 450-452. Omniscience, iv. 478 (see Foreknowledge, Knowledge, Wisdom). Eternity, ii. 474, 475; iv. 452; v. 168. Omnipotence, i. 568, 570, 571; ii. 698 n. 2; iv. 452-457, 459; v. 152, 167, 372. Immutability, i. 568, 569; ii. 474, 475, 561 and n. 3; iii. 473, 474, 482; iv. 451, 453. Indivisible essence, iv. 462 n. 4. Sovereignty, i. 567; iv. 477 (see Predestination). Goodness, i. 561, 562, 564. Anger, i. 563; iv. 501. Condescension, i. 562. See Justice, Holiness, Logos. Love, Trinity,

Relation of the creation to, i. 559; ii. 663-666; iv. 275, 472, 473, 477-485. Of the rational creatures to, i. 622, 623; iv. 443, 450-452, 473, 485-487, 490. Of man to, i. 559, 623, 629; ii. 625, 662-664; iv. 443, 485-492; v. 396-401, 408 -410 (see Likeness). The indwelling, ii. 499-501, 503. Communion with, ii. 714, 719, 724, 738; iv. 491 (see Contemplation). Longing for, iv. 310. Life in, v. 383, 392, 396, 397, 398, 402, 411. Reconciliation with, iv. 497, 505. See Creation, Likeness, Predestination, Redemption.

Images of, iii. 204, 207, 237. Image of God, see Image.
Goda, iii. 304 n. 2.
Godalsacius, iii. 62 n. 5.
Godehard, bp. of Hildesheim, iii. 408, 413 n. 6, 446 n. 1. See Acta S. May.
Godfathers and godmothers, iii. 53, 61.
Godfrid, duke. iii. 383 n. 4.
Godlike, the, in Gnosticism, i. 422, 426, 428. With Mani, i 497. Clement, i. 530. Tertullian, i. 615, 616.
God-man, the, ii. 51, 485, 486, 489, 492, 495, 513. See Person of Christ.
Godofredus on Libanius, ii. 95 nn. 1, 5.
Gods, pagan, appearances of the, i. 12, 106; ii. 106. Anger of, i. 12, 22. Mecænas on, i. 87. Marcus Aurelius, i. 106. Celsus, i. 163. Basilides, i. 409. Valentine, i. 427. In Buddhism, i. 496 n. 2. Regarded as n alignant spirits, i. 427; ii. 14, 21, 24. Appeals of Licinius to the, ii. 20. Images dismantled, ii. 27 (see Images). Gods of the nations, i. 163, 383, 427; ii. 51, 54, 107. Julian and the, ii. 50, 54, 58, 65, 68, 80, 87. Simplicius on the, ii. 107, 108. Forsaken, ii. 114. Exalted spirits as gods, Origen, i. 587.
Goetæ, i. 30, 33, 67, 161. See Magicians.
Γοητεία, i. 34 n. 1.
Gog and Magog. Druthmar on, iii. 458 n. 2. Militz, v. 179.
Goisfred, iv. 294.
Goldast.
Apolog. of Waltram, iv. 98 n. 1. Letter of Alboin, iv. 100 n. 2. Monarchia sacri imperii, t. 2, bull of Boniface VIII., v. 13 n. 2; John of Paris, de potest. reg. et papali, v. 15 n.; f. 246, Defensor Pacis, v. 25 n. 1; f. 391, Wm. Occam, Octo Questiones, 38 n. 2; f. 402, "Dialogue " of Occam, 40 n. 6.
Golden age, i. 12, 65, 177; ii. 347.
Golden calves, the, v. 191.
Golden rose, the, v. 106.
Golden rule, iv. 23.
Golden verses, i. 145 n. 1.
Gollnow, iv. 16 n. 3.
Γονυκλινόντες, ii. 30 n. 3, 357.
Good, the supreme, i. 623; iv. 466. Rational, iv. 521.
Good Friday. See Friday.
Good works. See Works.
Goodness, in human nature, Origen, i. 630. Isidore, ii. 722. Lombard, iv. 495. See Original condition.
Gorasd, disciple of Methodius, iii. 320 n. 2.
Gordian, emperor, i. 126 n. 7, 709.
Gorgias, of Plato, ii. 740
Gorze, St., monastery, i i. 336 n. 2, 345. Abbot of, 508 n. 4.
Goslar, sect there, iii. 592 n. 4, 606.
Gospel, in Hebrew (Aramaic), i. 81, 82. Of the Egyptians (κα— Αἰγυπτίους), i. 83, 458 n. 3, 600, 601. Gospel (καθ' Ἑβραίους, of the Nazarenes) used by Ebionites, i. 348 and n. 3, 350, 361 n. 3, 411 nn. 1, 2, 458 n. 1, 708; translated

into Latin by Jerome, i. 350; ii. 712 n. 3; commentary on, i. 708 and n. 2. Apocryphal, used by the Ophites, i. 446. Of Judas, i. 448 n. 4. Διὰ τεσσαρων, i. 458 n. 1. Used by Marcion, i. 473. Apoc. gospel used by Dionys. Alex., i. 712. Gospels used by Bogomiles, iii. 591 nn. 1, 2, 595 nn. 1, 2, 597 n. 2; iv. 553 nn. 5, 6, 554 n. 1, 558. Gospel used by Catharists, iv. 576. Everlasting gospel, iv. 220 n. 2, 229, 230, 291, 618–620; v. 150. See John the Apostle.
Gospel, the, with Jewish Christians, i. 62, 64. Power of the, i. 75, 670. Spirit, i. 62, 719.
Gospels, preached by apostles, i. 203. Read in churches (by deacons), i. 201; ii. 188. On the Sabbath (Saturday), ii. 334. On Good Friday, ii. 352 n. 1. Celsus on the, i. 165. Reverence paid to the, iii. 210 n. 1, 232, 268, 534 (72 n. 3, 89). Sergius, iii. 251. Used by Paulicians, iii. 268, 269. Authority, iii. 372. With heretics in Spain, iii. 430 n. 3. Catharists, iv. 588. Appeal of Huss to the, v. 342. Translated, i. 350; iv. 606; v. 150 (see Translation, Bible). Paraphrased, iii. 425. See Commentaries, Harmonies.
Gotha, Christianity in the dukedom of, iii. 50 n. 2.
Gothenland, Christianity in, iii. 285.
Gothic language, literature, ii. 152, 158. Bible translated into, ii. 152. Commentary, iii. 281 n. 1. Gothic war, i. 135.
Gothico-Spanish liturgy, iii. 157.
Goths, i. 720 n. 2; ii. 593, 594; iii. 4 n. 1. Christianity among the, ii. 149–160, 761. Arianism, ii. 156, 472, 473; iii. 5 n. 4. Bible study, ii. 159, 160. Become monks, ii. 298. Audians, ii. 767. See Visi-Goths.
Gottfrid of Tours, priest, iii. 516.
Gottfried, abbot of Clairvaux, Life of Bernard, iv. 153 nn. 2, 5, 156 n. 4, 157 n. 1. Miracles of Bernard, 256 n. 4. See Mabillon.
Gottfried, bp. of Chartres, iv. 198, 382, 393.
Gottfried, bp. of Lucca, iv. 129 n. 4.
Gottfried, duke, iv. 85.
Gottfried of Beaulieu, life of Louis IX., iv. 285 nn. 4–5. See Du Chesne.
Gottfried of Lukina, Polish abbot, iv. 43.
Gottfried of Vendome, abbot and cardinal, iv. 121 n. 1, 128, 135, 142, 194, 247, 249.
> Ep. 6, to Paschalis II., iv. 135 n. 3. Ep. 7, to the same, 135 n. 2; (on Gregory VII.) 121 n. 1. L. i. ep. 8, to the same, 128 n. 2. L. ii. ep. 11, authority of Roman ch., 194 n. 2. Opusc. III. to pope Calixtus, and tract. de ordinat. et invest., 142 nn. 3–5, 143 nn. 1–4. Opp. iv. 46, Robert of Arbrissel, 249 nn. 2, 3.

Gottfried of Viterbo.
> Chronicle (Pantheon.), iv. 172; f. 16, Conrad III., 172 n. 1; Gift of Constantine, 215 n. 3. See Muratori.

Gottingen.
> Sec. Reg. commentationes recentiores, dissertationes of Walch., ii. 145 n. 2, 838 n. 5. T. v., Diss. of Tychsen, 141 n. 6.

Göttingschen Anzeigen.
> Review of the Liber Adami, i. 376 n. 3.

Gottleben, castle of, v. 112, 340, 342, 363.
Gottschalk, founder of a Christian empire of the Wends, iii. 325, 326; iv. 32.
Gottschalk, monk, iii. 472–492. His doctrine, 474. Rabanus Maurus opposed to him, 473, 475. His defence of himself, 477. Declared a false teacher, 478. Confessions, 474 n. 4, 479 and n. 5, 490. (See Mauguin.) His death, 480. Controversy excited by, 366, n. 1, 471–494. Words addressed to Maurus (in Hinkmar on predestination), 477 n. 2. Defence of church hymn (in Hinkmar), 479 n. 3.
Government, basis of, v. 351–353.
Government, gift of, i. 182, 187, 188, 211, 212.
Gozachin, scholastic, ep. to Walcher, iii. 515 n. 6.
Gozbert, duke, iii. 38.
Grabe.
> Spicoleg. t. ii. p. 89, Heracleon, i. 430 n. 1.

Grace of God, i. 392, 564. And nature, 614. Gnostics on, 416, 432, 435. Hermogenes, 617. Tertullian, 618, 619. In Montanism, 614, 619. With Clement, 620, 621. Origen, 630.
In the Eastern church, ii. 641–643 (iii. 554). Theodore of Mopsuestia, 717. Chrysostom, 720. Isidore of Pelusium, 722. Maximus, iii. 172.
In the Western church, views of Augustin, ii. 495 n. 2, 627, 628, 663–665, 674, 675, 678, 679, 682–687. Hilary, 621. Ambrose, 622, 623. Pelagius, 638, 644 n. 1, 645, 646. Innocent I., 646. Council of Carthage (an. 418), 650. In the Pelagian controversy (384), 663–666, 671–679, 682–687. In the Semi-Pelagian controversy, ii. 687–712. Jovinian, ii. 304, 307, 308, 311.
With Alcuin, iii. 83. Gregory the Great, 144–146. Isidore, 151. Felix, 162. Claudius of Turin, 431, 432. In the Gottschalkian controversy, 472, 476, 478, 482 n. 3, 490, 492 n. 1, 493 (Servatus Lupus, 483. Scotus, 485, 487, 488). Sect at Orleans, 593. At Arras, 598.
With Gregory IX., iv. 76. The schoolmen, iv. 478, 485–495, 509–519. Janow on, v. 214, 215.
Irresistible grace, ii. 630, 631, 682, 684, 705, 712, 722; iii. 145. Superveniant, ii. 665; iv. 487, 512. Prevenient, ii. 682, 689, 705, 711, 722; iv. 516, 517. Coöperans, ii. 683; iv. 486, 487. Operans, ii. 683; iv. 487. Donum perseverantiae, ii. 684. Special grace, ii. 701, 702, 703. Gratia gratis data; gratum

faciens, iv. 489, 511; v. 214 n. 2. Informans, reformans, iv. 489. Justificans, iv. 514. Efficax, iv. 516.
Conditions of Grace, ii. 674; iv. 489. State of, ii. 304, 307, 308, 311; iv. 513-515. Marks of, iv. 514. Freedom and grace, iv. 515-519. Two doctrines, iv. 518. Grace and works, iv. 579 (see Works). Recipiency for, iv. 518, 519. Gifts of, iv. 522, 523 (see Charismata). Growth in, iv. 512. See Freewill.
Graces. See Charismata.
Gradations of existence, with the Gnostics, i. 549; Basilides, 401, 406, 413; Valentine, 421, 422, 426-428. With Origen, 624. Julian, ii. 50, 59. Priscillianists, 776 n. 4.
Græculi, i. 103 n. 1.
Grammar, study of, iii. 156 n. 1, 471. Improvements in, iii. 503; iv. 357. Anglo-Saxon, iii. 469 n. 2. Bacon's universal, iv. 425. Grammarians, iv. 559. Grammatical interpretation, i. 54, 388; ii. 389.
Γράμματα πασχάλια, ii. 338 n. 4.
Γράμματα συστατικά, iii. 564 n. 3.
Γράμματα τετυπωμένα, κοινωνικά. See Epistolæ.
Gran, abp. of, v. 373.
Granada, iv. 191.
Gratian, archpriest, iii. 377. See Gregory VI.
Gratian, emperor, ii. 91, 92, 94, 99, 206, 215, 257.
Gratian, monk, collection of ecclesiastical laws, iv. 204.
Graticia (Garz?), castle, iv. 16 n. 1.
Gratifications in expectancy, v. 125.
Gratus, bp. of Carthage, ii. 228 n. 3.
Graves of saints, honors paid to, iii. 42 (i. 334.) See Miracles at the.
Great Britain, iii. 9, 10. See Britain, England, Ireland.
Great Sabbath, the, ii. 341; iv. 551.
Great week, the, ii. 340-342.
Grecian spirit, i. 340, 368, 369, 565.
Greece, Christianity in, i. 79. Church synods in, i. 206.
Greek and Roman national characters, their influence in the development of Christianity, i. 508; ii. 166, 204, 383, 384; iii. 553.
Greek art, i. 4; ii. 75.
Greek character, ii. 166, 204. Insincerity, iii. 115, 531, 578. See Byzantine, Greek and Roman.
Greek church, traditions, i. 82. Acolytes, 201. Freedom of the, 215. The sermon, 303 (ii. 352). Tendencies of the, 508. See Doctrine, Church teachers.
In the second Period, Subordination of church to state, ii. 166, 20- (see Emperors.) Jurisdiction of bps., 171 n. 3. Theological schools, 183 (see Alexandrian, Antioch.) Contentious, 198. Confession, 216. Ecclesiastical laws, 252 n. 2; iii. 266. Monasticism, 284-293; iii. 169; iv. 528-530, 532. Infant baptism, 355. Times of baptism, 360. Pelagius and the Greek church, 678, 679.
Rise of Mohammedanism, iii. 84-90.
Gregory I. and the Greek church, iii. 113, 115. Feasts, iii. 133, 134. History, iii. 169-270, 330-551 (see Eastern church). State of learning, iii. 169, 530. Influence of monachism, iii. 169. Dialectic tendency, iii. 169. Mystical tendency, iii. 169-175. Relations with the Latin church, iii. 179, 184-194, 210 -212, 227, 233-243, 316, 551-586; iv. 536-551; v. 86, 133, 232, 308, 373, 374. Gerson on union with Greek church, v. 92. Jerome of Prague on, v. 373, 374. Relations with the Bulgarian, iii. 307-310, 314; with the Moravian, iii. 317, 318, 320 n. 2; with the Russian, iii. 328 -330; with the German, iii. 320. Compared with the Latin, iii. 553. Court influence, see Court. Doctrine of the Holy Ghost, iv. 458, 460, 536-538. Sects, iv. 552-565. Image worship, ii. 330; v. 233 (see Image Controversies). Greek church in Lithuania, v. 373. For other particulars, see Eastern church, Alexandria, Antioch, Bread, Greek church Fathers, Table of Contents.
Greek church fathers, teachers, i. 657-677, 691-723; iii 150 n. 4, 461. And Pelagius, ii. 632. See Church Fathers.
Greek colonies in Egypt, i. 83. In France, ii. 343. In Italy, see Greeks.
Greek culture, learning, i. 4, 65, 83, 368, 533, 662; ii. 264; iii. 169, 456, 530, 585; iv. 536-538, 545 and n. 2. Its influence on the Jews of Alexandria, i. 50. With the Catechists of Alexandria, Clement, i. 528, 533-539. And study of Scripture, i. 533. Logos doctrine, i. 585. With Origen, i. 698. See Greek language, literature, philosophy.
Greek customs, ii. 39.
Greek despotism, iii. 169, 531, 537, 543. See Byzantine.
Greek discipline, i. 391.
Greek emperors, iii. 327; iv. 177, 533, 539. See Byzantine.
Greek empire, and the Bulgarians, iii. 310. Moravians, 316. Hungarians, 330. See Byzantine.
Greek fire, iii. 209.
Greek homilists, ii. 367, 368.
Greek language, i. 79, 201, 303, 318, 662, 663, 713; ii. 116, 158 iii. 152, 320 n. 2, 576, 584. Ulphilas, ii. 152. Anthony, ii. 264. Gregory I., iii. 141. Abelard, iv. 378. Liturgical, iii. 318.
Greek literature, i. 696, 713; ii. 41, 52-54, 75, 77, 485; iv. 373, 530. Poets, ii. 62, 116.
Greek of N. T., ii. 116; iii. 460.
Greek philosophy, i. 4, 5-35; ii. 24 n. 3, 76, 116, 740. In Gnosticism, i. 366, 368, 369, 374-380, 390-393, 408, 409, 417, 418, 449, 456. Scythianus, i. 485. At

Alexandria, Clement on, i. 534, 535–539, 691, 692. Relation to Christianity, i. 538, 666, 672, 673, 674, 701, 717. Relation to Judaism, i. 666. Origen and, i. 698, 701, 717. Philosophers, iv. 378. See Celsus, Porphyry, Plato, Neo-Platonism.

Greek religion, i. 5–35, 36, 71, 170–173; ii. 117. Knowledge of it necessary to the Alexandrian catechists, i. 528. See Mysteries.

Greeks, ancient, iii. 130. At Alexandria, i. 528, 529. Of Calabria, iii. 376, 420. And Sicily, iii. 448 n. 1.

Greenland, Christianity in, iii. 307.

Gregoria, iii. 145.

Gregorius, cardinal, iv. 144. See Innocent II.

Gregorius, governor in Africa, iii. 184.

Gregorius, governor of Frascati, iii. 424 n. 1.

Gregory, abbot in Utrecht, iii. 47 n. 2, 73 (iv. 36). His first acquaintance with Boniface, 72. In Friesland, 73, 79, 80. His death, 74.

Gregory, abp. of Syracuse, iii. 558.

Gregory, Arian bp. of Alexandria, ii. 434, 436.

Gregory, bp. of Nazianzus, sketch of his life, ii. 459, 462–466. In Athens, education, 39 n. 2, 45, 183. Firmness of Gregory the father, 79. His mother, Nonna, 261, 262. Origen's influence, 387, 738, 741. Jerome and Gregory, 744. Under Julian, 77. Discourses of pagan priests, 62 n. 3. Julian's imitation of Christian institutions, 63 n. 3. Christian soldiers under Julian, 75 n. 1. Marcus, 81 n. 1. Lessons derived from the persecution, 87. Pomp of the bishops, 168. Basilias, 169. Education of the clergy, 182 and n. 3. Description of the clergy, 182 n. 3, 185 n. 1. Election of Basil, of bishops, 186 n. 1. Transfer of clergy, 187. Contention about rank, patriarchs, 196 n. 3, 198. Œcumenical councils, 209, 210 n. 1. Influence of the monks, 282 n. 1. Epiphany, 343 n. 2. Vanity of preachers, infant and adult baptism, 355, 726, 730. Oriental theology, 384–386. Doctrine of the Holy Spirit, 467, 468. Person of Christ, 483, 484. Against Apollinaris, 492. Intermediate state, 730. The Lord's Supper, 735. On the Apostle Thomas, i. 82.

Citations from his writings:—

Carmen de episcopis, ii. 185 n. 1, 196 n. 3, 182 n. 3. Carmen 47, ad Hellenium (opp. t. ii. f. 107), 273 n. 6.

Chrestomathy, 741.

Epigrams (see Muratori), Nonna, 262 n. 1.

Epistles (opp. vol. i.), ep. 18 (22) and 19 (23) election of Basil, ii. 186 n. 1; ep. 55, ad Procop., Synods, 209 n.; ep. 240, ad Amphilochium, consecration of the Lord's Supper, 735 n. 9; ep. ad Cledon., Person of Christ, 492 n. 1.

Orationes (opp. t. i.), orat. i. f. 15, topics of public instruction, ii. 385 n. 1; f. 18, skepticism arising from the doctrinal tendency, 767 n. 2; f. 35, enemies within, 87 n. 1; f. 38, the eucharist, 735 n. 5. Orat. ii. in Pascha, the Great Sabbath, 341 n. 8. Orat. iii. (stelitent. i.), f. 58, education of Julian, 40 n.; f. 60, Constantius, 45 n. 1; f. 85, Christian soldiers under Julian, 75 n. 1; f. 102, Julian's imitation of Christian institutions, 63 n. 3; f. 103, discourses of pagan priests, 62 n. 3. Orat. iv. (stelitent. ii.), ff. 130, 131, advice after the death of Julian, 87 n. 2. Orat. x. funeb. in Cæsar, f. 165, 68 n. 2. Orat. xvii., f. 273, eucharist, 735 nn. 6, 8. Orat. xix. f. 292, Nonna, 262 n. 1; f. 308, Gregory the father, 79 n. 2; f. 310, election of bishops, 186 n. 1. Orat. xx. (funeb. in Basil), Valens and Basil, 460 n. 3; f. 331, their life at Athens, 39 n. 2; f. 342, election of Basil, 186 n. 1; f. 348, the chief cook, 165 n. 5; f. 353, Basil and the asylum, 177 n. 1. Orat. xxv., Thomas in India, i. 82 n. 3. Orat. xxvii., institutions of Basil, 109 n. 4. Orat. xxviii., f. 484, ambition among the clergy, 198 n. 2. Orat. xxx., works of Basil, 149 n. 4. Orat. xxxii., farewell discourse at Const., applause, 353 n. 1; short-hand reporters, 353 n. 5; f. 526, pomp of the bps., 168 n. 3; worldly qualifications sought for in candidates for spiritual offices, 185 n. 1; f. 527; name Nazarene applied to monks, 129 n. 3. Orat. xxxiii., f. 536, topics for religious instruction, 385 nn. 2, 3. Orat. xl., de baptismo, unbaptized infants, 730 n. 1; f. 640, efficacy of baptism, 726 nn. 1, 2, 4; f. 643, delay of baptism, 356 n. 2; f. 648, consecration of children, infant baptism, 350 n. 1, 726 n. 5; f. 671, glorified body of Christ, 484 n. 3. Orat. xlii., the Great Sabbath, 341 n. 8. Orat. li., person of Christ, 492 n. 1. Five discourses on the Nicene doctrine, 463.

Gregory, bp. of Nazianzus, the father, ii. 79, 261, 462, 768 n. 1.

Gregory, bp. of Neo Cæsarea, iii. 231.

Gregory, bp. of Nyssa. Influenced by Origen, ii. 387, 741. Contributes to the victory of the Nicene doctrine; in the second œcumenical council, 459, 466. The forty soldiers in Sebaste, 19 n. 3. Education of daughters, Macrina, 262 n. 4, 316 n. 5. Christmas festival, 346 n. 1, 348 n. 1. Delay of baptism, 356. Enrollment of candidates for baptism, 358 n. 2. Pilgrimages, 378. The common people in the Arian controversy, 431, 432 n. 1. Eunomius, 444 n. 2, 447. Person of Christ, 483, 484, 490. Ordination, 725 n. 2. The Lord's Supper, 733–735. Ἀποκατάστασις, 738. On the Montanists, i. 682. Gregory Thaumaturgus, i. 718 n. 1, 719. Influence of his writings on Maximus, iii. 171, 175. Germanus, iii. 203 n. 2. John Scotus, iii. 461.

Citations from his writings:—

Antirrhetic. c. Apollinar. (see Zacagni), on the person of Christ, f. 126, ii. 489 n. 4; f 130, 485 n. 1; f. 135, 486 n. 4; f. 138, 487 n. 4; ff. 140, 177, 489 nn. 2, 4; ff. 184, 185, 486 nn. 5, 7, 8; f. 191, 489 n. 3; f. 194, 490 n. 3; f. 201, 490 n. 6; ff. 209, 215, 486 nn. 5, 1; ff. 220, 221, 489 nn. 6, 5; ff. 223, 225, 487 nn. 1, 5; ff. 232, 237, 486 nn. 5, 6; f. 241, 489 n. 9; f. 245, 486 n. 2, 489 n. 3; f. 255, 486 n. 2; f. 264, 489 n. 8; ff. 277, 284, 286, 490 nn. 1, 2.

Contr. Eunom. l. i. t. ii. f. 291, Eunomius on Basil, ii. 445 n. 2; f. 306, E. on asceticism, 445 n. 3.

De baptismo, t. ii. f. 216, roll of the candidates for baptism, ii. 358 n 2; f. 221, magical efficacy of baptism, 256 n. 2.
Ep. ad Theophilum, ii. 484 n. 1. Ep. canonica ad Letojum, penitents, i. 213 n. 2.
Expos. 1 Cor. 15: 28, ii. 738 n. 2.
Hom. in natal. Christi (t. iii. ed. Par. 1638), f. 840, ii. 348 n. 1: f. 352, ii. 346 n. 1.
Life of Gregory Thaumaturgus, i. 738 n. 1, 719; c. 27, 720 n. 1.
Λόγος κατηχητικός, cc. 8 and 35, ii. 738 a. 3.
Orationes. Orat. de deitate Filii et Spir. Sanct. (t. iii. f. 466), ii. 482 n. 1, Orat. in Abrah. (t. iii. opp. Par. 1638), f. 476, figures of Abraham and Isaac, 324 n. 5. Orat. ii. f. 440, doctrine of Eunomius, 449 n. 3; f. 482 (t. ii.), confession of Eunomius 478 n. 1; c. Eunom. f. 470, 449 n. 1. Orat. iii. f. 548, Eunomius, 449 n. 2. Orat. iv. c. Eunom., f. 573, E. on the being of the Logos, 478 n. 2; f. 580, G. on the two natures in Christ, 484 n. 1 Ornt., viii. f. 650, E. on the generation of the Son of God, 448 n. 1. Orat. xi. f. 794, E on accuracy in doctrine, 447 nn. 1, 2; G. on the same, n. 3. G. de baptismo Christi (t. iii.), doctrine of the Holy Spirit, 469 n. 2; f. 370, transubstantiation, 733 n. 2.
Tracts, on the soul, and on the death of children, ii. 738 n. 2.
Vita Macrinæ, ii. 262 n. 4, 316 n. 5.

Gregory, bp. of Pisinus in Galatia, iii. 229 n. 3.

Gregory, bp. of Tours, iii. 7 n. 1, 91 n. 1.
De gloria martyrum, l. i. c. 4, death of Mary, iii. 134 n. 1.
De miraculis S. Martini, ii. 7 n. 1. L. i. c. 8, iii. 7 n 2; c. 34, the vineyard, 133 n. 2. L. ii. c. 32, on doubts, 7 n. 3. L. iii., the miracles at Martin's tomb, ii 132 and nn 3, 4; c. 8, invocations of S. Martin, 133 n. 1; c. 18, amulets, 133 n. 2.
Hist. Francorum, l. ii. c. 27, Clovis, iii. 6 n. 2; c. 37, Clovis and the oracle, 129 n. 2. L. iv. c. 11, Crato, 93 n. 3; c. 19, Chramn, 104 n. 2; c. 26, Charibert, 91 n. 2; c. 35, picture of a pious bishop, 105 n 4. L. v. c. 3, cruel treatment of slaves, 100 n. 7; c. 4, 104 n. 2; c. 14, sortes sanctorum, 120 n. 3; c. 21, authority of the pope in the Frankish empire, 119 n. 1; c. 45, Chilperic, 91 n. 1. L. vi. c. 8, the monk Eparchius, 104 n. 1: c. 46, Chilperic on the wealth of the churches, 101 n. 3. L. viii. c. 15, Wulflaen the stylite, 28 n. 4. L. ix. c. 6, fanatics, deceptions practised upon the people, 56 n. 5, 59 n. 3, 133 n. 4.
On Dionysius the Areopagite, Christianity in Gaul, l. 84; iii. 467 n. 1.
Vitæ patrum, c. 1, superstition, iii. 133 n. 3; c. 6, f. 1171 (ed. Ruinart), life of Gallus, Theodoric, 93 n. 2.

Gregory, comes, imperial commissioner, ii. 228 n. 3, 229 and n. 3.

Gregory I. (the Great), pope, life and character, iii. 112-119, 141-151). Zealous for the conversion of the Anglo-Saxons, 11, 12. His principles with regard to conversion, 13 and n. 1. The Jews, 13 n. 1 (iv. 75.) Success of Augustin, 13 n. 2. His warnings addressed to Augustin, 14, 15. On miracles, 14, 15 n. 1, 146-148. His judgment with regard to the diversity of church customs, to idolatrous temples, and seasons of festival, 15, 16 n. 1. Founds archbishoprics in England, 16. Ascribes to himself sovereign power in the Western church, 16. His letter to Ethelbert, 22 n. 1. Columban, 32. His influence, 60 n. 2, 427, 456. Seeks to abolish abuses in the bestowment of benefices among the Franks, 94. Frankish synods, 95, 96. On admission to the spiritual order, 97 n. 2. His controversy with the emperor Maurice, 97. On the manumission of his slaves, 100. As pope, 112-119. His manifold activity, 112. His conduct towards princes, 113 n. 1, 116. His pains to support the authority of the Roman church, 113. His procedure with Natalis of Salona, 114. On the use of Scripture, 115. Recognizes the equal dignity of bishops, 115. His controversy with Johannes νηστευτής, 115-117. Exercises supreme judicial authority in Spain, 118. His relations with the Frankish church, 119. Arrangement of texts, 120. Friend to the notion of a magical influence connected with the Lord's Supper, 135, 136. Sacrifice in the mass, 499. His influence on church Psalmody, 142. His zeal for preaching, 142. Regula pastoralis, 142, 468. Influence of Augustin on him, 143. His doctrine of predestination, 144. On the relation of grace to free will, 144-146. His treatment of ethical science; his Moralia, 148 and n. 2. On love, and the cardinal virtues, 148. Against mere opus operatum, 149. On false humility and truthfulness, 149, 150. On the relation of "reason" to "faith," 150. On the ancient literature, 150. Bibliotheca Palatina, 150 n. 7. Use of his writings by Isidore of Seville, 151. On image worship, Serenus of Marseilles, 191, and notes, 200, 233, 552 (ii. 330.) Longobards, 386. Epithet cardinalis præcipuus, 387 n. 7. Defensores, ii. 192 n. 1. Donatists, ii. 238. Collection of his sayings in the sentences of Lombard, iv. 409. His life, see Johannes Diaconus.

Citations: —
Dial., l. iv. cc. 57, 58, on the Lord's Supper, iii. 135 nn. 2-5.
Epistles. L. 1. ep. 10, treatment of Jews, iii. 13 n. 1; ep. 25, on preaching, 142 n. 2; ep. 35, treatment of opponents of Christianity, 13 n. 1; ep. 36, ad Petrum, subdiaconum, on maintaining the authority of the Roman ch., imitation of good, 113 n. 4, 114 nn. 4, 5; ep. 66, presents, 114 nn. 1, 2. L. ii. ep. 18, to Natalis of Salona, 114 nn. 7, 8, 115 nn. 1, 2; ep. 54, qualifications of clergy. 143 n. 2. L. iii. epp. 65, 66, on entering spiritual offices, and monastic life, 97 n. 2. L. iv. ep. 26, taxation of pagans, 13 n. 1; ep. 108, Augustin, 11 n. 4. L. v. ep. 7, baptism of Jews, 13 n. 1; ep 18, to John (νηστευτής), on the title œcumenical, 116 n. 4; ep. 19, to his plenipotentiary on the same, 116 nn. 1, 3. L. vi. ep. 7, the Anglo-Saxons, 11 n. 3; ep. 12. deed of manumission, 100 n. 5; ep. 24, appeals from Const. to Rome, 115 n. 3; ep. 51, to the missionaries in England, 12 n. 1. L. vii. ep. 1, slavery, 100 n. 6; ep. 5, descent into Hades, 61 n. 2; ep. 25, assurance, 145 n. 4; ep. 27, to Anastasius of Antioch (t tle œcumenicus), 116 n. 2. L. viii. ep. 18, treatment of pagans,

13 n. 1; ep. 25, of Jews, 13 n. 1. ep. 30, to Eulogius of Alexandria, conversion of the English, 13 n. 2, title "Papa universalis," 115 n. 4.   L. ix. ep. 12, his relation to the Greek ch., 113 n. 2; imitation of R. ch., 114 n. 3; ep. 47, to bps. of Arles and Marseilles, the Jews, 13 n. 1; ep. 52, to a hermit, images, 199 nn. 1-3; ep. 85, pagans, 13 n. 1; ep. 105, to Serenus, use of images, 199 n. 4, 200 n. 1; ep. 106, to Frankish bps. and princes, on the holding of synods, 94 n. 3; ep. 112, his own change of life, 112 n. 1.   L. x. ep. 37, his times, 112 n. 3; ep. 38, study of Augustin, 143 n. 3; ep. 63, his times, 112 n. 2. L. xi. ep. 13, to Serenus, use of images, 200 nn. 2, 4; ep. 28, to Augustin, on miracles, 15 n. 1; ep. 44, servus omnium, 117 n. 1; ep. 54, to Desiderius of Vienne, studies of the clergy, 150 nn. 5, 6; ep. 56, Irenaeus, 150 n. 4; ep. 58, *et seq.*, to the Frankish bps. and princes, on synods, 94 n. 3, 96 n. 1; ep. 65, Eng. archbps., 16 n. 2; epp. 66, 76, pagan temples, 15 nn. 2, 3, 4.   L. xiii. ep. 12, to the bp. of Naples; Jews, 13 n. 1; ep. 31, to the emp. Phocas, 113 n. 1.

Homilies in Evangelia (h. 26, on faith, iv. 396). L. i. h. 4, § 3, miracles, prayer for temporal things, iii. 147 n. 1; h. 17, § 9, preaching, 142 n. 3, § 14, n. 4.   L. ii. h. 27, miracles, 148 n. 1, love, n. 4; h. 29, § 3, miracles, 147 n. 4; h. 30, §§ 8, 9, communication of divine life, 145 n. 2, 146 n. 3; h. 32, asceticism, 149 n. 4; h 34, grace, 146 n. 1.

Homilies on Ezechiel. L. i. h. 3, § 8, unity of virtue, iii. 149 n. 1; h. 10, § 9, morals, 149 nn. 2, 3; h. 11, § 6, external business, 141 n. 2; it interferes with preaching, 142 n. 6; § 7, n. 7; § 25, God's hardening of men's hearts, 144 n. 4.   L. ii. h. 6, § 21, his times, 112 n. 2. Other homilies, iv. 317 n. 5. See above.

In Job. L. iii. c. 2, § 15, causality of evil, iii. 144 n. 3.   L. viii. in c. 8, § 72, preaching, 142 n. 7.   L. xix. § 45, external business, 141 n. 3; c. 23, § 28, unity of virtue, 148 n. 3.   L. xx. in c. 20, cap. 7, § 17, miracles, 147 n. 5; in c. 30, § 18, study of scripture, 143 nn. 4, 5; § 63, predestination, 144 n. 1. L. xxiv. in c. 33, § 21, grace, 145 n. 1.   L. xxvii. in c. 36, § 7, incomprehensibility of God's providence, 144 n. 5; § 21, conversion of the Anglo-Saxons, 13 n. 2; in c. 37, § 36 (ed. Ben. t. i. f. 869), miracles, 147 n. 3.   L. xxix. in c. 38, § 77, assurance, 144 nn. 6-8. L. xxxi. in c. 39, § 26, God's hardening of men's hearts, 144 n. 4.   L. xxxiii. in c. 41, § 40, reward, 145 n. 3.   L. xxxiv. in c. 3, § 7, miracles, love, 147 n. 7.

In I. and II. Kings. L. v. in I. K. c. 4, § 30, study of ancient literature, iii. 150 n. 7.

Life of Benedict of Nursia, ii. 296, 298 n. 1, 299 n., 300 nn. 2, 3.

Moralia, iii. 148 n. 2; sermonizing, 142 n. 7. L. viii. § 3, faith and reason, 150 n. 3.   L. xviii. § 5, falsehood, 150 n. 2.   L. xxii. c. 1, unity of virtue, 148 n. 5.   L. xxiv. § 22, insincere confession, 149 n. 6.   L. xxvi § 5, falsehood, 150 n 2.   L. xxvii. § 78, mock humility, 149 n. 5.

Gregory II., pope, relations with Boniface, and the Bavarian mission, iii. 47, 48, 65 n. 4. His letter to Leo the Isaurian. 210-212 (213 n. 3 ?)

Ep. 8, ad Bonifaciam, 50 n. 3. Ep. 24, to the same, 54 n. 3.

Gregory III., pope, iii. 55. On the mission of Boniface, 50. Creates him abp., 65. Invites him to choose a successor, 67.

Ep. ad Bonifaciam, 48 n. 4; to the same (f. 66), on the eating of horseflesh, 295 n. Ep. 6, to the German bps. and dukes, 49 n. 1. Ep. 10, to the Germans, 49 n. 1. Ep. 45, ad episcopos Bavariæ et Alemanniæ, 49 n. 1. Ep. 46, ad Bonifaciam, 50 n. 4. Ep. 70, to the same, on Cologne as a metropolitan see, 65 n. 6.

Gregory IV., pope, iii. 277, 352, 362.

Letter to the French bishops (see Agobard, opp., ed. Baluz., t. ii. p. 60), 352 nn. 2, 3.

Gregory V., pope, iii. 374. Banishment and restoration, 422.

Gregory VI. (Gratian), pope, iii. 377 and notes, 380; iv. 84.

Gregory VII., pope, as Hildebrand, monk, iii. 379-382, 384 n. 4, 386-389, 395-399. Age of, 378 n. 2. Friend of Gregory VI., 380. His journey to Rome, 381. His influence, efforts to promote a reformation, 382, 384 n. 4, 386-388, 514 (iv. 82-84). Made subdeacon of the Roman church, 386. Damiani, 393 n. 6, 399. Favors the judgments of God, 449 (384 n. 4). In the controversy on the Lord's Supper, 510-512, 515-518 (iv. 92). His principles as to relation of church and state anticipated, i. 365 n. 1. Lucifer of Cagliari compared to, ii. 442 n. 2. The clergy of Liege on, iv. 132. See Hildebrandian.

As pope, election, iv. 82-86, 106. His times, 85, 86 (iii. 378 n. 2.) Principles, 86-92, 141. On penance, 91, 348. His name (iii. 381) 92 n. 4. Regulations, contest against simony and marriage of priests, 93-100, 146, 206, 293. Demagogical tendency, 96, 99, 107. Contest with Henry IV., respecting investiture, 2 n. 2, 4, 101-121, 134, 136, 233, 303. Imprisonment by Cintius, 108. (Berengar, iii. 518-521. On Leo IX., iii. 384 n. 4. Guitmund, iii. 529 n. 3.) Crusades, 123. Sigebert, 130. On excommunication, 132. Placidus, 140 n. 1. Consecration of popes by consent of the emperor, 151. Oath of bishops, 200. Hugo of Cluny, 249. His "Dictates," 120. His reign a crisis in the history of the papacy, 194; v. 8, 15. See Acta S. (Bolland.) May, Acta S. (O. B.) S. vi. P. ii., Hildebrand.

Citations:—

Epistles. Epp. making known his election, iv. 85 nn. 2, 3. L. i. ep. 7, ch. of Spain, feof of the Roman, 88 n. 3; ep. 9, to Gottfried, 85 n. 4; ep. 15, authority of R. ch., 89 n. 1: ep. 16, to a legate, report due to the pope, 89 n. 3; ep. 17, authority of legates, 89 n. 2; ep. 19, authority of king and pope compared, 88 n. 1; ep. 30, to Gebhard of Salzburg, 96 n. 3; ep. 42, letter missive for the fast synod, an. 1074, 93 n. 1; ep 47, to the margravine Mathilda, on the Virgin Mary, 87 nn. 1, 2; ep. 50, to Beatrice and Mathilda, love and good works, 91 n. 3; ep. 63, authority of St. Peter, 87 n. 3.   L. ii. ep. 5, to the French bps., 102 nn. 1-3: ep. 11, on piety among the laity, 97 n. 7: ep. 31, the crusade, 104 n. 1; ep. 45, to Rudolph of Suabia and Bertulph of Carinthia, 96 n. 6, 97 nn. 1-6; ep. 49, to Hugo of Cluny, on his own conflicts, 84 nn. 1, 2, 86 nn. 1, 2; ep. 55, piety among the people, 97 n. 7; ep. 63, authority of Peter, 87

n. 3; ep. 67, authority of R. ch., 83 n. 5; ep. 69, to Cunibert of Turin, freedom of monasteries, 93 n. 1; ep. 70, to Geusa of Hungary, 88 n. 2. L. iii. ep. 3, to Henry IV. of Germany, 103 n. 1; ep. 4, to Sigfrid of Mentz, 95 n. 4, 96 n. 1; ep. 10, to Henry IV., 104 n. 2, 105 nn. 1-3. L. iv. ep. 2, 110 n. 4; ep. 12, to the Germans, 106 n. 1, 112 n. 1, 114 nn., 116 n. 4. L. v. ep. 2, authority of legates, 89 n. 2; ep. 21, to Hugo of Cluny, 92 n. 1. L. vi. ep. 13, to Olbf of Norway, 90 n. 2; ep. 17, to Hugo of Cluny, 91 n. 4; ep. 35, authority of Roman ch., 88 n. 4. L. vii. ep. 1, to a legate, on reporting to the pope, fast synods, 89 nn. 4, 5; bread in the Sacrament, 92 n. 3; ep. 6, authority of Peter 87 n. 3; ep. 10, reformatory synod in Eng., 91 n. 2; ep. 21, to the king of Denmark, 90 n. 5, 100 n. 1; ep. 23, to Wm. of Eng., 83 n. 3, 87 n. 3; ep. 25, to the same, 88 n. 1; ep. 26, to Matilda of Eng., 90 n. 4. L. viii. ep. 1, to the king of Sweden, 90 n. 1; ep. 21, to Hermann of Metz, 87 n. 4, 130. L. ix. ep. 1, visitors to Rome, 96 n. 2; ep. 3, indulgent construction of the laws concerning celibacy, 129 n. 4; ep. 11, while besieged in Rome, 129 n. 1; ep. 22, to a count of Angers, 90 n. 3; ep. 142, ed. Eccard, to Otto of Constance, 94 n. 3, 96 n. 4; ep. 150 (Eccard script. rer. Germ., to the Romans, 84 n. 1; ep. 149, cod. Babenberg (Eccard. t. ii. f. 151), on the contest with Henry IV., 117 n.
Comm. on Matt. ! iii. 511 n. 1.
Ordinances of reform, iv. 94 nn. 1, 2. See Pez., t. v, Mansi Concil., xx.

Gregory VIII., pope, iv. 141.
Gregory IX., pope, conflict with Frederic II., iv. 178-183. The Jews, 76. His exactions for the crusades, 188 n. 5, Digest of ecclesiastical law, 205. To the university of Paris, 417, 418. Germanus, 539 and n. 2. Catharists, 590. Inquisition, 643.
Epistle to Univ. Paris, iv. 417 n. 6, 418 nn. 1, 2.

Gregory X., pope, election, crusades, union with the Greek church, iv. 188, 544. Mission to China, 56. Regulation with regard to papal elections, 192. Mendicants, 628.
Gregory XI., pope, election and death, v. 44, 102, 127. Suspends the ordinances regarding the papal elections, 45. Benedict XIII., 56. Embassy from England, 137. Bulls against Wicklif, 146, 147. Militz, 182.
Gregory XII., pope, election of, v. 71. And Benedict XIII., 72-77. Council at Aquileia, 76. Deposed at the council of Pisa, 84. Ladislaus of Naples, 73, 75, 90. The council of Constance and, 106, 107. 112. Abdication, 112. Wenceslaus, 253, 255, 256. Huss on, 281, 303.
Gregory Thaumaturgus, disciple of Origen, i. 287, 701, 706. Life and writings, 716-720. Canonical letter, 720 n. 2.
Gregory the Enlightener, ii. 136, 139, n. 1.
Grenoble, iv. 265.
Gretser.
His edition of Gerhoh, de statu ecclesiæ topp. t. vi.], iv. 134 n. 1, 138 n. 3, 140 n. 2, 147 n. 1, 163 n. 2. Scriptores contra sectam Wal-

densium prolog., Gerhoh, de investigatione Auti Christi (opp. t. xii. f. 12), iv. 148 n. 3, 162 n. 2.

Grieshaber, Prof. F. K.
Edition of German Sermons, iv. 318 n. 2.

Grimkil, English ecclesiastic, bp. in Iceland, iii. 291, 297 n, 305.
Grimm.
Deutsche Mythologie, &. 378, n. d. f., iv. 15 n. 3.

Gröningen, iii. 72 n. 2. Willehad in, 80.
Grosshead, see Robert.
Grotta (Crypta) Ferrata, iii. 376 and n. 2, 424.
Grottos, sacred, i. 481, 488.
Groves, ii. 139.
Grusinia, ii. 138.
Gualbert, abbot of Vallombrosa, iii. 398, 399 n. 1.
Gubbio, iv. 206 n. 2.
Gudbrand (Gudbrandsdalen), [Stift Aggershaus], iii. 298, 299.
Gudensberg, iii. 51.
Guelphs, v. 3, 412.
Guenrich, scholastic writer, on obedience to princes. iv. 109 n. 1.
Guhsciatazades, martyr, ii. 131, 132.
Guibert, abp. of Ravenna (Clement III.), iv. 101 n. 2, 113 n , 118-129.
Guibert of Nogent sous Coucy, on Peter of Amiens, iv. 124. His mother, 234. Bruno and the Carthusians, 265 and n. 3. On preaching, 313. John of Soissons, 325. Answers of Catharists, 587 n. 3. Influence of the Jews on Christians, 591 n. 2 (325). His life, c. 3, 234 n. 1; c. 8, 234 nn. 2, 3.
Citations: —
De pignoribus Sanctorum, iv. 330. L. i. c. ii. § 5, false saints, 329 n. 3, 330 n. 1; stories of miracles, 330 n. 4; § 6, false relics, 330 n. 2; c. 8, § 1, false legends, 330 n. 3; c. 4, § 1, relics, 330 nn. 5, 6. L. ii. c. 6, § 4, 331 n. 1. De vita sua, c. 3, his mother, iv. 234 n. 1; c. 6, worldliness in monasteries, 234 nn. 2, 3; c. 9, Ebrard of Breteul, 235 n. 1. L. i. init. enthusiasm preceding the first crusade, 125 n. 3; c. 7, f. 462, effect of the ordinances of Hildebrand, 146 nn. 2, 3; f. 477, origin of his work on Genesis, 314 n. 1; c. 11. Manasseh, abp. of Rheims, 26 n. 2; f. 507, imposture connected with the crusades, 127 nn. 5, 6; f 508, martyrdom, 128 n. 1. L. ii. c. 5, Jews at Rouen, 71 n. 3. L. iii. c. 4, Paschalis II., 132 n. 4; c. 4, f. 498, bribery at Rome, 196 n. 2; c. 15, John of Soissons, 325 n. 1.
Hist. Hierosolymitana (see Bongars), f. 482, iv. 124 nn. 2. 3.
On the Exposition of Genesis, introd., on preaching, iv. 313 nn. 3-6, 314 n. 1.
Tractat. de incarnatione contra Judæos, c. 1, iv. 325 n. 2.

Guido, abp. of Milan, ii. 389, 393 and n. 5, 394.
Guido, brother of Bernard, iv. 253 n. 1.
Guido, cardinal, iv. 150, 151, 341. See Cælestin II.
Guido, Cistercian, iv. 640.
Guigo, prior of the Carthusians, "Meditations," iv. 413. See Bibl. Patr. Lugd.

Guilt, existence of, i. 561. Consciousness of, i. 611; ii. 617. Propagation of, ii. 622, 669. Freedom of, Augustin, ii. 685. Bernard, iv. 516, 517. Transfer of, Abelard, iv. 494. See Sin, Traducianism.

Guiscard of Cremona, iv. 49.

Guitmund, abp. of Aversa, disciple of Lanfranc, iii. 529 and n. 3. Berengar and Hildebrand, iii. 512 n. 1.

De Corporis et Sanguinis Christi veritate. L. i. f. 441, Berengar at Chartres, iii. 503 n. 1; at Tours, 470 n. 4; Lanfranc, 470 n. 5. De Eucharistiæ Sacramento. L. ii. f. 464, practical importance of the doctrine of transubstantiation, 539 n. 1. L. iii. f. 459, 460, accusations against Berengar, 526 nn. 5, 6, 527 nn. 1-4; f. 461, impanation, 528 n. 1; f. 463, B. accused of altering his views, 528 n. 4; B. and Augustin, 504 n. 2; f. 464, unworthy communicants, 528 n. 3. See Bibl. Patr. Lugd., t. 18, and Orderici Vital. Hist. eccles., l. v. c. 17.

Gundobad, king of the Burgundians, iii. 5 and n. 2, 6, 9 n., 39 n. 3. Defends judgments of God, 130.

Gundobald, law concerning duels, iii. 429 n. 4.

Gundulf, founder of a sect in Arras, iii. 597.

Gunild, wife of Harald Blaatand, iii. 288.

Gunthert, monk, iii. 479.

Günther, abp. of Cologne, iii. 354, 356.

Günther Ligurinus, poem on Fred. I., iv. 148 nn. 1, 2, 149 n. 4.

Guntramm, king of the Franks, iii. 119 n. 1.

Gurm, king of Denmark, iii. 288.

Gushtasp (Hystaspes), i. 176.

Gützkow, history of the conversion of, iv. 21–24.

Gylas, Hungarian prince, iii. 330, 331.

Gyrovagi, ii. 283 n. 2, 298 n. 2.

II.

Habitus, iv. 443, 512.

Hacon, prince of Norway, iii. 293–296.

Hacon, Yarl, iii. 296.

Hadeby (Schleswig), iii. 275.

Hadelbod, bishop of Cologne, iii. 275.

Hades, i. 653, 667 n. 2. Baptism in, i. 646. Christ's descent into, i. 654, 656; ii. 491; iii. 61. The apostles in, i. 656 n. 1.

Hadrian, abbot, iii. 25, 152.

Hadrian I., pope, his warnings addressed to Charlemagne, iii. 121 n. 4. Zealous for church psalmody, 128. Adoptianism, 165. On the apostolical decree, 166 n. 6. Conduct in the image controversy, 227. Reply to the libri Carolini, 243, 552. Appeals to forged writings, 350. Letter to Constantinople, 563 n. 1.

Citations:—
From his letters to Charlemagne (Cod. Carolin. ed. Cenni. t. 1.) f. 352, gifts of Constantine, iii. 122 n. 1; ff. 371, 390, 506, 121 n. 4; ff. 389, 443, 510, 519, on the power of the Roman See, 120 n. 1. Reply to the Libri Carolini, 243 nn. 1-3. (See Mansi concil., t. 13).

Hadrian (Adrian) II., pope, iii. 361, 402. Cyril and Methodius, 316 and n. 4. Contends for the recognition of the Pseudo-Isidorean decretals, Hinkmar, 361–366, 402. His position towards the Greek church, 569.

Hadrian IV., pope, v. 301. See Adrian IV.

Hadrian, Roman emperor, i. 101–103, 174, 313, 344 and n., 449, 455, 661, 663 and n. 2, 664, 673 n. 2, 675.

Ep. ad Cons. Servianum, ap. Flav. Vopisc. in Saturnino, c. 8 (religious syncretism in Alexandria), i. 102 n. 6.

Hadrian's temples, i. 103.

Haimo, bp. of Halberstadt, iii. 458.

Halberstadt, iii. 458; iv. 400.

Halicarnassus. See Dionysius, Julian.

Halinardus, abp. of Lyons, life of, iii. 377 nn. 1, 4, 378 n. 4. See D'Achery, Spicileg., t. ii.

Halitgar, abp. of Cambray, iii. 272. Directions respecting penance, 137, 138 n. 1, 140. At Constantinople, 553 n. 3.

Citations:—
Liber pœnitentialis, iii. 272; compositions, 138 n. 1; satisfaction, 140 and nn. 1, 2.

Hallam, Robert, bp. of Salisbury, v. 121.

Halle, iv. 18, 30. Heretics at, 610.

Hallr, of Sido, iii. 303.

Ham, revelations of the patriarch, i. 408.

Hamann, letter to Herder (the Apocalypse), iv. 617 n. 2.

Hamar, Saracen, iv. 69 n. 2.

Hamburg, Gottschalk the Wend in, iii. 325, 326. Bishopric, 271. Central point of Northern missions, 84, 277, 279, 280. United with Bremen, 279, 290. Archbps of, 279, 290, 307, 325, 326.

Hamyares. See Homerites.

Hands, imposition of, i. 316. See Confirmation.

Hanke.
De Byzant. rer. Scriptorib. Græcis, persecution of Photius, iii. 568 n. 3.

Hanno, abp. of Cologne, iii. 396.

Hans, lord of Baden, v. 326.

Happiness, Aquinas on, iv. 432, 444. Anselm, iv. 500. Eternal, iii. 482 (485, 488). And blessedness, iv. 521.

Harald Blaatand, king of Denmark, successor of Gurm, iii. 288. Becomes a Christian, 288, 289. Death of, 290. Unni, 291. Seeks to introduce Christianity in Norway, 296.

Harald Klag, king of Denmark, iii. 271, 272, 288. Becomes a Christian, and is banished, 275, 277.

Hardaschir, Mares of, ii. 610. See Ibas.

Hardt, Hermann, v. d. See Van der Hardt.

Harduin.
Acta concil. (f. 217, pretended synod under Diocletian, iii. 372 n. 1).
T. i. f. 706. *council at Sirmium* (an. 357), symbol, ii. 450 n. 2; f. 959, *council at Tyrin*, 775 n. 5; f. 1271, Nestorius and P. of Samosata compared, 511 n. 4; f. 1280, *synod under Nestorius*, 511 n. 5; f. 1335, petition against N., 511 n. 3; f. 1337, N. on the epithet θεοτόκος, 512 n. 1; f. 1338, the disorderly monk, 511 n. 6; f. 1346, *council of Ephesus* (an. 431), imperial letter, 527 n.; f. 1347, commonitorium of Coelestin, 539 n.; f. 1348 (conc. Eph. P. i. c. 21), ep. of John of Antioch. 529 n. 1; f. 1382, admittance refused to the bps. at the house of N., 530 n. 2; f. 1391, which is surrounded by guards, 528 n. 1; f. 1391, words of Euoptios, 530 n. 4; ff. 1392, 1399, words of N., etc., perverted, 530 n. 5; f. 1422, sentence against N., 531 n. 1; f. 1435, ep. of Cyrill, 529 n. 2; f. 1438, report of N. to Theodosius II., 528 n. 2; f. 1440, ep. of N. and others to the same, 532 n. 1; ff. 1441, 1442, ep. of the Cyrillian party to the same, 528 n. 3, 531 n. 4; f. 1444, discourse of Rheginus, 531 n. 2; f. 1447, Dalmatius, 535 n. 2; f. 1452, publication of the sentence, 531 n. 3; f. 1459, ep. of John to the emperor, 528 n. 4; f. 1515, N. and Theodore, 500 n. 3; f. 1540, declaration of the emperor, 534 n. 2; f. 1548, ep. of comes Irenaeus, 537 n. 2; f. 1588, Dalmatius, 535 n. 1; his address to the people, 536 n. 2; f. 1593, declaration of the party of Cyrill, 538 n. 2; f. 1596, report of Memnon, 532 n. 2; f. 1669, edict banishing Nestorius, 552 n. 3; f. 1694 (P. 4), time of Christmas, ii. 346 n. 2.
T. ii. f. 34 (act. i.), *council of Chalcedon*, protest of Hilarus at Rome against II conc. Ephes., ii. 574 n. 3; ff. 48, 49, ep. of Marcion to the synod (at Nice), 577 n. 5; f. 48, the Roman delegates and Dioscurus, 577 r. 3; f. 74, B. Pulcheria, 519 n. 2 (578 n. 1); f. 90, reading of the "sacra" at the synod of Flavian, 574 n. 1; ff. 94, 102, the bps. on their intimidation at II. conc. Ephes., 571 nn. 2 3; f. 106, reply of lay dignitaries, 578 n. 3; f. 110, neglect of Leo's letter at II. conc. Ephes., 574 n 1; f. 111 E, Eusebius and Eutyches at the synod of Flavian (an. 448), 564 n. 1, f. 130, change of majority, 578 n. 2; f. 149, Eutyches, 560 n. 2; f. 160 D, ep. of Theodosius II. at the Flavian conc., 565 n 1; f. 161, E, Eusebius of Doryleum at II. conc. Ephes., 571 n. 1; f. 162 C, Eutyches and Chrysaphius at the synod of Flavian, 565 nn. 1, 3; f. 176 D, anticipation of a general council, 567 n. 2; f. 182, Eutyches on the ch. teachers, 565 n. 2; f 213, Basil of Seleucia on his conduct at II. conc. Ephes., 570 n. 1; f. 216, violence of Dioscurus there, 571 n. 4; f. 255 E, letter of Leo there, 574 n. 1; f. 258, protest of Hilarus at Rome, 574 n. 2; f. 286, opposition to the proposal for a new symbol at conc. Chalcedon., 579 n. 1; f. 322, complaints of his clergy against Dioscurus there, 559 n. 1; f. 346 (act. iii.), the Roman delegates, 577 n. 3; f. 426 (act. iv.), Leo and Anatolius, 577 n. 4; f. 449 (act. v.), discussions on the creed, 579 n. 3; f. 530 (act. x.), letter of Ibas, 529 n. 3; f. 672, petition of the monks from Palestine, 583 n. 2; f. 731, the bps. of Pamphylia on the determinations of conc. Chalcedon., 585 n.; (f. 1163, collatio. Const. (an. 533), on the Dionysian writings, iii. 170 n. 1); f. 1193, *council under Mennas* (an. 536) (act. i.), 593 nn. 1, 4; f. 1243, act. 4, 593 n. 2; f. 1334, 1337, 1339, 1355, 1356, 1359, popular hatred of Monophysites, Anantius, 591 n.
T. iii. f. 108, V. conc. œc. (an. 553), *II. œc. concil. Constantinop.* (act. v.) Cyrill's work, "there is but one Christ," and reply of Theodore, ii. 557 nn. 5, 6; f. 139, sermon of Theodoret after Cyrill's death, ii. 557 n. 7;

f. 176, Vigilii, ep. ad Rusticum et Sebastianum, ii. 403 n. 2; f. 198, condemnation of Origen at the V. conc. œcum., ii. 704 n. 4; f. 675, Martin I. ep. 14 ad Theodorum, iii. 187 n. 1; f. 677, *et seq.*, the same; Martin's sufferings, iii 189 n. 1; f. 724, *Lateran council* (an. 658), Maximus and others on the "type," iii. 185 n. 3; f. 796, the Ecthesis, iii. 180 n. 3; f. 824, the Type, iii. 185 n. 2; f. 913, *council of Arles*, instructions of Theodulf to his clergy, iii. 125 n. 5; f. 1181, *I. Trullan conc.* (act. viii.), confession of Macarius, iii. 195 n. 1; f. 1258 (act. xi.), circular letter of Sophronius, iii. 179 n. 5; f. 1309, reply of Sergius to Cyrus of Phasis, iii. 177 nn. 2-4; f. 1315 (act. xii.), ep. of Sergius to Honorius, 178 n. 3, 179 n. 1; f. 1319, reply of H., iii. 179 nn. 2, 3; f. 1338, Cyrus bp. of Phasis, his ep. to Sergius, iii. 176 n. 2, 177 n. 1; f. 1342, compromise of Cyrus with the Monophysites, iii. 177 n. 7; ff. 1343, 1344 (act. xiii.), fragments of Theodore of Pharan, iii. 181 nn.; f. 1354, ep. ii. of Honorius to Sergius, iii. 179 n. 4; f. 1386 (act. xvi.), petition concerning the anathema, and f. 1393 (session 18), anathema pronounced, iii. 195 n. 2; f. 1535, the archivarius of Constantinople on Phillippicus, iii. 196 n. 2; f. 1838, John of Const., ep. to op. of Rome, iii. 197 nn.
T. iv. f. 11, acts of the iconoclasts, iii. 213 n. 3; f. 25, efforts to prevent the assembling of council, 229 n. 2; f. 26, address of Tarasius at Constantinop., an. 786, 227 n. 2; f. 28, Irene bids the council dissolve, 230 n. 1; f 38, her proclamation for its reassembling at Nice, imperial sacra, Tarasius, 225 n. 1, 227 n. 1, 230 n. 2; ff. 39, 41, 48, 60, 62, 77, 128, confessions of bps. converted to image worship, 229 n. 1, 230 n. 4, 231 nn. 1-5, 7, 8; f. 42, form of recantation, 232 n. 2; f. 47, list of bps. conspirators against image worship, 229 n. 3; f. 137, writing of the Syrian monks concerning the false plenipotentiaries, 228 n. 2; f. 187 (act. iv.), ep. of Nilus read at the council of iconoclasts, 216 n. 3; (f. 194, fragments of the apology of Leontius, iii. 330 n.); f. 208, decree in regard to oaths 231 n. 6; f. 211, testimony of a presbyter, 230 n. 2; ff. 258, 259, letter of Germanus to Thomas of Claudiopolis, 205 nn.; f. 300 (act. v.), garbled extracts from the ch. fathers at the council of iconoclasts (an. 754) 216 n. 3; (f. 306, fragm. hist. eccles. of John the Schismatic, Philoxenos, ii. 331 n. 4; f. 310, testimony against the iconoclasts, 219 n. 1; f. 319, the oriental plenipotentiary on Constantine bp. of Nacolia, 203 n. 1; f. 322, the image kissed, 232 n. 4; f. 422, disorders of the iconoclasts, 217 n. 1; f. 423, confession of faith at the conc. of iconoclasts, 217 n. 4; f. 456, respect paid to images distinguished from the worship due to God, 232 n. 6 f. 476, burning of lights and incense, 233 n.; f. 521, ep. of Tarasius to the abbot John, 232 n. 1; f. 970, Charlemagne and Leo III., 555 n. 1.
T. v. f. 95, *council at Paviæ* (an. 853), on private chapels, iii. 413 n. 2; f. 125, ep. ii. of Nicholas I. to emp. Michael III., 502 n. 2; f. 135, to Photius, 565 n. 4; f. 145, ep. vii. to Michael, 566 n. 1; f. 147, to Constantinople, 563 n. 1; f. 160, to Michael, 550 n. 3; f. 164, ep. iii., 566 n. 3; f. 179, to his legates, 562 n. 3; f. 180, to Constantinople, 563 n. 1; f. 232, ep. 18, to Charles the Bald, 353 n. 1; f. 237, ep. 22, ad episc. Galliæ et Germaniæ, 354 n. 2; f. 248, ep. 28, to Hincmar, 361 n. 4; f. 268, to the French bps., 361 n. 3; f. 263, ep. 49, to the bps. of Lothar ngia, 355 n. 3; f. 273, to Charles the Bald, against duels, 450 n. 2; f. 288, ep. 55, to Lewis of Germany, 354 n. 3; f. 591, to the French bps., 359 n.; f. 752, council (an. 869) VIII. œcumen., *IV. œc. concil. Const.*, preface, Constantino the Philos., Photius, 314 n. 5, 550 n. 3; f. 757,

Bulgaria, 310 n. 1; f. 875, burning of records of synods, Const. an. 859, 561 n. 2; f. 876 (act. vii.), false envoys, 575 n. 2; ff. 951, 953, 955, 966, 974, life of Ignatius, 541 n. 3, 549 n. 3, 55* n. 1, 563 n. 2, 561 n. 1; f. 987, the same, signing of the sentence against Photius, 571 n. 2; f. 999, the same, on the 11. council of Nice, 532 n. 3; f. 1013, appeal of Ignatius, and his report of synod Const. an. 861, 595 n. 3; ff. 1014, 1015, report of Ignatius, 543 nn. 2, 4; f. 1035, priests of Photius' party suspended, 570 n. 3; f. 1036, the false envoys at the previous council (an. 867), 575 n. 3; f. 1058, defence of Photius by Zacharias, 570 n. 5; f. 1086, the testimony against Ignatius at the synod of 861, 564 n. 1; f. 1087 (act. vii.), the false envoys, 575 n. 3; f. 1089, Theodore Κριθινος, 551 n. 1; f. 1095, profanity of emp. Michael III., 561 n. 1; f. 1096, the witnesses against Ignatius, 564 n. 1; f. 1101 (can. 10), anathema against those who suppose man to possess two souls, 559 n. 3; f. 1165, ep. of John VIII. to Basilius, 574 n. 2; f. 1171, the same (Greek version), 576 n. 2.

T. vi. p. i. f. 61, John VIII., ep. 90, to Methodius, iii. 317 n. 1; f. 87, ep. 108 to Photius, 575 n. 1; f. 126, complaint of Tucotmar to John IX., 319 n. 3; f. 207, *synod of Rouen* (an. 879), 420 n. 5; f. 208, commonitorium of John VIII. to his legates, *Concil. Const.* (an. 867), 574 n. 3; ff. 223, 224, 228, 231, 242, 243, 254, papal legates at the council, 574 n. 4, 576 nn. 1, 3, 4; ff. 224, 244, friends of Photius, 573 n. 2; ff. 251, 283, 310, Photius on the pope's demands in regard to Bulgaria, 577 n. 1; f. 254, the legates, 576 n. 3; f. 255, Photius and Basilius, 572 n. 2; f. 283, Bulgaria, laity in clerical offices, 577 nn. 1, 3; f. 286, family of Photius, 559 n. 1; f. 290, on the false envoys at previous council (VIII. oecum.), 575 n. 5; f. 294, commonitorium of the pope to his legates, 576 n. 5; f. 415, *council of Soissons* (an. 899), 427 n. 3; f. 722, ep. of Hugo Capet to John XV., 368 n. 1; f. 726, Gerbert's confession of faith, 371 n. 2; f. 731, his ep. ad Constantinum abbatem, 371 n. 3; to Saguin, n. 5; ff. 733, 734, to Adelaide of France, 374 nn. 2, 3; f. 735, his defence at the *council of Muson*, 373 n. 1; f. 740, Gerbert and Gregory V., 375 n. 1; f. 760, G. as Sylvester II., 375 n. 2; f. 919, treuga Dei, 407 n. 3; ff. 927, 943, reply of Leo IX. to the attack of Michael Cerularius, 580 n. 2, 582 n. 1; f. 944, the same, term cardinal, 387 n. 7. P. ii. f. 1796, ep. of Paschalis II. to Pontius of Cluny against withdrawal of cup, iv. 315 n. 1.

T. vii. f. 471, *concil. Burdegalense* (Bordeaux) (an. 1255), can. 5, against the communion of children, iv. 342 n. 4; f. 1087, *concil. Melfitanum*, c. 16, Urban II. on false penance, iv. 348 n. 2.

T. viii. f. 409, *concil. Biterrense* (at Beziers) on preachers of indulgences, iv. 353 n 2.

Harkh, province of, iii. 588.
Harmonies of the Gospels. Harmonists, i. 171, 458 n. 1, 699 n. 1.
Haroun Al Raschid, iii. 458 n. 2.
Hartmann, master of the school at Paderborn, iv. 33.
Hartwig, abp. of Bremen, iv. 35, 37.
Haruspices, ii. 22, 23, 34, 90.
Harz, district, iii. 592.
Hase, Script. Byzant., ii. 111 n. 1.
Hasenburg, v. 237.
Hasselbach.

De Schola. quae Alexandriae floruit. catechetica, part 1, p. 15, i. 527 n. 2.

Hatto, abp. of Mentz, iii. 321 n. 4.

Hautvilliers, monastery, iii. 479.
Havel, river, iv. 18.
Havelburg, bishopric, iii. 324.
Havi, Horik's governor, iii. 286.
Haymo, abbot, life of Wm. of Hirschau, iv. 86 n. 4.
Healing, gift of, i. 73, 74, 119 n. 6, 510, 659; v. 266. Remedies taught in dreams, i. 107. See Miracles, Sick.
Heathen, preparatory development among the, ii. 708. Fate of heathen ancestors, iii. 314, 602. Heathenism under the first Christian emperors; reaction, persecution of, decline, ii. 1–110. See Paganism, Virtue.
Heaven, iv. 319, 364–367, 408, 429, 448; v. 38, 401. With Paulicians, iii. 257 and n. 4, 258, 261. See Kingdom of, Seven Heavens, i. 445.
Hebraism, i. 45, and Judaism, i. 352.
Hebrew Bible, ii. 160, 745. Text, i. 700, 708. (See Gospel.) Religion, i. 3. See Judaism, Languages.
Hebrews, epistle to the, i. 83, 657.

Heb. 1: 14, ii. 714. 2, i. 382 n. 2: 13, i. 563. 3: 2, ii. 405 n. 3. 4: 12, i. 707. 9: 13, 14, iii. 347 n. 5. 9: 14, ii. 498 n. 5. 11: 1, iv. 397, 402, 430. 11: 3, i. 872, 565. 12: 14, i. 715. 13: 4, ii. 306; iii. 557.

Hebrides, iii. 10.
Hedges of the Mosaic law, i. 39.
Heerbann, iii. 102, 385 n. 2, 404, 405.
Hegemonius, i. 485 n. 3.
Hegesippus, i. 343 n. 3, 376 n. 3. History and character, i. 675, 676.

Quoted by Euseb. l. 2, c. 23, i. 675 n. 1. L. iii. cc. 19, 20, i. 96 n. 6. L. 4, c. 22, i. 676 n. 1.

Heidelberg, university of, v. 372, 375.
Heinrich, bp. of Upsala, iv. 45.
Heinrich der Lette, priest.

Chronicon Livonic., iv. 39 nn., 40 nn., 41 nn. 1, 2. See Chron. Livon.

Heinricus ("mobilis"), v. 119 and n. 2.
Heisterbach, monastery, iv. 155 n. 5, 239 n. 1. See Caesarius of.
Held, J. Th.

Illustratio rerum, etc., v. 253 n.

Helena (Olga), iii. 328.
Helena, mother of Constantine, ii. 7, 31, 377.
Helenopolis, ii. 30, 170 n. 2. See Palladius of.
Helgaldi, vita Roberti regis, iii. 450 n. 5. See Du Chesne.
Helgoland, Willibrord there, iii. 45. Lindger, planter of Christianity there, iii. 79.
Heliopolis, ii. 26.
Helios, ii. 8 and n. 3, 13. See Sun.
Hell, i. 471; iii. 442; iv. 364, 365, 448, 555 n. 1; v. 383, 401. Sermons, iii. 486, 487. Cathurists concerning, iv. 575. See Hades.
Helladius, bp. of Tarsus, ii. 548 n. 3, 549
Hellenic culture, its relation to Christian-

ity, i. 4, 339, 342, 662 ; iv. 61. To Judaism, i. 49-59. And religion, ii. 52-54, 77. Principle, i. 351. Hellenism, ii. 104-106, 264. See Greek culture, etc.

Helmold, priest.

Chronica Slavorum, on the conversion of the Slaves, iii. 323 n. 3, 324 n. 2. Vicelin, iv. 35 nn. L. i. c. 1, iii. 325 n. 1. L. i. c. 6, early missionaries, iii. 323 n. 3 ; c. 12, Magdeburg, iii. 324 n. 3 ; c. 16, iii. 325 n. 4 ; cc. 19, 20, Gottschalk, iii. 325 n. 5, 326 n. 1 ; c. 22, iii. 326 nn. 2, 3, 5 ; c. 142, Vicelin, iv. 35 n.

Heloise, iv. 397, 400.
Helvidius, ii. 376, 377.
Hennegau, iv. 238.
Henoticon at Jerusalem, i. 342. Zeno's, ii. 588-590, 592.
Henricians, iv. 603 n. 4, 604. See H. of Cluny.
Henry, abp. of Mentz, iv. 74.
Henry, abp. of Ravenna, iii. 387 n. 3.
Henry, bp. of Speier, letter against Gregory VII., iv. 92 n. 6, 99 nn. 2, 6, 113 n. See Eccard.
Henry, count of Luxemburg, v. 22. See Henry VII.
Henry, duke of Bavaria, iii. 332, 334.
Henry I., emperor of Germany, iii. 288, 324.
Henry II. (Saint), emperor, iii. 334.
Henry III., emperor, iii. 377, 378, 380 n., 404 n. 1, 592 n. 4 ; iv. 89, 92 n. 6, 167.
Henry IV., emperor, iii. 380 n. 1, 395, 396. The bp. Bernard, iv. 2 n. 2. Otto of Bamberg, iv. 4 and n. 2. Election of Gregory VII., iv. 92 n. 6. Waltram of Naumberg, iv. 98 n. 1. Reconciliation, contest with Gregory, iv. 103 n. 1, 103-121, 233, 303. Goes to Italy, iv. 112-115. Supports Guibert, iv. 118, 121. Contest with Gregory's successors, iv. 129-132. Rebellion of his sons, iv. 129 and n. 3, 133, 134 n. 3. F. to Theodoric (Dieteric) of Verdun, iv. 120 nn, 2, 3.
Henry V., emperor, iv. 133-143, 245. Joachim, 223 n. 3.
Henry VI., emperor, iv. 172, 173, 176-223 n. 3, 226.
Henry VII., emperor, v. 22.
Henry (Emmerich), Hungarian prince, iii. 334.
Henry I., king of England, iv. 364.
Henry II., king of England, iv. 168 n. 2, 169-172.
Henry I, king of France, iii. 507, 509.
Henry, son of prince Gottschalk, iv. 32, 33.
Henry Knighton. See Knighton.
Henry of Constance, iv. 155 n. 5.
Henry of Ghent.

On writers of his own time, c. 24, iv. 418 n. 3.

Henry of Hessia. See Langenstein.
Henry of Nordlingen, v. 222 n. 1, 383 n. 2. See Heumanni opusc.
Henry Percy, v. 147.

Henry Suso, v. 388, 411.
Henry the Cluniacensian, iv. 597-604. Tract of, iv. 602 n. 5.
Henry the Lion, conqueror of the Wends, iv. 32, 35.
Heptanome, in Egypt, ii. 264.
Heptarchy, Anglo-Saxon, Christianity in the, iii. 11-25.
Heraclas, disciple of Origen, i. 698, 700, 712.
Heraclea, ii. 197, 591 ; iii. 195, 570.
Heracleon the Gnostic, on faith, i. 307. Valentine, 427. The cross, 431. His doctrines, 434-437. Scientific tendency, 440. Origen, 702.

In Evang. Joann. apud Orig. In Joann., t. 2, c. 15, the Soter, i. 423 n. 2. T. 6, c. 12, revelation, 441 n. 2 ; c. 23, the Soter, 430 n. 1. T. 10, c. 14, the marriage feast, 399 n. 2, 431 n. 3 ; c. 19, the cross, 441 nn. 1, 2. T. 13, c. 10, the pneumatici, 432 n. 5 ; c. 11, æon, 873 n. 3 ; syzygy, 432 n. 2 c. 16, the psychici, 422 n. 4 ; c. 20, pneumatici, 432 n. 4 ; cc. 25, 30, psychici, 422 n. 4 ; c. 48, Christ and the Soter, 423 n. 2 ; cc. 51, 59, and t. 20, c. 20, the psychici, 422 n. 4, 432 n. 3. In evang. Lucæ, apud Clement, Strom. L. 4, f. 503, 434 n. 4.

Heracleopolis, ii. 264.
Heraclian, bp. of Chalcedon.

Ap. Phot. cod. 95, acts of Mani, i. 485 n. 3.

Heraclitus, i. 71. Knowledge of God, ii. 117. The Sibyls, i. 177.
Heraclius, governor, i. 115.
Heraclius, Greek emperor, iii. 213 n. 2. Conquers the Persians, 84. In the Monotheletic controversy, 176-184. His formula for the union of the Monophysites with the Catholic church, 176. See his edict Ἔκθεσις τῆς πίστεως
Herard, bp. of Tours, "pastoral instructions," iii. 426.
Herbelot. See Bibliothèque.
Hercules, worship of, ii. 100.
Herculius. See Maximinus.
Heresies, heretical tendencies, i 337-506 ; iv. 315, 325. Celsus on, i. 164. Distinguished from Schisms, i. 221. Their relation to the development of Christianity, i. 337-339, 573 ; iv. 315. In the newly converted nations, iii. 38, 39 and n. 1. In monasticism, iv. 268 (see Franciscans). In the south of France, iv. 257 (see Sects). Sources of, iii. 602 ; iv. 99, 268, 313, 565, 582. Yves on, iv. 137. Innocent III., iv. 322. In the Greek church, iv. 537. In the pope, iv. 135 ; v. 19, 20. Heretical teachers in Bulgaria, iii. 308 n. 2, 309. In Spain, iii. 430 n. 3. See Sects.
Heretics, baptism of, i. 317-323 ; ii. 219 n. 2. Writings of, i. 150. Ordination, ii. 169 n. 7. Laws against, ii. 235. Condemnation of, as a condition of ordination, ii. 597 n. 1. Opinions as to the treatment of, ii. 601 (584, 767 n. 4) ; iii. 62, 63, 254, 255, 480, 491, 541, 544 ; iv. 604, 640 ; v. 28, 29, 353. Punish-

ment, suppression of, ii. 234, 249-252; iii. 62, 63, 478, 479, 541, 542; iv. 604, 640 and n. 2; v. 15, 119. Churches of, iii. 5 n. 4. False accusations against, iii. 265, 595 n. 3. Zeal of, iv. 315. Abelard on, iv. 391. See Inquisition, also the articles, Augustin, Cyprian, Dionysius of Alexandria, Stephanus, Tertullian.
Herewald, iv. 363.
Heribald, bp. of Auxerre, iii. 497 n. 1.
Heribert, abp. of Milan, iii. 600.
Heribert, ecclesiastic, iii. 595.
Heribert, monk, report of the sects near Perigneux, iv. 594 n. 2. See Mabillon.
Heribert of Boscham, life of A Becket, iv. 169 n. 3, 170 nn.
Hericlac, priest, iii. 271.
Herigar (Hergeir), iii. 276, 280-282.
Herigar, abbot of Laub, iii. 501.
Herluin, abbot of Bec, iv. 364. Life of, iii. 410 n. 4, 415 n. 2. See Acta S. (O. B.), S. vi.
Hermann, abbot, hist. of abbey at Tournay, iv. 357 n., 359 n. 2.
Hermann, bp. of Augsburg, iv. 143 n. 5.
Hermann, bp. of Bamberg, iv. 102, 103.
Hermann, bp. of Metz, iv. 87 n. 4, 105 n. 4, 107, 109 n. 3, 110, 130.
Hermann, bp. of Toul, iii. 385 n. 2.
Hermann, Jewish convert, iv. 71, 72, 79-81. Account of his own conversion 79 and n. 1, 81 n. 1.
Hermann. See Van der Hardt.
Hermannus Contractus.

Chronicle, an. 1052, Manicheans, iii. 592 n. 4; an. 1053, Leo IX., 386 n. 3.

Hermas, the shepherd of, i. 278. Creation from nothing, 565 n. 2. Baptism in Hades, 646. Criticism, 660.

L. iii. Similitud. V., fasting, i. 278 n. 2; statio, 206 n. 2; S. IX. (in Fabric. cod. apocr. cod. 3, p. 1009), Christ in Hades, 646 n. 4.

Hermeneutical canons, the first, i. 388.
Hermeneutics, i. 388, 722; iii. 458. See Bible Interpretation.
Hermes Trismegistus, i. 176; ii. 268 n. 4; iv. 461, 463 n. 7. Hermetic ideas, ii. 438.
Herminue. See Facundus of.
Hermias, apologist, i. 673.
Hermitages, iii. 419.
Hermits, in Britain, iii. 17. On the Rhine, 28. In Bavaria, 40. In Italy, 418, 419. In France, 504 (iv. 236). Ardgar, iii. 280. Berengar on, iii. 504, 505. Lull on, iv. 310. See Anchorets.
Hermogenes, doctrine of Creation, i. 565-568. Anthropology, 616-618. Tertullian, 684 n. 2. See Creation, Tertullian, Theodoretus.
Hermopolis, ii. 752.
Hermupolis, lower, ii. 587.
Herod I., v. 16.
Herod Agrippa, v. 36.
Herod Antipas, v. 191, 314.

Herodotus.

L. i. c. 136, 138, 140, on Persian customs, ii. 128 nn. 3, 4, 129 n. 1.

Heroism, Christian, effect on Pagans, i. 76, 77.
Heron, mathematician, ii. 104.
Heron, monk, ii. 275.
Heros, bp. of Arles, ii. 643 and n. 1, 648.
Hersfeld, monastery, iii. 74.
Hertford, iii. 25.
Herulians, iii. 28 n. 3.
Hesiod, ii. 85.
Hessia, Christianity there, iii. 47, 50 and n. 2, 51, 72, 74, 75.
Hesychius, Egyptian bp., reviser of the Bible, i. 722. Martyr, i. 722; ii. 254 n.
Hesychius, priest at Antioch, ii. 67 n. 2.
Hetaeriae, Trajan's law against the, i. 97, 98, 120.
Heumann.

Opuscula, f. 331, seq., f. 393, friends of God, Henry of Nördlingen, v. 222 n. 1, 383 n. 2.

Heuwald, brothers, iii. 44.
Hexapla, i. 708 and n. 4; ii. 745. See Origen.
Hezekiah, iii. 203, 211.
Hiallti, of Iceland, iii. 302-304.
Hiberuia, ii. 146. See Ireland.
Hieracas, Egyptian ascetic, i. 713-716.
Hierapolis, iii. 229 n. 3. See Alexander of Hierap., Xenayas.
Hierarchical element, i. 657.
Hierarchy, church, ii. 48. Arrogance of the, ii. 175, 176. Opposition to the, iii. 24, 269 n. 6, 270; iv. 578; v. 31, 134, 138, 158, 240. Wm. of St. Amour on the permanence of the, iv. 619. See Gerson's idea of the, v. 79. Janow, v. 197, 204, 210. Huss, v. 296, 352. See Church Constitution, Papacy.
Hierocles, i. 173, 174.

Λόγοι φιλαλήθεις πρὸς τοὺς χριστιανούς (ap Lact. inst., l. 5, c. 2; de mort persecut., c. 16), i. 173 n. 1.

Hieronymus. See Jerome.
Hierotheos, iii. 330.
Hierotheos, mystic, ii. 615. Apoc. writings of, 615 n. 1.
Hilarianus, the martyr, i. 152.
Hilarion, monk, ii. 142, 271, 378; iii. 420.
Hilarius (the Ambrosiast), ordination of deaconesses, ii. 190 n. 4.

In ep. ad Ephes. c. 4, v. 12, apostolic church constitution, i. 182 n. In ep. ad Tim. I. c. 3, bishops and presbyters, i. 190 n. In Tim. II. c. 3: 7, edict of Diocletian, i. 506 n. (144 n. 3).

Hilarius, bp. of Arles, ii. 206, 207.
Hilarius, Prosper's friend, ii. 691, 695, 697, 710.
Hilarius, rhetorician, ii. 397.
Hilarus, Roman deacon at Conc. Ephes. II., ii. 573, 574 and n. 1.
Hilary, bp. of Poictiers, on the favor of princes towards the church, ii. 35.

Freedom of belief, 165. Author of church hymns, 354 and n. 4. Participation in the Arian controversy, 441. Preparation for the Nicene creed among the people, 466. Doctrine of the Holy Spirit, 467. Person of Christ, 483 n., 608. Anthropology, 618–622. Doctrine of the Lord's Supper, 731, 732.

Citations: —
Ad Constant., l. i. §§ 2, 7, freedom of belief, ii. 165 nn. 3, 4. C. Auxentium, § 6, "sanctiores aures plebis," 466 n. 1. C. Constant., § 10, use of force in religion, 36 n. 1; § 15, sermon at Antioch, 457 n. 1 (De synodis, § 86, ὁμοούσιον at the council of Antioch an. 269, i. 606 nn. 1, 2). De trinitate, l. i. § 35, grace, 621 n. 2; l. viii. § 13, union with Christ, 732 n. 1; l. ix. and x., person of Christ, 483 n. 1. Ep. 156, ad Augustin, the oath, 635 n. 6. In Matt. 8, § 6, justification, 620 n. 1; 9, § 2, sense of sin, 619 n. 7; 10, § 24, evil, 619 n. 2; 11, § 13, the yoke of Christ, 621 n. 1; 18, § 6, the lost sheep, the human race, 618 n. On Matt. 5: 8, corporality of the soul, 706 n. 2. Opus hist. fragm., iii. § 25, Constantius, 452 n. 1; § 26, bps. at Antioch, 205 n. 1; vi. § 6, the Sirmian creed, 151 n. 1. Tract in Ps. i. § 4, natural bent towards sins, 619 n. 1; Ps. li. § 20, dependence on God, 621 n. 4; § 23, human righteousness, 619 n. 6; Ps. lii. § 11, the same, 619 n. 6; Ps. lvii. § 3, freewill and predestination, 621 n. 5, 622 nn. 2, 3; Ps. lxviii. § 24, rightcousness of the law, and of faith, 620 n. 2; Ps. cxix. § 12, the image of God, 619 n. 3; Ps. cxxix. § 6, spirit and sense, 619 n. 4.

Hildebert, abp. of Mans or Tours, on the contest between the pope and the emperor, iv. 134, 136, 141. Appeals to Rome, 199. Hypocritical monks, 244. Robert of Arbrissel, 247. Pilgrimages, 306. Tractatus Theologicus, 401 n. 3. Henry of Cluny, 599–602. Gesta, 599 n. 1, see Mabillon. On the Lord's Supper, v. 270.

Citations: —
Ep. 11, monks, iv. 244 n. 2. Ep. 15, to a count of Angers, 306 n. 3, 307 nn. 1, 2, 343 n. 3. L. ii. ep. 21, on Henry IV., 134 n. 3. Ep. 22, Paschalis, ii. 136 nn. 1, 2, 140 n. 4. Ep. 23, Henry of Cluny, 601 n. 2, 602 n. 4. Ep. 24, the same, 602 nn. 1, 2. Ep. 41, to Honorius II. on appeals, 199 n. 2. Ep. Marbod, f. 1408, Robert of Arbrissel, 248 nn.

Hildebold, abp. of Cologne, iii. 80.
Hildebrand, priest of Threida, iv. 41.
Hildebrand. See Gregory VII.
Hildebrandian epoch, iv. 205, 233, 592. Movement, iv. 246. Party, school, iv. 118 n. 2, 140, 141, 149, 248, 361. Principles, system, iii. 394 n. 2, 396, 399, 402 n. 1, 411 n. 7, 414, 599; iv. 118, 128, 130, 132, 143, 200, 205, 208, 361, 364, 593. Reform, iv. 195, 348, 565, 598; v. 159. Anti-Hildebrandian party, iv. 92 n. 6, 98 n. 2, 99 n. 4, 104, 118, 130; two classes, iv. 98.
Hildegar, bp. of Cologne, iii. 71.
Hildegard, abbess, iv. 216–220, 225, 586. Prophecies of, 219, 220, 462 n. 4; v. 222, 381. See Acta S. Sep.
Epistolæ (Colon. 1566), f. 115, to Elizabeth of Schönau, iv. 218 n. 1; ff. 121, 138, to the clergy of Mayence, 219 n. 1, 587 n. 1; ff. 160, 166, to the clergy in Cologne, 219 nn. 2, 3, 5, 586 n. 7; f. 169, 220 n. 1. In Martene et Durand, coll. ampliss. t. ii. f. 1017, from Berthold, 217 n. 2; f. 1029, ep. 11, 217 n. 3; f. 1053, to an abbot, 218 n. 3; f. 1055, to an abbot, 218 nn. 4, 5; f. 1058, to an abbess, 218 n. 6; f. 1060, on ascetieism, 217 n. 5; f. 1068, the same, 217 r. 4; f. 1098, ep. 66, on the divine essence, 462 n. 4.

Hildesheim, iii. 278; iv. 33, 421. See Bernward, Godehard.
Hilduin, abbot of St. Denis, iii. 466.
Areopagitica, in Acta S. of Surius, f. 638, iii. 467 n. 1; f. 653 *et seq.*, 466 n. 7.
Hillegenbach, iii. 289 n. 2.
Hiltibad, deacon, iii. 35.
Himerius, bp. of Tarraco, ii. 181, 360. Ep. to Damasus, 181.
Hindoo mysticism, i. 44, 450. Gnosis, 382. Antinomianism, 385. Maia, 386 n. 1, 481. Idea of the absolute, iii. 461 n. 2. Religions, iv. 275, 581.
Hinkmar, abp. of Rheims, for the supremacy of the church, iii. 354. For the rights of the bps., 358–368. For freedom in the election of bps., 400 n., 401, 402. His pastoral instructions, 427. His views of image worship, 440. Favors judgments of God, 449. His proceedings against Gottschalk, 478–482, 489–494. Scotus, 500.

Citations: —
Capitula ad presbyteros parochiæ suæ, iii. 427 n. 4. Epp. ad Amulom, 490. Sentence against Gottschalk, let er on the assembly at Chiersy (in Mauguin), 478 n. 2.
Opp. t. i., on predestination, c. 21, iii. 477 n. 2; cc. 24, 27, 29, 478 n. 1; c. 31, 500 n. 3. T. ii. f. 140, ep. to Lewis II. of Germany, 402 nn. 3, 4; f. 180 (opusc. xii.), cc. 3, 4, ep. to Lewis III. of France, on church elections, 400 n., 401 nn. 1–3, 402 n. 3; f. 261, ep. to Nicholas I., 481 n. 1; f. 290, ep. to Egilo, 481 n. 2, Guntbert, 479 n. 2; ff. 413, 429, 456, 459, 490, 483 (opusc. lv.), capitulorum adv. Hincmar Laphdunensem, 365 nn.; f. 457, the same, 441 n. 1; f. 476, the same, on decretals, 366 n. 2; f. 676, opusc. a l Hildegar, 449 n. 5; f. 697, ep. ad Adrian II. 362–364, 402 n. 2; ff. 706, 709, on the synod of Douzi (an. 871), 364 nn. 2, 3.
Sentence of Gottschalk; ep. on assembly of Chiersy (see Mauguin), iii. 473 n. 2.
Tract against the synod of Aix, iii. 354 n. 1.

Hinkmar, bp. of Laon, ii. 364, 365.
Hippolytus, life and writings, i. 681–683. On the celebration of the Sabbath, 297. The Lord's Supper, 383. On the charismata, 526.
C. Noëtum. § 1, i. 584 nn. 3, 4. Against heresies (apud. Phot. cod. 121), 682 n. 3. On Daniel (cod. 202), 682 n. 5. See Fabricius.
Hipporegius, church at, Augustin, ii. 167, 118, 232. Besieged, 695. See Councils (an. 393).
Hirsau, monastery, iv. 233.
Hirsch, Commentatio, Sigebert, iv. 130 n. 2.
Hirschau, iv. 86 n. 4; v. 374.
Hispalis (Seville). See Isidore.

Hist. Byzant.
   Continuatores post Theoph. f. 100, Basil. Macedo, iii. 307 n. 4.

Hist. Copt. Christianor.
   Ed. Wetzer, 1828, f. 89, iii. 89 n. 4.

Hist. des ducs, etc., de Narbonne. See Besse.

Hist. du diff. d'entre le pape Bonif. VIII. et Phil. le Belle, etc.
   Ep. of Phil. to Boniface, v. 7 nn. 2-4; f. 46, opinion of Peter de Bosco, 7 n. 5; f. 48, the pope to the king, 7 n. 6, 8 n. 1; f. 61, letter of the barons, 9 n. 3; ff. 63, 75, 76, replies from Rome (consistory. an. 1302), 7 n. 1, 9 nn. 4, 5, 10 nn.; f. 328, infidelity of the pope, 11 n. 1.

Hist. Edesseua e nummis illustrata.
   (Auct. Bayer) l. 3, p. 173, i. 80 n. 1.

Hist. générale de Languedoc, iv. 639 n. 3.

Hist. Hieronym. See Huss, opp.

Hist. Hussi, v. 344 n. 1.
   Opp. i. f. 6 seq., v. 322 n. 1, 338 n. 3; f. 13, i. 345 nn.; f. 27, 2, 369 n. 1. See Huss, Opp. i.

Hist. lit. de la France.
   (By the Benedictines of St. Maur.) Cæsarius of Arles, ii. 709 n. 2. T. v., Druthmar, iii. 458 n. 2. T. xii. f. 132, Abelard's dialogues, iv. 399 n. 3. T. xvi. f. 394, Simon of Tournay, iv. 418 nn. 3, 4.

Hist. of crusade against Albigenses, in verse, iv. 639 n. 2.

Hist. of the East Moguls.
   (In German, Schmidt, p. 271) Buddhism, i. 482 n. 1.

Historical criticism, iii. 170; iv. 520. Culture, sense, ii. 395, 402. Facts in Christianity, i. 368 (550, 551), 557; ii. 123 n. 1. Interpretation, i. 54-56; ii. 402, 493.

Histories, church (see Bede, John Cinnamos, John the Schismatic, Joseph Genesius, Gieseler, Julius Africanus, Lambert of Aschaffenburg, Lappenburg, Ledebur, Mosheim, Ordericus Vitalis, Raynaldi annales, Socrates, Sozomen, Strahl, Theodoret, Viguier, Wilkens, etc.) See Chronicles.

History, relation of Christianity to, i. 1-5. Attitude of Plato towards, i. 19; of the Neo-Platonists, i. 20, 368. Prophetic character of, i. 35, 36. Christ in, i. 36, 64, 65, 75, 169, 409. Significance of Christianity in, i. 64, 365, 379 (538), 539. Marcion on, i. 460, 462. Christian conception of, i. 218. Historical significance of Gnosticism, i. 365, 366, 368 (390), 460. Gnostic views of, i. 384, 391, 394, 407. Nature and, i. 379; v. 380. Philosophy of, Gnosticism and, i. 371 n. 1, 382. Historical Christianity with Paul, i. 551. Africanus, first Christian hist. of the world, i. 709 n. 1. Epochs of, iv. 216; v. 246, 274. Joachim on the periods of, iv. 223, 227-232. Fundamental tendencies in, iv. 444. Knowledge of, iv. 532. Forces in, v. 240, 275. See Ages, Christianity, Epochs.

History. See Hist., etc.

Hoffman.
   Nova Script. ac. monument. coll., t. ii., Lips. 1733. Liber Diurnus R. pontif., iii. 48 n. 5.

Högelsdorf, monastery, iv. 35.

Hohenstaufen, house of, contests of the popes with, iv. 163-169, 172-185, 215, 582, 610. Prophecies of Joachim concerning, 226 and n. 8.

Holiness of God, i. 22, 35, 58, 561, 562; ii. 109, 737; iii. 476, 477, 489; v. 392. Of man, i. 610, 644; ii. 181, 243; iii. 147, 148. Huss on, v. 336. Ruysbroch, v. 403. Tauler, v. 407. Mock, iv. 529, 531. Of the law, i. 36.

Holland, iii. 275.

Holm, in Liefland, iv. 37, 39.

Holstein, iii. 278, 325; iv. 34, 36.

Holum, episcopal see in Iceland, iii. 306.

Holy Sepulchre, iii. 398; iv. 70, 124, 179, 191, 298, 349.

Holy Spirit, doctrine concerning the, in the church, i. 608-610; ii. 466-471; iii. 554-556; iv. 458-461, 463-465. Opposition between the Latin and Greek churches concerning the procession of the, ii. 469-471; iii. 554-556, 567, 577, 585, 586; iv. 458, 536, 537, 540, 541, 544, 546, 549, 550. Sabellius on the, i. 599. Origen, i. 590, 609, 630. Justin, i. 609, 670. Hieracas, i. 716. Marcellus, ii. 439. Athanasius, ii. 468. Ulphilas, ii. 472 n. Photinus, ii. 482. Hilary, ii. 621. Augustin, ii. 627. Methodius, iii. 318. Joachim, iv. 227-232. Anselm, iv. 458. Abelard, iv. 459. Aquinas, iv. 464. Janow, v. 208. Eckhart, v. 394. See Trinity.

In the sects, with the Ebionites, i. 350. Cerinthus, i. 398. The Montanists, i. 511, 514-519, 525, 526, 673, 680. Artemonites, i. 582. Sabellius, i. 599. Paulicians, Sergius, iii. 253. Sect at Mortfort, iii. 600, 601. Thondracians, iii. 588 n. 2. Sect of the Holy Ghost, iv. 447, 448. Bogomiles, iv. 555 and n. 3. Catharists, iv. 569, 571, 574. See Apostolicals, Franciscans.

In particular relations. In the Trinity, i. 590, 599-602, 608-610; ii. 469-471; iv. 537, (see Trinity). Procession of the, ii. 469-471; iii. 554, 555; iv. 458-460, 463-465, 540, 547, 549. Uncreated, ii. 467, 468, 469, 471 (472 n.). Personality of, i. 608; ii. 467; iii. 157 n. 1. Relation to Christ (Ebionites), i. 350, 351, (Monarchians), i. 589 (Theodore), ii. 497-500, (Priscillianists), ii. 778. In the baptism of Christ, i. 347, 348, 351, 398, 411 and nn.; ii. 500; (iv. 575). In inspiration, revelation, i. 55, 56, 599, 657; ii. 391; iii. 172; iv. 391; v. 391; Clementines, i. 356, 357, 359; Clement, i. 533; Artemonites, i. 582; Montanists (see above).

In the apostles, i. 657; witness of the, i. 72. Relation to the church i. 180, 181, 209, 308, 516–519, 526, 609 (Irenæus, 678, 679), ii. 357, 369; iv. 537; v. 308, 309; to synods and councils, i. 206, 207; ii. 209, 210, 212; v. 27, 33, 88, 109, 115, 119, 132, 133, 2 7. In baptism, i. 646; ii. 728; Catharists, iv. 575. In imposition of hands, i. 315, 316 and n. 3, 318, 321, 322; Catharists, iv. 576. Relation to individuals, ii. 277, 278; iii. 172, 173, 483 n. 4; iv. 273, 562; v. 206, 396; to the πνεῦμα in man, i. 629, 630. Temples of the, i. 264, 654; ii. 304, 314. In regeneration, i. 250, 251; iii. 145; iv. 23. In grace, ii. 645. In justification, iv. 510. Teaching of, i. 320. Assistance, i. 624. Relation to the laity, ii. 179; v. 221. Source of divine love, ii. 460, 675, 678. Outpouring of the, iv. 293; v. 43, 140; Sabbath commemorative of, v. 140. Bestowal of the, v. 18, 170, 283. Gifts of the, iv. 522 (see Charismata). Conditions of his presence, v. 33, 115, 410. In the choice of popes, v. 117, 125. Relation to doctrine, v. 127, 128. To the Scriptures, v. 391 (see Inspiration). Leading, drawing of the, v. 177, 179, 187, 222, 309, 391. Janow on the, v. 208–210, 226. Huss, v. 267, 283, 308, 309. Sins against, i. 157; v. 186. Age of the, iv. 291, 448, 617, 618, 622, 623, 636–638. Representations of the, ii. 331. Church of, at Prague, v. 250.
Holy water, iii. 15.
Homage, iv. 49, 50, 143. Of the emperor to the pope, 163 n. 2.
Homer, ii. 41, 85. Comm. on, iv. 530. Ilias, l. 2, v. 204, i. 154 n. 2.
Homerites (Hamyares), ii. 142, 143.
Homiliaria, the ancient, iii. 124 n. 5. Falsified, iii. 126. That of Paul the deacon, 126.
Homiletic method, ii. 754.
Homilies read in churches, ii. 333; iii. 124, 126, 127, 586; iv. 317 n. 5; v. 195. Bulgarian, of Clement, iii. 315 n. 1.
Homoiousian doctrine, ii. 420, 421, 444, 453, 455, 472.
Homoousion, i. 578 n. 1, 590 n. 3, 606, 608; ii. 157 n. 4, 164 n. 2, 403, 404, 409 n. 4, 410, 415 n. 1, 416–424, 428, 429–440, 444, 452–456, 459, 461–468, 470, 472 n., 473, 478.
Honoratus, archdeacon, iii. 114.
Honoratus, bp. of Sicilibra, Donatist martyr, ii. 229 n. 2.
Honoratus, ep. of Augustin to, v. 312.
Honorius, emperor, ii. 92 n. 3, 100–102, 235, 236, 649 n. 1, 651 n 2.
Honorius I., pope in favor of Monotheletism, Sergius, iii. 178 n. 3, 179, 184. 193. Anathematized, 195. His name restored, 196.
   Epp. to Sergius, iii. 176 n. 2, 177 n. 1, 179 n. 4.
Honorius II., pope, iii. 396; iv. 6, 199.

Honorius III., pope, iv. 41, 177, 178, 270, 276, 341.
Honorius IV., pope, iv. 65, 627.
Hope, as motive, iv. 522. Means of salvation, 615.
Horace, iii. 602.
   L. I. epp. 18 et 84, iv. 409 n. 2.
Horæ canonicæ, iii. 106.
Horik I., king of Denmark, iii. 277, 279, 283, 285, 286.
Horik II., his successor, iii. 285, 286.
Hormisdas, bp. of Rome, ii. 592. Reply to Possessor, 710.
Hormisdas, Persian Christian, i. 134.
Hormisdas I. (Hormuz), Persian emperor, i. 488; ii 125 n. 2.
Hormisdas II., Persian emperor, ii. 125.
Hormuz, ii. 142.
Hormuz. See Hormisdas.
Horse-flesh, eating of, iii. 295 and n., 305.
Horses, sacred, iv. 15 and n. 3, 37.
Horus, with Valentine, i. 419, 420, 423.
Hosea, 8:4, iv. 160. 13, iv. 332.
Hosius, bp. of Cordova, ii. 31, 32, 187, 337, 414, 418 n. 1, 419, 443, 450.
Hospitality, among the Essenes, i. 40. In the early church, i. 197, 205, 255, 286. Julian on it. 63. Among monks, ii. 288, 289. Among the laity, iv. 294, 295. Catharists, iv. 583 and n. 2, 584. See Basilius.
Hospitals, ii. 169, 192, 593; iii. 408 n. 3; iv. 267, 296.
Host, iv. 336, 343 n. 4. Elevation of the, ii. 363, 364; v. 274. Kneeling before the, ii. 364; iv. 341; v. 156. See Lord's Supper.
Hottinger.
   Hist. Orient., f. 156, iv. 555 n. 1.
House, place of assembly for the church, i. 185, 186, 290, 291. Communion, i. 332. Church in the household, ii. 315. See Marriage.
Houses of Catharists, iv. 484 n. 1.
Hoxter, the river, iii. 273.
Hübner, v. 246.
Hugo, abbot of Cluny, reformer of monachism, iii. 418; iv. 84, 86, 91, 92 n. 1, 114, 249.
Hugo, abp. of Lyons, iv 123.
Hugo, bp. of Langres, iii. 506.
   Tract. de corp. et sang. Christi (see Bibl. patr. Lugd., t. 18), iii. 506 and n. 3.
Hugo, Franciscan, iv. 282.
Hugo, monk of Fleury, iv. 141, 142
   De regia potest. et Sacerdot. dignitate (see Baluz), iv. 141 n. 2, 142 n. 1. L. i. c. v., 142 n. 2.
Hugo of St. Victor, life and character, iv. 400–407, 408, 411, 413. On doubt as a means of transition to faith, 327, 328. On empirical science, 401. Communion of infants, 342 and nn. 1–3. Love to God, 386, 407. Rules of study, –01, 402. Faith, 402–407 (i. 415 n. 1). Omnipresence of God, 450, 452. Omnipo-

tence of God, 455, 456. Trinity, 460. Freewill and providence, 475. Original state, 487. Sinlessness of Jesus, 496. His works, 401 n. 3. The Lord's Supper, v. 270.

Citations from his writings: —
De Cærimoniis, etc., ecclesiasticis, 1. i. c. 20, infant communion, iv. 342 nn. 1-3. De Sacramentis fidei, 401 n. 3. L. i. c. 22, against curious speculations, 455 n. 6; P. iii. c. 28, the Trinity, 461 n. 1; P. v. c. 20, freewill, 476 n. 1; P. x. c. 4, faith, 327 nn. 1-3; P. x. c. 6, 405 nn. 1, 2. L. ii. P. xiii. c. 8, love, 407 n. 4. Erudit. didascalica, L. vi. c. 3 and l. vii. c. 20, 401 nn. 1, 4-6. Miscellan. l. i. tit. 18, faith, 403 n. 3; f. 47, 827 nn. 4, 5. Summa Sententiarum, iv. 401 n. 3. Tr. i. c. 4, omnipresence of God, against Abelard? 450 nn. 5, 6, 452 nn. 6, 7; c. 6, image of the Trinity in man. 460 n. 8, 461 n. 1; cc. 13, 24, omnipotence of God, against Abelard, 455 n. 7, 456 nn. 1-5. Tr. iii. c. 7, original state, iv. 487 n. 1. See Stud. und Krit. 1831, 2tes Heft.

Hugo Blancus, iv. 106, 107.
Hugo Capet, king of France, iii. 368, 369, 374, 450.
Hugo de Flavigny, Chronicon, council of Poictiers, iii. 518 n. 2.
Hugo de Paganis, master of the order of Templars, iv. 258.
Hugo of St. Caro (de St. Chers), iv. 426, 618 n. 1. Emendation of the Vulgate; Concordance; Comm., 426.

Sacra Bibl. recognita et emendata, etc., iv. 426 n. 4.

Huguenots, ii. 104.
Hulagu, khan of the Mongols, iv. 56.
Human and divine, separation of the, i. 26. In Christianity, ii. 245. See Inspiration.
Human life, sacredness of, iii. 102-104. See Punishment of death.
Human nature, power of Christianity over, i. 1-3, 75, 76; ii. 1. Its relationship to God, ii. 662-666, 718; iii. 171, 172; iv. 488, 506 (see Grace, Image of God, Redemption). Corruption of, i. 36, 630; ii. 637, 638, 641, 659-662, 671. Deterioration, 671, 675. Gnostics on, i. 372, 415. See Anthropology, Equality, Fall, Man, Original state, Sin.
Human sacrifices under Aurelian, i. 141, 142. Among the Saxons, prohibited by law, iii. 78.
Humanity of Christ. See Person of Christ.
Humbert, cardinal, validity of sacraments, iii. 379 n. 1. Berengarius, 513 and n. 2. In the controversy with Michael Cerularius, 581-584. Fasting on the Sabbath, 581 n. 4.

Adversus Simoniacos. L. ii. c. 35, iii. 404 n. 3. L. iii. c. 1, 404 n. 1; c. 11, 402 n. 1.
Defense of the Roman church, iii. 582 nn. 3-6, 5-8. Second defense, 583. Report of the embassy to Constantinople, 583 n. 3. See Canisius, Martene and Durand.

Humbert de Romanis, general of the Dominicans, schedule for the council of Lyons, iv. 189. The crusades, 190.

Care of lepers, 267. On preaching, 314-317 and n. 5, 332, 582, 589 n. 1. On the Catharists, 582, 583.

De Eruditione Prædicatorum, c. 12 (in Bibl. Patr. Lugd., t. 25), iv. 267 n. 2. L. i. cc. 2, 4, 16, 20, 21, 31, 314 nn. 8-5, 315 nn. : c. 6, 316 nn. 2-6, 317 n. 5; cc. 17, 26, 316 nn. 1, 7; c. 41 (f. 452), 583 n. 5. L. ii. 332 nn. 4, 5; cc. 36, 83, 91, 101, 317 nn. 1-4; c. 48, 584 n. 4; c. 62, 589 n. 1. L. v. c. 31, 583 n. 1. De his quæ tractanda, see Ortuinus Gratius. See Mansi Concil. xxvi.

Humiliates, iv. 630.
Humility in Platonism, i. 19, 34. In Phariseeism, i. 40. In the ancient world, i. 611; ii. 53. Celsus on, i. 166-168. In martyrs, i. 114, 229, 230. In the church, i. 207, 232, 236, 237; ii. 210, 211, 215. Of Christ, v. 199 (see Christ). In penance, i. 220. Origen on, i. 167 n. 2. Julian on, ii. 48, 53. In monasticism, ii. 282, 284, 299; v. 363. Augustin on, ii. 398, 401, 475, 683. Pelagius, ii. 634. Gregory the great, iii. 14 (17), 143, 144, 147, 149. Anschar, iii. 287. Benedict of Aniane, iii. 410. Bernard, iv. 262. Berthold, iv. 320. Abelard, iv. 379. Aquinas, iv. 526, 527. Gerson, v. 82. False, iv. 286, 308, 320; v. 59. Externalized, iv. 284, 285, 514 n. 5. Janow, v. 219, 224. Huss, v. 263. R. C. idea of, v. 268 n. 2, 363. Safeguard against error, v. 392.

Hunerich, king of the Vandals, ii. 473, 770.
Hungary, spread of Christianity in, iii. 39, 82, 316, 330-335. Reformation of clergy, iii. 384. Hungarians, iii. 321, 404, 405; v. 51, 237. King of, iv. 88 and n. 2. Jerome of Prague in, v. 246, 373 n. 2. See Schwandtner.
Hunns, ii. 156. See Avares.
Hunting, iii. 35.
Huss, John, v. 48. Forerunners of, 173-235 (174, 178, 183 n. 2, 192). Life and character, 235-371. Education, 235. Placed as preacher at Bethlehem chapel, 236. His hearers, 288 n. 1. The Wilsnack miracles, 237-239. Huss and Wicklif, 240-248, 258. On transubstantiation, 242, 247, 270, 337, 343. Discourse before the Diocesan Synod, 248-250. Nicholas of Welenowitz, 250, 251. Huss chosen rector of the university of Prague, 253. Departure of the Germans from Prague, 253, 254 (122). Huss on the council of Pisa, 255-259. In contention with the clergy, 255. Bull of Alexander V. against the doctrines of Wicklif, 259-262. Appeal of Huss to Alexander, 260. To John XXIII., 262. Writings of Huss, De Trinitate, 263. On tithes, 264, 274 n. 1. Defense of some articles of Wicklif, 264. On right of property, 268-270, 146. The goose, 271 n. 1, 311, 314, 333, 336. Huss cited to appear

before the pope, 271. Excommunicated, 272, 273. Confession of faith, 273. Summoned before the legate, 276. Against the indulgence of John XXIII., 276-285. The martyrs of Prague, 288-290. The eight doctors, 291-293 Huss placed under the ban and interdict, 294, 295. Leaves Prague, 295. Synod of Prague, 295-297. Commissioners appointed for the restoration of concord, 297-299. Docility of Huss, 306, 307 (263). Writings of Huss in exile, De ecclesia, 299-307. Against Stanislaus of Znaim, 307-310. Letters of Huss, 310-316, 315 n. 2. Safe conduct, 317 n. 1, 318, 323, 328, 329, 335, 348, 359, 369. Journey to Constance, 316-321. Arrival in Constance, 321. Discourse giving an account of his faith, 323-326. Imprisonment, 326. Committee appointed for preliminary examination of Huss, 330. His sickness in prison, 330, 331, 340. Letters, 331-337, 340-342, 349, 358-367. Tracts composed in prison, 336. Flight of John XXIII., 339. Huss removed to the castle of Gottleben, 339. On withdrawal of the cup, 339, 340, 342. New commissioners appointed, 340. Huss removed to the Franciscan convent, 342. First audience before the council, 342. Second audience, 343-348. Third audience, 349-356. His unknown friend, 349, 360-362, 366. Further proceedings of the council, 356, 357. Last days of Huss in prison, 357-368. Degradation and martyrdom, 368-371. Hist. Hussi (Opp. i.), 322 n. 1. See Jerome of Prague, Palacky.

Citations: —
Adv. indulgentias papales (opp. 1, f. 175 1), v. 278 n. 3.
Apellatio ab Archiepisc. ad Sedem apestol. (opp. i. f. 89), v. 263 n. 1.
Confession, v. 274 n. 4.
De ablatione bonorum (opp. i. ff. 119-122), v. 269 nn. 1, 2, 268 n. 5.
De arguendo clero, etc., v. 258 n. 1.
De Corpore Christi, v. 270, 336 n. 3.
De decimis, f. 252, sources of knowledge, v. 264 n. 1; truth, 268 n. 1; f. 128 2, law, 264 nn. 2, 3; f. 134 1, validity of sacramental acts, 274 n. 1.
De ecclesia, (opp. 1), ff. 196-206, the church, v. 303 n. 1; f. 202 2, Christ's guidance of, 304 n. 1; f. 206, prayer to Christ, 306 n. 2; f. 207 2, 304 n. 4; f. 210 1, the Rock, 304 n. 3; f. 212 2, individuality in the ch., 306 n. 4; f. 224 2, papacy, 304 nn. 5, 6, 305 n.; f. 225, 305 n.; f. 227 1, the final appeal in matters of faith, 306 n. 5; f. 230 2, 306 n. 3; f. 231 1, principles of reform, 307 n. 2; f. 244 2, 301 n. 2: f. 215 2, the martyrs at Prague, 290 n. 3, 306 n. 1; f. 247 1, docility, 307 n. 1; f. 249 2, 301 n. 1.
De fidei sine elucidatione, v. 323 n. 3.
De mandatis; de matrimonio, v. 336 n. 3.
De pace, opp. i. f. 52 *et seq.*, corruption of clergy, v. 321 n.
De regno, etc. Antichristi (opp. i.), f. 368, Janow on the future renovation of the ch., v. 200 n. 2; f. 370 2, 212 n. 2: c. 21, f. 374 2, his experience as prebendary at Prague, 194 n. 1.

De sufficientia legis Chris.i (opp. i.), v. 325 n.; f. 44 2 *et seq.*, 326 n. 1.
De trinitate (opp. i.), f. 105, v. 263 n. 2; his submission to truth, 253 n. 3; f. 106, and devotion to it, 267 nn. 2, 3; f. 107 2, on open disputation on matters of faith, 268 n. 3.
Defens. quor. art. J. Wickliff, f. 111, v. 264 n. 4; f. 115, 265 n. 3, 266 n. 2; f. 116 2, 267 n. 1.
Determinatis ques., etc., on the glorified blood of Christ, v. 238 n. 2.
Discourse before the diocesan Synod (opp. ii.), v. 248, 249.
Epistolæ. (Opp. i. f. 93), ep. to the college of Cardinals at Rome, v. 255, 259. (Opp. i.), cp. 1, to Martin, 320 n. 2. Ep. 2 (Mickowee 1), to his flock, 320 n. 1. Ep. 3, 320 n. 5. Ep. 4, of Joh. Cardinalis, 322 n. 2, 326 n. 2. Epp. 5, 6, his desire of a public hearing at the council, 323 nn. 1, 2. Ep. 6, 322 nn. 3, 4, 323 nn. 1, 2. Ep. 10, 332 nn. 4, 5. Ep. 15, account of his second hearing, 343 n. 2, 344 n. 1. Ep. 17, to Christann, shortly before his martyrdom, 367 nn. 3, 4. Ep. 18, to the members of Prague university, 366 n. 3, 4. Ep. 19, the council and the pope, 364 n. Ep. 21, to the Bohemian knights, 359 n. 3. Ep. 22, to Chlum, 360 n. 1, 307 n. 1. Ep. 23, 367 n. 2. Ep. 24, 367 n. 5. Ep. 27, before his second hearing, 343 n. 1. Ep. 29, to Peter of Mladenowic, 332 n. 8. Ep. 30, written on the vigils of St. John; Paletz 363 n. 3; his comfort in tribulation, his prayer, 366 n. 1. Ep. 31, false confession refused, 363 n. 4; last confession of Huss, 366 n. 2; last visit of Paletz, 366 n. 5. Ep. 32, 358 n. 2, 363 n. 1. Ep. 33, words of the Polish tailor, 319 n.; of Paletz, 331 n. 4; visit of Chlum, 350 n. 2; his dreams, 365 n.; counsel to prudence, 359 n. 4. Ep. 34, the emperor and his safe conduct, 317 n. 1, 318 n. 3, 329 nn. 2, 5. Ep. 36, 342 n. 2, 349 n. 1. Ep. 37, to his friends in Constance, his condition in prison, his books, Gerson, 336 n. 6, 340 nn. 2, 3. Epp. 38, 39, 40 and 41, his last days in prison, 362 n. 3. Epp. 44, 45, 46, to Chlum his dream, 333 n. 2. Ep. 45, 333 n. 2 (marginal note), the doctor of Biberach, 321 n. 1. Ep. 46, 330 n. 4, 331 n. 4, 332 n. 3, 333 n. 2. Epp. 47 and 48, withdrawal of the cup, 342 n. 1. Ep. 47, 334 n. 3, 342 n. 1. Ep. 48, betrayal by old friends, 331 n. 3; confidence in the truth, 332 n. 9, 334 n. 4. Ep. 49, refuses an advocate, desire to be heard, appeal to Christ, 330 n. 4, 334 n. 5, 335 nn. 2, 7. Ep. 50, 340 n. 4. Ep. 51, to Chlum, sufferings in prison, 331 n. 1, 332 n. 6; the emperor, 335 n. 5; Chlum's expenses at Constance, 336 n. 2. Ep. 52, to Chlum, 331 n. 2, 332 nn. 2, 7, 334 n. 1, 336 n. 5. Ep. 53, to Chlum, 335 n. 1; desires a Bible, 336 n. 5. Ep. 54, 332 n. 1, 334 n. 2, 335 nn. 3, 6, 336 n. 1. Ep 55, flight of the pope, 339 n. 2. Ep. ad Mag. Martinum et Mag. Nicol. de Miliczin (o p. i. f. 93 2, and 94 1), 311 n. 2. Ep. to his flock at Bethlehem chapel (ff. 96-100), 312-316 Ep. to a priest in Prachatic (f. 93 2), 316 n. 3. Ep. of June 231, Paletz, 363 n. 2. Ep. to Prague univ., June 27, 366 n. 3. Ep. to a foreign community (f. 100 2), 316 n. 2; unpublished letters in Palacky, 111., 1, ff. 297, 298. v. 310 n. 2. For other letters see Mickowee.
Opp. i. 1 2, terms of the safe conduct, v. 317 n. 1; f. 3 2, interview with abp. Conrad, 317 n. 3; f. 6, 322 n. 1; the Supper under both forms, 338 n. 3; 12 2, realism, 333 n. 3; f. 13 1, 345 nn.; 14 1, 346 n. 4; 18 1, 351 n. 1; 27 2, his appeal to Christ, 359 n. 1; ff. 29 2-44 1, treatises written in prison, 336 n. 4; ff. 31 1, 38 2, 337 nn.; f. 48 2 323 n. 5; f. 51 2, confession of faith, 323 n. 4; f. 86 *et seq.*, proceedings against Huss at Prague and Bologna, 272 n. 2, 273 n. 1; f. 37 2, ep. of Zbynek to the pope, 273 n. 2; f. 93, notice of

Zbynek, 255 n. 2 ; f. 94, Huss on the papacy, 311 n. 1 ; f. 162 2, the miraculous wafers, 228 n. 1 ; f. 247 2, on the interdict, 256 n. ; f. 255 2, mock genealogy of Huss, 245 n. 3 ; his party at Prague, 318 n. 1 ; f. 332, protest of Jesenic, 272 n. 1 ; f. 332 2, Zbynek on the Wickliffite heresy, 252 n. 3 ; f. 349 *et seq.*, Jerome of Prague, 374 n. 2 ; f. 350 1, his safe conduct, 375 n.
Pro defens. libri de trinitate Joann. Wicleff. (opp. i. f. 106), on the burning of books, v. 262 n. 4.
Protocol of his trial at Prague. See Mladanowec.
Quæstio de indulgentiis, etc. (opp. i. f. 174 *et seq.*), v. 279 n. 4, 279-285.
Reply to Paletz (opp. i.), f. 255 2, v. 245 n. 3 ; f. 256, 270 n. ; f. 256 1, his appeal to Christ, 295 n. 1 ; f. 259 2, 291 n. 1 ; f. 260, 245 n. 2, 248 n. 4 ; f. 260 1, 286 n. 2 ; f. 260 2, the true church, 263 n. 2 ; f. 262, 245 n. 2, 286 n. 3 ; f. 264 1, 287 n. 1 ; f. 264 2, 277 n. 2.
Reply to Stanislaus (opp. i.), v. 307-310 ; f. 265 1, 279 n. 3, 292 n. 2 ; f. 267, 245 n. 1 ; f. 277 1, 307 n. 3 ; f. 284 1, 278 n. 2 ; f. 288, 245 n. 1, 247 n. 1, 278 n. 1.
Reply to Stokes (opp. i.), ff. 108, 109 1, v. 242 nn.
Responsio ad Script octo doctor. (opp. i.), f. 292 2, v. 293 nn. ; f. 293 2, 277 n. ; f. 294 1, 278 n. 4 ; f. 298 1, 265 n. 2 ; f. 305 2, 258 n. 2.

Hussinetz, v. 235.
Hussites, Hussite movements, etc., v. 121, 122, 128, 129, 130-133, 272, 332, 336, 356, 357. At Basle, 130.
Huzitis, ii. 131.
Hy, island of, iii. 10.
Hyde.
Hist. relig. vet. Pers., p. 276, i. 487 n. 1 ; p. 295, Shahristani, 489 n. 4.
Hyginus, bp. of Cordova, ii. 772.
Hyle. See Ὕλη.
Hymns, used by the Essenes, i. 47. Therapoutæ, i. 61. Christian, i. 98, 304, 575, 604, 605 ; ii. 354 ; iii. 446 ; iv. 28, 40 ; v. 207, 243 n. 1, 379. Of Nepos, i. 653. Hieracas, i. 714. Ambrose and Hilary, ii. 354 and n. 4. Means of propagating doctrine, i. 604, 605 ; iii. 479 n. 3 ; v. 243 n. 1. In the image controversy, iii. 543. Latin, iii. 127. Emperor Theophilus, author of, iii. 546. Nilus, iii. 579. See Church psalmody, Poets, Song.
Hypatios, bp. of Nice in Bithynia, iii. 229 n. 3.
Hypocrisy, i. 142, 250, 251, 290 ; ii. 30, 89, 106, 118, 119 ; iv. 395. Among monks, ii. 284, 296 ; iv. 283, 284, 285, 310, 529. Nicetas on, iv. 530. Pelagius on, ii. 634. Janow on, v. 196, 224. Ruysbroch, v. 399, 401, 404.
Hypomnesticon, iii. 366 n. 1.
Hypostases, ii. 404, 439, 482, 501, 614. In Gnosticism, i. 400, 419, 437, 549, 588. In the doctrine of the Trinity, i. 576, 585, 591-593, 597-599, 606.
Hypostatized powers, in Basilides, i. 400.
Hypsistarians, ii. 768 n. 1.
Hystaspes, interpolated writings of, i. 176.

I.

Ialdabaoth, i. 443-446.
Ibas, bp. of Edessa, history, ii. 610, 611. In the Monophysite controversy, ii. 595, 597, 599. His letter to Mares, 529 n. 3, 539 n., 607, 610 and n. See Harduin, t. ii. f. 530, and Controversy of the Three Chapters.
Iberians, spread of Christianity among them, ii. 138, 139 ; iv. 46 n. 3.
Ibn-Wahab, on China, iii. 89 n. 4. See Renaudot.
Iceland, spread of Christianity in, iii. 300 -306. Character of Icelanders, 306. Mission to Greenland, 307.
Icia (Ida), iii. 278.
Iconium, ii. 327 ; iii. 229 n. 3. Council at, i. 318.
Iconoclasts, iii. 199, 200, 212, 213, 216-219, 235, 236, 250 and n. 1, 256, 440, 532, 533, 537-543, 549 ; iv. 557. See Councils (an. 754), Image controversy.
Idacius of Emerita, ii. 772, 773.
Idatii Chronicon, ii. 97 n. 1.
Idealism, Idealists, Jewish, i. 56, 58, 59, 66, 377. Christian, i. 292 ; iii. 170. Gnostic, i. 386. Platonic, i. 377 ; ii. 122, 123. With Augustine, ii. 399, 476. And realism, in the image controversy, iii. 539. See Alexandrian.
Idealistic sects, i. 208, 476. See Antinomian.
Ideals, moral, ii. 633.
Ideas, universal, in Alexandrian Judaism, i. 54, 56, 65, 66. In Platonism, i. 378, 379, 380 ; Wicklif on, v. 165 n. 2, 166-168. Reality of, iv. 369, 444. Of the absolute, iv. 441-445. Of God, iv. 441-444, 457, 481. Ideas of reason, iv. 458, 459, 470, 471, 481. The divine idea, ii. 476 ; iv. 457, 481, 482. Ideas in Gnosticism, i. 389, 420, 423. Ruling, iv. 271, 638. Force of, v. 275. Ideal and real, v. 396.
Idoler.
Manual of Chronology, i. 149 n. 1, 681 n. 4 ; ii. 106 n. 1, 125 n. 7, 338 n. 5.
Ἰδιωτεύοντες, i. 132 n. 6.
Idleness, iii. 443.
Idolatry, iii. 9, 51, 84, 307. Janow on, v. 211. See Paganism.
Idols, faith in, i. 71, 73. Sacrificed to by Christian priests, iii. 53 n. 7. Of the imagination, iii. 444. See Images.
Ἱερά, ἱερεῖς, iii. 264.
Ignatius, bp. of Antioch, narrative of his death, i. 100 n. 4, 661. Genuineness of his epistles, 191 n. 2, 196 n. 1, 661. To Polycarp, slaves, 269. Festival of Sunday, 295, 296 n. 4. Against Docetism, 631. Doctrine of the Lord's Supper, 647. Life and writings, 660, 661 (iii. 170).
Epistola ad Ephes. cc. 11, 42, κλῆρος ; appointment of ch. officers, i. 196 n. 1 ; c. 20, 647 n 3. Ep. ii. ad Polycarp, § 5, marriage, 284 n

1; c. 4, 269 n. 3. Ad Magnes. c. 8, 295 n. 3, 296 n. 4. Ad Smyrn. § 2, 631 n. 1.

Ignatius, deacon.
Life of Tarasius, iii. 225 n. 1. Of Nicephorus, 532 n. 1, 533 n. 1, 535 nn. 1, 2, 538 n. 2.

Ignatius (Nicetas), patriarch of Constantinople, iii. 327, 549 and n. 3, 550, 558–573. His origin, 558. Controversy between the Greek and Roman churches respecting his patriarchate, 561–579. Life of. See Nicetas David.

Ignis purgatorius, ii. 121 n. 1. See Purgatorial fire.

Ignis Sacer, iii. 408 n. 1; iv. 266.

Ignorance. And Christianity, i. 78, 79. Cause of heresies, ii. 751, 766, 767. In England, iii. 468, 469 n. 5. Huss on the plea of, v. 282, 283. See Clergy.

Igor, Russian Grand Prince, iii. 327.

Ilchester, iv. 424.

Ildefonsus, Spanish bp.
Diss. de azymo et ferment., vision of, iii. 581 n. 3. See Mabillon.

Illgen.
Zeitschrift für die historische Theologie. Bd. 2, 2tes St. p. 48, Kist's essay (see Kist), i. 185 n. 2. J. 1832, Bd. 2, 4tes St., Hist. of treatises on the Paschal Supper, by Dr. Rettberg, i. 298 n. 1. J. 1834, Bd. 4, St. 1, Neumann's trans. of Esnig., i. 463 n. 3; iii. 257 n. 4. J. 1839, Heft. 2, p. 61, Merswin, v. 388 n. 2. J. 1840, Bd. 2, Speiker on Anselm of Havelburg, iv. 536 n. 3.

Illumination of books, iii. 201.

Illus, ii. 587.

Illyria, bps. of, ii. 204, 377, 601, 604–607. See Councils (an. 347 and 375).

Illyricum, i. 80.

Image controversies, iii. 197–243, 531. General participation in them, 197. In the time of Leo the Isaurian, 202–214. Of Constantine Copronymus, 214–223. Of Leo IV., 223, 224. Of Constantine the Younger and Irene, 224–233. Participation of the Western church in them, 233–243. Renewed in the Greek church, 532–551. Participation of the Western church, 551–553.

Image of God, i. 46, 65, 86, 400, 428, 456, 562, 575, 612, 613, 614, 641 and nn. 2, 4; ii. 287, 411 n., 438, 494, 508, 664, 713–715, 751; iii. 98, 100, 103, 171 n. 2. 205, 515; iv. 412, 457, 460, 487, 488, 490, 491, 554, 623. Distinguished from likeness, i. 613, 641 n. 2; iv. 491. Of Christ, i. 434; iv. 623, 624. See Likeness.

Image of the Demiurge, i. 468.

Image of the emperor, i. 90, 99; ii. 112. As asylum, ii. 176.

Images, image worship, i. 71, 291–293; ii. 322–331; iii. 197–243, 532–553.
Superstitious use of them in the Greek church, iii. 170, 201, 546. As sponsors in baptism, 201–546. Images specially worshipped, 201, 213 n. 2. Miracles wrought by, 201, 230, 240. Inscriptions on, 545 n. 7. Substitute for Scripture, 199, 546. Gradual origin of image worship, 198; in the Greek church, 170, 200. Reaction against the extravagance of, 198–200, 201. Opposition to in the Greek army, 224, 533–535, 537, 538. In the Romish church, 199, 200, 233, 441, 584 n. 1. Gregory the Great on, 199. In the Frank church, 199, 200, 233–243, 428–437, 439–441, 584 n. 1. In Germany and Italy, 439. In the Sects, 250 and n. 1, 256, 598, 603, 604. Three tendencies, 545, 552 n. 7. Destruction of (ii. 28), see Iconoclasts. Combated by Agobard of Lyons, 428, 429. By Claudius of Turin, 430 n. 4, 433–437. Jews and Mohammedans on, 201, 203 n. 1, 431. Views of Jonas of Orleans, 439. Of Walafrid Strabo, 440. Hinkmar, 440. Michael II., 546. Ignatius, 558.

In the Fifth Period. Jews on, iv. 77, 79. Joachim, 225. Bernard, 264. Lull, 307. Innocent III., 317. Sects, 557, 578, 594. Niphon, 564.

In the Sixth Period. Wicklif on, v. 140, 156. Huss, 250 Janow, 233; on miracles wrought by, 198, 199, 233, 234.

Images of Christ, i. 125, 292, 451; iii. 201, 213 n. 2, 557. Of God, iii. 204, 207. Of Ormuzd, ii. 138 n. 3. Of Peter and Paul, i. 292 n. 2. Of Philosophers, i. 451. Of Sergius and Honorius, iii. 196. Others, i. 125.

Images, pagan, pagan writers on the worship of, i. 9, 21, 27. Valentine, i. 425, 427. Julian, ii. 50, 60, 61, 74. With educated pagans, ii. 27. Removed by Constantine, ii. 27. Forbidden, ii. 28, 34. Restored, ii. 66. Renounced, destroyed, ii. 98, 100, 101 and n. 5, 227; iii. 19, 20, 28, 51, 292, 297, 301, 302, 329; iv. 3, 14, 15, 22, 29, 31, 32, 34. See Iconoclasts, Idols.

Imagination, iii. 444; iv. 276. Dangers of the, v. 392, 394.

Immaculate conception, doctrine of the, iv. 331–333.

Immersion, i. 310. See Baptism.

Immortality, Demonax on, i. 10. M. Aurelius, i. 17. In Platonism, i. 19, 34. Clementines, i. 32, 33. Sadducees, i. 41 and n. 1. Faith in, i. 158. In Gnosticism, i. 421, 456. Hermogenes, Tertullian, i. 618. Irenæus, i. 641 and n. 3. Christian doctrine of, i. 644. Origen, i. 710, 711. Julian, ii. 58. Simplicius, ii. 108. Denial of, i. 600, 710, 711; ii. 763 n. 3; iii. 588 n. 2; v. 11. See Soul.

Immutable condition of spiritual life, Theodore, ii. 715.

Impanation, iii. 528 nn. 1, 4; v. 153.

Imposition of hands, i. 310 n. 1, 315, 316; ii. 30 n. 2, 190 n. 2, 359, 360, 725; iii.

63 n. 4. With the sect at Orleans, iii. 595. Bogomiles, iv. 562. Catharists, iv. 575–577. See Confirmation.
Imposts, iv. 41.
Imputation of guilt, ii. 669. Of original sin, iv. 517.
Ina, English king, on punishment in the church, of criminals who took refuge there, iii. 104.
Incantation, iii. 420, 444, 448; iv. 252 n. 3.
Incarnation, the, i. 592, 597, 602; iii. 158, 172, 261, 262, 465 n. 2; iv. 369, 451, 473, 498, 507, 508; v. 218. In the Supper, ii. 731–733 (iii. 215). In the image controversy, iii. 204, 205, 215, 217, 539. Of the Holy Ghost, iv. 448. Of Buddha, i. 483. See Christ, Docetism, Logos, Redemption.
Incense, i. 73. Burning of, before images, ii. 206 n. 1, 210, 233, 239, 546.
Incorruption, principle of, ii. 735 n. 4.
Incubations, ii. 26, 47 and n. 4, 59, 371.
India, spread of Christianity in, i. 81, 82; ii. 140, 141; iii. 89, 90 n. 2; iv. 57; v. 86 (iii. 51 n. 4). Ascetics in, i. 442. Mani in, i. 488. Judgments of God in, iii. 130. Antinomianism, v. 399.
Indiculus luminosus. See Paulus Alvarus.
Indifferent actions, iv. 524, 525.
Individuals, influence of, in great movements, i. 509; iv. 629; v. 158.
Indulgences, iii. 5 n. 2, 441, 451, 452; iv. 349–353; v. 47. Origin of, iii. 52 n. 6, 137 n. 3, 138. In connection with the crusades, iv. 124, 125, 156. Sale of, iv. 350–353; v. 52, 122, 123, 274 n. 3, 279, 283, 284, 285 n. 2. For the building of churches, iv. 350. Preachers of, iv. 351–353; v. 52, 183, 288. Berthold on, iv. 351, 352. Joachim, iv. 222. The Troubadours, iv. 604 n. 3. Sects, iv. 610, 614. Wiclif, v. 164, 171. Conrad, v. 183, 184. Huss, v. 250, 274 and n. 3, 277, 279–285, 291, 323. Jerome of Prague, v. 285 n. 2.
Industry, among the Essenes, i. 45, 46. In Parsism, ii. 129, 130. In monastic life, ii. 272, 277, 283, 286, 287, 289, 295, 298; iii. 29, 415; iv. 283, 286, 287. Ratherius on, iii. 443. See Manual Labor, Occupations.
Infallibility, papal, iii. 35. Of the fathers, iii. 485.
Infant baptism, i. 311–315, 461 n. 3, 498, 504, 615, 648, 715, 716; ii. 344, 355–357, 645, 726–731; iii. 496; iv. 587 n. 5, 593, 595, 601, 615. See Cyprian, Dionysius of Alexandria, Hieracas, Irenæus, Stephanus, Tertullian.
Infants, communion of, i. 333, 648; iii. 496; iv. 341–343, 345.
Infidelity, in Paganism, reaction against, i. 11–15. Plutarch on, i. 21. Relation to Christianity, i. 33. Of ecclesiastics, ii. 763 n. 3. Reactions of, iv. 324, 325,

531; v. 401 (68). Pantheistic, iv. 431. Of Frederic II., iv. 179–182. Of Boniface VIII., v. 11. Of John XXIII., v. 111.
Infidels reclaimed, iv. 287.
Infinite and finite, i. 372, 373, 417. Scotus on, iii. 465. Infinite series, i. 571.
Inflexibilis obstinatio, i. 90.
Informers, i. 96, 100–102, 104, 105, 118, 121. Laws against, i. 137. See Slaves.
Inge Olofson, Swedish king, iii. 291.
Ingelheim, iii. 272.
Ingeltrude, iii. 358 n.
Initiation, Symbolum, i. 307. Gnostic, i. 388, 437, 446. Into sects, iv. 556, 561, 576.
Innocence, i. 503. State of, iii. 490. See Original State.
Innocent I., bp. of Rome, presbyters of the filial churches, ii. 195 nn. 1, 2. The Roman primacy, 203. Fasting on the Sabbath, 335, 337 n. 1. Anointing, 360 n. 1. Celebration of the Lord's Supper, 367 n. 4, 368 n. 2. In the Pelagian controversy, 643, 644 n. 4, 645–647. Chrysostom, 756 n. 2, 761. Letter of Pelagius to, 730 n. 4.

Epistles, ii. 644 n. 4. Ep. ad Concil. Carthag., §§ 3, 7, providence, grace, 646 nn. 2, 3. Ep. 25, ad Decentium (Decretales), § 5, intercessions connected with the Lord's Supper, 367 n. 4, 368 n. 2; § 6, prerogatives of bps., 188 n. 2; 360 n. 1; § 7, fasting on the Sabbath, 335 n. 3; § 8, filial churches at Rome, 195 nn. Ep. ad quinque episcopos., 647 n. 1.

Innocent II., pope, election, takes refuge in France, Bernard, iv. 144–146, 153, 255, 503. Returns to Rome, Arnold, death, 146–151, 398. The Jews, 75. Peter of Cluny, 194. Fraudulent collectors of alms, 267. Abelard, 395, 396, 398, 503. Council of Pisa (an. 1134) 603.

Epp. l. i. ep. 450, iii. 267 n. 6.

Innocent III., pope, his administration, iv. 173–177, 178. Mission in Prussia, 43–45. The Jews, 75, 76. Appeals, 199. Interpolated bulls, 204 and nn. 2, 3, 5, 205. Roskild, 206 n. 5. Plurality of benefices, 207. Vicarii, 212. Joachim, 221 n. Bernard, 253 n. 3. Collection of alms for Spitals, 267. Order of Trinitarians; law against multiplication of monastic orders, 268. The Sects, 269. Lateran council (v. 153), see Councils, an. 1215. Order of Dominicans, 270. Francis of Assisi, 272. Franciscans, 277. Sermon on almsgiving, 306. As preacher, 317. Bible-reading among the laity, 321–324. Doctrine of Transubstantiation, 339–341 (v. 153, 270). Auricular confession, 353. Scholasticism, 411. Almaric of Bena, 446. Doctrine of redemption, 505, 506. Catharists, 582 n. 4, 583 n. 2. Waldenses, 609. Pauperes Catholici, 612, 613. Albigenses, punishment of heretics, 640. Peter of Castelnau, 641 n. 4. Inquisition, 643. Relations with England, v. 134.

Citations from his writings:—
De Eleemosyna, c. iii. f. 201, iv. 306 nn. 1, 2. De mysteriis missæ, l. i. c. 44, f. 395, the Bible, the eucharist, iv. 322 n. 1; l. iv. c. 16, 339 nn. Epistles. Ep. to French bps. against Catharists, iv. 583 n. 2. L. i. ep. 93, to the abp. of Aix, persecution of Catharists, 640 n. 2; ep. 171, to the king of France, 173 n. 3; ep. 235, falsified bulls, 204 n. 5, 205 n. 2; ep. 237, appeals, 199 n. 4; ep. 249, to a legate, 174 n.; ep. 324, decision on right of property, 174 n. 1; ep. 349, ungenuine bulls, 205 n. 2; ep. 358, on his multiplicity of business, 173 n. 4; ep. 481, Trinitarians, 268 n. 2. L. ii. epp. 13, 99, appeals, 199 n. 4; ep. 29, bulls, 204 n. 3; ep. 141, to the Waldenses, 321 n. 2, 323 n. 2; ep. 142, to the bp. and chapter at Metz, Waldenses, 322 nn. 2, 3; ep. 134, provision for converted Jews, 76 n. 2; ep. 235, religious societies at Metz, 324 n. 1; ep. 302, the Jews, 76 n. 1. L. v. ep. 23, appeals, 199 n. 4. L. vi. ep. 10, the forged bull, 204 n. 3. L. xi. ep. 26, Peter of Castelnau, 641 n. 4; ep. 198, Waldenses, 613 n. 1. L. xii. ep. 7, to the abp. of Milan; the same, 613 nn. 2, 3. L. xiii. ep. 78, to the bps. of Tarraco, 613 nn. 4, 5; ep. 128 to the abp. of Gneseu, 43 nn. L. xv. ep. 102, to his legates, the crusade against the Albigenses, 642 n. 1; ep. 147, to the Cistercian abbots, 43 n. 1, 44 n. 1; ep. 148, to the dukes of Pomerania and Poland, 44 n. 2. L. xvi. ep. 12, legates, 173 n. 5; ep. 84, the converted Jew, 76 n. 3.
Expositions of 2d penitential psalm, f. 241, iv. 349 n. 3.
Registr., ed. Baluz, disposition of the imperial crown, i. f. 697, iv. 176 n. 2; f. 715, 177 n. 1.
Sermo i. (opp. ed. Colon. 1575), f. 6, vicarious atonement, iv. 506 n. 1; f. 40, on preaching, 317 n. 6. S. iii. in dedicat. templi, f. 75, image worship, 317 n. 7.

Innocent IV., pope, embassy to the Mongols, iv. 49-51. The Jews, 76. Frederic II., 183, 184. The begging monks, 282. Heretics under, 610.
Innocent VI., pope, v. 44.
Innocent VII., pope, bull against the Wicklifite heresies in Bohemia, v. 247. Death, 70.
Inquisition, inquisitors, ii. 252; iii. 256; iv. 581 nn. 6, 9, 582, 585, 614 nn. 4, 5, 628, 629, 631 and n. 2, 640, 642-644; v. 180, 392. Directorium inquisitionis (see Nicholas Eymericus), 618 n. 1. Protocol of, see Philip of Limboreh.
Insabbatati, iv. 609.
Insanity, i. 75; iii. 102 n. 4; iv. 325.
Inscriptions, Chinese-Syrian, iii. 89. Nubian, iii. 90 n. 1. On images, iii. 545 n. 7. In Bethlehem chapel, v. 301, 321, 333.
Inscriptionum Latinarum ampliss. coll., ii. 92 n. 2.
Insignia, episcopal, obtained by abbots, iv. 201, 202.
Insincerity, oriental, iii. 561 and n. 3, 563 and n. 1, 564, 570 n. 2, 578, 583 n. 3 (235). See Rhetoricians.
Inspiration, views of, among the Alexandrian Jews, i. 55, 56. Charisma, i 181,
510. In the Clementines, i. 356. In Gnosticism, i. 371 n., 389, 427, 439; iv. 574 n. 1. Among the Montanists, i. 511, 515, 519. In the Catholic church, i. 518-520. Irenæus, Tertullian on, i. 679, 680. Antiochian school, ii. 389-394. Prædicians, iii. 265. Agobard, iii. 460. Abelard, iv 376, 377, 391, 392, 496 n. 1. Bernard, iv. 371. Catharists, iv. 574. See Charismata, Holy Spirit, Language.
Instantius, bp., ii. 772, 773.
Instruction, Christian, iii. 9, 11, 13, 21, 22, 41, 42, 51, 52, 55, 79, 80, 123-125, 152, 326, 330; iv. 4, 31, 39, 41. 90, 215, 276, 277, 282 n. 4, 287, 297, 298, 425, 426, 611, 612. Of the young, iii. 11, 23, 29, 53, 70, 72, 73, 153, 315 n. 1, 325, 330, 408 n. 1, 425. Family, iii. 108. Counsels of bp. Daniel, iii. 52. Alcuin on, iii. 76, 124. Lack of, iii. 323, 334. Through images, iii. 198, 199 (see Images). Alfred on, iii. 468. Wicklif on, v. 142. See Preaching, Schools.
Insufflation in baptism, ii. 359.
Insurrections, iii. 278. In England, v. 159, 160, 161, 163.
Intellectualism, i. 550, 556; ii. 400, 447; iv. 181.
Intention, in morals, Raymund Lull on, iv. 308, 309, 484, 485. Abelard, iv. 387-390, 392, 399, 528. Aquinas, iv. 528. Huss, v. 350.
Intercession, of the brethren, i. 219, 416. Of martyrs, i. 229, 231; ii. 373, 375. For martyrs, i. 334 n. 4; ii. 373. In connection with the Lord's Supper, ii. 367, 368. Of monks, ii. 285. Of the saints, iii. 7, 429, 433, 437; iv. 593. Huss on, v. 284, 323 324. Of Christ, v. 301.
Intercessiones, of the clergy and monks, ii. 29, 118, 173-176, 187, 230 n. 2, 285; iii. 28 and n. 3, 103, 104 n. 1, 422 and n. 3; iv. 243, 547, 548.
Interchange of predicates, ii. 489, 501, 502, 523; iii. 159-162, 183; iv. 340; v. 153. See Ἀντιμετάστασις.
Intercourse of nations and Christianity, i. 79. See Commerce, Crusades.
Interdict, against Lothaire and the synod of Metz, iii. 355, 356. Early use of, iii. 454. Threatened against Philip I., iv. 102. At Rome, iv. 131. In England, iv. 174, 176. Against Frederic II., Hildegard on the, iv. 219. The Catharists, iv. 582. The Sect at Halle, iv. 610. Against the Albigenses, iv. 640. Threatened against Philip the Fair, v. 6. Against Charles VI. of France, v. 77. Interdict against Louis IV. of Germany, v. 24, 42, 43, 380, 383 n. 2, 407. Against Huss, v. 272, 273, 275, 294-296, 300, 301, 312, 313, 322. Huss on the, v. 301. Tauler, v. 383. Margaret Ebnerin, v. 383 n. 2. See Ban.

Intermediate state, i. 654, 667 n. 2; ii. 730.
Interpolated writings, i. 172 n. 4, 176, 177, 355, 457 n. 4, 582; iv. 221. See Bulls.
Interpretation of the Bible, literal, i. 36, 41, 42, 49, 53, 54, 56, 57, 60, 460, 463, 547, 552, 652, 694, 696, 700, 711, 722; ii. 375 n. 1, 388, 666; iii. 443, 459; iv. 77, 78, 601, 614. Allegorical, i. 39, 40, 44, 47, 54, 59, 61, 171, 348 n. 2, 355, 460, 463, 700, 714; ii. 388, 389, 778; iv. 77, 78, 220, 230-232, 571. Arbitrary, i. 39, 49, 53-55, 379-389, 460, 501, 502, 582, 700; ii. 388; iii. 459; iv. 78. Logical, Scientific, Grammatical, Historical, i. 54, 533, 722; ii. 389-394, 402, 673, 754; iii. 458, 459; iv. 377. Spiritualizing, i. 546-548, 552-557 (see above, Allegorical). Mystical and mythical, i. 44, 331, 347, 460, 557; ii. 389, 393, 394, 616; iii. 459, 601. See Bible interpretation.
Interpreters, i. 303; iii. 12, 21, 36, 367, 576 n. 1; iv. 6, 7, 17, 20, 29, 39, 55.
Interstitia, iii. 93.
Introspection, iv. 304, 305, 514.
Intuition, Mystic, i. 64. Gnostic, i. 371, 372, 382, 387, 389, 414, 415, 426, 432. Clement on, i. 541. Origen, i. 546, 547, 552. Abelard, iv. 375 n. 4, 377, 380 n. 3. Oliva, iv. 623. Of God, Origen on, i. 623, 626, 636; Servatus Lupus, iii. 473; Bernard, iv. 371, 372; Richard de St. Victor, iv. 411-413; Aquinas, iv. 429, 431, 514; Pullein, iv. 486; John XXII., v. 37; Friends of God, v. 393; Pantheistic, iv. 230. Intuitive bent, iii. 466.
Inundations, ii. 528.
Investiture, iii. 400-404. Contests concerning, iv. 35, 36, 101-120, 133-143, 147, 172, 198, 593. Symbol of, iii. 402; iv. 134, 142. Per sceptrum, iv. 143. Three parties, iv. 141.
Invisible, the, iii. 236, 237. Power of becoming invisible, i. 448 and n. 1.
Ion, Irish bp., iii. 307. Martyr in North America.
Iona, St., iii. 10, 21.
Ionia, Julian there, ii. 44 and n. 1.
Ireland, spread of Christianity thither, ii. 146-149. Seminary of Christian culture, iii. 10, 43, 152. Mission among the Picts and Scots, iii. 10. Monasteries in (ii. 149), 10, 20, 23, 29, 43, 460, 461. Strict asceticism, 20, 21 and n. 31. Missions in England, 23. Influence of English church on, 25. Missions among the Germans, 29-38. In Brabant, 43. In North America, 307. Missionaries, their relation to Rome, 23, 32-35, 37 n. 6, 53, 60-63. Hospitality, 43. Theological culture, 43, 60, 62 n. 2, 63 n. 4. 152, 460, 461, 468. Spirit of freedom, 49, 53, 121, 461. Mission in Iceland, 300 n. 1. On the Orcades, 306 n. 3.

Migratory tendency, 300 n. 1, 460. Art in, 460 n. 6. Dialectic tendency, 461 n. 1. Bernard's monks, iv. 254. See Books, British Church.
Irenæus, bp. of Lyons and Vienne, disciple of Polycarp, life and writings, i. 677-681, 682. Transplants the theology of Asia Minor to the West, 508, 509. His relation to Montanism, 524, 525. Chiliasm, 651. Hermeneutics, 388, 613 nn. 1, 2. On the miracles of the Christians, 74. Christianity in Germany, 84; among barbarous tribes, 84, 85; in Spain, 85. Persecutions, 119. The gift of tongues, 186 n. 2. Presbyters, bishops, 192. Ecclesia apostolica at Rome, 204. Cathedra Petri, 213. Conception of the church, 209. Victor of Rome, dispute about the passover, 215, 299 nn., 300. Gladiatorial shows, 263. Fasts, 300. Infant baptism, 311, 312. Christ as archetype, 311. Oblations, 330 and n. 1, 331 n. 1. Ebionites, 344, 345, 348 and n. 2. Antinomian Gnostics, 385, 452, 453. Doctrine of accommodation among the Gnostics, 388. Arrogance of Gnostics, 393. Cerinthus, 396 and n. 1, 397 n. 1. Basilides, 401. Basilideans, 409, 447 n. 3. Ptolemæus, 437. Saturnin, 455 n. 1. Tatian, 456. Marcosians, 476 and n. 1. Alogi and the Gospel of John, 526, 527. Knowledge of God, 560. Doctrine of creation, 568. Monarchianism, 579. Soul of Christ, 634. Redemption, 640-642. Sanctification, 645. Baptism, 646. The Lord's Supper, 647; ii. 731, 732 n. 1. Hermas, i. 660. Hippolytus, i. 681. His writings at Rome, iii. 150 n. 4.

Citations from his writings: —
Epistola ad Florinum, ap. Euseb. l. v. 20, Polycarp, 667 n. 3. Ep. ad Victorem, ap. Euseb. l. v. 24, independence of communities, i. 215 n. 1; the fast, 300 n. 1; the Lord's Supper carried to the absent, 332 n. 2.
Hæres. (ed. Mas-uet.) L. i. c. 1, § 3, Valentinians, Bythos, 418 n. 1; c. 3, Ptolemæus, 489 n. 2; c. 3, § 5, Valentinians, the cross, 420 n. 1; c. 5, § 2, creation of man, 424 n. 3; c. 6, gladiatorial shows, 263 n. 1; c. 7, §§ 3, 4, Valentinians, the prophets, 426 n. 2; c. 8, § 4, Christ and the Soter, 423 n. 2; c. 10, Christianity in Germany, 84 n. 3; c. 11, § 2, Secundus, 438 n. 4; c. 12, § 3, Valentinians, man, 424 n. 2; c. 21, Marcosians, extreme unction, 477 n. 5; c. 21, § 4, knowledge, with the Gnostics, 476 n. 1; c. 24, Basilides, peace, 400 n. 4; Pseudo-Basilideans, 448 n. 2; Marcion, the redemption, 471 n. 1; c. 25, Carpocratians, 459 n. 1; c. 26, the Ebionites, 348 n. 2; Cerinthus, 397 n. 1; Nicolaitans, 452 n. 2; c. 26, § 2, Ebionites, 348 n. 4; c. 27, § 2, Marcion, 471 n. 1; c. 28, Tatian, 456 n. 4; c. 31, Cainites, 448 n. 5. L. ii. c. 4, matter, with Gnostics, 375 n. 5; c. 10, § 1, hermeneutical canons, 613 n. 1; c. 13, § 4, attributes of God, 560 n. 3; c. 16, Basilides, 400 n. 4; c. 22, § 4, Christ's relation to the different stages of human nature, 311 n. 3; c. 28, § 3, a principle in hermeneutics, 613 n. 2; c. 32, § 4, miracles of Christians, 74 n. 2. L. iii. c. 2, Gnostics on the discourses of Christ, 389 n. 3; c. 3, κλῆρος, 190 n. 1; church of

Rome, 204 n. 3; c. 3, § 4, Polycarp and Marcion, 465 n. 3; c. 4, conversion of barbarians, 85 n. 1; c. 5, against accommodation, 389 n. 1; c. 7, hyperbata in Paul's writings, 679 nn. 2, 3; c. 11, Nicolaitans, 452 n. 2; c. 11, § 9, Montanists, John's gospel, 527 n. 1; c 14, bishops and presbyters, 192 n. 1; c. 15, complaints of the Gnostics, 390 n. 1; their arrogance, 393 n. 2; c. 17, baptism, 646 n. 1; c. 18 (20), 20 (alias 22), 31, redemption, 642 n. 1; c. 22, person of Christ, 634 n. 3; c. 24, § 1, the church, 209 n. 1.
L. iv. cc. 13, 14, obedience and freedom, 645 n. 1; c. 18, thank-offering in the Lord's Supper, 330 n. 1, 331 n. 4; c. 26, bps. and presbyters, 192 n. 1; c. 30, Commodus, 119 n. 3; Christians in the world, 274 n. 1; c. 33, § 6, false prophets, 678 n. 1; § 7, separatists, 209 n. 3; § 9, martyrs, 119 n. 4.
L. v. c. 1, § 1, person of Christ, 635 n 1; the redemption from the dominion of Satan, 641 n. 1; c. 16, the Logos, 642 n. 1; c. 3, opponents of the Chiliasts, 654 n. 1; c. 32, the same, 651 n. 3; c. 35, the millennium, 651 n. 2.

Irenæus, comes, friend of Nestorius, ii. 527, 534, 537 and n. 2. Tragedy, 553 n. 3.
Irene, Greek empress, iii. 536 n. 2. Friend of images, her character, 223. Obtains the government, 224. Favors Monachism, 225. Her efforts to promote image worship, 224-233, 234. See Harduin, t. iv.
Irnerius (Guarnerius), at Bologna, iv. 203.
Irregulares sæculares, iv. 208.
Irresistible grace. See Grace.
Isaac, martyr, iii. 339.
Isacios, monk, ii. 535 n. 2.
Isaiah, Conrad on, v. 185, 186. Gregory I. on, iii. 150 n. 7. Catharists, iv. 571 n. 5.
Is. 1 : 2, ii 499 n. 3. 1 : 11, i. 281. 1 : 14, i. 300. 2 : 4, ii. 159. 6 : 3, ii. 500. 7 : 9, i. 530; iv. 551. 7 : 14, i. 348. 7 : 16, ii. 496. 8 : 23 (9 : 1, 2), i. 349. 9 : 6, iv. 554. 11 : 2, iv. 522; v. 198, 21 (31) : 7, 8, i. 350. 28 : 19, v. 340. 29 : 13, ii. 244, 315. 40 : 18, ii. 533. 43 : 19, i. 531. 45 : 7, iii. 144. 53 : 2, i. 169 n. 5, 271, 291, 631, 633. 53 : 4, 5, i. 643 n. 1. 53 : 7, i. 230. 53 : 8, ii. 450 n. 2. 65 : 4, ii. 47. 65 : 25, ii. 158. See Commentaries.
Isancios, iv. 564 n. 2.
Isaurea, bps. of, ii. 757. Robbers of, 761. See Seleucia.
Isidore, bp. of Hispalis (Seville), character, iii. 151, 152, 457. On predestination, 151, 474. The Jews, 152.
Abbreviatures, iii. 153 n 3. Chronicle of the Goths, iii. 152. De officiis ecclesiasticis, iii. 151. L. i. c. 40, fasts in January, ii. 351 n. 3. Decretals, iii. 347 and n. 1 Origines, iii. 347 n. 1. Sententiarum libri tres, iii. 151. L. ii. c. 6, predestination, twofold, iii. 151 n. 2; c. 30, falsehood, iii. 152 n. 1. See Pseudo-Isidorean.
Isidore, presbyter in Alexandria, ii. 748, 750, 752, 753.
Isidore of Pelusium, abbot, ii. 165, 189 n. 8, 289, 320, 355, 514 n. 1, 727, 743 n. 1. On slavery, 287 (iii. 99). Anthropology, doctrine of the church, 722. Controversy on the origin of souls, 764 n. 2.

Citations from his Epistles:—
L. i. ep. 37, validity of sacraments, ii. 766 n. 2; ep. 52, Manichean monks, 771 n. 1; ep. 63, pagan writers, 743 n. 1; ep. 90, theatrical singing, 355 n. 2; ep. 142, in behalf of a slave, 287 n. 5 (iii. 99 n. 1); ep. 152, Theophilus of Alexandria, 753 n. 1, 759 n. 2; ep. 262, rude monks, 289 nn. 3, 4; ep. 306, slaves, 288 n. 1; ep. 311, to Theodosius, ii. 165 n. 1; ep. 370, to Cyrill, 514 n. 1. L. ii. ep. 2, grace, 722 n. 6; ep. 3, use of pagan writers, 743 n. 1; ep. 127, Cyrill, 512 n. 3; ep. 246, church buildings, 320 nn. 2, 3. L. iii. epp. 13, 165, 171, 204, grace, 722 n. 6; ep. 235 et 295, infidel presbyters, 763 n. 3; ep. 340, validity of sacraments, 766 n. 2. L. iv. ep. 163, Origenistic doctrines, 764 n. 1; ep. 188, archdeacons, 189 n. 8. L. v. ep. 131, worldly-minded clergymen, 766 n. 1; ep. 195, infant baptism, 727 n. 3.

Isidorus, pagan philosopher, ii. 110.
Isidorus, son of Basilides, i. 400, 402 n. 2, 406, 408, 409, 415, 416.
Comment. in proph. Parchor. ap. Clem. Strom., l. vi. f. 641, demon of Socrates, i. 406 n. 3.
Isis, the priestess of, i. 22. Worship of, ii. 47 n. 4, 105 n. 3, 307.
Isle de France, iii. 459.
Isleif, iii. 305.
Islep, abp. of Canterbury, v. 135, 136.
Ἰσόχριστοι, ii. 764 n. 3.
Isolated efforts, iii. 25, 45.
Israel, abp. of Cologne, life of, iii. 460 n. 6. See Leibnitz.
Israel, spiritual, iv. 568.
Istria, ii. 608.
Italians, in France, iii. 42; v. 232. At the council of Constance, 103, 106, 118, 119, 126. Promoted to offices in the church, 137.
Italy, Christianity in, i. 80, 84. Maxentius, ii. 9 n. 1. Diocese of R., bp. in, ii. 199. Monachism in, ii. 294. Intended council, ii. 574, 576. St. Martin, iii. 7. Columban in, iii. 33, 34. Oath of Italian bps. to the pope, iii. 48. Relation to the East Roman Empire, iii. 112, 113, 117, 181, 186, 187, 234. Culture in, iii. 151. Church psalmody, iii. 242. Adalhard, iii. 273 n. 1. Lewis the German in, iii. 355. Political disturbances, iii. 366, 375, 378, 394, 403, 422; iv. 299, 627. Influence of Benedict IX., iii. 376. Henry III in, iii. 377. Orders of monks in, iii. 418-424, 451. Corruption and ignorance, iii. 432 (169); iv. 84. Penance in, iii. 451. Sects in, iii. 592, 594; iv. 99, 225, 582, 583 n. 2, 584 and n. 2, 585, 590, 609, 613, 626-639. Henry IV. in, iv. 104, 113-120. Henry V., iv. 133. Bernard, iv. 146, 254, 259. Influence of Arnold in, iv. 148 n. 2, 150-152, 160-162. Frederic I. in, iv. 161-163, 166-168, 173. Authority of the popes in, iv. 172. Frederic II. in, iv. 179. Worship of the host, iv. 341. Anselm, iv. 364. Students from, iv. 373. Louis IV. in, v. 24, 36, 37. Church in, depressed, v. 44. Janow in, v. 192, 223. Flagellants, v. 412. See Rome.
Ithacius, bp. of Sossuba, ii. 772-775.

Itineracy, iii. 108, 109; iv. 286, 290, 608. See Mendicants, Preachers.

Ivo (Yves), bp. of Chartres, his relations with Philip I. of France, iv. 121-123. On lay investiture, 136, 137, 141. The Roman church, 194, 196. Legates, 197, 198. Exemptions, 201. Collection of Ecclesiastical Laws, 203. On asceticism, 241, 242. Penance, 347.

Citations from his Epistles: —
(Ed. Paris 1610), ep. 5, iv. 121 n. 2. Ep. 12, to Urban II., legates, 198 n. 3. Ep. 15, to Philip of France, 121 n. 3. Ep. 20, to the men of Chartres, 122 n. 1. Ep. 35, on the council at Rheims, 123 nn. 1, 2. Ep. 46, to Urban II., 123 n. 3. Ep. 47, to Dapifer, 122 nn. 2-4. Ep. 60, to a legate, 198 n. 4. Ep. 63, priesthood, 502 n. 1. Ep. 65, exemptions, 201 nn. 2, 3. Ep. 67, appeals to Rome, 199 n. 1. Ep. 74, judgments of God, 588 n. 2. Ep. 87, corruption at Rome, 197 n. 1. Ep. 109, legates, 197 n. 5. Ep. 126, the canonical clergy, 207 n. 2. Ep. 133, Rome, 196 n. 1. Ep. 158, the same, 196 n. 2. Ep. 192, asceticism, 241 nn. 3, 4. Ep. 195, authority of the pope, 194 n. 1. Ep. 205, judgments of God, 588 n. 2. Ep. 228, penance, 347 n. 1. Ep. 233, on Paschalis II., 136 nn. 3, 4, 140 n. 3. Ep. 236, to John of Lyons, the same, 136 n. 5, 137 nn. 1, 2, 140 n. 3. Ep. 256, anchorets, 242 n. 1.

Ized, caliph, iii. 203 n. 1.
Ized, genius of the sun, i. 493.

J.

Jabdallaha, Nestorian missionary, iii. 89.
Jacob, and Esau, iv. 569 n. 1. Jacob's well, i. 435.
Jacob, bp. of Harkh, Thondracian, iii. 588. His doctrine, 589.
Jacob, dean, v. 298.
Jacob (James), king of Majorca and Minorca, iv. 65.
Jacob (Baradæus), Monophysite bishop, Jacobites, ii. 612.
Jacob, Persian martyr, ii. 134.
Jacob, steps of, i. 352.
Jacob Amund, Swedish king, iii. 292.
Jacob Boehmen, i. 482 n. 1.
Jacob of Edessa, bp., ii. 345 n. 1.
Jacob of Vitry (à Vitriaco), bp. of Acco, at Damietta, iv. 60. Canonici sæculares, 208. Fulco's influence, 211. Care of lepers, 267. Life at the University of Paris, 413. Peter Cantor, 414.

Epistle on the capture of Damietta (see Bongars), iv. 60 n. 3.
Hist. occidentalis, cc. 6, 9, f. 287, Fulco, iv. 209 n., 210 nn., 211 n. 1; c. 7, f. 277 et seq., univ. of Paris, 413 n. 7; f. 338, societies for the care of lepers, 267 n. 4; f. 339, fraudulent collections, 267 n. 5; c. 29, forged bulls, 204 n. 4; c. 30, canonici, 206 n. 5, 208 n. 6; c. 32, Francis at Damietta, Franciscans, 60 nn. 2, 4.

Jacob Tollius.
Insignia itinerar. Ital., Anathemas, f. 106, Marcionites, iii. 245 n. 1; f. 114, Tychicus (Sergius), 254 n. 3, 269 n. 1; f. 122, Euchites, 264 n. 1; f. 142, Aristocritus, ii. 771 n. 4;
f. 144, Paulicians, iii. 262 n. 4, 265 n. 2; f. 146, the same, 266 n. 2.

Jacobellus of Mies, v. 297, 331, 337, 338 and n. 1, 367.
Jacobi.
Auserlesene Briefwechsel, Bd. ii. s. 55, ii. 123 n. 1.
Jago di Compostella, iii. 394; iv. 298, 306, 640.
Jahrbücher für Wissenschaftliche Kritik.
Mai 1837, Nr. 85, Critique by Dr. Baur, i. 697 n. 1.
Jamblichus, the Neo-Platonist, i. 173; ii. 613 n. 2.
James, the apostle, i. 63, 461, 675.
Epistle of. —
1 : 2, 3, and 1 : 12, v. 365. 2 : 10, iv. 348. 2 : 19, ii. 122. 4, iii. 362. 5 : 14, i. 119 n. 6; iii. 448. 5 : 15, iii. 448. 5 : 20, iv. 588.

Janduno, John of, v. 25, 147.
Janow, Matthias of, life and character, v. 192-194 (93). On Militz, v. 174-178, 183 n. 3, 236. Conrad, 183 n. 3. De regulis V. et N. Test., 194-232. On frequent participation in the Lord's Supper, 193, 213, 217-231, 335. Under both forms, 217, 231, 233, 338. Vices of the clergy, 194-199, 202-206, 215, 256. Antichrist, 196-201, 231-234, 266. Faith, 199, 201. Elias, 201. Law of Christ, 207-210. Christ the head of the church, 210-214. Equality of clergy and laity, 213-217. Consilia and præcepta, 213, 216, 249. Persecution of preachers, 258. The schism, 231. The Synod of Prague; image worship, 233. Letters of fraternity, 250 n. 1. Angels, 257. Huss, 235, 238, 239, 240, 242, 248-250, 256, 257, 290, 291, 325, 337, 364. His writings, 193 nn. 1, 2, 194 and notes.

Citations: —
From manuscript, De regulis V. et N. Testamenti, preaching of Militz, v. 176 nn. 1, 3, 177 n. Beneficence of M., 182 nn. 1, 2. Death of M., 183 n. 1. M. and Conrad, 183 n. 3. His motives in writing, 195 n. Antichrist, 196 n., 197 nn., 232 n 3. Satan, 199 n., 199 n. 1. Faith, 199 nn. 2, 3. The spirit of Elias, 200 nn., 201 n. 1. The parish priest, 203 nn., 204 nn. Confession of Jesus, 205 nn. Human ordinances, 206 nn., 208 n. 1. Law of Christ, 208 nn. 2, 3, 209 nn. The Jewish law, 210 n. 1. Headship of Christ, 210 nn. 2, 3. Unity of the ch., 211 nn. 1, 2. The day of light, 211 n. 3. Self-righteousness, 212 n. 1. The church, 212 n. 2, 214 nn. Piety in the laity, 214 n. 1, 216 n. On frequent participation in the Supper, 217 nn., 218 nn., 221 n., 223 nn. 4, 5 224 n., 225 nn., 226 nn., 228 nn., 230 nn., 231 nn. 1, 2. Pride in dress, 223 nn. 1-3, 192 n. 2. The Schism, 231 n. 3, 232 nn. 1, 2.
Published fragments of the same (Huss, Opp. De regno, etc., Antichristi), 194 n. 2; c. 21, f. 374, p. 2, clergy at Prague, 194 n. 1. Future restoration of the church, 200 n. 2. De sacerdot. et monach. curualium abominatione (Huss, Opp. Norib. 1558, i.), f. 376 et seq., the fire within him, 193 nn. 2, 3 ; f. 398, p. 2, c. 22, the abomination of desolation, 193 n. 1 (196 n.).

Jansenists, ii. 724.
Japan, iii. 130.
Jaroslaw, Russian prince, iii. 330.
Jean Benoist.
  Hist. des Albigeois, t. 1, apochryphal gospel of John, iv. 553 n. 5.
Jehoschua Ben Meir, Jewish chronicle of, iv. 74 n. 1.
Jehovah, i. 57, 477.
Jenaischen Literaturzeitung.
  J. 1817, Nos. 48-51, Gesenius on the Liber Adami, i. 376 n. 3.
Jeremiah, iii. 150 n. 7; iv. 333.
  Jer. 1 : 5, ii. 629. 1 : 10, iv. 251. 3 : 10, v. 285. 17 : 5, i. 230; iii. 429. 31 : 33, 34, i. 308; iv. 231 and n. 2. 48 : 10, iv. 29, Lam. 3 : 25, ii. 135.
Jeremiah, abp. of Sens, iii. 552.
Jericho, i. 708; iv. 189.
Jeroboam, v. 191.
Jerome, history and character, ii. 742–750. Promotes monachism, 294. As a controversialist, 645, 646 and n. 1. In the Pelagian controversy, 640, 641, 644–646, 665, 670. In the Origenistic controversy, 748–750, 753. Jerome and Augustin, 750, 779 (iv. 424).
  On Thomas in Ethiopia, i. 82. Apollonius and his slave, 118. Equality of bishops and presbyters, 190 n. 1 (ii. 188). Nazarenes, 350. Gospel of the Nazarenes, 350. Acts of Mani, 485 n. 3. Xerophagiæ, 521 n. 1. Origen and Candidus, 589 n. 3, 703 n. 3. Beryll and Origen, 594. Quadratus, 661. Justin, 670. Hippolytus, 681, 682. Tertullian, 684. Cyprian, 685 and n. 4. Arnobius, 688. Novatian, 690 and n. 2. Minucius Felix, 690. Origen, 693 n. 2, 703 n. 3, 704 n. 3 (ii. 744, 750). Gnomes of Sextus, 697 n. 2. Ambrosius, 709. Rufinus, 722 n. 2.
  On the study of Scripture among the Goths, ii. 159, 160. Rome, 167 n. 4. Vigilantius and celibacy, 181 n. 2, 182. Equality of bps. and presbyters, 188. Deacons, 189 and n. 5. Ursinus, 256 n. 5. Paul and Anthony, 246 nn. 1, 2, n. 5. Sarabaites, 284. Jovinian, 305 and n. 5, 307, 313. Reading of the Bible, Laeta, 316, 317. Festivals, 332. The Sabbath, 334. Epiphany, 346 n. 3. Gregory Nazianzen as preacher, 353. Against theatrical singing in church, 355. Daily communion, 364. Against Vigilantius, 374–376. Helvidius, celibacy, 377. Pilgrimages, 378 (iii. 131). Interpretation of Scripture and inspiration, 388, 391, 392. Cœlestius, 659 n. 1. Human character; character of Jesus, 646 n. 1. With Cassian, 688 n. 3. With Theodore, 712. Labors on the Bible, 745, 746.
  Authority in the Western church, iii. 60 n. 2. His translation of the Bible, 347 (ii. 745). On fasting, 442.

Berengar on, 506. Catharists, iv. 578 n. 5. Commentaries, Wicklif, v. 149. Huss on, v. 303, 332.

Citations from his writings:—
Adversus Luciferianos, § 8, confirmation, ii. 360 nn 1, 2. T. iv. f. 295 (ed. Martianay), the same, 188 n. 1.
Adv. Pelag. ff. 496-497 (= iv. ed. Mart.), imperfection of human nature, ii. 646 n. 1.
Adv. Rufinum. L. i. ff. 358, 359 (t. iv. ed. Mart.), Euseb. on Pamphilus, i. 721 n. 6; f. 359, on Methodius, 720 n. 3; (f. 385, his dream, ii. 744 n. 1). L. ii. f. 41., accusations against Origen, 734 n. 3; f. 413, generation of the Son of God, with Origen, 589 n. 3; ff. 413, 414 (ed. Vallarsi, t. iii. p. 1, f. 512), dispute of O. with Candidus, 589 n. 3, 704 n. 1; f. 425, Bible, revision of, Hesychius, 722 n. 4; of Lucian, 722 n. 6.
Chronicle, Ursinus, ii. 256 n. 5.
Comm. in Ephes. l. 3, c. 5, t. 4, f. 387, ed. Mart. (t. vii. 1, f. 652, ed. Vall.), church singing, ii. 355 n. 3.
Comm. in Ezek., c. 1, ii. 346 n. 3, 350 n. 1.
Comm. in Galat., 5 : 12, ii. 391 nn. 1–3. L. ii. c. 4 (ed. Mart. t. iv. f. 252; ed. Vall. t. vii. 1, p. 457), seasons of worship, 332 n. 1, 337 n. 2.
Comm. in Isaiam, l. i. c. 1, t. 3, f. 71 (ed. Vallarsi, Venet. 1767, t. iv. p. 21), the Nazarenes, i. 349 n. 5. L. ii. c. 5. t.d 1s. 5 : 18, f. 83 (ed. Vall., p. 130), the same, n. 2. L. ix. c. 29, v. 18, f. 250, the same, n. 3. Ad. Is. 7 : 6 (ed. Vall., p. 130), the same n. 4. Ad. Is. 31 : 7, 8 (ed. Vall., p. 425. ed. Mart., t. iii. pp. 79, 83, 259, 261), i. 350 n. 1. L. iv. c. 11, t. 4, f. 156, i. 350 n. 4.
Comm. in Jer. L. ii. c. 11, v. 16 (ed. Mart., t. iii. f. 584, ed. Vall., t. iv. 2, f. 921), intercessions at the Lord's Supper, ii. 367 n. 4. L. iii. præfat., Pelagius, 652 n. 1, 639 n. 1, 641 n. 2.
Comm. in Matt. in c. 23, L. iv. (ed. Vall., t. vii. f. 184), ii. 259 n. 1.
Comm. in Micha. L. ii. c. 7, t. 6, f. 520, citations from Gospel of the Nazarenes, i. 350 n. 3.
Comm. in Titum, ii. 188 n. 3 (t. vii. f. 702), persecution of pious laity 261 n. 3.
Contra errores Joann. Hierosolomyt. ii. 670 n. 3.
Contra Jovinian. L. i. § 2, ii. 305 n. 6 : Jovinian on the church, 311 n. 3; § 3, on marriage, 304 n.; on abstinence, 306 n. 1; on the regenerate, 308 nn. 3, 6; § 5, to a virgin, 306 n. 2; § 34, on celibacy, 182 n. 1; § 40, Jerome on Jovinian, 305 nn. 3, 4. L. ii. § 1, Jov. on baptism of the spirit, 308 nn. 2, 4; § 5, abstinence, 307, 1–4; § 18, quare justus laboret, 307 n. 5, 311 n. 2; § 19, union of the church with Christ, 305 nn. 1, 2, 306 n. 3, 312 n. 1; on John 14 : 2, 311 n. 1; § 20, on stages in the religious life, 310 n. 3; § 37, sins after baptism, marriage, 309 nn.
Contra Vigilantium, c. 1, on celibacy, ii. 182 n. 2; cc. 4, 9, on martyrs and relics, 374 nn., 445 n. 1. Ed. Vall., t. iii. ff. 391, 395, the same, 375 nn. 1, 2; § 16, V. on Monasticism, 314 n. 1.
De viribus illust., c. 3, the Nazarenes, i. 349 n. 1; c. 20, Aristides, 661 n. 4; c. 25, Comm. of Theophilus, in Evang., 674 n.; c. 36, Alexandrian school, 527 n. 3; c. 42, the slave of Apollonius, 115 n. 2; c. 47, Maximus, 721 n. 3; c. 53, Cyprian and Tertullian, 227 n. 1, 685 n. 4; c. 63, Julius Africanus, 709 n. 1; c. 67, Cyprian, 222 n. 1; c. 72, Acts of Mani, 485 n. 3; c. 77, Δουκιανέω, 722 n. 6; c. 79, Arnobius, 688 n. 1.
Epistles. Ep. 5, ad Ctesiphon., Gnomes of Sextus, i. 697 n. 2; Pelagius, ii. 641 n. 3. Ep. 11 (or 94), ad Ageruchiam, ii. 744 n. 3. Ep. 17, ad Innocent., fossores, ii. 193 n. 1. Ep. 18, ad Eustochium, his vision, ii. 743 n.

2. Ep. 22, to the same, clergy at Rome, ii. 167 n. 4; Sarabaites, ii. 284 n. 1. Ep. 27, ad Marcellum, Quadragesima, i. 521 n. 1. Ep. 29, ad Paulum, the condemnation of Origen, i. 705 n. 1. Ep. 40, ii. 749 n. Ep. 41, ad Pammach. et Ocean., Lactantius, i. 608 n. 2; Origen's retractations, i. 702 n. 2. Ep. 48, ad Pammach., § 16, house communion, ii. 365 n. 4. Ep 49, ad Paulin., pilgrimages to Palestine, ii. 378 n. 3. Ep. 52, ad Nepotian., corrupt clergy, ii. 167 n 4; § 8, popular applause, Gregory, ii. 353 n 2. Ep. 53, ad Paulin., § 5, popular interpretation of Scripture, ii. 317 n. 4. Ep. 71, ad Lucin., § 6, frequency of communion, i. 333 n. 1; ii. 364 n. 4; fasting on the Sabbath, ii. 334 n. 6. Ep. 72, ad Vital., Hippolytus on this point, i. 297 n. 2. Ep. 75 (26), ad Vigilantium, and 76, ad Tranquillinum, ii. 747 n. Ep. 81, Synod of Diospolis, ii. 646 n. 1. Ep. 83, ad Magnum, Aristides, i. 661 n. 4. Ep. 93, ad Sabinian., ii. 189 n. 1. Ep. 95 (or 4), ad Rusticum, ii. 744 n. 2. Ep. 96, ad Principiam, ii. 750 n. 3. Ep. 99, ad Asellum, Babylon, ii. 745 n. 1. Ep. 101 (or 146), ad Evangel., bps. and presbyters, i. 190 n. 1; ii. 188 n. 3, 189 n. 2. Ep. 102, ad Marcellum, ii. 745 n. 3. Ep. 106 (in Vallarsi, elsewhere, 98), to the Goths, ii. 159 n. 3. Ep. 107, ad Lætam., § 2, the Goths, ii. 160 n. 2; § 12, her education of her daughter, ii. 316 nn. 4, 5. Ep. 109, ad Riparium, Vigilantius on relic worship, ii. 373 n. 3. Ep. 125, ad Damasum., Bible manuscripts, ii. 745 n. 2. Ep. 145, ad Evangel., position of deacons, ii. 189 nn. 5, 7. Ep. 146, ad Damasum. (Martianay, t. iii. f. 160), study of ancient authors, ii. 742 n. 2 Ep. 148, India, i. 82 n. 4. Ep. 202, ad Alypium et Aug., Annianus, ii. 657 n. 1. Ep. ad Algasiam (t. iv. f. 197), Theophilus, harmony of gospels, i. 674 n.

Life of Paul the Hermit, ii. 264 nn. 1, 2.

Præf. in reg. Pachom., § 7, ii. 272 n. 1; § 8, 273 n. 1; § 49, 273 n. 3; f. 957, 272 n. 5.

Præf. ad Philemon. (ed. Vall., ff. 741, 742), ii. 392 n. 1.

Preface to his edition of the Bible, ii. 745 n. 4.

Vita Hilarion (t. iv., ed. Mart., p. 2), ii. 271 n. 2; f. 82, 142 n. 4.

Jerome of Prague, character, v. 245, 246, 253. Connection with Huss, 245, 246, 253, 254, 279. Discourse at Prague, the papal bulls, 285 and n. 2, 286 and n. 1. Dream of Huss, 364. Labors and martyrdom, 371–380 (285 n. 2, 286 n. 1). Hist. of Jerome, v. 377 n. See Van der Hardt.

Jersey, isle of, iv. 236.

Jerusalem, destruction of, i. 38, 343; v. 57, 313. Temple at, i. 65, 67, 407 and n. 2; ii. 314, 321; iv. 555 n. 1. Attempt to rebuild the temple, ii. 69, 70. Philo on the restoration of the Jews to, i. 65. Ælia Capitolina, i. 153, 344. Apostolic council at, i. 159; v. 209. Apostolic church, i. 216 (ii. 295). Church at, i. 299; iii. 35; v. 31. Two parties, i. 342–344. Flight from and return, i. 343, 344. Pilgrimages to, i. 691; ii. 378; iii. 131, 448 n. 1; iv. 126, 155, 298, 298. Patriarchate, ii. 197. Monks at, from, ii. 270, 301, 314. Convent, iii. 207, 458 n. 1. Christmas, ii. 346. Church of H. Sepulchre, ii. 427. Prayer at, iii. 311. "Complaint of," iii. 375 n. 3. The crusades, iv. 124–126, 189, 349. Kingdom of, iv. 153, 179. Clement at, i. 691. Epiphanius, ii. 747. Jerome of Prague, v. 246. Bps. of, ii. 583 n. 1. See Cyrill, John, Juvenalis, Peter, Praylus, Sophronius, Temple. See, also, Councils, an. 415, Crusades.

Jerusalem, the heavenly, i. 153, 651 n. 5; iv. 126, 130, 155, 222, 238, 307, 621; v. 301. Catharists on, iv. 572.

Jesenic, v. 252 n. 3, 272 and n. 1, 294, 297, 298, 317, 334 n. 3. Repetitio pro causa Joann. Huss, v. 252 n. 3.

Jesters, iv. 384.

Jesuitism, ii. 301 n. 4.

Jesus, with the Jews of his own time, i. 38. With Jewish Christians, 62, 64. Justin Martyr, 74, 363. Worship of, 145 n. 3. Story concerning, Celsus, 162 n. 1. Apollo and, 172. Origen on the work of, 250; on belief in, 251, 545. Nativity of, 302. As God-man, 302, 410. As Messiah, 305 (see Messiah). In the Clementines, 354, 359, 360. With Gnostics, 476. Cerinthus, 398. Basilides, 410, 412. Ophites, 446. Sabæans, 447. Carpocratians, 449. Simonians, 454. Marcion, 469, 470. Mani, 500, 501. Monarchians, 577. Mohammed, iii. 86. Birth of, with Valentine, i. 429. Birth of, with later sects, iii. 594, 601; iv. 554, 571. Genealogies of, i. 709 n. Brethren of, ii. 376. With Julian, ii. 46, 49, 50, 73. Theodore, ii. 496, 500. Union with the Logos, ii. 500, 507, 508. Bernard on power of, iv. 261. Trust in, v. 140. And Antichrist, v. 197. See Christ.

Jewish Christians, i. 339–365, 159, 458 n. 3. In Ethiopia, 83. Observance of Sabbath, 296; ii. 334. Festivals, i. 297, 302. Two parties, i. 342–344, 363, 394. Jewish element, principle, in the church, i. 194–196, 212, 226, 235, 257, 273, 286, 289, 294, 302, 338–365, 367 n. 1, 390, 463, 478, 507, 548, 551, 645, 654, 657, 659, 674, 675; ii. 48, 314, 315, 337; iii. 270; iv. 264. In the Roman church, i. 365. In the church theocracy, ii. 166, 779; iii. 2, 263, 264, 351; iv. 110 n. 1. In the Clementines, i. 360. In Gnosticism, i. 369, 380–387, 396–442, 456. In Montanism, i. 511, 512, 513, 519, 520. In other sects, iv. 553, 571, 590–592. In Paul of Samosata, i. 603, 604. Aërius, ii. 379. Apollinaris, ii. 484–486. Mohammed, iv. 59, 637. Opposition to, iii. 263, 264, 431. See Anti-Jewish Gnostics, Jewish Christians, Judaism.

Jewish passover, i. 324. See Easter.

Jewish people, prophetic character of the, i. 35, 36, 52. Religious condition of the, 35–68. Punishment of the, 170. In the Clementines, 359. With Cerinth and Philo, 397. With Gnostics, 397, 408, 426, 427, 447, 448, 468. 'Iou-

δαϊκὸς βίος, 97 n. 1. See Jewish element, Jews, Judaism.
Jewish religion, Frederic II. on the, iv. 179-181. See Judaism.
Jewish theologians, theology, i. 574, 576, 597. Three tendencies of, 39. See Alexandrian Judaism.
Jews, Varro and Stral o on the, i. 9. Restoration of, 65. Dispersion, 67, 79. Influence, 67. In Arabia, 81. Malabar, 82. Egypt, 83 (see Alexandria). Rome, 89, 690. Banished by Claudius, 94. Revolt under Barcochba, 103. Opposition to Christians, 128 n. 5, 164 n. 4 (iv. 384). Pagan opinion of, 172 and n. 2. Sybilline prophecies, 177. On Peter and Paul, 203. Speculative tendencies, 394. Stories concerning Christ, 668.
In the second Period. Julian and the Jews, ii. 63, 69. Synagogues protected, 95. In Persia, 125. Suppress Christianity in Arabia, 142, 145. On image worship, 330. Jerome, 746.
In the third and fourth Periods. Conduct of Gregory I. in relation to the, iii. 13 n. 1. Influence in Arabia, 84. Isidore on the treatment of, 152. Intercourse with, 166 n. 6. Accuse the Christians of idolatry, 201, 202, 203 n. 1. Forced to receive baptism, 202. Chazars, 315, 329, 458 n. 2. Traffic in Christian slaves, 322. In Spain, 345. Judaism in Armenia, 588, 589. In Phrygia, 592.
In the fifth Period. Among the Mongols, iv. 57. Majorca, Raymund Lull, 68. Situation, polemics, conversion, 70, 71-81, 621. Persecution of, 71-77. In France, crusades, 71 n. 3, 72, 76. Accusations against, 72, 73. Their wealth, 72, 73, 144, 591. As witnesses of the truth, 73, 76. Defended by Bernard, 73-75, 77 n. 1, 154. By the popes, 75-77, 129. Oppose image and saint worship, 77, 79 (v. 233). Influence of intercourse with, 325, 326, 591. Enstathius, 531 n. 5. Pasagii, 590-592. Oliva, 624. God of, with the Bogomiles, iv. 554, 556. Niphon, 563 and n. 3. See Saturnin.
Jews and Christ, v. 38, 39, 44, 133, 349, 386. Papacy, 305. Conrad 185, 186. Janow, 196, 197. Merswin 388.
Jezdegerdes I., king of Persia, ii. 133, 134.
Jezdegerdes II., king of Persia, ii. 126 n. 5, 133, 135 n. 4, 136.
Jezedaners, iv. 558 n. 2.
Jistebnitz, Sigismund of, v. 250.
Jitzin, Master von, v. 289.
Joachim of Calabria, abbot of Floria, iv. 135, 189, 216, 220-232, 244, 268, 291, 292, 411, 447, 617, 618 and n. 1, 619 nn. 1, 3, 620, 625, 626, 636; v. 135, 381. His works, iv. 221 n., 619 n. 1. Life, iv. 220 n. 2. See Acta S. May.

Citations from his writings: —
Comm. in Apocalyps. f. 3, on the apostle John, iv. 228 n. 3; f. 5, the trinity, in revelation, 227 n. 2; f. 7, Paschalis II., 223 n. 3; f. 9, time of the Holy Spirit, 229 n. 5; f. 13, the same, 227 n. 1, 230 n. 2; f. 45, the same, 231 n. 3; f. 48 operations of the Trinity, 227 n. 4; f. 49, teaching of the spirit, 231 n. 1; f. 55, 230 n. 3; f. 77, the contemplative order, 228 n. 4; f. 78, false monks, 225 n. 4; f. 83, c. 2, obscure beginnings, 224 n. 1; f. 84, last times, 227 n. 3, 228 n. 2, 229 n. 3; f. 85, the spirit, 229 n. 4; f. 88, graces answering to the periods of the church, 229 n. 2; f. 91, sacraments, 225 n. 2; f. 95, the everlasting gospel, 230 n. 1; f. 103, symbols, 231 n. 4.
Comm. in Esaiam, f. 4, prophecy of Silvester, iv. 226 n. 3; f. 7, Almaric of Bena, 221 n.; the temporal sword, 223 n. 7; f. 28, Mongols, 221 n.; the church and the princes, 224 n. 1; f. 39, judgment against the papal court, 222 n. 7.
Comm. in Jerem. (ed. Colon. 1577), f. 56, humiliation of the ch., iv. 224 n. 2; ff. 61, 65, ch. of Rome, 222 n. 1, 223 n. 1; f. 81, Franciscans, 221 n.; f. 85, Cistercians, 221 n.; f. 86, the house of Hohenstaufen, 226 n. 5; f. 98, ch. of Rome, 222 n. 3; f. 104, confidence in externals, 224 n. 3; f. 108, 222 n. 4; ff. 123, 143, Patarenes instruments of judgment, 226 n. 1; f. 151, persecution predicted, 221 n.; f. 250, Paschalis II., 135 n. 1; f. 262, 222 n. 6; ff. 284, 292, the crusades, 189 nn. 1-3; f. 299, predictions concerning Frederic II., 226 n. 8; f. 310, the popes and the princes, 223 nn. 5, 6; f. 312, Paschalis II., 135 n. 1; f. 330, 223 n. 4; f. 331, 226 n. 4; f. 370, confidence in man, 223 n. 8.
De concordia nov. et vet. test., ff. 53, 54, corruption of the ch., iv. 222 nn. 8, 9; f. 71, 225 n. 6; f. 101, 225 n. 5; f 130 2, final attack of Antichrist, 226 n. 2.

Joan, pope (fabulous legend), iii. 367 n. 1; v. 285, 307.
Joannes Ozincusis. See John of Ozunn.
Job, ii. 378, 619 n. 3; iv. 250, 321, 611.
1 : 21, iii. 278. 2 : 10, iii. 278. 14 : 4, i. 412, 620. 19 : 25, iv. 325. 31, ii. 287.
Jocelin, biographer of Patrick, ii. 147 nn. 1, 2, 148 n. 1, 149 n. 1.
Joel.
2 : 25, ii. 406. 2 : 28, 29, i 518.
Joh. de Thwrocz. See Schwandtner, t. i.
Johann von Müller, von den Reisen der Päpste, iv. 197 n. 4.
Johann von Winterthur. See Winterthur.
Johannes, bp. of Constance, iii. 36.
Johannes, bp. of Nice, ii. 347 n. 1.
Johannes, monk, biographer of Odo, iii. 417 n. 1.
Johannes Beccus, iv. 545-550.
Discourse i. c. 3, iv. 549 n. 1. Dis. ii., 547 n. 3. Controversial writings, 547 n. 1. See Leo Allatius.
Johannes Cantacusenus, iii. 201 n. 3.
Johannes Cinnamos. See John.
Johannes Diaconus.
Life of Greg. I. L. ii. c. 1, Servus Servorum. iii. 117 n. 1; chair of G., 42 n. 1. L. iv. c. 80, the pallium, 119 n. 2.
Johannes Eleemosynarius, patriarch of Alexandria, on the treatment of slaves,

iii. 99. Life of, 99 n. 2. See Acta S.
Jan. t. ii., Anastasius.
Johannes Moschus.
    History of the monks, c. 110, Sophronius, iii. 178 n. 2.
Johannes νηστευτής, patriarch of Constantinople, iii. 115, 116.
Johannes Ozniensis. See John of Ozunn.
Johannites, party of Chrysostom, ii. 762. Of Strassburg, v. 392 n. 1.
John. See John the Apostle, John the Baptist.
John, abbot, iii. 232 n. 1.
John, abbot of Gorze, iii. 345.
    Life of, c. 1. § 4, iii. 445 n. 2; § 120, iii. 336 n. 2; § 122, f. 713, 345 n. 2. See Acta S. Feb.
John, abbot of Vallombrosa, iii. 419.
John, abp. of Lyons, iv. 136, 137. Ep. to Yves of Chartres, 137 n. 3.
John, abp. of Placenza (Philagathus), iii. 422.
John, apocryphal gospel of. See Gospel.
John, associate of Peter Waldus, iv. 606 n. 4.
John, bp. of Heraclea, iii. 570.
John, bp. of Jerusalem, ii. 328, 329 n. 2, 641, 642, 746-748, 750 n. 2.
John, bp. of Lubec (Lebus), v. 330.
John, bp. of Mecklenburg, iii. 327.
John, bp. of Sabino (Silvester III.), iii. 376.
John, bp. of Synnada, iii. 205, 206.
John, bp. of Trani, iii. 580.
John, bp. of Veletri (Benedict X.), iii. 387.
John, comes Sacrarum, ii. 537-540.
    Ep. to Theodosius II., ii. 538 nn. 1, 3. See Lupus.
John, count of Soissons, iv. 325.
John, disciples of. See Sabæans.
John (Sansterre), king of England, iv. 174, 175 and n. 2, 178, 182, 325; v. 136.
John, legend of the Tartarian priest-king, iv. 46, 47, 52.
John, martyr in Prague, v. 288-290.
John (the merchant), martyr, iii. 338, 339, 341, 343.
John (Ion), missionary to North America, martyr, iii. 307.
John, monk, pretended Syncellus, iii. 228.
John, Nestorian patriarch, iv. 47.
John, patriarch of Antioch, ii. 519, 521-523, 528-534, 537-539, 541 n.-557 and n. 7.
    Ep. to Nestorius, ii. 522 n. 1. Ep. to Theodosius II., conduct of Cyril, delay of his journey, 528 nn. 2, 4. See Harduin, t. i. f. 1469.
John, patriarch of Antioch, at Constance, v. 108.
John, patriarch of Constantinople, under Justin, ii. 591.
John, patriarch of Constantinople, under Philippicus and Anastasius II., iii. 196.

His letter to Constantine of Rome, 197. See Harduin, t. iii. f. 1838.
John, patriarch of Constantinople, at the council of Constance, v. 330.
John, presbyter, plenipotentiary of the oriental patriarchs, iii. 203 n. 1.
John III., pope, iii. 119 n. 1.
John VIII., pope, succeeds Hadrian, iii. 366. Obtains an organ at Freysingen, 128 n. 4. His transactions with Methodius, 316 n. 4, 317 n. 1, 317-321. Bestows the imperial crown on Charles the Bald, 366. His position in relation to the Greek church, 572-578.
    Commonitorium (see Baronius), iii. 574 n. 3. Epistles to the emperor Basilius. 574, 578 n. 4 (see Baronius). Ep. 89, ad Turentarum de Marauna, 318 n. 1. Ep. 90, ad Methodium, 316 n. 4, 317 n. 1, 320 n. 3, 321 n. 1. Ep. 107, on the liturgical use of the Slavonian language, to Swatopluk, 318 nn. 3-5, 319 n. 1; Methodius, 319 n. 2. Ep. 108, to Photius, 578 nn. 1, 2. Ep. 268, to Methodius, 321 n. 2. Harduin, t. v. and vi., Mansi Concil., t. xvi.
John IX., pope, iii. 319 n. 3, 321 n. 4.
John XII. (Octavian), pope, iii. 367, 370. Deposed on account of his immorality by Otho I., iii. 368; v. 18.
John XIII., pope, iii. 324.
John XV., pope, contends for the Pseudo-Isidorean Decretals, iii. 368-374. Canonization of Ulric, saint worship, 447.
John XVIII., pope, iii. 403.
John XIX., pope, iii 580.
John XXI., pope, iv. 192.
John XXII., pope, election, v. 23. Contest with Louis, iv. 23, 24, 30, 35-38, 40, 380. In the Franciscan controversy, 24, 33, 36. Propositions condemned by, 147. Bull concerning the doctrines of Eckhart, 395. Oliva, iv. 620 n. 3.
John XXIII., pope (Balthazar Cossa), election, v. 90. University of Paris, 90, 93. His reformatory council, 90. Incident at Whitsuntide, 91. Gerson on, 96-99. Flight from Rome, 100. At Bologna, 100, 101. His journey to Constance, 100, 101, 102. Arrival, 103. Letters of D'Ailly to, 102. At Constance, charges against, 104, 105, 106, 108, 110. Conditional abdication, 105. Flight to Schaffhausen, 106, 107, 339, 364. Proceedings of the council in relation to, 109-111. At Ratolfzell, 111. Deposition, 111, 112, 127, 352. At Gottleben, 112. Huss and, 262, 263, 271-273, 276-285, 293, 302, 303, 321, 322, 326-330, 333, 339, 352, 363, 364. Bull against Ladislaus, 276-290 (see Huss). Wenceslaus, 287. Bribery, 293.
John, presbyter at Alexandria, ii. 574 n. 1.
John, son of Callinice, iii. 244. Whether rightly called founder of the Paulician Sect ? 246.

GENERAL INDEX.

John, son of George, Tartar prince, iv. 58.
John, Syncellus of Cyrill, ii. 537.
John, the Apostle, his character, i. 212 (v. 306). His first epistle, 63 n. 1, 221. Relation to the communities, 183. In Asia Minor, 191 and n. 2, 194 n. 1, 342, 463, 508, 674. Peccata, 221. Passover festival, 297-299 and n. 2 (iii. 584). His age, 340. Relation of his gospel to the Clementines, 361 n. 3. To Justin Martyr, 364 n. 2, 585 n. Gnostics, 452. Cerinthus, 396. Heracleon, 436. Nicolaitans, 452, 453. Marcion, 463. With the Anti-Montanists (Alogi), 526, 527, 583, 678. The everlasting gospel, 448, 549. Doctrine concerning Christ, 574, 575. Logos, 575, 585. Artemonites, 580 n. 1. Noëtus, 584, 585. Polycarp on, 677. Julian on, ii. 56. His use of the term " world," ii. 242. Arius, ii. 408 n. 1. His logos doctrine, with Marcellus, ii. 439. His gospel translated by Bede, iii. 153 n. 2. With the Paulicians, iii. 246 n. 1, 248. In the controversy concerning the Lord's Supper, iii. 496, 498, 523. His last days, iv. 36. With Joachim, iv. 227 n. 1, 227-229, 231, 625. The Holy Spirit, iv. 537. With the Catharists, iv. 570, 575 and n. 7. Oliva, iv. 625.

Citations: —
John, 1 : 1, i. 251, 575. 1 : 5, i. 499. 1 : 9, iii. 268. 1 : 11, iii. 267. 1 : 14, i. 560, 574 ; ii. 56. 1 : 27, i. 430 n. 1 : 30, iv. 578 n. 1. 1 : 32, ii. 390 n. 4. 1 : 49, ii. 497. 2 : 4, iv. 674. 2 : 18, i. 169. 3 : 1, ff., i. 166. 3 : 5, i. 648 ; ii. 447. 3 : 6, v. 213. 3 : 10, iii. 506 n. 1. 3 : 16, iii. 267, 412 ; iii. 161 n. 1. 3 : 29, i. 434. 4, i. 435, 436. 4 : 21, iii. 443 ; v. 403. 4 : 22, iv. 72. 4 : 23, 24, i. 284, 288, 342. 4 : 24, i. 560 ; iii. 443 ; iv. 232. 4 : 34, i. 436. 4 : 42, iv. 290, 428. 4 : 48, i. 432. 5 14, i. 227, 229, 258. 5 : 17, ii. 476, 665 and n. 2 ; iii. 14 ; iv. 227 n. 1. 5 : 22, 27, i. 230. 5 : 23, ii. 425. 5 : 30, ii. 646 n. 1. 5 : 35, iii. 142 n. 7. 5 : 37, iii. 257. 5 : 43, i. 38. 6, i. 333 ; iii. 498, 523 ; iv. 342 ; v. 270. 6 : 15, v. 14. 6 : 26, ii. 118. 6 : 28, iv. 579 n. 1. 6 : 35, i. 623, 649. 6 : 37, iii. 538. 6 : 40, iv. 382. 6 : 44, ii. 248. 6 : 45, i. 177. 6 : 52, v. 223. 6 : 53, i. 648 ; ii. 447 ; iii. 496 ; v. 337. 6 : 54, i. 324. 6 : 56, ii. 304 ; v. 230. 6 : 60, v. 223. 6 : 62, ii. 783. 6 : 63, ii. 480, 736 ; iv. 262, 406, 576 ; v. 155, 156, 222. 6 : 67, ii. 36. 7 : 5, ii. 50. 7 : 10, ii. 646 n. 1. 7 : 37, iv. 259. 7 : 39, iv. 575 n. 7. 7 : 49, i. 364. 7 : 51, v. 325. 8, ii. 173 ; iv. 577 n. 3. 8 : 12, i. 49, 413. 8 : 24, i. 541. 8 : 36, i. 88. 8 : 42, i. 590 n. 1. 8 : 43, i. 545. 8 : 44, iv. 567. 8 : 45, i. 545. 8 : 46, i. 166, 658. 8 : 59, i. 590. 9 : 3, i. 412. 10, v. 316. 10 : 3, i. 227. 10 : 5, iii. 267. 10 : 9, ii. 446. 10 : 11, 12, ii. 131 ; v. 312. 10 : 16, iv. 568. 10 : 30, i. 584. 10 : 35, iii. 162. 10 : 38, v. 267. 10 : 39, v. 312. 11 : 25, i. 334. 11 : 27, ii. 497. 11 : 34, ii. 407, 436 n. 4. 11 : 54, v. 312. 12, v. 162. 12 : 19, v. 219. 12 : 24, v. 156. 12 : 28, ii 479 n. 1. 12 : 35, iii. 526 n. 2. 13, iv. 612 n. 3. 13 : 8, i. 690. 13 : 21, i. 636 n. 4. 13 35, i. 255. 13 : 33, iii. 14. 14 : 2, ii. 311 n. 1. 14 : 6, i. 530 ; ii. 446. 14 : 9, i. 584 ; iv. 381. 14 : 13, iii. 58. 14 : 16, iii. 23, ii. 305. 14 : 27, ii. 155, 248 ; v. 305. 14 : 28, iv. 534. 15, i. 176, 583 ; iv. 406. 15 : 1, i. 171. 15 5, i. 650 ; v. 308. 15 : 15, v. 382. 15 : 2, i.

230. 15 : 26, ii. 471 ; iii. 318 n. 3. 16 : 2, v. 310. 16 : 7, iv. 330 ; v. 308, 410. 16 : 12, i. 514. 16 : 13, iv. 382. 16 : 23, iii. 58 ; v. 309. 16 : 33, i. 128. 17 : 3, i. 572 ; iv. 381. 17 : 21, ii. 305. 18 : 10, iv. 215. 18 : 20, v. 293. 18 : 31, iv. 214. 18 : 36, i. 69 ; ii. 390 n. 2. 18 : 38, i. 8. 19 : 23, iv. 285. 20 : 22, ii. 497. 20 : 28, ii. 497. 20 : 29, iv. 375. 21 : 15, i. 212 ; v. 202. 21 : 21, iv. 228. 21 : 23, iv. 228. 22 : 21, iv. 229.

I. John, 1 : 7, i. 523. 1 : 8, iv. 228 ; v. 351. 2 : 1, 2, i. 246. 2 : 2, i. 643. 2 : 3, iii 444. 2 : 16, i. 266. 2 : 19, i. 341. 2 : 23, i. 545. 3 : 9, ii. 305. 4 : 3, v. 197. 4 : 18, ii. 299. 5 : 7, i. 572. 5 : 16, i. 221 ; iii. 314.

See Apocalypse, Apocrypha, Commentaries, Revelation.

John Balle. See Balle.
John Cardinalis. See Reinstein.
John Cassian, ii. 283, 284, 296, 656, 697 n. 3, 708, 751 n. 2. History and controversy, 637-690. Collationes, 296 n. 2.

Citations: —
Collat. 18, c. 8, Sarabaites, ii. 283 n. 3. Coll. t. 10, Serapion, 751 n. 2, c. 2, Epiphany and Christmas, 346 n. 2. De incarnat. Christi. L. i. c. 4, Leporius, 655 n. 3. Institut. Cœnob., 296. L. iii. cc. 9, 10, fasting on the Sabbath, 334 n. 6. L. x. c. 22, benevolence in the cloisters, 289 n. 3.

John Cinnamos, iv. 533, 534 n. 2.

L. ii. c. 64 (ed. Meineke), Niphon, iv. 563 nn. 1, 3 ; Cosmas, 564 n. 1. L. vi. c. 2, Byzantine spirit, 533 n. 6, 534 n. 2.

John Comnenus II., emperor, iv. 536.
John de Brogny. See Brogny.
John de Lugio, iv. 565.
John de Monte Corvino, iv. 57-59. His letters, 57 and nn. 2-4 58 nn., 59 n. 1. See Wadding, Mosheim.
John de Plano-Carpini, iv. 50.

Report of his visit to Tartary, iv. 48 n. 2, 50 n. 2 ; § 12, iv. 51 n. 1.

John Ducas Vatazes, Greek emperor, iv. 539, 541, 544.
John Eremita the Second, life of, iv. 254 n. 2.
John Gratian, arch-priest (Gregory IV.), iii. 377.
John Gualbert, founder of the Congregation of Vallombrosa, iii. 398, 399. See Acta S. (O. B.), S. vi. p. ii.
John Huss. See Huss.
John Lascaris, iv. 543.
John Malala.

Chronicle, Pars II., ff. 184, 187 (ed. Oxon.), Justinian, ii. 106 nn. 1, 3. L. xi. f. 273 (ed. Niebuhr), Trajan's edict, i. 100 n. 4.

John Militz. See Militz.
John Nieder, Dominican v. 391, 392 n. 3.

Formicarius (ed. v. d. Hardt), v. 381 n. 1 ; f. 304, v. 392 n. 3.

John of Bilombar, v. 129.
John of Chlum. See Chlum.
John of Damascus, his origin, iii. 206 n. 3. Defence of Christianity against the Mohammedans, iii. 88. Doctrinal manual, 169, 197. His opposition to tales

of dragons and fairies, 207 n. 1. Discourses in favor of image worship, 206–210. On the doctrine of the Holy Spirit, 554, 556. His relics, the Arsenians, iv. 550.

Citations: —
Dialogue between a Christian and a Turk, opp. t. i. (ed. Le Quien), f. 496, iii. 88 n. 1; f. 471, fragments on fairy tales, iii. 207 n. 1. Haeres., frgm. Philopon., ὁ διαιτητής, ii. 614 n. 1. Haeres., § 6, Euchites, ii. 278 n. 2; f. 997, the same, ii. 281 n. 2. H. 88, γνωσίμαχοι, ii. 767 n. 4. Manual of doctrine (ἀκριβής ἔκδοσις τῆς ὀρθοδόξου πίστεως), iii 169. L. i. cc. 7, 8, the Holy Spirit, iii. 554 nn. 2–4. Orat. adv. Constantin. Cabalin., f. 613, iii. 218 n. 2; f. 622, iii. 221 n. 1. Orat. ii. § 12, edict of Leo, iii. 209 n. 2.

John of Falkenberg, v. 127.
John of Fidanza, iv. 421.
John of Gaunt. See Lancaster.
John of Janduno. See Janduno.
John of Jesenic. See Jesenic.
John of Kebel, v. 250.
John of Leitomysl (the Iron), v. 294, 296, 297, 326 n. 3, 340, 341.
John of Lubeck, v. 330.
John of Matha, iv. 267.
John of Milheim, v. 235.
John of Oznun, iii. 250 n. 1, 265, 266.
Against the Paulicians, ff. 76, 89, iii. 250 n. 1: f. 85, 265 n. 5; f. 87, 244 n. 4. Armenian canons (Venet. 1834), f. 61, 589 n. 1. Contra fantasticos, f. 111, Monophysites, 261 nn. 5, 6

John of Paris, Dominican (Pungens asinorum), on transubstantiation, iv. 340, 341; v. 153. On the Papacy, v. 13, 15–19.

De potest. reg. et papali. (Goldast. t. ii.), v. 15 n. 1, 15–19. Determinatio (ed. Allix, Lond. 1686), iii. 511 n. 1; iv. 340 n. 7, 341 n. 1.

John of Parma, iv. 618 n. 1.
John of Ragusio, v. 129.
John of Salisbury, on papal absolutism, iv. 194. Conversation with Adrian IV., 195 n. 2. Effects of the enthusiasm for dialectics, 357, 358, 415.

Citations: —
Ep. 48, to Henry II. of Eng., iv. 168 n. 2. Ep. 58, Frederic I. in Italy, symbolical paintings, 163 nn. 1, 3. Ep. 80, archdeacons, 211 n. 4. Ep. 83, forgery of bulls, 205 n. 1. Ep. 193, to Alex. III., 194 n. 5. Ep. 222, Yves of Chartres, 197 n. 1. Ep. 254, the peace of Venice, 189 n. 1. Epp. 286, 287, miracles at Becket's tomb, 171 nn. (conduct of Becket, 169 n. 4). Metalog. l. i. cc. 3, 4, ambition at Becket's tomb, 358 nn. Polycratic, l. ii. 26, burning of Bibl. Palatina, iii. 150 n. 7; l. v. 115, Eugene III., iv. 197 n. 2; l. vi. 24, Adrian IV. on the stomach and the members, iv. 195 n. 2.

John of Stekna. See Stekna.
John of W'll arod, bp. of Riga, at Constance, v. 348, 368, 375.
John of Winterthur. See Winterthur.
John Parastron, iv. 544.
John Peter de Oliva, iv. 620–626. Comm. on Apocalypse, 620 n. 3. See Baluz.
John Philoponus, character of, ii. 613,
614 (iv. 461). Against Proclus, 105 n. 8, 613 n. 2.
De Creatione, ii. 613 n. 3. L. vi. cc. 10, 17, fragment of Theodore, 494 n. 1, 714 nn. 1, 3. Against Jamblichus, 613 n. 3. Ὁ διαιτητής (in Johann. Damasc. de haeres.), 614 n. 1.

John Phocas, Greek monk, on the holy places, Carmel, iv. 266.
John Ruysbroch. See Ruysbroch.
John Scotus Erigena. See Scotus.
John Strick, priest, iv. 40.
John Talaya, ii. 587, 588.
John Tauler. See Tauler.
John the Baptist, i. 272; ii. 56; iii. 59 n. 5, 595; iv. 312, 333, 405; v. 143, 154, 188, 200, 366, 377, 392. His reception by the Jews, i. 38. With the Ebionites, i. 347. With Gnostics, i. 420, 430 n., 434, 441 n. 2. With Mani, i. 504. Festival of, ii. 369; iii. 134; iv. 68. Picture of, iii. 547. With the Bogomiles, iv. 556, 559. Catharists, iv. 574. Disciples of. See Sabaeans.

John the Grammarian, iii. 533. Patriarch of Constantinople, 547, 548. Tutor of the emperor Theophilus, 547.
John the Schismatic, church history, ii. 331 n. 4. See Harduin, Concil., iv. f. 306.
John Trevisa, v. 149.
John Tzimisces (Zimisces), Greek emperor, the Paulicians, iii. 587; iv. 564.
John Villani. See Villani.
Joinville.
Memoires of Louis IX., dispute with the Jews at Cluny, iv. 77 n. 2; p. 175 (ed. Pelitot), Louis on dress, 285 n. 4; p. 177, on temptation, 326 nn. 3, 4; t. ii. p. 381, Hugo, 282 n. 2.

Jol. See Yule.
Jonah, v. 332, 358.
Jonas, bp. of Orleans, contends against Claudius of Turin, iii. 430 and n. 1, 432 n. 6, 437, 439. Against reliance on outward works, 452. His writings, 449, 459, 460. Envoy of Louis the Pious to the pope, 552.

Citations: —
His work against Claudius, on image worship, pref., iii. 432 n. 4 (n. 6, 433 n. 2), 439 nn. 3, 6; f. 168, 439 n. 7. L. ii. f. 183, 440 n. 1. L. iii. 438 n. 3; f. 180, 440 nn. 2, 3; f. 190, 438 n. 3 (see Bibl. Patr. Lugd.). De institutione laicali, 459 n. 5. L. i. cc. 14, 15, prayer, 460 n. 1; cc. 20, 23, 459 nn. 6, 7. L. ii. c. 17, on works, 452 nn. 2, 3; c. 22, treatment of servants, 459 n. 8. L. iii. c. 10, indulgences, 452 n. 4; c. 10, priestly mediation, 452 n. 5. See D'Achery, Spicileg., t. i.

Jonas, monk, life of Columban, 29 n. 3. Of Eustasius, iii. 38 n. 2, 39 n. 2. See Acta S. (O. B.), S. ii.
Jordan, P.
Die Vorläufer des Hussitenthums in Böhmen, v. 183 n. 2, 194 n. 2; s. 62, 222 n. 2.

Jordan, the river, ii. 31; iii. 207.
Jordanus, general of the Dominicans, life of Dominick, iv. 269 n. 1.
Joseph, Armenian patriarch, ii. 137.

Joseph, head of the Paulicians, iii. 250.
Joseph, œconomus of the church in Constantinople, iii. 536 n. 3
Joseph, patriarch of Constantinople, iv. 543-551.
Joseph, prayer of, i. 66 n. 3; iv. 568 n. 5.
Joseph Genesius.
  Reg. l. 1. f. 26 (ed. Lachmann). Leo the Armenian, iii. 582 n. 4. L. iv. f. 97, Bogoris, 308 n. 3.
Josephus, on the infatuation of the Jews, i. 38. On the three Jewish Sects, 39 n. 1, 41 n. 2, 42, 43, 44, 48. The Messiah, 65. The Temple, 407 n. 2.
  Archæol. L. xvi. c. 2, § 4, plea of Marcus Agrippa, i. 88 n. 2. L. xviii. c. 1, Judas of Gamala, 38 n.; § 4, Sadducees, 41 n. 2; Essenes, 48 n. 1. Contra Apionem, l. I. § 8, the canon, 41 n. 1. De bello Judaico, l. ii. c. 8, § 1, Judas of Gamala, 38 n.; § 4, Essenes, 43 n. 3; § 6, 12, 13, the same, 45 nn. 2, 2; §§ 8, 9, their reverence for the sun, 47 n. 3; § 10, their orders, 43 n. 2; § 13, prophecy among them, 45 n. 3.
Joshua, iii. 457.
  2 : ii. 219. 4 : 6 et seq., iii. 207. 6 : 26, iv. 189.
Josiah, ii. 607 n.
Jourdain.
  Recherches, etc., sur les traductions latines d'Aristote, iv. 417 n. 4, 445 n. 1.
Jovian, emperor, ii. 87-89, 87 n. 4, 92, 117, 132, 459, 487.
Jovinian, monk, ii. 182. On the unity of the divine life, asceticism, celibacy, the church, 304-313, (v. 350). At Milan, 312. Jerome, 305, 313, 377, 641. Pelagius, 632, 635, 641, 646. See Jerome, contra Jov.
Jovius, comes, ii. 101 n. 5.
Joy, iv. 623; v. 337. See Enjoyment.
Jubilee of Boniface VIII., v. 3. Reduction of the time of the J. to 50 years by Clement VI., 41, 51 (183, 184). Reduction to 33 years by Urban VI., v. 51.
Judaism, its relation to Christianity, i. 3-5, 62-66, 194-196, 289, 337, 339, 340, 352, 353, 381, 382, 386, 506, 507, 519, 548, 556. Preparatory character of, 35, 36, 536, 537, 548, 672. Influence on Christianity (see Jewish). Among the Greeks and Romans, 22, 67. National pride in, 36. Among the Romans, religio licita, 89. Caracalla, 119 n. 6. Law of Severus against, 120. Galen, 164 n. 1. Jewish view of life, 273. Essential element of, 352. With Gnostics, 366, 379-383, 407, 435, 436. As kingdom of the Demiurge, 382, 383. Cerinthus, 399. With Origen, 548. Zenobia and Paul of Samosata, 603, 604. Barnabas on, 638. And Greek Philosophy, Justin Martyr, 666-669. Under Julian, ii. 50, 52-57, 69. Gospel in the form of, iii. 50. Relation to Mohammedanism, iii. 85-87; iv. 59, 627. In the church, iii. 87, 208. Spiritualized,

iii. 170 (see Alexandrian). Reactions against, iii. 244, 269, 270, 431, 586, 588, 589, and n. 1, 592. Idea of God in, iii. 171 (i. 22; ii. 54). Abelard on, iv. 383, 384. Hamann on, iv. 617 n. 2. See Jewish people.
Judaizing, Latins charged with, iii. 581 and n. 4, 582.
Judaizing sects, i. 331, 341-365, 394. Tendency, 339, 340. See Gnostics, Gnosticism.
Judas Iscariot, i. 448, 622, 650 n. 2; ii. 704; iii. 544; iv. 116, 352, 482; v. 156, 221, 350, 370. Gospel of, i. 448 n. 4.
Judas of Gamala, i. 37.
Judgment of God, iii. 36; iv. 132. The final, i. 515, 650; iii 429, 444; iv. 617, 621, 635; v. 37, 68, 151, 179, 196, 199, 398. Expected, iii. 470 n. 2. Picture of iii. 308. Threefold, Catharists, iv. 571.
Judgments, divine, v. 199. On a corrupt church, iv 224, 621; v. 215. Predicted, iv. 219, 224, 225, 226, 632, 636; v. 102, 380, 412. Human, iv. 275, 391; v. 408.
Judgments of God, iii. 5 n. 2, 17, 80, 129, 130, 289, 384 n. 4, 399, 429, 449, 450, 480, 519; iv. 9, 16, 60 n. 2, 80, 86, 115, 145, 169, 550, 551, 588; v. 162, 275, 346, 347, 363. Entered into by proxy, iii. 452.
Judicial authority in the church, iii. 120, 349, 358-366, 368-375.
Judith, sister of Emp. Henry IV., iv. 4 n. 1.
Judith, wife of Louis the Pious, iii. 272.
Judith, wife of Wladislav, iv. 4.
Jugglery, i. 157, 161; ii. 42.
Julia Domna, i. 174.
Julia Mammæa, i. 125.
Julian, Apollinarist, ii. -91 n. 2.
Julian, bp. of Halicarnassus, ii. 608, 613.
Julian of Eclanum, Pelagian. Character and writings, ii. 652-654. Against the use of force in religion, 650 n., 651 notes 1, 2. Zosimus, 651 n. 3. Reason and religion, 653, 654. The popular consciousness, 654. Humanity of Christ, 655. Importance of the questions in dispute, 659. The first sin and its consequences, 666, 669, 670. Reason and Revelation, 673, 674. Grace, 675. Love, 677. Ethics, virtues of Pagans, 681 and n. 1, 682. Augustin's reasoning, 683, 685. Theodore, 712, 713. Nestorius, 721. On infant baptism, 727-729. See Augustin, c. Julian.
Julian the Apostate, Life of, ii. 40-87. Course of education, 40-45, 396. Conversion to Paganism, 34, 40-44. Oribasius, 45. His religious position, 45-59. Steps towards the restoration of Paganism, 35, 37, 59-69, 92. Conduct toward the Jews, 69. Towards the Christians, 70-86, 456. Death, 86-88 n. 1. Valentinian, 90. Libanius on

96 n. 3. Simplicius, 107. Polemic, — enemy of the monks, 111. The Donatists, 231. Epiphany, 343. His works, ii. 45. See Cyrill of Alexandria.

Citations: —
Epistles. Ep. 6, to the prefect of Egypt, ii. 74 n. 1. Ep. 10, ad Alexandrinos, 37 n. 2. Ep. 17, ad Oribasium, 45 n. 3. Ep. 25, f. 397, to the Jews, on the rebuilding of Jerusalem, 70 n. 1. Ep. 27, to Labanius, 86 n. 3. Ep. 31, Aëtius, 71 n. 2. Ep. 37, on death, 58 n. 2. Ep. 42, rescript concerning the Christians, 71 n. 1, 75 n. 3. Ep. 49, to the high priest Arsacios, 86 n. 4. Ep. 51, to the Alexandrians, edict against Athanasius, 73 nn. 2–4. Ep. 52, ad Bostrenos, 68 n. 1, 71 n. 4. Ep. 58, ad Alexandrinos, the obelisk, 47 n. 4. Ep. 62, to an officer, 66 n. 1. Ep. 63 (ed. Heyler, f. 132), to the high priest Theodore, 54 n. 7, 55 n. 1, 58 nn. 2, 3, 4, 62 n. 1. Ep. to Arsaces, 86 n. 3. Ep. ad Athenieuses, 45 n. 3. Ep. to Photinus, fragm., 71 n. 2 Fragm. epist. ed. Spanh., on his attempt to rebuild the temple, 69 n. 3.
Instruction for priests, f. 293 et seq., images, ii. 60 n.; f. 295; the prophets, 53 n.; f. 305; benevolence, 63 n. 2; the priest outside of the temple, 64 nn.
Misopogon, to the people of Antioch, ii. 83 n. 4; ff. 344, 357, 82 nn. 1, 2; f. 361, 84 nn. 2, 3; f. 363, reproaches them with their indifference, 8 nn. 5, 6.
Orationes. Orat. 4, f. 130, eulogy of Helios, ii. 49 n. 2. Orat 7, f. 228, Helios, 8 n. 3. Orat. 8, Salust., 45 n. 3.
Rescript., ii. 65 n. 2. See Muratori.
"The Cæsars," ii. 32 n. 3.
Works, f. 115, national characters, ii. 51 nn. 2, 3; f. 131, the same, Hellenic culture, 52 nn.; f. 206, the Christians reproached for persecuting, 46 nn.; f. 292, national gods, 51 n. 1.

Juliana of Cæsarea, i. 707, 708.
Juliano Cesarini, cardinal, at the council of Basle, v. 128–133.
Ep. ad Eugen., iv. f. 64 et seq., v. 128 n.; f. 67, 130 n. 2.
Julin, Pomeranian town, iv. 3, 9–11, 16, 30. Bishopric, 16.
Julius, bp. of Puteoli, ii. 573.
Julius, bp. of Rome. Athanasius, ii. 205, 433, 434. Council of Sardica, 199 n. 2, 205; of Philippopolis, 436. Marcellus, 440. Ursacius and Valens, 449 n. 5. Reply to the Oriental bps. 433 n. 2.
Ep. 1., ad Eusebianos, §§ 4, 5, ii. 205 n. 1.
Julius Africanus, i. 709.
Epistola ad Aristidem, ap. Euseb., 6, 31, i. 709 n. See Routh.
Julius Capitolinus.
Vita Antonii Pii, c. 9, i. 103 n. 5; cc. 11. 24, Marcus Aurelius, 105 nn. 1, 2; cc. 13, 21, the same, 107 nn. 2, 5.
Julius Cassianus, i. 458 n. 3.
Julius Firmicus Maternus, ii. 36.
De errore profan. relig., ii. 36 n. 6; c. 30, 37 n. 1.
Julius Krone.
On Fră Dolcino and the Paterenes, iv. 609 n. 3. 629 nn. 2, 3, 633 nn. 1, 2.
Julius Paulus, i. 87.
Sententiæ receptæ, i. 109 n. 2. L. 5, tit. 21, law concerning new religions, i. 87 nn. 2, 3.

Junilius, North African bp.
De partibus div. leg., ii. 183 n.

Jupiter, i. 116, 117; ii. 29, 49, 74, 84 n. 6. Jupiter Philios, Maximin, ii. 4. See Zeus.
Jura, iv. 214.
Jurisdiction, ecclesiastical, ii. 171, 172; iii. 95–97, 108, 452, 453; iv. 83, 390. Of the pope, iii. 120, 452; v. 9, 10, 13–19, 38. Of the emperor as against the pope, v. 18, 30. Of church and state respectively, v. 24, 25–30, 78. See Boniface VIII., Gerson, Papacy.
Jurisprudence, v. 113. See Law.
Justice, with Basilides, i. 402 n. 3, 404, 405, 412. Ptolemæus, 438. Marcion, 466, 467, 472. Aquinas, iv. 521, 524. Civil, iii. 102–105, iv. 40, 302. Of God, i. 57, 58, 561, 564, 642; iii. 474, 476, 477, 487; iv. 498, 506, 507.
Justification, with Basilides, i. 413. With Carpocrates and Epiphanes, i. 450. Constantine, ii. 32. Doctrine of with Hilary, ii. 620, 621. In the Pelagian controversy, ii. 677–679; Semi-Pelagian, ii. 688. In the sense of Augustin, ii. 678, 688; iv. 509; v. 302. Chrysostom, ii 720. By works, iii. 130–132. With Gregory the Great, iii. 146. Subjective mode of apprehending in the Middle Ages, iv. 304, 305. In Scholasticism, iv. 508–515. Abelard, iv. 502. Bernard, iv. 510. Different operations in, iv. 512, 513. Wicklif's views of, v. 172. Huss, v. 302, 347.
Justin, emperor, ii. 139, 145, 277 n. 3, 591, 606, 710.
Justin Martyr, his life and writings, i. 661–671. The philosophers of his time, 9. Development of his religious experience, 34 n. 3. Jewish deniers of angels, 42 n. 2. Jewish construction of Christianity. Jewish converts, 62, 63. Proselytes, 67. Miracles of the Christians, 74. Virtues of Christians, 76. Country communities, 79. Crescens, 93. Extension of Christianity, 129. On conversion, 250. Defects of Christians, 254. Magistrates, 259. Euelpistus, 270. Philosopher's cloak, 275. Christian places of assembly, 290, 291. Divine worship, 303. Instruction of catechumens, 305 n. 1. Baptismal formula, 310. Agapæ, 325. Baptism and the Supper, 328. Consecration of the Supper, 329 n. 2. Idea of Sacrifice, 330. Doctrine of the Lord's Supper, 647, 648 n. 1 (ii. 731). Bread in the Lord's Supper, 331. Celebration of the Supper, 332. Two classes of Jewish Christians, 342, 343 n. 2, 349. Elias, 347 n. Gentile Christians become Jewish, 362. Harsher and milder tendencies among Gentile Christians, 363. Ebionitism, 364, 674. Simon Magus, 454 n. 1. Tatian, 456, 672. Logos doc-

trine, 585, 586. The Gospel of John, 585 n. 1. Holy Spirit, 609. Christ's humanity, 635. Satisfaction, 642. Chiliasm, 651. The Trinity, 716. See Semisch.

Citations: —
Apologia, i. f. 45 (ed. Colon. 1686), Christian exorcism, i 74 n. 1; f. 48, Christianity the absolute religion, 586 n. 1; ff. 50, 51, his conversion, 662 n. 1; § 66, the Logos in the Supper, 648 n. 1. Apolog. II., change of character produced by Christianity, 250 n. 1; tribute, 259 n. 1; ascetics, 275, n. 1. Christian wives of pagans, 283 n. 2; exhortations in public worship, 303 n. 5; f. 56, objects of Christian worship, 609 n ; c. 58, the kingdom of Christ, 96 n. 5; f. 63, influence of Christian character, 76 n. 2; f. 74, on Gen. 49: 11, 670 n. 1; f. 75, Theodotus, 580 n. 4; f. 81, source of truth, one. 667 n. 1; f. 88, more converts from paganism than from Judaism, 63, n. 2; f. 98, country churches, 79 n. 2; § 10, person of Christ, 685 n. 4; § 61, instruction of catechumens, 395 n. 1; Ed. Ben. §§ 4, 6, 8, references to Apol. 1., 665 n. 4.
Cohortatio (παραινετικὸς πρὸς Ἕλληνας) f. 15. Greek philosophy indebted to Judaism, i. 666 n. 2.
Dialogus c. Tryphone Judæo, i. 34 n. 3; f. 218, skepticism of philosophers, 9 n. 2; philosopher's cloak, 275 nn. 5, 6; ff. 247. 264. 220, the teachings of conscience, 669 n. 1; ff. 249, 338, day of Christ's passion, 298 n. 4; f. 255, two parties among Jewish Christians, 342, nn. 3, 4, 343 nn. 1, 2; Pagan Christians become Jewish, 362 n. 3; f. 267, Ebionites, 363 n. 3; Christ teaches his own divinity, 585 n. 1; ff. 268, 336, Elias, 347 n.; f. 273, Gen. 49: 11, 670 n. 1; f. 291, Jewish view of the Messiah, 347 n.; of the supernatural birth of Jesus, 348 n. 1. f. 315, baptism of Jesus, 348 n. 3; f. 317, redemption, 642 n. 3; c. 39, f. 322, the same, 642 n. 2; ff. 327, 331, the apostolic commentaries, 585 n.; f. 344, the "Angel of God," 609 n. 1; f. 345, spread of Christianity, 129 n. 3; spiritual sacrifice, 330 n. 3; f. 340, citation from Apolog. II., 608 n. 2 f. 350, proselytes, 67 n. 3; f. 358, deniers of angels, 42 n. 2; the church and the world, 130 n. 1; church and state irreconcilable, 130 n. 1; f. 370; repentance necessary to forgiveness, 62 n. 2.
Λόγος πρὸς Ἕλληνας, operation of the Logos, i. 667, 668.

Justina, empress, and Ambrose, ii. 472; iv. 111.
Justinian, emperor, persecutes paganism, ii. 106. Spread of Christianity under him, 139, 140 (iii. 90). Elesbaan, 145. Imperial papacy, 166. Bps. are to care for prisoners, 173. Deacons in Constantinople, 189. Despotism, 215 (iii. 91 n., iv. 151). Marcian, 277 n. 3. In the church controversies, 553 n. 3, 592–609, 611, 612, 763–765, 710. Manicheism, 770. Founder of rights of patronage, iii. 109. Gregory II., on, iii. 212. Laws of, iv. 158, v. 87.

Novell, rights of patronage, iii. 110 n. 1. L. l. N. 3, ii. 180 n. 3. L. i. t. 3, N. 3, filial churches in Constantinople, ii. 194 n. 8.

Justinian II., emperor, iii. 196, 248.
Justus, English bp., iii. 18.
Justus, Paulician, iii. 248.
Justus, St., iii. 5 n. 2.

Jutland, iii. 271, 279, 286.
Juvavia, iii. 40.
Juvenal, iii. 602.

Sat. 2, i. 16 n. 3; Sat. 3, v. 75, i. 103 n. 1.

Juvenalis, bp. of Jerusalem, ii. 529, 569, 576, 583.

K.

Kaaba, at Mecca, iv. 535 n. 1.
Kaiserswerth, cloister, ii. 44.
Kajomorts, of the Zendavesta, i. 491 n. 4.
Kalendæ, ii. 349, 350.
Καλλιάνη (Calcutta), ii. 141 n. 4.
Kammin, iv. 9.
Kämpfer.

Amœnitates exoticæ, iii. 130 n. 1.

Kanngeiser.

Geschichte von Pomern, iv. 16 nn. 1, 3, 5.

Κανόνες ἀποστολικοί, i. 660. See Apostolic.
Kant, ii. 465 n. 2.
Kantzow, Thomas.

Chronicle of Pomerania, iv. 31 n. 1.

Kappenberg, monastery at, iv. 71, 80, 81.
Karamsin.

Hist. Russia, trans. by Hauenschild, Bd. i. p. 169, Nestor, iii. 329 n. 1

Καθαροί, i. 2–7.
Kathle, iii. 282.
Kebel, John of, v. 250.
Κένωμα, i. 374.
Kent, converted by Augustin, iii. 11–13. Christianity in, 11–19, 24. Suppression of Christianity in, 18 Revival of, 19.
Κεντουκλαδική αἵρεσις, iii. 545 n. 6.
Kerrsan (Cherson), iii. 329.
Keraït, Tartarian Kingdom of, iv. 46–48.
Κήρυγμα ἀποστολικόν, i. 306.
Κεστοί, i. 709 n. 1.
Keys of the kingdom of heaven, ii. 200; iii. 24, 35, 59, 585; iv. 159. Power of the, iv. 616; v. 146, 291, 296, 357.
Kiew, iii. 327, 328 and n. 2, 330.
Kil-Patrick, ii. 146.
Kingdom of God, i. 35, 36, 180, 194, 197, 324, 440, 521, 649, 652 653; ii. 51, 114; iii. 2, 98, 123, 174, 257. Prophetic spirit in relation to the, iv. 216. Stages of progress, Dolcino, iv. 634. Kingdom of Christ, i. 523, 601, 652; ii. 481. And of Antichrist, v. 199. Of the Messiah, i. 398, 399, 429. Of Heaven, i. 715; ii. 729; iv. 319, 366, 367, 581. Kingdom of light, in Parsism, i. 369, 376, 378, 402 n. 3, 483; with the Sabæans, i. 377; with Gnostics, i. 401, 402 n. 2, 404, 420, 455; with Manicheans, i. 480, 482, 489, 490–501, 503; with Priscillian, ii. 776. Kingdom of darkness, in Parsism, 376, 483; with the Sabæans, i. 377; with Gnostics, i. 402 n. 2, 403, 404, 413, 420, 455; with Manicheans, i. 490–493, 500, 505; with Priscillian, ii. 776. King-

dom of good, i. 481, 482. Of evil, i. 376, 401, 481, 482; ii. 776 n. 4; iv. 572. Kingdom of Ahriman, i. 402 n. 3. Of nature, i. 405. Of the Demiurge, i. 432, 653, 654; iii. 257–263 (see Demiurge). Of ὕλη, i. 429. Of Jaldabaoth, i. 444. Of Satan, i. 463, 644. Of Earth, i. 471.

Kings, the books of, ii. 152.
I. Kings 3, iii. 334 n. 4. 16 : 34, iv. 189. 18 : 19, iv. 266. 18 : 40, ii. 234. 19 : 11, iv. 316. 19 : 18, ii. 243. II. Kings 2 : 11, i. 265. 2 : 25 ; 4 : 25, iv. 266. See Commentaries.

Kings, their anointing, iii. 96 and n. 3. Gregory VIII. on the power of, iv. 88. Divine right of, iv. 88, 109, 110, 131, 132, 141, 142. Right and worthiness, v. 351–353. Right of revolution, v. 50.

Kionites, iv. 529 nn. 1, 2.
Kirdigar, ii. 127 n. 1.
Kirton, iii. 46.
Kiss, i. 124. Fraternal, 255, 262; ii. 362. In baptism, i. 313, 314, 317.
Kist, Dr.
Essay on the origin of the Episcopal power in the Christian ch. (see Illgen), i. 185 n. 2.
Κλῆρος, κληρικοί, i. 195, 196.
Klonkot, v. 182.
Kneph, i. 444.
Knighton, Henry, v. 150.
Chronicle (in Hist. Anglic. Script. antiq., Lond. 1652). T. ii. Wicklif, v. 150 nn. 1–3, and John Balle, 158 nn., 159 n. 4. The earthquake council, 162 n. 3.

Knights, iv. 125, 164, 233, 577 n. 5. Order of German, 45; Spiritual, 38, 41, 70, 127. See Crusades. Lull on spiritual knighthood, 191 (70); Bernard, 258.

Knights Templars, iv. 258. Suppression of, v. 23, 171.
Knin, Matthias Pater of, v. 250.
Knowledge, in Platonism, i. 21. In Christianity, 186, 187, 238, 367, 368, 476; iii. 124. Charisma, with Paul, i. 510. Clement on, i. 541. Paul and Origen, i. 544. Augustin on, ii. 475. Joachim, iv. 227, 229. Bernard, iv. 241, 258, 259, 371–373. Eustathius, iv. 532. Militz, v. 177. Tauler, v. 409. Mani, i. 487. Knowledge in relation to faith, i. 366, 530, 531 ; ii. 269, 307; iii. 463; iv. 64, 427; with Abelard and his school, iv. 376, 377, 380, 381, 385; Hugo, iv. 402–404; Peter of Blois, iv. 415; Alexander of Hales, and other scholastics, iv. 427–440. Knowledge, opinion, and faith, iv. 372. Relation to obedience, i. 531; to Scripture, i. 532. Knowledge and charity, ii. 650; and action, iii. 174; and intuition, iii. 174, 175. Zeal without, iv. 73. Harmony of life and, iv. 361, 364, 367, 411, 412, 427. Relation to salvation, iv. 405–407. Relation of the affections to, iv. 411–413, 427. In act and in habit, iv. 443, 444. Unity

of, iv. 431, 432. Limits of, ii. 450; (Lull on) iv. 438, 439. Pride of, i. 476; iv. 561. Opponents of, i. 535, 536. Self knowledge, iv. 263, 411, 412, 458. Spiritual knowledge, iv. 370, 372, 385, 428. Efforts to diffuse Christian, iv. 39 (see Instruction). Sources of, iii. 2; v. 264. Low state of, v. 387. See Clergy, Culture, Faith, Gnosis, Gnosticism, Ignorance, Monasticism, Schools.

Knowledge of God, with the Therapeutæ, i. 62. Eunomius, ii. 446, 447. Maximus, iii. 175. Scotus, iii. 463. Ægidius, iv. 312. The Scholastics, iv. 411–413, 429, 430, 438, 457. Huss, v. 336. In Christ, Theodore, ii. 496, 425. Knowledge in God, Gregory I. on, iii. 144; Scotus, 461, 465; Aquinas, iv. 480. In the Trinity, iv. 457, 465. Identity of knowledge and being in God, iv. 478, 480; v. 166. See Gnosis, Knowledge and Faith.

Koblai khan, founder of the Mongol Empire in China, iv. 56, 57.
Kolberg (Colberg) history of the conversion of, iv. 16.
Κοπιᾶται, ii. 193.
Kopts. See Copts.
Koran, iii. 336, 337; iv. 181 n. 3; v. 299. Moral element in the, iii. 85, 86. Gnostic elements in the, iii. 86 n. 1. On the mission of Mohammed, iii. 86 n. 2. Divinity of Christ, iii. 87 n. 1, 159, 337.
Sura, v. (ed. Maracci) f. 236, worship of Christ and Mary, iii. 87 n.; Sura, v. f. 296, S. vi. f. 262, S. xiv. f. 375, national religions, iii. 86 n. 2.

Kosegarten. See Taberistanensis annales.
Κοσμᾶς ὁ μελῳδός, iii. 206 n. 3.
Κόσμος νοετός and αἰσθητός, ii. 49.
Kozi-hradek, v. 299, 310.
Kristni-Saga, Introduction of Christianity into Iceland, iii. 300 n. 2; c. ii. 301 n. 3.
Krohn, missionary operations in the South Seas, iii. 39 n. 1.
Krone. See Julius.
Κρόνος, ii. 127.
Κρότος, ii. 353. See Applause.
Krzivousti, iv. 1. See Boleslav III.
Kulm, bishopric, iv. 45.
Kupan, Hungarian prince, iii. 333.
Κυριακὴ ἐν λευκοῖς, ii. 342 n. 2.
Kushanians, ii. 141 n. 3.
Kyllean. See Cyllena.
Kyrie Eleison, iii. 324.
Kyrknjolsa (Slavonian), iii. 324.

L.

Labarum, ii. 10, 13 n. 1, 20, 24 n. 4.
Labaun, Zdenek of, v. 298.
Labbe.
Nova Bibliotheca Manuscriptorum, t. i. f. 673, Adalbero of Metz, iii. 408 n. 1; f. 677, the same, 411 n. 4; f. 678, the same, 403 n. 1, 405 n. 5. Scoti, 460 n. 6. T. ii., Chronicle of Ademar, 593 nn. 1, 3; f. 212, Chronicon Maxentii, 618 n. 1.

Labeo. See Notker.
Labor. See Manual Labor.
Labors for the salvation of others, Francis on, iv. 274, 275. Mendicants, 278, 279. See Missions, Monks, Preaching.
Lachmann, iv. 173 n. 1, 216 n.
Lactantius, on the Holy Spirit, i. 608; ii. 467.
Institutiones. L. iv. c. 27, pagan rites hindered by the cross, i. 145 n. 3. L. v. c. 2, Hierocles, 174 n. 1; c. 11, Ulpian's collection of rescripts, 126 n. 2. L. vi. c. 13, oracle concerning Christ, 172 n. 4. De mortib. persecutor., c. 10, 145 n. 3, 153 n.; c. 16, 155 n.; Hierocles, 174 n. 1.
Ladder, the, ii. 276.
Ladislaus of Naples, v. 73, 75, 94, 100, 276, 281 and n., 283.
Laeta, ii. 316. See Jerome (ep. 107).
Laity, permitted to teach in public assemblies, i. 186, 187, 196, 197, 703. Participation in church government, 189, 190, 199, 200. In the choice of church officers, 189, 199, 200. Administration of sacraments, 196. Doctrine among the, 578, 583. In the epistles of Clement, 659. Justin Martyr, 662. Instruction of, 686. Commodian, 687.
In the Second Period. Arbitration, ii. 171 n. 3. Dependence on the priesthood, 179. Elevated to church dignities, participate in church elections, 185. As monks, in relation to the clergy, 284. In theological disputes, 432 and n. 1. And the Bible, 317. See Bible.
Third and Fourth Periods. Christian knowledge among the, iii. 124, 125. Pilgrimages, 131. Participation in communion, 136. In the image controversy, 198, 200, 207 n. 1, 229, 5-2 n. 1. Knowledge of Scripture (207 n. 1), 251, 252, 469 n. 4, 600, 604. Sects among the, 599, 600. Lay missionaries, 302. Pretended priest, 309. And priesthood, 348. Administration of church property, 351. Bring causes to Rome, 359. Preaching, 391 n. 4. Lay abbots, 416. Ignorance and corruption, 441, 592. Piety, 445. Saint worship, 446 n. 1, 448. Unction imparted by, 448. Rules for, 459. Elevated to church offices, 559, 574, 577. In the Greek church, 577.
The laity and the Jews, iv. 77. And Gregory VII.; as censors of the clergy, 96, 97, 99, 107, 112, 146, 149, 592. Perform priestly offices, 99, 592, 614. Right of investiture denied to, 101 (see Investiture). Asceticism, 112. Pious societies, 286, 302, 303, 607, 609, 612, 627, 628. Bible among laymen, 320-324, 425 (see Bible). Relation to the clergy, 224, 320, 354, 509, 514. Withdrawal of cup, 343-347. Neglect of the Lord's Supper, 343, 344, 346, 353. Bacon, 425. Influence of pantheistic doctrines among the, 447, 450. Interest in theological questions, 498, 534, 547. Eustathius to the, 532. Superstition, 577 (v. 239, see Superstition). Effect of interdict on, 582. Forbidden to dispute concerning the faith, 590. Separatist tendencies, 592.
Laity in councils, v. 33, 34. Mysticism, 42. Contempt for clergy, 123, 129, 131, 148 n. 1, 215. Wicklif on their relation to the clergy, 139, 146. On their right to the Scriptures, 149-151. Knighton on, 150. Compared with clergy, 34, 159, 221, 224, 230, 231. Contempt of the clergy for, 193, 194. Laity and clergy, 195, 200, 202, 203, 205, 213, 214. Participation in the Lord's Supper, 212, 213, 217-231, 337, 338. Piety, 213-218, 221, 224, 381. Societies, 42, 213, 381. Persecuted by monastic orders, 213, 216, 217. Increase of piety, 218, 236, 306, 381. Reform and anti reform parties, 232. Image worship, 233, 234. Right to preach, 250. Huss and the, 256, 257, 260 n., 288, 306, 307, 321, 352. Huss on the responsibility of the, 282, 283. Discussion before, 321. Friends of God and the, 42, 383, 387, 389, 391. Books among, 391.
Lamaism, iv. 47, 56.
Lambecius, sermons of Otfrid, iii. 425 n. 3.
Lambert, iv. 344 n. 4.
Lambert of Aschaffenburg.
History of Germany, ff. 44, 156, Hermann of Bamberg, iv. 102 n. 5, 103 nn. 1, 2; f. 89, Greg. VII., 92 n. 5, 6; an. 1074, decrees of, 94 n. 4, 95 n. 1; f. 136, witchcraft, 91 n. 1; an. 1075, f. 154, ignorance of clergy, 102 n. 4. Greg. VII. and Henry IV., 105 n. 4; and Hugo Blancus, 106 n. 2; and the Margravine Mathilde, 113 n. 1.
Lambeth, v. 148.
Lamentations, 3 : 25, ii. 135.
Lampetios, Lampetians, ii. 276. The testament of, 279 n. 1.
Lampon, presbyter, ii. 516.
Lampridius. See Ælius.
Lampsacus, ii. 319 n. 2.
Lancaster, Duke of, v. 93, 136, 147, 148, 159, 162.
Landlords, selfishness of Christian, ii. 90, 91, 100, 175. Pagan, 100 and n. 3.
Landrich, among the Frieslanders, iii. 79.
Landulph de Cotta, advocate of reform at Milan, iii. 391-394, 392 n. 3, 393 nn. 4, 5, 397.
Landulph de S. Paulo.
Life of Ariald, iii. 389 n. 3, 390 n. 2, 392 n. 5, 397 n. 2; c. 2, 389 n. 3; c. 3, 39) n. 3, 391 n. 5; c. 6, 391 nn. 1, 3, 6; c. 16, Anselm of Lucca, 393 n. 3; Erlembald, 395 nn. 1-3.
Landulph, Junior.
Hist. Mediolan, c. 30, Irnerius, iv. 203 n. 2. See Muratori.
Landulph the elder.
L. iii. cc. 1, 23, arguments of the opponents of

celibacy, iii. 297 n. 2.   Sect at Montfort, 600 n. 4.   See Muratori.

Lanfranc, at Bec, iii. 470, 471, 506 ; iv. 361, 362. In the controversy on the Lord's Supper, iii. 506, 507, 509 n. 4, 511 n. 2, 512 nn. 1, 2, 4, 513 nn. 1–3, 513–515, 519, 526 ; iv. 355. Archbp. of Canterbury, iv. 329. Guitmund, iii. 529 n. 3. Life of, in his works, iii. 506 n. 5, 510 n. 1. In Acta, S. (O. B.), S. vi. P. ii., iv. 329 n. 1.

De corpore et sanguine Domini, ed. Venet., f. 171, iii. 507 n. 1 ; c. 2, 512 n. 4. Opp. f. 170, 513 n. 1. See D'Achery.

Lanfrick, iii. 382.

Lange.

Dogmengeschichte, vol. i., "Dialogue" of J. Martyr, refutation of Muenscher, i. 668 n. 3.

Langebeth, iii. 272 n. 3.

Langenstein, Henry of, from Hessia, v. 49, 119.   Consilium pacis, 49, 50.

Consilium pacis, c. 3, the schism an admonition from God, v. 49 n. 4 ; c. 13, 49 n. 2 : c. 15, right of revolution, 50 n. De Schismate, 49 n.   Epistola pacis, 48 n., 49. See Boulaeus.

Langham, Simon, abp. of Canterbury, v. 136.

Langres, iii. 506 ; iv. 354, 355.

Langton, Stephen, cardinal, iv. 174.

Language, in preaching, i. 79, 83. In the public reading of the Scriptures, 303. Laws of, 387. Of Scripture, ii. 116. Origin of, ii. 449. Liturgical, dogmatic and ascetic distinguished, ii. 524 n. 1. Homiletic and dogmatical, ii. 546.

Third and fourth Periods. Use of the vernacular language in instruction, iii. 53, 72, 73, 126, 127, 129, 316 and n. 4, 317–319, 323, 324, 334, 425, 427, 468, 469, 598 n. 4. Insincere in the Greek church, 115, 235, 531, 559, 561, 570 n. 2. Hyperbolical, 252. Liturgical, 127 –129, 316 and n. 4, 317, 318, 323, 324, 326. Of church psalmody, 127. Simeon, 448 n. 1.

Fifth Period. Teaching and preaching in the vernacular, iv. 4, 29, 31, 56, 58, 62, 90, 186, 200, 201, 214, 313, 314, 317 and n. 5. The liturgy, 58, 318. Nestorian clergy, 52. Peter of Savoy on, 214. Knowledge of language and missionary work, 242. Formation of, 313, 320. Bacon on the knowledge of, 425.

Sixth Period. The vernacular in preaching, v. 175, 195, 236, 254, 256, 305, 383, 390 ; in writings, 297, 388, 390, 391, 401. Huss on the Bohemian, 243 n. 1, 244, 254–256, 320, 369 ; on abusive, 286, 287. Jerome of Prague, 374, 379. See Languages, Latin Language, Linguistic.

Languages, references to different. Anglo-Saxon, iii. 153 n. 3, 468, 469 and nn. 2, 4. Arabic, iii. 335, 448 n. 1 ; iv. 62, 63, 65, 68, 70, 417, 420, 436. Bohemian, v. 175, 176, 236, 241 n., 243 n. 1, 244, 254, 256, 297, 320, 369, 374. Catalonian, iv. 641 n. 2.   Chaldee, iv. 70. Chinese-Syrian, iii. 89.   Coptic, i. 83 ; iii. 448 n. 1. English, v. 149, 150. Ethiopic, ii. 776 n. 4.   French, iv. 55, 155 n. 5, 447, 448. German, iii. 425 ; iv. 6, 155 and nn. 4, 5, 313, 318 ; v. 149, 175, 241 n., 320, 371, 374, 379, 383, 390, 391, 411. Gothic, iii. 281 n. 1. Greek, i. 79 ; ii. 77, 116 ; iii. 448 n. 1 ; iv. 58, 378, 417, 425 ; v. 149 (judicial), 362 n. 1. Hebrew, i. 345, 700 ; ii. 744 ; iv. 70, 425, 426 ; v. 149 (see Hebrew). Icelandic, iii. 300 n. 2, 301. Italian, iv. 300 n. 1, 317. Latin (see Latin). Persian, iv. 50, 58. Provençal, iv. 320, 321, 639 n. 2, 641 nn. 3, 4, 5. Romance, iii. 425 ; iv. 605, 606, 607. Semitic, iv. 47 n. Sanskrit, i. 82 n. 2. Slavonian, iii. 315 n. 1, 316–319, 320 n. 2, 323, 324, 326, 330 ; iv. 6, 7, 20, 31. Spanish, iii. 430 n. 1. Swedish, iii. 281 n. 1. Syriac, i. 486 ; ii. 589, 610 ; iii. 448 n. 1 ; iv. 48 n. 1, 52. Tartar, iv. 47 n., 50, 56, 57, 58. Turkish, iv. 48 n. 1.

Languedoc, iii. 414, 415 ; iv. 597. Sects in, 639, 642.

Hist. gen. de (t. iii. an. 1787), 639 n. 3.

Laodicea, in Phrygia, ii. 451. See Councils, an. 363.

Laodicea, in Syria, ii. 77, 484.

Laodiceans, ep. of Paul to the, iii. 268.

Laon, iii. 364, 404 n. 2, 490 ; iv. 373.

Lapides uncti, iii. 300 n. 4.

Lappenburg.

Hist. England, Bd. 1, p. 400, Dunstan, iii. 411 n. 5.

Lapsi, controversies respecting their restoration to the fellowship of the church, i. 226–235, 239–246. Decision of the council of Carthage, 234.

Lascaris II., Greek emperor, iv. 542, 543.

Last judgment. See Judgment.

Last things. See Eschatology.

Last times, the, v. 42. Militz on the, 178, 179. Janow on the, 196–202, 211. See Joachim.

Lateran council. See Councils, an. 648, an. 1112, an. 1123, an. 1139, an. 1170, an. 1179, an. 1215.

Lateran palace, church, iii. 186 ; iv. 128, 163 n. 3.

Latin church. See Western church.

Latin church fathers, iii. 459, 461. See Church fathers.

Latin language, use, knowledge of, instruction in, i. 79, 303, 717 ; ii. 28, 152 ; iii. 36, 152, 317, 335, 408 n. 1, 459, 467–469, 602, 604 ; iv. 58, 81, 287, 378 n. 3, 425 ; v. 175, 241 n., 320, 374, 390. (Preaching, v. 175, 390). Tertullian and the Punic, i. 684. Pronunciation of, iii. 48, 503. Alphabet, iii. 91 n., 281 n. 1. Liturgical language, iii. 126–129, 316–319. Ignorance of, among the

GENERAL INDEX. 133

clergy, iii. 126; iv. 52, 287; v. 58. In Spain, iii. 165, 335, 430 n. 1. Methodius, iii. 317 n. 2. Laity ignorant of, iii. 129, 317, 468, 604; iv. 74, 3 4. In England, iii. 467-469. The Greeks and Nicholas I. on the, iii. 566, 567. Theophylact on the, iii. 586. Study of Latin authors revived, iii. 459, 602. In France, iii. 604. Scientific, iv. 357. Judicial, v. 362 n. 1. See Bible translation, Translation.
Latins accused of barbarism, iii. 566, 585.
Λατρεία and προσκύνησις, iii. 205, 233 n. 1, 545.
Latzemboek, Henry of, v. 328.
Laub, monastery of, iii. 501.
Lanf. See Studien und Kritiken.
Lauingen, iv. 421.
Laurac, iv. 639 n. 2.
Λαΐραι, ii. 271.
Laurentius (Lawrence), presbyter, among the Anglo-Saxons, iii. 11. Sent to Rome, 14. Augustin's successor, 18. His vision, 19.
Lausanne, iv. 598.
Lausiacum (Lorch?), iii. 26 n. 2. See Palladius.
Law, of God, holy, i. 35, 499. Relation to Christ, 63. And the Gospel (Marcion), 468, 472. To sin, Epiphanes, 450. Original and Mosaic, 354 n. 6. Fulfilment of the, ii. 634, 635, 637, 642, 643, 678. Law and grace, Hilary, ii. 620; Augustin, ii. 675, 678. Theodore on, ii. 715, 716. Common law of Catholic church, Gerbert on, iii. 372. Relation of law to evangelical perfection, Aquinas, iv. 524, 526. Old and new, Waldenses on, iv. 616. Occam, v. 38, 39. Of Christ, ii. 332; v. 151, 208 209, 242; Huss, v. 242, 204, 265, 278, 280, 285, 304–307, 325, 326, 338. Relation of the law of the spirit to positive law (Chrysomalos), iv. 502; (Janow), v. 206–209. Essence of things, v. 208. Evangelical and civil, v. 26, 27. Civil and ecclesiastical, v. 49, 50. See Ecclesiastical Law.
Law, of Moses, Jewish, i. 354 n. 6; ii. 55, 620; iv. 78; v. 38, 39. See Judaism, Gnosticism.
Law, political, relation of Christianity to, i. 70, 259; iii. 102, 103. Influence of Christianity on, ii. 171-178; iv. 40, 41. Influence of legates or civil order, iv. 198. Study of, ii. 590; iv. 172, 203, 204, 415. See Civil.
Lawgivers, Julian on, ii. 51.
Law school, ii. 590.
Law suits, ii. 91.
Lawrence, St., iv. 589.
Laws, national, ii. 51. Roman, i, 137. Of M. Aurelius, concerning the Christians, i. 107, 108. Of Severus, close associations, i. 120. Of Decius, against the Christians, i. 131. Of Diocletian, against Manicheans, i. 144, 506; ii. 769.

Of Constantine against heathen rites, ii. 21-23, 28. Of Constantius, the same, ii. 33-35. Of Julian, recalling bishops from exile, ii. 71. Of Jovian, ii. 88 n. 1. Of Valentinian, ii. 90. Of Valens, ii. 91. Gratian, ii. 92. Of Theodosius, soothsaying, temples, etc., ii. 94, 95 and nn. 4, 5, 97, 99. Of Arcadius and Honorius, ii. 100-103. Of Gratian on the execution of the death sentence, ii. 215. Of Constantine in the Donatist controv., ii. 223, 225; on festivals, ii. 333 and n. 4, 336. Of Theodosius II. against the Nestorians, ii. 554. See Capitularies, Codex, Edicts, Rescripts.
Lay abbots, iii. 416.
Laying on of hands. See Imposition of hands.
Lazan, Henry of, v. 315.
Lazau, Leli of, v. 317.
Lazarus, ii. 496 n. 4; v. 189, 353, 358.
Lazarus, bp. of Aix, ii. 643 and n. 1, 648.
Lazarus, monk, iii. 547
Lazians, spread of Christianity among them, ii. 139. Maximus banished among the, iii. 192. See Cyrus, bp. of Phasis.
Leander, bp. of Seville, iii. 118.
Learning, ii. 149; iii. -82; v. 32, 59, 86. See Culture.
Lebanon, iii. 197.
Lebheim, iv. 16 n. 1.
Lebus, bp. of, v. 330 n. 2.
Lech, river, iii. 37.
Lectores, i. 201; ii. 184, 354 n. 2. See Prelectors.
Lectures, university, iv. 281, 282, 418. Of Abelard, 373, 374, 383, 393 and n. 1, 398, 452. Copies of, 393 and n. 1, 415. Of Aquinas, 422. Of Almaric, 446.
Ledan, ii. 131.
Ledebur, A. von.

Algemeine Archiv, vol. viii., f. 97, iv. 536 n. 3.

Legacies, right of pagan priests to receive, ii. 92. Of the church, ii. 166, 167. Of heretics, ii. 235. To the church, iii. 101.
Legality, Jewish, i. 39, 40, 41 n. 1, 61, 63. Christian, ii. 291; iii. 50; iv. 510.
Legates, papal, iii. 55, 65, 67, 71, 354, 373, 374, 510, 511, 516 n. 2, 562, 563, 574, 576, 577, 583; iv. 41, 59, 123, 141, 150, 166, 200, 382, 540, 585 n. 2, 590 n. 6, 603; v. 6, 89, 272, 276. Importance of, iv. 89, 197, 198. Gregory VII. and, iv. 89, 91, 94, 117, 119. Exactions of, v. 131, 166, 167, 197, 198 False, iv. 204. Frederic I. and the, iv. 166, 167. Innocent III., iv. 173, 174 n., 176, 177, 269. Joachim on, iv. 222.
Legates a latere, iv. 131.
Legends, i. 66, 84; ii. 143, 371; iii. 19 n. 1, 101, 134 n. 1, 289, 300 n. 1, 467 n. 3; iv. 46, 60 n. 2, 187, 188, 332, 345. Of martyrs, i. 139. Moravian and Russian,

iii. 321 n. 5. Of pope Joan, iii. 367 n. 1. Of Robert Grosshead, iv. 187. Gift of Constantine, iv. 216 n.; v. 18, 42. Concerning Frederic II., v. 43, 44. Origin of, iv. 330. Use of by preachers. v. 383.

Leger.
Histoire des Vaudois, la nobla Leyczon, iv. 616 n. 1.

Legio fulminea, i. 115, 116.
Legislation, church, iii. 55, 56. See Councils, Ecclesiastical laws.
Legists, iv. 204.
Leibnitz.
Script. rerum Bohem., t. i., Ditmar's Chronicle, iii. 324 n. 1, 422 n. 4; Bernward, iii. 408 n. 2; f. 275, life of bp. Ismel, iii. 460 n. 6. Accessiones hist., t. ii. f. 543, chronicle of Alberic, iv. 643 n. 3; f. 568, Frederic II., iv. 181 n. 2.

Leidrad, abp. of Lyons, iii. 167, 168.
Leif, Icelander, iii. 307.
Leinster, iii. 29.
Leipsic, founding of the university of, v. 254.
Leitmeritz, Conrad at, v. 184.
Leitomysl, the bp. of, v. 294. See John of.
Lemnos, iii. 222.
Lenfant.
Hist. Conc. Const., v. 360 n. 2.

Lent, synods at Rome during, iii. 520; iv. 105 n. 4, 598, 599. In the Greek church, iii. 557, 581. See Quadragesima.
Lentzen (Leontium), iii. 326.
Leo, abbot, legate, iii. 371, 373.
Leo, bp. of Achris (Achrida), iii. 580.
Leo, bp. of Iconium in Phrygia, iii. 229 n. 3.
Leo, bp. of Phocæa, iii. 219 n. 1.
Leo I., bp. of Rome. See Leo the Great.
Leo, bp. of the island of Carpathus (Scarpanto), iii. 229 n. 3.
Leo, bp. of the island of Rhodes, iii. 229 n. 3.
Leo, consul, iii. 571.
Leo, deacon, ii. 111 n.
Leo I., Greek emperor, iii.
Leo III., Greek emperor (the Isaurian), enemy of image worship, iii. 202-214, 227, 229, 535. His first ordinance against the idolatrous worship of images, 204. His transactions with Germanus, 204. His law against all religious images, 209. Why he was favorably disposed to the Paulicians? 249, 250. The image of Christ, 535. Letters to Gregory II., 211, 212.
Leo IV., Greek emperor, enemy of images, iii. 223 and n. 2. His conduct towards the friends of images; his death, 224.
Leo V., Greek emperor (the Armenian), in the second image controversy, iii. 532-543, 549, 558. His attempts to abolish image worship, 533. His controversy on this subject with Nicephorus and Theodorus, 533-537. His measures for abolishing the images, 538, 539.
Leo VI., Greek emperor (the Philosopher), iii. 578.
Leo III., pope, crowns Charlemagne emperor, iii. 120, 235 n. 4. Complaints against him, 122. Doctrine of the Holy Spirit, 555, 556. Supposed assassination, Alcuin on, 103 n., 121 n. 3, 122. Life of, 122 n. 2. See Anastasius.
Leo VIII., pope, iii. 368.
Leo IX., pope, iii. 378, 379, 381, 384-386. Founds a new epoch in the history of the papacy, 378, 400 (iv. 83, 97, 146, 223). Hildebrand, iii. 381 n. 2. Fights against the Normans, 385, 386. Canonized as a saint, 386. Simony, 389 n. 2. Berengarius, 507, 511-514 (508 n. 3). Against Michael Cerularius, 580 n. 2, 581-583. Life of, see Bruno, bp. of Segni, Wibert.
Epistle to Michael Cerularius, iii. 387 n. 7, 580 n. 2, 582 nn. 1, 2. See Harduin, VI. i. f. 927.

Leo Allatius, on the transactions of Concil. Const. an. 879, iii. 572 n. 2.
Citations: —
Collection of Symmicta, John Phocas on the holy places, iv. 266 n. 1.
De eccles. occident. atque orient. perpetua consensu. L. ii. cc. 11, 12, acts of Synod Const. an. 1140, the Bogomiles, iv. 562 n. 5, 563 n. 2; ff. 682, 686, Niphon, Cosmas, iv. 563 n. 3, 564 n. 3; c. 13, persecution on the isle of Cyprus, iv. 589 n. 1; c. 14, letter of Blemmydes, iv. 542 n. 3.
De libris et rebus eccles. Græcis (Paris, 1646), f. 161, conference Const., report of Michael Cerularius, iv. 583 n. 3.
Græcia orthodoxa, t. i., treatises of Blemmydes, iv. 541 n. 2; t. ii., writings of Beccus, iv 547 nn.
Life of Clement, fragm. iii. 320 n. 2.

Leo Diaconus.
Hist. (ed. Hase), iv. 7 (or new coll., p. 64), and v. 5. Greek monks, prophetic gifts, iii. 590 n. 3.

Leo the Grammarian, on Photius, iii. 568 n. 3.
Leo the Great, bp. of Rome. De vocatione Gentium; conversion of the barbarians, ii. 124, 699 n. 3. The primacy of the Roman bp., 199, 202-204 (iii. 32, 350, 580). Hilarius of Arles, 206, 207. Fasts, 340. Sun-worship, 347 n. 4. Pagan element in relation to the Christmas festival, 348 and n. 1; to the New Year's festival, 350 n. 4. In the Eutychian controversy, 567, 568, 573-582. In the Monophysite controversies, 584, 585, 588. In the Pelagian, 657, 699-703. The Manicheans, 769, 770. Priscillianists, 776 nn. 1, 5, 577 Works, 580 n.
Citations: —
De vocatione gentium, grace and free-will, ii. 699-702, nn. L. ii. c. 6, Rome, 202 n. 1; c. 32, 124 n. 2.

Epistles. Ep. 5, ad metropolitanos Illyr., ii. 204 n. 2. Epp. 9 and 10, primacy of Peter, 207 n. 1. Ep. 15, ad Turribium, Priscillianists, treatment of heretics, 775 n. 2, 776 n. 1; cc. 3, 6, 9, 10, 13, 776 nn. 2, 5, 777 n. 3, 778 nn. 2, 3. Epp. 69-71, to Theodosius, Pulcheria, etc., 575 n. 1. Ep. 78, to the emp. Marcian, on the primacy, 202 n. 2. Ep. 80, c. 5, to Anatolius, 203 n. 1. Epp. 82, 94, to Marcian, 576 n. Ep. 93, to the Synod at Nice, 577 nn. 1, 2. His letter to Flavian, on the person of Christ, 573-580, 582.
Opp., f. 80, Rome, 202 n. 1.
Sermones. S. vii., fasts opposed to pagan festivals, 349 n. 1. S. xv., the Manicheans, 769 nn. 5, 6; c. 5, 770 n. 2. S. xxii. c. 5, Christmas, 348 n. 3 (350 n. 4). S. xxv. § 1, the same, 348 n. 1. S. xxvi. c. 3, sun worship, 347 n. 4. S. xli., Lord's Supper in both kinds, 366 n. 3.

Leocritia, Spanish Christian, iii. 342.
Leon, i. 122.
Leonardo Bruno. See Aretino.
Leonides, father of Origen, i. 593, 695.
Leonis, Peter, Cardinal, iv. 144.
Leonists, iv. 611.
Leontius.
Life of Johannes Eleemosyn., iii. 99 n. 2.
Leontius, abp. of Bordeaux, iii. 94.
Leontius, bp. of Arles, ii. 706 n. 3.
Leontius, bp. of Neapolis, apology, against the Jews, ii. 330, 331. See Harduin, t. iv. f. 194.
Leontius, imperial commissioner, ii. 228 and n. 3.
Leontius of Byzantium (or Jerusalem).
C. fraudes Apollinarist. (see Canisius t. 1.), ii. 491 n. 1. C. Nestorium et Eutychem., Greek fragm. Pauli Samosat. (see Erlich), s. 23, i. 602 n. 2. L. iii. f. 701 (Bibl. patr. Lugd., t. ix.), Theodore, de incarnat., ii. 496 n 3. C. Nestorianos et Eutychianos (see Mansi Concil.), reply to Monophysites, ii. 583 n. 1. L. iii., ii. 563, n. 5.

Leporius, Pelagian, ii. 655-657.
Leprosy, iv. 266, 267.
Lerina (Lerius), cloister, ii. 210, 296, 696, 706, 709. See Vincentius of.
Lessing.
On the Council of Paris, iii. 509 n. 4.
Letronne.
Memoires sur des inscriptions grecques, ii. 105 n. 3, 140 nn. 2, 3. Materieaux pour l'hist. du Christianisme en Egypt, etc., iii. 99 n. 1.
Letter and spirit, i. 36, 54, 56, 59; i. 269, 678, 701, 754; iv. 569. See Interpretation.
Letters of recommendation, i. 691. See Libellum, Libellus, Libelli, Literæ, Circular Letters.
Letters of Christ, pretended, i. 80; iii. 59.
Letters of fraternities, v. 250.
Letti. iv. 40.
Leuderich, bp. of Bremen, iii. 279.
Leutfrid, bp. iii. 102 n. 3.
Leuticia, iv. 18.
Leuthard, fanatic, iii. 603.
Levelling tendencies, v. 158-160.
Levites, i. 53 n. 1, 60, 195.

Leviticus, 15, iv. 306; 20 : 7, ii. 181; 20 : 9; 24 : 20, i. 439. See Commentaries.
Lewis.
Hist. Life and Sufferings of J. Wicklif, Lond. 1720. New ed. 1820 (Oxford), v. 135 n., 137 nn., 141 n., 144-155 nn., 161, 161-165 nn.

Lewis. See Louis.
Lewis Clifford, Sir, v. 148 n. 4.
Liafdag, bp. of Ripen, iii. 290, 291.
Libana, iii. 163, 164.
Libanius, pagan rhetorician. Enemy of Christianity, ii. 39, 41. Constantine, 10, 27. Constantius, 35, 87. Julian, 41, 42, 81, 86 n. 3, 87. Intercedes for the Christians, 67. 70, 84, 85. To the Antiochians, 83 n. 6, 85. Valentinian and Valens, 91. Defence of the temples, 94, 95, 96. Oppressive landlords, 230 n. 2. Neglect of education, 288. Monasticism, 290. Intercession for the Manicheans, 769.

Citations: —
De accusatorib. L. 3, f. 436, plundering of the temples, ii. 35 n. 1
De vita sua, ii. 81 n. 2, 82 n. 1, 91 n. 3.
Εἰς Ἰουλιανὸν αὐτοκράτορ. ii. 44 n. 1.
Ἔκφρασις Καλανδῶν, ii. 350 n. 3.
Epistles. Epp. 622, 624. Pagan festivals under Julian, ii. 66 n. 3. Epp. 636, 669, 673, 731, to Hesychius, Bacchius, and Belæus, intercession for Christians, 67 n. 2. Ep. 649, Julian, 87 n. 3. Ep. 681, to Seleucus, 66 n. 3. Ep. 714, to Modestus, 68 n. 4. Ep. 730, Marcus, 70, n. 3, 81 n. 1. Ep. 1057, 1375, to Alexander, 84 n. 6. Ep. 1346, 84 n. 6. Ep. 1522, 76 n. 5.
Epitaph Julian., ed. Reiske, vol. i f. 526, Ecebolius, ii. 42 n. 1; f. 528, Julian's conversion, 44 n. 1; f. 562, on persecution, 70 n. 3; f. 574, the old religion and the old culture, 39 n. 1; f. 578, Julian's efforts to bribe the soldiers, 69 n. 1; f. 619, Jovian, 88 n. 1. Vol. ii. p. 529, spoliation of the temples, 35 n. 1.
Monodia in Jul., ff. 508, 510, ii. 87 nn. 3, 4; f. 513, 81 n 3.
Θεοδόσ. περὶ στάσεως, ii. 22 n. 1.
Orat de fortuna sua, ii. 66 n. 1.
Περὶ τῆς τοῦ βασιλέως ὀργῆς, ii. 85 notes.
Πρεσβευτικὸς πρὸς Ἰουλιανόν, f. 459, Nicocles, ii. 41 nn. 1, 2; f. 476, Julian at Antioch, 81 n. 4.
Pro Aristophane, f. 430, ii. 34 n. 2; f. 446, 66 n. 2: f. 448, 37 n. 2
Πρὸς τοὺς εἰς τὴν παιδείαν, ii. 613 n. 1.
Προσφωνητικὸς Ἰουλιανῷ, ρ. 405, ii. 41 n. 3; f. 408, 43 n. 1.
Ὑπὲρ τῶν ἱερῶν (de, pro, templis), (ed. Reiske, vol. ii.) f. 160, ii. 10 n. 1; f. 162, 28 n. 3; f. 164, 88 n., 91 nn. 5, 6; f. 164, 95 n. 1; ff. 180 et seq., 94 n. 4, 27 nn. 2, 3, 32 n. 3.

Libations, to the emperors, i. 99, 154.
Libellatici. See Libelli pacis.
Libelli pacis, Libellatici, i. 131, 132 n. 1, 216, 227, 229 n. 2, 230, 234 n. 1, 242, 244, 245. See Church Divisions.
Libelli pœnitentiales, iii. 137.
Libellus paschalis (circular letter), ii. 338 n. 4, 513, and notes 1, 2.
Libentius, abp. of Hamburg and Bremen, iii. 290.
Liber Adami, i. 376 n. 3.
Liber c. Fulgentium Donatistum, ii. 223, n. 4.

Liber diurnus, Romanorum pontif., iii. 48 n. 5, 49 n. 1, 117 n. 3. See Hoffman.
Liber pastoralis, iii. 142, 143 n. 1.
Liber pœnitentialis, iii. 272.
Liber pontificalis, iii 351 n. 1.
Liberal tendencies, v. 235.
Liberatus Diaconus.

Breviar. causæ, Nestorian. et Eutychian., c. 11, synod of Flavian, ii. 566 n. 2; c. 12. Robber Synod, 572 n. 3; c. 13, Conc. Chalc., 577 n. 5; f. 108, ed Garnier, cc. 16, 17, Monoph. controv. 587 notes; c. 21, Mennas, 593 n. 4; c. 24, three chapters, 598 n. 1, 599 nn. 1, 2; c. 33, Origenistic disputes, 596 nn. 3-5; towards the end, 600 n. 4.

Liberius, bp. of Rome. Exiled, subscribes Arian creed, his return and death, ii. 256, 443, 451, and n. 1; iii. 166 n. 6, 515; v. 85. Christmas, ii. 344.
Liberty, of conscience, i. 86; ii. 15, 88, 130, 217. Roger de Foix on, iv. 642. Christian liberty, ii. 347; iv. 635; v. 38, 162, 212. Of the clergy, v. 5, 54. Political, iv. 175. See Freedom.
Libraries, i. 143, 696. 721. At Cæsarea, ii. 745. In Ireland, iii. 10. In Rome and Italy, iii. 150 nn. 4 and 7 (Cassiodorus), 151 and n. 1, 470 n. 3. Vatican, ii. 774 n. 1. Ambrosian, iv. 639 n. 1, 769 n. 6. In France, iii. 415; iv. 265, 637 n. 1. Paris (Simon of Tournay), iv. 418 n. 4. Sorbonne, iv. 606 n. 4, 618 n. 1. Munich, iv. 393 n. 1 (works of Lull), iv. 190 n. 3. Prague, iv. 279 n. 1. Bodleian, i. 602 n. 2; iv. 608 n. 1. Manuscripts of Abelard, iv. 399 n. 3 (at Vienna), 388 n. 1 (at Munich), 393 n. 1. Of Spain, iv. 637 n. 1. Destruction of, 467; iv. 529; burning of (the Palatine), iii. 150 n. 7; in Hamburg, iii. 278. See Books.
Libri Carolini, iii. 235-243. Their author, 235. Against fanatical destruction of images, 235. Against superstitious worship of images, 236. On the design and use of images, 236. On the opposition of the standing points of the Old and New Testaments, 237. On the Holy Scriptures: on the sign of the cross, 238; on relics, 239; on the use of images and of incense, 239. Against miracles said to be performed by images, 240. Against the argument in favor of image-worship derived from dreams, 240. On the worship of saints, 241. Against Byzantine Basileolatry, 241. Hadrian I. on the, 243, 552. Hinkmar, 441. See Charlemagne.
Libya, Libyan desert, i. 138; ii. 124, 196, 288, 289, 322 n. 2, 421, 552, 559 n. 1.
Licinius Cæsar, religious edicts issued in connection with Constantine, ii. 14, 15. War with Maximin, 17. First war with Constantine and persecution of the Christians, 8 n. 1, 18, 19. Second war and death, 20, 21, 23, 25, 351 n. 1, 413, 422. Son of, 31.

Liebner, Dr.
Monograph on Hugo of St. Victor, iv. 401 n. 3
Liefland, History of the conversion of, iv. 36–41, 45.
Liege, bp. of, iii. 125 n. 2. Diocese of, 458, 501; iv. 129, 256 n. 4, 341. Sect there, iii. 597, 598. School at, iii. 502 n. 3. Church at, iii. 606. Canonicals of, iv. 60. Letter of the clergy of, to Paschalis II., iv. 130-132 (see notes). Preaching of the crusades in, iv. 155 n. 5. Greg. X., iv. 188. See Adelmann, Alger Deoduin, Ratherius, Rudolph, Walcher, Wazo.
Life, human, influence of Christianity on, i. 69, 76-78. Power of Christian, ii. 63.
Life, principle of, in Christianity, i. 1, 69, 75, 77; iii. 1. Life and knowledge, ii. 400, 401; iv. 361, 385, 414 (see Knowledge). Unity of the Spiritual, ii. 681. Its development, ii. 682. Eternal, iv. 380 n. 3, 381 (see Immortality). Future iv. 382. See Christian Life.
Light nature, in Gnosticism, i. 403 n. 3, 405. In Manicheism, 499, 500. Light Spirit, 498. Light and darkness, 403, 500. See Kingdom of Light.
Lights burned before images, iii. 206 n. 1, 210, 233, 239, 546.
Liguria, ii. 472.
Likeness of God, i. 613, 614; iii. 99. To God, iv. 485, 488, 491; v. 397. Compare Image of God. Original State.
Lille, ab Insula, iv. 417.
Limina apostolorum, iii. 57.
Limit, in Gnosticism, i. 373, 417, 418, 419. See Horus.
Limmat, river, iii. 34.
Limousin, iv. 243, n. 1; v. 46.
Lincoln, plots at, v. 163. Bp. of, see Robert Grosshead.
Linus, Roman bp. v. 19.
Liodgarde, wife of Charlemagne, iii. 155 n. 1.
Lisle, school at, iv. 357.
Lisoi (Lisieux), ecclesiastic, president of the sect at Orleans, iii. 595.
Literæ formatæ, i. 205. See Epistolæ.
Literal interpretation. See Interpretation.
Literary culture, iv. 301; v. 71, 113. See Culture.
Literature, pagan. Christian use of, i. 143, 150, 176, 535-539, 692; ii. 52, 53, 75-77, 183, 742-744, 754. Forbidden to the clergy, ii. 61 n. 2. Its connection with the pagan religion, ii. 39, 41, 52, 53, 76, 77. Study of ancient, iii. 150 and n. 7, 156 n. 1, 459, 471; iv. 563. In the Greek empire, iv. 530. Origen, creator of Christian, sacred, i. 700. Popular, iii. 425. Restoration of ancient, v. 71. Bohemian, v. 244. See Books, Greek Culture, Libraries.
Lithuania, pagan tribes in, iv. 36. Lithuanians at Constance, v. 127. Jerome of Prague in, v. 373.

GENERAL INDEX. 137

Little Jerusalem, v. 176.
Liturgical element in worship, ii. 170 n. 3, 188, 352, 354 and n. 4, 353 n. 1, 361–364, 373, 658; iii. 142, 427. Tendency, ii. 447, 728.
Liturgy, i. 303. First traces of the, i. 329 n. 1. Aramæan, Marcus, i. 440. Roman, iii. 49 n. 1, 114; iv. 601; v. 205. Priests required to understand the, iii. 126. Latin, iii. 127, 324, 324, 326; iv. 52, 58, 314. Missæ privatæ, iii. 136. Improved by Gregory I., iii. 142. Charlemagne, iii. 154. Gothico-Spanish, iii. 157, 158 and n. 1. In the vernacular, iii. 316 and n. 4, 317–319, 323, 326.
Lindger, his education, iii. 79, 81. His labors among the Frieslanders and Saxons, 79, 80. His death, 80. Life of, 45 n. 1, 80 n. 2 (see Pertz). His life of Gregory of Utrecht, § 6, 47 n. 2.
Linthard, bp. iii. 11.
Liutolf, bp. of Augsburg, iii. 447.
Livin, missionary in Brabant, iii. 43. Life of, 43 n. 1. Poetical epistle to Florbert, 43 n. 2.
Lockum, Cistercian monastery at, iv. 37.
Löffler, celebration in remembrance of the first ch. in Thuringia, iii. 501. 2.
Logic, i. 533, 534 n. 3; ii. 471, 488, 526; iv. 357. Neglected, ii. 488. See Dialectics.
Logical element, ii. 447, 472, 473. Augustin, 625. See Interpretation.
Logomachy, ii. 382.
Logos, among the Alexandrian Jews, with Philo, i. 55 n. 1, 57, 66, 397, 424 n. 1, 575, 641 n. 4. Gnostics, 373 n. 2, 400, 423, 440, 441. Νόθος, 375 n. 4. Church doctrine of the, 469; in the New Testament and the oldest ch. teachers, 575, 584–586; in the Alexandrian School, 564, 586–591; with the Monarchians, 576–586, 591–603, 610; Justin, 585, 586, 635, 666–670; Clement, 541, 632, 692; Origen, 545, 547–553, 587–591, 594, 622, 623, 633–636, 640, 643; Tertullian, 635, 685 n. 2. Ἐνδιάθετος, 585, 586 n. 4. Προφορικός, 585, 586 n. 4, 588. Σπερματικός, 586 and n. 1, 666–670. Eternal generation of the, 588, 589. Source of immortality, 644. Προτρεπτικός, παιδαγωγός, 692.
Second Period, Julian on John's doctrine of the, ii. 56. With the Platonists, 123. Oriental doctrine, 404 n. 1, 469. With Arius, 405–408 n. 1. Athanasian doctrine, 435 and n. Marcellus, 438, 439, 479–481. Ἐνδιάθετος καὶ προσφορικός, 438, n. 3, 482. Eunomius, 448, 449. Photinus, 482. Apollinaris, 485–491. Eternal generation of the, 608 (i. 588, 599). In the Lord's Supper, 733, 735.
In the Third and Fourth Periods. With Migetius, iii. 157 n. 1. Felix of Urgellis, 160. Maximus, 172, 183. In the Monotheletic controversy, 180–183;

Image controversy, 217, 539. With Monophysites, 261. Scotus, 464, 556 n. 4. In the Eucharist, 497–499, 523. With the scholastics, iv. 457, 459, 464. With the Bogomiles, iv. 554, 557. Eckhart, v. 394. See Word.
Lögsögu, iii. 304 n. 3, 305.
Lollards, v. 143–145, 150, 160, 163.
Lombardy, iii. 541 n. 3; iv. 117, 146, 168, 179, 182, 576 n. 2; v. 36 n. 1, 100.
Lombez. See Councils, an. 1165.
London, chosen by Gregory the Great for an archepiscopal see, iii. 16. Despises the interdict, iv. 176. Bp. of, v. 146, 148. Council at, v. 162, 163. See Courtney.
Longevity, iii. 37.
Longing, in Paganism, i. 30, 71.
Longinianus, pagan, ep. to Augustin, ii. 115 n. 5 (Aug. ep. 234).
Longobards, Arians, iii. 33, 34, 117. Come over to the Catholic ch. 117. Encroachments, 112, 117. Pope Stephen II. against intermarriage with the, 120, 121. In Italy, 112, 119–121, 210, 386. Their kingdom in Italy destroyed by Charlemagne, 120. Gregory VII. on the, iv. 86. Struggles with the empire, iv. 168. Wulflach, iii. 28.
Lorch (Laureacum), iii. 26 n. 2, 316, 330 n. 2, 332 and n. 1.
Lord's day, i. 202, 676. See Sunday.
Lord's prayer, iii. 53, 108, 126, 427; iv. 556, 576, 577, 627.
Lord's Supper, celebration and conception of in the first centuries, i. 304, 323–335, 647–649. Institution, 323, 324. United with the Agapæ, 325–327. Disjoined from the Agapæ, 327 (ii. 361). Dismissal of Catechumens, 327–329 (see Missa). Liturgy, 329. Consecration, thanksgiving, 329, 330. The elements a thank-offering, idea of sacrifice, 330, 331. Common and unleavened bread, 331. Wine mingled with water, 331, 332. Water used by the Ebionites, 331 n. 2. Daily communion, the absent, partaken of at home, 332. Preparation, seasons, communion of infants, 333. In memory of the martyrs, 333, 334. Offerings and prayers for the departed, 334 and n. 4. Doctrine, three grades in the conception of the ordinance, 647–649. N. African church and Origen concerning its necessity, 648, 649.
Second Period, ii. 361–369, 725. Doctrine, 731–736. Despised by fanatical monks, 274, 275. The Euchites, 279. Seasons for its celebration, 333, 341, 364, 365. Liturgy, 362–364. Thanksgiving, 363, 367. Consecration, 363. Sacrifice, 362 n. 7, 363 and n. 9, 366–369, 735. Frequency, 364, 365. Taken home, on voyages by sea, 365, 366 n. 1. In one kind, 365, 366. In both kinds, 366 and n. 2. Memorial, intercessions,

prayers and offerings for the dead, 366 -369. Viewed as an incarnation of the Logos, 731, 732. Adoration of, 732 (see Host). Transubstantiation, 732, 733. More spiritual views, 733-736. Gregory of Nyssa on the necessity of participation in it, 447.

Third Period, iii. 135, 136. Unleavened bread, 18 n. 2. Worthy participation, 52. In private chapels, 109 n. 1. Idea of sacrifice, change in the, 135. Magical effects of the, 135. For the dead, 135, 136. Mischievous influence of these notions, 136. Frequency, private masses, 136. Compared with images, 215. With the Paulicians, 249, 263.

Fourth Period. Doctrine and controversies concerning the, iii. 494-530. As an ordeal in the judgments of God, 450. Communion of infants, 496. Commemorative, 499, 500. Controversies on the doctrine, 494-530. Doctrine of transubstantiation according to Paschasius Radbert, 494-497. Struggle for its recognition, 496-501. Compared with the doctrine of Ratramnus, 498, 499. Conversio, 498, 499, 511 n. 1, 524. Doctrine of the Lord's Supper according to Scotus, 500. Ratherius of Verona, Gerbert, Herigar on this subject, 501. Three tendencies, 502. Doctrine of Berengarius, 502, 505. Hildebrand (Greg. VII.), 510-513 (iv. 92). Eusebius Bruno on the doctrine of transubstantiation, 516, 517. Triumph of this doctrine, 520. More particular account of the doctrine of Berengarius, 521-530. On its necessity, 524 n. 2. Impanatio, 528 nn. 1, 4. Use of unleavened bread, controversy with the Greek church, 581-585. Essentials and unessentials, 585. Sect at Orleans, 594, 595. See Wine.

Fifth Period. Doctrine of transubstantiation confirmed, and completion of the cultus, abuse in the mass, iv. 335 -347. Substance and accidents, 335-341, 447. Questions as to its possible desecration, 338-340. Mode of union, 338, 340. Deification of the symbols, 338, 341. Withdrawal of the cup, 343-346. Doctrine of concomitance, 344, 345. Neglected by laity, 343, 344, 346, 353. Celebrated by proxy, 344, 346. As a substitute for the Scriptures, Innocent III., 322. Unleavened bread in the, 92, 538, 541, 614 n. 5. In the sects, Bogomiles, 556, 559 n. 3; Catharists, 556 n. 2, 576, 587 n. 5, 589; other sects, 594-596; Waldenses, 614.

In the Sixth Period. Wicklif's doctrine, v. 151-157, 161, 162, 163. Impanatio, 153. Janow on the frequent participation in the Supper, 193, 213, 217-231. Huss on the same, 337. Spiritual participation, 218, 222, 229, 230, 270, 337. Janow on worthy participation, 222-224, 229. Dangers of neglect, 217, 218. Enjoyment of the, 223, 224. As worship, as festival, 224. Benefit of, 225, 226. Relation to baptism, 226. Under both forms, 217, 218 and n. 1, 223, 231, 233, 338. Order of distribution, 229. Jacobellus on the withdrawal of the cup, 337, 338. Huss on this point, 338 and n. 3, 339, 342. At Prague, 338 n. 3, 340, 341. Doctrine of Huss, 238, 242, 258, 270, 336, 337, 339, 342, 343. Pretended miracles connected with the, 237-239. Unleavened bread in the, 92. See Body of Christ, Communion, Transubstantiation.

Lot, iii. 347 n. 5; iv. 564.

Lot, the, iii. 284, 285.

Lothaire II., emperor, iv. 34, 35, 146, 164 n. 3.

Lothaire II., of Lotharingia, iii. 353-358, 361.

Lotharingia, iii. 279, 353.

Lothario of Anagni, cardinal, iv. 173, See Innocent III.

Louis I., emperor, and king (the Pious), of France, conversion of the Danes, iii. 271, 272, 273, 275. Adalhard, 273. Mission to Sweden, 276, 283. Founds Hamburg, 277. Death, 278. Ebbo, 278. His age, 351. The pope in the disputes between the emperor Louis and his sons, 352, 353. Benedict of Aniane, 414 n. 1, 415. Claudius of Turin, 432, 439. Rabanus Maurus, 457, 473. Dionysius the Areopagite, 466. Pepin, 460. Image controversy, 546, 551-553. Benefits conferred on the church, iv. 133; v. 304. Life of, iii. 553 n. 3. See Mansi Concil., Pertz, Monumenta.

Epistle to Hilduin on the Dionysian writings, iii. 466 nn. 4, 5, 6. See Mansi Concil., t. xv.

Louis II., emperor, iii. 323 n. 3, 355, 356, 361.

Louis IV., emperor (Louis the Bavarian), v. 24, 25, 30, 35, 36, 37, 40-43, 380.

Louis III., king of France, iii. 401 and nn. 1, 3, 402 n. 3.

Louis VI., king of France, iv. 145. Life of, 140 n. 4. See Du Chesne.

Louis VII., king of France, iv. 75.

Louis IX. (St. Louis), king of France, character, iv. 300-302. Embassy to the Mongols, 51, 55. On disputations with the Jews, 77 n. 2. The pragmatic sanction, 203. The begging monks, 281, 282, 285. On dress, 285 and nn. 4, 5. On temptations to unbelief, 326. Thomas Aquinas and, 423. Life of, 285 nn. 4, 5. See Acta S. Aug., Du Chesne, Joinville.

Ep. 35, delay of papal elections, iv. 183 n. 2. His last will, iv. 282 n. 1, 302.

Louis of Angers, prince, v. 73.

Louis of Bavaria, pfalsgrave, v. 112, 342, 351, 370.

Love, Christian, i. 76, 256, 257, 262, 269, 275, 276, 326; ii. 291, 303, 304, 305, 678, 682; iii. 42, 416; iv. 21, 615. Love, with the Therapeutæ, i 59, 61. With the Gnostics, i. 405, 450. Euchites, ii. 279. Doctrine of Augustin on, ii. 678, 682. Gregory the Great, iii. 4, 147–149. Maximus, iii. 173, 174.

Fifth Period. Innocent III. on, iv. 44, 45. Gregory VII. on, 91, 92. Joachim, 227, 229. Ivo, 241. Peter of Cluny, iv. 250, 264. Bernard of Clairvaux, 257, 259–262, 263. Francis of Assisi, 273. Bernard of Tiron, 308. Raymund Lull, 309, 310, 435–437. Richard of St. Victor, 310 Berthold, 319, 320. Anselm, 361–367. Abelard, 383–386, 390. Hugo of St. Victor, 407. Gerhoh of Reichersberg, 407, 408. Alexander of Hales, 490. Bonaventura, 429, 491. Aquinas, 522. Eustathius, 533. Hildebert, 602. Dolcino, 633–635.

Sixth Period. Janow on, v. 200, 207, 215, 229. Huss, 306, 336, 337. Friends of God, 381, 383. Tauler, 384, 407–409. Ruysbroeck, 385, 386, 397, 398, 403, 404–406.

Disinterested love, Philo on, i. 57, 58. Abelard and Hugo on, iv. 386, 407. Gerhoh, 407, 408. Friends of God, v. 381, 383. Acts of, v. 388 (see Benevolence). Natural and Supernatural, iv. 490, 491. Love and knowledge, ii. 650; iv. 435–437 (411–413) (see Knowledge). In the period of the Holy Ghost, iv. 227, 623, 624.

Love in God, Marcion on, i. 466, 467; and justice, i. 561–564. Origen, i. 621. Irenæus, i. 642. Cassian, ii. 687, 688. Scotus, iii. 464. In the Trinity (Abelard), iv. 459; (Alanus), 461; (Albert), 463; (Aquinas), 464; (Lull), 465. In the atonement, i. 642; iv. 501–508. In justification, iv. 510–513, 518.

Love feast, with the Therapeutæ, i. 61. Catharists, iv. 576, 587 n. 5. Peter of Savoy, iv. 213. See Agapæ.

Lubec, iii. 223 n. 3, 326; iv. 33, 34; v. 330.

Lubinum (Lebbehn?), iv. 16 n. 1.

Lucan, iii. 381 n. 1.

Lucas, bp. of Tuy, on the Pasagians, iv. 591.

Adv. Albigenses. L. i., iv. 584 n. 5. L. iii. c. 3, 591 nn. 1, 3; c. 8, 585 n. 2. See Bibl. Patr. Lugd., t. xxv.

Lucas, Marcionite, i. 474.

Lucca, iii. 393, 395, 397 n. 1; iv. 101 n. 2, 129 n. 4; v. 74, 75, 192.

Lucian, martyr, ii. 30.

Lucian, presbyter of Antioch. ii. 404.

Lucian, Satirist, opponent of Christianity, i. 8, 9, 10 n. 1, 13, 30, 92, 93 n. 1, 157–162; ii. 111, 557 n. 7.

Citations:—
Ἀλέξανδρος ἢ ψευδομάντις, § 12, i. 161 n. 2.

Ἁλιεύς, 9 n. 1. Demonax Cypr., 10 n. 1. Hermotimos, § 81, 16 n. 4. Jupiter Tragœdus, 88 n. 1. Peregrinus Proteus, 158 *et seq.* Ζεὺς ἐλεγχόμενος, 21 n. 1.

Lucianus, confessor, i. 230.

Lucianus, martyr, founder of the Antiochian school, i. 722.

Lucianus, præpositus cubiculariorum, i. 143.

Lucidus, presbyter, ii. 706, 707 n. 1.

Lucifer, v. 225.

Lucifer of Cagliari (Calaris), Luciferites, ii. 441, 442, 456. On Athanasius, 436 n. 4, 442. In the Antiochian schism, 458. His schism, 256 n. 6, 257, 458, 559.

Pro Athanasio, ii. 436 n. 4, 412 nn. Petition to Theodosius and Arcadius (Sirmond, t. i.), 256 n. 6.

Lucilla, a widow, in the Donatist schism, ii. 221–223.

Lucius, archdeacon, in Pelusium, ii. 189 n. 8.

Lucius, bp. of Rome, i. 136.

Lucius, Christian, i. 664, 665.

Lucius II., pope, iv. 151, 152.

Lucius III., pope, iv. 659.

Lucius, the British king, i. 85.

Lucius Ælius Verus, i. 663 n. 2.

Lucius Verus Antoninus, i. 663 n. 2, 665.

Lucretius, poet, i. 8.

Ludmilla, Bohemian Christian, iii. 321 n. 5, 322.

Ludolf, abp. of Triers, iii. 374.

Ludolf, companion of Vicelin, iv. 33.

Lugdunum. See Lyons.

Luitprand, bp. of Cremona, iii. 367.

De rebus imperatorum et regum. L. vi. c. 6, female pilgrims in Rome, iii. 367 n. 2.

Luke, Heracleon on, i. 434. Marcion, 473. Justin Martyr, 585 n. Julian. ii. 56, 76. Paulicians, iii. 269. Gerhoh, iv. 345 n. 3. Defensor Pacis, v. 32.

Citations:—
Luke 1, iv. 396. 1 : 6, ii. 642 n. 4. 1 : 18–20, iv. 396. 1 : 31, i. 580. 2 : 2, ii. 346. 2 : 25, iii. 133. 2 : 40, i. 680. 2 : 46, iv. 392. 2 : 52, ii. 407, 496. 3 : 7, 8, i. 618. 3 : 14, i. 272, 273. 3 : 23, ii. 346. 5 : 32, ii. 619. 6 : 22, 23, v. 395. 6 : 31, i. 125. 6 : 36, i. 245, 246. 7, i. 273. 8 : 18, i. 36. 9 : 50, ii. 248. 9 : 54, v. 281. 9 : 55, i. 153; ii. 37; iii. 255. 9 : 56, i. 313. 9 : 58, i. 271. 9 : 60, iv. 314. 10, iv. 406, 572. D : 4, iii. 77. 10 : 20, ii. 268; iii. 14. 10 : 23. iii. 209; iv. 406. 10 : 30 ff., i. 246, 718; iv. 572. 11 : 21, v. 198. 11 : 27, iv. 571. 11 : 28, v. 142. 11 : 41, iv. 306. 11 : 42, iii. 483 n. 4. 12 : 8, i. 434, 436. 12 : 13, 14, ii. 172; v. 14, 26. 12 : 47, ii. 739. 12 : 48, v. 73. 12 : 49, i. 707. 12 : 50, i. 707 n. 4. 12 : 51, i. 70. 13 : 2, i. 412. 14 : 10–24, ii. 231. 14 : 19, v. 224 n. 1. 14 : 26, i. 707. 15 : 4 ff., i. 245, 292. 15 : 8, i. 420. 15 : 29, ii. 193. 15 : 8, iv. 301. 16 : 15, iii. 426. 16 : 31, v. 201. 17 : 21, iv. 251. 18 : 1, v. 301. 18 : 8, ii. 243. 18 : 19, iii. 161. 18 : 22, iv. 283. 18 : 19, v. 262. 19 : 6, iii. 364. 19 : 28, i. 36. 20 : 34, 35, iii. 597 n. 2. 21 : 20, 21, i. 343. 22 : 24, i. 272. 22 : 25, iii. 484 n. 1; v. 95. 22 : 32, iv. 83 n. 2. 22 : 43, 44, ii. 498; v. 365. 22 : 51, v. 281. 23 : 34, v. 232.

Lukina, monastery at, v. 43.

Lull, pupil of Boniface, delegate to the

pope, iii. 69. Consecrated bp., Boniface appoints him as his successor, 70. Gives him last injunctions, 71. At disagreement with abbot Sturm, 75 and n. 1.
Lull. See Raymund.
Luna, Peter of. See Benedict XIII.
Lund, bp. of, iv. 39, 164.
Luneburg, school at, iii. 325.
Lupus.
  Synodicon (opp., t. vii.), c. 6, "Tragedy" of Nestorius, ii. 553 n. 3; f. 56, c. 17, ep. of John, the comes sacrarum, 538 nn. 1, 3; c. 94, ep. of Alex. Hierop. to Theodoret, 538 n. 4; c. 117, ep. of the Orientals to Sixtus II., 545 n. 4; ep. in name of Sixtus II., 547 n. 1; c. 203, ep. of Epiphanius to Cyrill, 541 n. 1 (518 n. 3).
Lustration, ii. 109; iii. 301 n. 1.
Luther, ii. 304; iii. 380 n.; iv. 232; v. 139, 149, 150, 158, 171, 172, 192, 202, 246, 260 n., 360, 377 n.
Lutterworth, Wicklif at, v. 142, 163, 164, 165.
Luxeuil (Luxovium), iii. 30, 31, 38, 39 n. 2.
Lycaonia, iii. 254.
Lyceum, the, ii. 106 n. 2.
Lycopolis, ii. 252 and n. 1, 255.
Lydia, paganism in, ii. 105 n. 3.
Lyons, introduction of Christianity there, i. 84. Persecution of Christians, 111–114, 276. Connection with Asia Minor, Montanism, 524. Letter of Cyprian to the church on the right of choosing bps., 200 n. 1. Epitaph at, 273 n. 3. Church of, in the passover controversy, 300. In the Gottschalkian controversy, iii. 478 n. 2, 479 n. 1, 491. Florus, iii. 489. Gregory VI. and, iii. 377 n. 1. Innocent IV. at, iv. 183. Grosshead, the papal court at, iv. 185. Feast of the immaculate conception at, iv. 331. Abelard at, iv. 398. Peter Waldus, iv. 606. "Leonists," iv. 611. Abp. of, iv. 607. Clement V. crowned at, v. 20. See Agobard, Halinardus, Hugo, Irenæus, John, Leidrad, Nebridius, Palinus, Remigius. See also Councils, an. 475.

M.

Mabillon.
  Analecta, t. i. f. 22, Charlemagne's exhortation to the bps., iii. 123 n. 4; f. 26, his preface to the homiliarium, 126 n. 3; ff. 38, 39, Claudius of Turin, comm. on Levit., 431 n. 5, 434 n. 1; f. 207, life of Odo of Canterbury, 501 n. 3 T. iii., letter of Everwin to Bernard, iv. 580 n. 1, 593 n.; f. 312 (acta episc. Cenomanens.), Gesta Hildeberti, iv. 599 n.; f. 467, Heribert on the Sect near Perigueux, iv. 584 n. 2. Bernard, Tract. ad Hugonem, iv. 465 n. 1.
  Annal. ord. Benedict, t. ii. f. 144, Charles Martel, iii. 55 n. 2.
  Museum Italicum, t. i. P. ii. f. 28, on abuse of indulgences, iii. 137 n. 3.
  Ildefonsus, ouvrages posthumes, t. i. f. 180, vision of I., iii. 581 n. 3.
  See Acta S. Ord. Ben.

Mabug, ii. 589.
Macarius, imperial commissioner, in N. Africa, ii. 228 n. 3, 229, 230 n. 5.
Macarius, patriarch of Antioch, iii. 193, 194, 196 n. 2.
Macarius, presbyter and monk in Palestine, ii. 275.
Macarius, several, the Roman, Egyptian, πολιτικός, ii. 748 and n., 752 n. 2.
Maccabæus, iii. 326 n. 4.
Maccabees, v. 361, 362.
  Citations: —
  2 Macc. 6, i. 151. 6; 18, II. ii. 219. 7, v. 302. 14, ii. 238.
Macedo, iii. 314 n. 4.
Macedonia, i. 135; iii. 315 ff. 1.
Macedonius, bp. of Constantinople, ii. 454.
Macedonius, judge, ii. 175 n. 5.
Macedonius, magister officiorum, ii. 772.
Macedonius, monk, ii. 285.
Macedonius, patriarch of Constantinople, ii. 589, 590.
Macellum, ii. 40.
Macrianus, i. 140.
Macrina, ii. 262 n. 4, 316 n. 5.
Macrizi.
  Hist. Copt. Christianor. (ed. Wetzer, 1828), p. 79, Chozru Parviz, iii. 84 n. 2; p. 89, Coptic patriarchate, 88 n. 4. Saracens, 89 n. 1; p. 93, Coptic patriarchs and ch. in India, 90 n. 2.
Macrob. Saturnal., l. 1, c. 11, ii. 347 n. 3.
Madura, iii. 51 n. 4.
Mæcenas, advice to Augustus, i. 87.
Maestricht (Trajectum), bishopric, iii. 41.
Maffei.
  Osservazioni letterarie, t. iii. (Verona, 1738), documents on the Meletian schism, ii. 254 n.; p. 15, ep. of Egyptian bps. to Meletius, 193 n. 6; p. 16, Arius, 409 nn. 2, 3; p. 69, life of Athanasius, fragm., 72 n. 2.
Magdalene, hospital at Prague, v. 176.
Magdeburg, archbishopric, iii. 322, 324, 325, 329. Norbert, iv. 246. See Meibom.
Magenfrid, iii. 76.
Magi, the, iv. 250.
Magians, i. 486, 488; ii. 125, 126, 133.
Magic, magical arts, i. 30, 33, 145 n. 2; ii. 21, 22, 23, 43, 44 and n. 1, 45, 428 n. 2. Laws against, 47, 88, 89, 90 n. 4, 94; iv. 55 n.; v. 61. Celsus on, i. 161, 162. With the Carpocratians, i. 450. Phrygian, i. 513. Magic formulas, i. 73. Fear of, iii. 12.
Magical efficacy, notions of, connected with the sacraments, i. 309, 313, 314, 322, 331, 332; ii. 31, 120, 322 n 2, 356, 366 n. 1, 724; iii. 18, 123, 135, 348, 351, 494 (301 n. 1). Catharists, iv. 577. Magical virtues associated with the priesthood, iii. 348. The cross, iii. 534. Francis, iv. 272. See Priesthood.
Magicians, i. 30, 33, 67, 71, 72, 73, 92, 104, 107, 145 n. 2. Lucian on, i. 157, 159. See Goetæ.

Magico-theurgical tendency, ii. 723.
Magistrates, authority of, v. 28, 29.
Magistri, Manichean, i. 504.
Magnanimity, iv. 526, 527 (i. 15).
Magnaura, iii. 233.
Magnentius, usurper, ii. 33, 35, 42, 437, 440.
Magnentius Rabanus Maurus. See Rabanus Maurus.
Magnetism, i. 162, 520; ii. 26; iii. 591 and n. 4; iv. 257.
Magnoald (Magnus), at Füssen, iii. 37. See Acta S. Sept.
Magnus, bp., ii. 773.
Magusæan sect, i. 489.
Mahomet. See Mohammed.
Main, in Buddhism, i. 386 n. 1, 481.
Maii.
  Citations: —
  Scriptorum veterum nova collectio, T. ii. (1828), f. 212, fragments of Arian sermons, ii. 467 n. 3. T. ii. (Rom. 1827), pp. 277, 278, Eunapii excerpta, ii. 157 n. 1. T. iv. (Rom. 1831), p. 4, acta Synod Constantinop. an. 1166, iv. 534 nn. 1, 5. T. vii. (1832), p. 16, Apollinaris, his letter to Jovian, ii. 488 nn. 1, 2; pp. 20, 70, 203, 310, his work against Diodorus of Tarsus, ii. 488 nn. 3-7, 490 n. 5, 491 n. 2; p. 69, Theodore on the person of Christ, 500 nn. 1, 5; fragment of Nestorius, 505 n. 2; p 301, 490 n. 4. Spicelog. Rom., t. iv. p. 525, Theodore, comm. on Rom., ii. 471 n. 1; p. 527, ii. 714 n. 2.

Maining, iii. 445 n. 4.
Maimon, S., autobiography, i. 448 n. 1.
Maitland.
  Facts and documents relating to the Albigenses and Waldenses (Lond. 1832), p. 112; Waldensian confessions, iv. 616 n. 7.

Majolus, abbot of Cluny, reformer of Monachism, iii. 418. Life of, 418 nn. 1, 2. See Acta S. May.
Majoralis, iv. 614 n. 6.
Majorca, Lull in, iv. 61, 63, 65, 68, 71. Monastery for missionaries, 65. Saracens and Jews, 68.
Majorinus, lector, ii. 223-225.
Majority, voice of the, Huss, v. 285.
Majuma, iii. 206 n. 3.
Malabar, church there, i. 81; iv. 141. Jews, i. 82.
Malachi.
  1 : 2, 3, ii. 629. 2 : 12 (2), iv. 94. 3, ii. 736. 3 : 15, i. 451.
Malachias, abp. of Armagh, life of, iv. 337.
Malalas. See John Malala.
Mälarn, lake of, iii. 276.
Malatesta, v. 112.
Malchion, presbyter, i. 603.
Male (Malabar), ii. 141.
Malek al Kamel, iv. 59.
Malek al Moaddhem Isa, iv. 60 n. 2.
Malilosa, Catharist festival, iv. 566 n. 2.
Malmedy, iii. 458.
Mamas, tomb of, ii. 40.
Man, the ideal, in Alexandrian Judaism, i. 64-66. Dignity of with the Essenes, 46. With Celsus, 167, 168. Plotinus, 392. Relation of Christianity to the nature of, 75 (ii. 1; iii. 98). Philo on the higher and lower natures of, 396 n. 3. Gnostics on the nature, origin, and destiny of, 372, 392, 402, 404, 409-416, 424-428, 431-434, 441, 442, 444-446, 449, 455, 456, 468, 474. In Buddhism, 481, 496 n. 2. With Mani, 491, 492, 494-501, 505. The primitive man in Manicheism, 491, 492, 494, 496, 505. Rights of man, 86 (see Slavery). Christ the new, ii. 480. Man's position in the universe, Theodore on, ii. 713-717. Relationship to God, ii. 718; iv. 506. End of, iv. 437. Natural and supernatural end, iv. 429, 430; v. 16. Autonomy of, iv. 485, 486. Bogomiles on, iv. 554. To take the place of apostate angels, iv. 554 n. 2, 573. See Anthropology, Fall, God, Psychical and Spiritual, Redemption.

Mananalis, iii. 247.
Manasseh, iii. 422.
Manasseh, abp. of Rheims, iv. 265.
Mandata, iv. 200.
Mandeans, i. 376 n. 3.
Mando di Chaia, with the Sabæans, i. 447.
Mangukhan, iv. 51-56.
Mani, i. 478-488, 81, 314, 401 nn. 2, 3; ii. 326; iii. 245, 246 and n. 3, 253. And Augustin, ii. 625.
  Citations: —
  Ad Addam. Fabric. bibl. græca., ed. nov., vol. vii. f. 316, i. 499 n. 5. Ad Patricium, ap. August. op. imp. c. Julian, c. 186, i. 497 n. 1. Disputation of Archelaus and Mani (Fabric. Hippolytus, f. 193), c. 55, i. 401 n. 2 (485). Ep. ad Scythianum (Fabric. bibl. Græc., vol. vii.), f. 316, i. 486 n. 1. Ep. ad virginem Menoch. ap. Aug. op. imperfect. c. Julian, c. 3, c. 172, i. 494 n. 1, 498 n. 1: c. 174. i. 496 n. 1; § 184, i. 498 n. 3; § 187, i. 498 n. 4. Epistola fundamenti. ap. Aug. de ep. fund. c. 13, i. 490 n. 2; ap. Aug. de fide contra Manich. (Euod. Uzal.), c. 4, i. 501 n. 3; c. 11, i. 490 n. 6. Epistolæ (Fabric.), f. 316, i. 502 n. 4. Thesaurus (see Euodius), 494 n. 1. L. 7, ap. Aug. de nat. boni, c. 46, i. 495 nn. 2, 3.

Mavía, i. 356.
Manicheaus, i. 478-506, 401 n. 3. Law of Diocletian against, i. 144, 506. Among the monks, ii. 276 n. 2. On image and Saint-worship, ii. 326, 329, 372; iii. 208. New, ii. 657. Charged with immorality, ii. 769 n. 6. Persecuted, i. 505; ii. 768-771; iii. 255; iv 587. See Manicheism.
Manicheism. System cf, i. 479-506, 376, 447, 567. Sources of religious knowledge, 501, 502. Constitution, worship, moral character, persecution, 502-506. Its history in the second period, ii. 768-771, 511, 646, 657, 659. Relations of Augustin with, ii. 239, 396, 397, 400, 625, 724. Wine in the Lord's Supper, ii. 366. Among the Monks, ii. 276 n. 2. In the Priscillianist doctrine, ii. 776, 777, and n. 1. In Paulicianism? iii.

244-246, 256, 257, 262. In other sects, iii. 269 n. 6, 591 n. 5, 593, 594. Nilus on, iii. 579. Aquinas, iv. 423. The Bogomiles, iv. 558. Traces of among the Catharists, iv. 566 and n. 2, 567, 575, n. 4, 579-581. Boniface VIII, v. 9. See Mani, Manicheans.

Manifoldness in the Catholic ch., iv. 578. See Unity.

Manna, iii. 499; v. 230.

Mans, Henry the Cluniacensian at, iv. 598-602. See Hildebert.

Mansi, Concilia.

Citations: —
T. i. f. 1034, synodal letter to Paul of Samosata, i. 603 nn. 1, 3. T. v., "Tragedy" of Nestorius, ii. 553 n. 3; f. 1182, Conc. Antioch, defence of Theodore, ii. 556 n. 5. T. vii. ff. 154, 171, Concil. Chalcedon, letters to Leo, ii. 580 n. 1; f. 799, Leontius against the Eutychians and Nestorians, ii. 583 n. 1. T. ix. f. 153, ep. of Rom. clergy to the Frankish envoys (controv. of the Three chapters), ii. 600 n. 3; f. 364, oath of Vigilius, ii. 605 n. 1 T. ix. 8, conc. Mentz and II. IV., iv. 119 n. 2. T. xii. f. 605, ep. of Paul I. to Charlemagne, iii. 234 n. 1; f. 614, n. 2. T. xiii. f. 167, Conc. Nic. II. Actio v., περίοδοι ἀποστολῶν, i. 500 n. 4; f. 175, capitulary (an. 789), iii. 59 n. 2; f. 181, capit. (an. 789), iii. 78 n. 3; f. 759, Hadrian's reply to the Libri Carolini, iii. 248 n. 2; f. 1054, capit. (an. 801), iii. 102 n. 2; f. 1073, capit. (an. 811), iii. 131 nn. 1, 2 (see Capitularies); f. 1084, pastoral ep. of Gheerbald, iii. 125 n. 2. T. xiv. f. 419, removal of images, iii. 546 n. 3; f. 424, the French bps. and image worship, iii. 552 n. 1. T. xv. f. 436, instructions of the emp. Louis to his envoys to the pope, iii. 552 n. 9; f. 437, ep. of Louis to Hadrian I., iii. 553 n. 2. T. xvi. f. 199, ep. of John VIII. to Methodius, iii. 321 n. 2. T. xvii., his condemnation of Photius, iii. 578 n. 5. T. xviii. ep. of bp. Hatto to John XI., iii. 321 n. 4. T. xix. f. 53, ep. of Benedict VII., iii. 330 n. 2; ep. of Pilgrim of Passau to Benedict VI., iii. 331 n. 2; f. 109, Conc. Remig (an. 991), iii. 369 n. 1; f. 166, ep. of Gerbert to Wilderod, iii. 369 n. 1; f. 552, synod of Limoisin, an. 1031, iii. 455 n. T. xx. f. 386 (vii. 3), ep. of Greg. VII. to the Germans, iv. 112 n. 1, 118 n. 1; f. 434, fast Synod (an. 1074), ordinances of Greg. VII., iv. 94 n. 2; f. 713, Urban II. to Gottfried, iv. 129 n. 4 T. xxi f. 109, ext. from Humbert de Romanis, conc. Lugdunens., iv. 189 n. 4.

Manso. The Labarum, ii. 13 n. 1.

Mansus ecclesiæ, iii. 101 n. 5.

Manual labor of monks and missionaries, ii. 263, 267, 277, 283, 289, 295, 744; iii. 29, 30, 31, 106, 286; iv. 233, 273, 283, 287. Products of, ii. 272, 288 Alcuin on, iii. 77. Sergius, iii. 252. The Waldenses, iv. 611, 612. Wiklif on, v. 141. Friends of God, v. 393, 407. See Labor.

Manuel, uncle of Michael III., iii. 547, 548.

Manuel Comnenus, iv. 529, 530 n. 1, 533-535, 560, 563, 564.

Manuscripts of the Bible, i. 201, 303, 582 n. 2, 700, 701, 707, 721; ii. 316, 317, 318 n. 8; iii. 15, 52, 81 n. 1, 118, 126, 155, 247, 310, 427; iv. 58, 426. Inscribed with the names of revisors, i. 582 n. 2. Manuscripts of ancient authors, i. 696; iii. 459. Of the Latin fathers, iii. 459. Of the Pseudo-Dionysius, iii. 466. Cassiodorus, iii. 151 n. 1. Correction of, iv. 362. Copied, iv. 301. Militz, v. 175, 181. See Abelard, Bible, Books, Libraries.

Maraunia, iii. 318 n. 1.

Marbod, bp. of Rennes, iv. 246, 247.

Marcella, friend of Jerome, ii. 750 and n. 3.

Marcella, sister of Ambrose, ii. 344 n. 3.

Marcella, wife of Porphyry, i. 170 n. 2, 172 n. 1.

Marcellinus, bp. of Rome, iii. 372 and n. 1; v. 85.

Marcellinus, comes.

Chronicon, ii. 98 n. 2.

Marcellinus, imperial tribune, ii. 236-238.

Marcellinus, Numidian bp. ii. 220 n.

Marcellinus, presbyter, petition of, ii. 256 n 6.

Marcellus, bp. of Ancyra, ii. 438-440, 486 n. 4. On the Person of Christ, 478-482. Against Origen, 740. See Eusebius, c. Marcellum.

Marcellus, bp. of Apamea, ii. 98, 99.

Marcellus, bp. of Rome.

Ep. 1. in Pseudo-Isidorean decretals, iii. 849 nn. 1, 2, 4.

Marcellus, the centurion, martyr, i. 147.

Marcesina, iv. 541, 542 n. 2.

Marci, Cardinal St., v. 104, 340.

Marcia, i. 118.

Marcian, — Marcianites, ii. 276, 277 n. 3.

Marcian, emperor, ii. 519 n. 2, 575-580, 584.

Ep. ad conc. Nic., ii. 577 n. 5.

Marcian, monk, ii. 291.

Marcianopolis, bp. of, ii. 507.

Marcion, his doctrine and school, i. 458-473, 379, 393 n. 3, 395, 401 n. 3. His sects, 473-476, 582 n. 3. Formula of baptism, 310. Against the dismission of catechumens before the Lord's supper, 327, 328. Forerunner of Protestantism, 367 n. Pauline tendency, 460, 461, 463, 464, 473. Decensus Christi ad inferos, salvation of the heathen, 471, 655. God's revelation in nature, 559. Against anthropopathism, 561, 562. Artemonites, 582 n. 3. Anthropology, 616, 617. Marcion and Polycarp, 465. Tertullian and Marcion, 616-618, 660. Doctrine of redemption, 640, 641. Faith, 645. Justin Martyr, 670. Rejection of the authority of St. Peter, ii. 269 (i. 461, 473). Three fundamental principles, iii. 257 (i. 466). Opposition between the Old and New Testament, iv. 574 (i. 463, 464, 467, 471).

Antitheses, apud Tertull. c. M., l. iv. cc. 9, 85, i. 470 n. 3.

Marcionites, i. 473-476, 478, 582 n. 3.

Marcionitism, opposed by "the Clementines," i. 395. Paulicianism compared

with, iii. 245-247, 257 and n. 4, 260, 268, 269, 589.
Marco Polo, iv. 56, 57.
  De regionibus Orientalibus, iv. 56 n., 57 n. 1.
Marcomannians, i. 107, 115.
Marcosians, i. 476.
Marcus, bp. of Arethusa, ii. 70, 80.
Marcus, deacon, life of Porphyry, ii. 103 n. 1.
Marcus, monk, ii. 290, 307. Tracts, 290 n. 4, 308 n. 1. See Bibl. patr. Gall.
Marcus, presiding officer of the ch. at Ælia, i. 344.
Marcus, the Gnostic, i. 440.
Marcus, the Marcionite, i. 474.
Marcus Antoninus Philosophus (Annius Verissimus), i. 663 n. 2.
Marcus Aurelius, stoicism of, i. 17, 105-107, 159. On exorcists, 73. Bardesanes, 80. Alexander of Abonoteichus, 92. Persecution of Christians, 104-117, 130, 160, 513, 524, 671. The legio fulminea, 115. Quadratus, 661. Apology of Justin, 664-666; of Athenagoras, 673; of Melito, 676 (101 n. 1, 102 n. 3, 104 n. 1, 105).
  Citations: —
  Εἰς ἑαυτόν. L. i. c. 6, i. 73 n. 3; c. 17, 106 n. 3, 107 n. 1. L. i. fin., 116 n. 6. L. x. c. 14, i. 17 n. 1. L. xi. c. 3. 105 n. 3; c. 18, 107 n. 4. L. xii. c. 28, 106 n. 2. Edict in Pandect., 107 n. 4.
Marcus of Memphis, ii. 771.
Mares, Persian ch. teacher, ii. 529 n 3.
Margaret, Dolcino's friend, iv. 633.
Margaret Ebnerin, v. 222 n. 1, 383 n. 2.
Marianus Scotus, iv. 445 n. 4.
Marinus, disciple of Proclus.
  Life of Proclus, ii. 104 nn. 4-6, 105, nn. 1, 2, 4 6, 117 n. 1.
Maris, bp. of Chalcedon, ii. 79.
Maris, bp. of Hardaschir, ii. 539 n. 610.
Maris, Nestorian patriarch, iv. 46.
Marius, the martyr, i. 140.
Marius Mercator, on the anthropology of Theodore of Mopsuestia, ii. 713. In Constantinople, 721. Eusebius of Dorylœum, 563 n. 5.
  Citations: —
  Commonitorium adv. Pelag. et Cœlest., on Pelagius, ii. 632 n. 2, 639 n. 1. Commonit. super nom Cœlest., 640 n. 4, 651 n. 4; c. 5, 652 n. 5. Cyrill's ep. 5, 517 n. 2. Excerpts from Theodore against Augustin (opp. ed. Garnier), ff. 97, 103 ; ii. 493 n , 712 n. 3, 715 nn. 1, 2, 738 n. 6. Letter of Nestorius to Cœlestius, 721 n. 3. Opp. t. ii., four sermons of Nestorius (lat. trans.), 720 n. 4; 8. i, 507 n. 2; f. 13, 509 nn. 1, 2; 8. ii., 506 n. 2. Sermon of Theodoret, 557 n. 7. Tract on the symbolum Theodori Mopsuest. pref., 713 n. 1.
Mark the Evangelist, traditional founder of the Alexandrian ch., i. 83 ; ii. 203, 559. Justin on, i. 585 n. 1. Julian on, ii. 56.
  Mark 2 : 17, ii. 619. 4 : 39, ii. 135. 6, iii. 448. 6 : 13, i. 119 n. 6 ; iii 448. 7 : 34, ii. 359. 10 : 46, i. 364. 13 : 32, iii. 163. 15 : 21, i. 447. 16 : 16, v. 173.

Marks, impressed during visions, iii. 19 n. 1; iv. 276, 624.
Marmorica. See Theonas.
Maronites, their Monotheletism, iii. 197.
Marozia, iii. 366.
Marriage among the Jews, Essenes, i. 45. Christian idea of, i. 280-284. Sanction of the church, 283, 333, 522. Mixed marriages, Tertullian on, 255, 282, 283, 332 n. 3. Views of marriage among the Ebionites, 353. Gnostics, 385, 386, 416, 417. Manicheans, 503. Second marriage, Montanists, 522 and n. 4, 565 n. 3, 673. See Syzygy.
  Second Period. Christians accused of forbidding, ii. 125. With the Euchites, 279. Among the Eustathians, 281. With Chrysostom, 302, 303. With Jovinian, 304-306, 309, 312, 313. Jerome, Augustin, 313. A sacrament, according to Augustin, 725. Marriage of clergy in the Nestorian ch., 611.
  Third and Fourth Periods. Christianity spread through, iii. 4. Of clergy, 53 and n. 6, 61, 382, 383, 392 n. 2, 410 and n. 4, 411. Laws of Boniface on marriage, 61. The pope and the Frankish princes, 120, 121 Consanguinity in, 61; the Paulicians, 265, 266. Severus of Prague, 323. Between Mohammedans and Christians, 335. Indissolubility, 353, 358. Marriage of priests in the Greek ch., 557. In the sects, 597, 601, 603, 604.
  Fifth Period. Otto on, iv., 8, 9. Of priests in Normandy, 97 n. 8. Ordinances of Gregory VII., 93-100. Sacredness of marriage maintained by Urban II. and Yves of Chartres, 121-123. Of fallen women, 216, 299, 318. Religious societies of married persons, 276, 303. Christian marriage in the Middle Ages, 294, 295, 297. Ambrose of Siena, 296. Raymund Palmaris, 298. Sacramental significance, 335. Eustathius, 531. Among the Catharists, 572, 579, 587 n. 5 (Spiritual. 579). Sect near Cologne, 593. H. of Cluny, 600, 601, 603 n. 4. Dolcino, 633, 634.
  Sixth Period. Ægidius on spiritual jurisdiction over, v. 1-. Marriage of priests in the Greek ch., Gerson on, 92. Of reformed women, 176. See Celibacy.
Mars, Julian on, ii. 49, 51, 74.
Marseilles (Massilia), ii. 296, 687, 708. iii. 13 n. 1, 139, 233 ; iv. 637 n. 1. Conference at, v. 72.
Marsiglio Ficino, on Socrates, i. 18 n. 2.
Marsilius of Padua, author of Defensor Pacis, v. 25-35, 38, 93, 147.
  Citations: —
  Defensor Pacis (see Goldast.) L. i. ff. 158, 161, the state, v. 26 nn. 2, 3; f. 168, on the Scriptures, 26 n. 1: f. 192, the clergy, 28 n. 2; ff. 203, 206, 211, ch. and state, 28 n. 3, 29 n. 4, 30 n. 1; ff 215, 216, law, civil and evangelical, 26 nn. 4, 5, 27 n. 1 : ff. 217, 218, punishments, civil and divine, 28 nn. 4, 5, 29 nn. 1, 2 ; ff.

241-245, the hierarchy, the apostles, equality of bps., 31 nn. 3, 4, 5, 32 nn. 1-4 : f. 242, priests responsible to the state, 29 n. 5; ff. 252, 254, authority of Scripture, 25 n. 3, 27 n. 2; f. 252, Univ. of Paris, 32 n. 5; ff. 253, 254, councils, 27 n. 3, 33 n. 4; f 255, testimony of the church, 28 n. 1; f. 257, John XXII. and Boniface VIII., 32 nn. 2, 3; f. 258, ignorance of Scripture among the clergy, 33 n. 5, 34 n 1; f. 262, simony, 34 n. 2; f. 295, priority of Rome, 93 n. 1; ff. 274, 279, 281, corruption there, 34 n 3, 35 nn. : ff. 284, 285, 286, on absolutions from the oath of allegiance, 30 nn. 3-5, 31 n. 1; f. 301, Christ the head of the church, 25 n. 2.

Martene and Durand.
Citations:—
Collectio amplissima. T. i. f. 449, ep. of Ulric to Nicholas I., iii. 411 n. . T. ii. f. 339, ep. 147, Wibald of Stavelo on Bernard, iv. 144 n. 1: f. 399, ep. 213, iv 152, n. 1; ep. 288, Bernard to Eugene III., iv. 152 n. 3; f. 554, Eugene on the mob at Rome, iv. 161 n. 1; ep. of Wezel to Fred. I., iv. 161 n. 2; f. 556, ep. 384, iv. 152 n. 2; f. 1017, Abbot Berthold, iv. 217 n. 2; f. 1029, Hildegard's epistles, ep. 11, iv. 217 n. 3; f. 1053, iv. 218 n. 3; ff. 1055, 1058, iv. 218 nn. 4-6 ; ff. 1060, 1068, iv. 217 nn. 4, 5; f. 1075, iv. 218 n. 2; f. 1098, ep. 66, iv. 402 n. 4. T. iv. c. 59, f. 899, *gesta episc.* Leodens, iii. 600 n. 2, 605 n. 1; f. 902, iii. 592 n. 4. T. vi. f. 7, *speculum stultorum*, iv. 266 n. 4. T. ix. Ratherii prœloquia, iii. 469 n. 6; f. 943, the same, iii. 442 n. 3; f. 948, iii 442 n. 2. Rabanus Maurus, comm. on Joshua, iii. 457 n. 2.

Thesaurus nov. anecdotorum. T. i. Guenrich on obedience to princes, iv. 109 n. 1; f. 130, Fulbert against military bishops, iii. 406 n. 3; f. 190, Berengar's exhortatory discourse, iii. 504 n. 1; f. 495, Berengar, iii 505 n. 2; f. 496, ep. to, iii. 508 n. 3. T. iv. f. 103, B. on his trial at Rome, iii. 518 n. 2; f. 107, iii. 522 n. 1; f. 163, acta conc. Paris, an. 1210, iv. 447 n. 3, 448 n. 2. T. v., Humbert adversus simoniacos, iii. 402 n. 1; ff. 217, 218, tract. of Theoderic of Verdun, iv. 84 n. 3, 99 n. 6; f. 1210 *et seq.* Abelard's Theologia Christiana, iv. 383 n. 2— 385 notes; f. 1315, the same, transubstantiation, iv. 337 n. 4 : ff. 1357, 1358, the same, iv. 454 n. 5, 455 n. 2 ; f. 1372, Abelard in Hexaëmeron, iv. 467 n. 1. 468 n. 1. Disputatio inter Catholicum et Paterinum, iv. 569 n. 5; ff. 1722, 1726, 1730, 1750, the same, iv. 270 nn. 1, 2, 575 n. 7, 577 n. 1.

Martha, ii. 497 ; v. 386.
Martialis, Spanish bp., i. 216.
Martin, cardinal, iv. 198.
Martin, disciple of Huss, v. 320.
Martin, martyr at Prague, v. 288-290.
Martin I., pope, in the Monotheletian controversy, iii. 185-192. Convokes the Lateran council (an. 648), 186. Defence of himself, 187. Political charges brought against him, 188. Deposed and imprisoned, 188, 189. His trial, 189, 190. His death, 191. His successors, 192, 193. Life, see Anastasius. Ep. 14 ad Theodorum, iii. 187 n. 1, 188 n. 1, 189 n. 1.
Martin IV., pope, iv. 548.
Martin V., pope, v. 126-129. Constitution of, 127.
Martin of Tours, favors monasticism, ii. 294. Intercessions for the Priscillianists, ii. 773-775; iii. 606. Consideration in which he was held ; miracles at his tomb, iii. 7, 131-133, 417 ; iv. 312. Church consecrated to him, iii. 104 n. 2, 129 n. 2, 131 (in England, iii. 12 ; in Utrecht, 60 n. 1). Festival of, iii. 134. Abbey of, iii. 154 n. 3, 155, 156, 507. His life by Sulpicius Severus, ii. 773 n. 2. See Gregory of Tours, St. Martin, Sulpicius.

Martinus Polonus, Supputationes to Marianus Scotus, iv. 445 n. 4.
Martyrdom, Dionysius on, i. 243. Commodian on, i. 280. Gnostics, i. 413, 436, 472. Montanists, i. 514, 521, 523. Tertullian, i. 654. Origen on, i. 706, 707. Jovinian on, ii. 307. Augustin, ii. 313. In Persia, ii. 125. Fanatical pursuit of, i. 151, 523 ; ii. 227, 253 ; iii. 338-342. Of missionaries, ii. 292, 326, 327 ; iv. 40, 42, 43. Anschar's desire for, iii. 274, 283, 284, 287. Adalbert, iii. 323. Eulogius on, iii. 343, 344. Otto, iv. 10, 24. Lull, iv. 71, 191 and n. 3, 192, 242. Francis, iv. 273. Lanfranc, iv. 329. Of Greeks, iv. 539, 540. With the Catharists, iv. 582, and n. 2, 589. See Persecution.
Martyrs, influence of, i. 77, 109, 113 ; ii. 155. Marcus Aurelius on the conduct of, i. 105. Irenæus and Origen on their number, i. 119, 127. Their joy, i. 146 and n. 3. Imprudent zeal, i. 148. Feasts of the, i. 334, 335, 720 ; ii. 328, 351, 352, 369, 371. With the Pseudo-Basilideans, i. 448. Veneration of, ii. 3, 44, 47, 82, 83, 106, 328, 349, 369-376, 445 ; iii. 288. Fanaticism, ii. 217, 218, 227, 229. Donatist, ii. 221. Churches of the, ii. 40, 106, 328, 370, 371, 372, 374. Odo on, iii. 444. Greek martyrs, iv. 539, 540. See Birthdays, Confessors, Persecutions, Relics, and the individual martyrs.
Marun, abbot, Maronites, ii. 197.
Maruthas, bp. of Tagrit, ii. 126 n. 2, 133, 761. See Assemann.
Mary, fanatic, iii. 340.
Mary, the virgin, with Valentine, i. 429. Worship of, ii. 376, 377, 524 n. ; iii. 132, 211 ; iv. 331; v. 323. Priestesses of, ii. 376. Θεοτόκος, ii. (482), 502, 506-515, 520, 523, 536, 538, 542, 543, 546, 555, 562, 582 n., 610 ; iii. 158, 162, 163, 172, 187 n. 1, 218 n. 4, 222, 249, 601 ; iv. 331-333. Ἀνθρωποτόκος, ii. 502, 510, 536. Χριστοτόκος, ii. 510, 516, 520 (iii. 222). Sinlessness of, ii. 672. Opponents to the worship of, iii. 86, 204, 205, 262 ; iv. 608. Festivals in her honor, iii. 133, 134. Legend respecting her departure from the world, iii. 134 and n. 1. Pictures of, iii. 199, 201. Images of, iii. 206, 208, 211, 216, 232 (miraculous, iii. 206). Council of Constantinople (an. 754), on her worship, iii. 216, 218. Constantine Copronymus, 218, 222. Churches, etc. dedicated to her, iii. 219 n. 2 ; iv. 38, 77 n. 2, 272. Constantine IV., iii. 224. With the

Paulicians, iii. 261, 262. Whether she had other children after the birth of Christ, iii. 38, 262. Vision of, ii. 293. Scriptural history of, iii. 469 ; v. 312, 396). Consulted as oracle, iii. 519. Worship of, in the Greek church, iii. 546. Gregory VII., iv. 86 and nn. 3, 4, 87. Immaculate conception, v. 331–333. Bogomiles, iv. 554, 557. Catharists, iv. 569–571, 574, 587. Oliva, iv. 620. Merits of, v. 41. As an example of the contemplative life, Wicklif on, v. 143.

Mary Magdalene, v. 141, 143.

Mass, iii. 102, 239, 285, 312, 379 n. 1, 413, 426, 443, 444, 452, 499, 589, 595; iv. 25, 42, 285, 641 ; v. 115, 218, 2 0, 322, 335. For the dead, iii. 102 n. 4, 136, 450; iv. 610. With the sects, iv. 557, 559 n. 3, 594, 596, 612, 614 and n. 5, 615, 641. Mock mass at Prague, v. 245. See Lord's Supper, Missa

Massa perditionis, iii. 492.

Massilia, ii. 296. See Marseilles.

Massmann.
Gothic comm. on John, iii. 281 n. 1.

Materialism, i. 364. Of Hermogenes, 617.

Maternus. See Julius Firmicus.

Mathfred, Count, iii. 459.

Mathilda, margravine of Tuscany, iv. 86, 91, 112 n. 1, 113 and n., 114.

Matilda, queen of England, iv. 90, 365.

Letter to Anselm, 365 and nn. 5–7.

Matins (matutina), iv. 25.

Matrices ecclesiæ, i. 203.

Matricula ecclesiæ, ii. 358 n. 2.

Matter, in Gnosticism, i. 372, 375, 380, 403, 427, 429, 443, 456 (see Ὕλη). With Marcion, 465, 466. Pantheistic view of, 481. Manichean, 489, 491, 495, 496, 500. In the doctrine of creation; with Hermogenes, 565–567. Sovereignty of God over, 567. With Origen, 624 and n. 5, 634, 639, 714. Metamorphoses of, 634. Redemption from the power of, ii. 115. Paulicians on, iii. 261. David of Dinanto on, iv. 446. Catharists on, 572. Imperishableness of, v. 152. See Hyle, Ὕλη.

Matthew the apostle, gospel of, i. 81, 348, 350 n. 2, 585 n., 708 n. 2 ; iii. 269 n. 1. Julian on, ii. 56, 76. Cassian, ii. 689. See Apocrypha, Gospels.

Citations:—
Matt. 3:10, i. 353; v. 401. 4:1, ff., ii. 494 n. 2, 498. 4:4, ii. 138. 4:6, iv. 249, 250. 5:3, i. 40, 64. 5:8, ii. 706 n. 2. 5:11, v. 367. 5:13, i. 5; ii. 42 n. 1; iv. 351. 5:14, i. 250. 5:16, i. 253; v. 267. 5:17, i. 3, 70, 181, 260, 336, 339, 341, 350; ii. 55. 5:19, ii. 55. 5:22, ii. 310 and n.; iii. 427. 5:26, i. 654 n. 3; ii. 739. 5:34–37, ii. 635; iv. 301, 304. 5:39, i. 271; ii. 94. 5:40, v. 282. 5:44, i. 250, 258, 705. 6:14, ii. 174. 6:16, iv. 285. 6:19, iv. 5. 6:22, iii. 253; iv. 389. 6:23, ii. 681. 6:24, ii. 94. 6:25–34, ii. 295. 6:33, iii. 148. 6:34, ii. 299. 7:1, iv. 391. 7:3, i. 237. 7:6, i. 328 ; ii. 121;
iii. 344 n. 3. 7:7, i. 287, 719; ii. 401 n. 1; iv. 392. 7:13, 14, ii. 243. 7:17, ii. 310. 7:18, i. 618. 7:22, 23, i. 253; iii. 14, 147, 251, 444; v. 267. 7:24, ff., i. 253. 7:26, ii. 247. 8, iii. 201 n. 2, 444. 8:5, ff., iii. 201 n. 2. 8:8, ii. 304. 8:12, iii. 251. 9:10–13, i. 166. 9:12, i. 246. 9:16, ii. 121. 9:17, i. 464; ii. 121; iii. 82 n. 5, 83 n. 5. 10, iii. 348. 10:8, v. 190. 10:9, 10, iv. 2, 272. 10:12, i. 287 n. 1. 10:13, ii. 175. 10:14, v. 312. 10:16, iv. 255; v. 301. 10:19, i. 140; iii. 115; v. 333. 10:20, iii. 464 n. 4. 10:21, 22, v. 310. 10:23, i. 134, 695 n. 1; ii. 247; iii. 81, 343; v. 312. 10:24, i. 230. 10:26, ii. 401 n. 1. 10:27, iv. 323. 10:28, v. 267. 10:30, i. 168. 10:33, i. 230, 27). 10:34, i. 70. 10:40, ii. 374; iii. 121. 10:42, iii. 421; iv. 365. 11, iii. 115. 11:6, iv. 574. 11:8, i. 271. 11:11, i. 339; iv. 405. 11:12, i. 621. 11:13, i. 525. 11:19, ii. 306; iii. 115. 11:25–30, ii. 128. 11:27, i. 377 n. 1, 574, 623; ii. 412; iv. 381. 11:28–30, ii. 32 n. 3, 149, 629; iv. 259 532. 11:29, ii. 123, 634; iv. 167, 261. 12, v. 32. 12:6, i. 574. 12:7, v. 206. 12:19, iii. 605. 12:27, i. 73; iii. 526. 12:29, i. 633. 12:30, i. 73; v. 219. 12:31, i. 157. 12:32, i. 227. 12:36, i. 264. 12:42, i. 574. 12:44, i. 74. 12:45, v. 227. 12:48, iv. 574. 12:50, v. 32. 13:3, i. 251; ii. 311. 13:7, iv. 22. 13:8, v. 401. 13:12, i. 36. 13:16, i. 675. 13:24, ff., i. 247; ii. 242; iv. 589. 13:29, iii. 255, 605. 13:31, i. 207. 13:33, i. 260, 336. 13:41, v. 196, 257. 13:43, i. 623 n. 1. 13:46, i. 261. 13:47, ff., ii. 242. 13:52, i. 300. 13:54, i. 631. 14:13, i. 695 n. 1. 15:8, ii. 244, 315. 15:14, i. 37, 67. 15:17, iii. 529 n. 1; v. 155, 15:24, iv. 568. 15:28, iv. 403. 16:3, i. 69. 16:6, v. 195, 196. 16:16, ff., i. 211, 212, 574; ii. 497; iii. 161. 16:18, ii. 247; v. 25. 16:19, iii. 438. 16:23, ii. 498. 16:24, ii. 36. 17:1, i. 553. 17:12, i. 347. 17:20, iii. 444. 17:24–27, iv. 172. 18:13, ii. 618. 18:17, iii. 372, 306 n 3; iv. 122; v. 127. 18:20, i. 184, 209, 211, 281, 289; v. 79, 303. 18:23, ff., iv. 572. 19:5, i. 281; ii. 306. 19:6, ff., i. 439; iii. 557. 19:11, ii. 722; iv. 94. 19:12, i. 607. 19:14, i. 312, 552; ii. 228. 19:17, i. 591. 19:21, i. 222, 274, 277, 279; ii. 205, 313. 19:23, i. 132; iii. 139. 20:9, ii. 310. 20:16, ii. 243. 20:22, f., i. 707. 20:28, i. 224; iii. 482. 21:16, i. 705 n. 4. 22:17, ii. 233. 22:19, 20, i. 699. 22:21, i. 121, 259; iii. 403; iv. 172; v. 26. 22:46, iii. 526. 23:2, 3, ii. 240; iv. 199, 558; v. 196, 257. 23:5, iii. 411 n. 7; iv. 59. 23:9, ii. 245. 23:11, iii. 412. 23:12, i. 167, 220. 23:13, iii. 438. 23:15, i. 67; iv. 284. 23:16, iii. 404 n. 1. 23:23, v. 187. 23:27, ii. 47. 24, i. 343; v. 178. 24:13, iii. 68. 24:15, v. 178, 196. 24:23, iii. 371; v. 262. 24:25, ii. 240. 24:36, ii. 496. 25, i. 715; ii. 310; iii. 131; iv. 298. 25:14, ff., i. 303 25:25, ii. 263. 25:31, ff., ii. 310. 25:33, ii. 305. 25:34, iii. 444. 25:35, 36, iv. 298; v. 346. 25:46, ii. 643 n. 2. 26:26, 27, i. 324, 325. 26:30, ii. 778. 26:38, v. 365. 26:39, ii. 646 n. 1. 26:41, i. 261. 26:52, i. 273; v. 7. 27:7, iii. 458 n. 2. 28:19, iii. 76. 28:20, iii. 76; v. 25, 27.

Matthew of Paris.

Hist. Angl., persecution of the Jews, iv. 72 n. 2, 73 n. 4. Interdict in London, 176 n. 1. Religious opinions of Frederic II., 180, 182. The Franciscans, 277, 278. An. 1197, f. 160, Fulco, 210 n. 2. An. 1202, f. 173, Simon of Tournay, 418 n. 4; f. 187, death of Innocent IV., 252 n. 3. An. 1207, the Franciscans, 278 n. 1. An. 1209, ff. 192, 224, John, king of Eng., 175 nn. An. 1223, f. 267, Catharist pope, 590 n. 6. An. 1228, f. 293, ep. of Fred. II. to k. of Eng., 178 nn. 1-3. An. 1234, f. 339, the mendicants, 280 n. 1 ; f. 340, the crusades, 186 n. 3. An. 1236, f. 354, influence of the mendicants, 280 n. 3. An. 1237, f. 385, opp. of Germanus to Greg. IX., 539 n. 2. An. 1244, f. 567 (ed. Lond. 1686), accusations against the Jews, 73 nn. 1, 2. An. 1246, f. 608, influence of mendicants, 280 n. 4. An. 1247, f. 630, R. Grosshead on the same, 279 n. 4. An. 1250, f. 672, failure of the crusades, effects of, 188 n. 4; f. 686, degeneracy of mendicants, 280 n. 1. An. 1251, f. 710, children's crusade, 342 n. 5. An. 1253, f. 752, R. Grosshead, his disappointment in the mendicants, 280 n. 2, 281 n. 3. An. 1256, f. 792, persecution of Jews, 73 nn. 3–5. An. 1439, f. 408, Frederic II., 181 n. 2; ff. 493, 527, the same, Greg. IX., 182 nn. ; f. 538, ep. of Yves of Narbonne, 583 nn. 2, 3; f. 570, R. Grosshead on the papal arrogations, 187 n. 1; f. 575, ban against F. II., 183 n. 3; f. 585, Thaddeus de Suessa, 188 n. 1; impression made by circular letter of F. II., 184 n. 2; f. 760, legend concerning bp. Grosshead, 187 n. 3; f. 796, Alexander IV., 188 n. 2.

Matthias of Janow. See Janow.
Matthias Pater of Knin, v. 250.
Matthias the Apostle, i. 622.
Mattium, iii. 51 n. 3.
Mauguin.

Vindiciæ prædestinat. et gratiæ. T. i., confessions of Gottschalk, iii. 479 nn. 4, 5 (p. 10, 474 n. 4). Ratramnus, De prædestinatione, 482 n. 2; Scotus De prædest., 485 n. 4. T. ii., Libellus Remigii, etc., de tribus epistolis, 478 n. 2, 479 n. 1, 491 n. 1; f. 107, c. 24, ep. of Hinkmar, 478 n. 2.

Maurice, Greek emperor, iii. 97.
Maurins.

Hist. de Languedoc, iv. 639 n. 3.

Mauritania, church in, i. 84, 122. Cæsariensis, ii. 671 n. 2. Montagne in Flanders, iv. 380 n. 1. See Walter of.
Mauritius, archdeacon, iv. 211 n. 5.
Mauritius. See Peter the Venerable.
Mauritius of Prague, v. 259.
Maurus, Benedict's disciple, ii. 300.
Maurus, bp. of Fünfkirchen, iii. 334 n. 2.
Mavia, Saracen queen, ii. 142.
Maxentius Cæsar, ii. 9–12, 220.
Maximianus, Donatist deacon, ii. 231.
Maximianus, patriarch of Constantinople, ii. 541 n. 1, 542, 547.
Maximianus Herculius, Cæsar, i. 142, 146, 147, 155; ii. 8, 9 n. 1, 17.
Maximilianus, the martyr, i. 146.
Maximilla, the prophetess, i. 514, 515.

Apud Euseb. l. v. c. 16, sayings of, i. 515 n. 3. Apud Epiphan., 515 n. 4.

Maximinus, Arian bp.

Polemical tract, essay on Ulphilas, ii. 150 n. 4; f. 20, 151 nn. 1, 2; f. 23, 157 nn. 3, 4. See Aug. collat. cum Maximin.

Maximinus, Caius Galerius Valerius, i. 155; ii. 2. Persecution under, 155, 722; ii. 3–6, 254 n., 268. Measures of toleration, i. 156; ii. 2, 3. Rescript of toleration, ii. 16, 17. Second rescript and death, ii. 18.
Maximinus, the Thracian, persecutions under, i. 126, 130, 706, 709.
Maximus, abbot, ii. 555, 556.
Maximus, bp. of Jerusalem, i. 721 n. 3.

Maximus, bp. of Turin, ii. 340, 344 n. 2, 348. On the Arians, iii. 5 n. 2, 137 n. 3.

Homilies, ii. 350 n. 4. H. V. in Kal. Jan., 348 n. 2. H. VI., VII., 344 n. 2. See Bibl. Patr. Gall.

Maximus, church teacher, i. 721.
Maximus, Platonist, ii. 42–44 and n. 1, 88 n. See Eunapius.
Maximus, the monk (abbot), iii. 171. On vassalage, 171 n. 2. On the end of the creation and of redemption, 171, 172. On the relation of the two natures in Christ, 173. On the progressive and continuous development of divine revelations, 173. On faith, 174. On love, 174. On prayer, 174. On the temporal and eternal life, restoration, 175. Head of the Dyothelete party, 181. His arguments against Monotheletism, 181–184. His disputation with Pyrrhus, 184. The type, 185 n. 3. His arrest, 191. His trial, banishment, and death, 185 n. 1, 192. Influence on Scotus, 461.

Citations from his writings:—
Aphorisms (ἑκατοντὰς τετάρτη, § 20), t. i. f. 288, restoration, iii. 175 n. 3. 'Ασκητικός, i. 378, prayer, 175 n. 1. 'Ερωτήσεις καὶ ἀποκρίσεις, c. 13, i. f. 304, restoration, 175 n. 3. Exposit. in orat. Dom. (opp. ed. Combefis), t. i. f. 354, nature and grace, 172 nn. 4–7, 173 nn. 1–4; f. 355, the Trinity, 171 n. 3; f. 356, slavery, 171 n. 2.
Opp. (ed. Combefis). T. i. f. 30 et seq., Acta Maximi, § 8, f. 36, the type, iii. 185 n. 1; § 30, spiritual power of the emperor, 192 n. 1; f. 606, theoretical and practical elements, 174 n. 6. T. ii. ff. 10, 11, 102, Dyothelism, 183 n. 4; f. 83, the same, 182 n. 1; f. 105, Disputat. contr. Pyrrho, 182 n. 3; f. 220, ep. on love, 174 nn. 4, 5.
Quæst. in Scripturam. Q. 21, f. 44 (opp. t. i.), restoration of fallen spirits, iii 175 n. 3; ff. 45, 157, 209, union of the two natures, 171 n. 4, 172 n. 2. Q. 31, 54, 59, ff. 74, 152, 199, divine and human elements in believers, 173 nn. 5–8 (see 183 n. 4). Q. 33, f. 76, faith, 174 nn. 1, 2; f. 157, redemption, 172 nn. 1–3; f. 210, knowledge and intuition, 175 n. 2. Thoughts on charity, i. f. 453, 174 n. 3.

Maximus, usurper, ii. 99, 772–775.
Mayence. See Mentz.
Mayfreda, nun, iv. 639.
Mazdejesnan, ii. 137.
Μὴ ὄν, i. 623 n. 5; ii. 626. Fredegis on, iii. 460. Scotus, iii. 461.
Means of grace, ii. 673, 687.
Means sanctified by the end, iii. 377, 380. Gerson, v. 95, 96.
Meat offerings in the Armenian church, iii. 589 n. 1.
Meaux, iv. 267.
Mecca, iv. 535 n. 1.
Mechanics, Christian, i. 78.
Mechitarists, iii. 250 n. 1.
Mecklenburg, iii. 326, 327.
Media, church in, i. 80.
Mediæval Catholicism, iii. 146, 200. Period, 243.
Mediation of the priesthood, i. 179, 194,

GENERAL INDEX. 147

646; ii. 179, 180, 308, 368; iii. 2; iv. 354, 509, 514. See Church, Priesthood.
Mediator, Christ as, i. 80, 591, 641, 644; ii. 51; iv. 615; v. 411.
Meditation, custom of religious, v. 381.
Medschusic, Thondracian, iii. 588.
Meekness, i. 76, 232; iv. 320.
Μεγαλοψυχία, i. 611. See Magnanimity.
Meibom.
  Script. rer. germ., t. 1 (Helmæstadii, 1688), f. 339, Gobelinus Persona on conc. Const. V., 109 n. 2; f. 660, Annals of Wittekind, iii. 289 n. 1; f. 734, Narratio de erect. eccles. Magdeburg, iii. 325 n. 3.
Meinhard, converter of the Lieflanders, iv. 36, 37.
Meissen, bishopric, iii. 324.
Melancthon, v. 246.
Melchiades (Miltiades), bp. of Rome, ii. 221 n. 4, 223, 224.
  Epistle of, in the Decretals, iii. 349 n. C.
Melchite party in Alexandria, iii. 88 n. 4, 228.
Melchizedec, i. 716; iii. 191, 566.
Meletius, bp. of Lycopolis, — Meletian schism in Egypt, ii. 193 n. 6, 196, 252–255, 409 n. 2, 414, 425, 432.
Meletius, bp. of Mopsvestia, ii. 546, 549, 551, 555 n. 2.
  Epp. 76 and 121, ii. 546 n. 3. Ep. 152 (opp. Theodoret, t. v. f. 832), 555 n. 2.
Meletius, bp. of Sebaste and Antioch, Meletian schism at Antioch, ii. 257, 324, 457, 458, 461, 464, 465.
Melitene, ii. 551; iii. 250 n. 2, 587. See Acacius.
Melito of Sardis, plea in behalf of the Christians, addressed to Marcus Aurelius, i. 104, 105. His books on the passover, 299. Apology, Catalogue, 676.
  Apology, cited by Euseb. (l. iv. c. 26), i 101 n. 1, 102 nn. 2, 3, 104 nn.
Mellitus, abbot, sent to the Anglo-Saxons, iii. 15. Archbishop of London, 16. Banished from Essex, 18.
Melrose, iv. 328 n. 1.
Melun, iv. 373.
Memnon, bp. of Ephesus, in the Nestorian controversy, ii. 527, 528 n. 2, 529, 532–534, 539, 540.
  Letter to the clergy at Constantinople, 532 n. 2. See Harduin, t. i. f. 1596.
Memoires de l'Academie de S. Petersburg.
  Vol. I., 1832, pp. 223, 235, and vol. ii., 1834, essays on Buddhism, i. 482 n. 1, 491 n. 1, 503 n. 5. T. vii., Frähn's Essay, iii. 315 n. 2.
Memoires de l'Academie des inscriptions. See Abel Remusat.
Memorius, bp. of Apulia, ii. 652 n. 3.
Menander, i. 454 n. 1.
Mendacium officiosum, iii. 54 n. 2. See Fraus pia.
Mendicant friars, ii. 277, 300. The Mendicant orders, their origin, iv. 268–276. Regulations and manner of life, labors, iv. 276–279, 293. As preachers, 276–279, 282, 284, 624. Influence, 278–282. Begin to degenerate, 280 (634, 635). Attractions of, 280. In the universities, 281. As confessors, 281. Favored by princes, 281, 282 and n. 4. Opposed by university of Paris, Wm. of St. Amour, against, 282–286, 289. De Romanis, 316. Defended, 286–289. Efforts for reform, 289–292. Scholasticism, 420, 421. Relations with the popes, 280, 281, 282 and n. 4, 287, 291. Ordinance of Gregory X. respecting, 628. Favor withdrawal of the cup, 345. Clemangis on the, v. 59. Gerson, 86. In England, 134. At Oxford, 134, 141. Wicklif and the, 136–138, 140, 141, 145, 149, 157, 161, 162 and n. 5, 171. Militz, 180, 181. Conrad of Waldhausen, 186–191. See Dominicans, Franciscans.
Menken.
  Script. rer. germ., t. iii. f. 1786, iii. 323 n. 2.
Mennas, patriarch of Constantinople, in the Origenistic disputes, ii. 193 n. 6, 593, 596–598, 600, 602, 607 n. 1, 764, 765.
Menoch, Mani's letter to the Virgin. See Mani.
Mensurius, bp. of Carthage, i. 150, 151; ii. 217–221, 222 n. 3.
Mentz, iv. 190 n. 3. Archbishopric of, iii. 65 n. 6, 66, 71 n. 2. Presbyter of, 56 n. 5, 63 n. 1, 66 nn. 1, 2. Gottschalk in, 477. Persecution of Jews at, iv. 74, 75. Hermann, iv. 79. Hildegard, iv. 219 (see Hildegard, epp.). Archbishops of, iii. 66, 521 n. 4, 446 n. 1, 457; iv. 102, 643. Benedict Levita, iii. 350 n. 1. Gozachin, iii. 515 n. 6. Probus, iii. 602. See Maycnce.
Mercenaries, Paulician iv. 552.
Merchants, Christian, iv. 10, 56, 58, 69, 71, 270. Catharist, v. 583.
Mercinus, iii. 21.
Mercury, ii. 51, 74.
Mercy, spirit of Christianity, Cyprian on, i. 245, 246. See Love.
Merida, ii. 773; iii. 111 n. 1. See Councils, an. 666.
Merit, works of, ii. 319, 495 n. 2, 690, 705; iii. 101, 432; iv. 399, 489, 490. Merit and freedom, iii. 484; iv. 484, 515, 516. Of angels, iv. 486. De condigno and de congruo, 489, 319 and n. 1; v. 167. Treasury of, v. 41. Merits of Christ, i. 246; iii. 484; v. 171.
Meroe, i. 83.
Meropius, ii. 143.
Merovingians, iv. 110.
Merseburg, bishopric, iii. 324. See Ditmar.
Merswin, Rulmann, v. 387.
Μέσον, μεσότης, i. 421 n. 1, 438 and n. 2.
Mesopotamia, church there, i. 80. Tem-

ple, ii. 95 n. 1, 610, 611. Adelphios, ii. 277 n. 4. Audius, ii. 766. Bishops in, ii. 133, 136, 761. Monastery, iii. 89. Euchites, iii. 590.
Mesori, ii. 273.
Messalians, ii. 277; iv. 552 n. 2.
Messenger of life, i. 447.
Messenia, iv. 530.
Messiah, idea of, in the Old Testament, misapprehension of it, i. 36, 37, 94, 346, 357, 358, 574; ii. 482, 497; iv. 78; v. 16, 44. Expectation repressed with Josephus and the Alexandrian Jews, i. 65, 66. Among the proselytes, i. 68. Among the Jewish Christians, i. 62, 340, 341–343. Testament of the twelve patriarchs, i. 194 n. 1. Among the Ebionites, i. 346–348, 350–352. In the Clementines, i. 356–358. Faith in Jesus as the, i. 62, 305, 363, 364. Cerinthus on the, i. 398, 399. Psychical, with Valentine, i. 426, 429–431. Heracleon on the Messiah, i. 441 n. 2. Ophites, i. 445, 447. Sethians, i. 448. Marcion, i. 463, 468–471. Marcosians, i. 476. Mani, i. 500. And the millennium, i. 348, 399 (see Millennium). Justin M., i. 668. Cyprian, i. 685. Julian, ii. 56. Theodore, ii. 496 n. 2. Lost in Mohammedanism, iii. 87. False, i. 103; v. 239.
Messina, iii. 113.
Metempsychosis, with Basilides, i. 410. With the Carpocratians, 450. In Manicheism, 480, 483, 496, 503. With Origen, 627. With the Catharists, iv. 568, 579. See Transmigration.
Method, of Scholastics, iv. 204, 420; v. 269. Of Lull, iv. 436, 437.
Methodius, monk, iii. 308. Missionary among the Slavonians, 314–321, 323, 329 n. See Acta S. Mar. Dobrowski.
Methodius, patriarch of Constantinople, iii. 548, 549.
Methodius of Tyre, i. 358 n. 1. Against Origen's doctrine of the creation, 569. Athenagorus, 673. His writings, 422 n. 2, 720, 721. See Bibl. Patr. Gall.

Citations: —
De libero arbitrio, i. 422 n. 2 (see Galland). On prophecy, 358 n. 1 (see Combefis). Περὶ κτισμάτων, ap. Phot. (cod. 235), i. 569 n. 5. Symposium, Orat. ii. (Theophil., § 5), 721 n. 1. Orat. ix. § 5, 721 n. 2.

Methone, iv. 530.
Metropolitan constitution, ii. 195–198; iii. 111, 349; iv. 88, 98, 99. In the German church, iii. 64. See Metropolitans.
Metropolitans, i. 203; ii. 187, 188; iii. 64, 65, 110, 119 n. 2, 349, 359, 365, 366, 400, 454.
Metz, Musical School at, iii. 128, 345. Synod at, 354. Charles the Bald crowned at, 361. Amalarius, 428 n. 2. Paulinus of, 509 n. 4. Societies at, iv. 321–324. Bible at, iv. 321. See Adalbero, Chrodegang, Hermann, St. Gorze.

Micha.
I., iv. 132; 6 : 8, iii. 443.
Michael (Bogoris), iii. 308–310.
Michael, archangel, iii. 444; iv. 554. Feast of, iii. 134.
Michael I., Greek emperor. See M. Curopalates.
Michael II., Greek emperor, iii. 543–546, 551, 552 n. 7, 553.
Michael III., Greek emperor (son of Theophilus), iii. 308, 315, 502 n. 2, 547, 549, 550 n. 3, 558–568 and n. 3.
Michael, patriarch of Constantinople, iv. 563, 564.
Michael, St., feast of, iii. 134.
Michael Cerularius, patriarch of Constantinople, iii. 387 n. 7, 580, 583 n. 3. Takes his stand against the Romish church, 581–584.

Ep. to John, bp. of Trani, iii. 581 n. 4. Ep. to Peter of Antioch, 583 n. 1. Ep. 2, 583 n. 2. On the Schism, 583 n. 3. See Coteler, Leo Allatius.

Michael Curopalates (Rhangabe), Greek emperor, iii. 558. Persecutes the Paulicians, 255, 256.
Michael Nicetas, bp. of Athens.

Monodia on Eustathius, iv. 531 n. 1. Ep. to Eustathius, 531 n. 3. See Tafel.

Michael of Chesena, general of the Franciscans, v. 25.
Michael of Dentschbrod, or de Causis, v. 293, 300, 321, 322, 327, 330, 331, 335, 338 n. 3, 356, 376.
Michael Paleologus, Greek emperor, iv. 533 n. 7, 542, 544, 546–548, 551.
Michael Psellus, on the Euchites, iii. 590, 591, 595 n. 3. Their morality, 588 n. 2.

Διάλογος περὶ ἐνεργείας δαιμόνων (ed. Gaulmin, Paris, 1615), f. 5, iii. 589 n. 2 (ed. Boissonade 1838; (f. 2, ἱερόν κόμμα, iv. 552 n. 3); f. 9, Satannel, 591 n. 2; f. 18, 591 n. 5; f. 21, immorality of one party of Euchites, 591 n. 3; f. 37, 590 n. 2; f. 61, 591 n. 6; f. 69, 591 n. 4.

Michaelis.

Orientalische und exegetische Bibliothek, Th. X. s. 61, the church at Edessa, i. 291 n. 3.

Middle Ages, source of their character, iii. 1. Ecclesiastical development, iii. 396; iv. 605; v. 13. Intellectual productions, iii. 470. Journeyings of the popes, iv. 197 n. 4. Plagues of the, iv. 266. Subjective tendency, iv. 509, 514, 515. Latin of the, iv. 572 n. 1.
Miecislaw, king of Poland, iii. 330.
Miesroh, Persian, ii. 136, 137.
Migetius, Spanish errorist, iii. 157 n. 1, 166 n. 6.
Migration of nations, ii. 146; iii. 3, 25, 26, 330.
Mihr Nersch, Persian general, proclamation to the Christians in Armenia, i. 489; ii. 125, 127, 129, 137. See Elisæus, St. Martin.
Mikowec, Ferd. B.

Letters of John Huss written at Constance,

Ep. 1, v. 315 n. 2. Ep. 2, 320 nn. 1, 4, 321 n. 2. Ep. 3, 332 nn. 4, 5. Ep. 6 (June 24), 363 n. 5. Ep. 7, 359 n. 1. Ep. 8, 356 n. 1. Ep. 27, 344 n. 1.

Milan, Edict of Constantine at (an. 313), ii. 15. Simplicianus, 77. Ambrose at, 214, 312 and n. 5, 33-. Donatists before Constantine at, 225. Augustin at, 294, 318 n. 8. Jovinian, 312 and n. 5. Seasons of worship, 333 n. 2. Sabbath, 334. Paulinus, 640. Controversies there concerning simony, iii. 383–398. Sects, iii. 602; iv. 180, 613, 638. Bernard, iv. 255. Philargi, v. 83. See Councils, an. 355 and an. 1060.

Milano Sola, iv. 632.

Miles Christi, i. 309, 644. See Militia Christi.

Miles Satani, i. 644.

Mileve. See Councils, an. 410. See Optatus.

Military service of Christians, i. 91, 116, 117, 146, 270–273; ii. 129. Exemption of clergy, ii. 169, 170 and n. 2, 153 n. 3; iii. 404. Entered into by clergymen, iii. 55, 385, 386, 406; iv. 219 (see Clergy). Of bishops, iii. 404–406; iv. 31 and n. 2, 200; v. 86 (see Bishops). Damiani on, iii. 385. Fulbert on, iii. 406. Waldenses on, iv. 612, 614.

Militia Christi, i. 199, 296, 306, 307, 309; v. 249.

Militz, John, life and character, v. 173–183, and nn. 1–3, 93. De Anti-christo, 178–180, 181, 291. Theological school of, v. 181, 182. Imprisonment at Rome, 180. Release, 181. Influence in Bohemia, 181, 183 n. 2, 232, 235, 236, 242, 249, 275. On the corruption of the clergy, 178, 249, 258. Death at Avignon, 183. His writings burned, 261. His followers, 182, 288. Janow on, 176 and nn. 1, 3, 177 n., 183 nn. 1, 3. And Janow, 192, 201. Life of, 174 nn. 2, 3, 175 nn., 176 n. 2, 183 n. 1. See Balbinus.

Citations from De Anti-christo, v. 179 n. 2, 180 nn.

Militzans, v. 182.

Milk and honey, given to the newly baptized, i. 316; ii. 360.

Millennium, i. 348, 399, 471, 513 n. 1, 649–653, 669, 687; ii. 315, 616. See Chiliasm.

Milo Crispin.

Life of Laufranc, iv. 329 n. 1.

Miltiades, against the Montanists, i. 519.

Mimigerneford, iii. 79.

Mind, Bacon on the power of, iv. 474. Self deification of, 618.

Minerva, ii. 51.

Mingarelli.

Anecdotorum fasciculus (Romæ, 1756), Alani regulæ theolog., iv. 417 n. 3; f. 287, Theophylact. περὶ ὧν ἐγκαλοῦνται Λατίνοι, iii. 584 n. 1.

Ministri sacri palatii, iv. 196.

Minorca, iv. 55.

Minorites (ordo minorum), iv. 221 n. 276.

Minors, iii. 105.

Mints, in the hands of the clergy, iv. 133, 138.

Minucius Felix, i. 11. Character, 690.

Octavius of, i. 88 n. 3; charges against the Christians, 92 n. 1; c. 8 78 n. 1, 271 n. 1; c. 9, 76 n. 4, 90 n. 8.

Minucius Fundanus, proconsul, i. 101.

Miracles, means of advancing Christianity, 72–76. Dionysius of Halicarnassus on, i. 12. Philo on, 55. Justin Martyr on, 74. Origen, 74, 544, 545, 570, 643. Irenæus, 7+, 677. Hierocles, 173. The Gnostics, 388. Valentine, 432. Carpocrates, 450, 484 n. 3. Marcion, 470. The Montanists, 523, 526. Miracles of Christ, 75, 445, 450, 170, 643. Celsus on the, 169. Hierocles, Quadratus, Irenæus, on the, 173, 661, 677.

Second Period. Augustin, on, ii. 120, 240. His conception of, 475–477. Anthony on, 267, 268. Euchites, 280. At the graves of martyrs 370, 371, 375.

Third and Fourth Periods. At the tombs of saints, iii. 7, 22, 132, 133, 147, 299, 386, 445 n. 1, 447 448. As an aid in the spread of Christianity, iii. 6, 12–14. Gregory the Great on, 14, 15 n. 1, 146–148. Wilfrid on, 24. Severinus, 27, 28. Amandus, 41. Of fanatics, 56 and n. 5. Boniface, 60. Wrought by relics, 22, 221. By images, 201, 206, 221, 230, 240, 241. By sacraments, 146, 263. In the Lord's supper, 495, 496, 501 (see Paschasius Radbert). Paulicians on, 251, 263. Anschar, 287. Eulogius on, 343. Ratherius, Odo on, 444, 445. Gottschalk, 480. Berengar, Guitmund, 526. Sect at Arras, 598.

Fifth Period. Connected with the spread of Christianity, iv. 26, 27, 32, 623. Rubruquis, 56. Fraudulent, 76, 127, 284, 529. Egbert on, 80. Gregory VII., 115. Clement III., 129. Bernard, 145, 146, 157, 256 and n 4, 257, 258 and n. 1, 603. At Becket's tomb, and others, 171, 328, 329. Humbert on, 190. Cessation of, 190, 468, 469, 551. Fulco, 210. Joachim on, 229 Norbert, 246. R. of Arbrissel, 247. Of mendicant orders, 284. Love of the wonderful in the Middle Ages, significance of the miracle, 312. Berthold, 318. Guibert on, 330. In the Lord's supper, 336, 341, 346. Abelard, 377, 378, 467–469. Hugo, 404. Doctrine of, with the scholastics, 466–474. Aquinas on, 471, 511; two conceptions of, 472. Bogomiles, 554, 557. Niphon, 564. Catharists, 569, 570, 584, 585. Waldenses, 615.

Sixth Period. Wicklif on, v. 152, 169. Janow, 198, 199, 201, 239. The Wilsnack miracle, Huss, 237–239, 266, 267, Gerson, 353. Suso, 411. Of Antichrist,

198, 199, 266. Of images and relics, 233, 234. Of the last times, 201.
Miraculous signs, ii. 10. Augustin on, ii. 240. Visitations, iii. 19 n. 1.
Miranmolin, king of Tunis, iv. 436.
Mirans, prince of the Iberians, ii. 139 n. 1.
Mirkhond, Persian historian.

Hist. of the Sassanides, i. 486 n. 2, 487 n. 2.

Misa. See Jacobellus.
Missa, catechumenorum, missa fidelium, i. 327 n. 1, 478; ii. 361 and nn. 2, 3, 365. See Dismissal.
Missæ privatæ, iii. 136.
Missi, messengers of the emperor, iii. 122.
Missionaries, Buddhist, i. 480. Arian, iii. 5 n. 2. British, iii. 10, 22, 23, 55. Irish, 10, 20, 23, 29–38, 43, 53, 55, 63 n. 4, 300 n. 1 (see Patrick). Roman, 11–19, 24. Scottish, 21–24. Fear of magical influence from, 12. Miraculous interpositions in favor of, 6, 12, 22 and n. 1 (see Miracles). English, 22–24, 43–73, 79, 82, 290–292, 297. Frankish, 9, 22–24, 40–43, 271–287. German, 37, 300. From Friesland, 79, 289. Ordination of, 103. Employed on embassies, 279, 283. Bishops as, 39–42, 44, 72, 300 (see Adalbert). Laymen as, 302. Greek (see Methodius, Cyrill). Icelandic, 300–306, 307. Bohemian, 322, 323, 332, 333.

In the Fifth Period. From Spain, iv. 2. Protected by the secular arm 7, 20. From Suabia (see Otto). German, 33–37, 42, 43. Cistercian, 37, 39, 44. Bohemian, 41, 42. Pomeranian and Polish, 43–45. Nestorian, 46–48. Franciscan, 51–60. Dominican, 56. Native, 58. Education of, 34, 58, 62, 63, 65, 70, 426, 435 n. 2, 436. See Missions, Monks, Eutyches, Ulphilas.

Missionary labor, enthusiasm for, iii. 39, 57 n. 1. Alcuin on, iii. 76, 77, 82.
Missionary register, an. 1832, iii. 6 n. 3, 39 n. 1, 51 n. 4.
Missionary schools, iii. 10, 73. See Schools.
Missions, i. 261; ii. 761. Favoring providences in the history of, iii. 12, 280. Centres of, iii. 328 n. 2. In Abyssinia, ii. 144. In Ireland, ii. 146–149. Among the Goths, ii. 149–160.

In England, iii. 10–25 (i. 85, 86). In Germany, 25–82. In Bavaria, 38–40. In Friesland, 40–45, 72–75. In Saxony, 75–82. In Hungary, 82–84, 330–335. In Denmark and Sweden, 271–293. In Norway, 293–300. In Iceland, 300–306. In the Orcades and Faröe Isles, 306, 307. In Greenland, 307. In Bulgaria, 307–314. In the Crimea, 314, 315. In Moravia, 315–321. In Bohemia, 321–323. Among the Slavonians, (Wends), 323–327; (Russia), 327–330; (Poland), 330; (Hungary), 330–335.

Among the Slavonians (in Pomerania), iv. 1–33; (Vicelin), 33–86; (in Liefland), 36–40; (in Prussia), 41–45 (see Wends); in Finnland, 45. Domestic missions, v. 144. See Missionaries, Christianity, spread of.
Mistiwoi, Wendish prince, iii. 325.
Mithras, in Parsism, i. 493; ii. 128. Temple of, ii. 80.
Mitre, iv. 201.
Mizlav, Pomeranian governor, iv. 22–24.
Mjesco (Miccislaw), Duke of Poland, iii. 330.
Mladanowec, accompanies Huss to Constance, v. 320. Rumor of Huss's escape, 326 n. 3. The bp. of Lebus, 330 n. 2. Ep. of Huss to, 332. Befriends Huss, 342, 343. His record, 344 n. 1, 349 n. 2. Legacy of Huss to, 367. Befriends Jerome of Prague in prison, 375.

Protocol of the trial of Huss at Prague, an. 1414 (see Studien und Kritiken, 1837, H. 1), v. 243 n. 1, 250 n. 4, 317 n. 4; pp. 129, 130, v. 259 n. 1; p. 181, v. 255 n. 1.

Mobed, Christian, ii. 125, 126.
Modern civilization and Christianity, iii. 1.
Modestus, officer of state, ii. 64 n. 4.
Modestus, præfectus prætorio, ii. 460.
Mœris, Lake, i. 60.
Mœsia, ii. 449, 507, 547. Settlement of Goths in, 152.
Mohammed, i. 350 n. 3, 487. His appearance, iii. 84. His religious tone of mind, iii. 85. His first intentions, iii. 86. His opposition to idolators, to Judaism, and Christianity, iii. 86. His ground in opposition to the essence of Christianity, iii. 87. His use of apocryphal gospels, iii. 87. Polemics against, iii. 338; iv. 60, 436. And Dolcino, iv. 637. And Antichrist, v. 197. See Koran.
Mohammed, Arabian Caliph in Spain, iii. 342.
Mohammedan literature, iii. 335.
Mohammedanism, precursor of, i. 395. In Armenia, ii. 137. Its character, iii. 85. Its relation to Christianity, 85–88 (iv. 59). To Judaism, 87, 88 (iv. 59). Means of its advancement, 88. Among the Bulgarians, 329.
Mohammedans, in Spain, iii. 156, 164 and n. 6, 335 (see Spain). Apologetics against, 159. Opposed to image worship, 201, 202, 203 n. 1, 431. In the Crimea, 315. Intercourse with, 335 (166 n. 6.) Marriage with Christians, 335, 336, 339, 341. (See Saracens.) Favor the Nestorians, iv. 45, 46. In Persia, iv. 56. Mission among them, Lull, iv. 59–71, 465. Arguments of, iv. 69 and n. 2. And Frederic II., iv. 179, 180–182, 184. And the Greek church, iv. 531 n. 5, 535, 536.
Möhler, Dr.

Essay of, iii. 98 n. 3 (see Theologische Quartelschrift), on Gnosticism, i. 367 n. 1.

Momenta of Inspiration, i. 54.

GENERAL INDEX. 151

Monachism, i. 39, 274 n. 1, see Essenes, Therapeutæ.
Its origin, ii. 262–284. Criticism of, in the East, 284–293, 504, 505. In the West, 293–300. Different tendencies, 260, 300–314, 633. Patrick, 149 and n. 2. Mysticism in Oriental, 615. Pelagianism, 632. Morality of, 634. Jerome, 744.
History of, in the Third and Fourth Periods. Favored by Gregory the Great, iii. 15, 141, 149. In Ireland, 29; (ii. 149). Its decline in France, 30. Revived by Columban, 30, 31. Restrictions against, in the Frankish empire, 97. Its influence in the Greek church, 169, 414–424. Corruption of, 414, 416. Reforms of, 414–424. Resistance to despotism in the East, 536, 537. See Monks.
History of, in the Fifth Period, iv. 232–292. Gilbert on, 78. Gregory VII. on, 91. Monachism and the crusades, 126, 127. Enthusiasm for, Bernard on, 155, 258, 371. Gerhoh on, 205, Joachim, 220, 228. Reformatory influence, 232, 233, 318 (v. 171). Motives for entering the monastic life (ii. 356), iv 233–238, 358, 374, 514 (v. 177). Causes of corruption in, 234, 242, 243. Dangers of, 239–244. Lull on, 310. In the Greek church, 528–530, 532. Eastern and Western compared, 528. Evangelical poverty, 593 (see Mendicants). Wicklif on, v. 142, 143, 171, 172. Conrad, v. 186–191. Janow, v. 210, 213. See Asceticism, Monastic Orders, Monks.
Monachus Sangalli.

Gesta Caroli M., l. i. c. 20, iii. 133 n. 3.

Monad, i. 449, 450, 595, 596 n. 5, 598–601.
Monarchians, monarchy in the doctrine concerning God, i. 575–586, 588, 590–606, 608–610, 680; ii. 403, 405, 411 n. 1, 482, 777.
Monarchy, in the church, i. 183, 185, 190–193, 222.
Monasteria, ii. 271.
Monasteries, as a means of Christian education, iii. 10, 23, 29, 30, 73, 126 152, 273, 277, 415, 468, 472; iv. 62, 238, 249, 287, 532. Of reclaiming the wilderness, iii. 29, 30, 37, 53, 106, 273. In Ireland, ii. 149; iii. 10, 29 (see Ireland). Enriched by gifts, etc., iii. 9, 106; iv. 529, 530. Property, use of, ii. 272, 283. Confiscated, iii. 55. Wasted, iii. 414, 416; iv. 234. Hoarded, iv. 364. Temples converted into, iii. 41. Founding of, iii. 141, 273, 322, 330, 420; iv. 5, 65 (see particular Monasteries). Location of, iii. 36, 53. Privileges, iii. 75, 370 n. 4. Destroyed, iii. 84; (in Hamburg), iii. 278; (in England), iii. 467. Freeing of bondsmen, iii. 415. Ignorance in, iii. 468, 469 n. 5. Independence of, iv. 98. Immorality in, iv. 201. Worldliness of, iv. 244, 529, 530. Centres of arts, iv. 239. Of beneficence, ii. 272; iv. 239, 254. Decoration of, iv. 252. Poverty of Cistercian, iv. 252. Splendor of, iv. 264, 291. And the mendicant orders, iv 276. As reformatories, iv. 299. Plundered, v. 54. Decay of, 123. See Particular monasteries.
Monastic consecration as a sacrament, ii. 725.
Monastic orders, Benedictine, ii. 296–300, 283 n. 2, 287 n. 1 (reformed), iii. 415, 416. Camaldulensian, iii. 419. Carmelite, iv. 266. Carthusian, iv. 264, 265. Cistercian (see Cistercian). Cluniacensian, iii. 417, 418, 419; iv. 249-251, 263, 264. Dominican, iv. 268–270. Franciscan, iv. 270–276 (Minorites, order of Clara, Tertiarii, or Fratres pœnitentii, 276). Pauperes Christi, iv. 247. Premonstratensian, iv. 244–246. Trinitarians, iv. 267, 268. See Dominicans, Franciscans, Mendicants, Preaching Orders.
Monastic rules, ii. 287 and n. 1 (see Basil, Benedict, Francis). Of Columban, iii. 30, 31 nn.; 32 and notes.
Monastic Societies, iv. 244–247. See Monastic Orders.
Monasticism, i. 480. See Monachism.
Mone.

Anzeiger für Kunde der Teutschen Vorzeit Jahrgang, 1837, p. 72, sermons of Eckhart, v. 304 n. 4.

Moneta (Dominican), on the Catharists, iv. 566 n. 1. Birth of Cain, 573 n. 1.

Citations from his work, Adversus Catharos et Waldenses, iii. 597 n. 2; iv. 567-579 nn., 583, n. 4, 589 n. 2.

Money, accumulation of, v. 2 n. 1. See Contributions, Mints.
Mongols, Mongolian empire, iv. 48–56. Relation to Christianity and Mohammedanism, 48–59, 221 n. Joachim, 221 n. See Tartary.
Monica, mother of Augustin, ii. 239, 262, 317, 396, 754.
Monism, Platonic, i. 375, 391. Neo-Platonic, of Plotinus, 391, 392. In Gnosticism, 375, 438, 489 In Mani, 481. In Buddhism, 482. In Parsism, 489. Augustin, ii. 398. Of Scotus, iv. 444. Of Aquinas, iv. 445, 480. Of Almaric, David of Dinanto and others, iv. 446–449, 474, 566. Lull, 481. See Pantheism.
Monks, in the second period, fanatical, ii. 95 and nn. 1, 4, 5. Julian and the, 111. Extend the Gospel, 124, 142. Called Nazarenes, 120 n. 3. Attachment to Rome, 148. Irish, 149. Pretended, among the Goths, 157. Care of benevolent institutions, 169 n. 2. Societies of, 183. Basil, 186 n. 1. Judged

by a separate religious standard, 259. Cared for by women, 262. Egyptian, 270–276, 283, 289, 513–515, 583, 585, 741, 751–754. Pambo on, 355 n. 1. In the Nestorian controversy, 513–515, 524 n. 1, 527. 535, 536, 539, 540, 555. In the Eutychian controversy, 560–564, 570. In the Monophysite controversy, 583, 585. In the Pelagian controversy, 644. In the Origenistic disputes, 741, 751–758, 764. Worldly, 755. From Spain, 775 n. 6. Differing characters of, 633. See Monachism.

In the Third and Fourth Periods. Monks as teachers and missionaries, iii. 4, 10–38, 46, 51, 53, 70, 73, 89, 106, 272, 274, 275, 277, 300 n. 1, 323 n. 3, 331, 332, 334. Opponents of, 86, 221, 536 n. 1. Oriental, their principle to hold no persons as slaves, 99. Rising estimation of, 106, 223. Intercessions (see Intercessiones). Artists, 201, 308, 547. Their resistance to the iconoclasts, 219, 220, 223–225, 232, 536–538, 540–542, 548, 549. Paulician, 252. Irish, 300 n. 1, 306 n. 3. Employed in negotiations, 335. Promote the papacy, 369, 373. Euchites, 590. Extravagance of fanatical monkish asceticism in Italy, longevity, 418.

In the Fifth Period. As missionaries, iv. 1, 2, 5 and n. 3, 36, 37, 39, 43, 49, 50, 56, 57, 59, 60, 62. Vagabond, 44. Preachers of repentance, 97, 238, 243, 276–282 (see Mendicants). In the crusades, spiritual order of knights, 126, 127. Allies of the popes, 97, 98, 168, 180, 280, 281, 640. Exemptions, 201, 202. Joachim, 220, 225, 228. Menial employments of, iv. 233. Degeneracy in the older orders, 278 and n. 2. Respect for, 294. Sale of relics, 330. Doctrine of immaculate conception with the, 331. Of the Trinity, 333. Low morals among, 374. Hostility to reform, 374, 382, 383. Hugo's rules of study for, 401. Classes of in the East, 529 and n. 2. Hypocrisy, etc., 529, 530 n. 1. Persecuted, 539. Bogomiles among, 559–564. Dolcino, 635. Inquisitors, 640, 643.

In the Sixth Period. Mysticism among the, v. 42. Vagabond, at Rome, 52. At Oxford, 135, 136. At Avignon, 136. And pious laity, 213, 216, 217. See Manual labor, Mendicants, Monachism, Scholastics.

Monogenes, Valentine, i. 418, 423, 549.
Monogram of Christ, ii. 10, 13 n. 1, 24 n. 4.
Monophysite controversy, ii. 583–589, 581 n. 1, 583 n. 1. Monophysite party favored by the Mohammedans, iii. 88.
Monophysitism, ii. 583–589, 484 n. 1, 542. Monophysites as separate churches, ii. 611–616; iii. 197. Severus, ii. 279 n. 1.

Third Period. In Egypt, iii. 88 and n. 4, 228. In the Greek church, 169, 176–180, 228. In the Armenian church, 261 and n. 4. See Gobarus.
Monotheism, Hadrian on, i. 103. Of Ebionites, i. 347. In India, i. 442. Apelles on, i. 475, 476. Relation to Monarchianism, i. 576. Constantine, ii. 21, 29. Julian, ii. 51, 53. From the position of Parsism, ii. 127. Among the Arabs, iii. 84. With Mohammed, iii. 85, 87. Of the Mongols, iv. 48, 55.
Monotheletic controversies, iii. 175–197, 198, 171. Internal and external causes of the same, 175. Dogmatic interests of the Monotheletic party, 178.
Monotheletism, its approximation to Docetism, iii. 182 n. 2. Condemnation of it, 195. Its supremacy under Phillippicus, 196, 203 n. 3. Among the Maronites, 197.
Montacute (Richard Montague), bp. of Norwich.
Letters of Photius, iii. 309 n. 1, 530 n. 2, 550 nn. 1, 5. See Photius.

Montanism, Montanists, i. 206, 508–527, 715. General characteristics, 508–513, Doctrine of church development, 511, 512, 515–519 (ii. 210, 211). Doctrine of inspiration, of the Holy Spirit, 514–519, 680. Female prophets, 182, 514, 515, 520. Asceticism, resistance of the evangelical spirit to them, 280, 294, 520–523. Figures of Christ, 292 n. 3. Baptism of heretics, 318, 320 n. 6. Chiliasm, 513, 515, 523 (see Chiliasm). External history, 513, 514. On martyrdom, 521, 523. Views of marriage, 521, 522 (ii. 180). Absolution, 522. Position of the church towards Montanism, 517, 519, 520, 524–527, 651, 676. Ultra Anti-Montanists, 682. Clement, 525, 610. Origen, 544. Art, 565 and n. 3. On grace, 614, 619. Tertullian, 616, 683–685. His importance, 509 (see Tertullian). Athenagoras, 673. Irenæus, 677–679. Ordination of deaconesses, ii. 190 n. 4. Results in North Africa, ii. 217. Leo the Isaurian and the, iii. 202. Abelard on, iv. 375. See Praxeas.
Montanus, his importance as the founder of a sect, i. 509, 516. Life and character, 513, 514. Pepuza, 523.

Apud Epiphan. hæres., 48, oracular saying on inspiration, i. 515 n. 1 (2).

Monte Cassino, monastery, ii. 298, 553 n. 3; iii. 75, 79, 126, 375 n. 4, 384 n. 4, 387, 519, 579; iv. 85 n. 1, 121, 421.
Montenses, Donatists at Rome, i. 233 n. 3.
Montfançon, ii. 327 n. 6.

Collectio nova patrum. T. ii. f. 521, Euseb Comm. in Jesaiam, ii. 142 n. 3. See Cosmas Indicopleustes, Chrysostom.

GENERAL INDEX. 153

Montfort, sect there, iii. 600. Its doctrines, 601.
Montpellier, iii. 414; iv. 65, 269, 321, 436.
Montreal, conference at, iv. 641. See Nicole Viguier.
Monumenta eccles. Græc. See Cateler.
Monumenta res Allemann. illust. See Blas.
Moon, worship of the, ii. 104, 105. With the Catharists, iv. 572.
Mopsuestia. See Meletius, Theodore.
Moral element, preserving power of the, v. 402, 404.
Moral government of the world, iii. 130.
Moral systems, in Gnosticism, i. 377, 378, 384–386, 439 (Plotinus on, 393); Isidorus, 415; Basilides, 415, 416; Ptolemæus, 439, 440; Tatian, 457; Marcion, 468, 472. In Platonism, 378, 379. In Manicheism, 505. In Montanism, 514, 517, 520–523. Christian, 631, 632, 644, 645, 685, 686, 695, 714. Connection of the doctrine of creation with, 467, 472, 564, 565; of faith, ii. 121, 122, 385, 386, 634, 767. Jovinian, ii. 311. Relation of doctrine to, ii. 385, 386; iv. 434, 435. Pelagian system, ii. 634–638 (666, 676, 679, 681, 682). Of Augustin, ii. 666–668, 679–683, 779. Quantitative morality, ii. 634, 667; iii. 148. Priscillianists, ii. 778. Of Gregory the Great, iii. 148–150. Paulician, iii. 259, 266, 267. Of Abelard, iv. 384, 386–390, 398, 399. Of the scholastics, iv. 488, 519–528. Teleology and morals, iv. 466. Theology and, iv. 519. Catharists, iv. 579. Gerson, v. 95, 96. Janow, v. 205, 212. Huss, v. 350, 351. Tauler, v. 408. See Antinomians, Ethics, Morality, Sin, Virtue.
Morality, relation of the Greek and Roman religions to, i. 6. Of Judaism, 59. Christian, 76, 98, 175, 250, 254, 328 n. 4, 673; ii. 113, 114. Natural, i. 354, 669. In Gnosticism, i. 384, 393, 448, 450–454. Pagan, ii. 66 and n. 2, 115, 637; iii. 45 (see Virtue). Relation of faith and, ii. 121, 122. Penance and, ii. 216. In Monasticism, ii. 300, 301, 634. Efforts of missionaries in behalf of, iii. 21, 23, 32, 33, 36, 42, 52, 53, 55, 58 n. 1. Effect of pilgrimages to Rome on, iii. 57, 58 n. 1, 118. Alcuin on, iii. 77 n. 2. Sends, iii. 108. Outward, iii. 130, 131 (see Works). Of Paulicians, iii. 259, 265–267. Photius on, iii. 308, 309. At Rome (10th cent.), iii. 366, 367 and n. 2. Celibacy and, iii. 411 n. 7. Low state of, iii. 414, 416, 422, 441; iv. 304. Of the Nestorian clergy, iv. 52. Of the clergy, iv. 205, 206 (see Clergy). Militz, v. 178. See Asceticism, Christian life, Corruption, Good works, Love, Moral systems, Preachers of repentance.
Moravia, spread of Christianity in, iii. 315–321. Hungarians in, 330. Militz,

v. 174. Heresies in, v. 102, 316, 371 and n. 2, 376.
Morawa, iii. 318 n. 1.
Moriu.
De pœnitentia, ii. 216 n. 1.
Moritz, bp. of Paris, iv. 325.
Morocco, iv. 273.
Mortification, self, ii. 291, 292; iii. 287; iv. 239, 241, 249, 250, 264, 273, 314, 529; v. 388, 399, 407.
Mosaic law, i. 65. Among the Jewish Christians, 341–344, 349, 351, 352. In the Clementines, 354 n. 6, 355. Among Gentile Christians, 362, 363. In Gnosticism, 380, 381 n. 1, 397, 399, 439, 440, 468. Barnabas, 657. And image worship, iii. 202, 204, 207. Abelard, iv. 384. Bogomiles, iv. 553. Pasagians, iv. 590. And the papacy, v. 38, 39.
Mosaic work, iii. 232.
Mosburg, iii. 316.
Moses, with the Essenes, i. 49. Philo, 51. Clementines, 355, 358–360, 395. Gnostics, 395, 404, 407. Wish of, 179 (v. 219). Song of, i 409 n. 2. Polity of, 439. And Greek philosophy, 666, 667 n. 1. With Julian, ii. 54–56. Mohammed, iii. 86. Nilus, iii. 422. Learning of, iii. 150 n. 7; v. 262. Example of, iv. 136, 157; v. 262. Frederic II., iv. 179. Bogomiles, iv. 554. Catharists, iv. 568, 573, 574.
Moses, monk, ii. 242.
Moses of Chorene, his History of Armenia, ii. 138.

L. ii. cc. 77, 88, ii. 136 n. 3; c. 83, 138 n. 3, 139 n. 1. L. iii. cc. 47, 52, 137 n. 1.

Mosheim.
On Novatus, i. 242 n. 1. Commentationes, etc., Apolog. of Athenagoras, i. 673 n. 1. The Apostolicals, iv. 628 n. 1. Hist. Eccles. Tartarorum, Letters of Monte Corvino, iv. 57 n. 3 (App. N. III.); Chinese-Syrian inscription, iii. 80 n. 5. Quotations from Salembenus, iv. 629 n. 3.

Moslesme, forest of, iv. 251, 252.
Mother of life, Æon, with Mani, i. 491.
Mothers, Christian, influence of, i. 78; ii. 7, 85, 239, 261, 262, 396, 754; iii. 6, 282; iv. 233, 234, 249, 250, 252, 253, 295, 300, 301, 361, 422. Heathen, iv. 8. Mother of Marcus Aurelius, i. 106.
Motives, imputation of, i. 224 n. 1, 241, 242. See Intention.
Mount Lebanon, ii. 80.
Mountains, iv. 361.
Mourning for the dead, i. 333.
Moustier en Tarantaise, iv. 213.
Moymar, Moravian prince, iii. 316.
Mueuscher.
On J. Martyr's "Dialogue," i. 668 n. 3.

Mufti, iv. 68.
Mulieres prefecæ, i. 333.
Müller, J. von, Reisen der Päpste, iv. 197 n. 4.

Mundane soul, with Plato, i. 376, 380. Valentine, 423. The Ophites, 443–446. Mani, 491–496. Origen, 624.

Mundus intelligibilis, with Augustin, ii. 399 n. 2. Abelard, iv. 467.

Munich. See Libraries.

Münster, in Westphalia, monastery at, iii. 79. Ecclesiastic of, iii. 72 n. 4.

Münsterdorf. See Welanno.

Münter.

Fragmenta patrum Graecorum, fascic. i., Theodore's work against Julian, ii. 494 n. 1.

Münter.

Geschichte der Einführung des Christenthums in Dänemark u. Norweg., Bd. i. s. 520, Iceland, iii. 300 n. 1; s. 523, 304 n. 1; s. 558, Greenland, 307 n. 2; s. 561, John, missionary to America, 307 n. 3.

Muratori.

Anecdota (from the Ambrosian library, Mediolan., 1698). T. ii., confession of Bachiarius, ii. 775 n. 6; p. 112, old form of condemnation against sects, ii. 769 n. 6.

Anecdota Graeca (Patav., 1709), p. 92, Epigrams of Greg. Nazianz., ii. 262 n. 1; p. 332 (ed. Heyler, p. 134), rescript of Julian, ii. 65 n. 2; p. 334, Julian's letter to Arsaces, ii. 86 n. 3.

Antiquitates Ital. med. aev. L. i. (fol. ed.), Benvenuto of Imola, Comm. on Dante, iv. 629 nn. 4, 5; t. v., acts relating to Punzilovo, iv. 589 n. 1; f. 131, the same, 584 n. 1; f. 151, G. of Bergamo, on the Pasagians, iv. 590 n. 7.

Scriptores. rerum Ital. T. iv., Landulph the elder (l. iii. c. 23, etc.), iii. 397 n. 2; f. 29, Arnulph's Hist. Mediolan. (l. ii. c. 27), iii. 600 n. 3; f. 29 (l. iii. c. 12), iii. 389 n. 3; f. 403, Chronicon. Casinense, iii. 386 n. 6; f. 502, Landulph Jun. Hist. Mediolan., c. 30, iv. 203 n. 3. T. vii. ff. 360, 361, Pantheon of Gottfried of Viterbo (p. xvi.), iv. 172 n. 1, 215 n. 3. T. ix., Hist. Dolcini, iv. 629 n. 2, 633 n. 2, 636 n. 3, 637 n. 1; f. 436, 631 n. 1. Additamentum ad Hist. Dolcini, iv. 629 n. 2, 632 n. 3, 636 n. 3; f. 448, 628 n. 3; f. 450, 629 n. 1; f. 456, 635 n. 1; f. 457, 631 n. 3, 635 n. 3, 636 n. 2; f. 826, Chronicle of Parma, iv. 626 n. 4. T. xiii., Boniface VIII., v. 2 n. T. xix. f. 928 C, D, Aretini Commentarius, v. 100 nn. 2, 3. Vita Stephani, p. 482, Trullan Council, iii. 193 n. 2.

Murder, Christian view of, iii. 103. Punishment of, iii. 103, 137, 140.

Mursa, Valens of, ii. 449.

Music, i. 61; ii. 78. The Euchites, ii. 279. Schools of, iii. 128, 419. Ethelwold instructs in, iii. 408 n. 1. See Church music, Song.

Scriptores. eccles. de Musica (ed. Gerbert. 1784). T. i. p. 3, Pambo, ii. 355 n. 1.

Muson (Mosomense), council at, iii. 373 and notes.

Musonianus, ii. 16 n. 3, 769.

Μυστήριον, ii. 723, 725.

Mutilation, i. 114.

Mysteries, pagan, Demonax on the, i. 10. Philo, 52, 58. Hadrian, 101. Taste for tracing analogies with, 307 and n 1, 308. Conception of, transferred to the Lord's Supper, 327 n. 1, 328, 329; ii. 723, 725. In Gnosticism, i. 384, 389, 446, 448. Tatian on, i. 672. Traffic in, ii. 39. Brought into contempt, ii. 97.

Mysteries of faith, ii. 725; iv. 416; (the mystery, with Paul), i. 572. Huss on, v. 337.

Mystical element, i. 385. In Christianity, i. 64, 581; iv. 446, 447. In the system of the Alexandrian Jews, i. 64, 66, 394. In Manicheism, i. 493, 502, 503. In the Monophysites, ii. 614–616. Opposition to the, ii. 445–447. See Francis of Assisi, Mystical writings, Mystics, etc.

Mystical interpretation. See Interpretation.

Mystical sects, i. 44–49, 352, 362, 394, 399; iii. 590, 593, 594, 600, 601; iv. 557. See Bogomiles, Catharists, Euchites, Friends of God.

Mystical symbolism, ii. 388, 723 n. 1.

Mystical table, i. 477.

Mystical tendency, ii. 502; iii. 170, 463, 590, 593; iv. 275, 283, 371–373, 410, 563. Relation to the dialectic, iv. 411–413, 419, 421. In the Greek church, iv. 552–561.

Mystical theology, ii. 740 n. 3; iv. 220, 227, 231, 232, 411, 421.

Mystical writers, writings, iv. 411–413, 421, 447, 516–518. In the vernacular, iv. 447; v. 401. See Dionysian writings, Maximus, Richard of St. Victor.

Mysticism, characteristic position of, i. 39; iv. 231, 561. Fruits of, i. 46; iv. 407. Neo-Platonic, i. 27; ii. 27. In Christianity, i. 64. Jacobi on Christian, ii. 123 n. 1. In Monachism, ii. 276–282 (see Euchites). Of Adalbert, iii. 58, 59. Maximus, iii. 171–175. In Germany, v. 381. One sided, v. 398. See Mystics, Mystical sects, writings, etc., Pantheism.

Mystico-ascetic spirit in Ebionitism, i. 352, 362 (see Monachism, ii. 262–271, 273–283; iv. 239). Mystico-contemplative element, iv. 401. Mystico-dialectic, iv. 419. Mystico-rationalistic, i. 64. Mystico-theurgical, ii. 723.

Mystics, iv. 305, 411–413. Chrysomalos, 561, 562. Niphon, 563. Principle of obedience, v. 360. See Friends of God, Mysticism.

Mythical faith, i. 368. Doctrines, i. 502. Personifications, i. 509 n. See Interpretation.

Mythology, Myths, i. 78. Polybius on, i. 6. Strabo on, Greek, i. 7. Aristotle, 7 n. 1. Pausanius, 12. Plutarch, 23. Dionysius of Halicarnassus, 29. Ebionites, 347. Interpretation of, 16, 171. Hindoo, 386 n. 1. Pagan, in Mani, 493. Julian on the, ii. 54. Mixed up with Christian legends, ii. 371. Historical facts converted into, ii. 389. Christian, iii. 282 n. 3. See Legends.

N.

Nacolia, iii. 203, 205.
Nalgod.
  Life of Majolus, iii. 418 nn. 1, 2.
Nantes, iv. 373.
Naples, Neapolitan, iii. 28 n. 2, 541 n. 3; iv. 67, 193; v. 50, 51, 73. Bp. of, iii. 13 n. 1. University at, iv. 421, 422.
Narbonne, iii. 167. See Yves of.
Νάρθηξ, ii. 213, 321 n. 1.
Nas, Doctor, v. 272, 288 n. 2.
Natales. See Dies.
Natalis, bp. of Salona, iii. 114, 115.
Natalis, the Theodotian, confessor, i. 580.
Natalitia ecclesiæ et episcopatus, ii. 372 n. 2. Martyrum, i. 334 and n. 3.
Nathaniel, i. 382 n.; ii. 497.
National characteristics, Julian on, ii. 51. Themistius, 158, 159.
National customs, v. 92. Nations, rise and fall of, i. 5.
National religion, ii. 51-54, 107, 117.
Native teachers, i. 79 (iv 58). See Missionaries, schools for.
Natural and divine, i. 292. See Nature.
Naturalistic views, i. 570; iv. 181.
Nature, M. Aurelius on, i. 17. Deification of, i. 26. Relation of. to man, i. 65 and n. 2. To the Christian, i 329. Of God to, i. 570. Gnostic view of, i. 330, 369, 370, 379, 383, 384, 394, 462 (Basilides, i. 405, 406. Epiphanes, 450). In Manicheism, i. 480, 490, 492-494, 497, 503. In Pantheistic dualism (Buddhism), i. 481. Christianity and, i. 372, 536; v. 166. Tertullian on, i. 536, 559. Miracles and, i. 570. Julian and, ii. 48, 51. Redemption from, ii. 115 (see Parsism). Heraclitus on, ii. 117. Meaning of the term in relation to Christ, ii. 614. Nature and grace (Hilary), ii. 619; (Ambrose), 622; (Augustin), 624, 625; (Theodore), 713-718. State of, iv. 11. Feelings of, iv. 250. Bernard, iv. 259. Francis, iv. 275. Moral law and, iv. 384. Manifoldness of, iv. 479. Laws of, i. 406, 450, 570; v. 136. And history, v. 380. Tauler on, v. 409. See Nature and the supernatural.
Nature, human, i. 75, 369. Natural and supernatural in relation to, iv. 485-492, 495. Dona naturalia and superaddita, iv. 522; v. 26. Bona naturalia and gratuita, iv. 487, 495. Pura natura in, iv. 488-490, 491, 522, 528. Grace and, iv. 552 (see Grace, Nature). Change of, iv. 561 (see Regeneration). Higher and lower, iv. 562. With the Catharists, iv. 567. Doctrine of, see Anthropology.
Nature and the supernatural, i. 507, 570. Augustin on, ii. 476, 477; and the Pelagians, ii. 664, 672. Apollinaris, ii 485. Maximus, iii. 173, 174. Scholastics, iv.

378, 420, 467-474. See Human nature.
Nature-religion, i. 4. Esthetic position of, 35. Relation to Christianity, 176 and notes, 347, 462, 467, 479. To Judaism, 347. In Phrygia, 513. Necessity in, 570.
Naugard, iv. 16 n. 5.
Naum, disciple of Methodius, iii. 320 n. 2.
Naumberg, bishopric, iii. 324. See Waltram.
Navarre, Collegium of, v. 53.
Nave, ii. 321 n. 2.
Naxos, iii. 189.
Nazareans, i. 376 n. 3.
Nazarenes, i. 346, 349, 350. Name applied to monks in the East, ii. 129 n. 3. Gospel of the (see Gospel). See Paul, Sects.
Nazareth, bp. of, inquisitor, v. 317.
Nazarites, iii. 106 n. 1.
Nazarius, bp. of the Catharists, iv. 566.
Nazarius, preaches in Milan against the corruption of morals, iii. 391, 392.
Nazarius, rhetorician, ii. 11.
  Panegyr. in Const., ii. 11 n. 3.
Nazianz, ii. 462, 463, 465. See Gregory Nazianzen.
Neander, A.
  Apostol. Zeitalter, Bd. i. s. 169, et seq., i. 342 n. 2; s. 304, et seq., i. 340 n. 1; s. 384, et seq., i. 395 n. 2. Bd. ii. s. 532, et seq., i. 840 n. 2; s. 558, i. 483 n. 2. Chrysostom, Bd. i. s. 376, et seq., iii. 98 n. 2. Denkwürdigkeiten, Bd. ii. s. 253, iii. 98 n. 3. Dissertation on the Paschal Supper (see Vater), i. 208 n. 1. Genetische Entwickelung der Gnostische systeme, i. 447 n. 2; ss. 125, 205, iii. 86 n. 1; s. 149, i. 430 n. 1; s. 205, i. 422 n. 2. Kleine Gelegenheitschriften, s. 223, v. 193 n. 2. Monograph on Tertullian, iii. 684 n. 2. Planting and training, Bd. i., i. 81 nn. 1, 2, 185 n. 3, 186 n. 1, 187 n. 3, 210 n., 290 n. 2, 294 n. 1, 295 n. 1, 302 n. 2, 310 n. 2, 311 nn. 1, 2, 316 n. 2, 325 n. 1; iii. 467 n. 1, 557 n. 6. Bd. ii., i. 191 n. 1, 212 n.
Neapolis. See Leontius.
Nebridius, abp. of Lyons, iii. 416.
Nebuchadnezzar, dream of, v. 35.
Necessity, in nature, with the Gnostics, i. 383 (Basilides on, i. 404). Neo-Platonic doctrine, i. 406. With Hermogenes, i. 566. In nature-religion, 570. Origen on, i. 589 and n. 3, 590, 637, 638 n. 4. Of evil, in Stoicism, i. 611. Proclus, ii. 106. Augustin, 626, 684. Scotus on necessity, iii. 485. "De Causis," iv. 445. Lull, iv. 483. Unconditioned and conditioned, iv. 476. Moral, iv. 495. Of evil, iv. 508. In redemption, iv. 508. In God, iv. 453-455, 461, 465, 478; v. 167, 168.
Nechites (Nicetas), abp. of Nicomedia, iv. 536-538.
  Dispute with Anselm of Havelburg, ignorance of the Latins, 587 nn. 3, 4. Authority of the pope, 538 n. 2. See D'Achery, t. i.
Necromancy, i. 116; iv. 594.

Nectarius, patriarch of Constantinople, ii. 216.
Nefridius, bp. of Narbonne, iii. 167.
Negran, persecution there, ii. 145.
Neitra, iii. 318, 319.
Neo-Cæsarea, the church there on Monachism, ii. 293 n. 5. Bp. of, iii. 256. See Councils, an. 314.
Neo-Platonism, i. 19–35, 160, 161. Two stages in religion and worship, 25–29. The supreme essence, the absolute, 26, 27, 391, 417, 418, 589. Mysticism, 27, 308. Demons, 28. Aristocratic spirit, 29, 34. Relation to Christianity, 30–35, 160, 308; ii. 122, 123. With Porphyry, 170. Mundane soul, 376. In Gnosticism, 375, 379, 406, 417, 418. With Clement, 532, 586, 587. With Origen, 571, 589 (see Platonism). In Asia Minor, ii. 39, 44. With Julian, ii. 44, 59, 62. Victorinus, ii. 77. At Alexandria, ii. 97. Proclus, ii. 105, 106, 117. At Athens, ii. 106 n. 2. In the Pseudo-Dionysian writings and Scotus, iii. 170, 461 and n. 2, 466, 467; iv. 420, 444. In the Aristotelian philosophy, iv. 420. Translations of Neo-Platonic writings, iv. 420, 444. In the book "De Causis," iv. 445 and n. 1. Almaric, iv. 449. Influence in Christian theism, iv. 444, 449. Ethics, iv. 520, 523. See Platonism, Plotinus, Simplicius.
Nepos, Egyptian bp., Chiliast, i. 652, 653.
Nepotism, iv. 169 n. 4, 207; v. 3, 9, 21, 34, 36 n. 1, 40, 51, 77, 122.
Nequinta, pope of the Catharists, iv. 590.
Nero, persecution under, i. 94–96, 664. St. Paul and, iii. 83; iv. 172. Simon Magus, iv. 226. St. Peter, v. 304.
Nersetes Clajensis.
> Opera (vol. i. p. 40). Armenian fire-worship, iii. 589 n. 1.

Nerva, i. 96, 97, 99.
Nestor, Russian monk.
> Annals of (Schlozer's trans.). Vladimir, iii. 329 n. 1. Vol. iii., p. 171, Methodius, 308 n. 1. Vol. iv., p. 95, treaty of peace between Russia and the Greek empire, 327 n. 4; p. 99, ch at Kiew, 328 n. 1. Vol. v., pp. 60, 106, Olga, 328 nn. 3, 4.

Nestorian controversy, ii. 504–555, 557 n. 7, 563, 566, 598, 712; iii. 158, 170.
Nestorian schools, ii. 183 n., 610, 611.
Nestorianism, ii. 555, 556. And Pelagianism, ii. 495 n. 2. Dioscurus on, ii. 559, 562. Eutyches, 567. In the Eutychian controversy, 561, 562, 568 n. 2, 581, 582. Zeno's Henoticon, 588. Severus, 590. In Persia, 610, 611 (see Controversy of the Three Chapters). Columban, iii. 34 n. 2. In Adoptianism, iii. 157 n. 1, 163. Honorius, iii. 179. Martin I., iii. 187 n. In the image controversy, iii. 215, 218, 222.
Nestorians, history of the, ii. 554, 555, 610, 611. Leontius against the, ii. 583 n. 1. Catholics forced to become, iii. 84. Active in promoting the spread of Christianity, iii. 89, 90; iv. 45–48. Favored by Mohammedans, iii. 88; iv. 56. Among the Mongols, iv. 51, 52, 54, 56–59.
Nestorius, patriarch of Constantinople, history of, ii. 504–554, 164 n. 3, 184. Anthropology of, 720, 721. Cassian against, 688 n. 3.
> Ep. to Cyrill, ii. 511 n. 5. Ep. 3, to Cyrill, 516 n. 3. Ep. to the patriarch John, 522. Ep. to the prefect of Thebais, 552, 553 n. 1. Epp. to Coelestin, 721. Tragedy, 553. Sermons, 720 n. 4 (see Chrysostom). S. i., 507 n. 2. S. ii., 506 n. 2, 511 n. 1. S. iv., 720 n. 4. S. v., 510 n., 511 n. 2. See Harduin, Lupus, Maii, Mansi Concil., Marius Mercator.

Netherlands, Christianity in the, iii. 40, 43, 44, 45, 65, 71–73. Sects in, iii. 603. Students from the, iv. 357, 373. Friends of God, v. 381.
Netze, river, iv. 7.
Neumann, C. F.
> Memoires sur la vie et les ouvrages de David, ii. 613 n. 1.

Neumann, Prof.
> Trans. Esnig. (see Illgen's Zeitschrift), i. 463 n. 3; iii. 257 n. 4.

Neumünster, iv. 34 n.
New birth, the, ii. 617. See Regeneration.
New Platonism. See Neo-Platonism.
New Rome, ii. 197.
New Testament, Coptic version, i. 83. Bishops and presbyters in the, i. 188. With the Gnostics, i. 387–389. Marcion, i. 473. With the Manicheans, i. 502. Doctrine of creation, i. 565. Revisions of the. i. 582 and n. 2, 708 n. 4, 722 n. 6. Origen on the, i. 556. Read in churches. i. 658. Study of the, i. 688. With Julian, ii 41. Syrian translation, 589. In the image controversy, iii. 201, 203. With the Paulicians, iii. 245, 246, 247, 266, 269. Influence of, iii. 403, 431. Servatus Lupus, iii. 483. Relation to the old, iv. 405; v. 26, 39. With the Catharists, iv. 584, 587 n. 5. Henry of Cluny, iv. 597, 602. Waldenses, iv. 609. Dolcino, iv. 630. Wicklif on the, v. 151, 173, 242. Militz, v. 178, 235. See Old and New Testaments.
New Year's festival, ii. 350, 351; iii. 64, 134.
Newman, Prof. See Elisæus.
Nice (in Bithynia), residence of the Greek emperors at, iv. 539, 542. Council of (see Councils, an. 325). Council of Chalcedon first assembled at (see Councils, an. 451). Second council of Nice (see Councils, an. 787). Bp. of, iii. 229 n. 3. See Nicene creed.
Nice (in Italy), v. 105, 106.
Nice (Nicæ, in Thrace), symbol of, ii. 454, 455.
Nicene creed, formation of the, ii. 415–422. Its subscription by Arius, 428 n.

4. Various forms of opposition to, 434, 435, 444, 473. With the Western bps., 434, 435. At Rimini, 453, 454. The three church teachers of Cappadocia, 459, 460, 463–466. Law of Theodosius in support of, 461, 462, 464. Confirmed at II. œc. conc. Const. with an additional clause relating to the Holy Spirit, 468, 469. Addition to, confirmed at Toledo, 471. Cyrill on the, 555. At the II. council of Ephesus, 568–572. Philostorgius on the, 140 n. 5. Frumentius, 144. Ulphilas, 157, 472, 473. With the rude nations, 471–473. Adherents of, persecuted by the Vandals, 238, 473. Writings of Origen and the, 740. Embraced by the Burgundians, iii. 5. Nicetas on the, iv. 537. See Arian Controversy, Semi-Arians, Councils at Antioch and Sardica, Ursacius and Valens.

Nicene-Constantinopolitan creed, ii. 466, 468, 585, 588; iii. 318 and n. 3, 554–556, 577.

Niceno-Ephesian creed, ii. 564, 570–572, 574 n. 1, 585, 588.

Nicephorus, Catenæ of. See Catenæ.

Nicephorus, Greek emperor, iii. 536 n. 2. Conduct towards the Paulicians, 254, 256.

Nicephorus, patriarch of Constantinople, the Paulicians, iii. 255. His controversy with Leo the Armenian on the abolition of images, 532–538. Deposed and banished, 539, 540. Return from exile, 543, 544. Emperor Nicephorus and, 536 n. 2. His origin, 533 n. 1. Life of, 533 n. 1. See Ignatius, deacon, and Acta S. March 13.

Nicephorus Blemmydes, Greek abbot, iv. 541–543, 546.

Nicephorus Callistus, tract by, iii. 315 n. 1.

Nicephorus Gregoras.

Hist. l. ii. c. 7, Blemmydes, iv. 542 n. 4; f. 795, ep. of Euseb. of Cæsarea to Constantin, ii. 326 n. 4. L. iii. c. i., n. 5. L. iv. c. 8, M. Paleologus, iv. 544 n. 1. L. v. c. 2, 2. 129, Beccus, iv. 545 n. 2.

Nicetas (Ignatius), iii. 558. See Ignatius.

Nicetas, abbot, friend of image worship, iii. 541. Life, 218 n. 1. See Theosterict and Acta S. April.

Nicetas, abp. of Nicomedia, ii. 383 r.

Nicetas, bp. of Athens.

Monodia on Eustathius, iv. 531 n. 1.

Nicetas, bp. of Chonæ (Colosse), iv. 530. Dogmatism of the emperors, 533, 534 n. 6.

Hist. Manuel Comnenus. L. ii. f. 106 (ed. Bekker), Cosmas, iv. 564 n. 2. L. vii. c. 3, f. 370, law of Phocas concerning monasteries, 530 n. 1; c. 5, dogmatism of emperors, 533 nn. 5, 8; c. 6, f. 276 et seq., controversy concerning the person of Christ, 534 nn. 3, 6; c. 6, oath prescribed to converts from Mohammedanism, 535 n. 1; edict against the same, n. 2.

Nicetas, bp. of Nicomedia. See Nechites.
Nicetas, ecclesiastic, iii 550.
Nicetas David, of Pophlagaria.

Life of Ignatius (Harduin, t. v.), iii. 532 n. 3, 541 n. 3, 549 n. 3, 558 n. 1, 560 n. 2, 561 nn. 1, 3, 563 n. 2, 564, 568 n. 3, 570 n. 3, 571 n. 2, 572 nn. On the deposition of Photius, 568 n. 3. See Harduin, t. v.

Nicetas Pectoratus, iii. 583.
Nicetius, bp. of Triers.

Ep. to Clodeswinde, iii. 8 n. 1.

Nicholas, bp of Methone, iv. 530.
Nicholas, English monk, iv. 331, 332.

On a progressive development of the church, iv. 332 n. 7. Ep. 9, sinlessness of Mary, 332 n. 3.

Nicholas, patriarch of Constantinople, iv. 560.

Nicholas I., pope, begins a new epoch of the papacy, iii. 353, 509 n. 2. His prescripts to the Bulgarians, iii. 310–314. Cyrill, 316 n. 4. His conduct towards Lothaire of Lotharingia, 353–358. Hinkmar of Rheims, 358–361. His principles for the foundation of the papal monarchy, 359–361. Letter of Ulric, 411. Against judgments of God, 450. Pilgrimages to Rome, 453. Dionysius the Areopagite, 467. Gottschalk, 479–481. On the Lord's Supper, 502 n. 2. His conduct in the controversy between Photius and Ignatius, 559 and n. 1, 561–569, 572, 574. Letters of, 566 n. 3.

Citations:—
Epp. 17 and 21, iii. 453 n. 1. Ep. 20, to Charles the Bald, 458 n. 1. Ep. 27, ad Ludovicum Germ., et Carol. Calvum, 353 n. 2, 356 n. 6. Ep. 30, ad Carol. Calvum, 360 n. 5. Ep. 32, ad Episc. Synod. Silvanectensis, 361 nn. 2, 3. Ep. 37, to Hinkmar, 356 n. 5. Ep. 55, to Lewis of Germany, 354 n. 3, 356 n. 6. Ep. to the Bulgarians, 309–314 nn. (iv. 90 n. 6). Ep. to Thietberga, 357. Ep. to Charles the Bald on the publication of books, 467 and notes 4–6. Ep. to Emp. Michael, 562 n. 2, 561 n. 3. Other epistles to Constantinople, 562 n. 3, 563 n. 1. For other epistles, see Harduin, t. v.

Nicholas II., pope, iii. 387, 388, 393, 395 and n. 2, 396 n. 1, 397. Berengar and, 512, 514. See Pertz.

Nicholas III., pope. Bulls of (an. 1297), on the Franciscan rule, iv. 291; (an. 1288), the Jews, 591 n. 2.

Nicholas IV., pope, the Apostolicals, iv. 628.

Nicholas V., pope, v. 36, 37.
Nicholas, protospatharius, iii. 421.
Nicholas de Baya, v. 114.
Nicholas de Pistorio, iv. 57.
Nicholas Eymericus, Dominican.

Directorium Inquisitionis, iv. 618 n. 1, 626 n. 3, 628 n. 2.

Nicholas Krebs (of Cusa), v. 130.
Nicholas Peraldus (Peraalt), archbishop of Lyons. Summa de virtutibus et vitiis, iv. 519 n. 2.

Nicholas of Basle, v. 390–392.
    Letter to the Strassburg Johannites, v. 392 nn. 1, 2.
Nicholas of Clemangis. See Clemangis.
Nicholas of Faulfisch, count, v. 243, 245 n. 4.
Nicholas of Leitomysl, v. 246.
Nicholas of Lyra, v. 149.
Nicholas of Welenowitz (Abraham), v. 250, 251.
Nicocles, teacher of Julian, ii. 41, 84 n. 6.
Nicodemus, conversation of Christ with, ii. 728–730; v. 325.
Nicolaitans, i. 452, 453. Name applied to priests living in wedlock, iii. 392 n. 2, 394; iv. 98 n. 2.
Nicolas, deacon, i. 452, 453.
Nicolaus, abbot, scholar of Theodore Studita, iii. 100, 542. Life of, 542 n. 2.
Nicolaus, bp. of Hierapolis in Phrygia, iii. 229 n. 3.
Nicolaus, pretended founder of a sect, i. 452, 453.
Nicole Vignier.
    Histoire de l'Eglise, protocol of the conference at Montreal (an. 1207), iv. 641 n. 2. See Usher.
Nicomedia, meeting of Diocletian and Galerius at, i. 145, 147. Edict against the Christians, 148, 149 n. 1. Conflagration at, 153. Pagans at, ii. 3, 4, 5, 8, 19, 42. Constantine near, ii. 30, 425, 426. Julian at, ii. 42, 43 n. 1, 44 n. 1. Arius at? ii. 422 n. 4. See Eusebius, Nicetas.
Nicopolis, iii. 256.
Niebuhr.
    On the dialogue Philopatris. ii. 111 n. Corpus Hist. Byzant., iii. 308 n. 3, 328 n. 3.
Nieder, John, Dominican, religious life of his times, v. 381.
    Formicarius, p. 133, lay piety, v. 381 nn.; p. 304, Nicholas of Basle, 392 n. 3.
Niem. See Theodoric of.
Nierses, ii. 612.
Nigellus Witeker, monk.
    Brunellus, or Speculum Stultorum; the Carthusians, iv. 265 n. 4.
Nihilism, i. 482 n. 1; ii. 276. See Nirwana.
Nile, river, ii. 98, 272.
Nilus, Greek monk, ii. 286. Peristera, 262. Temptations of monks, 273, 274. On continual prayer; the Euchites, 277, 279. Benefits of the monastic life, 286. Slaves, 287. Rude classes of men in the monasteries, 289. Works, 290. Suppression of natural feelings, 291. On spiritual pride, 293. Causes of opposition to monachism, 300. On the ornamentation of churches, 328. Doctrine of the Lord's Supper, 731, 732 n. 6. Letter read at conc. Const. an. 754, iii. 216 n. 3.

    Citations: —
    De monastica exercitatione, c. 9, worthless monks, ii. 300 n. 4, 301 n. 1; c. 21, against the employment of monks in agriculture, 287 n. 1; c. 22, rude monks, 289 n. 3, 301 n. 2. Epistles. L. i. ep. iii. 286 n. 3; ep. 44, 782 n. 6; ep. 295, 275 n. 2; ep. 326, 274 n. 2. L. ii. ep. 46, 286 n. 2; ep. 62, 272 n. 3; ep. 114, 293 n. 3; ep. 140, 273 n. 5; ep. 188–190, Origenistic opinions among monks, 764 nn. 1, 2; ep. 310, 285 n. 3. L. iii. ep. 224, 274 n. 4; ep. 284 (expos. Rom. 2: 15), 289 n. 3; ep. 290, 291 n. 2. L. iv. ep. 4, 287 n. 2; ep. 61, 328 nn. 2, 3. Opp. l. 111, f. 73, the hermit life, 283 n. 1. Peristera, c. 3, 262 nn. 2, 3; § 9, c 1 (f. 134), 287 n. 4; § 10, c. 6 (f. 165), 287 n. 3. Tractatus ad Magnam (opuscula, Romæ, 1673); c. 21, The Euchites, 277 nn. 4, 5; c. 22, 277 n. 6; c. 30, spirit of gain, among monks, 284 n. 2; c. 30 (f. 279), Jewish monks, 270 n. 4; f. 297, rude monks, 289 n. 2.

Nilus the younger, Greek monk, in Italy. His life, iii. 376, 420–424, 441, 579. His death, 424 n. 1. See Acta S. Sep.
Ninyas, among the Picts, iii. 10.
Niobes, — Niobites, ii. 613.
Niphon, monk, iv. 563 and n. 3, 564 and n. 2.
Nirwana, in Buddhism, i. 481–484 and n. 3, 496, 503.
Nisibis, ii. 86 n. 3, 132, 612. School there, Barsumas, bp. of, 183 n., 611.
Nismes, iii. 433.
Nitria, anchorites there, ii. 275, 289, 752, 753.
Nitzsch, Dr., i. 204 n. 3.
Nivard, brother of Bernard of Clairvaux, iv. 253 n. 1.
Noah, iii. 445; iv. 573. Seven precepts of, i. 67 n. 2.
Noble lesson, the, Waldensian writing, iv. 616 and n. 7. See Leger.
Noητά, with Plotinus, i. 391.
Noetus, Patripassian, i. 584, 682.
Nogaret, Wm. of, v. 12.
Nogent sous Coucy. See Guibert of.
Nola, see Paulinus of.
Nomadic life, unfavorable to the spread of Christianity, i. 81.
Nominalism, Roscelin and, iv. 356, 359–361, 369, 461. Raimbert, 357. Opposed by Anselm, 361, 369. Applied to the doctrine of the Trinity, 360, 461, 462. Incarnation, 369. Hildegard on, 462 n. 4. Revived by Occam, v. 135. Opposed by Wicklif, v. 135, 165, 166, 168, 347 n. 1. D'Ailly, v. 343, 344. In Prague, v. 244, 245. In Paris, v. 372. See Realism.
Nomination of church officers, ii. 193.
Nomus, officer of state, ii. 566 and n. 1.
Non obstante, formula used by the popes of the thirteenth century, iv. 186, 200.
Non-residence, iv. 207, 286. See Absentees.
Non-resistance, of Christians under persecution, i. 127. Yves of Chartres, iv. 122.
Nonantula, monastery, iii. 553 n. 3; iv. 137.

GENERAL INDEX. 159

Nonna, mother of Gregory Nazianzen, ii. 261, 317.
Norberg, ed. Liber Adami, i. 376 n. 3.
Norbert, founder of the Premonstratensians, iv. 208, 244-246, 312. Life of, c. 13. Tanchelm, 592 n. 2. See Acta S. Junc.
Norden, iii. 79.
Nordlingen, Henry of, v 222 n. 1, 383 n. 2.
Noricum Ripense, iii. 27 n. 3.
Normandy, marriage of bps. and priests in, iii. 410 n. 4; (iv. 97 n. 8). Berengar in, 510. William, duke of, 529 n. 3. Heribert, 595. See Ascelin, Bec. St. Evreuil. St. Lenfroy.
Normans, desire of Lin Iger to visit the, iii. 80. Efforts of Anschar for the, 277. Inroads of, 278, 293, 323, 363, 385, 405. Planting of Christianity among the, 293-300. In Iceland, 300 n. 1 (see Iceland). Rurik and the Waragians, 327, 328. Gregory VII. on the, iv. 86. Guiscard, iv. 120. In England, iii. 529 n. 3; iv. 141, 329. Roger of Sicily, iv. 364. See Norway.
North Africa, persecution in, i. 150, 151. Pestilence in, i. 258. Montanism in, i. 565. Maxentius, ii. 9 n. 1. Paganism in, ii. 100, 102, 115 n. 5. Agonistici, ii. 227, 263 (see Circumcelliones). Monachism in, ii. 294, 295. Manicheans in, ii. 769, 770. Saracens in, iii. 89 124. Crusade preached against, iv. 12- 349. Crusade in, iv. 59, 60. Lull in, iv. 65, 68, 71, 190. See Carthage, Donatists, Egypt, Hippo, N. A. Church, Numidia, Reginus.
North African church. Contributions in the, i. 198. Synods, 207. Stepanus of Rome and the, 214-217, 318, 319. Schism of Felicissimus, 222-237. Of Novatus, 241, 243. Deacons, 233 and n. 2. Infant baptism, 313, 333. Milk and honey in baptism, 316. Baptism of heretics, 318-320. Daily communion; the supper under one form, 332 (iv. 343). Communion of infants, 333. Montanism, 509, 516. Doctrine of human nature, 614-620. Theology, 683-689. Doctrine of the Lord's Supper, 648, 649; ii. 734.
Second Period. Ascetic spirit, ii. 180. Church ordinances? 19: n. 2. Spirit of freedom and principle of unity, 197, 198, 200-202, 207, 208, 600, 603 607, 649 (i. 214-217). Traditores, 222. Donatist schism, 216-252 (v. 158). Observance of Sunday, 336. Holy week, 341 n. 5. Scripture reading, 352 n. 1. Scientific spirit, 394. In the Monophysite controversy, 600-607. In the Pelagian controversy, 645-652 (see Augustin). In the Semi-Pelagian controversy, 709-711. Persecuted by Vandals, 473, 709. Doctrine of the Lord's Supper, 734. Of baptism, 726, 729-731. See Arnobius, Augustin, Carthage, Church

Theology, Commodian, Cyprian, Novatian, Persecutions, Tertullian.
North Albingia, iii. 271, 277, 286, 325.
North America, Christianity introduced there, iii. 307.
North Friesland, iii. 289.
Northumberland, Christianity there, iii. 19-22, 80. Bede, 152.
Norway, spread of Christianity there, iii. 292, 293-300, 302, 305, 306. Gregory VII. and Olof, iv. 9C. Pilgrims from, v. 237.
Notarii, ii. 192. Νοτάριοι among the Paulicians, their business, iii. 264, 265.
Notitia dignitatum imperii Romani, Sect. 27, i. 116 n. 2; Sect. 45, Diocese of the Roman bps., ii. 199 n. 2.
Notker (Labeo), monk of St. Gall, his German paraphrase of the Bible, iii. 471.
Notting of Verona, iii. 475-477, 491.
Nous of Plato, i. 575 n. 1. In Gnosticism, 373 n. 2, 375, 380, 389. The highest Æon, 381 n. 3; with Basilides, 400, 410 and n. 1, 447 n. 4, 448. With Saturniu, 455. Neo-Platonic, Clement, Origen, 585 and n. 6, 587-590, 637. In Neo-Platonism, ii. 123.
Nova Comment. Soc. Reg. Gottingensis, ii. 338 n. 5.
Novara, iv. 409, 629, 632.
Novatian, i. 237-248, 560, 581. Writings of, 690 (581).

De trinitate, cc. 6, 8, i. 560 nn. 4, 5. Epist. ad Dionys. Alexandr. ap. Euseb., l. 6, c. 46, 241 n. 2.

Novatian schism, controversy. Novatians, i. 222, 237-248, 320 n. 4, 687; ii. 205, 213, 216, 225, 238, 252, 433, 505.
Novatus, exciter of the Carthaginian schism, ii. 224, 225, 233. Participation in the Roman, 241, 242.
Novem-populonia, iv. 565.
Novitiate, ii. 298.
Novus Comm. Reg. Soc. Gotting. See Walch.
Noyon, iii. 42. See Eligius.
Nubia, Christian realm of, under the Coptic patriarchs, iii. 90.
Nuits, monastery of, iv. 383.
Numbers.

11: 29, i. 170 n. 1; 23: 19, i. 57, n. 2, 25, 1 452.

Numen dominorum nostrorum, ii. 2 n.
Numidia, church there, i. 84. Persecution, 122, 146, 150-152. Ransom of Numidian captives by the N. African ch., 256. Murder of Christians in, ii. 102 n. 2. Numidian bps. in the Donatist schism, ii. 213-225. Victor, ii. 473. In the Pelagian controversy, ii. 645.
Numidicus, confessor, i. 133.
Nunia, Christian captive, ii. 139 n. 1.
Nunneries, ii. 273; iv. 210.

Nuns, as missionaries, iii. 51, 53. Order of, iv. 276. In the Sects, iii. 252; iv. 594.
Nuremburg, v. 129, 342. Pious women in, 222 and n. 1. Friends of God in, 320, 321, 381.
Nurses for the sick, iv. 267.
Nursia, ii. 296.
Nus. See Nous.
Nutescelle, convent at, iii. 46.

O.

Oak, Augustin's, iii. 17 n. 2. Oak of Geismar, iii. 51. Sacred oaks, iv. 15.
Oasis, ii. 566 n. 1. Nestorius banished to an, 552.
Oath, rejected by the Essenes, i. 46. Basil against the misuse of the, ii. 175. Renounced at baptism, ii. 356. Pelagius, ii. 635. Of Boniface to the pope, iii. 48, 49, 54. Of deans, iii. 108. Irene, iii. 223. Breach of, iii. 231. In the preparations for a universal peace, iii. 407. Contradictory oaths, iii. 449. Berengarius, iii. 511, 514. Required by Henry IV. against Gregory VII., iv. 107. Oath of allegiance, iv. 109, 110, 131, 147, 166, 167; v. 15, 28, 30, 99. Binding nature of the, iii. 231; iv. 109 n. 1, 131; v. 99. Of bishops to the pope, iv. 110, 200. Required of Henry IV., iv. 119. Of Paschalis II., iv. (134), 139-141. Of the pope, v. 56, 99. Arnold, iv. 150. A Becket, iv. 170. Louis IX., iv. 300, 301. Pious laymen, iv. 304. For converts from Mohammedanism, iv. 535. Among the sects, iv. 574, 580, 587, 588, 614, 631 and n. 2. Waldenses, iv. 611, 612, 616. Benedict XIII., v. 56. Huss, v. 249, 361, 362. Welenowitz, v. 250.
Obaize. See Stephen of.
Obedience to magistrates, with the Essenes, i. 46. Christian principle of, i. 259. Tatian, i. 673. Monastic obedience, ii. 279, 282, 283 n. 2, 284; iii. 31, 473; v. 278; (Bernard on), iv. 255; (Dolcino), iv. 635, 636; (Mystics), v. 360, 361, 400. To the Roman church, iii. 48, 49; v. 268 n. 2. To God, iii. 443. Relation to knowledge, iv. 370. Of Christ, iv. 499, 500, 507; v. 403. Huss, v. 278, 296, 305, 334. Friends of God on, v. 383, 384, 385, 387.
Obelisks, ii. 47 n. 4.
Objective power in sacraments, iv. 514 n. 5. See Sacraments, Subjective.
Oblati, iii. 472, 473; iv. 234, 251.
Oblatio, iv. 196.
Oblations, i. 330, 331; ii. 63 n. 3, 109; iv. 138; v. 161. Pro defunctis, i. 334 n. 2. Pro martyribus, i. 334 n. 4. In the Armenian ch., iii. 589. See Offerings.
Obotrites, iii. 324, 326.
Obscurantes, iv. 98 and n. 1.

Obstacles to Christianity, i. 72. As means of advancement, i. 69.
Occam, William, v. 25. On the papal power, 38-40. Definition of the church, 40. Nominalism, 135. Transubstantiation, 245.

Citations:—
Dialogue, v. 40. L. i. c. 4, the church, 40 n. 6. Octo quæstiones, f. 314, 38 n. 3; f. 327, 39 nn. 1, 2; f. 385, 39 n. 3, 40 n. 1; f. 390, 40 nn. 2-4; f. 391, 38 n. 2. See Goldast.

Occupations of Christians, i. 262, 263, 267, 270, 274, 279.
Oceanus of Rome, ii. 749.
Octava infantium, ii. 342 n. 2.
Octavian (John XII.), iii. 367.
Octavian, cardinal (Victor IV.), iv. 167.
Octavius. See Minucius Felix.
Odenatus, i. 603 n. 6.
Oder, river, iii. 323; iv. 16.
Odia tree, the sacred, iii. 51 n. 4.
Odilo, abbot of Cluny and reformer of monachism, iii. 418.
Odilo, duke of Bavaria, iii. 55, 63.
Odin, iii. 294, 295, 328.
Odinear, bishop, iii. 291.
Odo, abbot of Cluny, iii. 444, 445. Reformer of monachism, 417.

Collationes, iii. 417 n. 2. Life of Count Gerald, of Aurilly, 444 nn. 4, 5, 445 nn. 1, 3-5. See Bibl. Cluniacen. and Acta S. (O. B.), S. V.

Odo, archbp. of Canterbury, iii. 288.
Odo of Tournay (Udardus), scholastic, iv. 357, 358, 359 n. 3, 493. Life of, 359 n. 3.

De peccato originale, iv. 493 n. 3.

Odoacer, iii. 28 n. 3, life. See Sirmond, opp., t. i.
Œcumenical. See Ecumenical.
Œcumenius, bp. of Tricca, iii. 531.
Oertel, John, v. 299.
Ofen, v. 275, 373.
Offa, English king, iii. 121 n. 4.
Offerings. Apollonius of Tyana on, i. 26, 30. Plutarch and Porphyry on, 28. Notion of offering in connection with the Lord's Supper, i. 330, ii. 366-369. For the dead, 334 nn. 2, 4; ii. 369; iv. 597. In pagan temples, iv. 14. See Oblations.
Offices, election to church. See Ecclesiastical elections, Ecclesiastical offices.
Officiales, iv. 212, 213.
Officium Mozarabicum, iii. 157 n. 2.
Ohrdruf (Orthorp), church and monastery at, iii. 50 n. 2.
Οἱ καθαροί, i. 247.
Οἰκονομία, with the Orientals, ii. 557 n. 7, 572 n. 6; iii. 178, 179, 197, 224, 532, 533 n. 2, 536 n. 2, 541 and n. 5; iv. 549. Paulicians, iii. 269.
Οἰκονόμος (steward), ii. 191, 272.
Oil, anointing with, among the Essenes, i. 49. In healing, i. 119 n. 6. With the Gnostics (in baptism), i. 477. Con-

secrated by bishops, ii. 188. In baptism. See Anointing.
Oktaikhan, iv. 49, 50.
Old age, care for, iv. 363. See Longevity.
Old and New Testament positions, their relation, i. 179, 180, 394, 464, 672; ii. 391; iv. 77, 595. Origen on, i. 546, 556, 633; Sabellius, i. 599 and n. 4, 600; Antiochian school, ii. 392, 393. *Confounded*, i. 171, 194-199, 209, 220, 226, 227, 272, 365, 463, 519, 538; ii. 181, 329; iii. 201, 202, 605; iv. 257; by Montanists, i. 280, 294, 512, 513, 515, 519, 525 (see Ebionites); in the Western church, ii. 181, 679; iii. 2, 101 n. 2, 103, 411 n. 7, 605; iv. 82, 83, 88. *Distinguished*, i. 209, 525, 526; iii. 131, 237, 255, 257; by Tertullian, i. 272, 562; by the Artemonites, i. 582; by the Donatists, ii. 219, 234, 243; by Pelagius, ii. 672, 673; by Hugo, iv. 404, 407; Priscillianists, ii. 778; Aquinas, iv. 526; Waldenses, iv. 614; Occa n, v. 39. *Separated*, in Gnosticism, i. 371 n. 1, 380-390, 440, 441, 457, 475. (Marcion), 459, 463, 464-469, 470 n. 3, 562, 618 n. 1 (see individual Gnostics); by Julian, ii. 55, 56. Paulicians, iii. 257, 267. Bacon on the, iv. 425. The Catharists, iv. 567, 569. Old and New Testament Periods, Joachim, iv. 227, 228; Oliva, iv. 622, 625; Dolcino, iv. 631, 634. Old and New Testament in the doctrine of Inspiration, i. 371 n. 1, 511, 515, 520, 680; sacraments of, iv. 514 n. 5; v. 217. See Old Testament, Janow de Reg.
Old Testament, the, with the Pharisees, i. 39, 53; the Sadducees, 40-42; the Essenes, 44, 45, 46, 47; the Alexandrian Jews, Philo, 53-58, 397. Greeks, 53. Porphyry, 171. In the Synagogue worship, 302. With the Nazarenes, 349. In the Clementines, 355, 356, 361 n. 1. With the Ebionites, 358 n. 1 (see Ebionites). In Gnosticism, 381, 383, 407, 408, 409, 426, 437-440, -48, 459. J. Martyr on the, 672. With the Montanists (see Old and New Testaments). Chilperic, iii. 91 n. With the Paulicians, iii. 257, 267. Priesthood, iii. 384. Image worship in the, iii. 202, 203, 535. With the Jews, iv. 77, 78, 81. Gregory VII., iv. 82, 86, 88. Bogomiles, iv. 558. Catharists, iv. 571, 573. Peter of Bruis, iv. 595. God of the, i. 22. With Julian, ii. 53, 54. Bogomiles, iv. 553, 554, 563. Catharists, iv. 573. Logos of the, i. 588; ii. 482. Salvation in the, ii. 643 n. 2. Old Testament position discarded, v. 25, 26, 38. Old Testament law, v. 140, 233. Version of Symmachus, i. 708. See Interpretation, Janow de reg., Old and New Testament, Septuagint, Theocracy, Theophanies.

Old world, the, and Christ, i. 77. Ideas of the, i. 86.
Oldenburg (Altenburg), bishopric, iii. 324, 326; iv. 35, 643.
Olga (Helena), Russian grand princess, iii. 328.
Oliva, monastery, iv. 48.
Oliva. See John Peter de.
Olmutz, v. 247 n. 4, 251. Militz at, 177. Bp. of, 295.
Olof, king of Norway, iv. 90.
Olof, king of Sweden, i i. 283-285.
Olof Stantkonnung, king of Sweden, iii 291, 292.
Olof the Thick, king of Norway (saint), iii. 297-299, 305, 306, 307.
Olof Tryggweson, king of Norway, iii. 296, 297, 302, 303, 306, 307.
Olopnen, Nestorian priest in China, iii. 89.
'Ολοσφυρος, iv. 535 n. 1.
Olympias, ii. 191.
Olympius, exarch of Ravenna, iii. 186-188.
Olympius, pagan, ii. 97.
Omar, mosque of, iv. 181 n. 3.
Omens, belief in, ii. 12, 23, 350. Eligius on, iii. 42.
Omnipotence. See God.
Omnipresence of Christ, ii. 490. See Christ, God.
Omniscience of Christ, ii. 496, 656. See Christ, God.
'Ομοιούσιον, ὁμοούσιον. See Homoiousion, Homoousion.
'Ωμοφόριον, iii. 570 n. 2.
'Ον, ὤν, with Plato, i. 25 (ii. 412 n. 2). In Neo-Platonism, 27, 163, 417, 489, 571 and n. 5, 586 and n. 3, 589, 590 (Julian, ii. 50). In Alexandrian Judaism, 57 (with Philo), 373 n. 1, 397, 597, 601 n. 1. With Origen, 551, 571. Praxeas, 585. Clement, 586. With Eusebius, ii. 412 n. 2. With John Scotus, iii. 461.
Onesimus, i. 269 n. 1.
Only begotten God, ii. 449.
Ontological proof. See Anselm.
Ophiomorphus, i. 377 n., 443, 444.
Ophites, i. 375 n. 1, 377 n., 442-447, 477, 484 n. 3, 494 n. 2; ii. 776 n. 3.
Opinion distinguished from faith by Clement, i. 530, 540. By Bernard, iv. 372, 397. By Hugo, iv. 403. By Aquinas, iv. 512.
Opposition, between the church and the world, i. 70. Of natural and divine, 379. Oppositions within the church, 506-513. In general tendencies, and particular doctrines, ii. 383. Dualistic, iii. 247, 248. See Dualism.
Optatus of Mileve, number of churches in Rome, i. 203. Primacy of Peter, ii. 200. Efforts to win over the Donatists, ii. 228 n. 3.

De Schismate Donatistarum, ii. 228 n. 3; f. 174 (ed. Du Pin), i. 150 n. 2, ii. 218 n. 1; f. 184, ii. 163 n. 1. L. i. c. 16, ii. 221 n. 2; c. 22, l.

155 n.; ii. 225 n. 4. L. ii. c. 2, ii. 200 n.; c. 24; ii. 231 n. 2. L. iii. c. 3, ii. 229 nn. 3, 4; c. 4, ii. 230 n. 5. 231 n. 1; c. 12, ii. 231 n. 1. L. vi., ii. 231 n. 2. L. vii. c. 3, ii. 200 n.

Opus operatum, i. 62, 229, 235, 252, 280, 314, 317, 326, 436, 706; ii. 32, 120, 290, 356, 636; iii. 131, 149, 442; iv. 224, 225, 302, 306-312, 387, 514 n. 5; v. 217. See Works.

Oracles, Plutarch's defense of the, i. 23. Porphyry's collection, i. 31, 171, 172. Oracles relating to Christianity, i. 171, 172. Constantius and, ii. 34. Julian and the oracle at Daphne, ii. 82. Arcadius, ii. 103. Simplicius, ii. 108. Sought for in the Scriptures; of the saints; laws against, iii. 129. Compare Montanism, Sibylline.

Orange (Arausio). See Councils, an. 441 and an. 529.

Oratories, iii. 57, 58, 264; iv. 243 n. 1.

Orbais, monastery, Gottschalk at, iii. 473.

Orcades, islands, spread of Christianity in, iii. 306 and n. 3.

Ordeal, iii. 450, 480, 519; iv. 80, 115, 588 n. 6. See Judgments of God.

Ordericus Vitalis.

Historia eccles. L. i. c. 17, Guitmund, iii. 529 n. 2. L. iii. f. 468, false penitence, iv. 236 n. 1. L. vi. f. 536, the pious nobleman, iv. 297 n.; f. 628, Goisfred, iv. 295 n. 1; f. 639, Greg. VII., iv. 92 n. 5. L. viii. ff. 712, 713, Robert of Citeaux, iv. 252 nn. 1, 2; f. 714, spread of the Cistercian order, iv. 254 n. 1, 263 n. 3. See Du Chesne.

Orders, monastic, iv. 244-292. Jealousies between, 263. Multiplication of, 268. See Monastic orders.

Ordibarii, iv. 571.

Ordinances, papal, iv. 93-97, 101, 102. Grosshead on, 186. Respect for ordinances, 294.

Ordination, i. 188, 225, 316; ii. 182, 188, 190 and notes, 193, 352. Conditions of, ii. 184. Of bishops, ii. 195; iii. 48, 89, 371 n. 2. Name given in, iii. 277. Validity of, iii. 379 n. Sacrament, iv. 335. Of Origen, i. 703, 704 n. 3. Compare Donatist controversy, ii. 222, 224, Meletian schism, ii. 253-255.

Ordinationes absolutæ, iii. 57 n. 1, 108, 412.

Ordo, i. 184, 195.

Ordo dominarum pauperum, iv. 276.

Ordo fratrum militiæ Christi, iv. 38.

Ordo minorum, iv. 221 n. See Minorites.

Ordo predicatorum, iv. 270.

Ordo rationis, iv. 521, 522, 524.

Orestes, presbyter, ii. 615 n. 3.

Organ, the, iii. 128 n. 4.

Oribasius, body physician of Julian, ii. 45. See Eunapius.

Oriental church. See Eastern church.

Oriental despotism, ii. 130. See Byzantine.

Oriental languages, iv. 70. See Languages.

Oriental monachism. See Monachism.

Oriental sects, i. 366-506; ii. 768-779; iii. 586-592; iv. 552-593 (see Manicheans, Paulicians). Their influence in the West, iii. 592-602, 603 and n. 2; iv. 565-593. See Oriental Spirit.

Oriental spirit, oriental Theosophy, i. 5. Influence of upon the Essenes, 44, 45, 47. In the preparation for Christianity, 50. In heresies of the first period, 338. In Ebionitism, 351, 352. In Gnosticism, 366, 368, 369, 371, 377, 379, 382, 390, 400, 433, 443; ii. 768. Relation to Platonism, i. 368, 390; ii. 117. In Manicheism, i. 81, 479, 485; ii. 768. In other heresies, ii. 771. In Paulicianism, iii. 244, 269 n. 6, 587. Arevurdis, iii. 587. Catharists, iv. 565, 566, 582. In relation to the theocratic system, iv. 592. See Insincerity, Oriental Sects.

Origen, life and works of, i. 693-712. Correspondence with Julia Mammæa, 125. Expounds the Scriptures before ordination, 197, 703. As a catechist, 528. Scholar of Clement, 528 n. 1, 543, 692. As representative of the Alexandrian school, 543-557. Effects wrought by Christianity, 71, 72, 250. Miracles of the Christians, 74. Miraculous conversions, 75. On the preaching of Christianity in the country, 79. Origen in Arabia, 81. Thomas among the Parthians, 82. Situation of the Christians under Philip the Arabian, 127. On the persecutions, and the condition and prospects of the church, 127-130. Origen and Celsus, 71, 72, 127, 129, 160, 161, 163 n. 1, 165 n. 2, 167 n 2, 169, 177. Humility, 167 n. 2. The Sibyllists, 177. Exorcists, 201 n. 3. Church discipline, 219. Hypocritical profession of Christianity, 251. Profit of baptism, 253. The Christian's service to the state; military service, 272. Prayer, 284, 285. Prayer in the study of Scripture, 287. Posture and place of prayer, 288, 289. Spiritual worship of God, 289. Pentecost, 300 n. 2. Feasts, 300 n. 2, 301. Catechumens, 305. Infant baptism, 314. Ebionites, 345, 346, 348, 364. False Gnosis, 367 n. 2. Gnostic Bible interpretation, 387 n. 1, 388. Heracleon on John, 434, 436 n. 1. The Ophites, 446, 447. Simon Magus, 454 n. 1. Apelles, 475. The second marriage, 522 n. 4. Gnosis and Pietis, 544-551. Faith in miracles, 545. This present life "in part," 546. The eternal spiritual gospel, 547-549. Various standing points of Christians, 547, 548, 587 n. 3. Various forms of revelation of the Logos, 549, 634. Origen and Paul, 550. Tolerance, 551, 552. Interpretation of Scripture, 552-557, 613 n. 2. The creation and the Scriptures, 553, 554. His aim, higher truths, 554,

555. Threefold sense of Scripture, 555. Idea of God, 559, 560. Anthropopathism, Accommodation, 563. Doctrine of creation, 568-571 (553 ; ii. 474). Emanation, 568, 587-589, 621 (ii. 403). Omnipotence of God, miracles, 570, 571 (iv. 453). Monarchians, 576 n. 4, 578, 593 n. 1. Doctrine of the Logos, 587-592. Subordination, 589, 590 (ii. 403). Dispute with Beryll, 594. P'ride of church officers, 603 n. 5. Origen and Tertullian, 605 (ii. 384, 561). Doctrine of the Holy Spirit, 609. Anthropology, 621-631 (ii. 670). Christ's servant form, 633. Humanity of Christ, 635-640 (ii. 561). Redemption, 640, 643. Death of Christ voluntary, 644. Baptism and the Lord's Supper, 648, 649 (ii. 735). Against Chiliasm, 652. Resurrection, 655. Eschatology, 656. Hippolytus, 682. Influence of Origen, 607, 608 653, 711-722.

His influence in the second period, ii. 380, 386-389. His relation to Arius, 404, 405, 407 n. 3, 740. To Semi-Arianism, 410. Eusebius, 411 n., 422. Compared with Augustine, 394, 395, 475. Opposition to his school, 386. In the Western church, 388, 595, 739, 746. Vigilantius, 375 n. 1. Marcellus, 438, 740. His influence on the doctrine concerning the Holy Spirit, 466. The person of Christ, 478, 483, 484, 485, 490, 491. On Anthropology, 617, 670. In the Pelagian controversy, 641, 643 n. 2. Origen with Jerome, 641, 712 n. 3, 745 -750, 753. With other church teachers, 740, 741. Doctrine of Restoration, 737, 738. In the Monophysite controversy (see Origenists). Περὶ ἀρχῶν, 740. Translated by Rufinus, 748, 749. In the Irish monasteries, iii. 461. Abelard, iv. 351. Joachim, iv. 318. Huss, v. 263, 362. See Alexandrian theology, Ammonius, Catechetical schools, Clement, Leonidas.

Citations from his writings : —
Commentaries, Comm. in Exod. 10 : 27, 1. 629 n. 4 ; ed. Lommatzsch, p. 299, 613 n. 2 ; p. 300, 564 n. 1. Comm. in Genesin. init., on creation, 568 n. 2 (ed. de la Rue) ; t. 2, f. 25, Hegesippus, 676 n. 4. Comm. in Rom. L. i. (ed. Lomm., t. 5), f. 250, the soul of Jesus, 636 n. 5 ; f. 251, the possible and the actual, 571 n. 4. L. ii. (t 6), f. 107, the πρεσβύτεροι in man, 628 n. 2 ; c. 9, f. 108, 629 n. 1. L. v. (ed. de la Rue, t. 4, f. 549), Basilides on Rom. 7 : 9, 404 n. 2. L. v. (Rufini. trans.), infant baptism an apostolical tradition, 314 n. 2. Comm. series in Matt., § 62 (ed. Lomm., t. 4, f. 352), severance of the spirit from the soul of the disobedient, 629 n. 1 ; § 100 (f. 446), the Logos, manifoldness of his manifestation, 634 n. 1 Comm. in Titum, fragm. (Rufin. trans.), Patripassians, 578 n. 6, Monarchians, 593 n.
Contra Celsum. L. i. c. 1, Celsus accuses the Christians of secret compacts, I. 88 n. 1, 108 n. 1 ; c. 2, Greek culture, 4 n. O. on miracles, 74 n. 5 ; c. 4, λόγος ἀληθής of Celsus, 160 n. 1. O. on the idea of God, 559 n. 1 ; c. 9, C. on the place of faith in Christianity, 164 n. 2. O. on the necessity of faith in daily life, 544 n. 2 ; c. 17, C. on allegorical interpretations, 171 n. 2 ; c. 28, C. on the miracles, 161 n. 3, fable concerning Jesus, 162 n. 1 ; c. 32, O. on Christ's glorified body, 639 n. 3 ; c. 46, conversions through visions, 75 n. 3 ; c. 57, Simon Magus, 454 n. 1 ; c. 67, C. against Christ's miracles, 169 n. 8 ; O. on the work of Christ, 250 n. 2. L. ii. c. 1, Ebionites, 345 n. 2 ; c. 9, the soul of Christ united with the Logos through its merit, 636 n. 5 ; c. 10, sources of information used by Celsus, 169 n. 1 ; c. 16, transmigration, 627 n. 3 ; c. 23, glorified body of Christ, 639 n. 3 ; c. 27, Celsus on alterations of the gospels, 165 n. 2 ; cc. 13, 34, 41, 42, C. on the authority of the gospels and the sinlessness of Jesus, 169 nn. 2-4 ; cc. 55, 63, 67, C. on the resurrection and miracles, 169 nn. 7, 9. L. iii. f. 55, C. on the response of the lower classes to Christianity, 70 n. ; c. 7, Christianity a revolt from Judaism, 89 n. 4 ; c. 8, O. on the persecutions, 127 n. 3 ; c. 9, the gospel in the country, 79 n. 3, among the rich, 128 n. 3 ; c. 10 *et seq.* C. on sects. 164 nn. 5, 6 ; c. 14, 89 n. 4 ; c. 15, O. foresees new persecutions, 128 n. 6 ; c. 24, miracles in Origen's time, 75 n. 1 ; c. 27. Lucas on the mortality of the psychical, 474 n. 5 ; c. 29, O. on the character of the Christians, 250 n. 3 ; c. 41, merit of the soul of Christ, 536 n. 5 ; c. 42, his glorified body, 639 n. 3 ; c. 44, C. on the appeal of Christianity to the simple, 164 n. 3 ; c. 46, O. on the gift of knowledge, 544 n. 6 ; c. 50, 305 n. 1 ; c. 51, O. on penitents, 219 n. 4 ; on catechumens, 305 n. 2 ; cc. 59, 62, 65, C. on the call to sinners, 166 nn. ; c. 70, O. on the omnipotence of God, 570 n. 4 ; c. 76, transmigration, 627 n. 3. L. iv. c. 15, glorified body of Christ, 639 n. 3 ; c. 16, transfiguration, 633 n. 4 ; c. 36, writings of Celsus, 160 n. ; c. 40, O. on the story of the fall in Gen., 627 n. 1 ; c. 57, on the ὕλη, 655 n. 1 ; cc. 62, 69, C. on redemption, 168 nn. 4, 5 ; c. 69, O. on the repetition of redemption, 656 n. 2 ; cc. 69, 75, 76, 81, C. on man compared with brutes, 167 nn. 3-5, 168 nn. 1, 2 ; cc. 73, 75, C. on the uncomeliness and weakness of Christ, 169 nn. 6, 10 ; c. 90, C. on man as only a part of the whole, 168 n. 3. L. v. cc. 14, 23, omnipotence, 570 nn. 3-7, 571 n. 1 ; c. 25, C. on Christianity as a revolt from Judaism, 89 n. 5 ; c. 54, Apelles on the O. T., 475 n. 4 ; c. 61, Sibyllists, 177 n. 5, Ebionites, 348 n. 6 ; c. 63, C. on the disagreement of sects, 164 n. 7. L. vi. c. 12 *et seq.*, O. on faith, 544 n. 2 ; c. 13, wisdom, 544 n. 4 ; c. 15, C. on humility, 167 nn. 1, 2 ; c. 24, journeyings of Origen, 699 n. 2 ; c. 28 *et seq.*, reports of Jews against the Christians, 128 n. 5, Ophites, 447 n. 1 ; c. 41, C. on magic, 161 n. 5 ; c. 42, Lsidorus, 402 n. 2 ; c. 44, O. on goodness as derived from God, 623 n. 3 ; c. 75 *et seq.*, glorified body of Christ, 639 n. 3 ; c. 77, the transfiguration, 634 n. 1. L. vii. c. 26, O. on the spread of Christianity, 128 n. 1 ; c. 35, O. on the resurrection, 169 n. 7 ; cc. 36, 42, C. on the Christians, 165 n. 1 ; c. 56, C. and O. on the interpolation of the Sibylline writings, 177 n. 4. L. viii. c. 12, Monarchians, 576 n. 4, the Logos, 588 nn. 1, 2 ; c. 17, C. and O. on the absence of altars, images, etc., among the Christians, 90 n. 2, 289 n. 1 ; c. 21, C. on the absence of Christians from the public festivals, 265 n. 4 ; c. 22, Pentecost, 300 n. 2 ; c. 41, on the persecutions, 108 n ; cc. 63, 67, on swearing by the emperor, 91 n. 1 ; c. 68, C. and O. on the results if all should do as the Christians, 91 n. 5, 129 n. 2 ; c. 69, C. on the concealment of the Christians, 108 n. 1 ; c. 70, O. on the victory over the world, 129 n. 1 ; c. 72, C. on the impossibility of all men agreeing in one religion, 90 n. 1. Fir. service of Christians to the state, 272 n. 2.

De martyribus, § 4, i. 706 n. 2; § 7, restoration, 625 n. 2; § 12, 637 n. 1; § 37, Heb. 4:12, Luke 12:49, 707 n. 1.
De oratione dominica, c. 7, souls of the planets, i. 624 n. 5; c. 12, prayer without ceasing, 286 n. 3; c. 13, efficacy of, n. 1; c. 15, difference of the Son from the Father, 590 n. 5; c. 22, the Lord's prayer not a form, 285 n. 4; c. 20, temptation, self-determination, 629 n. 4, 630 n. 1; c. 31, 288 n. 1.
Dialogus de recta in Deum fide, opp. ed. de la Rue, t. 1, Marcus, i. 474 n. 3; f. 807, Marcion's gospel, 473 n. 4.
Epistles, ep. ad Greg. Thaumaturg., prayer, in the study of Scripture, i. 287 n. 2. Ep. ad Jul. African., § 4, on the Alexandrian version, 709 n. 2; § 5, necessity of a knowledge of the Hebrew, 708 n. 1. Ep. ad Demetrium (apud. Hieron. adv. Rufinum, 2, f. 411, ed. Mart.). 704 n. 3. Ep. ad Synodum (Hieron. adv. Ruf. 2, f. 411), 705 n. 4. Ep. t. i. f. 3 (ed. de la Rue), Ambrosius, 701 n. 1.
Homiliæ. In Isaiam, h. 4, § 1, i. 626 n. 1. In Jeremiam, h. 2, § 16, metempsychosis, 627 n. 3; h. 8, § 8, 705 nn. 2, 3; h. 9, § 3, eternal becoming, 599 n. 4; h. 14, Adam, 627 n. 1; h. 15, § 6, soul of Christ, 636 n. 5; h. 18, § 6, on anthropomorphism, 563 n. 2; h. 18, § 12, Ebionites, hostility to Paul, 346 n. 4; h. 19, § 4, celibacy, 277 n. 1. Hom. 14, in Lucam, infant baptism, 314 n. 2.
In Joannem, t. i. § 9, revelation of Christ under the O. T., i. 548 n. 2. Spiritual Christianity, 552 n. 1; § 11, 550 n. 3; § 16, final intuition of God, 623 n. 1; § 17, the incorporeal life, 624 n. 5; § 22, the redeemer, "all things to all men," 549 nn. 3, 4, Adam, 627 n. 1; § 24, the Gnostics on Rom. 8:20, 21, 411 n. 3; § 30, soul of Christ, 636 n. 5; § 32, time, in the generation of the Logos, 588 n. 4; § 40, Christ the "just one," 564 n. 3; § 42, περιγραφή, 593 n. 1. T. ii. § 1, eternal generation of the Logos, 588 n. 4; § 2, the Monarchians, 576 nn. 2, 4; the Logos, 587 n. 4; ἑτερότης τῆς οὐσίας, καὶ τῆς ὑποστάσεως, 590 n. 5; § 3, subordinate position in regard to the Logos, 578 n. 3; § 4, sufferings of Christ, 552 n. 4; § 6, citation from the gospel of the Nazarenes, 350 n. 3; § 7, μὴ ὄν, 623 n. 5; Satan, 624 n. 2; § 15, Heracleon on the Soter, 423 n. 2; the πνευματικοί, 628 n. 3; § 18, classes of Monarchians, 576 n. 4; § 21, infirmities of Christ, 643 n. 1; § 25, προσευχὴ Ἰωσήφ, 66 n. 3 (ed. Lomm.); f. 146, the Father first revealed by Christ, 591 n. 2. T. v. § 4 (ed. Lomm., t. i. f. 172), Gnosticism, 367 n. 2; Marcion on the gospels, 473 n. 4. T. vi. § 1, 704 n. 2; § 2, prophets of the O. T., 520 n. 3; § 12, Heracleon on the self-expression of the godlike, 441 n. 2; § 17, baptism, agency of the Logos in the Sacraments, 253 n. 1, 648 n. 8; § 23, Heracleon on the pneumatic principle in the Messiah, 430 n. 1; § 24, 703 n. 2; § 34, power of holy self-sacrifice, 643 n. 1. T. x., unity of essence, 590 n. 4; § 4, criticism of the gospels, 556 n. 3; § 13, περὶ ἀρχῶν, 702 n. 1; § 14, Heracleon on the "wedding feast," 369 n. 2, 431 n. 3; § 19, H. on the cross, 431 nn. 1, 2; § 21, Monarchians, 576 n. 4; § 27, the perfect faith, 547 n. 1. T. xii. § 3, development of Theism, 587 n. 3. T. xiii. § 5, relation of the Scriptures to the Gnosis, 551 n. 1; § 10, faith of the spiritual men, 432 n. 5; § 11, αἰών, with Heracleon, 373 n. 3; Syzygy, 432 n. 2; § 16, Satan, 421 n. 2; the psychici, 422 n. 4; the Jews and pagans, 427 n. 1; § 20, the pneumatici, 432 n. 4; § 21, idea of God as a spirit, 569 n. 1; § 25, psychici, 422 n. 4; O. on emanation, 568 n. 3; comparative exaltation of the Father, Son, and Spirit, 590 n. 2; God in Christ, 591 n. 1; §§ 25, 30, 51, 59, H. on the psychici, 422 n. 4; § 34, O. on Adam, 627 n. 1; §§ 38, 41, Heracleon's expositions of Scripture, 436 nn. 2-4; § 48, the Soter in relation to Christ, 423 n. 2; § 51, 422 n. 4; § 52, belief on testimony, 307 n. 2; O. on pistis and gnosis, 546 n. 1; § 58, effect of Christ's appearance, 563 n. 2; § 59, Gnostics on the psychalci, 422 n. 4, 432 n. 3; O. on τὸ ὑλικόν, 624 n. 5. T. xv. § 3, i. 6 (f. 367), i. 698 n. 1. T. xix. § 1, the Father revealed by the Son, 545 n. 2, 591 n. 2; § 3, seekers of Jesus, 251 n. 1; § 4, death of Christ voluntary, 644 n. 2; § 5, creation of the corporeal world, 624 n. 4; the κόσμος νοητός, 624 n. 5; the preëxistent soul of Christ, 636 n. 5, 638 n. 2. T. xx. § 16, on emanation, 568 n. 4, 590 n. 1; § 17, soul of Christ, 636 n. 5; § 18, the same, 637 n. 2; § 20, H. on the evil principle, 421 n. 4, 422 n. 1; § 25, O. on the sinlessness of Christ, 638 n. 3; § 28, Christ, all things to all men, 549 n. 2, 633 n. 3. T. xxii. § 18 (ed. Lomm., t. ii. f. 470), the personality of God, 571 n. 5. T. xxviii. § 14, redemption, 643 n. 2. T. xxxii. § 5, the sects, 709 n. 1; § 11, the pneuma, 627 n. 5; in saints, 628 n. 4; and in Christ, 639 n. 4; § 16, the Lord's Supper, 649 n. 2; § 18, eradication of God's glory in the world of spirits, 569 n. 1, 587 n. 4, 622 n. 3.
In Matt., ed. Huet., t. ii. § 10, evil as voluntary, i. 623 n. 5. T. iii. (f. 827, ed. de la Rue), the persecutions, 126 n. 4. T. iv. (Lat. ed. Lomm., p. 73 et seq.), death of Christ voluntary, 644 n. 2, (ed. de la Rue, f. 887) ubiquity of His glorified body, 639 n. 3. T. x. § 2 (f. 207), final intuition of God, 623 n. 1; § 9 (ed. Lomm., vol. iii. f. 26), pistis and gnosis, 546 n. 2; § 23, avoidance of danger, 695 n. 2. T. xi. § 12, the Ebionites, 346 n. 3; § 14, the Supper, 649 n. 2; § 17, interpretation, 694 n. 2. T. xii. § 6, the perfect faith, 547 n. 1; § 37, Christ's various revelations of himself, 633 n. 3. T. xiii. § 1 (ed. Lomm., vol. iii., p. 310), a determinate number of created beings, 571 n. 3; § 2, dependence of the spirit in man on the divine spirit, 629 n. 2; § 7, exorcism, 201 n. 3; § 22, necessity in relation to evil, 630 n. 3; § 26 (ed. Lomm., f. 257), free will, 622 n. 1; in Christ, 636 n. 5, 639 n. 1. T. xiv. § 16, advice to catechists, 528 n. 6. T. xv. § 1 (ed. Huet., f. 378), anger and goodness of God, 563 n. 3; § 3 (ed. Huet., ff. 367, 369), on Matt. 19:12, 694 n. 2, 697 n. 1, 698 n.; § 7 (ed. Lomm. vol. iii., p. 340), on Matt. 19:14, 552 n. 2; § 23, baptism, 648 n. 8. T. xvi. § 1, on avoidance of danger, 695 n. 3; § 8 (ed. Lomm., p. 24), the soul of Christ, 593 n., 636 n. 5, 640 n. 1, 644 n. 1; proud bishops, 663 n. 5; § 9, faith and knowledge, 520 n. 2; § 12, the Ebionites, 345 n. 2, 364 n. 4; § 22, covetous deacons, 233 n. 2; § 25 (f. 445), Origen's charity, 705 n. 4. T. xvii. § 14, the Patripassians, 578 n. 2; § 26, opinions of the multitude, 699 n. 3; § 30, bodies of the angels, 624 n. 5; f. 213, the souls under tutelage, 548 n. 1: f. 208, revelation of the Logos to different stages of faith, 550 n. 2; f. 290, the same, 550 n. 1; f. 344, soul of Christ, 636 n. 5; f. 363, second marriage, 522 n. 4; f. 402, hint at a repetition of the apocatastasis, 656 n. 2; f. 423, soul of Christ, 636 n. 5, opp. vol. lii., f. 898, the Lord's Supper, 649 n. 2.
Περὶ ἀρχῶν, præf. f. 4, creation from nothing, i. 568 n. 2. L. i. c. 2, § 6, on emanation, 568 n. 4 (ed. de la Rue, t. i.), f. 76, transmigration, 627 n. 2. L. i. c. 8, § 3 (Rufin. trans.), possibility of not sinning, 638 n. 4. L. ii. c. 1, soul of the world, 624 n. 3; c. 1, § 4, creation from nothing, 568 n. 2; c. 2, § 2, matter a necessary limit for the creature, 624 n. 5, c. 4, repetition of the redemptive process, 656 n. 2; c. 5, § 5 (Rufin. trans.), sinless nature of Christ, 638 n 4; c. 6, the same, 636 n. 5; c. 8, soul transfigured into spirit, 639 n. 2; c. 8, § 3, the same, 637 n. 1; c. 9, the divine omnipotence, 570 n. 2, 571 n

3. L. iii. c. 4, the σαρκικός and the ψυχικός in relation to conversion, 620 n. 3; c. 5, creative power not conditioned by a preexistent matter, 568 n. 2. L. iv. c. 3, on literal interpretation, 463 n. 1.

Philocalia. L. i. f. 17, spiritualizing interpretation, i. 557 n. 1; literal, 680 n. 3; f. 28, higher truths, 554 n. 2; f. 51, the Scriptures, 554 n. 1; c. 2, ff. 10, 61, analogy between the Scriptures and the creation, 558 nn. 3, 4; c. 18, ep. to Greg. Thaumaturg., 718 n. 3; c. 14, Gnostic interpretation, their ignorance of language, 387 n.; c. 15, growth of knowledge through faith, 544 n. 3; the word, 553 n. 1; p. 139, hermeneutics, 556 n. 1; c. 24 (ed. Loumn., t. ii., p. 450), grace and freewill, 630 n. 5; c. 26 (ed. de la Rue, t. ii. f. 111; Lomin., t. viii., p. 305), God's use of temptation, 626 n. 4.

Selecta in Psalmos, Ps. 4: 1, the Logos in the O. T., i. 588 n. 3 (ed. de la Rue, t. ii.) p. 570, effects of Chiliasm, 651 n. 1; (ed. Loamm., t. ii.), p. 388, identity of the body, 655 n. 2.

Origen, school of. See Origen, Gregory Thaumaturgus, Pamphilus.
Origen, the pagan, i. 699 n. 1.
Origenistic controversy, ii. 595–598, 641. Renewed, 739–765.
Origenists and their opponents, i. 713–722; ii. 387, 595. Two parties, ii. 764 n. 3.
Origin of evil. See Evil.
Origin of man. See Anthropology, Creation, Man.
Original condition, i. 626, 627; ii. 666–668; iv. 485–495; v. 15. Compare Anthropology, Image of God, Sin, Grace, Gnostics, Paulicians.
Original righteousness, iv. 492.
Original sin, i. 313, 314, 626, 627; ii. 344. In the Pelagian controversy, ii. 666–684. Hilary of Poictiers on, ii. 618, 619. Ambrose, ii. 622. Augustin, ii. 625, 626. Pelagius, ii. 638. Theodore of Mopsuestia, ii. 717, 727, 728. Immaculate conception, iv. 331–333. Scholastics, iv. 359, 491–495. R. of St. Victor, iv. 517. Catharists, iv. 573. Fomes peccati, iv. 332 n. 1. Compare Original condition, Sin.
Orion, ii. 67 n. 2.
Orleans, sect there, iii. 593–596, 601. Docetic doctrine taught there, 594. Sacraments of the sect, 594, 595. Bp. of, 509 n. 4. University of, v. 32. See Councils, an. 511, an. 533, an. 538, an. 541, an. 1022.
Ormuzd, in Parsism, i. 369, 402, 479, 480, 482, 488, 489 n. 3, 493; ii. 126 n. 1, 127–129, 133, 136; iii. 587.
Orontius, Pelagian bishop, ii. 657 n. 2.
Ὅρος, i. 419. See Horus.
Orosius. See Paulus.
Orphan houses, ii. 169, 288.
Orphans, care for, ii. 288; iv. 299. Bishops protectors of, ii. 176, 288, 755.
Orpheus, i. 125, 255.
Orthodox, Orthodoxy, zeal for, ii. 507, 514, 536, 569, 570, 578, 593, 737, 746; iii. 49, 169, 252, 541, 544, 546; iv. 304. Efforts of Lull in behalf of, iv. 68. At Prague, v. 235. Feast of Orthodoxy, iii. 549.

Orthorp (Ohrdruf), church and monastery there, iii. 50 n. 2.
Ortuinus Gratius.

Fasciculus rerum (ed. Brown), f. 42, Benno on Greg. VII., iii. 380 n. 1; app. f. 185 *et seq.*, Opusc. tripartitum, Humbert de Romanis de his quae tractanda, etc., iv. 189 n. 4, 190 nn. 1, 2; f. 251, writings of Grosshead, iv. 185 nn.

Osbern, the boy, and Anselm, iv. 363.
Osborn.

Life of Dunstan, iii. 411 n. 6.

Osma, iv. 268, 269.
Osmund, bp., iii. 292.
Osservazioni letterarie.

T. iii. p. 16 (Verona, 1738), old acct. of the Meletian Schism, Arius, ii. 403 n. 2.

Ostia, bps of, iii. 379; iv. 121, 603; v. 344, 360 n. 2.
Ostiarii, i. 201; iii. 53 n. 6.
Ostrogoths, ii. 298. See East Goths.
Oswald, king of Northumberland, iii. 20, 21.
Oswin, Anglo-Saxon king, iii. 24.
Otfrid, German preacher, iii. 425, 457. Sermons of, 425 n. 3. Paraphrase of the Gospels, 425, 426 n. 2. See Schilter.
Othma, iii. 163.
Otho, duke of Saxony. See Otho IV.
Otho I., emperor, his influence in the spread of Christianity, iii. 288, 322, 324, 328, 330 n. 2, 331. Embassy to Spain, 336 n. 2, 345. Deposition of John XII., 367 (v. 18). Gerbert, 470 n. 3.
Otho II., emperor, iii. 332, 418.
Otho III., emperor, ii. 334, 375. Gerbert, 374, 375. Romuald, 419. Philagathus, 422. Bruno, iv. 43.
Otho IV., emperor, as king of Rome, iv. 176, 177. As emperor, 177, 226 n. 7, 582 n. 4, 609 n. 3.
Othos, the, iv. 133, 167.
Otto, bp. of Bamberg, his education and early life, iv. 3. At the Polish court, as bishop, 4–6. His preparations for his mission, 6, 2 n. 1. His missionary labors in Pomerania, 6–31. His life, 2 n. 1; 4 nn. 1, 4; 5 nn. 1, 2; 6 nn.; 11 nn., 16 nn., 22 n. 2, 23 n., 26 nn., 27 n, 1, 30 n. Account of Andreas, 2 n. 1, 4 n. 1, 7 n., 26 n. 2. See Canisius.
Otto, bp. of Constance, iv. 94 n. 3, 96.
Otto, bp. of Freisingen, on Hildebrand, iii. 381 nn. 1, 2. Gunther Ligurinus, iv. 148 n. 1. Arnold, iv. 148 n. 2, 149 n. 3, 151 n. 2. The crusade, iv. 155.

Gesta Friderici, l. i. c. 40, iv. 155 n. 1. L. ii. c. 20, Abelard and Arnold, iv. 147 n. 2: ashes of Arnold, iv. 162 n. 1. L. ii. c. 37, Bernard and Rudolph, iv. 74 n. 2. History, l. viii. c. 6, Urban II., his return to Rome, iv. 129 n. 1.

Otto, bp. of Ostia, iv. 121.

Otto, cardinal of Colonna. See Martin V.
Orcia, ii. 450–455.
Outward forms and inward essence confounded, ii. 200, 258, 259, 282, 355, 365, 378. Outward works, forms, i. 386; iv. 264, 348. See Works.
Ovid, iv. 448.
Oxford, university of, iv. 70, 408, 424, 608 n. 1. Philargi, v. 84. Theological tendencies, v. 93, 240. And the mendicants, v. 134. Wicklif at, v. 135, 136, 137, 142, 149, 157, 162, 163. Bull of Greg. XI., v. 146, 147 and n. 2. Scriptures at, v. 151 n. 2. And Prague, v. 241–244, 246, 248. Jerome of Prague at, v. 246. Seal of, v. 244 n. 1.
Ozilia, iv. 39.
Oznnn, iii. 250 n. 1. See John of.

P.

Pacatus Drepanius.
  Panegyr. on Theodosius, c. 29, Maximus and the Priscillianists, ii. 773 n. 3, 774 nn. 2, 3.
Pacianus of Barcelona.
  Ep. 3, c. Novat., i. 246 n. 2. See Bibl. patr. Galland.
Pachomius, founder of the cloister life, ii. 271–274, 424 n. 2, 741.
  Life of, § 15, ii. 271 n. 5; §§ 19, 73, 85, distribution of charities, 272 n. 5; § 52, Mesori, 273 n. 1; § 61, 274 n. 1; § 77, 271 n. 4. See Acta S. May, and Jerome, Præf. in Reg. Pachom.
Pachomius, martyr, ii. 254 n.
Pachymeres. See George.
Paderborn, Diet of, iii. 273. School at, iv. 33.
Padua, university of, iv. 421.
Pagan Christians. See Gentile Christians.
Pagan customs, observance of, differing views of Christians in relation to, i. 259–267; ii. 347–351. Transferred to or mixed with Christianity, i. 720; ii. 371; iii. 53 n. 7, 78, 129, 297 and n. 333, 497 n. 1, 589 n. 1 (see Pagan festivals). Suppression of, iii. 51, 56, 78, 95, 107, 108 (see Paganism). Spiritualization of, iii. 170.
Pagan elements in Christianity, ii. 48, 258; iii. 132 (see Pagan customs). In the sects, ii. 768 n. 1; iii. 603. See Oriental sects, Oriental spirit.
Pagan festivals, attitude of the church in relation to, i. 91, 265, 301 n. 1; ii. 347–351; iv. 334. See Yule.
Pagan literature. See Literature.
Pagan shows, i. 263–267, 309; ii. 258.
Pagan world, its state among the Greeks and Romans at the appearance of Christianity, i. 5–35.
Paganism, religion of the state, i. 70, 87–91, 99, 105, 108. Consciousness of God in, i. 4, 177, 178, 558. Points of union with Christianity, i. 5–35, 63, 170, 427, 470, 536; ii. 486. Of contrast, opposition, i. 17, 26, 33, 34, 70, 86, 249, 250, 462, 631, 649; ii. 48. Attempts to unite it with Christianity, i. 93, 172; ii. 38, 258; iii. 297 (see Pagan customs, 333). Its influence on Christian life and doctrine, i. 252, 260–262, 265, 276, 292, 337, 338; ii. 21, 258. Eunomius on, ii. 448. Influence of Christianity on, i. 106, 170; ii. 62, 63, 107. Relation of Montanism to, i. 513, 520, 521. Adhered to by men, i. 172. Zeal of Maximin for, ii. 2–6. Measures for suppression of, ii. 22, 26, 27, 33, 88, 89, 91–104 (see Constantine, Force, Pagan customs). Revival of (see Julian). At Athens, ii. 39. And literature (see Literature). Remains of, ii. 90, 100, 110, 298. In high places, ii. 93 n. 3, 94, 96; in the country, origin of the name, ii. 90, 91, 100; in the East, ii. 91, 94–99, 102, 103; in the West, ii. 92–94, 99–102; in Sardinia, iii. 13, n. 1, 603 n. 2. Revival of in Kent and Essex, iii. 18, 19; in Northumberland, iii. 20; in Germany, iii. 25, 50 n. 1; among the Saxons, iii. 76, 78, 79; in Denmark, iii. 290; in Norway, iii. 296–298; Hungary, iii. 334, 335; the Franks, iii. 78, 79; Faroe Isles, iii. 307; in Bohemia, iii. 322; among the Wends, iii. 323, 325. Photius on Western, iii. 566 n. 2. Condition of, iv. 11. Reactions of (see Reactions). See Idealism, Platonism, Heathen, Logos.
Pagans. Intercourse with, i. 218. Excluded from part of the church service, 328. Instruction of, 527–529. Hostility to Christians, ii. 3–6, 17, 18. Excluded from places of trust, ii. 102. Of Julian's time, ii. 111 n. (see Julian). And image worship, v. 233. Salvation of, iii. 314, 602; v. 388. See Apologies, Baptism (period iii.), Barbarians, Clement, Justin Martyr, Virtues of the pagans.
Paganus, Peter, v. 244 n. 1.
Pagi.
  On the edict of Aurelian, i. 108 n. 2. Council of Gangra, ii. 281 n. 1. Ep. of Boniface, iii. 65 n. 6. Ep. of Alcuin, iii. 77 n. 6.
Paintings, i. 293; ii. 328; iii. 198, 199, 212, 215, 219, 232, 237, 440. Religious use of, forbidden, iii. 216–218. Destroyed, iii. 219. Of Methodius, iii. 308. The monk Lazarus, iii. 547. In the temple at Stettin, iv. 14. Symbolic at Rome, iv. 163 and n. 3, 164 and n. 3, 165. Lull on, iv. 307, 308. See Art, Artists, Image worship, Pictures.
Palacky, Franz, v. 344 n. 1.
  Geschichte von, Boehmen, Bd. iii. Abth. 1, s. 24, Ann of Bohemia, v. 241 n. 2. S. 161 and n. 225, Conrad of Waldhausen, 183 n. 2. S. 164, Militz, 174 n. 1. S. 187, Thomas of

Stitney, 245 n. 5. S. 188, Lectures at Prague, 248 n. 2. S. 192, u. 2–5, Faulfisch, and Jerome of Prague, 245 n. 4 SS. 197, 198, Wicklif and Huss, 243 n. 1. SS. 213, 214, Chronicles of Prague University, 247 nn. 2, 3. S. 216, Ep. of Huss to Zbynek, 237 n. 1. S. 222, Convocation of the university, an. 1408; decrees relating to Wicklif's writings, 248 nn. 1, 3. S. 223, Consistory of Prague, an. 1408, Welenowitz, 250 n. 3, 251 n. 1. S. 224, declaration of Zbynek, 252 n. 3; exodus of Germans from Prague, 253 n. S. 246, charges against Huss, 258 n. 4. S. 258, Ep. of Wenceslaus to John XX. I., 271 n. 2. S. 264, Chron. Univ. Prag., 272 n. 1. S. 277 note, and 278, burning of the bulls, 286 n. 1; edict of Wenceslaus, 287 n. 2, 3. S. 281, action of the faculty of the univ., 292 n. 5. S. 282, propositions of the eight doctors, 292 n. 1. S. 286, Chron. univ. Prag., excommunication of Huss, 294 n. S 289 *et seq.*, Synod of Prague, an. 1413, 297 n. 1. S. 293, the same, 297 n. 2. S. 294, committee appointed by the king, 298 n. SS. 297, 298 note, letters of Huss, 310 n. 2. S 298 *et seq.*, Huss and the Bohemian literature, 244 n. 3. S. 301 note, 412, Jerome of Prague, 373 n. 3. S 304, secret visits of Huss at Prague, 316 n. 4. S. 312, and 313 note, ep. of Huss to Sigismond, 318 n. 2. S. 321 note, Huss at Constance, 326 n. 3. S. 330, 330 n. 2. S. 332 note, Jacobellus, 338 n. 1 S. 333 note, 448, efforts to liberate Huss, 339 n. 4.
Tour to Italy (Prague, 1838), s. 72 *et seq*, suppression of a sect at Milan, iv. 639 n. 1.

Palais, iv. 373.
Palenza, Spanish University at, iv. 268.
Palestine, Judaism in, i. 39–49, 62. Platonism, 44. Persecution in, 103, 146, 153, 154, 156. Christmas, 302. Marcus, 440. Origen in, 594, 704, 705, 716. Pagans in, ii. 95, 103. Terebon, ii. 143. Monachism in, ii. 263, 270, 271, 275, 741, 744, 745, 747, 748; iv. 266. Sacred places, ii. 31, 377, 378; iii. 457; iv. 266 (see Pilgrimages). In the Monophysite controversy, ii. 583 and n. 2, 589, 590. Influence of Origen, ii. 595, 596, 764. Pelagius in, ii. 640–645. Manichæans in, ii. 769. Conquered by the Persians, iii. 84. By the Saracens, iii. 180, 206. Sophronius, iii. 178, 180. Image worship in, iii. 206, 209. The crusades, iv. 125–127, 178, 191, 300. See Acco, Bethlehem, Cæsarea, Cosmas bp. of Majuma, Crusades, Holy places, Jerome, Jerusalem.
Paletz, Stephen, friend of Huss, v. 244 and n. 2, 245, 248 n. 4, 252 n. 2, 277, 286. Timidity of, 277–279. Change of relations between them, 279. Dean of the faculty at Prague; joins in the condemnation of the 45 articles, 291, and n. Writings of Huss against, 294, 299. Proceedings against Huss, 295–298, 303, 306, 310, 318 n. 1. At Constance, 118, 279, 321, 327–332, 336, 345, 351, 356, 363, 366. Jerome of Prague, 376.
Pall. See Pallium.
Palladius, archdeacon, ii. 147 and n. 2.
Palladius, bp. of Helenopolis, visit to the Egyptian cloisters, ii. 272.
Hist. Lausiaca, cc. 6, 38, Bibl. patr. Paris t.

xlii. ff. 909, 957, numbers of the Cœnobites, ii. 272 u. 1; hospitality, 289 n. 1; c. 26, f. 939, Anthony, 271 n. 1; cc. 31, 33, 95, effects of spiritual pride, 275 n. 1, 276 n. 1; c. 39, cloister of Panopolis, industry, 272 n. 4. Heron, 275 n. 3; c. 76, Serapion, 288 n. 3; c. 78, Jerome, 644 n. 3 c. 147, Origen, i. 708 n. 3; f. 300, nunneries, ii. 273 n. 4. Life of Chrysostom (opp. Chrysost. ed. Montf., t. xiii.), ii. 170 n. 2, 753 n. 2, 756 notes; acts of process against bp. Antoninus of Ephesus, ii. 170 n. 2.
Palladius, magistrianus, ii. 534.
Pallium, of the ἀσκητής, i. 239 n.; ii. 409 n. 2. Philosopher's cloak, mantle, i. 275, 661, 662, 668, 674; ii. 88 n. 97. Pall, badge of archiepiscopal dignity, iii. 15, 64, 65, 118, 119 n. 2, 124 n. 1, 277, 375, 574; iv. 43, 200; v. 276.
Palm Sunday, ii. 341; v. 39.
Palmyra, ii. 95 n. 5.
Pambo, abbot, ii. 354, 355 n. 1.
Pammachius of Rome, ii. 749.
Pamphylia, ii. 276, 584, 757.
Pamphylus, presbyter at Cæsarea. His zeal in behalf of science, and Biblical study, i. 721. Death of Origen, 711 n. 3.
Apologia Origenis (ed. de la Rue), i. 704 n. 3; t. 4, f. 35, 640 n.
Pandects, i. 137 n. 4.
Pandulf, prince of Capua, iii. 422.
Paunonia, ii. 18, 449, 450, 742; iii. 318 n. 1, 330 and n. 2, 332, 333. Lower, ii. 438. See Sirmium.
Panopolis, cloister of, ii. 272. Nestorius in, 552.
Pantænus, catechist, in Arabia, i. 81. In India, 82. In Alexandria, 529, 691, 694 n. 1.
Pantheism, of the stoics, i. 16, 17. Unity and end of heathenism, 31. Opposition of Judaism to, 347. Origin of evil in, 374. In Gnosticism, 374, 375, 443, 444 n. 4, 446, 450. In the religions of ancient Asia, 479, 481, 573. Mystic, 450 n. 2. Relation of the doctrine of the Trinity to, 572, 573. And of the Resurrection, 654. Modern, 370 n. In Scotus, iii. 461, 462, 464 n. 4, 465, 489; iv. 444. In the Thon Iracians, iii. 588 n. 2. In the sect at Orleans, iii. 594. The Euchites, iii. 601. Pantheistic interpretations of Joachim's doctrine, iv. 230. (See Franciscans.) In the school of Averrhoes, iv. 431, 449. Contest of Christian theism with, iv. 444–450. Almaric, iv. 446, 449, 618. In the sects, v. 179 n. 1. Pantheistic friends of God, v. 392, 393–402, 409, 411.
Pantheistic tendencies, ii. 279, 615; iii. 183, iv. 275; v. 167.
Pantheon, presented to Boniface IV., iii. 134.
Pantomimes, i. 264.
Pantoppedan.
Annales eccles. Danic., p. 158, Poppo, iii. 269 n. 2.
Papa universalis, iii. 115. See Papacy, Pope.

Papa urbis æternæ, ii. 207.
Papacy, germ of the, ii. 211; ii. 198-208. In Britain, i. 85, 86. Zacharias and the, iii. 63. Its development in the *Third and Fourth Periods*, iii. 111-122, 210 (see Boniface, Gregory I.). In Britain, iii. 292, 346-399.
In the Fifth Period, iv. 82-197. Opponents of, 2 n. 2, 628. Papal elections, 169 and n. 2, 192 (see elections). Triumph of absolutism, 194. Papal system, 194-197. Attacked, 211. Distinct branches of the papal church government, 197-205. Bernard on the, 158-160, 255, 256. Abbot Joachim on the corruption of, 222-226. Downfall predicted, 187 n. 2, 202.
History in the Sixth Period, v. 1-133. Foundation of its power, 1. Wicklif and the, 137, 162, 164, 172, 173. Janow, 204. Huss, 304-309, 311. Epochs in the history of the papacy, iii. 112, 353; iv. 82, 173, 194. See Absolutism, Popes.
Papal court, v. 13, 21. See Avignon, Roman court.
Papal monarchy, i. 211; iii. 447; iv. 194; v. 21. See Papacy.
Papellards, iv. 285, 286, 303.
Paphlagonia, ii. 71, 180, 281. Image worship in, iii. 206.
Paphnutius, abbot, ii. 751.
Paphnutius, bishop and confessor, ii. 180, 181.
Papias, bp. of Hierapolis, i. 513 n. 1, 650, 651.
Λογίων κυριακῶν ἐξηγήσεις, fragm. J. A. Cramer, Catena in acta apost., Oxon, 1838, p. 12, Judas Iscariot, i. 650 n. 2.
Pappenheim, Von, marshal of the empire, v. 371.
Parables of Christ, with the Gnostics, i. 388. Bogomiles, iv. 558. Wheat and tares, i. 501; ii. 242; iv. 589; v. 158 n. 2. Mustard seed, etc., v. 201 (i. 1).
Parabolani, ii. 192, 570.
Paraclete, Mani, i. 487, 501, 504. In Montanism, i. 511, 512, 515-517, 527, 565 n. 3, 678. With Photinus, ii 482. In the Oriental sects, with Sergius, iii. 253, 254. Catharists, iii. 595; iv. 571.
Paracondaces, abbot, iii. 256.
Paradise, with Philo, i. 54 n. 2. The Rabbins, 56. In Manicheism, 497. Montanism, 523 n. 2. With Origen and Hieracas, 627, 714. With Tertullian, 654; Chrysostom, ii. 719; Catharists, iv. 581. John xxii., v. 38.
Παράδοσις ἀποστολική, i. 306, 528, 532.
Paraphrases, iii. 425, 471.
Παρασκευή, ii. 333 n. 1.
Parchor, the prophet, i. 406 n. 3, 408.
Pardulus of Laon, iii. 490.
Parentalia, i. 720; ii. 371, 372 n. 2.
Paris, introduction of Christianity there. Dionysius, i. 84; iii. 466. Bps. of, iii. 567; iv. 201, 325, 409, 423. University of, iv. 3, 33, 70, 173, 210, 211, 282, 283, 289, 340, 409, 410, 411, 417, 418 and n. 4, 425; v. 25, 32, 37 and n. 3, 84, 93, 192, 232, 248, 254, 353, 354, 407.
Spirit of freedom at, iv. 282, 289. Lull at, 63, 65, 70, 437. Yves summoned to, 121. Peter Cantor, 202. Fulco at, 209. Abelard, 373, 383. Albertus, 421. Aquinas, 422. Almaric, 446. The Sorbonne, 303. Scholasticism, 357. Life there, 413 and n. 7, 414, 417. St. Genovese, 416. Catharists, 583. The eternal gospel, 619. Convention of the Franciscan order at (an. 1292), 621. See Councils, an. 557, an. 615, an. 825, an. 1050-1052, an. 1210, an. 1212, an. 1406. See St. Victor, William of Auvergne.
The university and the popes in Avignon, v. 21. And that of Orleans, 32. Of Oxford, 93. Of Prague, 248. In the schism, 46 n. 1, 48-50, 52-56, 62-66, 72, 77. In the Council at Pisa, 78-83. After the Council at Pisa, 91-100. At Constance, 107, 110, 375. Pious women in Paris, 222. Jerome of Prague at, 246, 372, 375. Hist. Univers. Parisiens., see Boulæus.
Parish, parochia, ii. 194 and n. 1. Parish churches neglected, iii. 413. Parish priests, i. 194, iv. 277; oppressed, iii. 413; incompetent, iv. 287; Janow on, v. 203-205.
Parisian theologians, v. 13, 254, 375, 382. See Paris.
Parma, iii. 154, 396; iv. 107. Segarelli at, iv. 626 and n. 4, 627, 629. See Chronicle of Parma.
Parmenianus, Donatist bishop, ii. 249, 251 n. 2.
Parochia, parochus, παροικία, ii. 194 n. 1. See Parish.
Pars Donati, ii. 226.
Parsism. Among the Pharisees, i. 40. Parsic elements in the Essenean mysticism, 44, 47. In Gnosticism, 369, 374, 376, 378, 382. With Basilides, 402 and n. 2, 403. In Manicheism, 376, 479-495, 501, 506. Relation to Christianity, 482-484. Purgatory, 654. Paganism and, ii. 110. Opposition of, to Christianity, ii. 126-130. In the Oriental sects, iii. 243, 244 n. 4, 266, 587, 588; iv. 553.
Partheney, iv. 145.
Parthenius, bp. of Lampsacus, life of, ii. 319 n. 2.
Παρθένοι, i. 275.
Παρθενών, ii. 266 n. 1.
Parthia, Christianity there, i. 79, 80, 487.
Parthians expelled from Persia, 487.
Particularism, i. 86, 87; ii. 680, 701. With Mohammed, iii. 85. Particular conscience, iv. 84.
Parties, church, ii. 609-616. In the

schism, v. 63, 64. In reference to reform, 232, 233, 235, 240, 253, 254, 258.
Party, passion, ii. 72; conscience, iii. 350.
Party, spirit of, iv. 84.
Pasagii, iv. 590–592.
Pascal, i. 359.
Pascha, ii. 341 nn. 3, 6.
Paschal festival. See Easter, Passover.
Paschal lamb, v. 228.
Paschalis I., pope, iii. 433, 546.
Paschalis II., pope, iv. 2, 97 n. 8. Crusade against Henry IV., 129, 130 Remonstrance of the clergy of Liege, 130–132. Contest with Henry V., 132–135. Imprisoned, concedes the right of lay investiture, 134. Opinions in regard to his conduct, 134–140, 142, 223. His repentance, 140, 141. Consequent schism, 141. On the regalia, 147. Court of, 196 n. 2. Confirms the rule of the Cistercian order, 252. Opposed to the withdrawal of the cup, 345. See Harduin, t. vi. p. ii.
Ep. 22, to emp. Henry V., iv. 133 nn. 1. 2.
Paschalis III., pope, iv. 135 n. 1, 168.
Paschasius, deacon, iii. 25 n. 3.
Paschasius Radbert, teacher at Corbie, iii. 272. Doctrine of the Eucharist, 494–497, 499, 508. Opposed, 497–502, 515, 527, 528. Berengar against, 505, 506, 521, 522. Stories of actual appearances of the body and blood of Christ, 496, 521; iv. 345; v. 238. Controversy on Matt. 15: 17, iii. 529 n. 1.

Citations: —
Address to Charles the Bald, iii. 497 n. 2. Comm. on Matt. l. ix, 501 n. 1. L. xii., 501 nn. 1, 2. De corpore et sanguine Domini, c. 14, p. 1595, Peswil, 521 n. 2. De sacramento corporis et sanguinis Christi, 495 n. 2, c. 2, 496 n. 3; c. 3, 496 n. 1; c. 5, 499 n. 4; c. 14, miraculous stories, 496 n. 2; c. 19, 495 nn. 3, 4, 496 nn. 4, 5; f. 1506, 499 n. 2. Second edition, 497, and n. 2. (See D'Achery Spicileg., t. i., A. S. (O. B.) S. iv, p. 2). Ep. to Frudegard (opp. f. 1619), 496 n. 6. Life of Wala, 352 nn. 1, 3. Life of Adelard (Acta S. Jan.), 449 n. 3.

Passau, iii. 26. Bishopric there, 55. See Altmann, Pilgrim, Wenzel Tiem.
Passio Donati et Advocati.
(See Du Pin, monumenta, f. 190), ii. 228 n. 3; § 3, 229 n. 1.
Passion, the, of Christ. See Christ.
Passions, victory over, i. 76, 621. Conflict with, ii. 276; iv. 236. Passio and propassio, iv. 496, 497. See Affections, Temptation.
Passive tendency, iv. 623, 624. See Mysticism.
Passover festival, controversies with regard to the, i. 297–300; ii. 337, 338; iii. 347, 585. In the east and in the west, i. 297–300; ii. 338. Council of Nice on the, ii. 337, 338. Jewish, i. 324, 325, 331; ii. 337, 379; iii. 436 n. 2. See Easter.
Pastoral care, iv. 276, 277, 278, 281, 284, 287.

Pastoral epistles, the, i. 64, 396.
Pastoral instructions, iii. 123–126, 142, 143, 154, 426, 427.
Pastoral office, Grosshead on the, iv. 185, 186.
Pastors, ii. 193 (see Presbyters). Among the Paulicians, iii. 264. Franciscans as, see Pastoral care.
Patarenes, iii. 393; iv. 99, 225, 226, 565, 592.
Pataria (Patarenes), popular party in Milan, iii. 393. See Patarenes.
Paternoster, ii. 361 n. 2; iii. 42. See Lord's Prayer.
Paternus, the proconsul, i. 137.
Patience, of Christians, i. 76, 123, 127. Gregory I. on, iii. 149. Militz, v. 180. Huss, v. 267. Suso, v. 411, 412. See Martyrs.
Πάθος, in error, i. 21, n. 5, 22.
Patinus, bp. of Lyons, iii. 39 n. 3.
Patres apostolici, i. 109 n. 1. See Apostolic fathers.
Patriarchs, ii. 196–198; iii. 349, 545, 557, 570, 575. The twelve, with the Priscillianists, ii. 777, 778.
Patrick, St., ii. 146–149; iii. 10. Life of, ii. 147 n. 1.

Confessiones (see Opuscula Patricii, ed. J Warœi), ii. 146, 147 n. 1; c. 3, 148 n. 1; ff. 16, 20, 149 nn. 2, 3.

Patrimonium Petri, iii. 120, 234. Enlarged, 122.
Patripassians, i. 469, 576 n. 4, 577, 578, 583–585, 590, 592, 593 n. 610; ii. 485.
Patronage, rights of, first establishment of them, iii. 109. Their enlargement, limitation, 110.
In the Fourth Period. Abused, iii. 351, 400–404, 413. See Investiture.
Paul, Armenian, teacher of the Paulicians, iii. 246, 249.
Paul, martyr, i. 230.
Paul, patriarch of Constantinople, iii. 185–187, 190.
Paul I., pope, iii. 234. See Mansi Concil. t. xii.
Paul, son of Callinice, iii. 244, 246.
Paul, the Apostle, on the Pagan world, i. 4; iv. 370, 379. At Athens, i. 17 n. 2, 176; ii. 133 n. 3. Pharisee, i. 40, Persecutor, ii. 705. Conversion of, i. 544; ii. 705; iii. 312; iv. 79, 80, 245, 375. Method of, i. 550, 551; iii. 21; iv. 136, 158; v. 301. Relation to the other apostles, i. 212. To Peter, i. 319; iii. 437 n. 3; iv. 132, 424; v. 18, 32, 95, 127. Liberal culture of, iii. 150 n. 7; v. 262. Use of dialectics, ii. 233. Of the miracle, iii. 147. Revelations to, iv. 345 n. 3, 371, 405. Inspiration of (Jerome on), ii. 391, 392. Janow, v. 207. Labors among Gentile Christians, i. 342, 343. Manual labor, ii. 295; iii. 77, 286; v. 141. In Arabia, i. 81. In Spain, i. 85. At Rome, mar-

tyrdom, i. 203, 204, 213 (695); ii. 199; iii. 35; iv. 90. Images of, i. 292 n. 2; ii. 324, 326; iii. 199, 219 n. 3. Festival of, ii. 369; iii. 134. Tomb of, iii. 423. Church of in Rome, v. 3. Alluded to by Lucian? i. 158 n. 2. Influence in the early church, i. 159, 289, 351, 645. In the church constitution, i. 182, 188, 189, 197; earlier and later time, i. 187, 191; retrogression from his position, i. 194, 195. The Jewish spirit and, i. 340, 342, 343. With the Ebionites, i. 346, 349, 675. The Nazarenes concerning Paul, i. 349. In the Clementines, i. 360–362. In Gnosticism, i. 371, 383, 385, 388. With individual Gnostics, i. 396, 398, 413, 415, 417, 433, 450, 453, 457, 458 n. 3; (Marcion), 460–464, 470, 471, 473, 474. Porphyry on, i. 171. Clement, i. 262, 621. Justin Martyr, i. 364 and n. 2. With Origen, i. 544, 546, 550, 551, 628 and n. 2, 695. With the Artemonites, i. 580 n. 1. Hegesippus, i. 675, 676. Clement of Rome, i. 676. With Irenæus and Tertullian, i. 679, 680 n. 2 (290, 294). With Julian, ii. 46, 55, 56. Augustin and, ii. 124, 398, 624, 627, 630, 678; iv. 376. Jerome, ii. 391, 392, 747. Hilary, ii. 620. Prædestinatus, ii. 704, 705. Bishop Daniel, iii. 54 n. 2. Desiderius, iii. 56 n. 5. Migetius, iii. 157 n. 1. With the Paulicians, iii. 245, 246 and n. 1, 247, 248, 251–254, 258, 268. Claudius of Turin, iii. 431. Awakening influence of Paul, iii. 593. Abbot Joachim, iv. 227–229. Catharists and, iv. 569, 570, 576. Wicklif, v. 157, 171, 172. Janow, v. 207, 209. Huss, v. 332, 362. Nicholas of Basle, 391, 392. On Judaism and Christianity, i. 62, 63, 64; iv. 72, 81; v. 238. Power of Christianity, i. 72, 129, 249. Evidence of the Gospel, i. 75, 176; v. 27. On Charismata, i. 170, 180, 186, 510, 544; iii. 174. Universal priesthood, i. 180. On lay preaching (in the Apostolic constitutions), i. 197. Church discipline, i. 218; ii. 24. On conversion, i. 249. The stadium, i. 265. On slavery, i. 269; ii. 288; iii. 99. Place, in worship; the church in the house, i. 290. On fasts and festivals, i. 294, 297, 299 and n. 2. Church singing, i. 304. On preaching (i. 197), 323 n. 1; iii. 77, 124. Divine service, i. 327. Jewish and pagan Christians, i. 341, 363. Gnosis, i. 366. Second marriage, i. 522 n. 4. Faith and sight, i. 546, 645. Historical Christianity, i. 550, 551. Creation, i. 564. Trinity, i. 572, 574, 575. The manifold operations of the spirit, i. 595; iii. 179. Resurrection, i. 655. Corinthian church, ii. 48. On marriage of clergy, ii. 180, 182, 309; iii. 383. On martyrdom, ii. 253 n. 2. Difference in usages, ii. 335; iv. 92. The natural and spiritual man, i. 628; ii. 487; iv. 428; v. 8. Dependence on God, ii. 488; iii. 465 n. 3. Against superstition, iii. 64. On knowledge of Christ, iii. 143. Assurance, iii. 146. On intercourse with unbelievers, iii. 157 n. 1. Headship in the church, iii. 116. The Gospel as final, iii. 192, 209, 371, 406. Church offices, iii. 209. Contentment, iii. 306. Number of the saved, iii. 421. Incomprehensibility of God's decrees, ii. 699; iii. 477. 1 Tim. 2 : 4, iii. 482. 2 Cor. 5 : 16, iii. 522. Kings, iii. 537. Sect in Col. 2 : 2, iii. 592 n. 1. Life without law, iv. 11. False teachers, iv. 73. Magistrates, iv. 109 n. 1, 142, 172, 202. Clergy in secular affairs, iv. 147; v. 86. On sorrow, iv. 250. On knowledge, iv. 377. Eternity in predestination, iv. 475. Freewill, ii. 689, 705; iv. 516. The law and sin, iv. 554; v. 206, 209. Armor of, iv. 532. With Chrysomalos, works, iv. 561. Inner man, iv. 562. Antichrist, iv. 615; v. 239. Authority of Scripture, v. 27, 28, 40. The last times, v. 42, 178, 211. Spiritual liberty, v. (8), 118, 212. The Lord's Supper, v. 157, 220, 225. Orders of the clergy, v. 170. The church, v. 171, 172. Grace, v. 214 n. 3. His epistles, i. 64, 72, 290, 297, 396, 574, 575; iv. 616; copied, iii. 81 n. 1. See Commentaries, Pauline, The several epistles.

Paul, the hermit, ii. 264.

Paul Bernreider.

Life of Gregory VII., § 11, iii. 381 n. 2.

Paul of Antioch, Gnostic, i. 695.

Paul of Samosata, bp. of Antioch. His doctrine, i. 601–603. His character and methods, 603–605. Banishment of the church hymns, 604 (304). Deposition, 605 (142). Lucian and, 722 n. 6. Arius and, ii. 404. Apollinaris on, ii. 486. Doctrines of Nestorius compared with his, ii. 511, 563 n. 5.

Cited in Epiphanius, hæres., 67, i. 602 nn. 1, 5. In Leont. Byzant. c. Nest. et Eutychen, 602 n. 2, (63) n. 2 (see Erlich). Synodal letter against (in Euseb.), 7, c. 30), 602 n 4, 603 n. 4. In Mansi, conc. i. f. 1034 (pub. by Turrian), 603 nn. 1, 3. See Logos, Malchion, Monarchians.

Paul Perrin.

Hist. des Vaudois, I. iii.; iv. 605 n. 2. Albigeois, 642 n. 2.

Paul Warnefrid (Diaconus).

Homiliarium, iii. 126, Gesta episc. Mettens. (See Perz Mon., t. 2), Chrodegang, iii. 128 n. 1.

Paulicians, iii. 244–270. Their origin, 244. Derivation of the name; their founder, 246, 247. Their adherence to the N. T., particularly to the writings of St. Paul, 247. Distinguished teachers among them, 249, 250. Their opposition to image worship, 250. Their spread in Asia Minor, 250. False accusations brought against them, 253. Their conspiracy and flight, 256. Their irruptions into the Roman provinces, 256. *Doctrines* of the Paulicians, 256–263. On the creation of the world, 257. On the Demiurge, 257–263, 266–268. On heaven, 257. On human nature, 258. On redemption and the person of the Redeemer, 260–262, 594 n. 3. Against the worship of the Virgin Mary, 262. On the passion of Christ, 262. Against the adoration of the cross, 262, 598. Against the celebration of the sacraments, 263, 595 n. 2. Their ecclesiastical institutions, 263. Church offices among them, 264, 591 n. 5. Their system of morality, 265–267. Written records of the faith among them, 267–269, 600. In Bulgaria? 309 n. 6.

In the Fourth Period, iii. 586–589, 598. Proceedings of Theodora and of Tzimesces against them, 587. Athinganians, 592.

In the Fifth Period. Their settlements beyond the limits of the Greek empire, iv. 552. In Philippopolis (iii. 587), 564. Publicani, 565. Allied sects, 552, 567. See Peter of Sicily, Photius, Rader.

Paulicius. See Paulitzky.
Pauline church, i. 328; development, 342. See Paul.
Paulinus, bp. of Antioch, ii. 458. 461, 464.
Paulinus, bp. of York, iii. 19, 20.
Paulinus, canonical at Metz.

Ep. to Berengar, iii. 508 n. 3.

Paulinus, deacon of Milan, ii. 640.

Life of Ambrose, ii. 95 n. 4, 215 n. 1.

Paulinus, magister, ii. 519 n. 1.
Paulinus, patriarch of Aquileia, iii. 167.
Paulinus of Nola.

Carmen 9 and 10, de Felicis natali, ii. 328 n. 1. Ep. 36, ad Macarium, 119 n. 4. Ep. 321, 317 n. 3.

Paulitzky (Paulicius), Polish commandant, iv. 7, 8, 10.
Paullinianus, brother of Jerome, ii. 748.
Paulus, bp. of Emesa. Homily at Alexandria, ii. 346 n. 2. Deputy of Orientals at A., 542.
Paulus, imperial commissioner, ii. 229.
Paulus, notary, Catena of, ii. 34.
Paulus, patriarch of Constantinople, resigns his office, iii. 225. Death, 226.
Paulus Alvarus, friend of Eulogius, bp. of Toledo, iii. 340. On confessing Christ, 337. His Indiculus Luminosus (in Florez, España Sagrada, t. xi.), 343, 344.

Citations from his writings:—
Indiculus Luminosus, iii. 343 n. 2, 344 nn. 1–3; § 5, John the martyr, 339 n. 1; § 6, Mohammedan law against blasphemy, 339 n. 2; § 9, f. 219, Christians at court, 335 n. 3. 327 uu. 2–4; f. 220, condition of the Christians before the persecution, 336 n. 1; § 11, 344 n.

4; § 15, 344 n. 5; § 23, on Mohammed, 345 n. 1. Life of Eulogius (see Schott, Hispaña Illust., IV. and Acta S. March), 340 n. 2, 342 n. 2; f. 148, ep. to Speraindeo, 439 n. 3.

Paulus Diaconus. See Paul Warnefrid.
Paulus Orosius, presbyter of Tarraco, his history of the world, ii. 114. Pelagius, 632 n. 2. In the Pelagian controversy, 641, 642. Priscillian, 776 n. 5.

Adv. paganos, hist. libri vii., ii. 114 n. 2. Pref., name Pagani, 90 n. 5. L. viii. 32, the Burgundians, iii. 4 n. 2. Apologia de arbitr. libertat. (ed. Havercamp, p. 607), ii. 665 n 2.

Pauperes Catholici, iv. 612, 613.
Pauperes Christi, iv. 247.
Pauperes de Lombardia, iv. 609.
Pauperes de Lugduno, i. 352; iv. 609.
Pauperes Sacerdotes Christi, v. 248.
Pausanias, defence of the myths, i. 12.

Arcadica, or l. vii. c. 2, § 2, i. 12 n. 1.

Pavia (Ticinum), iii. 28 n. 3, 29 n. 3, 34, 469, 470 and n. 3. See Councils, an. 850, an. 853, an. 1160, an. 1423.
Payne. See Petrus Paganus.
Peace, proposals for a universal, iii. 407, 454. Promoted by Christian missionaries, iv. 24. Peacemaking, iii. 505; iv. 213, 294, 299. Clemangis on the means of promoting. v. 115, 116. Jacobellus on, v. 297. Huss on, v. 324.
Peasant, vocation of the, v. 214.
Peasant war in Germany, v. 158. Insurrections of peasantry in England, 159, 160, 161.
Peccata mortalia, venal a, i. 221, 226, 227, 240, 244, 245; ii. 319. Occulta, publica, iii. 136 n. 4.
Peene, river, iv. 18.
Pegua. See Francesco
Pekin (Cambalu), iv. 57–59.
Pelagian controversy, ii. 638–658; iv. 485. The questions in dispute, ii. 658–687. See Semi-Pelagian controversy.
Pelagianism, and Arianism, ii. 408 n. 4. And Nestorianism, ii. 495 n. 2. Foothold for, in Hilary's doctrine, ii. 620. In the apologists against Mohammedanism, iii. 88. Opposition to, iii. 148, 431, 472. In the Greek church, iii. 554. In the sects, near Arras and Liege, iii. 597. Abelard and, iv. 390, 493.

Opposition to in the Fifth Period, iv. 485, 488, 509, 510, 523. *In the Sixth Period*, v. 167; v. 350.

Pelagians, on baptism, unbaptized infants, ii. 728–730.
Pelagius, account of his character, ii. 624, 631–639. Letter to Demetrias, 633, 634. Comm. on Paul's epistles, 638. Cœlestius, 639. In the controversy, 624, 639–651, 659, 662, 663, 666, 669–679, 697 n. 1, 721. On baptism, 730. Purgatory, 637, 643 n. 2, 736. Theodore of Mopsuestia and, 713. Berengar on, iii. 505 n. 1. Abelard and, iv. 493.

Citations from his writings: —
De lib. arbitrio, l. i., li. 661 n. 1. Ep. ad Demetriad., cc. 2, 3, obedience to the divine commands possible, 637 nn. 3, 4; c. 8, custom a second nature, 671 n. 3; c. 9, works of supererogation, 634 nn. 5, 6; study of the Bible, 635 n 3; c 18. on unity in the moral life, 634 n. 1; false humility, 634 nn. 2-4; c. 19, the oath, 635 n. 6. On Col. 1 : 22, 637 n. 3. On Eph. 4 : 4. 5, 636 n. 2. On Ephes. 5:5, 6, 636 n. 4. On 1 Cor. 3 : 13, 637 n, 1. On 1 Cor. 6 : 9, 636 n. 4. On 1 Cor. 10 : 1, 636 n. 3. On 1 Cor. 13 : 3, 635 n. 2. On 11. Cor. 3 : 6, 635 n. 4. On 11. Cor. 6 : 12, 635 n. 1. On 11. Cor. 11 : 3, 637 n. 2. On 11. Cor. 12 : 20, 636 n. 1. On Rom. 5 : 12, 670 n. 1, 671. On Rom. 7 : 8, 670 n. 2. On Rom. 7, 671 n. 3. On Rom. 16 : 1, deaconesses, 191 n. 2.

Pelagius II., pope, iii. 141.
Pelagius, Roman archdeacon, ii. 596.
Pella, i. 344.
Pelusium. See Isidore of.
Pelzel.

Life of Wenceslaus, v. 253 n., 273 n. Doc. No. 81, p. 103 (ed. Prag., 1788), Bethlehem chapel, 236 n. 1. No. 229 (in Urkundenbuch), p. 130, petition against the burning of Wicklif's writings, 261 n. Thl. 11. s. 568, 262 n. 1. Urkundenbuch, No. 221, ep. of Wenceslaus to the cardinals, 271 n. 2. No. 230, confession of Huss, 274 n. 4.

Penance, regulations in regard to in the First Period, i. 218–220. Controversies relating to, 220, 221, 226–246. Germ of the Catholic doctrine, 647. For sins committed after baptism, 647, 654. With the Montanists, 522, 523.
In the Second Period. Imitated by Julian, ii 63 n. 3. Classes of penitents, 213. Difficulties in administering, Ambrose, 214–216. In the Greek church, abolished, 216. In the Meletian schism, 252–254 n. 1. Letter of Peter of Alexandria, 252.
In the Third Period. In the new states, iii. 95. System of, 136–140. Defects in administration, 140. Private and public penance, 136, 137. Instructions with regard to the administration of it; pecuniary fines introduced, 137, 138. Severer kinds of penance, 140. Gregory the Great on, 212.
In the Fourth Period, iii. 450–454. In preparation for the universal peace, 407. Opposite tendencies, 450, 451 Public and private, 451, 454. Council of Mentz on, 451. Compensation, 451, 452. Substitution, 452. Self castigation defended by Damiani, 451. Grades of guilt distinguished, 453, 454. At the deposition of Photius, 570 and n. 1.
In the Fifth Period. Assassins of the excommunicated, iv. 129 n. 4. The pirates and Bernard, 237. St. Francis on the dangers of, 273. Life of penance, 276. Louis IX., 285 n. 4. A sacrament, 335, 347. System of, 347–354. Three parts of, 347. False penance, 348. Effect of indulgences on, 348, 349. Law of Innocent III., regarding, 353. Abelard on, 390. With the Catharists, 577, 587 n. 5.
In the Sixth Period. Power of Peter confined to, v. 39. Clemangis on the administration of, 54. Gerson, use of penance money, 81. Council of Constance, 113. Militz, 174. Huss, 281. Tauler, 384, 407. Ruysbroch, 385, 386. 404. See Penitence.

Penitence, i. 218–221, 684 n. 2. Proofs of, i. 218, 219; ii. 213. Ambrose on, ii. 215. Peter of Alexandria on, ii. 254. Principles of, ii. 254 n. 1. Gregory I. on, iii. 145, 146. Ratherins, iii. 441. Relation to redemption, iii. 451. To indulgence, iv. 350. To forgiveness, iv. 615; v. 30. Fruits of, in monasticism, iv. 234. Clemangis on the necessity of, v. 114, 115. Militz, v. 182. See Penance, Penitents, Repentance.

Penitents, treatment of, i. 218–221. Classes of, 213. Prayer for the, ii. 361 n. 2. See Donatist Schism, Meletian Schism, Penance.

Penny preachers, iv. 279, 351, 352.
Pentapolis, ii. 181, 196, 215, 388, 763.
Pentateuch, with the Pharisees, i. 39 The Sadducees, 41, 42. The Alexandrian Jews, 53. In the Clementines, 355, 358. Genuineness, 355. The Ebionites, 358 n. 1. Ptolemæus, 439 n. 1.

Pentecost, festival of, i. 300, 301 ; ii. 332, 342, 343, 360, 361, 452; iii. 134, 156. See Whitsuntide.

People, the, relation of, to the philosophical religions of antiquity, i. 29. See Aristocratic spirit.

Pepin of Aquitania, iii. 460. Adalhard, 273 n. 1.
Pepin of Heristal, maj. dom., iii. 44.
Pepin the Little, Boniface and, iii. 55. Sturm, 75 n. 1. Maj. dom., 68. Anointed king, 69 (v. 15). Gregory I., 73. General assemblies, 96. Increases the patrimony of St. Peter, 119, 120. Improves the church psalmody, 127. Organs, 128 n. 4. In the image controversy, 233, 234. Referred to by Nicholas I. (?), 360, 361. Supply of vacant bishoprics, 401 n. 4. Benedict of Aniane, 414.

Pepuza, Pepuzians, i. 513 n. 1, 525.
Peræa, flight to, i. 343.
Peraldus, iv. 519.
Percy, Henry, v. 147, 148.
Peregrinus Proteus, cynic, i. 158, 159.
Perfect, the, among the Manicheans, i. 503. See Elect.
Perfecti. See Perfects.
Perfectibility of Christianity, Gnostics on the, i. 389. Montanists, 512. Compare Development, Joachim, Abbot.
Perfection, moral, Pelagius on, ii. 642, 644 n. 1, 671, 672, 676. Augustin, ii. 683. State of, iii. 183. Evangelical, iv. 272, 291, 292; v. 25, 216. Monas-

tic idea of, iv 524-526. Janow on, v. 215. Christian, v. 249, 282, 403.
Perfects, among the Catharists, iv. 576 and n. 2, 579-581, 584, 585.
Perfectus, martyr, iii. 338, 343.
Pergamus, school of Platonists there, ii. 42. Julian at, 44 n. 1.
Pericopes, iii. 126.
Perigueux (Petragorium), sect at, iv. 594, 604.
Περιοδενταί, ii. 193 and n. 6, 221, 253.
Περίοδοι ἀποστολων, apocryphal writing. Act. conc. Nic. 2, actio 5 (ed. Mansi, t. xiii. f. 167), i. 500 n. 4.
Periods of excitement, i. 370. Of transition, v. 1, 274, 380. See Epochs.
Peristera, ii. 262.
Perjury, iv. 131. Of John XXIII., v. 111. Huss on, v. 361, 362. See Oath.
Permanence, in effects of the Christian faith, i. 72, 74.
Permission and causality, i. 374. See Evil, Predestination.
Pernan, v. 320.
Perpetua, the martyr, i. 123, 124.
Perrin. See Paul.
Persecutions, of Christians by Pagans, history of, i. 83, 84, 86-156; ii. 1-6, 80, 81, 83, 84, 99, 102 n. 2, 125, 126, 130-136, 137, 138, 141, 151, 152-156; iii. 42, 45, 72, 286, 301-303, 326, 327, 331; iv. 10, 38, 39, 40, 42. Causes of the early, i. 86-93. Occasions, i. 67, 76, 103, 104, 119, 126, 136, 153, 283. Conduct of Christians under, i. 76, 77, 109, 111, 114, 132-135, 151; ii. 19, 70, 80, 133, 135 n. 1. Impression produced by their conduct, i. 76, 77, 105, 109, 111; ii. 155. Salutary effects of, i. 130, 131, 135, 138, 143 n. 1, 208; ii. 86, 87, 141. Immunity purchased, i. 121. Withdrawal from, i. 132, 133, 134. Seeking of, wavering under, i. 132, 133, 135, 151 (see Lapsi, Sacrificati, Traditores). Consolations under, i. 138. In the provinces, i. 131. Intermission of, i. 142. Causes of cessation, i. 117, 140, 142, 156. See Diocletian, M. Aurelius, Maximin, Nero, Trajan.
Against the Manicheans, i. 505. Of pagans by Christians, ii. 34, 88 n., 95, 96-99, 104-110. Julian on, ii. 70, 80, 81-83, 84; in Norway, iii. 297, 298. See Force.
Of Jews, ii. 95, 512 (iii. 13 n. 1). Of Donatists, 226-238. Donatists on persecution, 247, 248. Augustin on, 249-252. Of Aërius and his party, 379. By Nestorius, 505, 553 n. 4. In the Nestorian disputes, 548-555, 572. By Vandals, 238, 473, 709 (iii. 5 n. 2). Of Athanasius, see Athanasius. Of Origenists, 753, 755, 756 (see Chrysostom). Of Audians, 767. Of Manicheans, 769, 770.
Of image worshippers, iii. 220, 224, 534, 536 n. 2, 538, 540-543, 546, 547.
Of Paulicians, 248, 254-256, 587, 589. Of the adherents of Ignatius, 560. Of sects, 591, 592, 596, 398, 599, 601-603. Branding, 588 n. 3, 589. Effects of, 586, 587. Of Christians by Mohammedans, 336-345; iv. 124.
In Pomerania, iv. 10. Liefland, 38. In Persia, 56 (ii. 125-136, 141, 143). Of Jews, 71-76. Of the adherents of Innocent II., 145. Of Saracens, 190. Of the sects. 448, 585 n. 1, 640-644; (Bogomiles), 557-560; (Catharists), 586, 589, 590; (Waldenses), 609; (Apostolicals), 628-633. Of Greeks by the Latins, 539. In the Greek church, 534, 546-550, 552. Burning, 448. Bernard, Hildegard, Peter Cantor on, 586, 587. The Catharists on, 589. Wm. of Paris, 589. Peter of Cluny on, 597.
Persecutions of the church foretold, v. 60, 113, 114, 180, 322 (see Hildegard). Of pious clergy and laymen, Janow on, 232, 233. Patience under, 180, 267. Of castigatory preachers, 258. Huss, 258, 267 (see Huss). At Prague, 288, 289. Henry of Nordlingen, 383 n. 2. Crucifratres, 412. See Fanaticism, Jerome, Martyrdom.
Perseverance, i. 630. With Augustin, ii. 684. Arnulph, iii. 445 n. 2. Florus, iii. 490. Synod of Valence on, 493. Of angels, iv. 486.
Persia, Jews in, ii. 125, 126. Mongol empire in, iv. 56. See Mani, Manicheans, Parsism.
Persian church, foundation of the, i. 80. Infant baptism in the, 314, 498. Connection with the Syrian church, 486. Persecution, ii. 112 n. 2, 125-136, 141, 143; iv. 56. Schism with the Roman church, ii. 136. Syriac version of the Bible, ii. 137. Activity in spreading the gospel, ii. 136, 141; iii. 89, 90 n. 2. Nestorianism, ii. 589, 610, 611; iii. 89. Under the Mongol rule, iv. 49, 56, 57. See Ebed Jesu., Ibas, Nestorians, Steph. Euod., Asseman.
Persian mysticism, i. 44.
Persian wars, i. 144, 149 n. 1; ii. 69, 86, 87 n. 3, 132, 136. With Armenia, ii. 137, 138. Conquest of Armenia, ii. 612. Conquests in the Roman empire, iii. 84. Provinces lost, iii. 176.
Persico-Jewish ideas, ii. 736.
Person of Christ, doctrine of the, i. 576, 577, 592, 593, 631-640. Sabellius, i. 597, 599, 601; ii. 478-504, 573, 708, 717. Controversies regarding the, ii. 504-616. Julian of Eclanum on the, ii. 655. Leporius, ii. 656, 657. Gnostic view, ii. 561. See Gnostics.
In the Third Period. Adoptianist controversy, iii. 157-168. In the Greek church, 169. With Maximus, 171, 173. Monotheletic controversy, 175-197. The Euchites, 591. Catharists, iv. 574. See article Christ.

Personality of God, i. 571. Of the Logos, i. 600–602; ii. 405. Essence of, v. 402. See Holy Spirit.
Persons, distinction of, in the Godhead, ii. 403, 439; iv. 360, 369, 462, 465. Person in Christ, ii. 500, 501. See Person of Christ, Trinity.

Pertz.
Citations: —
Italienische Reise, law of Nicholas II. on papal elections, iii. 388 n. 1. T. i. ff. 463, 465. Annales Bertiniani, Lothaire and Nicholas I., 356 nn. 1, 4. Monumenta hist. germ., t. ii., life of Sturm, 75 n. 3, 76 nn. 1, 2; life of Willehad, 82 n. 2; Gesta episc. Mettens. Chrodegang., 128 n. 1. T. ii. f. 30, Vita St. Galli, 29 n. 1; c. 1, f. 334, life of Boniface, 46 n. 2, 48 n. 1, 49 n. 1; Adalbert, 56 n. 5, 63 n. 1; f. 405, Lindger, 45 n. 1 (80 n. 2); f. 576, Corvey, 273 n. 2; f. 681, life of Louis the Pious (an. 828), 553 n. 3; f. 698, life of Anschar, Heridae., 271 n.; f. 706, Anschar (c. 22), 279 n. T. iii., Scriptores rerum Germanicum, life of Gallus, 36 n. 2.

Pescennius Niger, i. 119.
Pessinus, town in Galatia, ii. 86.
Pestilence in the reign of Marcus Aurelius, i. 104. In Alexandria and Carthage, conduct of the Christians, i. 257, 258. In the time of Gregory the Great, iii. 112. Of Constantine Copronymus. iii. 214. In Pomerania, hostility excited against the clergy, iv. 26, 100. Influence on mental development, v. 380.
Peswil, priest, iii. 521 n. 2.
Peter, abp. of Amalfi, iii. 583.
Peter, abp. of Moustier en Tarantaise, iv 213. Life of, 214 n. 1, 294 n. 3. See Acta S. May.
Peter, bp. of Alexandria, in the Meletian schism, ii. 252–255. Arius, 409 n. 3. Festival of, 423. Homoousion, 461. His pastoral ep. to the Egyptian church, 252 and n. 2. Ep. to the Alexandrian community, 254 and n. 1.
Peter, bp. of the Saracens, ii. 143.
Peter, monk, among the Anglo-Saxons, iii. 11. Sent to Rome, 14.
Peter, monk in Florence, iii. 399.
Peter, patriarch of Antioch. iii. 583 n. 1, 584 and n. 1, 585. On bread in the Lord's Supper, 584 n. 2. See Cotelerius, Monumenta, t. ii.
Peter, patriarch of Jerusalem, ii. 596, 597, Ep. to Constantinople, 596 n. 3.
Peter, the Apostle, in Babylon, i. 79 n. 4. In Parthia, i. 80. Primacy of, representative of church unity, i. 183, 211–213, 216, 319; (Aug. on), ii. 200, 201; iii. 116, 349, 386; iv. 175. Relations with Paul, i. 171, 319, 417, 461; iv. 132, 424; v. 95, 127; (Paulicians on), iii. 247. At Rome, i. 203, 204, 213; ii. 199; v. 32. Confession of, ii. 497; iii. 585. The rock, i. 211; ii. 200, 201; iii. 24, 166; iv. 88; v. 25, 304. Power of the keys, i. 517, 518; ii. 200; iii. 24, 35, 113 n. 4, 438; iv. 194, 195; v. 39, 108. Christ's rebuke to, ii. 498. Paying of tribute, iv. 167, 172. Command to (Matt. 26 : 52), i. 273; iv. 215 (v. 7). Denial, iii. 386, 514; iv. 139. Deliverance of, v. 358. At Cæsarea, ii. 155; v. 222. Wisdom of, iii. 83. Labors preparatory, i. 341. Poverty of, v. 14. Dispute with Simon Magus, i. 296 n. 5, 454 n.; ii. 335. Relation to the Alexandrian and Antiochian churches, ii. 203. Martyrdom, i. 203, 204, 213; ii. 199; iii. 35. Tomb of, pilgrimages to, ii. 199, 378; iii. 48, 118, 120, 140, 423, 437; iv. 157, 640. Churches named for, iii. 52, 81, 457. Church at Rome, ii. 160, 347 n. 4; iii. 191, 355, 367, 546; iv. 157, 298; v. 3; synod in, iii. 367; assemblies of Henry VII. before, v. 36; Militz at, v. 180, 181. Of Peter and Paul, iii. 19. Festival of, ii. 324, 369; iii. 113. Images of, i. 292 n. 2; ii. 324; iii. 219 n. 3. Picture of. iii. 199. Princeps apostolorum, iii. 349. Banner of St., iii. 398 and n. 3. Dignity of the Roman church connected with, i. 213, 216; ii. 202; iii. 24, 35, 310, 369, 376; iv. 90, 222; (John of Paris on), v. 18, 19. Roman bishops as successors of, ii. 202; iii. 48, 113 n. 4; iv. 158, 161, 166, 176, 183, 536, 540, 593; v. 18, 85, 95, 123, 301, 304, 350; (Gregory the Great on), iii. 112–114, 116; (Stephen II.), 121; (Gregory VII.), iv. 83 n. 3, 86; (Bernard on), iv. 158, 159; (Defensor pacis), v. 31, 32. Mediation of, iii. 191. In the Clementines, i. 353, 361, 362. Visions of, iii. 19, 56 n. 5. Boniface and, iii. 48, 52 (copy of the epistles of, 52). Bishop Daniel, iii. 54 n. 2. Claudius of Turin on, iii. 437 and n. 3, 438. With Joachim, iv. 227–229, 231. Abelard on, iv. 376, 377. Lull, iv. 482. Rejected by the Paulicians, iii. 247, 269. Patrimony of, iii. 120. See Cathedra, Petri, Keys.
On questions in baptism, i. 308 n. 5. Fasting on the Sabbath, ii. 335. Obedience, iv. 165. Salvation by faith, ii. 121, 122. Convocation of councils, v. 85. Ep. to James in the Clementines, i. 361.
I. Pet., 2 : 6, 8, i. 554. 2 : 9, i. 180. 2 : 13, ii. 283 n. 1. 2 : 18, v. 257. 3 : 21, i. 306 n. 2, 308 n. 5. 4 : 10, ii. 283 n. 1. 5 : 13, i. 79 n. 4.

Peter Alix, iii. 511 n. 1.
Peter Bernard, abbot (Eugene III.), iv. 152.
Peter Cantor, character of, iv. 414. On exemptions, 202, 203. Absentees, 207. Lectures at Paris, 209. Worldly bishops, officials, 212. Confessors, 212 nn. 2–4. Orthodoxy and morals, 304. Victorine, bp. of Tournay, against secularization in the church, 414. Against persecuting the Catharists, 587, 588. Judgments of God, 588.
Citations: —
Verbum abbreviatum. (Summa), iv. 207 n. 3, 414; f. 7, on arbitrary interpretation 414 nn. 3, 4; c. 24, officiales, 212 nn. 2, 3, 6, 213 n. 1; cc. 27, 28, sale of masses, 346 nn. 2, 5;

c. 34, absentees, 207 n. 4; c. 51, study of law, 204 n. 1; f. 114, exemptions, 202 n. 6, 203 n. 1; f. 171, Alex. III., on the papal office, 173 n. 2; f. 200, on persecution, 587 n. 2, 588 nn. 5, 6; f. 211, quibbling interpretation, 304 u. 4, 415 n. 1; c. 80, f. 212, orthodoxy and morals, 304 n. 3; c. 127, f. 201, oaths, 304 n. 2; f. 587, Henry of Cluny, 604 n. 2.

Peter Chrysologus, ii. 350 n. 2.
Peter D'Ailly. See D'Ailly.
Peter Damiani. See Damiani.
Peter de Bernadone, iv. 270.
Peter de Bosco, v. 7.
Peter de la Celle, abbot, iv. 331, 382, 488.

Epp. l. iii. ep. 4, image of God, iv. 488 nn. 1-3. L. vi. ep. 23, sinlessness of Mary, 322 n. 1. L. ix. ep. 10, the same, 332 n. 6.

Peter de Lucalongo, iv. 58.
Peter de Lugio, apostolical (Petrus Lucensis), iv. 636. Babylon, 635 n. 1. On perfect and imperfect poverty, 635 n. 2. See Philip of Limborch.
Peter de Luna, cardinal, v. 52, 55, 56. See Benedict XIII.
Peter de Rusia (Rossiaco), iv. 211.
Peter de St. Angelo, v. 293, 294.
Peter de Vineis, chancellor, iv. 180

Ep. ii., of Frederic II., iv. 180 n. 1.

Peter Gerber. See Peter the Clothier.
Peter Leonis, cardinal, iv. 142 n. 3, 144.
Peter Lombard, character, school of, iv. 409-411. Method of, 204. Three parts of penance, 347, 353. Aquinas, 422. Sentences of, 409, 421. Lull on the, 437. Being of God, 462. Man's original state, 487. Original sin, 495. Sinlessness of Jesus, 496. Doctrine of atonement, 505. Justifying faith, 511.

Citations from his writings:—
On absolution, iv. 347 nn. 2, 3. L. ii. Dist. 24, original state, 487 n. 3; determinations of the church on the being of God, 462 n. 6.

Peter Mongus, head of the Monophysite party, ii. 586-588.
Peter of Amiens (the hermit), iv. 124, 125, 154.
Peter of Blois, episcopal insignia of abbots, iv. 202. Officials, 212. Estrangement of theologians from the study of the Bible, 415.

Citations:—
Ep. 25, officiales, iv. 212 n. 5. Ep. 28, A Becket, 169 n. 4. Ep. 53, falsifying of bulls, 205 n. 1. Ep. 60, nepotism, 207 n. 1 Ep. 68, exemption of abbots, falsifying of bulls, 205 n. 1. Ep. 76, distaste for the Bible, study of law, 204 u. 1, 415 n. 7. Ep. 90, to an abbot, 202 nn. 4, 5. Ep. 101, unprofitable directions of theological culture, 415 nn. 2-4. Ep. 140, study of law, unfruitful speculations, 204 n. 1, 415 nn. 5, 6. Ep. 152, appeals to Rome, 199 n. 1.

Peter of Bruis, reformer in South France, iv. 595-597, 598, 602 and n. 5, 604.
Peter of Cluny on, 602 n. 5.
Peter of Castelnau, iv. 641 and n. 4.
Peter of Cluny (Mauritius), the Venerable, character of, iv. 249-251. The Jews, 75. Anaclete, 144. Admonition to Innocent II., 194. Pilgrimages, 238. To a recluse, 242. Mother of, 246, 249, 250. On asceticism, solitude, 249, 250. Christian communion, 251. Compared with Bernard as the man of love, 259 (75). Luxury in monastic life, 263. The church, love, 264. On the divinity of Christ, 328. Abelard, 398, 400. Peter of Bruis, 595. The Petrobrusians, 595 n. 2, 597, 603. Henry of Cluny, 602 n. 5.

Citations:—
Ep. to a prior, on excessive asceticism, iv. 250 n. 1. Ep. to his brother on the death of their mother, 250 n. 2. Ep. against the Petrobrusians (epp. f. 1119), 595 n. 2, 597 and n., 602 n. 5, 603. L. i. ep. 20, to a recluse, 242 nn. 3, 4. L. ii. ep. 15, to a knight, 238 n. 3; ep. 17, his mother, 247 n. 1, 249 n. 4; ep. 22, to a monk, on flying h s country, Christian intercourse. 250 n. 3, 271 n. 2; ep. 28, to Innocent II., 194 nn. 3, =. L. iii. ep. 7, the studious monk, 249 n. 5. L. iv. c. 36, ep. to Louis VII. of France, the Jews, 75 nn. 1, 2; ep. 4. Bernard and Abelard, 398 n.; ep. 21, to Heloise, last years of Abelard, 400 nn. 1, 2. L. vi. ep. 12, to Eugene III., 251 n. 3; ep. 15, luxury of the Cluniacensians, 263 n. 4.

Peter of Corvaro, v. 36.
Peter of Dresden, v. 338.
Peter of Mladanowec. See Mladanowec.
Peter of Morone (Celestin V.), iv. 193.

Autobiography of, iv. 193 n. 1. Tracts by, 193 n. 2. Life, 193 n. 3 See Acta S. May, t. 4.

Peter of Poictiers, iv. 410. Image of God, 487.

Libri sententiarum, iv. 410 n. 2. P. ii. c. 9, 487 n. 4.

Peter of Sicily, iii. 244 n. 1. Letter of Sergius, 258, 259 nn. The Paulicians on the Virgin Mary, 262. Ep. to the Laodiceans, 268. The Paulicians in Bulgaria, 537 n. 6.

Citations:—
His account of the Paulicians (see Hist. Paulic., ed. Bader., Ingolstadt, 1604), iii. 244 n. 1; f. 6, the Paulicians, knowledge of N. T., 252 n. 6; f. 16, on the creation, 257 n. 2; f. 18, on the Virgin Mary, 262 n. 3; on the Lord's Supper, 263 n. 2; on the O. T., 267 n. 3; on the gospels, 268 n. 2; f. 20, presbyters, 264 n. 4; f. 40, their relation to Mani, 246 n. 3; f. 54, Sergius, 251 n. 1; f. 60, epistle of, his labors, 252 n. 2; f. 62, his influence among monks and clergy, 252 n. 7, hostile inroads of the Paulicians, 256 n. 3; f. 64, language of S. concerning himself, 252 n. 8, 253 nn. 1, 2; f. 66, Argaum, 256 n. 2; f. 68, S. on the πορνεία, 1 Cor. 6:18, 258 nn., 259 nn. Marginal remark on the gospels used by the later Paulicians, 268 n. 3, 269 n. 2.

Peter of Vaux-Sernai. See Chronicle of.
Peter of Verona, Dominican, his life, iv. 585 n. 1.
Peter of Znaim, v. 244.
Peter Philargi, archbishop of Milan, v. 83, 84. See Alexander V.
Peter (Gerber) the clothier, patriarch of Antioch, ii. 589, 590.

Peter the hermit. See Peter of Amiens.
Peter the Venerable, iv. 249. See Peter of Cluny.
Peter Waldus, iv. 606, 607, 609.
Petermann, Dr., iii. 587 n. 8.
Petilianus, Donatist bishop, at the conference at Carthage, ii. 237, 245. Pastoral letters against the Catholic church, 246. On persecution, 247, 248. See Aug. brevic. collat. c. Donatistis and c. lit. Petil.
Petitions in favor of persecuting the Christians, ii. 3, 4.
Petra, ii. 552.
Petrarch, on the papal court at Avignon, v. 44, 67.
> Epp. senil. l. vii. 1 (oper. ed. Basil., p. 811). Ep. to Urban VI., v. 44 n.

Petrobrusians, iv. 595 and n. 2, 596, 602 n. 5, 604. See Peter of Bruis.
Petrus de Marca.
> De concord. sacerdotii et imperii, iii. 457 n. 6.

Petrus Paganus (Payne), v. 244 n. 1.
Petrus Passinus.
> Thesaurus asceticus (Paris, 1684), life of Bartholomæus of Crypta Ferrata, f. 440, abdication of Benedict IX., iii. 376 n. 2.

Pez.
Citations: —
> Thesaurus anecdotorum novissimus, t. i. f. 47, Dissert. Isagog., Abbreviatio de libro Petri Parisiensis, iv. 410 n. 1; f. 476, Alanus, Ars. Cath. fidei, iv. 417 n. 2. T. i. p. ii., f. 133, Gerbert de corp. et sang. Dom., iii. 502 n. 1; f. 221, Gerhoh de gloria et honore f. hom., c. Folmar, iv. 345 n. 3, 346 n. 1. T. ii. f. 482, Gerhoh de diff. cler. sæc. et reg., iv. 206 n. 3. T. ii. p. ii. f. 75, Placidus de honore eccles., iv. 137 n. 4; ff. 281, 359, Gerhoh de ædificio Dei, iv. 133 nn. 1, 3, 214 n. 3. T. ii. p. iii. ff. 204, 228, life of Courad of Salzburg, iv. 141 n. 1, 143 n. 6. T. iii. p. ii., Scito te ipsum of Abelard, ff. 652, 646, 666, 682, iv. 346 n. 3, 351 n. 4, 386 n. 4, 349 n. T. iv. p. ii., Anti-wickleffus, etc. (see Stephen of Dola). T. v. f. 157, Gerhoh in Ps. x., ordinance of Greg. VII., iv. 94 n. 2: f. 540, ep. to Alex. III., iv. 215 n. 2; ff. 792, 794, G. in Ps. 39, iv. 153 n. 4, 205 n. 4; ff. 1182, 1183, in Ps. 64, de corruptu statue ecclesiæ. iv. 83 n. 2, 151 n. 1; ff. 1352, 1353, in Ps. 67, iv. 208 nn. 4, 5: f. 1497, in Ps. 72, iv. 410 n. 3; f. 2034, in Ps. 133, iv. 143 n. 5; f. 2039, in Ps., iv. 208 n. 1.

Phædrus of Plato, i. 449, 623 n. 4.
Phalet, Prussian convert, iv. 43.
Pharan, iii. 181, 182 n. 2.
Pharaoh, ii. 627, 628.
Pharensis, synod of, iii. 24 n. 1.
Pharisaism, and the Essenes, i. 357, 396. Influence on Christianity, 351, 352.
Pharisees, i. 39, 40, 42 n. 3; iv. 559; v. 16, 59, 113, 114, 171, 189, 206, 212, 389. Relation to Christianity, i. 63, 538. Two classes, i. 63. With the Nazarenes, i. 349. Huss, v. 292 n. 4, 300, 319, 337.
Phasis, bp. of, iii. 177.
Phasitla, cloister of. ii. 612.
Pherecides Syrius, i. 402 n. 2.
> Fragmenta, p. 46, ed. Sturz, i. 402 n. 2.

Pherozes, Persian king, ii. 611.
Phidias, i. 27.
Philæ, worship of Isis at, ii. 105 n. 3.
Philagathus (John, archbishop of Placenza), iii. 422.
Philargi, cardinal Peter, v. 84. See Alexander V.
Philaster, on the Ophites, i. 447 n. 1.
> Hæres., § 91, the Rhetorians, ii. 767 n. 4.

Phileas, Egyptian bp., martyr, ii. 254 n.
Philemon, epistle to, ii. 391.
> V. 2, i. 185.

Philemon, the Roman presbyter, i. 712 n. 1.
Philip, companion of Christian, iv. 43.
Philip, companion of Gottfried, iv. 43.
Philip, duke of Suabia, iv. 176, 177, 582 n. 4.
Philip I., king of France, iv. 97 n. 8, 102. Repudiates his queen, 121. Firmness of Yves of Chartres, 121-123. The king under the ban, 123.
Philip, the apostle, v. 306.
Philip, the deacon, i. 316 n. 3.
Philip Augustus, king of France, iv. 175.
Philip of Limborch.
> Protocol of the inquisition at Tonlouse (Hist. Inquisitionis, app. Amstelodami, 1692), iv. 580, 581 n. 9, 584 n. 3, 614; ff. 15, 20, 22, 29, 59, 104, 111, 152, on the Catharists, 581 nn.; ff. 33, 76, 138; the same, 582 nn. 1-3; ff. 201, 207, 251, 290, the Waldenses, 614 nn. 4-7; f 360, the Apostolicals, 635 n. 2; f. 361, 631 n 2, 635 n. 1.

Philip of Sida, the catechist, i. 673.
Philip the Arabian, i. 126, 130, 683, 710; ii. 7.
Philip the Fair, king of France, his contest with Boniface VIII., v. 5-13, 19, 20. Clement, v. 20, 22. Abolition of the order of Knights Templar, 23. John XXII., council of Vincennes, 37, 38.
> Ep. to Boniface VIII., v. 7 nn. 2-4. See Hist. du diff.

Philippians.
> 1 : 1, i. 184. 1 : 16, i. 323 n. 1. 1 : 18, ii. 26 n. 4, 248, 767 n. 4; iii. 152 n. 2. 1 : 21, iii. 189. 1 : 23, ff., i. 266 : ii. 253 n. 2; v. 313. 2, ii. 407. 2 : 4, ii. 283 n. 1. 2 : 7, i. 224. 2 : 8, 9, ii. 407; iii. 160 n. 5. 2 : 10, i. 288; ii. 738 n. 1. 2 : 11, iii. 318. 2 : 15, i. 251. 2 : 13, ii. 675. 2 : 15, i. 253. 3, v. 142. 3 : 15, ii. 602. 3 : 18, 19, ii. 685 n. 1. 3 : 20, v. 575. 4 : 3, i. 658. 4 : 7, i. 707. 4 : 13, i. 129.

Philippicus, Greek emperor, friend of Monotheletism, iii. 196, 203 n. 3.
Philippopolis, in Thrace, seat of the Paulicians, iii. 587; iv. 564. See Councils, an. 347.
Philistines, iv. 39.
Philo, on the office of the Jewish people, i. 35, 52. On the Essenes, 44, 47, 48 n. 3. Relation of Judaism to universal history, 52. Against mysteries, 52. Paradise, 54 n. 2. As representative of the Alexandrian Judaism, 52-60, 65.

Allegorical interpretation, 56, 657. On miracles, 55. On rationalists, 53. On contemplation, 59. Therapeutæ, 60, 61. Perpetuity of temple and Messianic period, 65. Golden age of Jerusalem, 65. Number of Jews in and about Alexandria, 50 n. 3. On the Logos, 351 n. 1 (57), 397, 424 n. 1, 578, 585, 597. Angels, 380. Theophanies, 386 n. 2. Creation, 396 n. 3. Distinction between the masses and the enlightened few, 381, 397, 578, 587 n. 3 (48 n. 3, 57, 58; iii. 170 n. 3; v. 568 n. 5). The temple, 407 n. 2. Matter, 456. Anthropopathism, 563. Polytheism, 587 n. 3. Trinity, 601 n. 1. The Serpent, 620 n. 6. Image of God, iii. 641 n. 4.

Citations: —
De Abrahamo, § 19, f. 364 prophetic office of the Jews, i. 52 n. 2; f. 367, Trinity, 601 n. 1. De Caritate, § 2, f. 699, vocation of the Jews, 52 n. 1. De Cherubim, § 5, falsehood, 58 n. 2. De confus. ling., § 5, 54 n. 2. De decalogo, § 22, therapeutic and moral life, opposition between, 59 n. 3. 60 n. 1; f. 790, 61 n. 4. De excerationibus, § 9, restoration of the Jews, 65 n. 2. De migratione Abrahami, § 16, neglect of the ceremonial law, 58 n. 3; f. 402, 59 n. 1. De monarchia, l. ii., the temple, a symbol of the world, 407 n. 2; § 3, continuance of, 65 n. 1. De mundi opificio, § 24, 396 n. 3. De i ominibus mutatis, § 8, f. 1053, scoffers, 51 n. 4. De plantat. Noæ, t. ii. § 8, f. 219, Paradise, 54 n. 2; § 17, pagan accusers of O. T., 53 n. 1. De præmio et pœna, § 7, self manifestation of God, 57 n. 4; § 15, reconciliation of nature with man, 65 n. 2; § 19, 65 n. 2. De profugis, § 1, asceticism, the occasion of family divisions, 59 n. 4; § 6, f. 455, human virtue first, 60 n. 5; § 7, hasty entrance on the Therapeutic life, 60 n. 3; §§ 15, 18, eternal life, 66 n. 2. De sacrif. Abel et Caini, § 17, 61 n. 2. De somniis, l. i. § 17, f. 590, literal interpreters, 54 n. 1; § 41, subordinate position in religion, 397 n. 3. De victimis, § 3, f. 238, the offering, for the race, 52 n. 4. De victimis offerent, f. 854, Therapeutæ, 61 n. 4; § 12, f. 856, the mysteries, 52 n. 5. De vita contemplativa, diffusion of Therapeutæ, § 3, 62 n. 1. De vita Mosis, L i. § 7, f. 607, renegades, 51 n. 1; § 27, f. 625, the Jews a priestly people, 52 n. 3. L. ii. § 3, perpetuity of the Mosaic law, § 38, miracles, 55 nn. 3, 4. L. iii. § 17, universality of sin, 60 n. 1; f. 681, contemplative class, 61 n. 4. Legis allegor., i. § 12, Δυναμις ἀληθινης ζωῆς, 66 n. 2. L. ii. § 7, creation of woman, 56 n. 1; § 21, solitude, 59 n. 2. L i i. § 3, immediate knowledge of God, 57 n. 4; § 73, 397 n. 2. Opp. f. 186, eunuchs, 69 n. 1. Oratio in Flaccum, § 6, number of Jews, 50 n. 3. Quæstiones in Genesin (Armenian trans., ed. Lips., opp., t. vii.), l. i. § 55, on anthropopathism, 57 n. 2. L. iii. § 3, p. 5, pagan accusers of O. T., 53 n. 1. Quis rer. divinar. hæres., § 16, f. 492, arbitrary interpretations of Philo, 55 n. 1. Quod deus immutab., § 11, on anthropopathism, 57 n. 2; § 1, fear and love in religion, 58 n. 1; § 16, sin, 56 n. 1. Quod deterior potiori insid., § 6, interpretation, 56 n. 2; § 7, asceticism, 60 n. 2. Quod omnis probus liber, § 12, the Essenes, 43 n. 3, 47 n. 2, 48 n. 3.

Philogonius, martyr, ii. 3–5 n. 2.
Philopatris, dialogue, ii. 111.
Philoponus. See John.

Philosophers, Christian, i. 275, 278, 279.
Philosophers, Pagan, their relation to Christianity, i. 176; ii. 106–110, 163. To other religions, ii. 62, 117. Influence of, ii. 21. Under Julian, 88 n. 1. Christian, iv. 434. Tatian on the, i. 672. Odo of Tournay, iv. 359. Abelard on the, iv. 383, 384. See Philosophy.
Philosopher's cloak. See Pallium.
Φιλοσοφία διὰ συμβόλων, i. 47.
Philosophical education, necessary for the catechists at Alexandria, i. 528, 529, 698, 701. Clement on, 533–539, 558. Tertullian, 558. Influence on the exposition of the doctrine concerning Christ, the word Logos, 585. Of Clement, 559, 620, 691. Justin Martyr, 662. Origen, 698.
Philosophical religion, i. 367; ii. 116. Development, iv. 355. Life (ascetical), ii. 78.
Philosophy, its source, i. 5. Influence, i. 6–11, 368. Uncertainty, i. 11, 354. Particular systems, i. 8. 15–35. Of the Essenes, i. 47. Need of a more positive, i. 368. Christian, i. 542, 670. Relation of philosophy to Christianity, i. 533–543, 667 n. 2, 672, 719. To Judaism, 666, 667. Philosophy of religion, ii. 39 (see Neo-Platonism). In the Western nations, ii. 52. Julian's advice to priests in relation to, ii. 62. Relation to religion, ii. 62, 106–110. Augustin, ii. 396, 397. Synesius, ii. 763. Scotus on philosophy and religion, iii. 462. Study of, iv. 415. Relation to faith, Lull on, iv. 64. To theology, iv. 64, 70, 369, 419, 432, 434, 435, 474. Abelard on the supernatural and, iv. 377; on the ancient, iv. 383, 384, 385 n. 4, 399 n. 3. Anselm, iv. 369. Hugo on the place of, iv. 401. Bacon on the province of, iv. 434, –35. Moral and speculative, iv. 434. Faith and, iv. 64, 418, 450. Worldly, v. 113. Philosophy and theology in England, Wicklif, 135, 142, 241, 261; in the time of Huss, v. 235, 241, 308, 309, 375, 376.
Philostorgius, Arian historian, on Theophilus Indicus, ii. 140. Ulphilas and the Goths, 150. Omissions in Ulphilas' trans. of the Bible, 152. Constans and Athanasius, 436 n 4.

H. E., l. i. § 7, ii. 417 n. 8; § 8, Constantia, 422 n. 1; § 9, 421 n. 2. L. ii. § 3, doctrine of Arius, 408 n. 3; § 5, Christian captives among the Goths, 149 n. 4, migration of Goths under Ulphilas, 152 n. 1; § 6, Theophilus Indicus, 142 n. 2. L. iii. §§ 3, 4, 5, the same, (l. 83 n. 1), 142 n. 2; § 14, the Christianity in India, 140 n. 5.

Philostratus, the rhetorician, on Apollonius of Tyana, i. 30, 173, 174.

Vita Apollonii Tyanensis, l. iv. f. 200 (ed. Morell. Par. 1608, c, 40, f. 181, opp. Philost. ed. Olcar), prayer of Apollonius, i. 31 n. 1; l-

vi. c. 29, 174 n. 2. Ep. 58, of Apollonius, 31 nn. 2-5.

Philoxenos (Xenayas), bp. of Hierapolis, on images, ii. 331. Philoxeucan trans. of Old Testament, 589.

Philumene, Marcionite, i. 474, 475.

Phineas, iii. 255, 579.

Phocæa, iii. 219 n. 1.

Phocas, Greek emperor, Gregory I. and, iii. 113 n. 1. The Pantheon, iii. 134. Decree concerning monasteries, iv. 530.

Phocas, martyr, ii. 371.

Phœnicia, persecution in, ii. 6. Paganism in, 26. See Emesa.

Photinus of Iconium, his erroneous doctrines spread among the Waraskians, Bavarians, and Burgundians, iii. 38, 39.

Photinus of Sirmium, — Photinianism, ii. 71, nn. 2, 3, 78 n. 1, 438, 440, 492, 506 n. 1, 509. Person of Christ, 481–483, 486.

Photius Damaskios, patriarch of Constantinople, his erudition ; Bibliotheca, iii. 530. As patriarch, 559, 560. In the image controversies, 549, 550 and n. 1, 559–578. Controversy between the Greek and Roman churches respecting his patriarchate, 561–578 (356). On the Latin church, 567 ; iv. 547. See Harduin, t. vi.

On Justin's writings, i. 666, 670. On Hippolytus, 681, 682. On Clement, 692. On Origen, 693 n. 2, 703 n. 5, 711 n. 3. Pierius and Theognostus, 613. Stephanus Gobarus, ii. 614.

On the Paulicians, iii. 257, 258, 263, 268, 269. Bogoris, 308 and n. 2, 309. Constantine, the philosopher, 314 n. 5. The Russians, 327. See Wolf.

Citations: —

Bibliotheca, p. 1. Theodore on the Dionysian writings, iii. 170 n. 2.

Cod. 52, Eustathians ; Synodal acts against the Euchites, ii. 277 n. 3, 279 n. 1. Cod. 54, Pelagianism and Nestorianism, ii. 495 n. 2. Cod. 59, Synod of the oak, ii. 759 n. 1. Cod. 95, "Acts" of Mani, i. 485 n. 3. Cod. 111, on the Stromata of Clement, i. 692 n. 4. Cod. 118, Origen, i. 693 n. 2, 704 n. 3, 711 n. 3. Cod. 121, Hippolytus, i. 681 n. 1. Cod. 177, Theodore against Jerome, ii. 712 nn. 2, 3. Cod. 179, Agapius, ii. 771 n. 2. Cod. 181, Damascius, ii. 110 n. 4. Cod. 202, works of Hippolitus, i. 682 nn. 3, 4. Cod. 215, Philoponus, ii. 613 n. 2. Cod. 232, Gobarus, ii. 6, 14 n. 2. Cod. 233, Germanus on Gregory of Nyssa, ii. 738 n. 4. Cod. 235, Gobarus, quotation from Hegesippus by, i. 675 n. 2.

Epistolæ. Ep. to Nicholas I. (Baronius, Annal. an. 861), iii. 559 n. 1, 565 n. 2. Ep. 2 (correspondence, ed. Monticut), f. 58, circular letter, 327 n. 2, 567 n. 3. Ep. 6, f. 70, to Bardas, 559 n. 5, 560 nn. 3, 4. Ep. 22, against cruel punishments, 560 n. 4. Ep. 64, images of Christ, 560 n. 1. Ep. 84, against the Occidentals, 566 n. 2. Epp. 85, 97, 114, his misfortunes, separation from his books, 572 n. 1. Ep. 97, to Michael III., 568 n. 3, 572 n. 1. Ep. 98, to the emp. Basilius, 568 n. 3. Ep. 101, the earthquake, 572 n. 1. Ep. 113, family of Bardas, 559 n. 1 ; the anathema, 571 n. 3. Ep. 116, the anathema, 571 n. 3. Ep 118, f. 160, Basilius, 568 n. 3 ; false plenipotentiaries, 575 n. 4. Epp. f. 40, to the Bulgarians, 309 n. 1 ; f. 49, to the bishops of the East, conversion of the Bulgarians, 308 n. 2.

His work against the Manicheans (see Wolf). On the Paulicians, iii. 244 n. 1. L. i. c. 2, name Paulicians, 244 n. 2 ; c. 4, f. 13, their origin, 246 n. 2 ; c. 7, their doctrines, incarnation, 261 n. 3 : c. 7, f. 28, the cross, 262 n. 5 ; f. 24, O. T. teachers, 267 n. 2, St. Peter, 269 n. 3 : c. 8, f. 25, their principles with regard to veracity, 267 n. 1 : c. 9, sacraments, 263 nn. 1, 2 ; oratories, 264 n. 2 ; c. 9, f. 29, use of the cross, 263 n. 3 ; f. 31, their church officers, 264 nn. 3, 4 ; f. 33, reverence paid to the gospels, 268 n. 1 ; c. 16, death of Constantine (Silvanus) 248 n. ; c. 18, Paul, and his son Theodore, 246 n. 4, 249 n ; c. 22, the Virgin Mary, 262 n. 2 ; f. 95, Sergius, 251 n. 1 ; f. 98 (and 111, 115), his designations of himself, 254 un. 1, 2, 252 n. 8 ; f. 108, on the dominant ch., 252 n. 5 ; f. 111, Paraclete, 253 n. 4, 254 n. 2 ; f. 112, labors of Sergius, 252 n. 2 ; f. 114, intercession of the spirit, 253 n. 3 ; c. 21, f. 116, their apostles. 264 n. 5 ; f. 117, the first sin, 258 n. 1 ; c. 22, f. 120, moral character of Sergius, 252 n. 4 ; f. 128, inquisitors cut off, 256 n. 1 ; ἄστατοι, 265 n. 3 ; f. 130, trade of S., 252 n. 3 ; c. 25. f. 134, συνέκδημοι, 265 n. 1. L. ii. c. 3, origin of the evil principle, 257 n. 1 : self revealing power of God, 260 n. 2 ; c. 5, the Creator, 257 n. 3 ; f. 147, 261 n. 1 ; f. 169, John 1 : 9, 260 n. 1 ; c. 10, f. 190, name derived from St. Paul, 247 n. 1.

Photius on his relations with Basilius, and Ignatius (see Harduin, vi. p. i. f. 255), iii. 572 n. 2, 573 n. 1. See Councils, Const. an. 879.

Φωτιζόμενοι, ii. 358.

Φρόνησις, Basilides, i. 400.

Φροντιστήρια, ii. 317.

Phrygia, i. 109, 117, ii. 327, 451, 563 ; iii. 203, 205, 219, 229 n. 3 ; iv. 530. Seat of Montanism, i. 509, 513. Of Iconoclasm, iii. 229 n. 3. Paulicians, iii. 254. Upper, iii. 592.

Phthartodocetism, ii. 613.

Φθορά, i. 615.

Phusik, martyr, ii. 132.

Φύσις, ii. 614. See Nature.

Physical and spiritual phenomena connected, v. 380.

Physicians, ii. 169, 537 ; iv. 310 n. 7.

Picardy, iv. 235.

Piccolomini, Æneas Sylvio, v. 380 n. See Æneas Silvius.

Picts, pagans, ii. 146, 149. Conversion of the, iii. 10.

Pictures, in churches, ii. 328, 329. Devotional use of, iii. 198, 199, 237, 238, 239, 547 ; iv. 58, 79, 307. Symbolical of the papal system, at Rome, iv. 163 and n. 3, 164 and n. 3, 165. In monasteries, Bernard on, iv. 264. In Bethlehem chapel, v. 332, 333. See Art, Image worship, Mosaic.

Piedmont, Anselm, iv. 361. Waldenses in, 609.

Pierius, the Alexandrian, i. 713.

Pierre de Bères, knight, iv. 577 n. 5.

Pierre de Vaux, iv. 606. See Peter Waldo.

Pietism, in Montanism, i. 523, 565. Pietistic bent promoted by monks, iv. 285, 286. In the sects, iv. 594. "Pietists"

term of reproach, i. 273; iv. 206, 303; v. 143, 213, 288, 386.
Piety, ii. 628. Discouraged, ii. 260, 765, 766; v. 216-218, 221, 224. Among the laity, ii. 261, 766; iii. 445; v. 213-218, 221, 224, 306, 381. Caricature of, iv. 271, 303. See Laity, societies among the.
Pilate, i. 8, 74, 93, 451; v. 38, 39, 191, 301 n. 3, 314, 359.
Pileus, abp. of Genoa, v. 119.

Address to conc. Const., v. 119 n. 3.

Pilgrim of Passau, iii. 331, 332, and n. 3.

Ep. to Benedict VI., Hungarian mission, ii. 331 n. 1.

Pilgrimages, ii. 259, 377, 378; iii. 7, 20 n. 1, 276, 394; iv. 172, 236, 276 n. 2, 638. Opposer of, iii. 57. Cautions against trusting in, iii. 131, 443. As penance, iii. 140. To Rome, iii. 58 n. 1, 131, 132, 290, 322, 367 n. 2, 378, 433, 437, 438, 440, 452, 453, 475; iv 164, 165, 204, 222, 298, 640. Dangers of, iii. 58 n. 1, 367 n. 2. Advantages of, iii. 118, 440. To Jerusalem, iii. 398, 448 n. 1, 470 n 2; iv. 237, 298. Indulgences for, iii. 451, 452. Dispensation from, on taking monastic vows, iv. 237, 238. Raymund Palmaris, iv. 297, 298. Hildebert on, iv. 306. Lull on, iv. 307 (63). Benedict, iii. 414. Catharists, iv. 578. Buddhist, iv. 52. Wicklif on, v. 140. To Wilsnack, v. 237-239. Huss on, v. 324.
Pilgrims to Palestine, ill treated by Saracens, iv. 124, 125. At Rome during the Jubilee, v. 3.
Pilichdorf.

Tract against the Waldenses, c. 1, iv. 605 n. 1, 606 n. 4, c. 20 et seq., 614 n. 3. See Bibl. Patr. Lugd., t. xxv.

Pilsen, v. 174.
Piper, Prof. See Studien u. Kritiken, 1838.
Piracy, pirates, ii. 146, 147, 149; iii. 300; iv. 26, 236, 237, 294.
Pisa, Lull at, iv. 69, and n. 2, 70, 190. Bernard at, iv. 146. Frederic II. at, iv. 152. Papal court at, iv. 198. Flight of the cardinals of Gregory XII. to, v. 77. Appointment of the council at, v. 77, 78, 253. University of, v. 89. See Councils an. 1409, Bernard of Pisa.
Pisidia, ii. 590; iii. 206, 229 n. 3, 250.
Pisinus, in Galatia, iii. 229 n. 3.
Πιστικοί, i. 381, 692.
Πίστις and γνῶσις, i. 208, 305 n. 1, 413, 460, 529-557, 645, 698, ii. 395. Jewish conception of πίστις, i. 395 (381). See Gnosticism, Faith.
Pistus, Arian bishop of Alexandria, ii. 432, 433.
Pityus, ii. 761.
Pius, bishop of Rome, i. 660 and n. 2.

Ep. 2, in the Pseudo-Isidorean decretals, iii. 348 n. 1.

Placenza, church assembly at, an. 1095, iv. 125. Palmaris at, iv. 297-299.
Places, sacred, ii. 240; iii. 45. Francis of Assisi, and, iv. 271, 272. Peter of Bruis, iv. 597. Dolcino, iv. 636.
Placidus, disciple of Paschasius Radbert, iii. 495.
Placidus, Benedict's disciple, ii. 300.
Placidus of Nonantula, Liber de honore ecclesiæ, iv. 137-140. On the church, 138, 139. On the oath taken by Paschalis, 139.

Citations:—
iv. 138 nu. 1, 2. See Pez, Thesaurus, t. ii. p. 2.

Placita episcoporum, iii. 107 n. 6.
Plague, the, iii. 92 n. 3. See Black death.
Planetary spirits, empire, i. 455, 456.
Planets, the seven, i. 444, 445, 446. Origen on the, 625.
Planck, Hist. of the Papacy, ii. 1, p. 198; iv. 113 n. 2.
Plato, on the natural explanation of myths, i. 5. His philosophy, view of Socrates, 18. Ταπεινότης, 19, 166. His monotheism, 25. Idea of the absolute, as distinguished from the Supreme Spirit, 26 (586). Of God, 78. Timæus, 25 n. 1, 26 n. 3, 78. On falsehood, 58 n. 2. Busts of, 292. Μανία, 356. Mundane spirit, 380. The Symposium, 386. In Gnosticism, 390, 408 and n. 1. Θεός γενητός, 424 n. 1. Phædrus, 449, 623 n. 4. With Tertullian, 618. Μὴ ὄν, 623 n. 5. Justin Martyr, 662. And Moses, 667 n. 1. With Julian, ii, 50 n. 3, 62. Translated by Victorinus, ii. 77. Libanius, ii. 85. On the relation of passions to reason; Themistius, ii. 158, 159. Study of; the Monophysites, ii. 613. Abelard on, iv. 378 n. 3, 379, 384, 467. Janow, v. 212. With Wicklif, v. 165 n. 2, 166. See Νοῦς.

Citations:—
De legib., 1. iv. (ed. Bip., vol. viii., p. 185), ταπεινόν, i. 19, threefold relation of God to mankind, 572 n. L. x. (ed. Bip., vol. ix., pp. 87-91), conflict between προνοία and ἀνάγκη, 375 n. 2. De republica, 26 n. 2. L. ii. p. 257 and l. iii., p. 266 (vel. vi., ed. Bip.), on falsehood, 58 n. 2. Phædrus (ed. Bip., vol. x., p. 285), Sophists, 5 n. Philetus, 26 n. 3. Timæus, 25 n. 1, 26 n. 3 (ed. Bip., t. ix., f. 326), the mortal in man proceeds from subordinate gods, 396 n. 3.

Plato, monk, iii. 100, 230 n. 1, 536 notes 1, 2. See Theodore, Abbot.
Platonic philosophy, Platonism, i. 15. Its essence, 18. Relation to Christianity, 19, 33, 34, 379, 388, 391, 558, 559, 585. Original and derivative, 19-35. In later Judaism, 40, 51-54, 58, 64, 366, 377. Relation to the Essenes, 44, 47. In Alexandria, 51, 52, 53, 366, 377, 508, 542. With Celsus, 163, 166. In Gnosticism, 366, 368, 369, 374-380, 390, 391, 449, 456. Its place in the Alexandrian Gnosis, ii. 395. Two tendencies in Platonism: practical and contempla-

tive, i. 378, 379. In Asia, i. 479. With Clement, i. 540. With Origen, i. 543, 550, 569, 571, 622, 627; ii. 740, 764 n. 2. Aristotle, i. 611. With Constantine, ii. 24 n. 3, 163. In paganism, ii. 27. In the doctrine of the church, ii. 387, 388, 438, 445. With Augustin, ii. 124, 294, 295, 395–400, 401, 625, 626, 669. Synesius, ii. 763. In Scotus, iii. 461. Pseudo-Dionysian writings, iii. 466, 467. See Neo-Platonism, Platonists.
   Platonic philosophy in the thirteenth century, iv. 419, 420.

Platonic anthropology, i. 611. Μανία, i. 356.

Platonico-Aristotelian realism, ii. 669; iv. 356.

Platonists, the, on magnetic influences, i. 161, 162. And the oracles, 172 n. 4. The irrational soul, 376. On Homer, ii. 41. At the head of the pagan party, ii. 42, 102, 104, 106. Influence on Julian, ii. 42, 43, 44 n. 1. Toleration, ii. 163. Latin and Arabic translations of the, iv. 420, 444 (378 n. 3). See Neo-Platonism.

Platten, lake of, iii. 316.

Πλατυσμός, Sabellius, i. 599, see 595 nn. 2, 3, 596 n. 5.

Plaul, Master, v. 83.

Plays, Tertullian on, i. 264. Spiritual, iv. 39.

Pleroma, πλήρωμα, in Gnosticism, i. 373 n. 3, 374, 375 n. 5, 389, 393, 399 n. 2, 418, 420–427, 432, 434, 441, 442, 443, 477; iv. 571.

Plescow, v. 373.

Pliny the Elder, on religion, i. 10, 11. On the Essenes, i. 43.

   Hist. nat., l. ii. c. 4, *et seq.*, l. vii. c. 1, the Highest cannot concern himself about men, i. 10 n. 2. L. xx. c. 3, wild cucumber, iv. 582 n. 2. L. xxxiii. c. 24, holosphyratos, iv. 535 n. 1.

Pliny the Younger, on suicide, i. 16 n. 2. Report to Trajan, 79, 97–100, 105, 175. On the Christian hymns, 98, 304, 575. Testimony of slaves, 112 n. 3. Agapæ, 325.

   Epistles. L. i. 12, 22, l. iii. 7, l. vi. 24, suicide, i. 16 n. 2. L. x., ep. 97, i. 97 n. 2, 99 nn. 1, 2.

Plotinus, his intuition of the absolute, i. 27. Stages of development, 29. Pantheism, 31. Porphyry, 170. Relation to Platonism, 368, 391 (iv. 445). Against the Gnostics, 368, 390–394, 415, 472. Matter, 376 n. 1. Ethics, 379, 415. Relation to Christianity, 390, 391 and n. 1. Monism, 391 (iv. 445). Providence, reason, 406 and n. 2, 472. Clement and Plotinus, 586 n. 6. Anthropology, 611. Pupil of Ammonius Saccas, 698. Magic, ii. 43. Division of the virtues, iv. 523, 524 n. 1.

   Citations: —
   In anecdota græca, t. 2, p. 237 (ed. Villoison,

Venet. 1781), intuition of the absolute, i. 26 n. 4. Ennead I., l. ii., division of virtues, iv 523 n. 2. L. viii. c. 14, longing of the Ὕλη, i. 376 n. 1. II., l. ix., i. 369 n. 3. L. x. c. 9, classes of men, i. 29 n. 4. III., l. ii., providence, i. 406 n. 2. L. vii., endless becoming, i. 569 n. 2; νοῦς and ὄν, i. 586 n. 6. See Porphyry.

Ploughmen, iii. 426.

Plozk, v. 36.

Plurality of benefices, iv. 207; v. 50, 367.

Plutarch, against foreign religious customs, i. 13. Superstition and infidelity, 13–15, 21, 22, 71. Epicureanism, 15. Stoics, 18 n. 1. Relation of religions, 20, 21, 368. Hypocrisy of philosophers, 21. Anger of the gods, 22. The priest, 22. Natural causes, oracles, 23, 24. Demons, 28. Alexander the Great, his significance, 50. Moral freedom, 611.

   Citations: —
   Adversus Stoicos, c. 31, i. 20 n. 3. De anima procreatrice in Timæo, c. 9 (opp., ed. Hutten, t. 13, p. 295), 376 n. 2. De εἰ apud Delphos, c. 20, the only true Being, 25 n. 2. De Iside et Osiride, c. 1, αἰώνιος ζωή, 34 n. 2; c. 20, myths, 23 n. 1; c. 23, on unbelief, 21 n. 3; c. 37, relations of different religions to one another, 20 n. 2; c. 71, effects of false notions of the gods, 14 n. 5. De Pythiæ oraculis, c. 6, Sibylline oracles, 177 n. 1; cc. 7, 21, inspiration, 24 nn. 2–4; c. 9, Sibyl cited, 176 n. 2; c. 24, 514 n. 1. De sera numinis vindicta, c. 3, humiliation by punishment, 19 n. 2. De Stoicorum repugnantiis, c. 6, self-contradiction of the Stoics, 18 n. 1; c. 13, Stoical pride, 16 n. 1; c. 15, punishment, 22 n. 1; c. 35, Chrysippus on evil, 16 n. 7; c. 38, the God of Judaism, 22 n. 3; c. 39, cycles, 16 n. 5. De superstitione, c. 33, foreign ceremonies, 13 n. 1. Defectu oraculorum, l. i. c. 2, unity of religions, 20 n. 1; c. 9, decay of forms, 21 n. 1; c. 12, demons, 28 n. 1; c. 24, infinite series, 571 n. 2; c. 47, causes, divine and natural, 23 n. 2. Life of Alexander, c. 27, Psammon, on the kingdom of God, 34 n. 2. Non posse suaviter vivi secundum Epicurum, c. 20, reverence and faith, 15 n.; c. 22, hypocrisy, 21 n. 2. Oratio 1, de Alexandri virtute sive fortuna, §§ 6, 10, mission of Alexander, 50 nn. 1, 2. Quæstiones Platonicæ, qu., iv. 375 n. 2.

Πνεῦμα, i. 474, 492 n. 1, 636–639. Πνεύματα ὑλικοί, 456. See Spirit.

Πνευματικοί and ψυχικοί, among the Gnostics, i. 366, 381, 388, 389, 393, 395, 399 n. 2, 411, 413, 541. In particular systems, 411, 413, 414, 420–435, 441–447 456, 474, 476, 477, 502. With Origen, 546, 627, 628, 629. Ἰουδαϊσμὸς πνευματικός, 399.

Πνευματικόν, ii. 733 n. 4.

Pneumatology, i. 47, 612. See Anthropology.

Pneumatomachi, v. 186.

Po milni (Slavonian), iii. 324.

Pococke, specimen Hist. Arab., on Mani, i. 486 n. 2.

Pœnitentes, i. 219, 687. See Penitents.

Poets and poetry, consciousness of God in, i. 176. The Logos, i. 667. Study of, ii. 85, 116, 288; v. 113. Plato on, iv. 384. Rutilius, ii. 290 n. 1.

Christian; Alanus Magnus, iv. 417 n. 1. Alcuin, iii. 153 n. 4. Alphanus, iii. 399 n. 4; iv. 83 n. 1. Ambrose and Hilary, iii. 354 and n. 3. Arius, ii. 409. Damiani, iii. 399 n. 3. German national poets, iv. 180, 188, 215, 216. Sacred song, iv. 155, 313. Gregory Nazianzen, ii. 182 n. 3, 185 n. 1, 196 n. 3, 262 n. 1, 273 n. 6. Günther Ligurinus, iv. 148 n. 1, 149 n. 4. Κοσμᾶς ὁ μελωδὸς, iii. 206 n. 3. Livin, iii. 43 n. 2. Nigellus Witeker, iv. 265 n. 4. Otfrid, iii. 425. Paulinus of Nola, ii. 328 n. 1. Prosper, ii. 691 n. 1, 693 nn. 1, 2, 694 n. 1. Provençal, iv. 616 nn., 639 n. 2, 641 nn. 3, 4, 5. Roman de la Rose, iv. 289 n. 2. Rudolph of Liege, iv. 343 n. 4 Severus, ii. 13 n. 4, 323 n. 2. Synesius, ii. 371 n. 2. Theodulph of Orleans, iii. 132. Troubadours, iv. 604 n. 3, 616 n. 1. Walafrid Strabo, iii. 472 n., 474 n. 2. Walter von der Vogelweide, iv. 173 n. 1. See Hymns.

Poggio of Florence, v. 378 and n. 1, 379 and n. 2. See Van der Hardt, iii. f. 71.

Poictiers, council at (an. 1076), ii. 518. Bp. of, iv. 145, 408. See Gilbert, Hilary, Isidore, Peter.

Ποιμήν, i. 184; iii. 254, 264.

Poitou, iv. 247.

Poland, spread of Christianity in, iii. 330; iv. 1, 3, 4. Dukes of Poland and the Pomeranians, iv. 1, 6-8, 10, 11, 12, 14, 16, 24; and the Prussians, iv. 44. Otto in, iv. 3, 4, 17. Adalbert, iv. 41. Gottfried, iv. 43. Mongols in, iv. 49. Pilgrims from, v. 51. Poles at Constance, v. 127. Militz, v. 182. Polish nation at Prague, v. 247. Doctrines of Huss in, v. 357. Jerome in, v. 373.

Polemic, between Christians and pagans, i. 157-178; ii. 111-115. Against the Mohammedans, iii. 88; (Raymund Lull), iv. 61-71. Against Jews, iv. 77-81. Evil connected with, iv. 395. Mystics on, v. 360. Nicetas, iv. 530. See Apologists, Controversies.

Poli, merchants of the family of the, iv. 56, 57.

Political disturbances in the West, ii. 102. In North Africa, ii. 694, 695. Of the tenth century, iii. 425. In Oldenburg, iv. 643, 644. And religious, in England, v. 157-161. In Italy, see Italy.

Political idea, with the Romans, i. 85, 87, 100.

Political influences in choice of bps., ii. 185.

Polybius, on Roman superstition, i. 67.

Hist. 1. iii., 6, c. 6, cause, true and apparent, i. 3 n. L. vi. c. 56, superstition and the state, 6 nn. 2-4

Polycarp of Smyrna, the martyr, i. 109-111, 335 (v. 371). On the passover, 299 (iii. 32). Meeting with Marcion, 465. Ignatius, letter to the Philippians, 661. Irenæus on, 677, 680.

Polycrates, bishop of Ephesus, the apostle John, i. 194 n. 1. The passover controversy, 298, 299.

Ap. Euseb. h. eccles., l. v. c. 24, i. 194 n. 1, 298 n. 3.

Polycronius, monk, iii. 195.

Polygamy, in Bohemia, iii. 322. Among the Pomeranians, iv. 8, 9. Nestorian clergy in Tartary, iv. 52.

Polytheism, Pliny on, i. 10. According to the eclectic philosophy, 25. Tertullian against, 177. Judaism and, 347. Origen and Philo on, 587 n. 3. Of Julian, ii. 50, 51, 54, 57. Of Simplicius, ii. 106-110.

Pomerania, introduction of Christianity into, iv. 1-31, 130. Manners of the Pomeranians, 11. As missionaries, 43, 44.

Pomesanien, bishopric, iv. 45.

Pompa diaboli, i. 264, 509.

Pomponatius.

De natural. effect. admirand. causis, p. 142 et seq., iii. 591 n. 4.

Pontianus, North African bp., ii. 600.

Ponticus, the martyr, i. 114.

Pontifex Maximus, Constantine, ii. 23. Julian, 59. Gratian, 92.

Pontius.

Life of Cyprian, i. 139 n. 2, 222 nn. 2, 3, 225 nn. 1, 3. A. 1, 223 n. 1.

Pontius, abbot of Cluny, iv. 249, 345.

Pontoise (Pontisara), iv. 97 n. 8.

Pontus, Alexander of Abonoteichus in, i. 92. Pliny in, 97. Earthquakes in, 126. Influence of Origen, 716. Of Gregory Thaumaturgus, 719, 720. Persecution under Libanius, ii. 19. Asylum in, ii. 177 n. 1. In the patriarchate of Constantinople, ii. 196 n, 3, 197, 203. Eustathius, monachism, ii. 281 and n. 1. Evagrius, ii. 752. Chrysostom exiled to, ii. 761. See Amasca, Cæsarea, Comana, Pityus, Sinope, Trapezund.

Poor, goods bestowed on the, i. 222, 274. Agapæ, 325. Poor and rich principle, with the Gnostics, 402. Care of the poor, 232, 255, 256, 274, 278, 281; Constantine, ii. 26; Julian on, ii. 63; by bishops, ii. 168; iii. 103, 408 nn.; iv. 5, 213; Basil, ii. 169; council of Carthage on, ii. 192 n. 1; by women, ii. 262; in cloisters, ii. 272, 288; Crato, iii. 93 n. 3; by monks, iii. 104 n. 1, 415, 418; Alcuin, iii. 131, 132; Frideburg, iii. 282 n. 2; by spiritual societies, iv. 34; the laity, iv. 34, 255, 294, 296, 298, 299; by legates, iv. 198. Dominick, iv. 268. Berthold, iv. 318 n. 1. Eustathius on, iv. 533. The Catharists, iv. 577. Wicklif on, v. 138, 142. Militz, v. 182. Gifts of the, iii. 421. Fund for the, iv. 255. Bonaventura on the honor to be paid to poor and rich, iv. 288, 289. Gerson on the pope and the, v. 98. See Almsgiving, Poverty.

Poor priests, v. 143-145, 163. See Lollards.

Pope, the, authority of, law of Valentinian III., ii. 207.
Oath of obedience to the, iii. 48, 49, 54. Presents to the, 62 n. 3, 114. Relation to the metropolitan constitution, Boniface on, 64. Theocratical head over the nations, 68, 69, 111, 112, 355, 360, 361. Relation to the East Roman church and emperors, 112, 113 and n. 1, 117, 120, 210–212, 234, 536 n. 2, 545, 561–584. To bishops, 114. To the patriarchs of Constantinople, 115, 197, 576. To the Spanish church, 117, 118. To the English church, 118 (see Augustin, abbot). In civil affairs, 119. To the Frankish empire, 118–122, 351–358, 361, 362, 367, 377. Emperor crowned, anointed, by the, 120, 367. Declarations concerning their powers, 120, 349, 350. Supervision of the whole church, 113, 115, 120, 353, 359. Authority disputed or resisted, 121, 292, 351–382. Infallibility, Alcuin on, 122, 167, 350. Popes of the eighth century, 151. In the image controversies, 234, 551–553. Charlemagne and the, 242. Relation to the northern missions, 292. To the Bulgarians, 310–314. To the Moravians, 316, 319. In the Decretals, 346–351. Judge of bishops, 349, 369. Arnulph on the character and authority of the, 369, 370. Crimes of, in the tenth century, 366–368. In the eleventh century, 375, 376. Order of election, 387, 395 n. 2. Dominus apostolicus, 438. Absolution by the, 453. Supervision of books, 467.

In the Fifth Period. Connection with missions, iv. 43 n. 1, 44, 56 (see Innocent III., Innocent IV.). The Mongols, 49, 50, 56. Conduct towards Jews, 75. Imperial sovereignty over the world, 83, 87, 88–90, 120, 163 n. 1, 173–175. Head of the whole church, 87–89, 194. Consecrated by consent of the emperor, 92 n. 6, 151, 177. Coronation of emperors, 118, 119, 120, 161, 164 and n. 3, 177. Contests with the German emperors, iv. 103–121, 129–143, 161–169, 176–185, 582, 610. Appeals to the, 123 (see Appeals). Heretical, 135. Person of the, 140. In France, 144, 145, 152, 153, 157, 168, 183–185, 197. Bernard on the duties of the, 157–160, 255. On the secular authority of the, 158–160. Laws on papal elections, 169, 192. Emperor in papal elections, 92 nn. 4, 6, 151, 177. Abdication, deposition of, 193, 194. Journeyings of, 197 and n. 4. Relation to bishops, 200, 256. To abbots, 201. Predictions of Joachim concerning the, 223, 224. Mendicants and the (see Mendicant). Laws limiting indulgences, 352. Opposition to, 448, 610, 642. In the Greek church, 538–541, 544, 546. Relation to the period, 600. Wm. of St. Amour, 619. Dolcino, 636 and n. 3. See Extortions.

In the Sixth Period. Abdication, depositions of popes, v. 2, 4, 17, 18, 19, 64, 70, 71, 76, 94-96, 99, 101, 112, 125, 126, 352. Vicar of Christ, 13, 14, 17. Secular power contested, 14, 16, 146, 165. Power to bind and loose, 15, 98, 146, 171, 284. Church property, 16, 17. Dependence on France, 21, 22. Supreme authority on matters of faith and polity denied, 33, 40, 65, 92, 96, 107, 108, 127, 164, 165, 285 (see Occam). Simony, 34 (see Simony). Corruption, 35, 51. Secular possessions of, 39. Subtraction of allegiance to the, 63–65, 69, 70, 95, 96, 253. Power to convoke councils, 76, 96 (see Œcumenical Councils). Relation to ecclesiastical laws, 97, 112. To secular tribunals, 146. Servus servorum, 98. The Germans on the, 122. Wicklif on the, 137, 146, 147, 164, 172, 173. Janow on the, 202. Huss, 278, 284, 285, 299, 304, 307–309, 363 (see Huss). The Sword, 281, 282.

See Abbots, Absolutism, Avignon, Benefices, Bulls, Church constitution, Extortions, Legates, Nepotism, Papacy, Peter, Roman court, Simony. See, also, the individual popes.

Popes, Catharist, iv. 590.
Pophlagaria, iii. 558 n. 1.
Poppenbüttel, iii. 289 n. 2.
Poppholz, iii. 289 n. 2.
Poppo, archbishop of Triers, ep. to Benedict IX., on the hermit Simeon, iii. 445 n. 2, 448 n. 1.
Poppo, bp. of Aarhus, iii. 289.
Poppo, bp. of Brixen (Damasius II.), iii. 378.
Populace, rage of, against the Christians, i. 71, 92, 93, 94, 101, 109, 112, 126, 130, 136, 513, 664; iv. 26. Gothic, protect Christians, ii. 154. Decisions of, in favor of Christianity, iii. 285, 304, 305; iv. 8, 16, 29, 31.
Πορνεία, with the Paulicians, iii. 258–260.
Porphyrius, martyr, i. 722 n. 1.
Porphyry, bp. of Gaza, ii. 103. Life of, 103 n. 1.
Porphyry, pagan philosopher, Neo-Platonic mysticism, i. 27. Defence of image worship, 27. Demons, 28. Oracles, longing of heathenism, 31. Against Christianity, 170–173. Antinomian Gnostics, 385. Gnostic writings, 393 n. 3. Origen, 699 and n. 1. Arius classed with, ii. 421, 552. On John 7:10, Pelagius, ii. 646 n. 1.

Citations: —
De abstinentia carnis, l. i. c. 40 *et seq.*, i. 385 n. 2; l. ii. c. 34, Apollonius of Tyana, 26 n. 1. Ep. ad Marcellam uxorem, p. 172, c. 18, national worship, 170 n. 3; c. 24 (ed. Maii, Mil. 1816), faith, love, and hope, 170 n. 1. Κατὰ Χριστιανῶν, ap. Euseb., l. 6, c. 19, Ammonius Saccas, 699 n. 1. Περὶ τῆς ἐκ λογίων φιλοσοφίας, Euseb. præparat., l. iv. c. 7, oracles, 31 n. 7; Euseb. H. E., l. vi. c. 19, on artificial interpretations of O. T., 171 n. 3; a. Aug. de civitate Dei, l. xix. c. 23, fragments, theology drawn from the oracles, 171 n. 4; ap. Euseb. demonstrat. evang., l. iii. p. 134 and ed. Maii, fragments, 171 n. 4 (see Theodoret, Græc., affect. curat.) Vita Plotini, intuition of the absolute, 27 n. 1; c. 2, death of Plotinus, 31 n. 6; c. 16, Plotinus on the Gnostics, 390 n. 2.

Portiuncula, church of Mary at, iv. 272.
Porto, iii. 562. Cardinal bp. of, v. 10.
Porto Venere, Benedict XIII. at, v. 75, 76.
Portugal, iv. 174 n.
Posen, bp. of, v. 109.
Posidonius, deacon, ii. 520.
Possession. See Demoniacal.
Possessor, North African bp., ii. 710.
Possibility and necessity, iv. 482–485. See Predestination, Foreknowledge.
Possible and actual, v. 166, 167, 168.
Possidius, life of Augustin by, ii. 168 n. 1, 192 n. 1.
Postills, v. 193.
Potamon, confessor, ii. 427 n.
Pothinus of Lyons, i. 112, 677.
Potho of Prum, iv. 331, 333 n. 6.
De Statu domus dei, l. iii., festival of the Immaculate conception, iv. 331 n. 5; of the Trinity, 333 n. 6. See Bibl. Patr. Lugd., t. xxi.
Poverty, of the early church, i. 197, 346. With the Ebionites, 352, 367. Voluntary, 222, 274, 457, 462; iv. 149, 235. Gilbert on, iv. 78. In Cistercian monasteries, 252. Carthusian, 265. Albigenses, 269. The mendicants, 268, 270, 272 (v. 188). Catharists, 580. Waldenses, 608, 609, 611, 616. See Evangelical Poverty.
Poverty of spirit, in relation to Christianity, i. 63, 64.
Power of God (see Omnipotence). Ordinaria et absoluta, iv. 457.
Powers of darkness, Mani on the, i. 491, 494, 495, 497–499.
Prachatic, Christann of, v. 298, 310, 367.
Prachatic, priest of, v. 316.
Prachin, circle of, v. 235.
Practical bent, in mysticism, i. 44, 45, 60; iv. 371; v. 393, 409. In the Clementines, i. 395. Of Marcion, i. 462–464, 466, 467, 474, 478. Of the Christian mind, i. 560. Practical realism, i. 529. Practical and theoretical, i. 367. Practical interest in the Pelagians, ii. 660. With Gregory the Great, iii. 143, 144. In the Carolingian age, iii. 156. In the Greek church, iii. 169. Sergius, iii. 252, The Latin church, iii. 553. Arnold, Abelard, iv. 148. Societies, iv. 302,

303. Berthold, iv. 318. Peter Waldus, iv. 607. Huss, v. 237. Practical theology, iii. 460, 471, 472. Practical element in theology, Clemangis on, v. 61 Practical reformers, iv. 209; v. 192, 240, 243, 264.
Præcepta and consilia, ii. 635; iv. 525, 526; v. 213, 216, 249. See Consilia.
Prædestinati, v. 302.
Prædestinatus, i. 685; ii. 702 n. 2, 703–706, 767 n. 4. Author of, ii. 767 n. 4. II. 26, and 86, Tertullian, i. 685, nn. 2, 3. II. 88, Cœlestius, ii. 639 n. 2. L. ii., ii. 703 n. 2, 705 nn.; ll. ii. et iii., ii. 706 n. 1.
Prædicatores, iv. 221 n.
Prælectors, ii. 354.
Præsciti, iii. 474, 476; v. 302, 350, 353. See Merit, de congruo.
Pragmatic sanction, iv. 203.
Prague, archbishopric, iii. 321 n. 5, 322, 323, 332. Library at, iv. 279 n. 1.
Sixth Period. Alp. of, v. 182, 183, 186, 191, 223, 237, 294 (see Albic, Zbynek). Militz at, 174, 175, 181–183, n. 1. Conrad, 184–192. Janow, 194, 233–235. Pious women, 222. Ordinance relating to dress, 223. Huss at, 235–295, 316–320. Trial of Huss at (an. 1414), 243 n. 1, 250 n. 4, 254, 256, 258, 288 n. 1, 317 and n. 4. Jerome at, 245, 372. Disturbances at, 255, 256, 261, 288–295. Burning of Wiclif's books, 261. Bull of John XXIII. at, 276–293. Martyrs of Prague, 288–290. Senate of, 294, 299. Hussite movements, 356. See Adalbert, Bethlehem Chapel, Huss.
University of, Militz at, v. 175. Huss and the, 235, 242–255, 263, 299, 310. Influence of Wiclif at, 241–248, 265. Oxford and, 241, 243, 244, 246. Foundation of, 244. Teachers at, 244, 245, 247, 252, 253. Convocation of (an. 1403), the forty-five propositions, condemned, 246, 247, 253, 278, 291. Paris, 248. Convocation (an. 1408), ordinance in regard to Wicklif's writings, 248. Withdrawal of the Germans from the university, 252–255, 274, 347. Convocation (an. 1410), on the burning of Wiclif's books, 261. Division in the Bohemian party at, 253, 279. Theological faculty, 279, 291–293, 295, 296. Banishment of four of its members, 298, 299, 347. Master Jesenic's publication, 294. Christann of Prachatic, 310. Delegate at Constance, 320. Jacobellus, 338 n. 1. See Palacky.
Pranger, v. 286.
Prato, iv. 629 n. 3.
Prato, cardinal da (du Prat), v. 20, 22.
Praxeas, against the Monanists, i. 513 n. 3, 525. Patripassian, 583, 584.
Prayer, Apollonius of Tyana on, i. 26, 31. With the Therapeutæ, i. 61. Prayer of M. Aurelius, i. 17, 73. Of Apollonius, 31. Simplicius on, ii. 110.

Christian use of prayer, power of, i. 73, 74, 284–288. Intercessory, Cyprian on, 135, 287. Important business begun with, 206, 286, 287. Without ceasing, 286. Seasons of, 286, 287. In the study of Scripture, 286, 287, 719. In the family, 286. Posture in, 288, 295, 300. And works of love, 288. In baptism, 315. At the Agapæ, 326. At the Lord's supper, 329 n. 2, 330. For the dead, 334 (iv. 594, 597; v. 324). Basilides, 416. The Prodicians, 451. Origen on prayer to Christ, 590. Through Christ, 591.

Second Period. Prayers of Constantine, ii. 23, 25, 28, 29, 30. Julian on, 61. Healing in answer to, 138, 240, 268, 285. Nilus on continual, 277. The Euchites, 277–279. Eustathians, 281. Intercessory, 284–286 (iv. 81). In the Cœnobiæ, 287. Chrysostom on, 315, 316. Athanasius, 322. Prayer for catechumens, 357, 358 n. 1. Church prayers, 361 and n. 2, 658. In the Lord's supper, 367, 368. Augustin, 638, 686.

Third and Fourth Periods. Remarkable answers to, in the history of missions, iii. 6 and n. 3, 8, 27, 28, 30, 284, 285, 300, 301. Undertakings begun with, 20, 27, 275, 284, 285, 299. Ministration of, 26. For temporal things, 28, 132, 148. Repetitions of, 139, 452 (iv. 302). Gregory the Great on, 147, 148. Maximus, 174, 175. John of Damascus, 210. For teachers of error, 255. Anschar, 286, 287. Place of, 311, 443, 460. Ratherius on, 442, 443. Indulgences for, 452. Scotus, 462 (prayers of, 462 n. 1). Berengar, 505.

Fifth Period. Answers to, iv. 13, 26, 28, 81. Undertakings begun with, 28, 423. Gregory VII. on, 91. Bernard on, 241, 260, 261. Francis, 273, 274. Lull, 309. Almsgiving and, 306. Preaching and, 314, 315. Aquinas, 423. Chrysomalos, 561. Repetition of, 572 n. 2. For departed souls, 594, 597. Waldenses on, 612, 616.

Clemangis on, v. 114. Wicklif on, 143, 163. In preparation for preaching, 175, 180. Janow on, 193. And the Lord's supper, 224. Seasons of, 207. Pantheistic Friends of God on, 395, 400. Particular, 395, 405. Distraction in, praying by memory, 407. See Worship.

Praying brothers and sisters, iv. 286.
Praylus, bp. of Jerusalem, ii. 648.
Preachers of the gospel, early, i. 72–79. Schools for, iii. 126 (see Schools). Boniface as, iii. 52. Willehad, 80. Gregory the Great, 142. Anschar, 274. Boso, 324. Elfric, 469.

Fifth Period, iv. 293. Otto of Bamberg as, iv. 4, 16, 20. Converts from heathenism, 13. Monte Corvino, 58. Francis of Assisi, 59, 273, 274. Innocent III., 173, 317. R. Grosshead, 186. Archdeacons as, 211. Peter of Savoy, 214. Mendicant orders, 276–279, 282, 284, 624 (v. 59) (see Mendicant Orders). Raymund Palmaris, 298. Aquinas, 317, 422. Wm. of Auvergne, 423. Berthold, 318–320. Anselm, 365. Catharists, 584. Waldenses, 607, 608. Sectaries, 610.

Preachers of repentance, iv. 97, 208–211, 238, 239, 245, 246–249, 272, 293, 313, 594, 598–604, 627; v. 158, 183, 184. Of indulgence (see Indulgences). Traveling preachers, i. 197, 504; v. 143–145, 162. Militz, v. 174–177, 179, 180. Angels of the last times, v. 179, 196, 200, 257. Persecution of, v. 258. Friends of God, v. 383. See Bernard, Chrysostom, Conrad, Gregory Nazianzen, Huss, Preaching.

Preaching, i. 75, 196–198, 302, 303. In the Roman church, 303 n. 6. Gift of teaching, 186, 187. Office of, 197. Of laymen, 186, 187, 196, 197.

Second Period, ii. 352–354. Athanasius on, 36. Augustin on, 122. Of women, 139 (iv. 13). Among the Goths, 158. Doctrinal, 384, 692.

Third Period. Alcuin on, iii. 76, 77, 123–125. Charlemagne on, 102, 123. Of bishops, 107, 123–125, 426. Rule of Chrodegang on, 123. Schools of, Homiliaria, 126, 127, 315 n. 1.

Fourth Period, iii. 425–428. Language of, 323–325 (v. 383) (see Language). Subjects of, 425, 426.

Fifth Period. Lull on, iv. 62, 191, 242, 310. Of bishops, 213. Lateran council on, 270. Francis on, 274. Guibert of Novigentum on, 313, 314. H. de Romanis on, 314, 317. Preparation, 298, 316, 323 (v. 61, 175, 180). Place, 278, 298, 316, 318, 323 (v. 184, 263). Neglect of, 317. Oliva on, 624.

Sixth Period. Clemangis on, v. 59–62. Gerson, 81. Wicklif, 141–143, 162, 173. Janow on, 195, 196, 199, 200, 224. Foundation of Bethlehem chapel for, 236. Huss on, 263, 265, 288 n. 1, 313–316, 321, 353. Wicklifite party in Bohemia, 251. Preaching in private chapels forbidden, 259, 260, 265. See Preachers, Laity.

Preaching orders. See Mendicant orders.

Prebends, iv. 206.
Preces, precistæ, iv. 200.
Predestinatians, Predestinationists, ii. 702–706, 711.
Predestination, in the Holy Scripture, i. 613. Absolute, Marcion on, 618 n. 1, 655. Florinus, 680 n. 3. Origen, 630. Of Christ, 592 (ii. 482).

In the Second Period. Theodore of Mopsuestia's views of, ii. 495. Hilary of Poictiers, 621, 622. Ambrose, 623, 624. Controversy on in the western

church; Augustin, 680, 684–711, 401 n. 3; earlier views, 627–630; later, 630, 631. Praedestinatio duplex, 711.
   Third Period. Clement, antagonist of Boniface, on, iii. 62. Injurious consequences of Augustin's doctrine, 77 n. 1. Gregory the Great on, 144–146. Isidore on, 151. Felix, 162.
   Fourth Period. Gottschalk, praedestinatio duplex, iii. 474 and n. 1, 479, 482, 483, 485, 492. The three questions, 482, 483. Probus, 602.
   Fifth Period, iv. 474–485, 515, 518. Bernard on, 509, 510. Catharists, 568. See Freedom, Grace.
   Sixth Period. Wicklif on, v. 167, 168. Huss on, 266, 302, 303, 337, 347, 350.
Predetermination, i. 612, 617. 622; ii. 482, 618, 638, 685, 686. See Predestination.
Predicates. See Interchange of.
Predictions. Simplicius on, ii. 108. Regarding Christianity, 102.
Preëxistence, of souls, doctrine, with the Essenes, i. 47. With Basilides, 402 n. 3, 404. Carpocrates, 449. The Manicheans, 494–497. Origen, 626, 627. Methodius, 721.
   Ground of the doctrine, ii. 618. Platonico-Origenistic doctrine, 763, 76‒ nu. 2, 3. Paulicians, on, iii. 258.
Pregel, river, iv. 41, 42.
Pregentia (Bregenz), iii. 34.
Prelates, v. 50, 53, 172.
Prelectors, ii. 188, 192, 530. See Lectores.
Premonstratensians, iv. 79, 80, 244–246.
Premonstre (Praemonstratum), iv. 245.
Preparation for Christianity, i. 2–68, 536; iii. 304 n. 1, 305 n. 2. See Missions.
Preparatory epochs, positions, become injurious to the higher stages of development, i. 34, 340, 341, 511. Left behind, 29, 30. Origen on, 548.
Πρεσβύτεροι among the Paulicians, iii. 264.
Πρεσβύτιδες, ii. 190 n. 3.
Presbyter, in the apostolic times, i. 184–186, 659; v. 31, 170, 173. After the time of the apostles, 190–195, 223. In Rome, 203. Sacred functions of, 135, 152, 219, 316. In the persecution under Valerian, 137, 139.
   In the Second Period, ii. 184, 188, 193, 194, 195, 216, 221, 379, 696. Condition of ordination, 64 n. 3. Pelagius among the, 642. See Presbyterianism, Priests.
Presbyterial college, i. 190, 192, 223, (584).
Presbyterianism, conflicts of, with episcopacy, i. 222–248.
Presents, sending of, ii. 347 and nn. 2, 3, 351. Use of in spreading Christianity, ii. 149; iii. 21, 69, 272, 284, 286, 296; iv. 6, 7, 13, 18, 38, 49, 50. To monks, ii. 275; iv. 243. To the pope, iii. 62 n. 3, 114; iv. 90; v. 272. To obtain benefices, iii. 93 and n. 2, 110. Of church property, iii. 114. For masses, iii. 136. To St. Peter's church, iii. 546. Francis of Assisi, iv. 60 n. 2. Obtained by fraud, iv. 127. To preachers, iv. 211. By the pope, v. 58, 105. See Bribery, Gifts.
Prester John, iv. 46, 47, 52 and n. 1.
Prevarication, iii. 267. See Veracity.
Pride, spiritual, i. 63, 199, 228–230, 252, 436, 524; ii. 123, 275, 279, 280, 291, 293; iii. 21 n. 149, 252–254, 287, 420, 505; iv. 242, 274, 285, 292, 296, 304, 305; v. 405, 408. Danger of, ii. 683. In the fall, iv. 505, 507. Of culture, i. 71; iv. 259. In Gnosticism, i. 392. Of the church, v. 57.
Priegnitz, iv. 18; v. 237.
Priesthood, universal Christian, i. 179, 180, 196, 198, 279, 284, 288, 315, 330, 519, 644, 662; ii. 259, 314, 362 n. 7; iii. 2; iv. 592, 609, 614; v. 212, 217, 221, 250.
   Priesthood of a caste, i. 179, 190, 193–199, 329, 331, 365, n. 1, 519, 686; ii. 179–182, 188, 259; iii. 2, 348, 383, 494, 577. Function independent of character, i. 321, 322 (see Validity of sacerdotal acts). Mediatorial function, i. 179, 194; ii. 179, 388; iii. 2. Sacrificial function, iii. 135, 136, 494. Training of priests, ii. 182–184 (see Schools). Unction, iii. 449. Worldly motives in entering the, ii. 184; iii. 9. Inviolability, iii. 348. With the Paulicians, iii. 264. In the Greek church, iii. 577 (ii. 183). Gregory on the authority of, iv. 87. Influence of the O. T. idea of the, i. 194, 195, 365, 519, 686; ii. 321. Janow on the, v. 212–217, 219, 221. See Clergy, Bishops, Presbyters.
   Pagan priesthood, privileges of the, ii. 35, 169. Julian's views of the, 61–66. Colleges of priests, 97, 99.
Priests, Egyptian, i. 83. Roman, i. 92, 107. Christian preaching of, iii. 24, 125. As missionaries, iii. 23, 43, 79, 331, 334. Requisitions concerning, iii. 126, 154. Sons of, iv. 97, n. 8, 361. Parish priests in England, v. 134. And mendicants, v. 134, 162. Wicklif on the duty of, v. 138, 144. Wicklif as, v. 142. And bishops, v. 170, 173, 202. Janow on the importance of, v. 202–204. See Poor priests, Presbyters.
Prignano, archbishop of Bari. See Urban VI.
Primal man, primitive man, i. 424, 425, 491, 493.
Primasius, bp. of Adrumetum.
   <small>Comm. on the epistles of Paul and Revelation, ii. 605 n. 2.</small>
Primasius, Donatist bp. of Carthage, ii. 605.
Primates, iii. 70, 119 n. 2, 203, 250 n. 1, 349, 366; iv. 169. Primacy over the English church, iii. 16. Of the pope.
Primeval state. See Original condition.

Primianus, Donatist bp. of Carthage, ii. 231.
Primicerius palatii, iii. 109.
Primitive Christianity, ii. 48; iv. 563, 621, 623. Religion, iii. 85.
Primsigning, iii. 301 n. 2.
Prince of darkness, i. 493–495, 500, 501.
Princes, divine right of, iv. 109. Calling of, iv. 310 n. 7. Deposition of, v. 10, 18. Relation to the State, v. 50. Worthiness, v. 351–353. Trust in, v. 359. See Rulers.
Principle, of divine life in the church, i. 1, 75, 78. Of Spiritual life, ii. 634, 635, 681, 714, 715. Highest, iv. 445 n. 2. Of Christianity, iv. 510. In grace, iv. 513.
Principles, necessary development of, ii. 179; v. 240, 275. Fundamental, iii. 3. With the Paulicians, iii. 257. David of Dinanto, iv. 446, 447.
Prisca, Priscilla, Montanist, i. 514. On celibacy of the clergy, i. 521.
Priscilla, i. 290 n. 2.
Priscillian, Priscillianists, ii. 354 n. 4, 771–779.
Letter of Priscillian, ii. 777 n. 2.
Priscus, pagan philosopher, iii. 88 n.
Prisoners, redeemed, ii. 136 (see Captives). Oversight of by bishops, ii. 178. Care for, ii. 272; iii. 105.
Prisons, visited, i. 123, 135, 255, 332; iv. 295, 299.
Private intercourse, in the propagation of Christianity, iii. 4 n. 1.
Private devotion, Janow on, v. 202. Private war. iii. 407.
Privileges of monasteries, iii. 75; iv. 201, 202. See Exemptions.
Privilegium, papal, iv. 202.
Privinna, Moravian prince, iii. 316.
Proæresius of Athens, ii. 76. See Eunapius.
Probus, priest, heretic, iii. 602.
Processions, ii. 97. Penitential, ii. 86; iii. 355; iv. 85; v. 43, 74, 113, 115, 116, 412. With relics, iv. 330. Of Henry VII. at Rome, v. 36.
Proclus, Montanist, i. 652.
Proclus, Neo Platonist, ii. 104, 105, 117, 613 n. 2; iv. 445 n. 1. Life of. See Marinus.
Comm. in Platonis Alcib., P. ii. (op., ed. Cousin., t. iii. Paris, 1821), pp. 125, 126, consent, il. 105 n. 7. See John Philoponus.
Proclus, patriarch of Constantinople, ii. 509, 510, 547, 555–557, 559 n. 2, 762.
Synodica, ff. 509, 805, ii. 547 nn. 2, 3. Homily of, 509.
Procopius.
De bello Goth., l. iv. c. 3, Abasgians, ii. 140 n. 1. De bello Pers., l. i. c. 20, Christian king of Ethiopia, 145 n. 1. Hist. arcana, c. 11, f. 90 (ed. Orelli), Justinian, 106 n. 1; c. 13, the same, 605 n. 3; c. 17, Theodora, 593 n. 3; c. 18, Justinian in doctrinal controversies, 608 n. 1.

Procopius, abp. of Cæsarea, iii. 576 n. 3 577.
Procopius, martyr, i. 303 n. 3.
Procopius, the presbyter, i. 154.
Proclus, Christian slave, i. 119.
Proculus, Montanist, i. 678 n. 2.
Procurator, the term, i. 119 n. 6.
Prodicus, Prodicians, i. 451.
Profanity, iv. 301.
Professions incompatible with Christianity, i. 262, 267. See Employments.
Prohibitory laws, ii. 184.
Promises, sacredness of, iii. 100 n. 8. Of O. T., Jews on, iv. 78.
Propagation of souls, of sin, ii. 640, 647, 670, 671. See Traduction.
Property, among the Essenes, i. 46. Of heretics restored by Julian, ii. 71. Of widows and orphans, ii. 176. Renunciation of, ii. 265, 266, 313, 314; iv. 208, 220, 525, 581, 594, 607, 634; v. 16. (See Dolcino.) Of mendicant orders, iv. 291. Of Greek monasteries, iv. 529, 530. Waste of, v. 21, 54, 123. Of the pope, v. 39. Possession of, v. 16, 24, 25, 132. Rights of, Wiclif's views respecting the, v. 136, 146, 170. Views of Huss, v. 269, 274, 335. See Church property, Evangelical, Poverty, Monasteries.
Prophecy, among the Essenes, i. 45, 47. Gift of, i. 175, 181, 186 n. 2, 358, 510; iii. 590; iv. 511, 598. Prophecy, with the Gnostics, i. 371 n., 441 n. 2. Valentine, i. 426. With the Montanists, i. 510, 511, 515–519. Opponents of Montanism, i. 519 520. Obscurity of, i. 649, 650. Irenæus on, i. 678; Julian, ii. 58, 59. Conscious and unconscious, twofold sense of, ii. 392, 393. Gregory VII., iv. 118. Anselm, iv. 368. Fulfilment of, iv. 78. Dolcino, iv. 632. Interpretation of, iii. 430 n. 3; iv. 601; v. 178, 194, 266. See Joachim, Franciscans, Inspiration, Prophets, Sibyls.
Prophetesses, Montanist, i. 182, 511, 514, 515.
Prophetic element in Judaism, i. 35, 36, 52. In paganism, i. 175–177. In the Aristotelian morals, iv. 520. Relation to the evolution of the kingdom of God, iv. 216. Prophetic warnings against the secularization of the church, iv. 215–232; v. 135. Utterances, iv. 284, 318 n. 1, 617; v. 60, 121; (Wiclif), 171; (Militz), 178; (Janow), 194, 207; (Huss), 311, 313, 314, 332, 333, 364, 367; (Jerome), 377 n.
Prophets, in the Old Testament, i. 35, 36, 347, 354, 371 n., 511, 519; iii. 372; v. 178, 194, 309, 380. Marcion on, i. 470. Paulicians on, iii. 267, 268. Hugo of St. Victor, iv. 405, 406. The Clementines, on the true prophet, i. 354–359. Ep. of Peter to James, on O. T. prophets, i. 361 n. 1. Christian, i. 343. With Valentine, i. 426, 427, 429. Heracleon on, i. 441 n. 2. Among the Monta-

nists, i. 182, 514-520, 524-525, 583. Persian, i. 487. Greek, Clement on, i. 537. Chrysostom on the, ii. 302, 303. Augustin, ii. 725. Bernard, iv. 258. Abelard, iv. 391, 496. Hugo, iv. 405. Catharists, iv. 574. Testimony to Christ, iv. 78, 574.
    Prophets in the Middle Ages, v. 215-232, 226 n. 3, 318, 617, 625, 632. False, i. 38; v. 186, 205, 230.
Proselytes, made by the Pharisees, i. 67. Of righteousness, of the gate, 67, 68. Laws against, 89.
Proselytism, i. 67; ii. 120, 121; iv. 248, 284.
Προσκλαίοντες, ii. 213.
Προσκύνησις, ii. 330; iii. 199 nn. 3, 4, 210 n. 1, 238, 268, 534. Σχετική, iii. 545. Ὁμώνυμος, συνώνυμος, 545 n. 7.
Πρόσωπα, i. 595 n. 3, 596 and nn. 3, 5, 599.
Prosper of Aquitania, letter to Augustin, ii. 691, 692. Augustus, writings in reply, 691-693, 710. Carmen de ingratis, ii. 693, 694. Against the Semi-Pelagians, 693, 695, 697-699, 701, 703. Appeal to Rome, 695, 697. Compared with the author of De vocatio gentium, 699 n. 3. Rabanus Maurus, iii 477. See pretended Prosper.

Citations:—
Adv. Cassian, ii. 697 n. 3.
Adv. Collator, ii. 696 n. 2, 697 n. 3.
Capitula objectionum Vincentianarum, ii. 697 nn. 1, 3.
Carmen de ingratis, vss. 92 685, 775-788, ii. 693 nn.; vss. 370, 384, ii. 698 n. 2; vs. 754 *et seq.*, ii. 699 n. 1; vs. 964, ii. 694 n. 1.
Chronicle, ii. 651 n. 2; ar. 431, Pallad us, ii. 147 n. 2; au. 443, Leo I. and the Manicæans, 770 n. 1.
Ep. ad Augustin, ii. 690 n. 3. Ep. ad Rufinum, 697 n. 3.
Liber contra Collatorem, ii. 697 n. 3; c. 21, § 2, Palladius, 147 n. 2; c. 21, § 4, 698 n. 1.
Poem ("a husband to his wife"), vss 23, 40 (ed. Venet., 1744, p. 450), ii. 691 n. 1.
Responsum ad capit. Gallor., ii. 697 n. 3; c. 8, 699 n. 2.

Prosper, pretended.
(Opp. Prosper. Aquit.). De promiss. et prædict. Dei, P. iii. prom. 38, banishment of Symmachus, ii. 99 n. 3. P. v. c. 7, prostration before emperors, 112 n. 4.

Prostitutes, v. 81, 113.
Prostrati, ii. 357.
Prostration, before the emperor, ii. 131. Before images, ii. 330; iii. 201, 204, 206, 210 n. 1, 213, 238, 534, 538, of the emperor, ii. 112; iii. 204, 233 n., 241. The Khan, iv. 48, 49.
Πρώτη ὄγδοος, i. 401.
Proterius, bp. of Alexandria, ii. 584.
Protestant spirit, principle, Protestantism, i. 367 n. 1, 459, 477, 461, 518; ii. 308; iii. 232, 249, 515; iv. 578, 595, 639; v. 25, 149, 157, 168, 210. Precursors of, iv. 578.
Proteus, ii. 104 n. 2.

Protocol, i. 102 n. 4. See Philip of Limborch.
Protoctetus, the friend of Origen, i. 706.
Ἡρωτόκτισται, ii. 764 n. 3.
Πρωτοπασκιταὶ, ii. 338 n. 2.
Protospatharius, iii. 201 n. 2, 421, 559 n. 4, 560 a id n. 4, 576 n. 1.
Πρωτότοκος τῆς κτίσεως, ii. 438 (764 n. 3).
Provence, Semi-Pelagian tendency in, ii. 687. John of Matha, iv. 267. Louis IX. in, iv. 281 (Novem populonia). Catharists in, iv. 565. Henry of Cluny, iv. 602. Oliva, iv. 620. Provençal language, Bible in the. iv. 320, 321. See Language, Lerins, Rhegium.
Proverbs, ii. 288.
3:5, v. 361. 8:16, iii. 362. 8:22, ii. 404 n. 1; iv. 569. 8:22, 23, ii. 480. 10:19, ii. 709 n. 2. 17:3, v. 269. 22:28, i. 710.
Providence, doctrine of in the dialogue of Minucius Felix, i. 11. With the Stoics, 16. Essenes, 42. Basilides, 405-407, 412. Neo-Platonists, 406. Ptolemæus, 438. Marcion, 472. Origen, 553, 571. Dionysius of Alexandria, i. 713 n. 1.
    Constantine on, ii. 24, 414. Julian, ii. 51. Simplicius, ii. 109. In the Pelagian controversy, ii. 646 n. 2. Schoolmen on, iv. 473, 476, 477. Leadings of, v. 410, 411.
Provincial bishops, ii. 186 n. 1.
Provincial synods, i. 206; ii. 195. Restored in the Frankish empire, iii. 55, 56. Participation of monarchs in, iii. 95. Go ot t of use, iii. 95.
Provins, iv. 256 n. 4.
Prozymites, iii. 584.
Prudence, iv. 521, 524.
Prudentius, Christian poet.
C. Symmachum, l. i. vs. 617, ii. 102 n. 4; vs. 620, name Pagan, 90 n. 5.

Prudentius of Troyes, iii. 460 n. 6, 481, 482, 489.
Letter to Hinkmar and Pardulus (see Cellot. Hist. Gotheschalci, Par. 1655, app. f. 429), iii. 482 n. 1. Adv. Scotus, 489; t. i. ff. 218, 404, God's working distinct from his being, 489 nn. 2, 3.
Prüm, iii. 108 n. 1; iv. 203. See Potho.
Prussians, Adalbert among the, iii. 323. History of the conversion of the, iv. 41-45.
Psalmody, Monastery of, iii. 433.
Psalmody. See Church Psalmody.
Psalms, singing, chanting of, i. 281, 304; iii. 74, 139; iv. 28, 42, 58; v. 371, 379. Committed to memory, iii. 281 n. 1; iv. 4 n. 2. Repetition of, iii. 139; iv. 4 n. 2; v. 370. Expositions of (see Commentaries). Versions, of Ulphilas, Swedish, iii. 281 n. 1. See Bible trans.
Ps., 2:7, i. 598. 8, ii. 494 n. 1. 18:40, 41, iii. 129 n. 2. 19:4, i. 568 n. 1. 20:7, i. 285. 22:22, iii. 362. 26:4, ii. 287. 31, v. 370. 31:2, iv. 500. 31:5, v. 370. 82, iii. 139. 33:17, i. 285. 34, ii. 363. 87:25, iii.

30. 37:27, iii. 416 n. 1. 33:9, ii. 57. 39:1, iii. 570. 42:2, ii, 249. 42:5, i. 706. 44:1, i. 588 n. 3. 45:5, i. 636. 49:20, ii. 671 n. 2. 51, v. 370. 51:5, i. 620; iv. 331. 51:17, i. 138. 53:1, iv. 441. 55:7, iv. 250. 58:4, 5, ii. 621. 68:30, iii. 130. 72:10, ii. 844 n. 1. 78:26, iv. 260. 78:24, iii. 499. 82, i. 466. 82:1, iii. 348. 82:6, ii. 499 n. 3. 83, 1, 2; iii. 337 n. 5. 89:32, 38, ii. 160. 90:4, i. 399, 650. 95:3, i. 543. 97:7, i. 409 n. 2; iii. 337 n. 5. 106:47, ii. 351. 110, i. 574. 110:1, ii. 481. 111:10, i. 411 n. 4; iv. 259, 386. 115, iii. 185 n. 3. 117:1, iii. 318; v. 301. 119:115, ii. 172. 133:1, ii. 457. 145:3, i. 563.

Psalter, iv. 4 n. 2, 42, 102 n. 4. Instruction in the, iv. 39. Translation, iv. 102 n. 4, 321.
Psammathia, ii. 425.
Psammon, i. 34 n. 2.
Pseudo-Basilideans, i. 447, 448.
Pseudo-Cynics, i. 93, 275.
Pseudo-Dionysian writings, theurgical system, mystical element in the, ii. 388, 725, 740 n. 3 : iii. 170. In the Greek monasteries, iii. 169 (176) Genuineness attacked, defended, iii. 170, 466. Platonic, Alexandrian elements in, iii. 170 ; iv. 420. Influence on Maximus, iii. 171. Ἐνέργεια θεανδρική, iii. 176. Expression of a tendency, iii. 351 n. 2. Influence on Scotus, iii. 461, 467 ; iv. 444. Translations, iii. 466, 467. See Vogt.
Pseudo-Isidorean Decretals, origin, authorship, iii. 346, 347, 350 and n. 1. 351. Benedictus Levita and the, iii. 350 n. 1. Relation to the papal system, iii. 346-351, 364, 369, 562 and n. 1; iv. 194 ; v. 78. Nicholas I. and the, ii. 353, 360, 565 n. 4. Influence on ecclesiastical law, iii. 122 n. 3, 347-351, 509 n. 2 ; iv. 203. Under Charlemagne, iii. 351. Spirit of, iii. 372 n. 1. Authenticity questioned, iii. 360, 364, 365 ; v. 78. Damiani, iii. 396 n. 3.
  Citations:—
  I. ep. Alexandri., iii. 347 n. 5. I. ep. Anacleti, 347 n. 5, 349 n. 3. I. ep. Marcelli, 349 nn. 1, 2, 4. Ep. Melchiadis, 349 n. 6. II. ep. Pii, 348 n. 1. II. ep. Sextii, 349 n. 5. Epp. Urbani, 348 n. 2.
Pseudo-Paulinists, i. 342.
Pseudo-Petrinists, i. 342.
Pseudo-Sibylline writers, books, i. 96 n. 2, 101 n. 1, 513 n. 1, 654.
Ψυχή, Valentine, i. 426, 428. Ἄλογος, iii. 559 n. 1. Mani, i. 497. Distinguished from πνεῦμα, Origen, i. 636, 637, 638 n. 4. Photius, iii. 559 n. 3. Νοερά, in Christ, ii. 483. Λογική καὶ νοερά, iii. 559 n. 3. See Soul.
Psychical, Messiah, i. 426, 429-431. Christianity, 433, 476, 477.
Psychici, psychical natures, ψυχικοί. See Πνευματικοί.
Psychological phenomena, i. 75, 236 ; ii. 133. Connected with the Lord's Supper, iii. 146 n. 2.
Ptolemæus, Christian teacher, i. 663.

Ptolemæus, Gnostic, i. 437-440, 441, 476. Epistle to Flora, i. 437-440, 438 nn. 1, 2 ; also, Note on p. 725.
Ptolemæus, monk, ii. 275.
Ptolemais, ii. 763. See Euoptius, Secundus, Synesius. Crusaders at, iv. 60, 188.
Public services, exemption of clergy, ii. 169.
Publicani, iv. 565.
Public works, Theodoret, ii. 169.
Pudens, i. 102 n. 4.
Pulcheria, sister of Theodosius II., in the Nestorian controversy, ii. 164 n. 3, 518, 519 and notes, 526, 540, 541 and n. In the Eutychian controversy, 566, 575 and n. 1.
Pulpitum, i. 291 n. 2.
Punishment, of sin, divine, Platonic doctrine of, i. 22. Fear of, i. 57 ; iv. 319. Deliverance from through Christ, i. 324. Gnostics on, i. 381, 412, 413, 438, 568 ; (Marcion), 467, 471, 472. Manichæans, i. 439, 501. Church doctrine, the Alexandrian school, i. 563. Simplicius on, ii. 109. After death, duration of, ii. 737-739 ; iii. 474-476, 482. Pelagius on, ii. 637, 643 n. 2. Council of Carthage on, ii. 650. In the Pelagian controversy, ii. 659, 667, 669, 677. Theodore on, ii. 716. Scotus on, iii. 486-488. Gottschalk on, iii. 474, 475, 479. Abelard on, iv. 494. Anselm, iv. 498. Fore-ordination to, iii. 474, 475, 482, 479. In the atonement, iv. 498, 506. Mitigation of, iii. 485. Civil and divine, v. 28, 29.
  Of children, Basil on, ii. 288. Anselm on, iv. 362. In monastic discipline, corporeal, iii. 31, 98, 107 n. 2, 108. Spiritual, iii. 108, 255. Janow on punishment, v. 207.
  Of death, Ptolemæus on, i. 439 ; Alcuin and others, iii. 103, 104 ; Nicholas I., iii. 312. Wenzeslav, iii. 322. Catharists, iv. 574. The Waldenses, iv. 614 ; In spreading Christianity, iii. 78. Against heretics, see Heretics.
Punzilivo, Armanno, iv. 585. See Muratori, t. v.
Pupianus, Florentius, i. 224 n. 1, 236, 237.
Πυρεῖον, ii. 133.
Purgatory, origin of the doctrine of, i. 654, 656. In the teaching of catechists, ii. 121 n. 1. Pelagius against, ii. 637, 643 n. 2, 736. Augustin on, ii. 736, 737.
  In the Third and Fourth Periods, iii. 135, 136, 442. Scotus, iii. 486.
  In the Fifth Period, iv. 348, 350, 594, 614. Assembly of Vincennes on, v. 37. Indulgences and, iv. 350 ; v. 280, 383. Deliverance from, iii. 139 n. 7, 282, 548 n. 1 ; iv. 350 ; v. 280, 324.
Puricelli,
  Records relating to the ch. of Milan (Milan

1657). Life of Ariald (c. ii.), iii. 330 n. 3 (c. iii.), 3.0 n. 3. Life of Erlembald, 390 n. 2.

Purification, Basilides on, i. 403, 405, 406, 415, 419. Mani, i. 492-503. Origen, i. 624, 626, 627, 629, 630. In Hades, i. 654-656. Pagan ideas of, ii. 109, 115. Through conflict, ii. 764 n.; v. 409. See Theodore of Mopsuestia.

Purification of the virg u, festival of, iii. 133, 134, 287.

Purity of the church, ii. 243-245, 248 n. Berthold on purity, iv. 319.

Purpureus, bp., ii. 219.

Puteoli, Julius of, ii. 578.

Puy, iv. 125.

Puy Lorent. See Chronicle of, and Du Chesne.

Pyritz, town in Pomerania, iv. 7, 9, 10, 16.

Pyrrho, ii. 62.

Pyrrhus, patriarch of Constantinople, iii. 183 n. 4. 184, 192.

Pythagoras, i. 173, 449; ii. 62, 85.

Q.

Quades, war with the, i. 115, 116.

Quadragesima, Quadragesimal fast, i. 300, 521 n. 1; ii. 338, 339, 379, 743.

Quadratus, bishop at Athens, i. 661.

Quadratus, the Apologist, i. 101, 661.

Quæstuarii, iv. 279.

Quantitative estimate in morality, ii. 634, 667; iii. 148.

Quartodecimani, ii. 338 n. 2, 505, 506 n. 3.

Querfurt, iv. 43.

Quernheim, iv. 33.

Quetif and Echard.

On writers of the Dominican order, t. i. f. 202. Processus in librum evangelii æterni, iv. 618 n. 1, 619 n. 1. Script. ord. prædic. (Paris, 1719), t. i. f. 507, t, Eckbart, v. 393 n.

Quietism in Montanism, i. 521. Pantheistic, v. 393. Ruysbroech and Tauler against, v. 396-401.

Quinisextum, council, iii. 196 and n. 1. See Councils, II. Trullan, an. 691 or 692.

Quintus, Phrygian fanatic, i. 109.

Quintus, the African bishop, i. 319.

Quintus Aurelius Symmachus. See Symmachus.

Quirinus, Cyprian's friend, i. 685, 686.

Quirinus, Roman procurator, census of, ii. 346.

R.

Rabanus Maurus, Magnentius, abp. of Mentz, iii. 457, 458. His rules of religious instruction, his writings, 427, 457, 458, 475. Opponent of Gottschalk's doctrine, 473-482, 490, 492. His doctrine of predestination, 476, 477. Bread in the Eucharist, 581 n. 3. Doctrine of the Lord's Supper, 497 n. 1. Life by Rudolph, c. 2 (Acta S. Boll. Feb.), 446 n. 1.

Citations: —
Comm. on Joshua (Martene et Durand. coll. ampliss., t. ix.), iii. 457 nn. 2, 3.
De ecclesiasticis officiis, l. i. c. 31, iii. 581 n. 3.
De institutione clericorum, 427, 457. De virtutibus et vitiis (see Wolfgang Lazius), ep. to Louis the Pious (see, also, Baluz), 457 and nn. 5, 6. Epp. to bp. Notting, against Gottschalk, 475, 490, 491 (ed. Sirmond), p. 35, 476 nn.; p. 39, 377 n. 1. Ep. to Count Eberhard, against Gottschalk, 475. Ep. to the abbot Egilo, against Paschasius Radbert, 497 n. 1. Letters to Heribald (liber pœnitentialis, see Stewart), 497 n. 1. Ep. to Hinkmar (Sirmond), concerning Gottschalk, 481 and n. 4.

Rabbanta, Nestorian monk, iv. 48.

Rabbinism, i. 54, 56.

Rabulas, bp. of Edessa, in the Nestorian controversy, ii. 555, 610, 611.

Rack, v. 23, 51. Nicholas I., against the use of the, iii. 312.

Radbert. See Paschasius.

Radbod, abp. of Utrecht, iii. 405. See A. S. (O. B.) s. v.

Radbod, bp. of Triers, iii. 408 n. 1.

Radbod, king of the Frieslanders, iii. 43, 44, 45, 47.

Radegast, Wendish idol, iii. 327.

Rader.
Hist. Paulicians (Ingoldstadt, 1604), Peter of Sicily, iii. 244 n. 1.

Radislav (Rastices), Moravian prince, iii. 316, 317.

Radla, disciple of Adalbert of Prague, iii. 332.

Radulf (Rudolph), monk, persecutor of the Jews, iv. 74, 75.

Radwic.
Hist., i. 10, picture at Rome, iv. 164 n. 3.

Raginfred, bp. of Cologne, iii. 65.

Rahab, ii. 219.

Raimbert of Lisle, iv. 357, 359 n. 3.

Raimund, count of Toulouse, iv. 641.

Rainald. See Raynald.

Rainer, Cistercian, iv. 640.

Rainer, Dominican, iv. 326.

Rainerio Sacchoni, on the Catharists, iv. 579. Their surrender of property, 581. Duration of the sect, 603 n. 1. The Waldenses, 611.

Citations: —
Contra Waldenses, cc. 3, 8 (Bibl. Patr. Lugdun., t. 25), their knowledge of scripture, iv. 611 nn. 1, 3. C. 4, Waldenses on the Roman ch., 611 n. 2. C. 5, Peter Waldus, 606 n. 4. C. 7, mode of living, 611 n. 5. C. 6, f. 266, the Catharists, their doctrine of the Holy Spirit, 571 n. 2; consolati, 576 n. 2; the church, 577 n. 4; f. 267, Catharists on the writings of the fathers; Bernard 578 n. 5; f. 268, Catharist asceticism, 579 n. 2; f. 269, ch. officers among them, 580 n. 2; f. 571, union of parties among them, 579 n. 5; f. 272, consolamentum, 576 n. 3, 577 n. 2; diet of the

perfects, 580 n. 3; surrender of property, imposition of hands at death, 581 n. 5; self inflicted death, 582 n. 2.

Raising of the dead, i. 74; iii. 195; iv. 246 n.

Rameshoe, iii. 278.

Ramihrd, president of the sect in Cambray and Arras, iii. 599.

Rank, secular, in clerical offices, iii. 390 n. 1, 409. Among the canonicals, iv. 207.

Ransom, by Christ, Abelard on the term, iv. 502. Of captives, see Captives.

Rasticcs, see Radislav.

Ratherius of Verona, his life and writings, iii. 469. Contends against the rudeness of the clergy, 366 n. 4, 382 n. 3, 409 n. 2, 410 and nn., 411, 412. His view of fasts, pilgrimages, 441-443. Contends against the sensuous anthropomorphism, 443. Against superstition, 443, 444. Defends saint-worship, 446. Penance, 452. His view of the Lord's supper, 501. Works, 469 n. 6. Compared with Gerhoh, iv. 208.

Citations: —

De contemptu canonum (D'Achery, Spicileg, t. i.), ff. 347, 349, crimes of the clergy, iii. 366 n. 4; f. 350 (ed. Ballerin, f. 355), 441 n. 3; p. ii. f. 354, clergy in Italy, 582 n. 3; f. 358, 441 n. 5. De discordia inter ipsum et clericos, f. 363, iii. 383 n. 1; f. 364 (opp., Ballerin, Verona, 1765, f. 487), dissolution of the canonical life, 410 nn. 1, 2. Ep. i. ad Patricium (ed. Ballerin, f. 523), transubstantiation, 501 n. 3. Itinerarium (D'Achery), 443 n. 1; f. 381, cardinals, 387 n. 7. Praeloquia, 469 n. 6; l. i. ff. 15, 21 (ed. Ballerin), on superstition, 444 n. 2; l. iv. f. 802, the dignity of the saints, 447 n. 1; l. vi. (Martene et Durand, t. ix.), ff. 943, 948, good works, 442 nn. 2, 3. Qualitatis conjectura (Ballerin, f. 376, D'Achery, t. i. f. 358), reproaches of the clergy, 409 n. 2 Sermo ii. de ascensione (D'Achery), 444 n. 3. Synodica ad presbyteros (D'Achery), f. 371, inheritance of church property, 411 n. 1; ff. 377, 378, rudeness of the clergy, 410 n. 3; § 8, absolution, 441 n. 4.

Rational element, relation to other spiritual forces, iv. 400. Relation of the rational creature to God, 436, 487, 490, 491.

Rationalism, rationalist element in Paganism, i. 8. Among the Alexandrian Jews, i. 55-58, 64, 66. In Gnosticism, i. 368, 387, 389. In Docetism, i. 387. In the development of Christian doctrine, i. 507. In Julian, ii. 57. Antiochian school, ii. 394. In Adoptianism, iii. 163. In Scotus Erigena, iii. 462, 463. In the theological school at Orleans, iii. 593. Absence of in Abelard, iv. 377. In the sects, iv. 570, 595. Friends of God, v. 393.

Rationalistico-pantheistic party, iv. 230, 431. See Pantheism.

Rationes causales, seminales, iv. 470-472.

Ratolfzel, v. 111, 112.

Ratramnus of Corbie, iii. 482, 497. His doctrine of predestination, 482. His doctrine of the Lord's Supper, 497-501, 505, 507, 523. Birth of Christ, 495, n. 4. Defends the Latin church, 567.

Citations: —

Contra Graecor. opposita Romanam eccles. informantium, libri iv., iii. 568 nn. 1, 2. De corpore et sang. Domini, 497-500, 505 n. 3, 498 n., 489 nn. 1, 3, 5, 6. De praedest. Dei, libri ii. (Mauguin, t. i.), 482 n. 2, f. 76, ordo praedestinationis, 482 n. 3.

Ratzeburg, iii. 326.

Ravenna, iii. 186, 374, 419, 602. See Guibert.

Raymund à Pennaforte, iv. 63, 205.

Decretalium, libri v., iv. 205 n. 3.

Raymund Lull. Life, character, and labors, iv. 61-71. His work on universal science, Ars generalis, Ars magna, iv. 62, 63, 65, 67, 427, 437. Necessity of linguistic education for missionaries, 62, 63, 65, 67, 70, 190; of scientific, 426, 435 n. 2. Tabula generalis, 67 n. His work on the contemplation of God, 191, 192, 307, 483, 519. On the conversion of the heathen and the crusades, 190-192. On the eremitic life, 242. On hypocritical monks, 244. External works and love, 307-311. The cross, 308. The immaculate conception, 333. Transubstantiation, 336 n. 1. His importance in systematic theology, 426, 427. Fides and ratio, 435-440. Trinity, 465. Miracles, 473. Foreknowledge and predestination, 481-485. Incarnation, 508, Fides formata, 512. Ethics, 519. His works, 68 n., Mayence edition, 190 n. 3. Life of, 61 n. (see Acta S. June 31, t. v. f. 661), 66 n. 1, 67 n.

Citations: —

Arbor philosophiae amoris, opp., t. 6, f. 56, hypocritical monks, iv. 244 nn. 3, 4.

Ars generalis, iv. 63, 65, 67, 68, 427, 437.

De anima rationali, p. 11 (opp., t. 6, f. 51), attitude of mind necessary to inquiry, iv. 436 n. 5.

De centum nominibus Dei, opp., t. 6, love and knowledge, iv. 436 n. 1; c. 2, f. 23, prayer, and temptation, 309 n. 3; c. 31, love, 309 n. 8; c. 90, 310 n. 3.

De contemplatione Dei (concordantiae et contrarietates inter fidem et rationem), iv. 439 and n. 6. Opp., t. ix. f. 39, creation, 473 n. 2; f. 125, prayer, 309 n. 2; f. 162, love, 309 n. 1; f. 184, intention, 308 n. 9; f. 219 (vol. i., 1, 2, Dist. 22, c. e.), the Trinity, 465 n. 6; f. 246, on missionary work, 242 n. 2; f. 247 (vol. ii., l. 3, Dist. 23, c. cxi.), for princes, physicians, 310 n. 7, 311 n. 1; f. 250, c. cxii., knights, 191 n. 4; f. 252, c. cxiii., pilgrims, 307 n. 3; f. 280 (Dist. 23, c. cxxiii.), image of Christ, 308 n. 5; f. 296 (Dist. 27, c. cxxx.), love to God, 309 n. 7; f. 299 (Dist. 27, c. cxxx.), desire of martyrdom, 71 n. 1; f. 301 (c. cxxxi.), the same, 191 n. 3; f. 349 (Dist. 28, c. cli.), the supernatural in Christianity, 473 n. 6; f. 354 (c. clvi.), faith and reason, 439 nn. 5-7, 440 nn. 1, 2; ff. 401, 402, nature and the supernatural, 473, nn. 3-5; f. 409 (Dist. 29, c. clxxiii.), freedom from prejudice essential to investigation, 437 n. 1; f. 420 (c. clxxvi.), the soul as an object of knowledge, 439 n. 1; f. 461, Christian virtue, 308 nn. 6-8; ff. 498, 499 (c. cc.), prayer, 309 nn. 4, 5; f. 512 (c. cciv.), on the crusades, 192 nn. T. x. Dist. 36, c. cexxxviii., and cexxxix.,

three kinds of faith, 440 nn. 3-7; f. 135 *et seq.*, vol. iii., l. 4, D. 38, c. cclxv., predestination, 483 nn. 2-5; f. 136, difficulty of stating the doctrine, 485 n. 2; f. 141, c. cclxvii., time and space, 482 n. 2; ff. 142, 143, 145, 147, predestination, 483 nn. 6, 7, 484 nn , 485 n. 1; f. 330 (vol. iii. l. 5, Dist. 40, c. cccxv.), prayer in the life, 309 n. 6
De convenientia fidei et intellectus in objecto, t. 3, story of Miramamolin, iv. 436 nn. 3, 4.
De eruditione interior. hom., P. I. l. 3, f. 107, love, iv. 310 n. 1.
Disputat. eremitæ et Raymundi, on the sentences; Theology, iv. 347 nn. 6-9, 348 nn.
Disputat. fidei et intellect., iv. 439 n. 2.
Disputat. Raymundi Christ ani et Hamar Saraceni, iv. 69 n. 2, 190 n. 4.
Lamentation, iv. 70 n.
Liber proverbiorum, the son of God, iv. 465 n. 2; the divine productivity, 465 n. 3; t 6, c. 17, f. 10, love, 310 n. 2; P. 1, f. 38, longing, 310 n. 3.
Liber super Psalmum, "quicunque vult." true mode of converting the heathen, iv. 111 n. 1.
Necessario demoustrat. articulor. fidei, introd., iv 64 nn. 1-5.
Proverb. moral., t. vi., p. 3, c. 51, f. 110, preaching, iv. 310 n 6; c. 69, f 119, excess re asceticism, 310 n. 5; c. 70, c. 119, almsgiving, 310 n. 4
Quæstiones super sententias, in lib. i. (opp., t. iv. f. 27), Q. 27, the idea, iv. 482 n. 4; Q. 33, immediate and mediate agency of God, 482 nn. 6, 7; Q. 36, predestination, 483 n. 1; Q. 38, creation and preservation the same, 482 n. 5. In lib. 2, Q. 96, f. 84, immaculate conception, 383 nn. 4, 5. In lib. 3, QQ. 113, 114, f. 98, faith, 512 nn. 3-6.
On transubstantiation, iv. 386 n. 1. The Trinity, 465 nn. The idea in God, 481 nn. 6, 7, 482 n. 1. The incarnation, 508 nn. 4, 5.
Tabula generalis, iv. 67, n.

Raymund Martini, Pugio fidei, iv. 79 n. 1.
Raymund Palmaris, iv. 297-300, 303, 607 n. 2. Life of, 300 n. 1. See Acta S. July.
Raynald.
Annales eccles., an. 1231, No 13, Catharists, iv. 590 n. 2; an. 1232, No. 24. Stephen of Mungary, iii. 333 n. 3; an. 1233, § 5, *et seq.*, report of legates to Constantinople, iv. 541 n. 1; an. 1236, § 48, Greg. IX and the Jews, iv. 76 n. 4; an. 1248, § 84, Innocent IV, and the Jews, iv. 77 n. 1; app. an. 1297, No. 34 protest of the Colonnas against Boniface VIII. v. 4 nn.; an. 1301, No. 28, ep. of Boniface VIII. to Philip the Fair, v. 7 n. 6; an. 1304, No. 13, bull, "Unam Sanctam," v. 8 n. 2; an. 1329, Nos. 70 et 71, bull of John XXII. against mystical preachers, v. 395, nn. 1, 2, 396 n 1; an. 1349, § 11, constitutiou unigenitus, v. 41 n 3; t. vii. an. 1374, Nos. 10 et 11, f. 351, Militia and Gregory XI. v. 182 n. 3; an. 1377, No. 4, f. 204, bulls against Wicklif, v. 1-6 n. 7; vol. i., an. 1414, s. 10 *et seq*, constitution of the comm. to examine Huss at Constance, v. 330 n. 3; t. ix , an. 1431, dissolution of conc. of Basle, v. 130 n. 1; t. xvii. f. 300, bull of Alexander V. against Wicklif, v. 259 n. 2

Raynald de Bergamo, iv. 629 n. 4.
Raynouard.
On the antique form of the "Noble Leçon," iv. 616 n. 7. Choix des poésies orig. des Troubadours, t. ii. p. 76, La nobla Leyczon, 616 nn. 1-6. Introductory Essay, iv. 604 n. 3.
Reactions, against the Christian principle, how called forth, i. 366-368, 390, 506 ; ii. 38. Against the natural course of development, i. 510. Of the Christian consciousness against foreign elements, i. 390, 461 , ii. 765; iii. 2. Against the Catholic element, the theocracy, the papacy, i. 461, 478; iii. 18, 60, 243, 244, 292, 468, 586; iv. 140, 146, 147, 174, 195, 446, 592, 605, 628; v. 21, 47, 48, 134, 380. Of Paganism, ii. 37, 38; iii. 603 n. 2 ; iv. 17, 25-28, 37, 38. In the East, against forcible imposition of doctrines, ii. 658; reformatory, iv. 563 Against saint worship, iii. 446. Of the iconoclasts, iii. 531, 532. Of Christianity, iv. 26, 27. Against the corrupt church, reformatory, iv. 82, 83, 146, 232, 592, 503. Against reform, iv. 92. Proceeding from monasticism, iv. 232, 528, 563 ; v. 24, 171. Of unbelief, understanding, sense, iv. 239, 324-328, 336, 380. Of the Christian spirit, iv. 298, 336 ; v. 1. Called forth by the zeal of the heretics, iv. 315. Against oppression, v. 158, 159. Against monasticism, foretold, v. 171. Effects of reactions, i. 506, 507 (390); ii. 38; iii. 518, 531.
Readers, church, i. 152, 201.
Realism, practical, i. 529. Of the Western ch., i. 557. Philosophical, iv. 356-361, 441, 461, 462 n. 4, 492. Wicklif's, v. 135, 152, 165 and n. 2, 166-168, 241, 242. In Prague, v. 241, 242, 244, 245. Of Huss, v. 242, 343, 347 n. 1. At Constance, v. 343, 344, 375, 376.
Realist tendency, i. 292. See Irenæus, Melito of Sardis, Montanus, Papias, Polycarp, Tertullian.
Realistic externalization of the sacrament, iv. 338, 339.
Reason, i. 375. The Supreme, i. 380. Absolute, Origen on, i. 587. The Montanists, i. 512. In Christ, Justin on, i. 635.
Reason and faith, Augustin on, ii. 401, 402 and n., 674 ; iii. 150, 463, 471. Apollinaris on, ii. 484. Julian of Eclanum, ii. 654, 673, 674. Cassian, ii. 690. Gregory I., iii. 150. Scotus, iii. 462, 463. Roscelin, iv. 360. Anselm, iv. 369, 370. Abelard, iv. 378-380. Hugo, iv. 402. Other scholastics, iv. 409, 411, 412, 415, 417, 427-431, 434, 435, 439, 440, 443. Wicklif, v. 157. (See Faith and Knowledge.) Reason and Revelation, ii. 673 ; iii. 463. And tradition, iii. 462, 463, 471. Boundaries of rational demonstration, iv. 430.
Practical and speculative, iv. 434. Common and particular, iv. 444. Unity of, iv. 449 (i. 412). God as, iv. 454. The divine, iv. 470, 481. End of, iv. 521. Ordo rationis, iv. 521, 522. Rationes seminales, causales, iv. 470-472. Huss on the use of, v. 264, 305, 306, 334. Ruysbrock, v. 385. Eckhart, v. 397. Deification of, v. 393.
Rebais (Resbacum), monastery, iii. 38 n. 1.
Reccafrid, abp. of Seville, iii. 340.
Reccared, king of the West Goths, iii. 96.

Goes over to the Catholic ch, ii. 471; iii. 118.
Recho, bishop, iii. 133 n. 3.
Recluses, iv. 366. See Anchorets.
Recognitions of Clement, i. 358, 376 n. 3.

L. 8, c. 53, i. 359 n. 1.

Recommendations, iii. 110.
Red sea, passage through the, commemorated, i. 61.
Redeemer, Redemption, doctrine of in the First Period, i. 640-645. Need of, in paganism, 33, 34, 252. In Alexandrian Judaism, 66. In Platonism, Celsus on, 168. Christian consciousness of, in relation to asceticism, 276, 277. The Ebionites on, 347. In Gnosticism, 370, 371, 379, 387, 477, 612-614, 630; iv. 507. With individual Gnostics, 398, 409-413, 419-432, 446, 457, 462, 470. In the old religions of Asia, 479. In Parsism, 483. Buddhism, 482, 483. With Mani, 500. Montanism, 512. Clement on, 537. Relation to Christian doctrine, 557 (ii. 386, 659). Presupposes guilt, 561. Connection of the doctrines of creation and of redemption, 564, 565. Sabellius on, 599. Anthropology in its relation to Christian and heathen views of, 610-614, 620, 630. Origen on, 549, 637, 638. Hieracas, 714. Redemption in relation to the heathen, 655.

In the Second Period. Doctrine of in the Pelagian controversy, ii. 655, 659, 660, 666, 673-679, 717. The emperor Julian on, 48, 50. Simplicius, 109. Need, presentiment of, 115, 116, 122, 398, 616, 617, 719, 720. In Neo Platonism, 122, 123. Relation to Christian faith, 616. Jovinian on, 304, 307. Augustin, 386, 398, 659. Completion of the, Marcellus, 480. Gratuitous, Ambrose, 622. Doctrine as held by Pelagius, 637, 638. Praedestinatus, 704. In the Eastern church, 617, 676, 718, 726. Relation to creation, Faustus, 707. With Theodore of Mopsuestia, 716-718. Chrysostom, 719, 720. Priscillian, 777, 778.

In the Second and Third Periods. Its place in Christianity, iii. 2. In Mohammedanism, 85, 86. As affecting slavery, 98, 100. Need of, 132. Doctrine of, with Maximus, 171, 172, 181, 182. In the Monotheletic controversy, 180-184. With Scotus, 465. Gottschalk, 477. Limited, 482, 483, 484, 492-494. With Servatus Lupus, 484, 485. In the Western church, 554. In the sects, 593, 598, 602.

In the Fifth Period. Doctrine of, with the scholastics, iv. 480, 497-508 (v. 172). Need of, 11, 488. Necessary form of, 497-499, 501, 503-505, 507. Relation to the rational end of man, 522. In the sects, 554, 555, 562, 568, 569, 573, 595, 596. Wiclif, v. 172.

Redeeming Spirit, Genius, in Gnosticism, i. 412, 413, 588.
Redepenning, Dr.

Monograph on Origen, i. 697 n. 1.

Reflection, Valentine on the power of, i. 426. Lack of, ii. 116. R. of St. Victor, on, iv. 412. Ruysbrock and Tauler on the dangers of excessive self reflection, v. 405, 409. See Contemplation, Self-examination.
Reformation of science, Bacon on the, iv. 424, 425.
Reformation of the church, Boniface on the, iii. 55, 64. In the Roman church, 378-388, 400, 402 n. 1, 408-414. Of the clerical and monastic orders, 106, 107, 379, 382-388, 409-412, 414-416, 468, 469 (see Celibacy). The Hildebrandian epoch of Reform, iv. 82, 120, 205 (see Gregory VII.). Tendencies towards, i. 39; iv. 401, 563, 594, 595, 604, 605. Eustathius, iv. 531. Movements towards, in the VI. Period, v. 1, 48, 50, 52, 65, 77, 84, 90, 91, 93, 112, 129, 171, 316, 360. Gerson on, v. 80-83, 87, 94. Alexander V. on, v. 87. D'Ailly, v. 94. At Pisa, v. 87, 88, 112. At Constance, v. 109, 112-128. Necessity of, iii. 408, 414; v. 130. Reform and anti-reform parties, v. 232, 240, 253, 254, 258, 275, 291. See University of Paris, Bohemia, Clergy, Dunstan, England, Gerson, Monasticism, Preachers of repentance.

The German, i. 194; ii. 386; iii. 380 n. 1; v. 139, 158. Premonitions of the, iv. 187 n. 2, 216. (With Grosshead), iv. 186; (Clemangis), v. 60; (Wiclif), v. 171; (Huss), 314; (Jerome of Prague?), 377 n. 1. Foretokens, precursors of, ii. 304, 307; iv. 318, 592; v. 14, 48, 121, 139, 202, 393. In England, Wiclif, v. 48, 134-173. Forerunners of Huss, v. 173-235. Huss, Jerome of Prague, v. 235-380. Friends of God, v. 393.

Reformation of individuals, iv. 236, 293, 294 (see Preachers of repentance).
Paulicians as reformers, iii. 247, 250, 253, 254.
Regalia, of bishops and abbots, iv. 134, 143, 147.
Regeneration, sins incompatible with, i. 221. Objective and subjective in, i. 246. Cyprian on, i. 249. J. Martyr on, i. 250. And baptism, i. 311, 312, 522, 646, 647, 655; ii. 35, 726, 728. Clement on, i. 620. Julian, ii. 48. Jovinian, ii. 308-310. Augustin, ii. 625. In Pelagianism, ii. 679. Of the world, Mani on, i. 482.
Regensburg, bishopric of, iii. 55. Assembly at, iii. 165. Boso, iii. 324. Bps. of, iv. 421. Bernreider, iii. 381 n. 2. Berthold, iv. 318. Abp. of, v. 133.
Reginald, bp. of Liege, iii. 598 n. 2.
Regino, abbot of Prüm, De disciplina, on

Sends, iii. 108 n. 1. Collection of ecclesiastical laws, iv. 203.
Reginus, comes, ii. 601 n. 1.
Reichenau (Augia) abbey, iii. 440 n. 4, 458.
Reichenthal, Ulrich, v. 326 n. 3.
Reichersberg, monastery at, iii. 331 n. 2. See Gerhoh.
Reinauld.
  Extraits relatifs aux guerres des Croisades, pp. 429, 431, 432, Frederic II., iv. 178 n. 4, 181 n. 3.
Reinstein, John Cardinalis of, friend of Huss, v. 272. Accompanies Huss to Constance, 320. At Constance, 326 n. 2, 327, 328. His name, 328. Warning of Huss to, 336, 360 n. 2.
  Ep. of (Huss), opp. i. f. 58, 1, ep. 4), v. 322 n. 2, 326 n. 2.
Relics, Julian on the veneration of, ii. 47. Lucilla, ii. 221. In Egypt, Anthony on, ii. 270. Sale of, ii. 296; iii. 445 n. 1; iv. 330. Magical effects attributed to; superstitious use of, ii. 329, 370; ii. 20 n., 22, 59, 80, 132, 445, 446; iv. 557. Janow on miracles wrought by, v. 198, 199. Vigilantius against the worship of, ii. 373–375. Eunomius, ii. 445. In the consecration of churches, iii. 15. Of Peter and Paul, iii. 35 (see Peter). Of living persons, iii. 58; iv. 210, 238. In the Western church, iii. 201, 584 n. 1. In the Eastern, Const. Copronimus on, iii. 201, 218, 221. Libri Carolini on, iii. 238, 239. Anschar, iii. 278. Opposition to, iii. 433, 460, 598; iv. 330. Otto, iv. 28. Arnold's, iv. 162. Gribert against, iv., 330. Processions with, iv. 330. Dissensions concerning, at Constance, v. 113. Conrad on, v. 189. Janow, v. 198, 199. Huss, v. 238, 250, 290. The eight doctors, v. 291, 296.
Religio (monasticism), iv. 284.
Religio Romana, i. 11. Religiones licitæ, publice adscitæ, i. 87, 88, 89, 93, 97, 102, 116, 125, 126. Novæ, i. 87, 93, 97. Illicitæ, i. 99, 100. Religio urbis imperatoris, ii. 93.
Religion. And national life, i. 5. Need of in man's nature, 11. Multiplicity at Rome, 88. Revealed and natural, 176 and nn. (iv. 20). Primitive, 353, 354, 395; (iii. 84, 85). Comparison of religions, 368. Christianity as the absolute, 382. Interests of science and, 427. Popular religions, 449. The ancient, ii. 1. State, ii. 9, 14, 15, 16, 21, 34, 35, 37, 91. Diversity of forms, ii. 117. See Church and State, Paganism, Pontifex.
Religious awakening, Causes of, v. 380, 381.
Religious instruction. See Instruction, Language.
Remigius, abp. of Lyons, iii. 491.
  Ep. to Gottschalk, iii. 491 nn. De tenenda veritate script. sanct., l. iii. p. 182, freewill, 492 n. 1. See Mauguin.

Remigius, bp. of Rheims, iii. 6 n. 2; 8. *Natales* of. 131.
Remoboth, ii. 283.
Remusat, Abel. See Abel.
Renatus, Roman presbyter, ii. 573.
Renaudot.
  Hist. patriarchar. Alexandrinor., Saracens, iii. 89 n. 1 (Page 40, Severus, i. 485 n 3). P. ii. The Copts, 88 n. 4; p. 154, Chozru-Parviz, 84 n. 2; pp. 178, 188, Coptic patriarchs and Abyssinia, Nubia, and India, 90 n. 2. Anciennes relations des Indes et de la Chine, p. 68, Travels of Ibn Wahib, 89 n. 4.
Rennes, bp. of, iv. 246, 247.
Renunciation, monastic, iv. 91, 266–269, 525, 526. See Poverty.
Reparatus, bp. of Carthage, ii. 605.
Repentance, and forgiveness, J. Martyr on, i. 62 n. 2. Simplicius on, ii. 109, 110. Tokens of required by the church, ii. 213, 214. Death-bed, i. 238; ii. 707 n. 1. Gregory VII. on true, iv. 91. Doctrine of, Abelard, iv. 390. The Catharists, iv. 569, 571. Wicklif, v. 171. See Penitence, Penance, Preachers of repentance, Indulgences.
Repertorium für bibl. u morgenländ Literatur.
  Bd. ii. s. 74, Stroth on J. Martyr's Dialogue, i. 668 n. 3.
Reprobation, ii. 704, 711; iii. 472. With Gottschalk, iii. 474, 479. Pardulus, iii. 482. Servatus Lupus, iii. 483, 484. Scotus, iii. 485–487. Hinckmar, 492. Aquinas, iv. 478, 479. Lull, iv. 483, 484. Wicklif, v. 167. Huss, 267, 302, 353. See Predestination, Præsciti.
Resbacum (Rebais) monastery, iii. 38 n. 1.
Rescript of Trajan against the Christians, i. 99, 100, 102, 105, 107, 122. Of Hadrian, 101–103. Of Antoninus Pius, 104. Of Valerian, and Gallienus, 137, 139. Maximin, ii. 17, 18. Of Constantine, against the Donatists, ii. 227. Collection of rescripts, by Ulpian, i. 126. See Du Pin.
Reservations, v. 98.
Resignation of Stoicism, i. 17, 105.
Responsales, iii. 117 n. 2, 141 n. 1. See Apocrisiarii.
Responses, i. 329; ii. 363.
Restitution, of all things, ii. 439, 481, 482. See Apocatastasis.
Restoration of human nature, ii. 616; iv. 623. Doctrine of universal, ii. 615, 616, 737–739; iii. 62. Theodore of Mopsuestia on, ii. 717, 728, 738, 739. Maximus, iii. 175 and n. 3. Scotus, iii. 461, 465, 466, 489. Almaric, iv. 445 n. 4.
Restoration to church fellowship, i. 218, 219; ii. 213. See Penance.
Resurrection, denied by the Sadducees, i. 41, 63. Pagans on the Christian hope of, 114, 158, 169. Of Christ, 169. Witnesses of the, 183. Festivals of the, 295–300 (ii. 339; v. 140). (See Easter,

Sunday). Relation of Christ's resurrection to Christianity, 342. Christian view of death, in hope of, 334. The Gnostics on, 398, 445, 655. Doctrine of the resurrection, 654, 655. Hieracus on the, 714. Justin M., 670. In Parsism, 482.
Julian on the resurrection of Christ, ii. 46 n. 1, 48 n. 1. Doctrine of Theodore of Mopsuestia, ii. 493–495, 497, 716. Athanasius on, in connection with the Lord's supper, ii. 733. Synesius, ii. 763. In relation to relics, iii. 238. To transubstantiation, iii. 495. Michael II., iii. 544. Catharists on the, iv. 571, 574, 575, 587. Oliva, iv. 621. Council of Vincennes, v. 37.

Retaliation, i. 439.
Rethre, principal seat of Wendish idolatry, iii. 325, 327.
Retirement, religious, iii. 286, 287. See Monasticism.
Rettig, i. 83 n. 5.
Revelation, need of, i. 17, 31, 558; ii. 117, 671, 701. The Jewish, i. 35, 42, 57, 666. The Clementines on the original, i. 354, 355, 358. The Gnostics on, i. 382, 549. In Platonism, i. 163. Revelation and reason, i. 507, 512; ii. 673; iii. 463, 464; iv. 412 (see Reason). In Montanism, i. 511, 512. Origen on, i. 549, 553, 717. In nature, i. 558 (176). Progressive, i. 562; iii. 173. Source of truth, i. 666; iii. 463. End of, ii. 52. Julian on, ii. 58. Eunomius on, ii. 449. Pelagians on, ii. 673–675. Outward and inward, ii. 675, 701. Gregory I. on, iii. 115. Doctrine of with Maximus, iii. 173, 174. The Paulicians, iii. 260, 261. Scotus, iii. 463, 464. The Euchites, iii. 590. Gregory VII., iv. 118. Frederic II. and, iv. 182. Revelations of Hildegard, iv. 217. Periods of, with Joachim, iv. 227–232. Of the Spirit, Joachim, iv. 230–232. Sought for, iv. 305, 514. Aquinas on, iv. 429, 430. Dolcino, iv. 631.
Revelation, the book of, i. 527, 676; v. 177, 195. Cains on, i. 652. Babylon in, iv. 624.
    Rev. 1 : 6, i. 197. 1 : 10, i. 295. 2 : 6, 15, i. 453. 2 : 27, i. 247. 3 : 15, i. 629. 3 : 20, ii. 623. 9 : 2, iv. 221 n. 10 : 10, iv. 625. 12 : 4, iv. 567 n. 4. 14 : 4, ii. 375. 14 : 6, iv. 618. 17 : 2, v. 359. 21 : 12, iv. 625. 22 : 17, iii. 124. See Apocalypse, Commentaries.
Revenge for bloodshed, iv. 278.
Reverie, v. 397.
Revival of spiritual life after the tenth century, iii. 368.
Revocatus, martyr, i. 123, 124.
Revolutionary ideas, v. 353.
Reward, as motive, i. 57, 381; ii. 290 n. 4, 677 (682); iv. 259, 260, 386, 407, 408. Heaven as, ii. 722, 739. Gregory of Nyssa on, ii. 738. Of Christ, ii. 407 n. 3. Earthly, iii. 22 n. Spiritual, iii. 145; iv. 624. See Eschatology.

Rhangabe. See Michael Curopalates.
Rheginus, bp. of Constantia, ii. 531. See Harduin, l. f. 1444.
Rhegium (Riez) in Provence. See Faustus of.
Rheims, iii. 8, 479. School at, iv. 265, 470. Archbishops of, iv. 265, 360, 398, 418 n. 4. Bernard, iv. 255. History of, iii. 440 n. 6. See Adalbero, Arnulph, Ebbo, Hinkmar, Samson. See Councils, an. 991, an. 996, an. 1148.
Rheinwald.
    Writings of Abelard published by, iv. 388 n., 393 n. 1, 399 nn. 2, 3, 493 n. 4, 503 n. 1, 524 n. 1.
Rhetorical culture of church teachers, i. 683, 684, 688, 717; ii. 45 n. 1, 76, 78, 183, 396, 754. In the western nations, ii. 52.
Rhetorical language of church teachers, ii. 723, 732, 735 n. 9. Tendency, iii. 472.
Rhetorical preachers, ii. 45 n. 1, 353, 367, 368, 506.
Rhetorical schools, their character and influence, ii. 42, 52 n. 3, 116, 183, 396.
Rhetoricians, rhetorical panegyrists, i. 688, 693; ii. 10, 11, 35, 37, 41, 42, 45 n. 1, 67, 96 n. 3; iv. 531 n. 1. Their influence, ii. 21. Privileges, ii. 169. Intercessions, ii. 173.
Rhetorius, ii. 767, 768.
Rhine, the river, iii. 275. Hermits on the, iii. 28. Boniface on the, iii. 72. Radulf, iv. 74. Sects in the countries on the, iv. 582, 609, 643. Fanatical persecutions, iv. 586. Friends of God along the, v. 42, 390, 401, 407. Adherents of Gregory XII., v. 303. Cloister on the, v. 328, 330, 331. Ashes of Huss cast into the, v. 371.
Rhodes, iii. 229 n. 3.
Rhodoald, bp. of Porto, iii. 562, 565 n. 5, 569.
Rhodon, church teacher, on Marcion, i. 467 n. 1. Against Apelles, 474, 475. Ap. Euseb. II. E., l. 5, c. 13, 467 n. 1.
Rich men, favored by the clergy, iv. 288, 289; v. 222. Clement on the use of riches, i. 279, 280. Ruysbrock, v. 404. Bonaventura on the rich and poor, iv. 288, 289. See Poverty, Property.
Richard a St. Victore, character, iv. 411–413. Purposes of repentance, 293, 294. Works, subjective experiences, 305. Sowing contentions, 310. Intention, 387. Knowledge of God, 411–413. On the Trinity, 460, 461. Freewill, 517, 518.
    Citations:—
    De contemplatione, c. 2, wisdom of this world, iv. 413 n. 4; c. 3, revelation and reason, 412 nn. 5–7; c. 6, self knowledge, 412 n. 2; c. 12, use of intuitions, 413, n. 2.
    De eruditione interioris hominis, l. ii. c. 25, iv. 293 n. 2, 294 n. 1. P. i. l. iii. c. 18, despair 305 n. 2; c. 38, good disposition, 412 n. 4.
    De præparat. anim. ad contemplat., c. 30, good works, iv. 305 n. 1; c. 72, the mind a mirror

for God's image, 412, n. 1; cc. 73, 74, 412 nn. 8-10, 413 n. 1.
De statu interioris hom., c. 3. f. 39, the Trinity, iv. 460 n. 5; p. i. t. i. cc. 13, 22, 23, grace and freedom, 517 nn. 3-7, 518 n. 1; c. 24, knowledge and inclination, 412 n. 3; c. 27, depression, 305 n. 4.
De tribus appropriatis personis in trinitate, f. 271, iv. 460 n. 6.
De trinitate, l. v. cc. 7, 8, iv. 461 n. 2.

Richard, abp. of Armagh (Armacanus), v. 134.
Richard, abp. of Canterbury, on the exemptions of abbots, iv. 201, 202.

Ep. (68), to Alex. III., iv. 201 n. 4, 202 nn. 1, 3. Ordinance of; false bulls, 205 n. 1.

Richard, ecclesiastic, ep. of Berengar to, iii. 508 nn. 1, 2, 510 n. 1, 526 n. 1. See D'Achery, t. iii.
Richard II., king of England, v. 14", 155 n. 2, 163. 241.
Richard Montague. See Montacute.
Richbald, arch-priest, iii. 317 n. 2.
Richbon, bp. of Triers, iii. 167.
Richelieu, ii. 301 n. 4.
Richer, Benedictine.

Chronicon Senonense, l. iv. c. 16, f. 634. cupidity of the mendicant orders, iv. 290 r. 1; c. 37, Louis IX., 285 n. 7.

Richmar, ecclesiastic, iv. 79.
Richmond, v. 135.
Riculf, bp. of Soissons, iii. 427.
Riedel, A. F. on Anselm of Havelburg, iv. 536 n. 3.
Riga, iv. 36, 38, 39, 40, 41. See John of Wallenrod.
Rigaltius.

[In Tert. de exhort. castitat., c. 11], i. 525 n. 1.

Right and wrong, iv. 494; v. 399.
Righteousness, by the law and by faith, Hilary, ii. 619, 620. Self, ii. 633. Stages of, the Pelagians, ii. 673, 676 (677), 679. Original, iv. 492, 495. Of man and God, iv. 509. Eckhart on, v. 394.
Rights, of conscience in ancient Rome, i. 86, 90, 144, 175. Human, ii. 217. See Freedom, Liberty.
Rigord.

De gest. Phil. August. an. 1195 et seq., Fulco, iv. 210 n. 2; an. 1198, Peter de Rusia, 211 n. 2; an. 1196 f. 40, Moritz of Paris, 355 nn. 3, 4.

Rimbert, disciple and biographer of Anschar, iii. 281. Missionary labors of, 287, 291. See Acta S. (O. B.), S. iv.

Life of Anschar, cc. 6, 9, Anschar at Corvey, his visions, iii. 274 nn.; c. 12, plans of Charlemagne in regard to the northern missions, 271 n.; c. 13, Ebbo, 272 n. 1; cc. 15, 36. Anschar's purchase and training of captives, 277 n.; c. 16, his resignation, 278 n. 1; c. 18, Gauzbert, 281 n. 1; c. 19, Herigar, 281 n. 3; c. 20, Kathle, 282 n. 3; c. 21, Anschar's labors, 278 n. 3; c. 22, the bishopric of Bremen, 279 n.; c. 24, Schleswig, 280 n. 3; c. 25, Anschar's dream, 283 n. 1; c. 27, Birka, 255 n.; c. 35, Anschar's humility, 287, nn. 1, 2.

Rimini, Catharists at, iv. 584 n. 1. See Councils, an. 359.
Ring, of bishops and abbots, iii. 402; iv. 134, 142.
Ripon, iii. 286, 291.
Rites, i. 49. Pagan, 78, 116. Foreign, at Rome, 88. Paulicians on external, iii. 263, 264. See Ritual.
Ritter, C.

Die Stupas (Berlin, 1838), s. 29, i. 485 n. 6; s. 30, u. d. f. i. 481 n. Erdkunde von Asien, Bd. i. f. 283, iii. 89 n. 4; Bd. iv Abth., i. ss., 443, 602, 603, Thomas in India, name India, i. 82 nn. 1, 2; Geographie, ii. ii. Bd. i. s. 257, Prester John, iv. 47 n.; Thl. v. ss. 443, 603, the Banians, ii. 140 n. 4; ss. 515, 603, Kalliana, ii. 141 n. 4; s. 603, Dioscorides, ii. 140 n. 3.

Ritter, H.

Christlichen Philosophie, Bd. I., Origen's view of matter, i. 624 n. 5; s. 317, Origen's doct. of Creation, i. 621 n. 3; § 524, Origen's view of evil, i. 623 n. 5.

Ritual, of the British church, i. 85; iii. 16, 17, 23-25. Differences in, iii. 15-17, 23, 24, 317, 318, 555, 580. Influence of general councils on the. ii. 212. Instruction in the, iii. 107. See Church usages.
Robe of the supreme pontiff, ii. 92.
Robert, cardinal bishop of Cambray (Clement VII.), v. 47
Robert, count of Flanders, iv. 129, 130.
Robert, king of France, iii. 374, 450, 596. Life of, 450 n. 5. See Du Chesne, t. iv.
Robert de Sorbonne, on conscience, iv. 303, 304.

(See Bibl. Patr. Lugd., t. 27), f. 348, iv. 303 n. 6, 304 n. 1; f. 350, the Beguines, 303 n. 5

Robert Grosshead (Greathead, Capito), bp. of Lincoln, character, iv. 185-187, 424. On the papal court, 185, 186. Predicts the Reformation, 186. Abuses in the bestowment of benefices, 186, 200, 207. The Benedictines, 278 n. 2. The Mendicants, 278, 280, 281 n. 3. Roger Bacon, 424. Influence on the reformatory movements in England, v. 134. Wicklif on, v. 157. Influence on Huss, v. 240. Writings, iv. 185 n. 1, 279 n. 1. See Ortuinus Gratius fascic. rerum, app. f. 251.

Citations:—
Address to his clergy, f. 260, iv. 278 n. 4. Discourse before the papal court, 185 n. 2, 186 n. Ep. 6, to the pope, the Dominicans, 279 n. 1. Ep. 7, to the cardinal de Ostia, Minorites, 279 n. 1. Ep. 40, f. 334, to the general of the Dominicans, 279 n. 3. Ep. 53, f. 343 and ep. 108, f. 382, the Benedictines, 278 n. 2. Ep. 107, to his archdeacon, 207 n. 5, 278 n. 5, 279 n. 1. Ep. 114, f. 388, favorable view of the mendicants, 279 n. 4.

Robert Guiscard, iv. 120.
Robert Hallam, bp. of Salisbury, v. 121.
Robert of Arbrissel, iv. 243, 246-249, 600. Life of, c. 4, § 23, 247 nn. 2, 3. See Acta S. Feb. 25, Baldrich.

Robert of Citeaux, founder of the Cistercian order, iv. 251, 252.
Robert Pullein, iv. 408. Merits of Christ, 349 n. 2. Doctrine of the original state of man, 486. Of atonement, 505. Freewill, 515. Sententiæ, 408 n. 4.
Rocca Sicca, castle of, iv. 421.
Roch, on Justin Martyr's Dialogue, i. 668 n. 3.
Rochester. See Ernulph.
Rock, the, i. 211; ii. 200, 201; iii. 24, 166, 334 n. 4; iv. 88; v. 25, 154, 304.
Rodoald. See Rhodoald.
Rodulf, bp. iii. 297 n. 1.
Roeskilde, iv. 31.
Roger II. bp. of Chalons, iii. 600 n. 2.
Roger, cardinal (Gregory XI.), v. 44.
Roger, count of Foix, on religious liberty, iv. 642.
Roger, duke of Sicily, iv. 364.
Roger, king of Sicily, iv. 144, 146, 157.
Roger Bacon, character, iv. 423–426. Opus majus, 424 and n. 5, 425 n. 4. Relation of theology to philosophy, 434, 435. On miracles, 474. Influence on reformatory movements in England, v. 134.

Citations: —
De laude scripturæ sacræ (see Usser), iv. 425 nn. 1–3. Corruption of the text, 426 n. 3. Opus Majus, iv. 424, 425; on Theology at Paris (see Boulæus), 425 n. 4, 426 n. 1. P. i. ff. 10–17, against dependence on authority, 424 nn. 6, 7; c. 6, f. 28, universals, 356 n. 1; f. 45, Grosshead, 424 n. 3. P. 2, c. 5, one source of truth, 434 nn. 2–4; f. 41 seqq., P. 3, f. 47, philosophy and theology, 434 nn. 5, 6, 435 nn. 1–3; f. 160, faith and reason, 435 n. 4; f. 189, education of missionaries, 426 n. 2.

Roger of Hoveden.
Annals of, an. 792, Alcuin in the image controversy, iii. 235 n. 4.

Roland of Siena, Cardinal, legate to Frederic I., iv. 164. Elected pope, 167. See Alexander III.
Roland of Parma (Eberhard), iv. 107, 108.
Roman bishops, objects of persecution, i. 136. Arrogant claims of, i. 214–217, 299; ii. 521, 533, 647. Wealth of, ii. 167 n. 3. Pomp of, ii. 168. Idea of the papacy, ii. 202. See Papacy, Peter, Popes.
Roman character, the, in relation to Christianity, i. 508.
Roman church, supremacy, i. 85, 86. Number of presbyters, 202, 203. Peter, 213. Irenæus on the superiority of the, 204. Schism of Novatian, 222, 237–248. Treatment of the Lapsi, 231. Learning, 240 n. 4. Passover festival, 299. Monarchical spirit, 299 (see Roman bps.). Preaching, liturgical pomp, 303 n. 6. Baptism of heretics, 317–323. Importance attached to tradition, 319, 320. Jewish element, 365, 579. Pauline origin, 365 n. 2, 464, 579, 675. Anti-Judaizing tendency, 464, 465. Fasting on the Sabbath, 521 n. 1. Monarchians, 579, 581. Anti-chiliastic tendency, 651. Doctrines, 689–691. Jerome, 684 n. 1. Origen, 705.
In the Second Period. Relation of the Irish church to the Roman, ii. 147, 148. Presbyters of filial churches, 195 n. 1. Patriarchate, eccles. apostolica, 196, 198. Primacy, 198–208. Property of the, 199. Diocese, 199. Schism in the, 255–257. Fasting on the Sabbath, 335. Times of baptism, 360. Daily communion, 364. In the Arian controversy, 433, 434. In the Nestorian controversy, 515, 519–521, 523, 526, 533, 534, 552, 697, 721 (see Cœlestin I.). In the Eutychian, 568, 573–583 (see Leo). In the Monophysite, 584, 591–596, 600–609 (see Vigilius). The three chapters, 600–608. In the Pelagian controv., 643, 645–652, 697, 721; in the Semi-Pelagian, 695–698, 710–712. Chrysostom, 761, 762.
In the Third and Fourth Periods. Ritual, iii. 15, 17, 23–25, 555. Claims, 16. Relation to missions, 11, 12, 32, 34, 35, 47–50, 53–56, 68, 243 (see Gregory VII., Zacharias). Adalbert, 59. Simony, 64. Property of the, 113, 120, 122, 234. Efforts to enlarge its authority, 113–122. Relation to the Greek church, 112, 113, 196 n. 1, 210–212, 545, 561–584. To the Spanish, 117, 118. To the English, 118 (see Augustin). To the Frankish (15), 118–122, 242. (In Germany, see Bouifnce.) To the Bulgarians, 310–314. In the Adoptianist controversy, 165, 167. In the Monotheletic controversy, 179, 184–194, 197. In the image controversy, 199, 200, 210–212, 227, 228 n. 3, 233, 545, 546, 550–553. Authority of, in the Decretals, 349. See Popes.
In the Fifth Period. Relation to missions, iv. 15, 43 and n. 1, 49, 50, 56. Wealth, exactions, etc., 184, 185, 195, 196, 222 (see Extortions). Abbot Joachim on the, 222–224. Relation to Greek church, 536–551. Attacked by Waldenses, 611. Compared with Babylon, Joachim and Oliva on, 222, 223, 624; Arnold Hot, 641. Dolcino, 636. See Roman court.
In the Sixth Period. Authority, Defensor pacis on the, v. 31–33. The Germans at Constance, on the, 122, 123. See Cathedra Petri, Popes, Papacy, Peter, Roman court, Rome.
Roman citizenship, i. 113.
Roman court, exactions of the, iv. 182 (see Extortions). Frederic II. on the, 184. Grosshead, 185–187. Corruption, 195–197; v. 34, 35, 98, 102, 113, 137, 160. As a tribunal, iv. 198, 199 (see Appeals). Interference with authority of bishops, iv. 201, 202, 256; with church elections, v. 137. Wenceslaus

and the, v. 252. Huss on the, v. 258, 271, 294, 300, 301, 331. See Avignon.
Roman culture, ii. 52; iii. 141, 576.
Roman curia. See Roman court.
Roman customs, ii. 39, 92.
Roman de la Rose, iv. 289 n. 2.
Roman emperors, their relation to the church, ii. 1–110, 162. Influence in the appointment of bps., ii. 92.
Roman empire, relation to the spread of Christianity, i. 49, 79 84, 85. Extension and limitation of the church within the, ii. 1–124, 146. Influence of, ii. 51, 52. Patriarchal constitution in the, ii. 196, 197. In ruin, ii. 146; iii. 3, 25. See East Roman empire.
Roman forum, ii. 13 (92).
Roman law, i. 126, 175. School of, i. 717. Arbitration, ii. 171; iii. 361. Study of, iv. 172, 204.
Roman life, pictured by Polybius, i. 6.
Roman literature, iii. 141, 150, 151, 335.
Roman liturgy, iv. 58. See Ritual.
Roman religion, i. 36, 126. See Religio, Roman state.
Roman republic, empire restoration of the, iv. 150, 151, 161.
Roman senate, i. 184. Paganism and the, ii. 92.
Roman state, relation of religion to politics, i. 6–8, 86–91, 144, 175. Toleration, 86, 88, 126.
Roman theocracy. See Theocracy.
Romans, epistle to the.
Ch., 1 : 19-32, iv. 370, 379. 1 : 28, ii. 669 n. 2; v. 212. 1 : 32, iii. 255 n. 1. 2 : 11, i. 313. 2 : 15, ii. 290 n. 3. 2 : 23, iii. 444. 3 : 12, ii. 293 n. 4. 3 : 23, iv. 509. 3 : 25, iv. 502 n. 2. 5 : 3, ii. 677. 5 : 12, ii. 618. 669 and n. 3, 670 n. 1, 671; iv. 493. 5 : 13, ii. 716. 5 : 18, i. 716. 5 : 19, ii. 719. 5 : 21, ii. 716. 7, i. 63. 7 : 5, 23, ii. 671 n. 3. 7 : 8, ii. 670 n. 2. 7 : 9, iv. 11. 7 : 20, ii. 671 n. 3. 7 : 23, ii. 391, 671 n. 3. 8 : 1, iv. 240. 8 : 3, i. 641. 8 : 8, 9, ii. 181. 8 : 9, iii. 242. 8 : 12, ii. 670 n. 1. 8 : 18, ii. 572 n. 6. 8 : 19, i. 625; ii. 716. 8 : 20, 21, i. 411 n. 3. 8 : 24, iii. 237. 8 : 26, i. 716; iii. 253, 483 n. 4. 8 : 28, iv. 475. 8 : 32, iii. 161 n. 1. 8 : 35 ff., ii. 137; iii. 372. 8 : 38, v. 198. 9, iv. 588. 9 : 5, i. 534. 9 : 11, ii. 627, 630. 9 : 13, ii. 622. 9 : 15, ii. 628. 9 : 16, ii. 628, 705; iv. 305. 9 : 18, i. 630. 9 : 20, ii. 628; iii. 477. 10 : 5, ii. 626. 10 : 8, iii. 237; iv. 431. 11 : 11, iv. 72. 11 : 17, 24, i. 638. 11 : 20, i. 230. 11 : 26, iv. 74. 11 : 33, ii. 690. 12 : 1, i. 138, 180; iv. 241. 12 : 7, 8, i. 187 n. 2. 12 : 19, iii. 130; v. 281. 13, v. 26, 164. 13 : 1, iv. 202. 13 : 1-3, iv. 160 : v. 17. 13 : 2, iii. 345 : v. 285. 13 : 4, ii. 173 ; v. 18, 29. 13 : 14, i. 138 ; ii. 302. 14 : 3, ii. 181, 579. 14 : 16, i. 326. 14 : 17, i. 278, 298, 299 ; iv. 241, 264. 14 : 20, ii. 306. 14 : 23, ii. 381. 15 : 24, i. 85. 16 : 1, ii. 191 n. 2. 16 : 5, i. 290 n. 2. 16 : 5-14, 15, i. 185. 16 : 14, i. 360. 16 : 23, i. 289. See Apocalypse, Commentaries.
Romans, the, in their relation to Christianity, i. 4–16, 49.
Romans, town in Burgundy, iv. 314 n. 2.
Romanus, monk, ii. 297.
Rome, early miracles in, i 74. Appearance of Christianity at, 77. Metropolis and ecclesia apostolica, diffusion of Christianity from, 84, 203, 204. Multiplicity of religions at, 88. Persecution at, 133, 136, 139. Cathedra Petri, 213 (see Roman church). Valentine at, 417. Tatian, 456. Marcion, 464, 465. Monarchians, 530. Artemonites, 581. Praxeas, 583. Justin, 663.
Second Period. Constantius at, ii. 35. Victorinus at, 75, 77. Paganism at, 92–94, 99, 100. Patrick at, 147. Proposed school at, 183 n. Churches at, 194. Monachism, 294. Morals at, 296, 297. Influence of Jovinian at, 312. Image worship, 324. Sabbath at, 334, 335. Christmas at, 344, 345 and n. 1, 347. Athanasius at, 434. Pelagius at, 639. Cœlestius at, 639, 647, 651. Jerome at, 742, 744, 745, 749, 750 (i. 684 n. 1). Clergy at, 744, 748. Rufinus at, 748–750. Manicheans, 769. Priscillianists, 772. See Councils, an. 342, an. 390, an. 419, an. 430.
Third and Fourth Periods. Visits to, iii. 44, 47, 55, 57, 58 n. 1, 79, 81, 114, 120, 154, 277, 316, 321 329 n., 541 n. 3 (see Pilgrimages). State of morals, superstitious practices, 58 n. 1, 64. Compared with Constantinople, 329 n. Corruption, 366–368, 375–378. Pope's secular power in, 349. Synods in, 353. Rome in the tenth century, 366–368, 370, 375–378, 403. Old and new, 399 n. 4. Manuscripts at, 459. Bigotry at, 512, 513. See Councils, an. 648, an. 745, an. 800, an. 863, an. 868, an. 963, an. 1046, an. 1050, an. 1059.
Corruption at in the Fifth Period, iv. 83, 84, 86, 184, 185, 187 and n. 2, 195, 196, 201, 604 n. 3. Visited, 43, 65, 96, 185, 593, 612. Lull at, 67. Sovereignty, 83. Besieged and entered by Henry IV., 119, 120. Assembly under Henry IV., 120. Urban II. expelled from, 121. His return, 128. Henry V. and Paschalis II., 134. Popes expelled by Henry V., 141. Innocent II. and Bernard at, 146. Frederic I., sovereignty of the emperor in, 163, 166, 172. Influence of Arnold of Brescia in, 150–152, 160, 161. Commotions at, 108, 151, 152, 161. Senate, 151, 161. People of, 159–161. Frederic II., 176, 182. Students from, 373. Robert Pullein at, 408. Greek embassy to, 546. See Councils, an. 1074, 1075, 1076, an. 1112, 1123, 1139, 1170, 1179, an. 1215, 1227, 1241.
In the Sixth Period. Jubilees at, v. 3, 51. Absence of the popes from, v. 20, 36, 41 (see Avignon). Ghibellines at, 36. Attempt of Urban V. to return, 44. Commotions, 44, 45. Gregory XI., election of Urban VI., 44–46. Clemangis on the fall of, 57. Election of Gregory XII., 70, 71. Ladislaus at, 73, 100. Militz at, 180. Conrad at, 184. Janow at, 192. Pious women in, 222. See Cardinals, Councils, an. 1412.

Romuald, founder of the Camalduleusian order, iii. 419, 446 n. 1. Life of, 419 nn. 1–4, 6.
Romulus, landlord, ii. 175.
Roncala, diet of, iv. 203.
Roscelin, Dialectician, iv. 247 n. 4, 356, 359, 360, 361, 369, 382, 461.
Rose, the golden, v. 106.
Rosenmüller.
Altes und neues Morgenland, Dd. ii. p. 226, judgments of God, iii. 130 n. 2.
Rossano, iii. 420.
Rothad, bp., iii. 358–361.
Rothe.
De disciplinæ arcani, etc., in eccles. Christian. origine, i. 305 n. 1, 327 n. 1, 328 n. 4. Ueber die anfänge der Christlichen Kirche, p. 197, i. 185 n. 3.
Rothrud, Frankish princess, iii. 234.
Rouen, iii. 595 n. 5; iv. 590 n. 6. Massacre of Jews in, iv. 71 n. 3.
Routh.
Reliquiæ Sacræ, vol. ii., ep. of Dionysius Alex. to Basilides, fragm., i. 712 n. 2; f. 115, ep. of J. Africanus to Aristides, fragm., i. 709 n.; vol. iii. f. 237, i. 296 n. 5. See Victorinus.
Rudbert (Ruprecht), bp. of Worms, among the Bavarians, iii. 40.
Rudebach.
Fragments of Claudius of Turin, iii. 436 n. 1.
Rudolph.
Life of Rabanus Maurus, c. 2, sale of relics, iii. 446 n. 1. See Acta S. Feb., t. i.
Rudolph, abbot of Liege, on communion under one form, iv. 343 n. 4.
Rudolph, archduke of Austria, v. 191.
Rudolph, duke of Suabia, iv. 96 n. 6. Elected emperor, 117, 118, 119.
Rudolph, priest, companion of Vicelin, iv. 33.
Rufianus, villa, ii. 540.
Rufinus, rescript of Hadrian, i. 101 n. 2. Edict of Diocletian, trans., 148 n. 1, 149 n. 1. Apostles creed, 307. Recognitions of Clement, 358. Origen, de principiis (see Origen, περὶ ἀρχῶν), 638 n. 4. Eusebius on Tertullian, 684 n. 1. Pamphilus, 722. Theophilus of Cæsarea, iii. 347. Collationes patrum, iv. 423.
Constantine and the Labarum, ii. 11, 13 n. 2. Theodorus the martyr, 83 n. 2. Conversion of the Iberians, 139 n. 1. The Abyssinian church, 144 and n. 2. Diocese of the Roman bishop, 199. Ambrose and Theodosius, 215 n. 1. Jerome and Rufinus, in the Origenistic controversy, 641, 743, 744, 746–750, 752. See Jerome adv. Rufin.
Citations: —
De adulteratione librorum Origenis (opp. Hieron., t. v. f. 251, ed. Martianay), i. 704 n. 3. Exposit. symbol. apostol., i. 306 n. 3, 307 n. 3. Hist. eccles., l. i. c. 5, adoption of the Nicene Creed, ii. 420 n. 3; c. 9, Ædesius, ii. 144 n. 1; c. 10, Bacurius, the Iberian, ii. 139 n. 1; c. 23, destruction of temples in Egypt, ii. 98 n. 2. L. ii. c. 6, Moses, Saracenian bp., ii. 142 n. 5. L. ix. c. 9, vision of Constantine. ii. 11 n. 1. Invectiva contr. Hieron., l. ii., ii. 744 n. 4, 746 n.; f. 285 (t. v. ed. Mart.), ii. 743 n. 3.
Translation of Euseb., i. 684 n. 1; ii. 13 n. 2; 83 n. 2. Of Origen, Comm. in, tit. i. 578 n. 6, 593 n.; περὶ ἀρχῶν, i. 638 n. 4; ii. 748, 749. Of i. ep Clement to James, iii. 347 n. 2.
Rufus, bp., enemy of the Priscillianists, ii. 773.
Rufus, bp. of Thessalonica, ii. 652.
Ep. of Pelagian bps. to, ii. 652 n. 2, 722 n. 1. (See Theodoret, opp., t. iv., ed. Halen, ep. 170.)
Rugen, island of, attempts to Christianize repelled, iii. 325, 328 n. 4. History of the conversion of, iv. 24, 25, 26, 30, 31, 32.
Rugi, Rugians, iii. 28 n. 3, 328 n. 4. See Rugen.
Ruinart.
Edict of Aurelius, i. 108 n. 2. Acta Martyrum, 122 n. 3. Acta Felicis, 151 n. 1.
Rulers, duties of, iv. 285. Hildebert of Mans on, iv. 306, 307. Authority of, v. 307. See Princes.
Rules. See Monastic.
Rulmann Merswin, v. 387, 388.
Rupert convent, iv. 217.
Rupert of Bamberg, iv. 109.
Rupert of Bavaria, emperor, v. 84, 252, 256.
Rupert of Deutz (Tuitiensis), German mystic, Hermann the Jew, iv. 79. Transubstantiation, 337, 338. His writings, 411.
Comm. in Exod., l. ii. c. x. t. 1, f. 171, transubstantiation, iv. 338 n. 1. In Johann., l. vi. t. ii. f. 308, the same, 337 nn. 6, 7. De victoria verbi Dei., l. ii. c. 7, image of God, 487 n. 5.
Ruspe. See Fulgentius of.
Russia, Russians, iii. 296. Spread of Christianity, iii. 327–330. Liefland and, iv. 38. Mongols in, iv. 49. Journey of the Franciscans, iv. 50. Jerome of Prague in, v. 246, 373, 374. See Karamsim.
Russian annals. See Nestor.
Russian legend, pub. by Wastokow, Drahomira, iii. 321 n. 5.
Russico-Waragian empire, iii. 327, 328.
Rusticus, deacon, ii. 603.
Rutilius, ii. 290.
Ruysbroch, friend of God, v. 382, 385, 386, 396–407.
Citations: —
De calculo, f. 283, v. 401 n. 2; f. 825, 386 n. 2. De ornat. spirital. nuptiar., f. 266 (or 486), 404 n. 6; f. 267, 404 n. 5; f. 274, 404 n. 4, 405 n. 3; f. 275, 399 n. 2. De præcip. quibusd. virtut. f. 170, obedience, 385 n. 3; f. 173, love, 404 n. 1; f. 175, desertion, 405 n. 3; f. 176, holiness, 403 n. 6; f. 179, pantheistic expressions, 402 n. 1; f. 180, the will, 404 n. 7; f. 181, the same, 404 n. 8; f. 185, confidence in God, 386 n. 1, 405 n. 1. De quatuor subtil. tentat., f. 196 (or 500), apathy, 398 n. 4; f. 195, external exercises, 404 n. 2;

De sept. amor. grad., f. 220, use of riches, 404 n. 3; f. 221, obedience, 385 n. 4; f. 224, against apathy, 399 n. 1; f. 226, repose in God, 402 n. 2. Speculum æternæ Salut., f. 11 (ed. 1600, p. 21), freedom from the world, 385 n. 2; f. 12, tempting thoughts, 407 n. 1; f. 13, 403 n. 1, spiritual dearth, 406 n. 2; f. 14, Christ, 402 n. 3, 403 n. 3; f. 15, 403 n. 2; ff. 25, 26, contemplation without action, 403 n. 5; f. 27 (or 50), quietism, 396 n. 2; fall of the angels, 398 n. 3; contempt for sacraments, 401 n. 3; f. 29, 396 n. 3; a good will, 405 n. 1; f. 31, the creaturely spirit not God, 397 nn.; f. 34, union with God by love, 398 nn. 1, 2.

S.

Saale, river, iii. 323; iv. 18.
Saba, convent, iii. 207.
Sabæans (disciples of John), i. 353 n. 1, 376 and n. 3, 382, 383 n., 444 n. 1, 447; iii. 257. Hamyares, ii. 142.
Sabaeism (Zabaism), i. 387 n. 3; ii. 768 n. 1. Among the Arabians, iii. 84.
Sabas, abbot, life of, ii. 271 n. 4, 76. n. 3. See Coteler, Cyrill of Scythopolis.
Sabas, the martyr, ii. 153-155.
Sabbas, disciple of Methodius, iii. 320 n. 2.
Sabbath, the (Saturday), among the Essenes, i. 49. Therapeutæ, i. 61. In Christianity, i. 294-297, 676; ii. 333-335, 338 n. 6, 339, 365; v. 140, 336. Fasting on the, i. 296 and n. 5, 521 n. 1, 684 n. 2; ii. 333 n. 8, 334, 335, 339 n. 6; iii. 407 (in the Greek church), iii. 557, 567, 579, 581. The millennial, i. 399. The Demiurge, ii. 411 n. 3. Ptolemæus on the, i. 440. The Prodicians, i. 451. In Montanism, i. 521 n. 1, 684 n. 2. Chrysostom on, i. 315. Gregory of Nyssa, ii. 448 n. 1. The Great Sabbath, ii. 341. The last period of Dolcino, iv. 621.
Sabellius, Sabellianism, i. 594-601, 606, 607, 610, 591 n. 4; ii. 385, 408 421, 439, 440, 479, 482; iii. 91 n, 157 n. 1, 479 n. 3; iv. 227 n. 1, 461, 462 n. 2, 556.
Citations: —
Ap. Athanas., c. Arian. orat., iv. § 8, i. 598 n. 4; § 11, i. 597 n. 1; § 12, i. 598 n. 5, 600 n. 2; § 13, i. 595 n. 3; §§ 20, 21, 22, i. 598 nn. 1-3; § 23, i. 599 n. 4; § 25, i. 595 n. 3, 597 n. 2. 598 n. 6 599 n. 1. Ap. Basilium epp. 210, 214 § 3, 235 § 6, i. 596 n. 4. Ap. Epiphan. hæres. 62. i. 596 n. 2. Ap. Justin. Mart. dial. c. Tryph. Jud., f. 358 (ed. Colon.), i. 597 n. 3. Ap. Theodoret. hæret fab. 2, c. 9, i. 600 n. 1. See Monarchians, Logos, Epiphanius, Athanasius.
Sabert, king of Essex, iii. 16, 18.
Sabigotha, enthusiast, iii. 341.
Sabina. See John, bp. of.
Sabinus, prætorian prefect, ii. 2, 17.
Sabotiers, iv. 609.
Saccendion, monastery, iii. 536 n. 1.
Sacerdotal acts, validity of, ii. 219, 224. See Sacraments.
Sacerdotal colleges, offices, ii. 5.

Säckingen, monastery near, iii. 37.
Sacra (sacred customs), i. 101, 141; ii. 21, 22, 66 n. 1, 76 n. 3.
Sacra, imperial, ii. 537, 557, 574, n. 1; iii. 225 n., 227 n. 1.
Sacraments, signification of, external conception, celebration, i. 304-335 (252). Doctrine of, 646-649. Marriage as a, 522. Right of laity to administer, 196.
In the Second Period. Objective validity of the, ii. 219, 224, 246, 247, 724, 766 n. 2. Superstitious views of the, 258, 259, 636, 724. Administration and apprehension of the, 355-369. Eunomius on the value placed upon the, 447. Doctrine of the, 722-736. Number of, 725.
In the Third and Fourth Periods. Magical notions connected with the, iii. 18, 123, 263, 351, 42., 495, 525. Miracles, 146. Objective validity, 379 n., 389, 392, 492, 493. Number of, 449, 496 n. 1. Berenger on the term as applied to the Lord's Supper, sacrament and res sacramenti, 523-525, 528 n. 4 (ii. 734). With the sectaries at Orleans, 593-596. At Arras and Liege, 597. At Montfort, 601.
In the Fifth Period. The number seven, iv. 8, 334, 335, 614. Administration by simoniacal and married persons, iv. 92-100, 592. Objective validity of, 100, 592, 593. Res sacramenti, 137, 337 n. 2. During the interdict, 174. Doctrine of the, 334-354. Unbelieving participation, 325, 327. First mention of the number seven, 335 (8). Joachim on the, 224, 225. Innocent III., 322. Followers of Almaric of Bena, 448. In relation to grace, 514. Of the Old and New Testament, 514 n. 5. With sectaries, 556, 557, 575-578, 593. Chrysomalos, 561. "Votum" a substitute for the, 578. Administered by laity, 592, 614. Waldenses on, 614.
In the Sixth Period. Abuse of, v. 54, 81. Duty of priests in regard to, 143, 146. Validity, Wicklif on, 163; Huss, 274, 345, 351; Cruci fratres, 412. Definition, 169. Wicklif on the multiplication of, 169, 170. Neglect of, 198, 199. Janow on the, 209, 214. Huss, 270, 274 and n. 1, 291, 296, 298, 340, 345, 351. Eckhart and the friends of God on the, 395, 396, 398. See the several sacraments.
Sacramentum militiæ Christianæ, i. 98 n. 1, 264, 309. Term sacramentum, i. 316 n. 3. Sacramentum crucis, ii. 621.
Sacred writings of the Essenes, i. 45. Sacred places, iii. 40 (see Pilgrimages). Pagan, iii. 45. Sacred poetry, iv. 155, 313. See Poets, Song.
Sacrificati, i. 234 and n. 1, 242, 244, 245.
Sacrifice, among the Essenes, i. 48. Marcus Aurelius, i. 107. To the emperors,

GENERAL INDEX.

i. 147, Tertullian on, i. 175. Prayer as, i. 284. Ptolemæus on, i. 440. Human sacrifices, i. 142; iii. 78, 304, 326, 327. Of Christ, see Christ.
Sacrifices in private dwellings forbidden, ii. 21, 22, 59. All sacrifices forbidden, 28, 33, 34, 35, 91, 251 (59, 95 n. 5, 106). Meat offered in, 52, 153, 154 (see Apostolic decrees). Libanius, 67 n. 2. Julian, 68, 81, 86, 87. Jovian, 83 and n., 89. Nocturnal, 90 n. 4. Soothsaying from, 89, 94, 95. Crimen majestatis, 99. Simplicius on, 107, 108.
Animal sacrifices in the Armenian church, iii. 589. To idols, by ignorant priests, iii. 53 n. 7. In Norway, iii. 294. In Iceland, iii. 304, 305. Sacrifices, with the Pasagians, iv. 590. Daily, v. 217, 218. Old Testament, iii. 16 n. 1; v. 231. Idea of sacrifice in the Lord's Supper. See Lord's Supper.
Sacrilege, iii. 101, 348, 402, 521; iv. 133, 138.
Sadducees, i. 39, 40–42, 351. Relation to Christianity, 63.
Sagittarius, bp. of Gap, iii. 119 n. 1.
Saguin, abp. of Sens, iii. 371 and n. 1.
Saintones. See Councils, an. 564.
Saints, worship of, history of the, ii. 369–373; iii. 123, 132, 133, 201, 445–448; iv. 328-333.
Julian on saint-worship, ii. 47. Adalbert, iii. 58. Mohammed, iii. 86. In the Greek church, iii. 170. Germanus on (Λατρεία), iii. 205. John of Damascus on, iii. 208. Decree of the council of Constantinople (an. 754), iii. 218. Libri Carolini, iii. 241. The Paulician woman, iii. 251. Agobard on, iii. 428, 429. In Italy, iii. 433. Claudius of Turin on, iii. 437. Reaction against, iii. 446. Change in, iii. 447, 448. In the sects, iii. 593, 598. The Jews on iv. 77. Francis, iv. 276. The Bogomiles on, iv. 557. The Catharists, iv. 578. Henry of Cluny on, iv. 601, 602. Waldenses on, iv. 614. Wilhelmina, iv. 638. Council of Constance, v. 113. Wicklif on, v. 140, 168, 169. Tauler, v. 408, 409. Huss, v. 323, 324, 349.
Nicephorus on the character of the saints, iii. 535 n. 3; Conrad, v. 189; Janow, v. 214, 215. Communion of, iii. 134, 135; v. 324. Condition of the, v. 37, 38. Churches in honor of, ii. 328, 370; iii. 12, 130; iv. 78. Days, i. 334, 335; iii. 15 (see Festivals). Intercession, merits of, iii. 535 n. 3; iv. 63, 78, 349, 350, 593; v. 323, 324, 349. Patron saints, ii. 371. Shrines, iii. 42. Glorification of the, iv. 621, 622. See Canonization, Miracles, Relics.
Saiset de Pamiers, papal legate, v. 6.
Salaberga, St., life of, iii. 38 nn. 2, 3.
Salamauca, university at, iv. 70.

Salamis (Constantia), ii. 328, 741. See Epiphanius.
Salaries of clergy, i. 198 n. 1.
Salawar, iii. 316.
Salerno, iii. 399 n. 4.
Salimbenus de Adam. See Francesco Pegna, Mosheim.
Salisbury, bp. of, v. 121. See John of.
Sallust, iii. 526 n. 6.
Salona, iii. 114.
Salonius, bp. of Embrun, iii. 119 n. 1.
Salt, in baptism, ii. 359.
Salt.
Voyage to Abyssinia, Greek inscription, ii. 144 n. 2.
Salustius, statesman, ii. 45 and n. 3. Prefect, 83.
Salvation, the ground of, i. 363, 645 (see Faith and). Straight gate, iv. 304. Order of, iv. 304, 511–513. Conditions of, iv. 446, 513, 514, 516, 517, 578, 579. Uncertainty in regard to, iv. 513, 514. See Grace, Justification.
Salvianus, bp., convert to Priscillianism, ii. 301, 772.
De gubernat. Dei, ii. 301 n. 3.
Salzburg, foundation of the bishopric of, iii. 40, 55. Archbishopric, iii. 332. Priest of, on the conversion of the Moravians, iii. 316 n. 2, 317 n. 2 (see Freher). Bps. of, see Arno, Conrad I., Eberhard, Gebhard, Theotmar, Virgil.
Samaneans, i. 278.
Samaria, the apostles in, iv. 576. The woman of, i. 435; iv. 428; v. 403. Religion of, i. 454. Goetæ in, i. 454 n.
Samaritans, the, i. 102, 316. The good Samaritan, iv. 572.
Same, Epiphanes at, i. 451.
Sameland, Adalbert in, iv. 42. Bishopric, 45.
Sammael, iv. 553 n. 1.
Samosata, ii. 71; iii. 244. See Paul of.
Samosatenian disputes, doctrine, i. 581, 601–605; ii. 205, 483, 506 n. 1; iii. 91 n. Clergy, ii. 190 n. 2.
Samson, abbot of Cordova.
Apologeticus, l. ii. f. 385, translator at the Arabian court, iii. 385 n. 4. See España Sagrada, t. xi.
Samson, abp. of Rheims, iv. 587, 604.
Samson, Irish priest, on imposition of hands, iii. 63 n. 4.
Samuel, v. 351.
1 Sam. 2: 25, i. 226. 3, iv. 162. 15: 11, v. 351 n. 2.
Sanctification, redemption and, i. 644, 645 (311). Doctrine of creation and, i. 564. Basilides on, i. 413. Justification and, i. 413; ii. 677, 678; iv. 304 509, 510, 513. Friends of God on, v. 383. See Justification.
Sanctuary. See Asylum.
Sandals, iv. 201.
Sanhedrim, i. 41 n. 1.

GENERAL INDEX. 201

Saniahs, i. 442 ; ii. 291.
Sansara, in Gnosticism i. 370, 484 n. 3.
  Sansara und Nirwana, in Buddhism, i.
  481–484 and n. 3, 503.
Sanskrit, i. 82 n. 2.
Sapor I. (Shapur I.), king of Persia, i.
  149 n. 1, 488.
Sapor II., Persian emperor, ii. 125-133,
  141.
Sarabaïtes, ii. 283, 284.
Saracens, churches among the, ii. 142,
  143. Influence of ascetics over the, ii.
  142, 143, 267.
  In the Third and Fourth Periods. In
  Asia and North Africa, iii. 83. In
  Egypt and Syria, 88, 89, 228, 453 n. 2
  (ii. 111 n.). In Spain, 152, 164 and n.
  6, 165, 335–345. In Palestine, 180,
  206. Intercourse with, 157 n. 1, 166
  n. 6. Martin I. and the, 188 n. 1. Maronites and the, 197. Hinder intercourse with the Roman empire, 218,
  575. The Paulicians and the, 247, 250,
  256, 587.
  Fifth Period. Among the Mongols,
  iv. 53, 57. Francis of Assisi and the,
  59, 60 and n. 2. Raymund Lull, 62–71,
  190–192. In Majorca, 68. In the East,
  104, 124, 153, 189, 190. In North Africa, 124. In Grenada, 191. Anselm
  and the, 364. Gerson, v. 86. Huss, v.
  308. See Mohammedans.
Saragossa. See Councils, an. 380.
Sardica (see Councils, an. 347). Bp. of,
  ii. 377.
Sardinia, belongs to the diocese of the
  Roman church, ii. 199 North African
  clergy in, ii. 709. Paganism in, ii. 13
  n. 1, 603 and n. 2. Roman church
  property in, iii. 113.
Σαρκικόν, Origen on the, i. 627.
Sarmatio, monk, ii. 312.
Sarolta, daughter of Gylas, iii. 331, 333.
Sartach, Mongol prince, iv. 51.
Σάρξ of Christ, in the church doctrine, i.
  634. With Marcellus, ii. 480. Apol-
  linaris, ii. 490.
Sasima, ii. 462, 465.
Sassanides, the, i. 81.
Satan, with the Ebionites, i. 352. In
  Gnosticism, 375, 377, 421, 422, 427,
  438, 455, 624 ; (Marcion), 466, 471. In
  Buddhism, 483. In later Christian
  sects, 489 n. 3. With Mani, 499. With
  Origen, 624, 704 n. 3. Tertullian, 617.
  In the doctrine of redemption, 635 n. 1,
  640–644 ; iv. 500, 501, 503, 505, 506.
  Renounced in baptism, ii. 359. Conflict with, ii. 479. With the Traducian-
  ists, according to Julian of Eclanum,
  ii. 659. In ancient literature, ii. 742.
  Priscillianists, ii. 776. In the Koran,
  iii. 86 n. 1. Power, working of, iv. 300 ;
  589 ; with Chrysostom, ii. 719, 720.
  Hildegard, iv. 218, 219 ; Wicklif, v.
  156, 171 ; Clemangis, v. 116 ; Paletz,
  v. 119 ; Janow, v. 193, 197–200, 204,
  205, 227, 232. Existence denied ? iii.
  544. As Antichrist, Joachim, iv. 226.
  Appearance of, iv. 296. The sin of, iv.
  486 and n. 4. The Bogomiles on, iv.
  555 and n. 1. The Catharists, iv. 567–
  569, 572–575. Peter, v. 165. Loosed,
  v. 171. Destruction of, v. 200.
Satanael, iii. 591 n. 2, 597 n. 2 ; iv. 553–
  559, 573.
Satisfactio, i. 220 n. 5.
Satisfaction, in the doctrine of redemption, i. 642–644, 647. With Anselm,
  iv. 498–500, 501, 506. Abelard, iv. 501,
  502. Aquinas, iv. 506. William of
  Paris, iv. 506, 507. Active and passive, i. 642 ; iv. 500. Vicarious, i. 643 ;
  iv. 505, 506. Paid to Satan, i. 542–544 ;
  iv. 505, 506. For sins after baptism,
  ecclesiastical, i. 647, 654 ; ii. 292 ; iv.
  577, 587 n. 5, 593 ; v. 39. See Pen-
  ance.
Saturday, ii. 365 ; iii 407. See Sab-
  bath.
Saturnalia, ii. 347.
Saturnin of Toulouse, martyr, i. 84.
Saturninus, Gnostic, i. 455.
Saturninus, proconsul, i. 122.
Saturnius, martyr, i. 123, 124.
Saul, i. 229 ; iii. 5 n. 2 ; iv. 624 ; v. 351.
Saul (Paul), ii. 704.
Saul, bp. of Cordova, i i. 340.
Savona, proposed abdication at, v. 72–74.
Savoy, iv. 213.
Saxo-Grammaticus,
  l. xiv. ed. Klotz, on bp. Absalom, iv. 31 n. 2,
  32 n.
Saxons, carried into slavery, iii. 41 n.
  4. First attempts to convert the, 44.
  Inroads of the, 47, 63, 74, 75, 76 n. 2,
  78, 79. In Thuringia, 50 n. 1. Chris-
  tianity among the, 75–81, 83 n. 1. Ed-
  ucation, 73, 273. Reasons of their opposition to Christianity, 75–78. Conquest of the, 78, 81, 272. Labors of
  Lindgar and Willehad, 79–82. Charlemagne and the, 75–81, 272, 273. Gottschalk, 472. At the university of Prague,
  v. 247. Eckhart, v. 393. See Anglo-
  Saxons.
Saxony, Thorwald in, iii. 300. Otto, iv.
  18. Conquered by Henry IV., iv. 104.
  Assembly at Tribur, iv. 111. Otho of,
  iv. 176. See Otho IV.
Scalds, Icelandic bards, iii. 301, 303.
Scandinavian tribes, spread of Christian-
  ity among the, iii. 271–307. Yule, 294,
  295. Exposure of children among the,
  305 n. 2.
Scapula, proconsul, i. 84, 101 n. 2, 122.
  See Tertullian.
Scepticism. See Skepticism.
Scetic desert, monks of the, ii. 276, 748
  n., 751–753.
Schaffhausen, iv. 233. John XXIII. at,
  v. 106, 110, 339.
Schelde, river, iii. 40.
Schelling, i. 176 n. 1.

Schelstrat, Em. a.
Tractat. de sensu et auctoritate decret. Constant. conc., etc., f. 226, the fourth session, v. 100 n. 1; f. 256, the Germans, 119 n. 4; f. 257, 120 n.; f. 269, 124 n. 2; f. 271, points settled by the council, 125 n.

Schenkel.
On the ep. of Barnabas, i. 658 n. 3.

Schilter.
Thes. antiquitat. Teutonicar., t. i., sermons of Otfrid, iii. 425 n. 3; 426 n. 2.

Schisms, i. 191, 208, 221–248. Irenæus on, 209. Cyprian, 211. Dionysius of Alexandria on, 243. Schism of Felicissimus, 222–237. Of Novatian, 237–248.
In the Second Period. Schism between the Roman and Persian church, ii. 136. Donatist schism, 216–252. Meletian schism in Egypt, 252–255. Of Damasus and Ursinus at Rome, 255–257. Meletian, at Antioch, 457, 458, 461, 464, 465. Of Lucifer, 458, 459. In the Eastern church, excited by Cyrill, 547. Between the Eastern and Western church, and in the Western, in the Monophysite controversy, 589, 608. Of the Johannites at Constantinople, 762.
Third and Fourth Periods. In the English church, iii. 18. Among the Longobard communities, 34, 35. In the Eastern church, 88, 176, 178. Between the Eastern and Western churches, 193, 196 n. 1, 558–584. In the Paulician sect, 249–251.
Fifth Period. Concerning lay investiture, iv. 104–143. Gottfried of Vendome on, 143. Concerning papal elections, 144–146, 167–169, 218. Under Innocent III., 177, 253 n. 3. Within the mendicant orders, 291 (v. 24, 36). Predicted, 284. Abelard, 380. Between the Greek and Roman church, 536–551. In the Greek church, 543–551.
Sixth Period. Power of the pope during, v. 15. During the papal election, 20. Occasioned by the interdict in Germany, 24, 42, 43. Among the Cardinals, 44. The forty years schism (22), 47–126, 164, 273; three parties, 49, 63; Janow on the, 231, 232; Huss, 306, 308, 324. Huss accused of causing, 347.

Schleiermacher.
On the conception of virtue (p. 21), ii. 681 n. 6. Cardinal virtues, iv. 521. Predigten. neue Ausgabe, B. iii. p. 590. Christendom as a revelation of Christ, i. 337 n. Diss. on the Monarchians, term περιγραφή, i. 593 n.

Schleswig (Sliaswig, Hadeby), iii. 275, 280, 286, 288, 289 n. 2.

Schliemann, i. 353 n. 4.

Schlosser.
Weltgeschichte, iii. ii. 1, s. 269, Prester John, iv. 47 n. 1.

Schlözer. See Nestor.

Schmidt.
Essays on Buddhism, pp. 223, 225, i. 482 n. 1. On the thousand Buddhas, p. 69, i. 491 n. 1; p. 88, i. 503 n. 5 (see Mem. Petersburg Academy). Hist. Eastern Moguls, trans. (ed. Petersburg, 1829), i. 482 n. 1. Essay on the affinity of gnostico-theosophic doctrines with Buddhism, etc. (Leipsic, 1828), i. 484 n. 1. See Ssanang Ssetzen.

Schmidt, Prof., of Strassburg.
"Johannes Tauler von Strassburg" (Hamburg, 1841). S. 25, n. 5, Nicholas of Basle, v. 329 n. 2. S. 29 n., 300 n. 3. S. 52, friends of God in the interdict, 383 n. 1. S. 165, 382 n. 1. S. 178 n., Merswin, 388 n. 1. S. 180, "Book of the Nine Rocks," 388 n. 3. S. 216, the popes, 388 n. 3. S. 219, salvation of unbelievers, 389 n. 1. S. 231, 300 n. S. 234, 235, letter of N. of Basle to the Johannites, 392 nn. 1, 2.

Schmölders, A.
Essai sur les écoles philos. chez les Arabes (Paris, 1842), iv. 444 n. 4; f. 95, 420 n.

Schnitzer.
Origines ueber die Grundlehren der Glaubenswissenschaft, i. 697 n. 1.

Schola Palatina, iii. 154.

Scholasticism, scholastic theology, i. 530; iii. 169, 456; iv. 220. Rise of, iii. 518. History of, iv. 181 n. 1, 355–528. Method of, iv. 420; v. 269. Authorities of, iv. 420. Representatives of, iv. 420–427. Joachim on, iv. 220. Rainer, iv. 326. In the Greek church, iv. 536, 549. Clemangis on, v. 61, 62. Wicklif and, v. 168, 172. And mysticism, v. 381, 382, 407.

Scholasticus, iii. 503.

Scholasticus, imperial chamberlain, ii. 536.

Schönau, iv. 217, 236 n. 2. See Eberhard, Ecbert.

Schonen, iii. 293.

Schools, theological, i. 527 and n. 2, 721; ii. 182, 183 and n., 610, 611. Gnostic, i. 389. Julian on, ii. 63 n. 3, 75, 76. Patrick, ii. 149. See Catechetical.
In the Third and Fourth Periods. Founded by missionaries, in Ireland, iii. 9, 10; England, 23; Germany, 51; Friesland, 73; Fulda, 75; among the Saxons, 78. Schools established in France, 126, 154, 156, 410, 417, 427, 460, 470, 502 n. 3, 503, 593. In England, 152, 153, 468, 469. In Denmark, 275. At Luneburg, 325. At Kiew, 330. Gregory II. on image worship in the, 211. Theological schools, 126, 470, 502, 593. For girls, 427 n. 2. In the Greek church, 543.
Fifth Period. Schools in Poland, iv. 3, 4 n. 1. At Paderborn and Bremen, 33. Nestorian, 45. For missionaries, among the Slavonians, 34. Lull on, 62, 65, 70 (see Lull). School at Augsburg, 143 n. 5. Rheims, 265. Compiegne, 356. At Lisle and Tournay, 357, 358.

Multiplication of, 358. At Bee, 362. Abelard, 374.
Sixth Period. Gerson on, v. 82. Of Militz, for preachers, at Prague, 181. See Monasteries, Schmölders, Universities.

Schools, musical, iii. 128, 419.

Schott.
Hispania Illustrata, vol. iv., Mem. Sanctorum of Eulogius of Cordova, iii. 335 n. 3.

Schwandtner.
Scriptores rer. Hungaricar., t. i. Joh. de Thwroez, Chronica Hungaror., cc. 42 et 46, iii. 335 n. 2.

Schwartzach, monastery, iv. 103.
Science and the Greek mind, i. 5, 672. In its relation to Christianity, 508, 510, 581. And Montanism 511. And the Alexandrian school, 529, 533–535, 538–540, 558. Origen, 701, 706, 719. The science of antiquity and its religious principle, ii. 39. Science in the service of the church, Apollinaris on, ii. 484, 485. Jerome, ii. 745 n. 3.
Third and Fourth Periods. In monasteries, iii. 10, 53, 460. Promoted by bishops, 408. In France, 470. Prudentius on, 490.
Fifth Period. Relation to missions, iv. 61–71, 426, 435 n. 2, 436. New enthusiasm for, 234, 246, 252, 253, 258, 281, 400. In monasteries, 239, 249, 251, 281, 529. Abelard on, 376–378. Peter of Cluny, 249, 398, 400. Bernard on, 258, 259. Roger Bacon on, 434, 435. Empirical, 401. Natural, 436. The Bogomiles, 559.
Sixth Period, v. 113, 123, 192, 262. In Bohemia, 245 and n 5. And Faith, 230. See Culture, Dialectics, Knowledge, Scholasticism.

Scientific culture, i. 533; ii. 52, 53, 34 n. 6, 183. Augustin on, ii. 401. Isidore of Seville, iii. 151. In Spain and Ireland, iii. 152, 156. In England, iii. 152–154, 467–469. France, iii. 154. In the Western church, iii. 156; iv. 565. In the Eastern, iii. 530; iv. 529, 537. Scientific element in reform, v. 192, 245. See Culture, Science.

Scillita, persecution at, i. 22.
Scilly islands (Syllina), ii. 774; iii. 296.
Scotia, ii. 632 n. 2.
Scotland, Christianity in, ii. 146; iii. 10, 20. Church usages, iii. 23–25. Masters from, iii. 152. Scots, ii. 147 n. 2, 149; iii. 10, 20. Scottish language, iii. 21. Missionaries, iii. 22–24. Dialectic tendency, iii. 461 n. 1. Scotica vasa, iii. 460 n. 6.
Scotus Erigena, John, iii. 461, 62 n. 2. His theological system, 461–466. On Dionysius the Areopagite, 467. His doctrine of predestination, 485–490, 493, 62 n. 2. His doctrine of the Lord's Supper, 500, 505–508. His view of the doctrine of the Holy Spirit, 556. His influence, 466; iv. 444, 445 n. 4.
Citations :—
De Divisione Naturae, l. i f. 37, on the Symbolism of the Scriptures, iii. 464 nn. 1–3; f. 38, on the absolute, 463 n. 3; f. 39, reason and faith, 463 n. 1; f. 42, God as creator, 464 n. 5; f. 44, interpretation of Matt. 10 : 20, 464 n. 4. L. ii. 1. 46, four kinds of being, end of redemption, 465 n. 1; ff. 63, 83, 84, God's knowledge one with his willing, evil not an object of knowledge to him, 465 n. 3. L. iii. f. 111, prayer for illumination, 462 n. 1; ff. 126, 127, self-creation of God, in the creation, 465 n. 2; f. 129, evil non-existent in relation to the whole, 465 n. 4. L. iv. f 163, restoration, 466 n. 1. L. v. c. 20, f. 242, humanity of Christ after the resurrection 500 n. 4; f. 243, appearances after the resurrection, 500 n. 6; f. 259, evil not an object of knowledge to God, 465 n. 3; c. 29, f. 265, on punishment, 486 n. 5; f. 275, evil only seems to exist in the parts, 465 n. 4; ff. 284, 286, 292, hell, 4–7 n. 1; c. 38, f. 296, ubiquity of Christ's glorified nature, 500 n. 5; f. 306, address to Jesus. 462 n. 1; f. 311, all things return to the divine nature, 465 n. 1.
De prædestinazione, c. 1, philosophy and religion. iii. 462 n. 2; c. 4, on necessity, 485 n. 5; on twofold predestination, 486 n. 1; c. 5, § 5; God a voluntary cause, 488 n. 4; c. 6, punishment 486 n. 4; cc. 9, 10, attributes of God, 486 nn. 2, 3; c. 17, § 8, the fire of hell, 487 nn. 2, 3; immutability of the divine law, 487 n. 4: c. 18, § 8, reward and punishment proceed from the relation of will to law, 488 n. 1. See Mauguin.
Letter to Charles the Bald, trans. of Dionys. Areop., iii. 457 and nn. 2, 4.
Tract on transubstantiation, iii. 500, 505 n. 3.

Scourgers, v. 412.
Scribes, i. 53; iv. 559.
Scriptores ecclesiast. de Musica. See Music.
Scriptores rer. Brunsvic. See Leibnitz.
Scriptores rer. Danicar.
Hafniæ, 1772, t. i. f. 453, life of Auschar, Ebbo, iii. 272 n. 3.

Scriptores rer. German. See Meibom.
Scriptores rer. Hungar. See Schwandtner.
Scriptores rer. Ital. See Muratori.
Scriptorum vet. nova Collectio. See Maii.
Scriptures, the sacred, i. 143, 159 n. 2. Burned, 148–150, 689. Public reading of, 201, 279, 303. Knowledge of, 283 n. 1, 287, 307. In the family, 286, 693. Origen on the study of, and prayer, 287 Basis of instruction, 302, 305, 307, 358, 532. Open to the heathen, 307, 308. At Alexandria, 527 n. 2, 528, 530 and n. 1. Source of knowledge, with Clement, 532. Scientific culture and, 552. And the works of creation, Origen, 553. Cyprian on the study of, 686. Pamphilus, 721.
In the Second Period. Julian's knowledge of, ii. 40, 41. His opinion of, 52. Style of, distasteful to rhetoricians, 116. Versification of, 77. Augustine on the, 116, 120, 351. Reading, study, knowledge of, 122, 123, 262 and n. 4, 265, 355, 743 n. 1. In public worship,

213, 333, 334. Surrender of, 217. Relation to the authority of the church, Augustine on, 240, 241. In the cenobiæ, 287, 288. Divine and human elements in the, 389, 391, 392, 394. Use of, by the apostles, 393. Authority of, 602. Augustin on, 671. Julian of Eclanum, 673 and n. 4. Marcellus, 740.
Source of purification to the church, iii. 2. Study of in the Third and Fourth Periods, iii. 10, 21, 31, 41, 48 n. 2, 52, 72, 73, 81, 124–126, 152–155, 153 n. 3, 201, 202, 207 n., 247, 275, 281 n. 1, 370, 427, 428, 431, 445, 462, 469, 471, 473, 483 and n. 4, 485, 503, 600, 602 n. 3, 604. Used in preaching, 52. At the meetings of the canonical clergy, 107. Read in churches, 251. Authority, 60, 210, 232, 485, 490, 506, 508, 533, 535. In amulets, 56. Ignorance of, 199, 207 n., 251, 252, 390, 427. Corruption of the text, 251. Committed to memory, 281 n. 1. Consulted for oracles, 309, 418 n. 2. Boniface on the, 60. Gregory the Great on the, 115, 143, 150 n. 7, 199. The Paulicians, 245–247, 251, 265, 267–269, 600. Charlemagne, 238. In the Isidorean Decretals, 347, 348. Ariald, 390. On the marriage of priests, 397 and n. 2. Scotus on the, 464. Florus, 490. Fredegis on the language of, 460. External marks of reverence to, 440. Among the sects, 600–604.
In the Fifth Period. The khan of Tartary on, iv. 55. Wresting of the, 98 n. 3 (v. 40). Peter Cantor, 209. Hildegard on the, 218. Joachim, 227–232. Letter and spirit, 232. Peter of Cluny, 251. Bernard, 258, 259. Ignorance of, 287, 611. Study of, 297, 314, 537, 540. In France and Germany, 320–324. In relation to the veneration of Mary, 332, 333. Bacon on the Scriptures, 424, 425. Exposition of, 584. In the sects, 320–324, 584, 594, 601, 604, 607, 609, 611–614. Oliva, 621, 623. Waldenses forbidden to expound the, 608. Reading suppressed, 324. Pauperes Catholici, 612. See Bible.
In the Sixth Period. Marsilius of Padua on the, v. 25, 27. Authority of, 25, 26, 31, 38, 127, 128, 296, 298 (see below, Huss). Knowledge of, among the clergy, 33, 34, 59, 195. Occam on the, 40. Neglect of, 59, 61, 62, 151 n. 2, 199. At the universities, 128, 151 n. 2. Wicklif, 136, 140, 141, 149–151, 242, 251. The laity and the, 149, 150. Janow, 193, 195, 199, 200, 201, 207, 233. Wicklifite party in Bohemia, 251, 296. Huss, 263, 264, 267, 280–285, 290, 291, 306, 310, 311, 323, 333, 334, 336, 338, 342, 346, 352, 368, 369. Pantheistic friends of God and the, 396, 398. See Bible, Interpretation, Old Testament.

Sculpture, iii. 440. Slavic, iv. 14. See Images.
Scythia, ii. 767. Scythian monks, the, 687, 710.
Scythianus, Saracen, merchant, source of Manichean doctrines, i. 485.
Seasons for holding divine worship, i. 293–302; ii. 331–352. See Festivals.
Sebaste, the forty soldiers at, ii. 19 n. 3. Meletius, 457. See Eustathius.
Sebastian, deacon, ii. 603.
Sects, origin of early, i. 64, 66. Number of, edict of Galerius on, 156. Celsus, 164, 165; Clement, 164 n. 4, 532. Idealistic, 208. History of in the First Period, 341–506.
In the Second Period. Edicts of Constantine and Licinius in their relation to, ii. 14, 15. Significance and origin of, 765, 766. History in this period, 765–779.
In the Third Period. As a reaction against the church system and corrupt Christianity, iii. 243, 244, 586. History in these periods, 243–270, 586–606; iv. 565.
In the Fifth Period. Rapid spread, iv. 99, 269. Origin, 99, 216, 233, 552, 565, 590–594. Frederic II. and the, 181. Hildegard, 219. Joachim, 225. In conflict with the church system, efforts to suppress, 269, 321–324. Transubstantiation, 336. Indulgences, 353. History, sects originating in the West, 321–324, 447, 448, 592–644. In the East, 552–592. Secret, 561. People of rank in the, 594, 603. See Particular sects.
Secular and spiritual powers, Gregory VII. on their relation, iv. 87, 88. Ægidius on, v. 14, 15. John of Paris, v. 15–19. See Spiritual.
Secular clergy, character of the, iv. 208, 209.
Secular direction of the religious sentiment with the Jews, i. 357.
Secular employments of the clergy. See Bishops, Clergy.
Secular nobles, Huss on, v. 249. Secular rulers and general councils, 96, 97, 99.
Secular power in church affairs, ii. 753, 7 6, 773; iii. 164, 202–209, 255, 380, 400, 527, 544. Nicholas I. on, iii. 566. Delh i ., iv. 634. Source of, v. 16, 17, 99. Of the pope, 16. See Benefices, Byzantine, Church and State, Investiture, Pope.
Secular sword. See Sword.
Secularization of the church, i. 70, 214; iv. 149, 195–197, 215, 284, 303, 414. Wicklif on, v. 162, 242. Reaction against in monasticism, iv. 232, 233.
Secundulus, the martyr, i. 123, 124.
Secundus, bp. of Ptolemais, ii. 421.
Secundus, bp. of Tisigis, ii. 218–220, 221.
Secundus, nephew of the above, ii. 220.
Secundus, Numidian bp., i. 150.

Secundus the Gnostic, i. 438 n. 4.
Sedes apostolicæ, i. 203, 215; ii. 202, 244.
Seeds of life, i. 492. See Germs.
Segarelli, iv. 626–629, 631. Life of, 626 n. 3. See Francesco Pegna.
Segeburg, iv. 34, 35, 36.
Segui. See Bruno of.
Seine, river, iv. 437.
Σειραί, iii. 169.
Selene, worship of, ii. 105.
Seleucia Ctesiphon, i. 79 n. 4. Bp of, ii. 125, 126, 130, 611.
Seleucia in Isauria, Gregory Nazianzen at, ii. 463 (see Councils, an. 359). See Basil.
Seleucus, ii. 66 n. 3.
Self, feeling of in Stoicism, i. 19.
Self-castigation, iv. 529; v. 412. Defended by Damiani, iii. 451.
Self-conceit, spiritual, iv. 562.
Self-deception, i. 251, 252.
Self-deification, v. 393, 396-399.
Self-denial, i. 270; ii. 115, 122. Ruysbroch on, v. 406, 407.
Self-determining power, iv. 516, 518. See Freedom, Will.
Self-examination, ii. 339, 364; iv. 303.
Self-knowledge, ii. 116; iv. 412, 457.
Self-love, ii. 661, 667; v. 231. In religion, v. 405.
Self-renunciation, i. 34, 72. Ruysbroch on, v. 406.
Self-righteousness, i. 63, 64; ii. 291. See Righteousness.
Self-sacrifice, ii. 368. Of monks, 276–278.
Self-will, ii. 661, 667; v. 402, 408. See Will.
Seligenstadt, iii. 450 n. 4, 453.
Selz, treaty at, iii. 78.
Sembat, Thondracian, iii. 588.
Semgallen, church planted in, iv. 38.
Semi-Arians, ii. 410, 415 n. 1, 416, 417 n. 3. Party opposed to the Nicene creed, 419–422, 434, 435, 444. At Philippopolis, 436 n. 1. Attack Marcellus, 439. Conflict with the Arians, 444, 449, 451–459, 460. Auxentius of Milan, 471. Among the rude nations, 472.
Semi-Pelagianism, Semi-Pelagian controversy, ii. 687–711; iii. 472, 477.
Seminal principles in nature, iii. 83; iv. 471, 472.
Semisch.

   Monograph on Justin Martyr, t. i. s. 105, ἶλεγχος of J. M., i. 666 n. 1; s. 146, 670 n. 2; s. 166, Λόγος πρὸς Ἕλληνας, 667 n. 1; s. 167, περὶ μοναρχίας, 668 u. 1. T. ii. s. 232, Justin on Ebionitism, 364 nn. 1, 2; s. 236, Anm. 1, 362 n. 3; s. 318, on the Holy Spirit, 609 n. 1. See Studien und Kritiken.

Semler.

   Ed. Dial. Tryph. (1764), f. 174, genuineness, 668 n. 3.

Senate, ii. 92; iv. 151, 161.
Sends, iii. 107, 108, 136 n. 4.

Seneca, on superstition, i. 7. On the spread of Judaism, 67. Ep. 41 ad Lucil., presence of God, 17 n. 2, 18 n. 1. Jerome of Prague on, v. 377.
Seneca, bp. in Italy, ii. 657.
Seniores, Seniores plebis, in the North African church, i. 192; ii. 222 n. 3.
Senglier, abp. of Sens, iv. 394.
Senlis (Silvanectensis), iii. 508 n. 1.
Sens, iii. 154. Archbishops of, iii. 44, 366, 371 and n. 1, 481 n. 2, 489, 552; iv. 394, 398.
Sense, evil referred to the power of, i. 620, 632; ii. 619, 634, 667, 668, 716; iv. 573. Contempt of, iv. 633. See Antinomian, Gnostic.
Sensible impressions used in the conversion of pagans, iii. 51, 52.
Sensible world, origin of, in Gnosticism, i. 373–378 (see Individual Gnostics). In Paulicianism, iii 257. With the Catharists, iv. 570, 573.
Sensuous tendencies in religion, i. 253, 254, 560; ii. 615, 616 iii. 2, 132, 198, 457; iv. 264, 271, 275, 317, 324, 328; v. 408. Element in paganism, ii. 115.
Sentences, of Lombard, iv. 409, 410 nn. 1, 2, 422, 425, 437, 492 (v. 269). Of Pullein, 408 n. 4. Of Abelard, 452 and n. 7, 455 n 3. Sententiaries, 417. Sententiæ, Peter Waldus, 607.
Separateness, Christian i. 92.
Separatism, conflict with, i. 211, 222–248, 318, 320; ii. 216; iii 389, 393; iv. 99, 147, 321, 592. See Church unity, Schism, Sects.
Septimius Severus, i. 174, 721. Law against change of religion, 89, 120. Persecution under, 83, 119–122, 691, 694.
Septuagint, i. 54, 68, 330 and n. 4, 409, 511, 530, 658, 707, 722; ii. 47, 496 n. 2, 745, 746; v. 269.
Serapion, abbot, ii. 288 n. 3.
Serapion, archdeacon, ii. 755.
Serapion, bp. of Thmuis, ii. 430, 468 nn. 1, 2, 469 n. 2.
Serapion, Egyptian monk, ii. 751.
Serapis, i. 102, 103, 696. Temple of, destroyed, ii. 97, 98.
Serennius Granianus, the proconsul, i. 101.
Serenus, bp. of Marseilles, iii. 199, 200, 233.
Sergius (Mansur), father of John of Damascus, iii. 208 n. 3.
Sergius (Paulus), ii. 46.
Sergius, patriarch of Constantinople, his judgment respecting the formulary of union of Heraclius, iii. 176, 177. His view of the Monotheletian controversy, 178. His good understanding with Honorius of Rome, 179. Ecthesis, 180, 184–186, 195 n. 2, 196.

   Reply to Cyrus bp. of Phasis, iii. 177 nn. 2, 3, 4. Narration to Honorius, 178 n. 3, 179 n. 1. See Harduin, t. iii. ff. 1309, 1315.

Sergius, pope, church of Utrecht, iii. 71.
Sergius (Tychicus), reformer of the Paulicians, iii. 251–256, 264–266, 269 n. 1. False accusations brought against him, 253. Opponent of the crusades of the Paulicians, 256. His assassination, 256. A fragment of one of his epistles, 258. His doctrine, 258–260, 268.
Sermon, the, i. 282, 303; ii. 213, 333, 339, 352–354; iii. 126, 413; iv. 209, 531. Written and extempore, ii. 353. Guibert on, iv. 313. Wm. of St. Amour, length, text, diction, etc., iv. 316. Wiclif on the, v. 142. German, iv. 318 n. 2. Militz, v. 175. See Berthold, Preaching.
Sermon on the Mount, among the Ebionites, i. 347. In the first centuries, i. 512. Julian on the, ii. 55. Appealed to by monks, as forbidding labor, ii. 295. Chrysostom on, ii. 302. Jovinian, ii. 310. Augustin and Pelagius, ii. 635. Peter Cantor, iv. 304. Aquinas, iv. 526. Catharists, iv. 574, 587. Waldenses, iv. 615. Huss, v. 249, 282.
Serpent, the, i. 444, 497. See Ophiomorphus.
Servant form of the true church, v. 266. Of Christ, see Christ.
Servants, kindness to, ii. 328, 340; iii. 459. See Equality, Slavery.
Servatus Lupus, abbot of Ferrieres, on exemption, iii. 404 n. 4. At Fulda, 457. Promoter of learning, clearness of his style, 459, 482, 483, 488. Gottschalk, 473. His doctrine of predestination, 482–485, 491 and n. 8. Probus, 602.

Citations from his writings:—
De tribus quæstionibus (ed. Baluz), iii. 483–485 nn. Ep. to Rabanus Maurus, 457 n. 4. Ep. 18, on exemption, 404 n. 4. Ep. 20, Probus, 602 n. 2. Ep. 30, to Gottschalk, 478 nn. Ep. 34, study of letters, 459 n. 2. Ep. 79, ad Ratramnum, 401 n. 4. Epp. 91 et 103, 459 n. 3.

Servianus, consul, i. 102.
Servus Servorum, iii. 117 n. 1; v. 7.
Seth, representative of the Pneumatici, i. 445, 448.
Sethians, i. 448.
Seven, sacred number, i. 61, 400. Seven heavens, angels, stars, 445. Planets, 444–447. Star spirits, 383 n., 445, 447.
Seventy, interpreters, the, i. 54; ii. 746. See Septuagint.
Severa, or Severina, empress, i. 127 n. 1, 683.
Severianus. See Severus.
Severinus among the Germans, iii. 25. His origin, 25 n. 3. His labors, 26. His miracles, 27, 28. Life of, see Eugippius.
Severus, poem of, ii. 13 n. 4, 323 n. 2.
Severus, Alexander, i. 125.
Severus, abp. of Prague, iii. 323.
Severus, bp. of Asmounia, i. 485 n. 3. See Renaudot.

Severus, emperor. See Septimius.
Severus, Gnostic — Severians, i. 458 n. 3.
Severus, Monophysite — Severians, ii. 279 n. 1, 280 n. 3, 590–594, 613; iii. 170. Fragment of Severus, ii. 279 n. 1.
Seville (Hispalis), bishops, archbishops of, iii. 118, 151, 340, 342.
Sex, iv. 445 n. 4.
Sextus, gnomes of, gn. 12, i. 697 n. 2.
Sextus Empiricus, definition of αἵρεσις, i. 338 n. 1.
Shahristani, i. 489 n. 4.
Shapur. See Sapor.
Shelters, on the Alps, iv. 214.
Shepherds, designation of clergy, i. 184. Rude, iii. 63 n. 1. Pastoral care for, iii. 426.
Shimnus, in Buddhism, i. 483, 496.
Ships, preaching in, iv. 317.
Shorthand writers, ii. 353.
Shrines, iii. 42.
Sibylline oracles, i. 141, 176, 177. See Pseudo-Sibylline.
Sibyllists, i. 177.
Sibyls, iv. 379.
Siciliba, ii. 229 n. 2.
Sicily, in the diocese of the Roman ch., ii. 199. Benedictines in, ii. 300. Jews in, iii. 13 n. 1. Property of Roman church, iii. 13 n. 1. 113, 114. Festival, iii. 113. Saracens in, iii. 187, 188 n. 1. Photius on, iii. 566 n. 2. And the empire, iv. 167, 173, 223 (548). Paterenes, iv. 225. Ladislaus, v. 73. See Roger of, Peter of, William of.
Sicininus, ii. 256.
Sick, absolution of the, i. 221, 231, 234, 235. Baptism of the, i. 238 and n. 2, 310 (see Clinici). Communion of the, i. 332; iv. 341; (under one form), 343, 345. Visiting the, i. 255. Care of the, ii. 169, 192; iii. 102, 408 n. 1; iv. 5, 34, 213, 266, 267, 294, 296, 298, 299, 363, 364; v. 138, 142, 186. Healing of the, ii. 26, 105 and n. 3, 106, 107, 108, 268, 272, 285, 286, 370; iv. 37, 638 (see Anointing, Healing). Among the Catharists, iv. 576, 580, 581, 582 and n. 2, 587 n. 5. See Consolamentum.
Sidereal world, in Platonism, ii. 44. Priscillian, ii. 776 n. 4, 778 n. 1. Paulicians, iii. 257. See Stars.
Sido-Hallr, iii. 303, 304.
Sidon, iii. 457.
Sidonius, priest, ii. 63.
Sidonius Apollinaris, bp. of Clermont.

Ep. 12 (opp., Simond. i. f. 582), Photinians among the Burgundians, iii. 39 n. 3.

Siebenbürgen, iii. 334.
Siegismund, king of the Burgundians, adopts the Catholic faith, iii. 5.
Sieledibu (Taprobane, Ceylon), ii. 141.
Siena, iv. 295; v. 44, 74. See Councils, an. 1423. See Roland.
Sigebert, Frankish king, iii. 95 n. 2.
Sigebert of Gemblours, opponent of the

Hildebrandian system, iv. 130. Hirsch on, 130 n. 2.

Chronicle of, iv. 130. Sects in Italy, 99 nn. 3, 4; an. 1085, death-bed of Gregory VII, 120 n. 5; an. 1089, St. Anthony's fire, 206 n. 4. De scriptoris ecclesiast. (see Bibl. ecclesiast., ed. Fabric., f. 114), op. in the name of the ch. of Liege, 130 n. 2.

Sigfrid, abp. of Mentz, iv. 94–96, 102, 109.

Epp. to Greg. VII., 95 and n. 3.

Sigfrid, English ecclesiastic, iii. 291, 297 n. 1.

Sigfrid, monk, iv. 39.

Siggo, pagan priest, iv. 42.

Sighard of Aquileia, patriarch, iv. 111.

Sigillaria, ii. 347.

Sigismund, emperor, and king of Bohemia and Hungary, interview with John XXIII., v. 100. Call for the council of Constance, 101. Friend of reform, 103, 106. Efforts in behalf of it, 105–108, 118, 121, 126. John XXIII., 111. Influence at C., 120 n. Zbynek, 275. Relations with Huss, 317, 318, 322, 323, 327, 328, 329, 334, 335, 339, 341–343, 351, 355–357, 359, 368–370. Jerome of Prague, 373 and n. 2, 374.

Sigmund Bresterson, iii. 306, 307.

Sigmund of Jistebnitz, v. 250.

Sign of the cross. See Cross.

Signaculum, i. 316, 503; ii. 188. Militiæ, i. 146 n. 2.

Signs, Plutarch on, i. 23. Of the times, i. 69. From God, ii. 69. Sought for, iii. 519 n.; v. 198, 266. Gregory VII, iv. 86. Of the last times, v. 178 200, 231, 232. Huss on visible, v. 266.

Signy, Cistercian abbey at, iv. 393.

Sigtuna, iii. 276.

Sigurd, Norwegian nobleman, iii. 295, 296.

Silentiarius, imperial secretary, ii. 564.

Silesia, iv. 6, 49; v. 182. Silesians at Prague, v. 247.

Silistria, ii. 150 n. 4.

Silvanus, bp. of Troas, ii. 171 n. 3.

Silvanus (Constantine), Paulician, iii. 248. See Constantine.

Silverius, bp. of Rome, ii. 594.

Silvester, bp. of Rome, ii. 225; iv. 132, 616, 634, 635; v. 85. Gift of Constantine, iv. 152, 166, 172, 215 n. 3, 6(5; v. 19, 42, 170, 345. Legends concerning, iv. 163 n. 2, 216 n. Viticinium cf. iv. 226 n. 3.

Silvester II. (Gerbert), pope, iii. 375; iv. 43, 104, 123.

Silvester III., pope, iii. 376.

Silvestre de Sacy.

Memoires sur diverses antiquitates de la Perse (Paris, 1793), Mani, in Mirkhond's Hist., i. 486 n. 2; p. 41, Ormuzd, ii. 128 n. 1; p. 42, efforts to restore the ancient religion, i. 487 n. 1; f. 209, Mani, i. 487 r. 1.

Simeon, sent against the Paulicians, iii. 248. Becomes head of the sect under the name of Titus, 248. His death, 248.

Simeon (Barsaboe), bp. of Seleucia, martyr, ii. 130–132.

Simeon, hermit, iii. 445 n. 2, 448 n. 1.

Simeon, monk, iii. 421.

Simeon Magister, Photius and Basilius, iii. 568 n. 3.

Simeon Stylites, ii. 1–2, 143, 292, 293, 324 n. 3. See Acta S. Jan.

Simon (Gauzbert), bp., iii. 277.

Simon, monk, iv. 235.

Simon Magus, i. 66 n. 3, 72, 454 n.; ii. 308, 552; iv. 226. Contest with Peter, i. 204, 296 n. 5, 361, 362, 454 n.; ii. 335. In the Clementines, i. 361, 395. Simonians, i. 453, 45-; ii. 326. Justin Martyr on, i. 454 n. 1. Image of, ii. 326.

Simon of Cyrene, with the Pseudo-Basilideans, i. 447.

Simon of St. Quintin, iv. 49 n.

Simon of Tournay, iv. 418 and nn. 3, 4.

Simonians. See Simon Magus.

Simonians, followers of Nestorius, ii. 554.

Simony, Monophysites on, ii. 583 n. 1. In the Roman church, iii. 64. In the Frank church, 93 and n. 2, 108. Of patrons, 110. Treatment of at the Conc. Const. (an. 786), 228 n. 3. Arnulph, 373 n. 1. Efforts to abolish, 377, 379 n. 1, 382, 384, 386, 388–399, 400, 403, 404. Ramihrd on, 599.

In the Fifth Period. Ordinances of Gregory VII. against, iv. 93, 94, 96, 97, 101. Defenders of, 98 n. 2. Henry IV., 103. Concordat of Worms on, 143. At Rome, 176, 222. Yves of Chartres on, 196. Robert of Arbrissel, 246. Sale of masses as, 346.

In the Sixth Period. Boniface VIII., v. 11. At the papal court, 21, 23, 34, 35, 122. In the schism, 47, 51, 52, 54, 58, 101, 102, 113, 336 John XXIII., 89, 110, 111. In Germany, 101. Council of Constance on, 125. The Germans at Constance on, 126. Wicklif on, 137, 144, 164. Militz, 178. Conrad, 186. Dola, 251. Huss, 283, 336, 363, 364.

Simplicianus, bp. of Milan, ii. 630.

Simplicianus, presbyter, ii. 77.

Simplicius, pagan philosopher, against Mani, i. 496. His views of philosophy and religion, ii. 106–110, 115 n. 5, 117.

Citations from his writings:—
Commentary on the Enchiridion of Epictetus, ii. 106; c. 13, f. 131 (ed. Schweighäuser), persecution, 109 n. 3; f. 351, on offerings, ii. 108 n. 1; f. 352, times and seasons, 107 n. 2; c. 38, f. 376, polytheism, 107 n. 1; c. 38, f. 392 et seq., offerings for sin, 109 nn.; c. 39, f. 408 et seq., divinations, 108 n. 2; f. 187 (in Epictet. ed. Salmas), Manichean doctrine, i. 491 n. 3.

Sin, the fall, recognition of in the Alexandrian Judaism, i. 66 and n. 1. Stoic view, 106. Views of Christians, mor tal and venial, against God and man, 221, 226, 227, 244, 245. Against the Holy Spirit, 227. Original, 313, 615, 626, 627. Deliverance from, 324, 483. Basilides on, 413. Relation to law, with Epiphanes, 450. Christian notion of sin absent from Buddhism, 483. Heathen notion of, 568. Christian doctrine of (see Anthropology). Origen, 626–630, 637, 638. J. Martyr on the universal recognition of, 669. After baptism. See Baptism.

Doctrine of, *in the Second Period.* Julian on, ii. 51. The Euchites, 278. Jovinian, 308–310. Athanasius, 492. Doctrine of in the Eastern church, 617. In the Western, 617 (see Anthropology); with Hilary, 618; Ambrose, 622; Augustin, 625, 626; Pelagius, 638; Cœlestin on the origin of, ii. 647; council of Carthage, 650. Julian of Eclanum, 666, 667. In the Pelagian controversy, 659–685. In the Semi-Pelagian controversy, 698–702, 704. Theodore, 715–718. Chrysostom, 719, 720. Isidore, 722. Final destruction of, 718.

In the Third and Fourth Periods. Scotus on, iii. 461, 465, 466, 485–488. Claudius of Turin, 432. In the controversy with Gottschalk, 474–477, 482. Florus on, 489. Synod of Valence (an. 855), 492. The Paulicians on, 258–260. Other sects, 597 and n. 2, 601.

In the Fifth Period. Berthold on, iv. 319. Mortal sins, 319, 353, 514. Sins of ignorance, 399, 494, 495. Imputation of, 493–495. Doctrines of the scholastics, 492–495. Abelard, 389, 390, 399, 493–495, 501. Peccatum naturale et personale, 493. Propagation of, posse et non posse peccare, 495, 496. As disorder, 495. Passio and propassio, 497. And punishment, 498, 499 (see Punishment). The first, 507. Extirpation of, subservient to good, 508.

Sixth Period. Relation to law, Janow, v. 209. In the Christian, Huss, 351 (compare Sins after Baptism, Jovinian). Consciousness of, 392. Mortal, 336, 401. See Evil, Fall, Original state, Peccatum, Redemption.

Sina (China), iv. 46.
Sinai, ii. 286. Monastery on Mt., iii. 448 n. 1.
Sincerity, v. 408.
Singidunum, ii. 449.
Singing, ii. 277 n. 4. Schools for, iii. 128, 419. Congregational, ii. 354 n. 3. Of children, iv. 58.
Sinibald of Anagni (Innocent IV.), iv. 183.
Sinlessness of the redeemed, iv. 509 (see Jovinian). Of Christ, see Christ. See Mary.
Sinope, Marcion at, i. 461, 463. Phocas, ii. 371.
Sinnessa, pretended synod at, iii. 372 n. 1.

Sirach. 18 : 1, iv. 568. 19 : 4, iv. 375.
Siricius, Roman bp., ii. 181, 204, 312, 377, 745, 750. Decretals, 212, 360 (iii. 346). On the punishment of heretics, 773–775.
Citations: —
Decretals, ad Himerium (an. 385), celibacy of clergy, ii. 181, 312; § 2, confirmation, 360 n. 1; § 3, times of baptism, 361 n. 1; § 4, apostates, 119 n. 2. Ep. ad Anysium, Mary, 377 n. 1. Ep. ad Gallos episcopos, laymen in the episcopal office, 185 n. 2. Synodal letter contr. Jovin., 312.

Sirmium, Hosius banished to, ii. 443. See Councils, an. 351, an. 357, see Photinus of.
Sirmond.
Opp., t. i., petition of Marcellinus and Faustinus, ii. 256 n. 6. Life of Epiphanius of Ticinum, iii. 28 n. 3. Epp. f. 582, Sidonius Apollinaris, ep. 12, iii. 39 n. 2. T. ii. f. 44, ep. 28, Avitus to Gundobad, iii. 39 n. 3; f. 228, Avitus and the Arians, iii. 5 n. 2; ff. 376, 407, Facund. Hermian, defensio trium capit., ii. 71 n. 2, 211 n. 4; f. 593 E, his ep. ad Mocian, ii. 595 n.; f. 760, gesta de nomine Acacii, ii. 563 n. 5. T. v. opp., Theodore Studita, life of, iii. 535 n. 1. Life of Plato, iii. 100 n. 1; f. 66, slaves, iii. 100 n. 4; f. 136, iii. 213 n. 4; f. 331. Theodori epp., ep. 21, iii. 198 n. 1. Ep. of Rabanus Maurus, to Hinkmar, f. 26, iii. 481 n. 4. Prædestinatus, ii. 708 n. 2.

Sisabut, king, iii. 152 n. 2.
Sixtus II., bp. of Rome, i. 320 n. 5, 321. Martyr, i. 139. Letter of the Orientals to, ii. 545 n. 4, 547 n. 1. See Lupus.
Sixtus III., bp. of Rome, ii. 147, 686, 698
Decretals, ep. 2, iii. 349 n. 5.
Skalholt, episcopal see in Ireland, iii. 306.
Skara, in West Gothland, iii. 292.
Skeptical method, v. 38. See Skepticism.
Skepticism, in paganism, ii. 27. Reactions of, iv. 239 and n. 2, 324–328. Skeptical tendency in nominalism, iv. 356, 357, 359, 360; v. 38. In Abelard, iv. 379, 380, 392, 501. See Infidelity, Unbelief.
אֲבַן רֹטֶב in Eisenmenger, Part i. c. 8, p. 336, i. 354 n. 5.
Slander, Bernard on, iv. 262.
Slanko, convert, v. 185, 186.
Slave, librarian of Julian, ii. 45. Of Lull, iv. 63.
Slavery, rejected by the Essenes, i. 46 and n. By the Therapeutæ, i. 62. And Christianity, i. 267–270; iii. 98–101. Christians reduced to (see Persecution). Captives sold into, ii. 146, 147; iii. 11, 26, 41, 286. In the Eastern church, iii. 99, 100, 171 n. 2. Theodore Studita and Gregory the Great on, iii. 100. Alcuin on, iii. 166 and n. 5. Nicholas I. on, iii. 312.
Slaves, testify against their masters, i. 92, 97 (110), 112, 118. Christian, i. 78, 119; iii. 84. Persecuted, i. 98, 139, 148, 155, 664. Forced to offer, in place of

GENERAL INDEX.

their masters, ii. 253. Right of asylum, ii. 176-178; iii. 100. Justinian on the traffic in, ii. 140. Patrick on, ii. 149. Treatment of, ii. 230; iii 100, 312. Donatists and, ii. 230. Peter of Alexandria, ii. 253. Become monks, ii. 287, 540 n. 2; iii. 99. Emancipation of on Sunday, ii. 336. Redemption, manumission of, iii. 4 n. 1, 26, 41, 99, 100. Selected for the spiritual order, iii. 97, 98, 101, 107, 109, 277, 412. Manumission of, 98, 99, 100, 101, 312, 415. Jewish traffic in Christian, iii 322.
Slavoni, iv. 565.
Slavonians, pagan in North Germany, iii. 41, 84, 404. Spread of Christianity among the, iii. 271, 277, 307-334; iv. 1-45. Euchites, iv. 552. Sects from the, iv. 565. Slavic religion, iv. 10, 14, 15, 20, 37. Huss and the Slavic peoples, v. 244. See Language.
Sleep, among the monks, ii. 274, 279.
Sliaswig. See Schleswig.
Smaragd, abbot, iii. 555 n. 1.
Smyrna, persecution of Christians at, i. 109-111. Church at, report of Polycarp's martyrdom, 109, 335.
Snorro, Icelandic priest, iii. 304.
Sobriety, of martyrs, i. 114. Of the understanding in Christianity, 513.
Social customs influenced by Christianity, iii. 313, 321 n. 5.
Societies, spiritual, benevolent, iv. 34, 266, 267, 276, 293, 302, 303, 607, 612, 613, 627, 628, 631; v. 143, 213, 250 n. 1, 381. For church building, iv. 293. For Bible reading, iv. 321-324.
Society, rudeness of, iii. 63 n. 1, 64, 70; iv. 293. Avoidance of, iv. 296. See Barbarism.
Society Islands, iv. 17.
Socinianism, i. 602 n. 6; ii. 387, 449, 494; iv. 450.
Socrates, the church historian, on Porphyry, i. 170. Novatian, 244, 245. Beryll, 593 n. Methodius, 720. Marcus, ii. 81 n. 1. Gothic martyrs, ii. 156. Meletian schism, ii. 254 n. Ursicinus, ii. 256 n. 5. Festivals, ii. 332, 333. Outbreak of Arian controversy, ii. 409 n. 4. Recall of Arius, his confession, ii. 422 n. 4. Death of Arius, ii. 430 n. 1. The confession at Philippopolis, ii. 436 n. 1. Recall of Athanasius, ii. 436 n. 4. Nestorius, ii. 505 n. 1, 506 n. 1. Palladius and, ii. 756 n. 1.

Citations: —
Hist. Eccles., l. i. c. 9, ep. of the Nicene conc. on the Meletian schism, ii. 225 n. 1; c. 11, Paphnutius on wedlock, 180 n. 4; c. 14. Eusebius and Theognis, 421 n. 1; c. 38, Arius and Constantine, 428 n. 4
L. ii., Arianism at the court of Constantius, ii. 431 n. 4; c. 15, 205 n. 1; c. 41, Theophilus the Goth, 150 n. 1; c. 43, Eustathians, 281 n. 1.
L. iii. c. 1, Ecebolius, ii. 42 n.; c. 7, Beryll, 593 n.; c. 16, ancient literature, ii. 77 n. 2;

c. 23, Porphyry, i. 170 n. 1; cc. 24, 25, Jovian, ii. 88 n.
L. iv. c. 13, Methodius and Origen, i. 720 n. 4; c. 23, Anthony, ii. 289 r. 2, 270 n. 3; c. 28, Novatian, i. 244 n. 1; c. 32, Orat. of Themistius, ii. 91 n. 4; c. 33, Athanaric, the Goths, ii. 151 n. 3, 156 n. 4; c. 36, Mavia and Moses, ii. 142 n. 5.
L. v. c. 8, Patriarchs, ii. 196 n. 3; c. 10, see Valesius; c. 16, Egyptian temples destroyed, 98 n. 2; c. 19, abolition of penance in Greek ch., 216 n.; c. 22, period of quadragesima, 338 n. 6.
L. vii. c. 7, Cyrill, ii. 512 r. 2; cc. 21, 22, Acacius, 136 n. 1; c. 25, schism averted, 762 n. 1; (c. 30, the Burgundians, iii. 4 n. 2); c. 32, Anastasius, 507 nn. 1, 2; c. 33, the slaves and the right of asylum, 178 n. 1; c. 34, banishment of Nestorius, 552 n. 4; c. 37, Silvanus of Troas, 171 n. 3; c. 41, Proclus, 556 n. 2; c. 45, and the Johannites, 762 n. 2.

Socrates the philosopher, against the rage for enlightenment, i. 5. His importance, i. 18. Demon of, i. 406. Julian on, ii. 60. Abelard, iv. 379. Aristotle and, v. 279. Jerome of Prague, v. 377, 380.
Sodom, iv. 564; v. 176, 200.
Sodrach, a convert, iv. 43.
Soissons, crowning of Pepin at, iii. 69. Musical school at, 128. Riculf of, 427.
Soldiers, of Christ, i. 199; v. 249. Christian, i. 146, 147, 272, 273; ii. 28, 74. Vocation of, v. 214. See Military service.
Solidarity, v. 47.
Solomon, i. 229, iii. 422; iv. 396. Song of, ii. 306 n. 3, 509 (see Bernard). Song, 5:2, ii. 36. Translation and exposition by Williram, iii. 471. See Proverbs.
Solomon of Bassora, ii. 738 n. 6.
Solstitia, ii. 347 n. 4, 349
Σῶμα θνητόν, ἐμπαθές, ii. 317 n.
Somme, iii. 420 n. 1.
Somnambulism, i. 513, 520; iii. 591 n. 4; iv. 368.
Son of David, i. 364, 574, 658.
Son of God, i. 382, 531, 586. Celsus on, 163. In Jewish theology, 574. With Origen, 548, 549, 554, 589-592, 622, 623. With the Monarchians, 577-586, 592. J. Martyr, 585 n. Sabellius, 595, 596, 598-601. Paul of Samosata, 602, 603. Tertullian, 605. Dionys. Alex., 606. As a creature, 607. Relation to the Holy Spirit, 608-610. Ep. of Barnabas, 658. Hieracas, 716.
Second Period. Julian on, ii. 56. The Apostles, 393. Augustin, 400. In the Eastern and Western systems of doctrine, 403, 404. With Arius, 405-408, 410, 416, 425. Eusebius of Cæsarea, 411, 412, 419, 420. Athanasius, 424, 425. Confession at Philippopolis, 436 n. 1. Marcellus, 439. Eunomius, 444, 446, 448, 478. Photinus, 482. Theodore, 500, 502. Nestorius, 508, 512. Eternity of, 411 n. 1, 412, 452. Platonico-Origenistic doctrine, 764 n. 2 (see Origen). Gerhard, iii. 600.

14

Fifth Period. Incarnation, iv. 66, 384. The Son of God with Joachim, 227–230. Scholastics, 458–465. Controversy concerning, 534. Bogomiles, 554. Catharists, 569. And law, v. 208. See Adoption, Christ, Logos, Trinity.
Son of Man, i. 157, 658; ii. 439; iii. 160. With Mani, i. 493, 494, 505 n. 1.
Song, sacred, ii. 83, 149, 354; iii. 74, 106, 311; iv. 28, 40, 42, 58, 212, 561; v. 371, 379. Use of in the family, i. 281, 286. In public worship, i. 304. At the Agapæ, i. 326. See Church Psalmody, Hymns, Music.
Songs, spiritual, ii. 354. Of Arius, ii. 409, 413. Of Cosmas, iii. 206 n. 3. German, iv. 155, 188. National, iv. 180. See Hymns.
Sons of God, with Philo, i. 57. In paganism, 586.
Soothsayers, soothsaying, i. 103; ii. 94, 108; iii. 56, 449; iv. 55, 359 n. 3, 462 n. 4.
Sopatros, rhetorician, ii. 21, 22 n. 1, 31, 428 n. 1.
Σοφία, in Gnosticism, i. 389 n. 2, 399 n. 2. With individual Gnostics, 400, 414, 420, 424, 426–428, 430, 431, 434, 443, 444, 446, 448, 477. Ἄνω and κάτω, 181 Φυλοκρινητική, 414. Origen, 544, 546.
Sophia, sister of Henry IV., iv. 4.
Sophia of Bohemia, v. 253, 271, 287.
Sophists, i. 5, 19; ii. 39, 288.
Sophronius, monk, opponent of the compact with the Monophysites, iii. 178. Is made patriarch of Jerusalem, 179. His circular letter expressing Dyotheletism, 179, 180. See Harduin, iii. 1258.
Sorbonne, the, iv. 303. Library, 606 n. 4, 618 n. 1.
Sorcery, i. 87; ii. 91; iii. 312.
Σωρός, iii. 248 n.
Sorrow for sin, iv. 240, 241, 390. See Penitence.
Sortes sanctorum, iii. 129.
Sossuba. See Ithacius.
Soter, bp. of Rome, i. 299 n. 4, 525.
Σωτήρ, Soter in Gnosticism, i. 399 n. 2, 492 and n. 5, 549. With Valentine, 423, 424, 426–434. Apelles, 475.
Soterich, diaconus, iv. 533 n. 9.
Soul, consciousness of God in the, i. 177 (see God). Soul in Platonism, 378, 618. With the Gnostics, Basilides, 403. Relation to spirit, with Valentine, 426; to the Soter, 428; to God, with Tertullian, 616, 618; Hermogenes, 616–618.
Origin of the, church doctrine as to, i. 714. Essenes, 47. Bardesanes on the, 441. Ophites, 444. Marcion, 468. The Manicheans, 491, 496–501. Philo, Sabellius, 597. Tertullian, 618. Apollinaris on the, ii. 487, 489. The Paulicians, iii. 258, 260 (redemption of), 261. David of Dinanto, iv. 447. Preëxistence of (see Preëxistence). Corporeality, Faustus of Rhegium, ii. 706 n. 2. Mortal, with Valentine, i. 426; Tatian, i. 456; Hermogenes, i. 618; Arabians, i. 710, see Immortality. Symbol of the Logos, with Sabellius, i. 597. Hieracas on the, i. 714. In ecstasy, Clement, i. 520. Λογική and ἄλογος, i. 618; iii. 559 n. 3. Doctrine of two souls, iii. 559 n. 3; iv. 562. Soul reunited to its guiding spirit (Catharists), iv. 567, 571. Heavenly garments of the, iv. 572, 575. See Metempsychosis, Traducianism.
Soul, mundane, of nature, of the world, i. 376, 624. With Valentine, 420, 421, 423, 428. The Ophites, 443–446. The Manicheans, 480, 491, 494–496. In matter, 376. In the stars, 392. Heavenly, iii. 260; iv. 567, 579. See Metempsychosis.
Soul of Christ, with Mani, i. 493. Irenæus, 634, 635. Tertullian, 635. Origen, 636–640. Apollinaris, ii. 487–489, 491. Theodore, ii. 498. The Origenists, ii. 764 n. 3. See Person of Christ.
Soul of light, ii. 769 n. 3. See Light nature.
Souls, in nature, purification of, Manicheaus on, i. 480, 492, 493. Of human souls, 496–499, 501. Guidance of, iv. 513.
South Sea islands, iii. 305 n. 2.
Sovereignty of God. See Predestination.
Sozomen, church historian, Julian and Marcus, ii. 81 n. 1. Abolition of penance in the Greek church, 216. Ursinus, 256 n. 5. Rise of Arian controversy, 409 n. 4. Arius and Constantine, 428 n. 4. Recall of Athanasius, 436 n. 4. Chrysostom and the Origenistic monks, 753 n. 2.
Hist. eccles., l. i. c. 5, Constantine and Hosius, ii. 31 n. 4; c. 7, Licinius, 18 n. 1; c. 8, law of Constantine against paganism, 28 n. 3 (court chapel of C., iii. 109 n. 1); c. 9, law of C. on arbitration of bps., 171 n. 2; c. 13, Anthony, 204 n. 3; c. 16, time of passover, 337 n. 3; c. 24, Meletian schism, 254 n.
L. ii. c. 11, Phusik, ii. 132 n. 1; c. 20, death of Arius, 430 n. 3. L. iii. c. 11, the creed of Philippopolis, 436 n. 1; c. 14, Hilarion, 271 n. 2; the Eustathians, 281 n. 1. L. iv c. 29, the Arians at Antioch, 455 n.
L. v. c. 4, Julian and Maris, ii. 79 n. 3; c. 5, restoration of temples, 67 n. 1; c. 7, fate of Georgius, 80 n. 2; c. 17, Julian's statues, 74 n. 2; Soldiers betrayed into offering, 75 n 1; c. 19, Babylas, 83 n. 1; c. 20, Theodorus, 83 n. 3.
L. vi. c. 1, Julian and Arsaces, ii. 86 n. 3; c. 2, γενέσια τοῦ σεισμοῦ, 351 n. 1; c. 3, Jovian, 88 n. 1; c. 32, Epiphanius, 741 n. 3; c. 33, the βοσκοί, 203 n. 4; c. 36, Themistius on toleration, 91 n. 4; c. 37, the Goths, 156 n. 4; c. 38, Mavia, 142 n. 5.
L. vii. c. 15, Egyptian temples destroyed, ii. 98 n. 2. Marcellus of Apamea, 99 n. 1; c. 16, penance in the Greek ch., 216 n. (c. 19, preaching in the Roman ch., i. 303 n. 6); c. 25, place of the emperor in the ch., 321 n. 6. L. viii. c. 11, Theophilus and the Anthropomorphites, 752 n. 1; c. 12, T. and Isidore, 753 n. 2.
Sozopolis, ii. 590; iii. 206.

GENERAL INDEX. 211

Space, in relation to God, iv. 451. See Omnipresence.
Spain, spread of Christianity there, i. 85, 122. In the Diocletian persecution, 154, 155. Conflict with Rome, 217. Power of deacons in the Spanish church, 233. Ascetic spirit, ii. 180, 181. Time of baptism, ii. 360. Daily communion, ii. 364. Nicene creed, doctrine of the Holy Spirit, 471 (iii. 555). Priscillianists in Spain, ii. 771, 772, 774, 775 n. 6. *Third and Fourth Periods.* Veneration of St. Martin in, iii. 7. Eligius, 42. Relation of the church there to the state, 95, 96, 105. Relation of the Spanish to the Romish church, 117, 118, 121, 152 (iv. 88 and n. 3). Culture, 151, 152, 165. Adoptianist controversies, 156–165. Condition under the Mohammedans, 152, 156, 164 and n. 2, 335–345. Addition to the creed, 555 (ii. 471). Sects, 603 n. 2.
Fifth Period. Merchants from, iv. 69. Feof of the Roman church, 88. Saracens in, 191. Bernard's monks, 254. Dominicans, 269. Arabian philosophy from, 325. Rationalism, 431. Waldenses, 613. Inquisition in, 643.
Sixth Period. The measures against the memory of Boniface VIII., v. 22 (303). The Spanish at Constance, 112, 118, 119, 126. Benedict XIII., 112, 303. Pilgrimages to, see St. Iago. See Schott.
Spanish bishops, letter to Charlemagne, and to the Frankish bps., defence of Adoptianism, iii. 164 n. 3, 165. See Alcuin, opp., t. ii.
Spartianus, i. 663 n. 2.
Spectacles, public, attitude of the Christians in regard to, i. 263–267, 719, 720; ii. 258, 336, 342.
Speculative tendencies, i. 394. Gregory the Great on, iii. 143. New awakening of, iii. 471; iv. 281, 324, 356, 373, 401, 444. Anselm, iv. 367. Thomas Aquinas, iv. 423, 430. At Oxford, v. 240. Danger, limits of, v. 392, 393. Mystico-speculative, iv. 283, 401–408, 411.
Speculators, Fulco and the, iv. 210.
Speculum Stultorum, iv. 265 n. 4.
Speier, iv. 74, 112.
Speraindeo, abbot, iii. 430 n. 3.
Speratus, the martyr, i. 122, 123.
Σοφίς, ii. 188.
Spicker, Dr.
On Anselm of Havelburg, iv. 536 n. 3.
Spirit, in Gnosticism, i. 426 (see Πνεῦμα), in Pantheistic dualism, i. 481, 482. Living, with the Manicheans, i. 492, 499, 505. Difficulty of conceiving the notion of, i. 560. Doctrine concerning, i. 612. Origen, i. 569, 587, 623–630, 636–639. David of Dinanto, iv. 447. Anselm, iv. 457. Spirit of man and the idea of God, iv. 443, 457. Absolute, iv.

445 n. 2. Church of the, i. 518. Flesh and, ii. 619, 624, 734; v. 384. See Πνεῦμα.
Spirit of God, i. 179, 180. See Holy Spirit.
Spirit of Jesus Christ, v. 200, 201, 206, 218, 227–229, 231.
Spirit of the universe, Pliny on the, i. 10.
Spiritales, in Montanism, i. 518, 524. In the Decretals, iii. 348. With Joachim, iv. 228, 230. Franciscan, iv. 291, 617.
Spirits, Jewish, oriental doctrine of, i. 66. World of, 66; with Origen, 587, 714; gradations in the, ii. 776 n. 4. Spirits of the earth, i. 449.
Spirits, proving of, i. 181. Evil, ii. 274 n. 2, 278. See Demons.
Spiritual and secular, placed in opposition, i. 198, 199; ii. 179, 180, 259, 262, 263; iv. 121, 166; v. 172, 213, 215, 216. Confounded, ii. 184, 185; iv. 133, 147, 174, 215; v. 28, 42. Separated, iv. 186. Inquiries into their relation, iv. 141; v. 24, 25. See Consilia evangelica, Monachism, Priesthood, Secular.
Spiritual dangers, v. 392. See Temptations.
Spiritual gifts, i. 516. With Gegnæsius, iii. 249. See Charismata.
Spiritual judicature, iii. 107, 108, 406, 407.
Spiritual knowledge, iv. 232, 370.
Spiritual natures, men (see Πνευματικοι, Spiritales). With Joachim, iv. 230–232.
Spiritual offices, motives for entering, iii. 97 nn. 2, 3. See Appointments, Benefices.
Spiritual order, ii. 259. See Clergy.
Spiritual societies. See Societies.
Spiritual tendency, i. 557; v. 390.
Spiritual trials, Hildegard on, iv. 218. See Temptations.
Spiritual world, i. 426. See Spirit.
Spiritus principalis, iv. 571.
Spitals, iv. 267.
Sponsors, i. 315; iii. 53, 61.
Sporacius, ii. 582 n. 1.
Sporting, among the clergy, iii. 53, 56.
Sports. See Spectacles.
Σπουδαῖοι, of Plotinus, i. 29.
Sprinkling, in baptism, i 238 n. 2, 310.
Ssanang Ssetzen.
Geschichte der Ost-mongolen (Schmidt, trans Petersburg, 1829), p. 87; iv. 46 n. 1.
St. Adalbert, church of, in Prague, v. 293.
St. Ægidius, church of, in Pragne, v. 175.
St. Agatha, convent of, ii. 423.
St. Aile (Agil), iii. 38 n. 1.
St. Andrew, festival of, iv. 105 n. 4.
St. Angelo, castle of (Domum Crescentii), iv. 120, 128, 129; v. 73, 74.
St. Anthony's fire, iii. 408 n. 1; iv. 266 Society of St. Anthony, iv. 266. See Acta S. Jan.

St. Augustin, order of, v. 183. See Augustin.
St. Barbara, v. 189.
St. Bernard, mount, iv. 214.
St. Blasen, monastery of, iv. 233.
St. Clara, order of, iv. 276.
St. Cosmas, isle of, iii. 521.
St. Cyran, ii. 301 n. 4.
St. Denis, church of, iii. 446. Abbey of, iv. 140 n. 4, 374, 382. See Dionysius.
St. Dominic, monastery of, at Pisa, iv. 69 n. 2.
St. Elizabeth, iv. 302.
St. Eloy, iii. 41 n. 2. See Eligius.
St. Emmeran, monastery, iii. 324.
St. Evreul, monastery, iv. 92 n. 5.
St. Gall, monastery, iii. 36, 471. St. Galli church in Prague, v. 134. See Monachus Sangalli.
St. Genovese, abbey of, iv. 416.
St. Gilles, iv. 597.
St. Gorze, monastery, iii. 336 n. 2, 345.
St. Hubrecht, monastery, iii. 37.
St. Jago di Compostella, iii. 394; iv. 298, 306, 640.
St. Lazari, island of, iii. 250 n. 1.
St. Leufroy, monastery, iii. 529 n. 3.
St. Malo, island of, iv. 236.
St. Marcel, priory of, iv. 400.
St. Marci, cardinal, v. 104.
St. Martin, iii. 333 and n. 3. Chapel of, ii. 298. Church in Kent, iii. 12. Monastery near Pontisara, iv. 97 n. 8. At Tours, iv. 359 n. 2. See Martin of Tours.
St. Martin.
   Memoires, etc., de l'Arménie (Paris, 1819), t. i. p. 323, Persian religious wars, ii. 138 n. 2. T. ii. p. 472, proclamation of Mihr Nerseh, i. 489 n. 1; ii. 127 n. 2, 137 n. 2. Nazarenes, ii. 129 n. 2.
St. Maum, monastery, iii. 315 n. 1.
St. Michael, festival of, iii. 303. Church of, at Prague, v. 337. See Michael.
St. Nicholas, church of, v. 175.
St. Paul, church of, at Rome, ii. 160.
St. Peter, church of. See Peter.
St. Riequier. See Centulum.
St. Salaberga, life of, iii. 38 nn. 2, 3. See Acta S. O. B. Sæc. ii.
St. Salvator, cloister in Schaffhausen, iv. 233.
St. Sebald, church of, v. 321.
St. Sophia, church of, iii. 329, 583; iv. 534, 555 n. 1.
St. Stephen, ii. 369; iii. 211.
St. Thierry, monastery, iv. 393.
St. Veronica, handkerchief of, v. 3.
St. Victor, foundation of canonicals at Paris, iv. 401, 410–414. See Hugo, Richard.
Staff, of bishops and abbots, iii. 402; iv. 134, 142. See Insignia.
Stagirius, monk, ii. 273.
Stake, death at the, i. (95), 109, 111, 506; ii. 19 n. 3; iv. 597, 629, 639, 643;
v. 371, 379, 392, 412. See Martyrdom, Persecution.
Stanislaus of Znaim. See Znaim.
Star Spirits, i. 382, 383 n., 447. See Ophites, Saturnin.
Stars, the, with Plotinus, i. 392. Bardesanes, 442. Ophites, 444, 445. Julian, ii. 48, 60. In Priscillianism, ii. 777. With the Catharists, iv. 572, 575. See Planets.
Stasek, martyr in Prague, v. 288–290.
State, idea of the Roman, i. 86. Relation of Christianity to the state, i. 259–262, 440; ii. 15, 16. Ptolemæus on the, i. 439, 440. Influence on the church, ii. 72. Ancient notion of the, i. 86; ii. 114 (53); v. 26. Influence on doctrine, ii. 382. Dependence on the church, iii. 92, 96. Independence, v. 134. See Church and state, Emperors.
State religion, i. 7, 70, 86–93; ii. 9, 14–16, 21, 34–37; iii. 251. See Religio.
Statesmen, Roman, i. 77.
Stationes, i. 296. See Dies Stationum.
Statues, of the Gods, ii. 27, 95 n. 4. Of Julian, 74. See Images.
Staudlin.
   Archiv. für alte und Neue Kirchengeschichte (ii. 1), essay on Berengar, iii. 505 n. 5, 509 n. 4. IV. 3tes St., § 549, German songs, iv. 188 n. 1.
Staupitz, v. 360.
Stauros, cross, with Valentine, i. 419, 420, 431.
Stavelo, monastery, iii. 458.
Stedingers, the, iv. 643, 644.
Stefner, lay missionary in Iceland, iii. 302.
Steiermark, church in, iii. 316.
Steinach, river, iii. 36.
Steinfeld. See Everwin of.
Stekna, John of, v. 183 n. 2, 258.
Stenkel, king of Sweden, iii. 292, 293.
Stephanus, abbot, iii. 196 n. 2. Vita Stephani (ed. Muratori), 193 n. 2.
Stephanus, leader of rebellion, iii. 209.
Stephanus, leader of the monks in favor of image worship, iii. 220. His conduct before the emperor, 220. See Stephen, monk.
Stephanus Euodias Assemani.
   Bibliotheca Oriental., t. i. f. 391, the Chronicle of Edessa, i. 80 n. 2, 291 n. 3. T. ii. f. 30, ep. of Xennyas, ii. 615 n. 3; p. 291, Abulpharagius on Bar Sudaili, ii. 516 n. 1; p. 1636, Jacob of Edessa on Christmas, ii. 345 n. 1.
   T. iii. P. i. pp. 20, 75, acta martyrum, persecution in Persia, ii. 126 nn. 2, 3; f. 35, Phusik, ii. 132 n.; f. 36, Ebed-Jesu, list of Syrian eccles. writers, i. 681 n. 5; ii. 553 n. 3; f. 95, Nestorian missions, iv. 45 n. 2; f. 152, accusations against Christians, ii. 126 n. 4; f. 158, Timotheus, Nestorian patriarch, ii. 89 n. 2; f. 183, iii. 89 n. 3; f. 181, ii. 127 n. 4; f. 186, ii. 188, ii. 129 n. 2; f 215, ii. 126 n. 6; f. 227, second persecution, ii. 126 n. 1; f. 243, Jacobus, ii. 143 n.; ff. 323, 324, extracts from Diodorus of Tarsus and Theodore on restoration, ii. 788 n. 6; f. 391 extracts from Jacobite historians, ii. 611 n

GENERAL INDEX. 213

1. P. ii. f. 79, celibacy of clergy abolished in the Nestorian church, ii. 611 n. 2; ff. 486, 488, Kerait, Prester John, iv. 46 n. 2.
Bibl. Vat., t. iii. P. 2, f. 927, school at Nisibis, ii. 183 n.
Kalendarin eccles. univers., t. iii. f. 175, Cyrill and Nicholas I., iii. 316 n. 4.

Stephanus Gobarus, i. 675, 682; ii. 614; iv. 390.
Stephanus Niobes, ii. 613.
Stephanus of Antioch, ii. 436 n. 4.
Stephen, author of the life of Stephen of Obaize, iv. 312 and n. 2.
Stephen, bp. of Rome, i. 214–217, 318–321, 323 n. 1.
Stephen, cardinal, iii. 395.
Stephen, enemy of images, iii. 213. Inscription by, 213 n. 4.
Stephen, Hungarian prince, iii. 333–335. See Acta S. Sep.
Stephen, monk, image worshipper, iii. 213 n. 3, 220. Life of, see Analecta Græca.
Stephen I. See Stephen, bishop.
Stephen II., pope, Boniface and, iii. 71 nn. 1, 2. Gregory of Utrecht, 73. Solicits the aid of Pepin against the Longobards, 119. Arrogates to himself the right of confirming marriages among princes, 120, 121. On church Psalmody, 242. Ariald, 390.
Stephen IX., pope, iii. 387.
Stephen, president of the sect at Orleans, iii. 595.
Stephen, son of Basilius, the Macedonian, iii. 568 n. 3.
Stephen, the martyr, i. 341; iii. 211, 212; v. 377. Festival of, i. 369.
Stephen de Ansa, iv. 606.
Stephen de Borbone (de Bella Villa), iv. 607 n. 1.
De septem donis spiritus sancti, Peter Waldus, iv. 606 n. 4.
Stephen Gobarus. See Stephanus.
Stephen Harding, Cistercian abbot, iv. 252.
Stephen Langton, cardinal, iv. 174.
Stephen of Dola, abbot, against the Wicklifites, v. 251. Friendly to Huss, 252. Opponent of Huss, 262. Flight of Zbynek, 275 nn. Huss and the martyrs of Prague, 289, 290.

Citations:—
Anti-Wickliffus (Medulla tritici), in Pez Thesaurus, t. iv., v. 247 n. 4; ff. 157, 158, Wickliffite doctrines in Bohemia and Moravia, v. 371 n. 2; f. 158, ordinance of Zbynek, 247 n. 4; ff. 184, 209, 213, 214, Wickliffitism in B., 251 nn. 2–6; f. 240, letters of fraternities, 250 n. 1.
Anti-Hussus, f. 373, closing of Bethlehem chapel, v. 265 n. 1; f. 380, former friendship with Huss, 252 n. 2; Edict of Wenceslaus, 287 n. 2; ff. 380, 381, the martyrs of Prague, 288 n. 3, 289 nn.; f. 381, Beguines, 288 n. 1; f. 383, Huss accused of pride, 268 n. 2; f. 386, burning of Wicklif's books, 262 n. 3; f. 390, friends of Huss, 260 n. 1, 288 n. 1; ff. 417, 418, burning of the books of Wicklif, 262 n. 2; ff. 418, 419, death of Zbynek, 275 n. 2. See Pez, t. iv.
Dialogus volatilis, f. 462, auditors of Huss, v. 257 n. 1; ff. 464, 465, 466, citation of Huss to Rome, 271 n. 1, 301 n. 3; f. 474, indulgences, 285 n. 1; f. 492, appeal of Huss, 295 n. 2; f. 492, Beguines, 288 n. L See Pez, t. iv.

Stephen of Obaize, abbot, iv. 312. On indulgences, 351.
Life of (see Baluz), f. 60, pref. iv. 312 n. 2. L. i. c. 4, charitable customs, 295 n. 5; the false anchoret, 243 n. 1. L. ii. c. 4, f. 106, 312 n. 4; c. 18, indulgences, 351 nn. 5, 6; church building, 293 n. 1.

Stephen of Prague, v. 118. See Paletz.
Stephen of Tournay, bp., iv. 416.
Ep. 79, Simon of Tournay, iv. 418 n. 4; ep. 221, forged bulls, 205 n. 1; ep. 241, on the theologians, 416 n. 1. See Bibl. Patr. Lugd.

Stephen Paletz. See Paletz.
Stettin, history of its conversion, iv. 11–16, 25–30.
Steuart.
Tomus singularis insign. auctarum (Ingoldstadt, 1616, c. 33, liber penitentialis, of Rabanus Maurus (letters to Heribald), iii. 497 n. 1.

Stewards, ii. 191, 272. Of Roman bps., 192 n. 1.
Stigmata, iv. 276 and n 1. See Marks.
Stilicho, ii. 102.
Stitney, Thomas of, v. 245 n. 5.
Stoa, the, ii. 106 n. 2.
Stobæus, Johannes.
Eclogæ, l. ii. c. i. 11 (ed. Heeren), P. ii. p. 10, saying of Demonax of Cyprus, i. 10 n. 1.

Stoicism, i. 10, 77. Its essence, 15–18. Of Marcus Aurelius, 105, 106. Of Novatian, 239. Cyprian on, 245. Anthropology, 611. Christian, ii. 719.
Stone, the, of Codran, iii. 300. At Mecca, iv. 535 n. 1.
Stoning, i. 93; iii. 326.
Stories, popular, iii. 19 n. See Legends.
Strabo, on mythology, i. 7. Moses, nature worship, 9.
Geograph., l. i. c. 2, i. 7 n. 2. L. xvi. c. 2, i. 9 n. 6.

Strahl.
Hist. Russian church, t. i. p. 61, Vladimir, iii. 329 n. 1.

Strangers, the Lord's Supper carried to, i. 332. Care for, ii. 169; iv. 294, 295 (214).
Strassburg, crusaders from, iv. 74. University, iv. 421. Friends of God in, v. 381, 383, 388, 389, 390, 401, 407. Johannites of, v. 392 nn. 1, 2. See Wilderod.
Strategius Musonianus, deputed by Constantine to make inquiries concerning the Manicheans, ii. 16, 769.
Streets, images in the, iii. 232.
Strenæ, ii. 347, 351.
Strick, priest, iv. 40.
Stridon, ii. 742.
Stridova, ii. 742 n. 1.
Stromata. See Clement of Alexandria.
Stroth.

i. 582 n. 3; on the Dialogue of Justin, i. 668 n. 3. See Repertorium.

Studien und Kritiken.
Bd. i. St. 4, Lauf's Essay, Scotus and Ratramnus, iii. 500 n. 2, 505 n. 3. 1828, i. 1, Geiseler on the mendicant orders, iv. 280 n. 4, 29 n. 1. 1829, Bd. ii. H. 1, on the Paulicians, iii. 244 n. 3. 1830, s. 397, Gieseler, critique of Neander, on the Gnostics, i. 401 n. 3, 402 n. 3, 403 n. 2, 447 n. 2. 1831, H. 2, monograph on Hugo of St. Victor, iv. 401 n. 3. 1833, H. 3. Ullmann, Greek ch. in the twelfth century, iv. 530 n. 5; s. 920, etc., Semisch. on the I. Apolog. of J. Martyr, i. 664 n. 3, 665 nn. 1, 6. 1836, 4tes St. s. 1073, Ullmann Hallischen Weihnachts-programm, Beryll, i. 591 n. 4 (593 n. 1). 1837, Protocol of the trial of Huss at Prague, 1414, v. 243 n. 1, 317 n. 4; s. 127, v. 274 n. 1; ss. 129, 130, v. 250 n. 1; s. 131, v. 255 n. 1; s. 132, v. 246 n.; ss. 139, 140, v. 250 n. 4; s. 143, v. 256 n. 2; s. 147, v. 288 n. 1. 1837, II. 2, Gieseler on Prester John, iv. 47 n. 1838, H. i., Prof. Piper on writings of the church fathers, i. 676 n. 6; Engelhardt on Origen, i. 697 n. 1. 1842, Thiersch (on Irenæus, iii. 3), i. 204 n. 3.

Studies, of the twelfth century, iv. 203, 204, 357. John of Salisbury on the methods of, 357, 358. Hugo of St. Victor on the same, 401, 402. Peter Cantor, 414. Peter of Blois, 415. Aquinas, 423. Monastic, 287. Conrad on study, v. 188. See Study, Dialectics, Law, Theology.

Studion (Studium), monastery, iii. 535 n. 1, 536 n. 1, 583.

Studius, officer of state, ii. 173.

Study of the ancients. See Literature.

Sturm, abbot, iii. 74. Founds the monasteries of Hersfeld and Fulda, 74, 75. Labors and death, 75, 76. Difficulties with archbishop Lull, 75 n, 1. Life of, 75 n. 3. See Pertz.

Stylites, ii. 142, 292; iii. 28, 571; iv. 529 and n. 2, 532. Stylite at Thessalonica, iv. 532. See Simeon.

Styria, ii. 742 n. 1.

Suabia, iii. 36, 37; iv. 3, 96 n. 6, 111, 176, 610. Friends of God in, v. 42, 411. See Rudolph of.

Subdeacons, Subdiaconi, i. 201; iii. 381, 384 n. 4, 386.

Subintroductæ, i. 277 n. 5; iv. 249. See Συνείσακται.

Subjective and objective, with Origen, i. 634. In salvation, iii. 183. In justification, ii. 621, 678; iv. 304, 305, 502, 509, 510, 513; v. 172, 302, 347. In atonement, iv. 497, 502. In morals, iv. 388. Subject and accident in the Lord's Supper, iv. 335, 336.

Subjective tendencies, i. 39; iv. 304, 305, 446.

Sublacus (Subiaco), ii. 297.

Subordination, with the Gnostics, i. 380, 469. In the tradition of the church, i. 575, 576, 608. In the Eastern church, i. 585, 716; ii. 404, 405. The Monarchians, i. 591, 592. With Origen, i. 589, 590, 605. In the Western church, i. 605–607 and n. 1, 610. With Arius, ii. 405, 408. Marcellus of Ancyra, ii. 438, 440, 478. Supplanted by the Nicene doctrine, ii. 473. With Catharists, iv. 569, 574. The Pasagii, iv. 590. In the doctrine of the Holy Spirit, i. 608, 609; ii. 466; iv. 569.

Substance and accidents, iv. 447. See Lord's Supper.

Substitutes, iv. 201, 206.

Substrati, ii. 213.

Succath (Patricius), ii. 146.

Succession in spiritual gifts, with Gegnæsius, iii. 249. See Apostolic.

Succendion, monastery, iii. 536 n. 1.

Sudbury, Simon, abp. of Canterbury, v. 148, 161.

Suenes, Persian Christian, ii. 134.

Sueno. See Sveno.

Suetonius, on Chrestus, i. 94.

Vita Claudii, c. 24, Ducenarius, i. 604 n.

Suevi, iii. 34. Education, 73.

Suffering, with Basilides, i. 402 n. 3, 403 n. 3, 412. In Parsism, ii. 129. Use of, iv. 260. As awakening thought, v. 380, 381. God's meaning in, v. 411. Patience in, v. 411, 412.

Sufferings of Christ, i. 301, 413, 471, 493, 552. See Christ, Redemption.

Suffetum, massacre of Christians at, ii. 102 n. 2.

Suffragan bps., iv. 215, 326 n. 1. In Germany, v. 101.

Suger, abbot of St. Denis.

Life of Louis VI., iv. 140 n. 4.

Σύγκελλος, iii. 209 n. 1.

Suicide, the elder Pliny on, i. 11. Stoics, i. 16. With the Donatists, Augustin, ii. 231, 238. Among the monks, ii. 273; iv. 239 and n. 2. Judgment of the church on, iii. 102 n. 4. In the sects, iii. 602 and n. 1, 604; iv. 582. Sellers of indulgences, v. 52.

Suidas, obscure passage in (Pulcheria), ii. 519 n. 1.

Suidger, bp. of Bamburg (Clement II.), iii. 378.

Sulmone, iv. 193.

Sulpicius Severus.
Ithacius and Idacius, ii. 772 n. 3, 773 n. 1. Biography of Martin of Tours, Dialogues, 773 n. 2. Dialog., i. c. 3, Origenists, 763 n. 3; cc. 6, 7, 753 nn. 3, 4; c. 8, parochin, 194 n. 1 Hist. Sacr., l. ii. c. 31, Hadrian's decree banishing Jews from Jerusalem, i. 344 n.; c. 46, Priscillian, ii. 772 n. 1; c. 50, Ithacius, ii. 772 n. 2.

Συμμορία, ii. 193 n. 2.

Sun, the, worship of, i. 125, 141; ii. 8 and n. 3; iii. 587. With the Essenes, i. 47. With Julian, ii. 49, 73. In Persia, ii. 128, 130, 131. With pagan Christians, ii. 347 n. 4. Paulicians? iii. 244 n. 4. In Norway, iii. 294. Olof on the, iii. 299. Creator of the, iii. 304 n. 1. Children of the, iii. 587. With the Catharists, iv. 572. Eclipse of the, iv. 37.

GENERAL INDEX. 215

Sun and moon, sun-spirit, with the Manicheans, i. 480, 493, 494, 497, 499, 500, 505; ii. 769 and n. 2.
Συνάσεια, ii. 503, 504, 523.
Sunday, observance of, i. 98, 295, 296, 298, 301 n. 1, 676; ii. 28, 332–336, 338 n. 6; iii. 95, 123, 126, 294; iv. 9, 209, 278, 296, 297, 300; v. 140, 336. Contributions on, i. 198. Places of meeting, i. 203, 290; ii. 194. Celebration of the Lord's Supper, i. 332; ii. 333. Visitation of prisoners, ii. 178; iii 105. Law of Constantine, suspending business on, ii. 333, 336. Fasting excluded from, i. 295; ii. 334; iii. 579. In Norway, iii. 294. Wicklif and Huss on, v. 140, 336. With the Manicheans, i. 505. Montanists, i. 521 n. 1. Millennial, ii. 616.
Συνείσακτοι, i. 277 n. 5, 659; ii. 182 n. 2; iv. 249 n. 1, 633.
Συνέκδημοι, iii. 264, 265.
Sunnia, ii. 159.
Σύνοδοι οἰκουμενικαί, ii. 209.
Supererogatory righteousness, i. 645, 714. Works of Supererogation, iv. 349, 350. See Indulgences, Merit.
Superior, the, in monasticism, ii. 282; iv. 276, 290. Magister, iv. 267. Generalis minister, iv. 268.
Supernatural, the longing for the, i. 11. Relation of the, to Christianity, i. 72, 507, 510. In Christ's life (Ebionites), i. 348; (Felix), iii. 163. The Clementines on the, i. 359. Constantine, ii. 21, 23. Alexandrian and Antiochian schools, ii. 394. Supernatural destiny of man, i. 614. Supernatural element in knowledge, iv. 429. Supernatural revelation, iv. 429, 430. Hostility to the, v. 393. See Miracles, Nature and the Supernatural.
Supernaturalism, Jewish, i. 55, 64, 680. Docetic, i. 387. Christian, i. 507, 570. Two tendencies, i. 614. Montanistic, i. 511, 512–515, 523. With Julian, ii. 57. In the Middle Ages, iv. 324, 338, 466 (312). In the doctrine of the fall, iv. 494. The Catharists, iv. 570.
Superstitio externa, i. 89; prava, ex tiabilis, 98.
Superstition, in relation to the Roman state religion, i. 6–8. Seneca on, 7. Lucian, 7, 8. Strabo, 9. Relation to unbelief, Plutarch, 13–15 (v. 401). And unbelief, efforts at conciliating, 27–31. Relation to Christianity, 33, 71, 78, 84. At Rome, 89. Of Galerius, 145.
In the Second Period. As a way to faith, ii. 13, 119. Constantine, 13, 21–23. Effects of disturbing, 27, 98. Connected with the delay of baptism, 356, 357. With the Lord's Supper, 365, 366. Eudoxia, 755, 756, 760.
In the Third and Fourth Periods. Remains of pagan, iii. 12, 42, 107, 123, 129, 130, 446 n. 1. Transferred to Christianity, 56, 78. Arabian, 84. In gifts to churches, 101. In the use of the Bible, 129, 309. Of the sacraments, 136, 280, 301. In the West, 146. In the Greek church, 169, 170, 309, 531. Connected with images (ii. 329), 201, 240, 428, 429 (see Image worship). Bulgarians warned against, 311, 312. Opposition to, 444, 446 457. Promoted by the clergy, 445, 446.
In the Fifth Period. Pagan, iv. 37. Connected with the sacraments, 45, 338, 343. Mongolian, 48. Opposition to, 317, 318, 328, 563, 564. Reactions from, 324. Spread of, 328. In the Eastern church, 531. Clemangis on, v. 61. Ridicule of the saints and, 81. Janow, 207. Huss on, 238, 250, 290. And immorality, 237, 238. And infidelity, 401. See Amulets, Images, Miracles, Relics, Saints, Witchcraft.
Support of the clergy, i. 197, 198 n. 1. See Tithes.
Supralapsarians, ii. 704 n. 1. System, iii. 475.
Supreme essence, Strabo on the, i. 9; Spirit, in Platonism, 13, 26; essence, in Neo-Platonism, 25. Absolute, substituted for, 26, 57, 578. Supreme God, with Plato, 396 n. 3; in Gnosticism, 373, 381–384, 388, 393, 394, 578; Cerinthus, 396–398; Basilides, 405–410; Valentine, 424, 427, 428; Ptolemæus, 437–439; Pseudo-Basilideans, 447; Carpocrates, 449; Prodicians, 451; Mani, 489–491; with Origen, 587 and n. 3; Paulicians, iii. 259; Euchites, iii. 591. Bogomiles, iv. 553, 554. Supreme light, i. 499. Supreme soul, i. 500.
Surius. See Acta Sanctorum of.
Sursum corda, i. 329 n. 1; ii. 363 n. 1; iii. 136.
Susa, ii. 133.
Susannah, v. 332, 358. History of, i. 709, v. 60; iii. 77 n. 4.
Susiana, Mani in, i. 488.
Suso, Henry, v. 388, 411. Life and writings (see Diepenbrock). Little book of eternal wisdom, 411 n. 3.
Sussex, Christianity in, iii. 22.
Sutri, council at, iii. 377. Treaty at, iv. 133.
Svautovit, idol of Rügen, iv. 31.
Sveno (Sven Otto). Son of Harald Blaatand, iii. 288, 290.
Svidbert, among the Boruchtuarians, iii. 44.
Swabia. See Suabia.
Swatoplnk. See Zwentibold.
Swätoslav, Russian prince, iii. 328.
Swearing, by the emperors, i. 90, 91, 109, 110.
Sweden, spread of Christianity in, iii. 276–287, 291–293. War with Norway, iii. 297. Crusade against the Finns, iv. 45. Gregory I., iv. 90. The bp. of Lund,

iv. 164. Forged bulls, iv. 204. Cistercian monasteries, iv. 254. Brigitta of, v. 44. Pilgrims from, v. 237.
Switzerland, Christianity in, iii. 34–37, 332. Arnold in, iv. 150. Berthold, iv. 318. Henry of Cluny from, iv. 597. Reformatory spirit, v. 128. See Basle, Constance, Thesaurus, Hist. Helveticæ.
Sword, i. 113; iv. 186. Power of the, iii. 255, 362, 363. Spiritual and secular, iv. 106 and n. 4, 130, 143, 151, 162, 165, 182, 186, 189, 190, 586, 643; v. 8, 10, 347, 353. Bernard on, iv. 159, 586. Humbert, iv. 190. Joachim, iv. 223.
Sword, order of the brothers of the, iv. 45.
Syleum, iii. 219.
Symbol, chanting of the, iii. 555. Changes in the, 555, 577. See Creeds.
Symbolism, in Neo-Platonism, i. 27. Alex. Judaism, 54, 56, 58, 59, 64. Therapeutæ, 61. Gnostic, 372, 376, 381, 387, 392, 420, 424, 435, 440. Mani, 482, 488, 495. Pagan, 672. Scotus on, iii. 463, 464.
Symbolizing tendency, iii. 170, 206 n. 1.
Symbols, early Christian, i. 292, 293; ii. 24 n. 4. Sacraments as, i. 304, 648; ii. 723, 724, 734; iii 495, 498, 500, 501, 505; v. 153, 154. In mediæval Catholicism, iii. 200. Symbolic rites in baptism, i. 315. Symbolic knowledge of the divine essence, ii. 445. Tendency to multiply symbols, ii. 723. Use of images as, iii. 198, 199, 200; John of Damascus on, iii. 207; Libri Carolini, iii. 238. Confusion between sign and thing signified, iii. 200, 238. Joachim on, iv. 231, 232. Of Christ, iv. 275. Deification of, iv. 338, 340.
Symbols of feudal tenure, iii. 401, 402. Of the Episcopal office (regalia), iii. 402; iv. 134, 142, 143, 147. See Insignia.
Symbolum, i. 306, 307.
Symeon, Metaphrast.
Collection of, martyrdom of Justin, i. 671 n. 3.
Symmachus, Ebionite, version of the Old Testament, i. 708.
Symmachus, Quintus Aurelius, ii. 92 and nn. 3, 5, 6, 93, 94 n. 1, 99 and n. 3, 117.
Ep. 7, to his brother, ii. 92 n. 6. L. x. ep. 61, Relat. ad Valentinian, 35 n. 4, 92 n. 3, 93 n. 2. Memorial, 92 n. 5.
Symphorian of Autun, the martyr, i. 115. Acts of, 108 n. 3, 115 n. 1.
Symposium of Plato, i. 386.
Synagogues, Jewish, i. 184, 218, 302, 303; iii. 13 n. 1; iv. 622, 624; v. 210. Demolished, ii. 95 and n. 4. Internal jurisdiction of, ii. 171.
Syncel, ii. 507 n. 2, 518 n. 3, 537 n. 1.
Syneisaktes. See Συνεισακτοι.
Synesius of Cyrene, bp. of Ptolemais, his conversion, ii. 116, 122, 123. Platonism,

388, 763. Election as bp., 181, 763. On celibacy, 181. On Athens, 106 n. 2. Contest with Andronicus, 177 n. 1, 215. Anthony, 268 n. 4. Amus (Ammun), 269 n. 2, 290. Character, 530 n. 3.

Citations: —

Dion [ed. Petav.], Amus, Anthony, ii. 290 n. 2; f. 48, 269 n. 2; f. 81, 268 n. 4. Ep. 58, Andronicus, 177 n. 1. Ep. 66, ad Theophilum, 762 n. 1. Ep. 67, ad Theophilum, 822 n. 2. Ep. 105 (ed. Basil), 181 n. 1. Ep. 136, ad fratrem, 106 n. 2. Ep. 137, ad Heraclian, 104 n. 2; f. 358, 763 n. 2. Hymns, 115 n. 4. H. iii. v. 438, 371 n. 2.

Synnada, council at, i. 318. Bp. of, iii. 205.
Σύνοδος πενθέκτη, iii. 196 n. 1.
Synods, provincial, i. 206, 207. Annual of North African bps., i. 234 (84). In Asia Minor, concerning Montanism, i. 524. Egyptian against Origen, i. 703, 704. Opinion of Origen consulted by synods, i. 710.
Second Period. Convened by Constantine, ii. 164. Synods, on qualifications for the episcopal office, ii. 184. On deacons, ii. 189. On deaconesses, ii. 190, 191. Of fourth century on chor-bishops, ii. 193. Greg. Nazianz. on, ii. 209. Of Egyptian and Lybian bps., against Arius, ii. 409. Favoring the Homoousion, before the Nicene council, ii. 417 n. 3. Against Athanasius, ii. 426, 427. Multitude convened by Constantins, ii. 452. Synodal articles, ii. 468, 492.
Third and Fourth Periods. Columban on, iii. 32. Synodal system of Boniface, 55, 56. Secularization of, in the Frankish empire, 95–97. Convened by Charlemagne, 122. Theodulf on, 125. Reforming, under Charlemagne, 143. Decretals on the power to convoke, 349. In Rome, 353. French, treuga Dei, 407. Of the ninth century, ecclesiastical elections, 400. On preaching, 425.
Fifth Period. Annual (Lenten), under Gregory VII., iv. 89. Of reform in England, 91. Provincial, authority defended, 131. Endemic at Constantinople, against sects, 563, 564.
Sixth Period. Henry of Langenstein on the renewal of provincial, v. 50. See Councils.
Syrens, the, i. 535 n. 2.
Syria, Gnosticism, Basilides, i. 400. Julian in, ii. 81–86. Temples on the borders of, ii. 95 n. 5. Armenia, ii. 136. Monachism, ii. 124, 263, 270, 276, 283, 291, 292. Desert of Chalcis, ii. 742. Saracens in, iii. 89, 228; iv. 153. Image worship, iii. 209. Paulicians, iii. 244. Marcionites, iii. 247. Francis in, iv. 60 n. 2. Pilgrimages to, iv. 276 n. 2. See Palestine, Pilgrimages, Syrian church.

Syriac. See Bible translation, Languages.
Syrian church, i. 79. Persecution of, i. 153-155. Epiphany, i. 302. Interpreters, i. 303. Monachism (see Syria). Theological schools, ii. 182, 183 (see Antiochian). Monophysites, ii. 331, 589; iii. 88. In the Nestorian controversy, ii. 521-525, 529, 547-549, 555-563. Contests with the Egyptians, ii. 522 n. 1, 523 n. 1, 557. Dogmatic use of language, ii 524 n., 546. See Controversy of the three chapters, Apollinaris.
Syrian devil-worshippers, iv. 558 n. 2.
Syrian Gnostics, i. 374, 377, 378, 478; iii. 258.
Syrians, ii. 117.
Syrianus, pagan philosopher, ii. 104.
Syro-Persian church, i. 81. Christians, 82.
Systematizing period, ii. 380.
Systems of doctrine, partial, their origin, i. 337.
Syzigia, i. 423, 426, 432, 434, 477; iv. 568.

T.

Tabennæ, ii. 271, 272, 587.
Taberistanensis.
   Annales regum atque legatorum Dei (Kosegarten's Lat. trans.), vol. ii., p. 1 (Gryph., 1835), f. 103, i. 350 n. 3.
Tablets, iii. 211.
Tacitus, concerning the Christians, i. 94 n. 2, 95 nn. 2, 3, 98. Nero, 95 nn. 1, 4, 96 n. 1. Tiberius, 112 n. 4. Roman laws regarding slaves, 268 n. 3.
   Citations.
   Annal., l. ii. c. 4, rector provinciæ, i. 106 n. 3; c. 30, testimony of slaves. 112 n. 2; c. 85, foreign rites, 89 n. 3. L. xi. c. 15; l. xiii. c. 32, superstitio, 89 n. 1. L. xiv. c. 42, 269 n. 3. L. xv. c. 42, Nero, 95 n. 4; c. 44, per flagitia invisos, 94 n. 2. Hist., l. ii c. 8, death of Nero disbelieved, 96 n. 1. Germania, c. 10, use of horses in divination, iv. 15 n. 3
Tafel, Prof., iv. 530 n. 6.
   Diss. Geograph. de Thessalonica, etc. (Berolin, 1839), p. 17, iv. 531 n. 5; app. Monodia of Nicetas, on Eustathius, 531 n. 1. Programme (1832), p. 10, formula of Manuel Comnenus, 533 n. 9; p 18, transactions of the synod under Manuel, 534 n. 1.
Tagrit. See Maruthas.
Tahal in Persia, ii. 589.
Talanos, Spanish monastery, iii. 339.
Talk, unprofitable, iv. 273.
Tall brothers, the, ii. 752.
Tanchelm of Flanders, iv. 592.
Tangiers, i. 147.
Tangmar, priest, iii. 408 n. 2.
Ταπεινός, i. 19, 166, 392 n. 3.
Taprobane (Ceylon), ii. 141.
Taraco, bps. of, and the Waldensians, iv. 613. Abp. of, v. 84. See Himerius, Orosius.
Tarasius, patriarch of Constantinople, in the image controversy, iii. 225-228, 230 n. 1, 231, 549. Constantine and Theodota, 536 n. 2. Great uncle of Photius, 559 n. 1. Biography, 225 n.; c. 3, 227 n. 2.
   Letter to the abbot John, iii. 232 n. 1. Letter to the empress Irene, 232 n. See Harduin, iv.
Tarsus, ii. 461 n. 1; iii. 25. See Diodorus, Helladius.
Tartary, Tartarian tribes, Christianity in, iii. 307-315; iv. 46-56. Language, translation of the New Testament and Psalms, iv. 58. Oliva, iv. 624. See Mongols.
Tascir, iii. 250 n. 1.
Tatian, the Gnostic, i. 456-458, 716. Apologist, 672, 673. Crescens, 671.
   Oratio contra Graecos, § 19, i. 671 n. 1.
Tauler, v. 360, 382-384, 386-389, 391, 393, 396, 407-411. Hist. Tauleri, 389 n. 2.
   Citations.
   Sermons, Basle, ed. an. 1522, f. 6 b (Frankfort ed., an. 1826, vol. i., f. 134), submission to superiors, 7 384 n. 1; f. 7 a (Fr. ed., i. 135), contemplation, 409 n. 1; f. 8 a (Fr., i. 141), self-righteousness, 407 n. 5, God's discipline, 411 n. 1; f. 8 b (Fr., i. 142), prayer, 407 n. 6; f. 14 a (Fr., i. 159), love, 384 n. 4; f. 15 b (Fr., i. 123), undue value placed on contemplation, 401 n. 1; f. 17 a (i. 127), use of works, 384 n. 2; f. 17 a, love, 405 n. 1; f. 19 b (Fr., i. 192), danger of works, 409 nn. 2, 3; f. 20 a (Fr., i. 194), comfort, 405 n. 4; f. 21 b (Fr., i. 199), Christian growth, 405 n. 5; f. 28 b (Fr., i. 261), victory through Christ, 411 n. 2; f. 3. a (Fr., i. 266), help from friends of God, 387 n. 3; f. 3. a (Fr., i. 266), God present with those who seek him, 410 n. 1; f. 32 b (Fr., ii. 57), jealousy towards good men, 386 n. 3; f. 34 a (Fr., i. 280), submission, 384 n. 3; f. 36 a (Fr., ii. 64), hidden presence of the spirit, 410 n. 2; f. 42 a (Fr., ii. 101), light natural and divine, 382 n. 4; f. 46 a (Fr., ii. 113), emotion, 409 n. 3; f. 48 a (Fr., ii. 121), dangers of spiritual enjoyment, 409 n. 4; f. 48 b (Fr., ii. 122), outward and inward comfort, 410 n. 3; f. 57 b (Fr., ii. 167), doctrinal disputes, 382 n. 3; f. 77 a (Fr., ii. 235), formal religion, 387 n. 1; f. 120 b (Fr., ii. 449), mendicancy, 407 n. 2; f. 134 a (Fr., iii. 217), despondency, 409 n. 6; (Fr., iii. 218), luxury of feeling, 409 n. 2; f. 135 a (iii. 220), kingdom of God within, 382 n. 5; f. 146 a (Fr. iii. 120), God our end, 407 n. 4; f. 146 b (Fr., iii. 122), friends of God, 387 n. 2.
Tauris (Tabris), iv. 57.
Taurus, pretorian prefect, ii. 548. See Theodoret, ep. 105.
Tavia, iii. 251.
Taxes, from temples, ii. 90, 91. Imposed on Persian Christians, ii. 130. Oppressive, ii. 174. Basil against the use of the oath in collecting, ii. 175. Imposed on pagans, iii. 13 n. 1. On church property, iii. 101. Taxgatherers, iv. 531. Wicklif on taxes, v. 160.
Teachers, under Julian, ii. 76. False, iii. 53. Paulician, iii. 264. Influence of, iv. 357. Anselm as teacher, iv. 362. Wicklif as, v. 141. See Church teachers.
Teaching, gift, office of, i. 181, 186-188,

510. Right of laity to teach, 196. See Laity, Preaching.
Tears, deemed disgraceful, iii. 291. Gift of, iv. 306, 533.
Tebald, life of Ubald, iv. 206 n. 2.
Teleology, rejected by Celsus, i. 168. By Plotinus, i. 391. By the Neo-Platonists, i. 589; ii. 106. In Basilides, i. 406. With Origen, i. 589, 627. Christian, i. 649. With the schoolmen, iv. 466. See End, Final Cause.
Temperance, iv. 521, 524, 611.
Tempestarii, iii. 429 n. 3.
Temple, at Jerusalem, i. 48, 65, 67, 80, 407 n. 2; ii. 53. Worship, i. 352. Destruction of the, i. 38, 343, 362, 671; ii. 314; iv. 555 n. 1, 590. Its restoration expected, i. 343. Attempted, ii. 69, 70. Christian churches modelled after, i. 80; ii. 321. Expulsion of the money changers, i. 431 n. 1.
Temple, order of knights of the, iv. 258. Abolished, v. 23.
Temples, Zeno on, i. 18 n. 1. Hadrian's, i. 103. Temple to Epiphanes, i. 451. Worship, dreams and cures in the, ii. 26, 88, 106. Destruction of, ii. 26, 27, 34, 41, 80, 88 n., 95, 98, 101 and n. 5, 103, 133, 289, 298; iii. 5 n. 4, 15, 34. 41, 80, 297, 302, 305; iv. 14-16, 21, 22, 30, 32. Plundered, ii. 27, 28, 32 n. 3, 34-36, 67 n. 2, 70, 95. Closed, ii. 33, 97, 103. Converted into churches, ii. 97, 98, 320; iii. 5 n. 4, 15, 134. And monasteries, iii. 41. Restoration, building of, i. 155; ii. 66, 80; iii 79, 284. Unfinished, ii. 88 n. Worship suppressed, ii. 95, 97 (see Pagan). Julian on the, ii. 65, 82. In the country, ii. 35, 90, 98, 298. Taxes from, ii. 90, 91. Estates confiscated, ii. 92. Of the Valentinians, ii. 95 n. 4. Defended by Libanius, ii. 95, 96. At Adrotta, ii. 105 n. 3. Fire temple, ii. 133 and n. 3. As asylums, ii. 176. Beauty of, ii. 320. Paulicians, iii. 264. Tribute to, iii. 301. At Caracorum, iv. 53.
Temples of God, men as, i. 136, 289; iii. 452; iv. 222.
Temptation, Basilideans on, i. 416. The first, Manicheans on, i. 497. Temptations of monks, ii. 266, 274-279; iv. 235, 239-244. Anthony on, ii. 266, 270. Jovinian, ii. 308. Theodore of Mopsuestia, ii. 715. Louis IX., iv. 300. Preaching on, iv. 313. In preaching, 315. Abelard on, iv. 389. Of mystics, v. 392. Ruysbroch, v. 405. Tauler on, v. 409-411. See Concupiscence.
Temptation of Christ. See Christ.
Temudschin (Dschingiskhan), iv. 48, 49.
Tenthyra, nome, ii. 272.
Tephrycain, city of the Paulicians, iii. 244 n. 1, 587.
Terebinth (Buddas), i. 485.
Terebinthus, island, iii. 558.
Terebon, Saracen chief, ii. 143.

Terminalia, i. 148.
Tertiani, iv. 276.
Tertullian, life and writings of, i. 683 685. As organ for the North African theology, 509. As a Montanist, 196, 213 n., 214, 297, 326 and n. 1, 335, 509, 514, 677, 678 and n. 2, 683-685 (ii. 294). Hindrances to faith, 72. Conversion by means of extraordinary psychological phenomena, 75. Mutual love of the Christians, 76. Christian heroism, 76, 77. Diffusion of Christianity increased by persecution, 77. Universal intelligibleness of Christianity, 78. Spread of Christianity in Africa, 84. Church in Britain, 85. "Non licet esse vos," 88. Reverence paid to the emperors, 90. Participation in heathen festivals, de corona. 91 nn. 3, 4. Tiberius favorable to Christianity, 93, 94. Domitian, 96 n. 7. Trajan's rescript, 100. To Scapula, 101 n. 2, 102 n. 4, 122 and n. 2. The legio fulminea, 117. Arrius Antoninus, 119 nn. 1, 2. Proculus, 119 n. 6. Septimius Severus, 119, 120. Extortion of money in the persecutions, 121. Christians under Caracalla, 122. Universal religious rights, 175. The testimony of the soul, 177. Presbyters and bishops, 192. Summus Sacerdos, 195. Universal priestly right, 196. Lectores, 201. Synods, 206 and n. 1. Cathedra Petri, 213. The Lord's words to Peter, Montanism, 213 n. Assumption of Roman bishops, 214. Excommunication, 218. Penance, 219, 220. Church penance as satisfactio, 220. Cyprian's study of, 226, 227. Assumption of confessors, 229 n. 2. Baptism, as opus operatum, delay of, 252, 253, 646. Deficiencies of the church, 254. The Christian matron; mixed marriages, 255, 281-283, 325 n. 3. Payment of tribute by the Christians, 259. Crowning, 260 n. Fabrication of idols. 262. Gladiatorial shows, 263. Spectacles, 264, 265. Pleasures of the Christians, 266. Slavery and Christian freedom, 269. Hatred towards Christianity, 269 n. 1. Civil and military service, 270, 271 n. 4, 272, 273. Following Christ in poverty, 274. Inconceivableness of the conversion of the emperors, 272 n. 1. Life of Christians in the world, 273. Philosopher's cloak, 275. Hypocritical asceticism, 277 n. 3. Christian marriage, 281, 286. Dress of women, 282. Consecration of marriage by the church, 284. Prayer, 284-288. Family devotion, 286. Worship not confined to place, 289. Images, 292. Stated festivals, 294. Observance of Sunday, 295, 296, 301 n. 1. Stationes, 296 n. 2. Fasting on the Sabbath, 296 n. 5, 297. Pentecost, 301 n. 1. Symbolum, 306 n. 4. Pompa diaboli, 309 n. 1. Infant baptism, 312, 315, 615. Anointing, 315.

GENERAL INDEX. 219

Baptism and confirmation, 316 and n. 1. Milk and honey, 317 n. 1. Baptism of heretics, 318. Agapæ, 325, 326. Publicity of Christian assemblies, 327. Catechumens and believers among the heretics, 328. Exclusion of unbelievers from certain parts of the service, 328. The fourth petition, daily communion, 332. Veneration of martyrs. 335. Ebion, 344. Gnostic Bible interpretation, 388. Ptolemæus, 437. Simon Magus, 454 n. 1. Marcion, 461 n. 1, 462, 463 n. 3, 465, 469 n. 2. Apelles, 474, 475. Caianians, 476 n. 1. Baptism by substitution, 478 n. 3. Resemblances of Christianity in the old religion, 479 n. 1. Prophetic ecstasy, 511 n., 520. The Paraclete, progressive development of the church, 516. The new revelations, 517. The church of the spirit and that of the bishops, 517, 518. Forgiveness of sin, and sanctification, 522. Absolution through confessors, 523. Against the enemies of Montanism, 525. Philosophy, 536. Inborn consciousness of God, 558–560. The real apprehended as corporeal, 560. Anger of God, Anthropopathism, graduated progress in revelation, 561, 562. 563. Against Hermogenes, art, second marriage, 565 n. 3. Creation, 568. Monarchians, 578, 582 n. 3. Praxeas, 583, 584. Trinity, 605. Anthropology, 614–620. Traducianism, infant baptism, 615, 626. On Docetism, Christ without comeliness, realism, 631. Humanity of Christ, 635. Baptism, 646. Satisfactio, 647 n. 1. Lord's Supper, 648. Chiliasm, 651 nn. 4, 5. Intermediate state, 654. Irenæus, 677, 678 n. 2. Inspiration, 679, 680 n. 2. Blastus, 680.
Seculo obstricti, ii. 169 n. 7. Saturnalia, 347 n. 2. Kalendæ Januariæ, 350. Brethren of Jesus, 376. Compared with Augustin, 394. Anthropology, 617, 670. Tertullian and Origen, 384, 561. Ratherius of Verona compared with, iii. 469.

Citations from his writings: —
Ad martyres, c. 1, i. 229 n. 2. *Ad Nationes,* 1. i. c. 5, apostates, i. 218 n.; morals of Christians, 254 n.; c. 18, the pagans on Christian heroism, 77 n. 1. *Ad Scapulam,* c. 2, on religious freedom, i. 175 n.; c. 4, the persecutions, 84 n. 2, 116 n. 1, 119 n. 6, 122 and n. 2; c. 5, 102 n. 4, 119 n. 1. *Ad Uxorem,* l. i. c. 7, ordination of deaconesses, ii. 130 n. 1. L. ii. c. 4, disadvantages of a mixed marriage, i. 255 n. 2, 385 n. 3; c. 5, 382 n. 3; c. 8, happiness of a marriage between Christians, 255 n. 3, 281 n. 4, 284 n. 2. *Adv. Hermogenem,* c. 15, II. on the origin of evil, 563 n. 1; c. 36, matter and soul, 617 n. 2. *Adv. Judæos,* c. 7, Britain, 85 n. 6; (c. 9, the three magi, ii 344 n. 1). *Adv. Praxeam,* relation of the Son to the Father, 605 n. 4; c. 1, P. in Carthage, 583 n. 3; c. 3. Monarchianism, 576 n. 3; c. 7, materialism, 560 n. 2; c. 10, 14, 26, 27, Logos doctrine of Praxeas, 584 nn 1, 2; c. 12, man as image of Christ, 641 n. 4. *Adv. Valentinianos,* c. 4, Ptolemæus, 437 n. 3; c.
5, Irenæus, 678 n. 2. *Apologeticus,* c. 1, ch. in N. Africa, i. 84, n. 1; c. 3, 269 n. 1; c. 5, Tiberius, 93 n. 2; Domitian, 96 n. 7; M. Aurelius, 116 n. 1; c. 7, 327 n. 2; c. 17, the Sibyl, 177 n. 6; c. 21, 93 n. 2; impossibility of the emperors becoming Christians, 272 n. 1; emanation of the Logos, 684 n. 2; c. 34, honor to the emperor, 90 n. 4; c. 39, Christian love, 75 n. 3; seniores, 192 n. 2; agapæ, 325 n. 4; c. 42, Christian honesty, 259 n. 2; Christian appropriation of the world, 273 n. 5. *Contra Marcionem,* l. i. c. 2, 684 n. 2; c. 5, 467 n. 2; cc. 7-15, 469 n. 1; c. 10, testimony of God in creation, 559 n. 5; c. 11, God first manifested in Christ, according to Marcion, 469 n. 3; c. 14, anointing in baptism, 315 n. 2; milk and honey, 317 n. 1; cc. 18, 19, witness of God in nature, 559 n. 5; c. 19, 469 n. 2, 559 n. 5; c. 20, progressive development of Paul, 680 n. 1; c. 28, M. on punishment, 472 n. 1; c. 34, M. on asceticism, 473 n. 1. L. ii. cc. 12, 13, T. on justice in God, 561 n. 2; cc. 16, 27, image of God, anthropopathism, 562 nn. 1-3; c. 29, relation of justice and love, in God, 562 n. 4. L. iii. c. 3, M. on Christ's self-manifestation, 470 n. 4; cc. 3, 4, 24, on the resurrection 471 n. 2; c. 15, on the Messiah. 470 n. 1; c. 24, rewards of the Demiurge, 468 n. 1, 471 n. 2. L. iv., Marcion, 462 n. 1: cc. 2, 3, his rejection of the gospels, 473 n. 4; c. 5, his ecclesiæ, 474 n. 2; cc. 9, 36, his conflicts, 465 n. 1; M. on Christ's miracles, 470 n. 3; c. 10, T. on Marcion's doctrine of God's forgiveness, 561 n. 1; c. 17, M. on the beginning of the gospel, 469 n. 3; c. 22, T. on ecstasy, 519 n. 2; c. 29, M. on the resurrection, 471 n. 2; c. 35, on the miracles of Christ, 470 n. 3; c. 36, 465 n. 1; c. 40, T. on the Lord's Supper, 648 n. 2. L. v. c. 1, symbolum, 306 n. 4; c. 10, baptism for the dead. 478 n. 3. *De anima,* c. 9, ecstatic visions, 520 n. 4; cc. 10, 19, traducianism, 615 n. 3; c. 11, Hermogenes on the origin of the soul, 617 n. 1; c. 12, dichotomy of T., 635 n. 6; c. 16, 618 n. 4; c. 19, 615 n. 3; c. 21. freewill, 617 n. 4; grace, 619 n. 1; c. 22, divination and prophecy, 616 n. 3, 618 n. 3; c. 41, the godlike not extinguished in the soul, 616 n. 2; effects of baptism, 649 n. 2; c. 47, conversion through visions, 75 n 2; c. 55, descent into Hades, 654 n. 2; c. 56, paradise, 523 n. 2; c. 58, intermediate state, 654 n. 3. *De baptismo,* c. 7, anointing, 315 n. 2; c. 8, imposition of hands, 316 n. 1; c. 15, validity, 318 n. 2; c. 17, " Summus Sacerdos," 195 n.; c. 18, denay of baptism, infant baptism, 312 n. 2, 615 n. 6; sponsors, 315 n. 1. *De carne Christi,* c. 5, 631 n. 2; c. 6, 641 n. 4; c. 9, 631 n. 5; c. 11 *et seq.,* 500 n. 2, 635 n. 7; c. 14. 631 n. 3. *De corona militis,* c. 2, 273 n. 1; c. 3, sign of the cross, 293 n. 5; answer at baptism, etc., 308 n. 5, 309 n. 1, 317 n. 1; offerings for the dead, 334 n. 2; church regulations, may be changed, 517 n. 3; c. 11, the believing soldier, 270 n. 2; c. 13, freedom in Christ, 269 n. 2. *De cultu fæminarum,* l. ii. c. 9, ναρθενοι, 275 n. 1; c. 11, dress, 282 n 1. *De exhortatione castitatis,* second marriage, 522 n. 3; c 5, inspiration of Paul, 680 n. 2; c. 11, prayer for the dead, 334 n. 2. *De fuga in persecutione,* 521 n. 2; c. 12, 121 n. 2, 123 n. 1; c. 13, 121 n. 4, 121 n. 6. *De idololatria,* c. 6, 262 n. 6; c. 11, 262 n. 1; c. 14, 277 n. 3, 301 n. 1; c. 15, 91 n. 3, 259 n. 2; c. 18, 271 n. 2, 272 n. 3; c. 19, 273 n. 2. *De jejuniis,* c. 11, 525 n. 2; c. 13, provincial synods in Greece, 200 n. 1; charity united with fasting, 256 n. 1; fasts of the Montanists, 280 n. 3, 521 n. 3; c. 14, 294 n. 2; Statio, 296 n 2; c. 17, the agapæ. 326 n 2. *De monogamia,* c. 1, 522 n. 3; Christian priesthood, 519 n. 1; c. 12, the same, 197 n. 1; c. 20, sanction of the ch. in marriage, 522 n. 2. *De oratione,* c. 6, the Lord's Supper, 648 n.

2; c. 19, taken home, 332 n. 3; c. 21, prayer for the guest, 287 n. 1; c. 23, Sunday, 296 n. 1, 301 n. 1; fasting on the Sabbath, 297 n. 1; c. 24, place of prayer, 289 n. 4; c. 25, seasons of prayer, 286 n. 6; c. 28 (Muratori Anecdota bibl. Ambros., t. 3), spiritual sacrifice, 284 n. 3. *De pallio*, 275 n. 7. *De patientia*, 616 n. 1; c. 1, grace, 619 n. 2. *De Pœnitentia*, c. 5, 220 n. 6; c. 6, delay of repentance, baptism, 252 n., 306 n. 4; c. 9, acts of penitence, 219 nn. 1, 2, 220 n. 1; c. 10, 219 n. 3. *De pudicitia*, c. 1, episcopus episcoporum, 214 n. 3; c. 4, sanction of the church in marriage, 522 n. 2; cc. 7, 10, images, 292 n. 3; c. 12, the new revelations, 517 n. 1; c. 19, mortal sins, 221 n.; validity of baptism, 318 n. 1; on 1 John, 1; 7, 523 n 1; c. 21, the church of the Spirit, 517 n. 4; 518 nn. 1, 2; c. 22, libelli pacis, 229 n. 2, 523 n. 4. *De resurrectione carnis*, c. 2, 474 n. 5; c. 8, sacraments, 315 n. 2, 316 n. 1, 648 n. 2; c. 48, 308 n. 5; baptism for the dead, 478 n. 3. *De spertaculis*, 265 n. 5; c. 1, 265 n. 3; c. 2, 72 n. 1; c. 15, 264 nn. 2, 3; c. 19, 263 n. 3; c. 24, 264 n. 1; c. 26, 265 nn. 1, 2 *De testimonio animæ*, 559 n 3; c 1, 177 n. 7. *De virginibus velandis*, the Roman bishops, 214 n. 4; Paraclete, 517 n. 2; c. 1, progressive development of the church, 516 n. 1; c. 9, deaconesses, 188 n. 2. *Præscriptio hæreticorum*, 684 n. 2; c. 19, 582 n. 1; c. 30, Marcion, 462 n. 1, 463 n. 3, 465 n. 4; Apelles, 463 n. 3, 474 n. 6; c. 41, 201 n. 1, 328 n 1, 478 n. 1; (ii. 169 n. 7); addit., 463 n. 3; addit., c. 53, Theodotus, 580 n. 6.

Tertullianists, i. 685.
Tertullus, præfect. urb., ii. 35.
Τεσσαρακοστή. See Quadragesima.
Τεσσαρεσκαιδεκατιται, ii. 338 n. 2.
Tesserants, iv. 565.
Testament of the twelve patriarchs, test. iii. (Levi), c. 8, i. 194 n. T. iv. (Jud.), c. 21, 365 n. 1; c. 23, 348 n. 5. T. vii. (Dan), c. 5, 348 n. 5, 352 n. 3.
Testament of Ulphilas, ii. 472 n.
Τετραδιται, ii. 338 n. 2, 764 n. 3.
Tetrarchy, i. 154.
Tetras, ii. 333 nn. 1, 2.
Teuffel, Dr.
De Juliano imperatore (Tubingæ, 1844), ii. 32 n. 3, 43 n. 2.
Teveste, i. 146.
Text, the, iv. 316. Roman arrangement of texts, iii. 126.
Teyn church, at Prague, v. 192.
Thaddeus, one of the seventy disciples, i. 80.
Thaddeus de Suessa, statesman, iv. 184.
Thalassius, bp of Cæsarea, ii. 569.
Thamurgade, ii. 238.
Thanet, island of, iii. 12.
Thangbrand, priest from Bremen, iii. 296. Goes to Iceland, 302, 303.
Thanksgiving, ii. 333, 337, 367.
Theatre, the, i. 264–267, 278; ii. 275, 336. Julian on the, ii. 64, 65, 82.
Thebais, ii. 252. Persecution in, i. 83; ii. 264. Nestorius and the prefect of, ii. 552, 553. Thebes, ii. 272.
Θεῖος παιδαγωγός, i. 541.
Theism, i. 3, 4, 35, 40, 58. And the doctrine of the Trinity, 571, 572. Development of, 587 n. 3. With Julian, ii.

49. Scotus, iii. 462. In conflict with pantheistic monism, iv. 444, 445.
Themistius, deacon at Alexandria, ii. 613.
Themistius, rhetorician, ii. 35, 88, 89, 91, 117, 158.

Citations: —
Ad Valentem. (ed. Harduin, f. 99, c. ed. Dindorf, p. 118), ii. 88 n. Orat. ad Valentem. (Socrat., iv. 32, Soz., vi. 36), 91 n. 4. De pace (f. 157), 159 n. 1 (f. 160), 151 n. 2. Orat. 6, de religionibus, 91 n. 4. Or. 15, τίς ἡ βασιλικωτάτη τῶν ἀρετῶν, i. 116 n. 4.

Theobald, count of Champagne, iv. 236, 245, 255, 374, 383.
Theobald, historian, v. 243 n. 2.
Theocracy, theism and the, i. 3, 35, 572. The Jewish, 35–38, 66, 574. Made outward, episcopal, 209, 235. Relation of Christianity to the, 339. Ebionites, 348. The prophets, 358. In Gnosticism, 379, 396. Relation of the doctrine of the trinity to the, 572. Development of the external, ii. 162, 163, 166, 172, 178, 200. The papal, iii. 68, 120, 121, 346, 380, 580. Its relation to the rude nations, iii. 2, 50, 68, 92, 96. Reaction against, iii. 60, 243, 292, 586; see Papacy, Popes, Roman church. Contest with the secular power, iv. 82–194; v. 5–10. Two parties, iv. 135. Bible reading and the, iv. 321. Dependence on the, iv. 509, 514, 515. Reactions of the Christian spirit against the, 446, 592, 605, 614; v. 21, 134. Efforts to purify the, v. 78. See Reform, Sects.
Theocritus, count, ii. 591 n.
Theoctista, mother of the empress Theodora, iii. 547.
Theoctistus, bp. of Cæsarea, i. 703.
Theoctistus, guardian of Michael III., iii. 547.
Theodelinde, Longobardian queen, goes over to the Catholic church, iii. 117.
Theodemir, abbot of Psalmody, iii. 433, 434, 437. Letter to Claudius, 434, 435. Apology to Claudius, 438. See Bibl. Patr. Lugd., Claudius of Turin.
Theodo I., duke of Bavaria, iii. 39.
Theodo II., duke of Bavaria, iii. 40.
Theodora, Greek empress, iii. 308, 547. Reintroduces image worship, 548, 549. Ignatius, 558. Paulicians, 587.
Theodora, mother of Thomas Aquinas, iv. 422.
Theodora, vicious Roman woman, iii. 366.
Theodora, wife of Justinian, ii. 592–595, 598, 599, 609.
Theodore (Κρόθνος), iii. 550.
Theodore (studita), abbot of Studion, character and education, iii. 536 and nn., 605. Against the holding of slaves, 100. The image controversies, compared with others, 198. Images as sponsors, 201 n. 2. On the œcumenical council under Irene, 228 n. 3. The court policy, 232 n. 1. Against bloody

persecutions of heretics, 255, 605. Number of the saved, 42. Contents for image worship, 533 n. 2, 534 u. 3, 536-545. His tendency to sensuous realism, 539. Biography, 535 n. 1. See Sirmond, opp. t. v.

Citations: —
Antirrheticus against the iconoclasts, iii. 213 n. 5. Antirrhet. i. f. 75 539 nn. 2, 3; f. 76, 534 n. 3. Antirrhet. ii. f. 84, 583 n. 2; f. 88, 534 n. 3. Antirrhet. iii. f. 108, 540 nn. 1, 2; f. 123, 540 nn. 3, 4.
Epistles, 1. i., his contests with the emperors, iii. 536 n. 2. L. i. ep. 10, slavery, 100 n. 3; ep. 17, images as sponsors, 291 n. 2; ep. 38, on the V. œc. conc Const., 225 n 3. L. ii. ep. 2, to the monks, 537 n. 1, 538 n. 2; ep. 14, spies sent out against image worshippers, 543 nn. 4, 5; f. 318, school books prepared by the iconoclasts, 543 n. 6; ep. 16, f. 320, to the patriarch of Antioch, 543 n. 7; ep. 18, to Nicephorus, 540 n. 5; ep. 21, on the Monotheletic controversies, 198 n 1; ep. 39, on falsehood, 541 n. 5; ep. 40, οἰκονομία, 541 n. 4: ep. 55, to a layman under persecution, 542 n. 1; ep. 71, 542 n. 1; ep. 87, προσκύνησις, 545 n. 7; ep. 94, his sufferings, 543 n. 1; ep. 124, 544 n., 545 n. 1; ep. 151. 545 nn. 6, 7; ep. 155, to Theophilus, treatment of heretics, 255 nn. 3-5; epp. 161, 171, on the use of images, 545 n 1. 4, 7; ep. 215, f. 583, 541 n. 3.
Life of Plato (Acta S. April, t. i. app.), iii. 100 nn. 1, 2, 4, 223 n. 3, 224 n 1, 230 n. 1.
Opp., f. 136, inscription of Stephen, iii. 212 n. 4.
Will of Theodore, iii. 100 n. 4.

Theodore, abp. of Canterbury, his origin, iii. 25. Promotes customs of the Romish church in England, 25. First exercises the rights of a primate, 25. Slavery, 99 n. 3. Suicides, 102 n. 4. Penance, 137. Promotes culture in England, 152, 467. See Acta S. (O. B.), S. ii.
Capitula, c. 8, slaves held by monks, iii 99 n. 3; c. 63, on suicides, 102 n. 4.

Theodore, bp. of Caria, ii. 570 n. 2.
Theodore, bp. of Mopsuestia, ii. 389. The forbidden fruit, 127 n. 3. On zeal for orthodoxy, 259. Exegesis, inspiration, Old and New Testaments, 389, 390, 392, 393. Holy Spirit, 470, 471. Person of Christ, 493-502, 505, 506, 545, 656. Agnoëtism, 496, 613. Creed of, 506 n. 3. Controversy relating to Theodore, 555-557. In the Eutychian controversy, 562. Influence among the Nestorians, 610, 611. Compare controversy concerning the three chapters. Philoponus, 613 n. 3. Anthropology, 653, 712-718 (493, 494). Baptism, 727, 728, 729. Apocatastasis, 738, 739. Influence on Adoptianism, iii. 158, 159, 162, 163, 430 n. 3. Sinlessness of Christ, iv. 495.

Citations: —
Address to Neophytes (Act. Concil. œcumen. V., Collat., iv. c. 36), baptism, ii 728 nn. 1-3. Confession, 470. Comm. in Gen. (see Catena Nicepb.), the forbidden fruit, 127 n. 3. Fragm. in Gen. (see John Philoponus), 494 n. 1. Comm. on the Minor prophets ed. Wegner), f. 501, application of passages from O. T. by the apostles, 393 n. 4; ff. 513, 539,

393 nn. 5, 6; f. 612, prophetic sense of Scripture, 393 n. 1; on Joel, f. 156, 393 n. 2; on Micah, f. 354, 393 n. 3 on Nahum, c. 1, f. 297, ecstasy, 390 nn. 1, 2. Comm. on the Gospels (see Asseman, . iii.), 738 nnd n. 6; on John (Catena Corderii), 390 n. 4 (738 n. 6). Comm. in ep. Rom. fragm. (Mail, Spicileg., t. iv. p. 525), the Holy Spirit, 471 nn. 1, 2; pp. 504, 506, 516, 517, 528, 529, the fall and its effects, 716 nn., 717 nn. Contr. Julian, fragm. (see Münter), temptation of Christ, 494 n. 2. De incarnatione (see Leontius Byzant.), 496 n. 3. Against the system of Augustin (Phot. cod., 177), 712 n. 2. In Marins Mercator, ff. 97, 103, 712 n. 3; f. 100, two states of the creation, 493 n., 715 nn. 1, 2; Ex. 4, restoration, 738 n 6. See Concil. Oecum. V. and Harduin, t. iii.

Theodore, bp. of Pharan, head of the Monothelete party, iii 181, 182 n. 2.
Fragments of his writings (Hardnin concil, t iii. ff. 1343, 1344), iii. 18 nn., 182 n. 2.

Theodore, bp. of Rome, iii. 184.
Theodore, friend of Martin I., iii. 189. Epistle of Martin to, 186-189 nn.
Theodore, head of the Paulicians, iii. 249.
Theodore, merchant, iii. 213 n. 2.
Theodore, monk (ὁ γραπτός), iii. 547 n. 1.
Theodore, patriarch of Antioch, iii. 587.
Theodore, patriarch of Constantinople, iii. 193.
Theodore, presbyter, defender of the genuineness of the writings ascribed to Dionysius the Areopagite, iii. 170.
Theodore, protospatharius, iii. 571.
Theodore, singer, iii. 128.
Theodore Abukara, defender of Christianity against Mohammedanism, iii. 88.
'Ερωτήσεις καὶ ἀποκρίσεις, ff. 431, 432, iii. 88 nn. 1-3. See Bibl. patr. Paris, t. xi.

Theodore Ascidas, ii. 595-597, 598 n., 599.
Theodore Lascaris II., iv. 542, 543.
Theodoret, bp. of Cyros, his public buildings, ii. 169. His intercession at court, 175. His mother, 262. Representative of the Antiochian school, 394. In the Nestorian controversy, 523-525, 540, 545-554. On defence of Theodore, 557. Death of Cyril, 557 n. 7. In the Eutychian controversy, 559 and n. 2, 561-563, 569, 572, 574, 578, 581, 582. In the controversy of Three Chapters, 595-608. Helena, 7 n. 2. Marcus, 81 n. 1. Christianity not dependent on the favor of princes, 112 and n. 1. Offence felt by miseducated pagans at the Holy Scriptures, 116. Abdias, 133 n. 3. Letter of consolation during the Persian persecution, 135. Simeon Stylites, 143, 292, 293. Precedence of the Roman church, 199. Ambrose and Theodosius, 215 n. 1. Euchites, 276 n. 2, 278 n. 1. Anachorets, 286. Consecration of churches, 321. Veneration of martyrs, 372. Theodoret as representative of the Antiochian school, 394. Constantine and Arius, 428 n. 4. Constan-

tius, 436 n. 4. Holy Spirit, 471. Ἐρανιστής, 561 and n. 3. On the Lord's Supper, 732.
On Cerinthus, i. 396. Tatian's εὐαγγέλιον διὰ τεσσάρων, 458 n. 1. Τέλειοι among the Manicheans, 503 n. 1. Hermogenes, 567, 568 n. 1. Noetus, 584, 585. Malchion, 605 n. 1. Hippolytus, 683. The Marcionites, iii. 245.

Citations: —
Defence of Theodore (see Harduin, t. iii. f. 108), fragments, ii. 557 n. 6.
Dial. II. inconfus., elements in the Lord's Supper, ii. 364 n. 2.
Epistles, ep. ad Alex. Hierop. (opp., t iv p. 1346, ed. Halens.), ii. 540 nn. 1, 4. Ep. 16, ad Irenaeum, 562 n. 1. Ep. 21, on his deposition, 572 n. 6. Ep. 42, intercession, 175 n. 2. Ep. 50, on the condemnation of the doctrine of Nestorius, 545 nn. 2, 5. Ep. 59, on the deposition of N., 546 n. 1. Ep. 60, to Dioscurus, 561 n. 2. Ep. 73, the doctrine of Cyrill, 545 n. 1. Ep. 78, to the Persian bp. Eusebius. 135 nn. 2, 3. Ep. 79, his plea for a hearing, 563 n. 1. Ep. 81, his public works, 169 n. 6. Ep. 82, 561 n. 1, 563 n. 2. Ep. 83, to Dioscurus, confession of faith, 562 n. 2. Ep. 86, to Flavian, on Dioscurus, 559 n. 2, 562 n. 3. Ep. 92, 562 n. 4. Ep. 101, discontent of the monks, 561 n. 1. Ep. 102, to Nestorius, 546 n. 2. Ep. 103, 549 n. 2. Ep. 112, to Domnus of Antioch, 572 n. 2. Ep. 113, to Leo the Great, 199 nn. 3, 4, 562 n. 3, 574. Ep. 122, on οἰκονομία, 572 n. 6. Ep. 123, declining gifts, 572 n. 5. Ep. 124, 572 n. 6. Ep. 125, on his acceptance of the articles of agreement, 549 n. 1. Ep 128, Cyrill's confession, 545 n. 2. Ep. 129, 572 n. 6. Ep. 134, cruelty of his enemies, 572 n. 4. Ep 138, to Helladius, urging reconciliation of the churches, 549 n 3. Ep. 142, 571 n. 3. Ep. 146, desire for seclusion, 582 n. Ep. 147, 572 n. 1, 573 n. Ep. 148, to Nestorius, concerning Alex. Hieropol., 550 n. 1. Ep. 150, to John of Antioch, 523 n. 6, 550 n. 2. Ep. 151, circular letter, against the anathemas of Cyrill, 524 n. 1 (471). Ep. 163, report of the judge of the Secunda Euphratesia. 550 n. 3. Ep. 170, the oriental delegates to Rufus, 722 n. 1. Ep. 180, to John of Antioch, on the death of Cyrill, 557 n. 7.
Ἐρανιστής or πολύμορφος, against Eutychianism, ii. 561 n. 3.
Grac. affect. curat. (fragments of Porphyry, i. 171 n. 4). Disputat. i, f. 696 (t. iv.), pride of superficial knowledge, ii. 116 n. 1. Disput. viii., f 899, language of N. T., 116 n. 3; f. 902, relics, 370 n. 3, 371 n. 2: f 922, 371 n. 1. Disput. ix., f. 935, spread of Christianity, persecutions in Persia, 112 n. 1, 135 n. 1.
Haeret. fab. i. 14, Ophites, the serpent, i. 444 n. 4; 19, Hermogenes, 567 n. 4, 618 n. 2; 20, Tatian, 458 n. 1; 21, Severians. 458 n. 3. II. 3, Cerinth, 396 n. 2; 9, Sabellius, 600 n. 1. III. 3, Noetus, 584 n. 3. IV. 2, Euchites, ii. 278 n. 1; 10, Audians, ii. 767 n. 1.
Hist. eccles. (I. i. c. 4, Lucian the martyr, i. 722 n. 6); c. 5, Arius on his opponents, ii. 413 n. 1; c. 7, Eustathius of Antioch, 416 n. 4, 417 n. 3; c. 18, Helena the mother of Constantine, 7 n. 2. L. ii. c. 6, council of Sardica, proposed confession, 436 n. 2. L. iv. c. 9, Audius and the Audians, 766 n. 5, 767 n. 1; c. 10, the Euchites, 278 nn.; c. 12, 280 n. 4; c. 19, Byzantine court, 167 n. 6; c. 23, Mavia, 142 n. 5. L. v. c. 39, Abdas, 183 n. 3. C. iii. ed. Halens., t. iii f. 1146, sect in Syria, 276 n. 2.
Hist religios., t. iii. f. 1146, Manicheisn among monks, ii. 771 n. 1; ff. 1188, 1214, consecration in childhood, 280 n. 1; c. 3, Marcian, 291 n. 1; c. 13, intercession of Macedonius, 285 n.

4; cc. 25, 26 (f. 1274), Simeon Stylites, 143 n. 1, 293 n. 1; c. 28, self-torture, 292 n. 1.
Lector., l. ii. f. 564 (ed. Mogunt., 1679), Almundar, ii. 143 n. 4.
On Philip. 1: 18, ii. 767 n. 4.
Quaest. in Gen. 20, ii 714 n. 1.
Refutation of Cyrill (see Ep. 151).
Sermon after the death of Cyrill (see Harduin, t. iii.), ii. 557 n. 7. See Maii, Marius Mercator.

Theodore Studita. See Theodore, abbot of Studion.

Theodoric, companion of Militz, v. 180, 181.

Theodoric, converter of Lieflanders, iv. 37.

Theodoric, East Gothic king, ii. 593.

Theodoric, son of Clovis, iii. 93 n. 2.

Theodoric of Niem, v. 51, 52, 56, 67 n. 2, 72, 74, 75, 85, 89, 91, 105 n. 1.

Citations: —
De fatis Joh. XXIII. (see Van der Hardt., t. ii.), cc. 9, 10, f. 348, Boniface IX., v. 89 n.; f. 375, the owl, 91 n. 2; f. 387, John on the way to Constance, 101 n. 1; f. 391, at Constance, 105 n. 1.
De schismate, l. i. c. 10, Clement VII., v. 47 n.; c. 68, Boniface IX., 51 n. 4. 52 nn. 1, 2. L. ii. c. 6, 51 n. 1; c. 7, 52 n. 3; cc. 11, 13, 51 nn. 2, 3; c. 33, Benedict XIII., 56 nn. 2, 3, 67 n. 2. L. iii. cc. 6, 12, 13, Gregory XII., 72 nn. 2-4; c. 15, 75 n. 3; c. 17, 73 n. 2; c. 25, 75 n. 2; c. 36, 76 n. 3; c. 51, Alex. V., 85 n. 1.

Theodoric of Thuringia.
Life of Elizabeth of Hessia, l. ii. c. 5, iv. 302 n. 2. See Canisius.

Theodoric of Verdun.
Epistle. Gregory VII., iv. 99 n. 6. See Dieteric, Martene and Durand, thes. nov., t. v.

Theodorus, confessor, ii. 83.

Theodorus, disciple of Origen, i. 717 See Gregory Thaumaturgus.
Panegyr. in Originem, c. 15, i. 717 n.

Theodorus, Egyptian martyr, ii. 254 n.

Theodorus, high priest, ii. 54 n. 7.

Theodosius, bp. of Constantinople iv. 535.

Theodosius, bp. of Ephesus, iconoclast, iii. 214.

Theodosius, patriarch of Jerusalem, ii. 583, 584.

Theodosius I. (the Great). Roman emperor, his measures for the suppression of Paganism, ii. 94-99. The temple at Edessa, 95 n. 4. Laws against apostates, 119. Ulphilas, 157. Intercession of Flavian, 174. Ambrose, 214, 215, 604 (iv. 110). Fine against heretics, 235. Intercession of Macedonius, 285. Place in the church, 321 n. 6. Victory of the Homoousion, 461, 464. See Cod. Theodos. Epiphanius, Pacatus Drepanius.

Theodosius II., Roman emperor, ii. 133, 164, 177. In the Nestorian controversy, 518, 525-528, 539-541, 548, 551, 552, 556. In the Eutychian, 564-569. Chrysostom, 762.
Sacra, addressed to the I. conc. Ephes., ii 164 n. 4.

Theodota, iii. 536 n. 2.

Theodotus, the Monarchian, i. 580, 693.
Διδασκαλία ἀνατολική, i. 693 (opp. C.em. cd. Par., 1641), f. 794, Basilides, 404 n. 1; f. 796, D., 411 n. 3; f. 797, B. Valentine, 424 n. 3, 425 n. 1, 433 nn. 1, 2; f. 800, col. 2, D. exorcism, 477 n. 5; f. 806, Tatian, 457 n. 1.

Theodotus Cassiteras, patriarch of Constantinople, iii. 539–541.

Theodrad, iii. 273.

Theodulf, abp. of Orleans, zealously promotes the cause of religious instruction, iii. 125. On external works, 131. On pilgrimages, 132. Against private masses, 136. On the forgiveness of sins and penitence, 139 n. 7. Alcuin, 154 n. 3. Adoptianist controversy, 167. Doctrine of the Holy Spirit, 555. See Alcuin, epp. 119, 193.

Citations: —
Capitulare ad parochiæ sum sacerdotes C. 7, on private masses, iii. 136 n. 2. C. 28, parochial instruction, 125 n. 5. C. 30, on confession, 139 n. 7. C. 44, on preparation for communion, 136 n. 3.
Poem (on pilgrimages), iii. 132 n. 2.

Theodulus, ii. 67 n. 2.
Theognis, bp. of Nice, ii. 421, 422.
Theognist, abbot, iii. 565, 567.
Theognist, bp., ii. 774.
Theognostus, i. 713.
Theogonic process, in Gnosticism, i. 371. Origen, 588, 589.
Θεοί γενητοί, i. 25. Φανεροί and ἀφανεῖς, 25 n. 3. Νοητοί, αἰσθητοί, ii. 50.
Theologians, v. 61, 62, 64, 283, 382.
Theological definitions, bps. of Pamphylia on, ii. 584.
Theological discussions, ii. 431, 432 and n. 1; v. 382. See Controversies.
Theological education, culture, ii. 182–184; iii. 126, 142, 143, 150 and nn. 4, 7, 156, 411, 415, 425–428, 456–471; iv. 204, 413–416; v. 58, 60–62, 149, 235, 382. In the Greek church, iii. 169, 530, 531. In the Frankish church, in the ninth century, iii. 456–467. Effort to improve, iv. 414. Clemangis de Studio Theologico, v. 60–62. Compare Canonical life, Charlemagne, England, Ireland, Scholastics, Studies, Theological schools.
Theological schools, the Alexandrian, i. 306, 527–557; ii. 182. At Cæsarea, i. 721. Antiochian, ii. 182 (see Antiochian school). At Edessa, ii. 610, 611. *Third Period*, iii. 126. At Chartres, 470, 502. Tours, 470. Orleans, 593. See Alcuin, Clerus, Cloisters, Monasteries, Schools, Theological culture, Universities, etc.
Theologische Quartel Schrift.
1834, 1. ii., Dr. Möhler's Essay, Christianity and slavery, iii. 98 n. 3.
Theologische Studien und Kritiken. See Stud. u. Krit.
Theology, birth of Christian, i. 529, 540, 542. Varro on theology, i. 7, 86 n. 1. System of Porphyry, i. 171. Theology in the more limited sense of the term, i. 557–610; ii. 403–478; iv. 440–466.
Third and Fourth Periods, iii. 141–243, 456–586. Practical, iii. 456, 457, 460 (v. 61). Negative and positive (Ἀποφατική and καταφατική), iii. 461, 463.
Fifth Period, iv. 355–528. And philosophy, 355–361, 367, 401, 431, 435 (see Dialectics, Knowledge, Speculation); relative points of view confounded, 359, 474. Mystic, 411. Dialectic, its transition from the twelfth to the thirteenth century, 417. Character of among the scholastics of the thirteenth century, inquiries as to its essence, 427–440, 519. Central point of, 428. Relation to Ethics, 519, 520. Aquinas on, 431, 432, 519. Bacon, 425, 434, 435. Lull, 437, 438.
Sixth Period, v. 134–412. Clemangis on, 60–62. Parisian, 93. And philosophy, 135. Friends of God on, 381, 382. See Church theology, Creation, Doctrine concerning God, Holy Spirit, History of Doctrines.
Theonas, bp. of Alexandria, i. 143.
Ep. to the chamberlain Lucianus (D'Achery, Spicileg., f. 297, Bibl. Patr. Gallaud., t. 4), i. 143 n. 1.

Theonas, bp. of Marmarica, ii. 421.
Theopaschites, i. 579 n. 1; ii. 609.
Theophanes, Chronograph.
Justinian, ii. 106 n. 1. Tzitthus, 139 n. 2. An. 524, Abyssinia, 145 n. 1. Nestorius, 507 n. 2. Θεοτόκος, 508 n. 1. f. 68 (ed. Venet.), Chrysaphius, 596 n. 3. Recall of Pulcheria, 575 n. 2. Amantius, 591 n. 1. Vigilius at Const., 602 n. 3, 606 n. 2. Manicheans persecuted in Persia, 768 n. 2. John Talaya and Acacius, 587 n. 2.
F. 199, persecutions under Chosru Parviz, iii. 84 n. 2. The Saracens, 29 n. 1. Legends relating to images, 201 n. 3. ff. 289, 291–296 Constantine Copronymus, 220 n. 3, 221 nn. 4, 6, 222 nn., 223 n. 1. Paulus and Tarasius, 225 n., 226 n. f. 412, cd. Paris, the Paulicians under Nicephorus, 254 n. 4. f. 419, treatment of heretics, 256 n. 1. Continuat. ed. Venet., f. 347, Nicephorus, patriarch, and Leo the Armenian, 534 n. 1, 535 n. 1; f. 348, 538 n. 1.

Theophanes, jurist, iii. 550.
Theophanes, the singer, monk, iii. 547 n. 1.
Theophanies, i. 381, 386 n. 2, 584, 597, 598. Pausanias, Dionys. Halicarnass. on, i. 12. M. Aurelius on, i. 106. Scotus on, iii. 462, 463, 465. Almaric, iv. 445 n. 4. Epiphany as Theophany, ii. 346.
Theophilus, bp. of Alexandria, ii. 97, 181, 320 n. 1. In the Origenistic disputes, 748–763. In the Decretals, iii. 347.
Theophilus, bp. of Antioch, on revelation, i. 559. Apology and Commentaries, 674.
Ad Autolycum, i. 71 n. 2; 1 1 c. 2, 559 n. 2. See Methodius.

Theophilus, bp. of Cæsarea, iii. 347 n. 4.
Theophilus, bp. of Ephesus, iii. 255.
Theophilus, Gothic bishop, ii. 150.
Theophilus, Greek emperor, iii. 546, 547. History of, 547 n. 2.
Theophilus, layman, iii. 550.
Theophilus, patriarch of Constantinople, ii. 322 n. 2.
Theophilus, protospatharius, iii. 560.
Theophilus Indicus, i. 83; ii. 140, 142, 144.
Theophrastus, i. 581.
Theophylact, iii. 375, 376. See Benedict IX.
Theophylact, abp. of Achrida, iii. 584–586; iv. 530.
 Life of Clement, iii. 315 n. 1. Tract in defence of the Latins (see Mingarelli), 584 n. 1, 586 n. 3; §§ 5, 6, 586 n. 1; § 9, f. 273, 585 n. 2; § 14, 586 n. 1.

Theophylactus Simocatta, stories about images, iii. 201 n. 3.
Theoretical and practical, in the charismata, i. 181. Opposition of, 367. Maximus, iii. 174. See Practical.
Θεός γενητός, i. 380 n. 2. See Θεοί.
Θεοσεβείς, ii. 768 n. 1.
Theosophic asceticism, i. 458. Idealism, 460. Theosophic schools, 208, 389. Sects, iii. 267, 590. Tendencies, i. 714; iv. 552, 559. See Oriental spirit.
Theosophists, i. 425 n. 3. Jewish, and Gnosticism, i. 381.
Theosophy, of the Jews, i. 381, 394 (ii. 767 n. 1). Pharisees, 40. Essenes, 44, 45, 47, 64. Carried over into Christianity, 64 (iv. 552). Platonic, 170. Gnostic, 389, 393, 434. See Oriental spirit, Theosophic.
Theostericf, monk.
 Life of Nicetas (Acta S. Apr., vol. i. app.), f. 23, iii. 535 n. 1; § 27, 545 n. 2; §§ 28, 29, 214 nn. 1, 2; § 40, 541 n. 1.

Theotecnus, bp. of Cæsarea, i. 141.
Theotmar, abp. of Salzburg.
 Complaint to John IX. (Harduin, t. vi. p. i. f. 126), iii. 319 n. 3, 321 n. 4.

Theotokos. See Mary.
Theramenes, ii. 89.
Therapeutæ, i. 59–62; ii. 263. Relation to Christianity, i. 64.
Thesaurus, Hist. Helvet. See Winterthur.
Thesaurus meritorum supererogationis, iv. 349; v. 41, 171, 284.
Thesaurus nov. anecdotor. See Martene and Durand.
Thesmophoria, ii. 376.
Thessalonica. Eustathias in, iv. 530, 531 nn. 1, 3, 532. Bps. of, ii. 152, 155, 204, 377 n. 1, 652.
I. Thessalonians.
 4:11, iv. 283. 4:13, iv. 250. 5:14, ii. 135. 5:17, i. 285. 5:21, ii. 602, iv. 255.

II. Thessalonians.
 2. v. 230. 2:3, iv. 202 n. 6; v. 199. 2:6, iv. 619. 2:9, v. 198. 3:8, iii. 77. 3:10, ii. 205

Thessaly, ii. 547.
Theurgy, ii. 39, 388.
Thibaritans, church of the, i. 136.
Thibault II., iv. 300.
Thief on the cross, ii. 690.
Thierri II., king of the Burgundians, iii. 33, 39 n. 2.
Thiersch. See Studien u. Kritiken, 1842.
Thietberga, wife of Lothaire of Lotharingia, iii. 353, 354, 357, 450.
Thietgaud, abp. of Triers, iii. 354.
Thile, ultima, iii. 300 n. 1.
Thilo.
 Cod. apocryph. Nov. Test., t. i., Marcion's gospel, i. 473 n. 5. Conversation between Christ and John, iii. 591 n. 1; f. 885, iv. 553 n. 5; f. 893, iii. 595 nn. 1, 2; f. 894, iii. 597 n. 2.

Thiven. See Councils, an. 536.
Thmuis, ii. 430.
Thoco. See Wm. of.
Thomas, bp. of Claudiopolis, enemy of image worship, iii. 205 n. 1, 206.
Thomas, bp. of Neo-Cæsarea, inquisitor over the Paulicians, iii. 256.
Thomas, ecclesinstic, iii. 575.
Thomas, monk, pretended Syncellus, iii. 228.
Thomas, the apostle, in Parthia, i. 80 n. 3. In India, i. 82. Confession of, iv. 375; v. 238.
Thomas à Becket, iv. 168 n. 2, 169–172. Lives of, letters, 169 n. 3. Life by Heribert, pp. 33, 75, 170 nn.
 Ep. to Henry II. (John of Salisbury, ep. 49), iv. 168 n. 2.

Thomas Aquinas, life and character of, iv. 280, 421–423. Writings, 422, 423. 519. Defence of the mendicant orders, 286–288. Preaches in Italian, 317. The immaculate conception, 332. Sacraments, 335 n. 3, 514 n. 5. Transubstantiation, 338, 339. The Lord's Supper under one form, 344 nn. 1–3. Indulgences, 350 and n. 1. On revelation, faith, nature of theology, 429–432. Knowledge of God, 444. Aristotle de Causis, 445. Almaric and David of Dinanto, 447. Against pantheism, 449. Against Averrhoës, 449, 450 and n. 1. Omnipresence of God, 452. Omnipotence, 456. Trinity, 463–465. Doctrine of creation, 466. Doctrine of miracles, 471–473. Foreknowledge and predestination, 477–481, 491 nn. 7, 8. Man's original state, 491 and nn. 7, 8, 492. Original sin, 495. Doctrine of atonement, 506. Incarnation and original plan of God, 508. Faith, 511, 512. Justification, 512, 513. Uncertainty with regard to the state of grace, 513, 514. Freedom and grace, 518, 519 and n. 1. Doctrine of morals, cardinal virtues, 519–528. Adiaphora, 524. Consilia and præcepta, 525, 526. Magnanimity and humility, 526, 527. The intention and the execution, 528. The everlasting gospel, 619 n. 1. Image worship, v. 233. Life of (Acta S. Mar.), 422 n. 1; c. iv. 450 n. 1; c. viii. § 48, 317 n. 8.

Citations from his writings:—
Comm. on " De Causis " (opp., Paris, 1660, t. 4), iv. 445 n. 1, 480.
Contra gentes, iv. 422, l. iii. c. 99, miracles and providence, 473 n. 1.
Contra impugnantes religionem, opusc. xvi. (ed. Venet., t. xix. f. 341 *et seq.*), defence of the mendicant orders, iv. 287 n. 2; f. 410, 288 n. 2; f. 411, 288 nn. 4–6; f. 415, the Everlasting Gospel, 619 n. 1.
De unitate intellectus, contra Averroistas, opusc. ix. (ed. Venet., t. xix), iv. 449 n. 3, 450 and n. 3.
In Sententias (ed. Venet., tt. ix., x.). L. i. Dist. 17, Q. 1, art. 4, assurance, iv. 513 n. 2; D. 25, Q. 1, art. 1, predestination, 481 nn. 1–3; art. 3, 481 nn. 4, 5; D. 38, Q. 1, art. 1, origin of evil, 480 n. 1; D. 42, Q. 2, art. 2, miracles, 472 nn. 3, 4. L. ii. D. 17, Q. 1, art. 1, David of Dinanto, 446 n. 1; Q. 2, art. 1, against the Averrhoists, 450 n. 2; D. 18, Q. 1, art. 3, two conceptions of the miraculous, 472 nn. 6–7; D. 29, Q. 1, art. 2, original condition, 492 nn. 1, 4–8. L. iii. D. 20, Q. 1, art. 3, atonement, 506 n. 2.
Summa theologiæ, on the miracle, iv. 473. L. i. P. i. Q. 3, art. 8, Almaric and David of Dinanto, 447 n. 2; Q. 8, art. 1 and 2, Omnipresence of God, 452 nn. 9, 10; Q. 14, art. 5, knowledge in God, 480 n. 2; Q. 23, art. 5 predestination, 479 n. 2; Q. 46, art. 2, creation, 466 n. 1; Q. 47, art. 1, manifoldness of the universe, 479 nn. 3–5; Q. 48, art. 2, evil and good, 479 nn. 6–8; Q. 95, art. 1, grace, 492 n. 2; Q. 105, art. 6, miracles, 471 n. 7, 472 n. 1; art 8, 472 n. 2; P. ii. Q. 112, art. 5 (t. xxi. f. 633), assurance, 514 nn. 1–4. L. ii. P. ii. Q. 1, art. 4, will and faith, 5–1 n. 7; P. (or I.), iii. Q. 1, art. 3, effect of sin, 508 n. 3. Supplement to P. iii. Q. 13, art. 1, merits of saints, 349 n, 1.
On the immaculate conception, iv. 333 nn. 1–3. Relation of the sacraments to Christian life, 335 n. 3.

Thomas de Celano.
Life of Francis of Assisi, iv. 60 n. 2.

Thomas of Cantipre, his experience as a mendicant, iv. 277.

Citations:—
Bonum universale, de Apibus, c. 1, f. 6, Mauritius, iv. 211 n. 5; l. i. c. 1, f. 120, Do to of Friesland, 278 n. 3; l. i. c. 5, f. 23, Catharists, 582 n. 4; c. 9, f. 39, 279 n. 5. L. ii. c. 3, § 14, children's crusade, 342 n. 5; c. 10, mendicants, 277 nn.; Rainer, 326 nn. 1, 2; c. 10, f. 171, mendicants, 281 n. 1; c. 10, § 21, f. 174, death of Innocent IV., 282 n. 3; the mendicants and the princes, 282 n. 4; f. 281, secular clergy as teachers, 281 n. 2; c. 16 (Duaci, 1627, f. 215), Hugo of St. Victor, 401 n. 2; c. 28, § 7, piety in children, 343 n. 1; c. 48, Simon of Tournay, 418 n. 4; c. 57, § 63, Louis IX., 285 n. 7; § 64, f. 585, Wm. de St. Amour, 285 n. 5.

Thomas of Stitney, v. 245 n. 5.
Thomists, v. 172.
Thondracians (sect), iii. 588. Their doctrines, 589.
Thor, iii. 51, 295, 299.
Thorault, monastery, iii. 277, 278. The boy of, iv. 343.

Thorgeir, priest in Iceland, iii. 304, 305.
Thormod, iii. 303.
Thorwald, Icelander, iii. 300–302.
Thorwald Spakbödvarsson, iii. 301.
Thoth, interpolated sayings of, i. 176.
Thought, laws of, despised, i. 387.
Thought and being, correspondence of, v. 166.
Thoughts, evil, Anselm and Bernard on, iv. 240, 241. See Temptation.
Thrace, Aurelian in, i. 142. Metropolitans of, relation to the bp. of Constantinople, ii. 197, 203. Christmas, ii. 345. Collyridianians in, ii. 376. Synod in, ii. 435. Liberius in, ii. 443. Maximus. iii. 192. Polychronius, iii. 195. Paulicians in, iii. 250 n. 2, 587; iv. 564. Œcumenius, iii. 531. Bisanthe, iii. 563, n. 4.
Thrand, islander, iii. 307.
Thrand, Norwegian province, iii. 298.
Three Chapters, controversy concerning the, ii. 595–608, 764; iii. 34, 176 n. 1.
Threida (Thoreida), iv. 37, 40.
Θρόνος. See Cathedra.
Thrudpert, missionary, iii. 37. See Acta S. Apr.
Thule, ultima, iii. 300 n. 1.
Thundering legion, the, i. 115–117.
Thurgot, English ecclesiastic, iii. 292.
Thurificati, ii. 223.
Thuringia, iii. 37, 66. Boniface in, 47, 50, 72. Erroneous teachers there, 49 n. 1. Destruction of the Thuringian empire, 50 n. 1. Berthold in, iv. 318. See Theodoric of.
Ουρωροί, i. 201.
Thursday of the Great Week, ii. 341.
Thyana, ii. 462. See Anthimus of.
Thyra, Harold Blaatand's mother, iii. 288.
Tiber, iv. 140, 162.
Tiberianus, prefect, i. 100 n. 4.
Tiberius, law against proselytism, i. 89. Attitude towards Christianity, 93.
Tichonius, Donatist grammarian, ii. 244, 245, 247 n. 3.
Hermeneutic rules of, ii. 244 nn. 2, 5, 6.
Ticinum (Pavia), ii. 192 n. 2; iii. 28 n. 3. See Epiphanius.
Tieck, " Der Schützgeist," v. 390 n. 1.
Tiem, Wenzel, v. 321.
Tiflis, iv. 49.
Tillemont.
On Nestorius, ii. 512 n. 1. Cassian, 688 n. 6. Mémoires, t. 14, life of Cyrill (note 80), on Theodoret's letter, 557 n. 7.
Timæus, of Plato, i. 380.
Time, in relation to God, iv. 451, 452. To freedom, iv. 475, 476, 481, 519. Time and space, Lull on, iv. 482 n. 2. Times and seasons, ii. 107.
Timocles, in Lucian's dialogue, i. 93 n. 1.
Timotheus.
De receptione hæreticorum (see Coleter, t. iii.), Euchite sects, ii. 277 n. 3; § 2, 278 n. 1; § 4, 279 n. 2; § 6, 280 n. 1; § 9, 278 n. 2.

Timotheus, Nestorian patriarch in Syria, iii. 89.
Timotheus, patriarch of Constantinople, ii. 590.
Timotheus Ailurus, patriarch of Alexandria, ii. 584–586.
Timotheus Salophaciolus, patriarch of Alexandria, ii. 585–587.
Timothy, iv. 136. Genuineness of II. ep. to, i. 85.

I. Timothy 1 : 7, iv. 587. 1 : 13, ii. 705. 2 : 1, i. 272. 2 : 4, iii. 482, 483. 2 : 5, ii. 386. 2 : 8, ii. 316 ; iii. 438. 2 : 15, ii. 306. 3 : 1, i. 184. 3 : 2, i. 197 ; ii. 182. 3 : 8, i. 184. 3 : 12, ii. 182. 3 : 16, ii. 494 n. 3, 498 n. 5. 4 : 3, ii. 306. 4 : 8, iv. 241, 262, 314. 5 : 14, ii. 306. 5 : 17, i. 188, 326 n. 1; iii. 124. 5 : 23, iii. 147 ; iv. 250. 6 : 8, iii. 306. 6 : 12, v. 306 n. 2.
II. Tim. 2 : 4, i. 199 ; iii. 97 n. 1; iv. 158 ; v. 86. 2 : 5, i. 715. 2 : 14, iii. 485 n. 3. 2 : 20, i. 247. 2 : 25, iii. 255 ; iv. 72. 3 : 7, i. 506 n. 3 : 12, v. 310. 3 : 16, v. 62.

Timothy (Gegnæsius), Paulician, iii. 249, 250.
Timur Khan, iv. 57.
Tingis (Tangiers), i. 147.
Tira (Tiron), monastery of, iv. 97 n. 8, 236.
Tiridates, king of Armenia, ii. 136.
Tiron. See Tira.
Tirovano, iv. 639.
Tisigis, ii. 218, 221.
Tithes, opposed by the Saxons, iii. 76–78. Alcuin on, iii. 77 and n. 2, 82. Laws respecting, iii. 101 n. 2. Leuthard, iii. 604. Wm. of Modena on, iv. 41. Clergy exhorted to be content with, iv. 138, 147, 149. To be applied to the crusades, Lull, iv. 191. Wiklif on the payment and use of, v. 159–161. Huss on, v. 264, 274, 335, 345, 346 (see Huss, de decimis).
Titular bishops, v. 103.
Tituli, ii. 195.
Titulus de Decurionibus, ii. 171 n. 1.
Titus.

1 : 5, i. 184, 189. 1 : 6, ii. 182. 1 : 7, i. 184. 1 : 9, i. 188. 1 : 15, i. 313 ; iv. 92. 2 : 4, iii. 242. 2 : 11, ii. 342. 3 : 5, i. 249, 646.

Titus, bp. of Bostra.

C. Manichæos, l. i. c. 12, i. 492 n. 3 ; c. 30, 500 n. 6 ; l. iii., præf., 496 n. 1, 497 n. 3 ; initio, 501 n. 4. See Canisius.

Titus, comes, ii. 551.
Titus (Simeon), Paulician, iii. 248.
Titus, Roman emperor, i. 174 n. 2.
Tocsin, iii. 394 ; iv. 610.
Tolbiacum, battle of, iii. 8.
Toledo, iii. 164. Bps. of, 340, 342. Liturgy, 158 n. 1. See Councils, an. 400, an. 589, an. 633.
Toleration, Roman, i. 86–88, 102–104. Claimed by the Montanists, i. 524. Under Constantine, ii. 14, 21, 25, 163, 223, 227, 228. Under Julian, ii. 70–72, 84–86. Jovian, ii. 88, 89. Valentinian, Valens, Gratian, ii. 90, 91. Theodosius, ii. 97. Themistius on, ii. 88, 89, 91 and n. 4. In Persia, ii. 132.
Tolle, J. (Tollius).

Itinerar. Italic., f. 112, tract of Euthymius against the Bogomiles, iv. 559 un. 2. 3 ; anathemas, f. 114, anath. II., against Tychicus, iii. 269 n. 1 ; f. 116, anath. of the Bogomiles, iv. 572 n. 1 ; f. 122, of the Enchites, iii. 264 n. 1, anath. 12, iv. 559 n. 3 ; f. 144, iii. 265 n. 2 ; f. 146, against the Paulicians, iii. 266 n. 2.

Tombs of the saints, iii. 7. See Miracles, Peter, Paul.
Tongues, gift of, i. 181, 186 n. 2, 510 ; v. 150.
Tonsure, iii. 17, 106 n., 577.
Tormod Torf.

Hist. Norveg., l. ii. c. 2, Olof the Thick and Iceland, iii. 305 n. 3 ; c. 21, in Thrand, 298 n. 1 ; c. 23, Gudbrand, 299 n. 1.

Torture, i. 98, 108, 109, 112 n. 4, 113, 131 ; iii. 326, 598. Nicholas I., on the use of, iii. 312 ; iv. 90 n. 6. Self-torture, iv. 514.
Toscana, party in Italy, iii. 375.
Totila, king of the Goths, ii. 298.
Toul, iii. 493. See Bruno, Hermann of.
Toulouse, sects at, iv. 257, 639. Bp. of, 270. Inquisition at, 580, 643 (see Philip of Limborch). Catharist council at, 590. Henry of Cluny at, 603. Counts of, 639, 641 and n. 4, 642 nn. University of, v. 63.
Tournay, iii. 42. School at, iv. 357, 359 n. 3. History of the abbey at, iv. 357 n. (see Hermann). See Odo, Simon, Stephen.
Tours, pilgrimages to St. Martin's tomb at, iii. 131, 132. Odo at, 417. School at, 470, 503. Gozachin on the, 515 n. 6. Berengar at, 502, 503, 507, 510, 511, 516, 521. Ep. of bishops of, 101 n. 2. Abp. of, 511, 521 (see Councils, an. 1054). See Berengar, Gregory, Hildebert, Martin.
Trade, iii. 408. Of Jews, iv. 72. Of monasteries, iv. 239. Huss on, v. 326.
Tradesmen, v. 214. See Merchants, Traffic.
Tradition, with the Jews, i. 39, 40, 41 n. 1. On the early dissemination of Christianity, 80, 82, 85. Irenæus on, 215. Cyprian on, 216, 319, 320. Firmilianus on, 216. Apostolic, 204 n. 3, 314, 319, 320, 437, 528. In Gnosticism, 388. Basilides on, 408. Ptolemæus, 437, 439 n. 1. Marcion, 459, 461, 462. Persian, 487. In Montanism, 517, 519. Church, 519, 530. Augustin on the authority of the church tradition, ii. 239, 402, 697, 725. Differing views of, ii. 723 ; iii. 555. In the spread of Christianity, iii. 2, 32, 48, 91 n. At Toledo, iii. 164. In the image controversy, iii. 210, 232. Icelandic, iii. 300. Scotus on, iii. 462, 463. The dialectic tendency and, iii. 471 ; iv. 355, 380. Anselm, iv. 370.

With the scholastics, iv. 420, 519, 520. Roman, iv. 536. Opposition to, iv. 575. Janow, v. 207. Huss, v. 264, 324.
Tradition of spiritual gifts, Paulicians on, iii. 249. Of the Christian spirit, iii. 445.
Traditores, i. 115; ii. 217, 219, 222–224, 230.
Traducianism, of Tertullian, i. 615, 626. Ambrose, ii. 622. Coelestius on, ii. 639 n. 2, 640, 647. Julian of Eclanum, ii. 653, 659. Annianus on, ii. 657. Pelagius, ii. 669. Augustin, ii. 668–671. Aquinas, iv. 495. The Catharists, iv. 573.
Traffic, in priestly functions, iii. 53, 108 (see Simony). Traffic, iv. 210. With the Eastern monks, iv. 529. Waldenses, iv. 611, 612. See Trade.
Tragedy, of Nestorius, ii. 553. Of Irenæus, 553 n. 3.
Training of souls, i. 406.
Trajan, Roman emperor, i. 27. Rescript of, 97–100, 102, 105, 107, 118, 122, 191, 664, 665 n. 6.
Trajectum (Mæstricht), iii. 41 (Utrecht), 44.
Trance, i. 513, 520; ii. 240.
Trani, iii. 580.
Transcendentalism, i. 26, 57; iii. 490.
Transfiguration. See Christ.
Translations, ii. 77, 103 n. 1. Of Chrysostom's homilies, 657, 727. Sermons of Nestorius, 720 n. 4. Of Origen by Jerome, 744–746; by Rufinus, 748–750. Of Evagrius, 752. Ascensio Isaiæ (Ethiopic), 776 n. 4 (Latin), iv. 572 n. 1.
In the Third and Fourth Periods. Bede, iii. 18 n. 1, 153 n. 3. Of the writings of Theodore, 158. John of Oznun, 250 n. 1. Of Kristni Saga, 300 n. 2. Liturgy into Slavonian, 326. From Greek into Slavonian, 330. From Latin into English, iii. 468. In transactions between the Greek and Roman churches, 563, 576 n. 2, 581, 584. Latin into the vernacular, 598 n. 4.
In the Fifth and Sixth Periods. Ep. of Innocent IV., into Persian and Tartar languages, iv. 50. Latin translations of the Platonists, etc., iv. 359, 420, 444. Of Aristotle, iv. 417. Ascension of Isaiah (Latin), 572 n. 1. Arabic, iv. 417, 420. Of Arabic philosophers, iv. 444, 445. Of various writings, iv 300 n. 1; v. 150, 411. See Bible translation, Rufinus.
Transmigration of souls, in Platonism, i. 34. With Basilides, 404. Origen, 627. See Metempsychosis.
Transplanting of peoples, iv. 1.
Transubstantiation, ii. 732, 733; iii. 494–530. Two parties opposed to, iii. 527.
In the Fifth Period, iv. 335–341. In relation to the priesthood, 336. Waldenses on, 614.
In the Sixth Period. Doctrine attacked by Wicklif, v. 151–157, 163, 242,

259. (Accidentia sine subjecto, 152, 153, 155, 156, 163, 243 n. 1, 337). Huss on, 242–244, 247, 270, 271, 274, 331, 337, 339, 343, 344. At Prague, 244, 247. Stanislaus of Znaim, 244, 245. Zbynek, 247. Pancitas a parte rei, 343. See Lord's Supper, Paschasius Radbert.
Trapezund, ii. 592.
Traufenstein, iv. 345.
Treasury of merit, v. 284. See Thesaurus.
Tree of knowledge, iii. 659.
Trees, worship of, ii. 139. Sacred, iii. 51; iv. 15, 30.
Trent, iv. 630. Bp. of, v. 326, 327.
Treugæ Dei (truces of God), iii. 407, 454.
Trevisa, John, v. 149.
Triad, with Sabellius, i. 595, 596 n. 5, 598. Gospel of the Egyptians, i. 601. Eastern church, i. 605, 608, 609. In Neo-Platonism, ii. 122. With the Euchites, ii. 279. Marcellus, ii. 438. Augustin, ii. 469. Photinus, ii. 483. See Trinity.
Triarchy, with Marcion, i. 467 n. 1.
Tribur, synod at, on marriage of priests, iii. 383, 411 n. 7. Assembly of princes at, iv. 111, 112.
Tribute, from the clergy, Philip the Fair on, v. 5, 6. To Cæsar 16. From England to the pope, 136. See Cæsar.
Tricca, iii. 531.
Tricennalia, ii. 25, 427.
Trichotomy, of Origen, i. 555, 627, 629. Sabellius, i. 596 n. 2. The Gnostics, i. 627 (420–422). Justin, i. 635. Apollinaris, ii. 487, 488.
Triers, Athanasius banished to, ii. 428, 433. Maximus, trial of Priscillianists at, ii. 772–775. Stylite in, iii. 28. Monastery, iii. 72, 325. Bishops. Archbishops of, iii. 167, 354, 374, 408 n. 1, 445 n. 2, 448 n. 1; iv. 111, 331; v. 37, 133. Heretical schools at, iv 609. Memorabilia of abps. of Triers, iv. 609 n. 5. See Nicholas Krebs.
Triglav, Slavic idol, iv. 14, 15.
Trimurti, the Indian, i. 573.
Trinitarians, order of the, iv. 267, 268.
Trinity, doctrine of the, i. 518, 571–610, 690, 720; ii. 111 n., 122, 384, 385, 403–473; iv. 334, 385 n. 4, 418, 430, 457–466.
In the First Period. With Justin Martyr, i. 585, 586; Alexandrian school, 586–594; Sabellius, 594–601; Paul of Samosata, 601–605. Tertullian, 605 (518). Dionysius of Alexandria, 606–608.
Third and Fourth Periods. Opposed by Mohammed, iii. 86, 87, 159; Chilperic on the, 91 n.; in Spain, 117, 118; in the Greek church, 169, 210; With Maximus, 171–174; in Ireland, 461 n. 1.
Fifth and Sixth Periods. Raymund Lull on the, iv. 66, 69, 465; Roscelin,

360; Anselm, 457, 458; Abelard, 377, 380, 385 n. 4, 396, 458, 459; Aquinas, 463, 464; the three ages, 227–232, 447, 448; Bogomiles, 556; Catharists, 571, 574; Pasagii, 590. Janow on the, v. 208; Huss, v. 337; Tauler, v. 382; Eckhart, v. 396, 397. See Arian controversy.
Trinity, festival of the, iv. 333, 334.
Tripoli, in Phœnicia, ii. 590.
Trisagion, additions to the, ii. 590, 609 n. 2; iii. 176 n. 1.
Trismegistus (Hermes), i. 176.
Tritheism, i. 607; ii. 422, 614; iv. 227 n. 1, 360, 461.
Troanne. See Durandus of.
Troutano, iv. 629 n. 3.
Troubadours, iv. 604 and n. 3, 616 n. 1.
Troyes, iii. 154, 481, 489; iv. 147, 211 n. 5, 383. Monastery near, iii. 154. See Councils, an. 1127.
Truces of God, iii. 407.
Trullan councils. See Councils, an. 680, an. 691 or 692.
Truth among pagan nations, Valentine on the, i. 427; Bardesanes, i. 442. Origen on the unity of, i. 588. Confidence in the, iii. 508, 515; iv. 67. Zeal for an idea, and, iv. 84. Absolute, and the human presentation of, iv. 331. Spirit of, iv. 410. Devotion of Huss to, v. 264, 267, 268, 277, 279, 292 n. 4, 310, 315, 319, 363, 368. Close connection of truth and error, v. 392.
Truthfulness, relation of Christianity to, i. 388, 389. Huss on, v. 363. See Veracity.
Trypho. See Justin Martyr.
Tschamtschean.
Hist. Armenia. P. i. f. 765, Arevurdis, iii. 587 n. 8. T. ii. ff. 884–895, Thondracians, 588 n. 2.
Tübinger Theol. Quartelschrift.
1834, ii. 14 n. 2.
Tudun, prince of the Huns, iii. 82.
Tuentius, bp., ii. 695 n.
Tuggen, iii. 34.
Tunis, iv. 301. R. Lull at, iv. 66, 67 and n., 71 n. 2.
Tununum, Victor of, ii. 605 n. 4.
Turholt (Thoroult), monastery in Flanders, iii. 277, 278.
Turin, sect near, iii. 600. Cunibert, iv. 98. Waldenses at, iv. 609 n. 3. Council of, ii. 775 n. 5. See Claudius, Maximus.
Turkistan, Mani in, i. 488.
Turks, iii. 187, 188, 375; iv. 300, 301; v. 388.
Turlepinus, v. 213.
Turribius, bp. of Asturica (Astorga), ii. 776 n. 1.
Tuscany, iii. 366.
Tuscoli, counts of, iii. 375.
Tusculum (Frascati), iii. 423.
Tuventar, Slavonian prince, iii. 318 n. 1.
Tuy. See Lucas of.

Tychæ, ii. 80.
Tychicus, iii. 254.
Tychicus (Sergius), Paulician, iii. 251, 254 and n. 3, 269 n. 1.
Tychsen.
Dissertat. de Inscript. Iudicis, ii. 141 n. 6.
Type, the (τύπος τῆς πίστεως), iii. 184–192.
Types, iv. 220. See Symbols.
Tyre, ii. 143, 144. Paganism in, ii. 3, 4. Irenæus, bp. of, ii. 553 n. 3. Hatred of Monophysitism in, ii. 591 n. See Councils (an. 335), Methodius, bp. of, William of.
Tyrol, Dolcino in the, iv. 629 n. 5, 630. John XXIII., v. 102.
Tzabians, iii. 257. See Sabians.
Tzanio, iii. 256.
Tzathus, prince of the Lazians, ii. 139.
Τζυκαλικὴ αἵρεσις, iii. 545 n. 6.

U.

Ubald, life of bishop, iv. 206 n. 2.
Ubiquity, iii. 500; iv. 345. See Omnipresence.
Uchomo, Abgar of Edessa, i. 80.
Udardus. See Odo.
Udo (Audius), ii. 766.
Udo, bp. of Triers, iv. 111.
Udo, Wendish prince, iii. 325.
Ὑδροπαραστάται, i. 458 n. 2, 505.
Ueberlingen, v. 374.
Ὕλη (Hyle), Platonic doctrine of the, i. 34, 44, 376, 378, 611. With Celsus, 163, 168 and n. 1. Plotinus, 391 n. 2. In Gnosticism, 374–379, 383, 384, 423 n. 2, 442, 492, 618, 620. Basilides, 402 n. 3. Valentine, 420–423 n. 2, 427–429. Other Gnostics, 438, 441, 443, 455, 456, 466, 468, 472. In the church, 565, 567. With Origen, 624 nn. 4, 5. Gilbert of Poictiers, iv. 462 n. 1.
Redemption from the power of the, ii. 115 (see Gnosticism), 122. Manicheans, ii. 769 n. 3. See Matter.
Ullmann. See Studien und Kritiken, J., 1833, and 1836.
Ulm, v. 125.
Ulphilas, ii. 150–159; iii. 129. His Arianism, ii. 472, 473. Life of, ii. 150 n. 4 (see Auxentius). His version of the Bible, ii. 152; iii. 281 n.
His Testament, f. 21, ii. 472 n.
Ulric, bp. of Augsburg, iii. 405, 408. Canonized, 447. His letter (perhaps not genuine), to Nicholas I., on celibacy, 411 and n. 7. See A. S. Jul., or A. S. (O. B.), S. v., Martene et Durand, t. i.
Ulric, companion of Otto of Bamberg, iv. 2 n. 1, 20, 21, 25.
Ulrich Reichenthal.
Hist. conc. Const. v., 326 n. 3.
Ultramontanes, v. 90

Unam sanctam, bull, v. 8.
Unbelief, in paganism, i. 11-15, 20-22, 33, 71. Clement on, i. 531. End of (Joachim), iv. 229. In the Fifth Period, iv. 239, 324-328. Louis IX. on, iv. 326, 327. See Infidelity.
Unbelievers, fate of, v. 388. See Pagans.
Uncharitableness, iii. 443.
Unction, extreme, i. 477; iii. 102, 448, 449; iv. 335. Unction, among the Greek mystics, iv. 562. Janow on, v. 214. Imperial, iii. 367. See Anointing.
Understanding, Christianity of the, i. 581. Tendency of the, ii. 493; iv. 257. Reactions of the, iv. 239, 336, 380. Faith and (Lull on), iv. 439, 440. See Reason.
Ung Khan, iv. 47.
Ungodlike nature, the, with the Gnostics, i. 420, 421, 456.
Uniformity of doctrine, ii. 382. Of law, i. 401.
Unigenitus, the Constitution, v. 41.
Unitarians of the second century, i. 304. See Monarchians.
Unity in multeity, with the Gnostics, i. 401, 421, 449, 450.
Unity of essence, in the Godhead with Origen, i. 590. In the Eastern and Western churches, i. 605; ii. 403, 404, 410, 439, 441. See 'Ομοούσιον.
Unity of nations, v. 211. Christianity and the, i. 411.
Unity of the church, original, through the spirit, i. 179-183, 207, 208. Relation of the doctrine of the Trinity to, i. 573; iii. 568. Outward forms of union, i. 201-207. Outward unity of the Catholic church, and its mode of representation, i. 207-217. God the source of unity; Origen on, i. 621-624. Spiritual, ii. 33. Ratramnus on, iii. 568. Under manifold forms, Joachim, iv. 225. Catholic idea of, iv. 268, 578; with Bernard, iv. 263; Peter of Cluny, iv. 264; Huss, v. 306. And papal absolution, v. 14, 19, 33, 70, 78 (see Papacy, Popes). And Christ, Janow on, v. 210, 211, 231. Huss, v. 302, 303, 306-308.
Unity of the spiritual life, in relation to Christian ethics, ii. 634, 635, 681.
Universal ideas, in Alexandrian Judaism, i. 54, 56. Moral, ii. 660. Of dependence, ii. 666. Conceptions, universalia, ii. 654; iv. 356, 461. Universalia ante rem, in re, iv. 356. See Realism.
Universality, as test of doctrine, ii. 210, 239, 697.
Universe, laws of the, i. 401. Manifoldness of the, Aquinas, iv. 479. Perfected through the redemption, iv. 507, 508.
Universitas prædestinatorum, v. 263.
Universities, iv. 68, 70, 421, 422; v. 128, 263. Monastic influence in the, iv. 270, 281, 284, 289. Condition of the, iv. 413-416. Theological discussions in the, iv. 416. Teaching compared with preaching, v. 61. See Bologna, Orleans, Oxford, Palenza, Paris, Pisa, Prague, Salamanca, Toulouse.
Unjust steward, parable of the, iv. 553 and n. 5, 572 and n. 2.
Unleavened bread. See Bread.
Unnatural crimes charged against the Christians, i. 92, 94, 95, 98 nn. 2, 4, 109 n. 2, 112, 113, 664. Against heretical sects, iii. 265, 591, 595 n. 3; iv. 586. Against the Jews, iv. 72, 73, 76, 77. Against the Templars, v. 23.
Unni, archbishop, iii. 288, 291.
Unvan, archbishop, iii. 292.
Ὑποπίπτοντες, ii. 213, 357.
Ὑπόστασις, ii. 614. See Hypostases.
Upsala, central point of pagan worship in the North, iii. 292, 233. Bp. Heinrich of, iv. 45.
Urban, bp. of Rome, e. in the Pseudo-Isidorean Decretals, ii. 348 n. 2.
Urban II., pope, Guitmund, iii. 529 n. 3. Banished from Rome, iv. 121. Philip of France, iv. 121-123. The Crusade, iv. 123-125, 153. Returns to Rome, iv. 128, 129, 140 n. 1, 163 n. 2. On assassins of excommunicated persons, iv. 129 n. 4. His successor, iv. 132. Lay investiture, iv. 136, 160. Yves of Chartres, iv. 198, 201. Robert of Arbrissel, iv. 246. Robert of Citeaux, iv. 252. On penance, iv. 348. Indulgence, iv. 349. Anselm, iv. 364. Council at Bari, iv. 536.

Ep. to Gottfried, iv. 129 n. 4. See Mansi Concil., xx.

Urban IV., pope, iv. 341, 421.
Urban V., pope, at Rome, v. 44. Assembly under, 102. Demands tribute of England, 136. Militz, 179-181.
Urban VI., pope, validity of his election disputed, v. 46-50. Besieged at Naples, release, death, 51. Bull against Clement VII., 164. Wicklif on, 165. Law on dress, 192, 223. Janow on, 232.
Urbicus, i. 664.
Urie, Zacharias of, v. 107.
Urgellis, iii. 156 n. 5, 167. See Felix of.
Urkundenbuch. See Pelzel.
Urolf, archbishop of Lorch, iii. 332 n. 1.
Ursacius, bishop of Singidunum, ii. 449, 451, 452, 454.
Ursacius, comes, ii. 226, 228 and n. 3.
Ursicinus. See Ursinus.
Ursinus, bp. of Rome, schism of, ii. 255-257.
Ursinus, monk, i. 322 n. 4.
Urstis.

German. historic. post Henric. IV. pars alt. Francof., 1585, f. 133, Chronicle of Albert of Strassburg, v. 41 n. 2.

Usages, uniformity of church, iii. 568. See Church usages, Ritual.
Usda (Uscz), castle, iv. 7 n.
Usedom history of its conversion, iv. 18.

230 GENERAL INDEX.

Assembly at, 18, 22. Otto and Wartislav at, 24.
Usher, archbishop.
  Britannicarum eccles. antiquitates, ed. ii. f. 362, Columba, iii. 10 n. 2; f. 429, Patrick, ii. 146 n. 1, 148 n. 1. De Christianar. eccles., etc., successione et statu (Londini, 1687, f. 112), Walter Mapes on the Waldenses, iv. 608 n. 1; f. 157, protocol of the conference at Montreal between Albigenses and Catholics, iv. 641 n. 2. Hist. dogmatica, de Scripturis (ed. Wharton, Lond., 1690), f. 377, extracts from Elfric of Malmsbury, iii. 469 nn. 3-5; f. 421, from Bacon's tract addressed to Clement IV., iv. 425 n. 1-3. Vet. epist. Hibernic. sylloge, f. 41, ep. of Scotus to Charles the Bald, iii. 467 n. 2.
Usury, ii. 766; iv. 52, 72, 74, 176, 184, 300; v. 52, 175, 185, 189, 223.
Utrecht, bishopric at, iii. 44, 65. Monastery at, 73. Willibrord at, 45. Boniface, 47, 71. Subordinated to Mentz, 71 n. 2. William of, iv. 109. Letter of the church of, iv. 592 n. 2. See Gregory, Radbod.
Utrecht, the priest of, sketch of Boniface, iii. 60 n. 1, 71 n. 3, 72 n. 3.
Uzziah, iii. 211, 385.

V.

Vagabond monks, iv. 44; v. 52.
Vagrant clergy, iii. 108, 109, 412, 413; iv. 52.
Vagrants, imposters, iii. 446 n. 1.
Vaison. See Councils, an. 529.
Val d'Ossola, iv. 629 n. 3.
Valence. See Councils, an. 529; an. 855.
Valens, bp. of Mursa, ii. 449, 451, 452, 454.
Valens, emperor, ii. 88 n., 91 and n. 4, 111 n. 151 n. 2, 152 n. 1, 155, 156, 165 n. 5, 174, 301, 459, 460.
Valens, monk, ii. 275.
Valentine, abbot, ii. 686.
Valentine the Gnostic, himself and his doctrines, i. 417–434, 377 n. 1, 385, 386, 401 n. 3, 437, 439, 443, 445, 492 n. 5.
Valentinian I., emperor, ii. 90–92, 162, 167, 459, 461, 471.
Valentinian II., emperor, ii. 92 n, 3, 93, 94, 99, 117, 472, 775; iv. 111.
Valentinian III., emperor, ii. 207, 575, 769 n. 6, 770.
Valentinian school (Gnostic), i. 393 n. 3, 417, 434–442, 635; iii. 261; iv. 569.
Valerian, emperor, i. 127, 136–140, 148 n., 320, 321; ii. 149.
Valerius, count, ii. 650.
Valesius.
  Notes to Socrates, l. v. c. 10, f. 61 (ed. Mogunt.), Eunomius' confession, ii. 449 n. 3.
Validity, of Sacerdotal acts, ii. 219, 224, 245, 246. Of sacraments, see Baptism, Sacraments.
Valley of Sessia, iv. 632.
Vallis Absinthialis (Valley of Wormwood), iv. 254.

Vallombrosa, Vallombrosians, iii. 398, 419.
Vain Khan, iv. 47.
Van der Hardt.
  Acta concil. Const., t. i. p. 3, f. 18, Clemangis, De ruina ecclesiæ, v. 66 n. 5; f. 179 et seq., Zacharias of Uric, 107 n. 1; f. 801, 119 n. 2; f. 833, speech of Stephen of Prague (Paletz?), 119 n. 1; f. 881, Baptisé, 113 n.; f. 1010, the Germans on indulgences, 126 n. 3; Martin V. on the same, 126 n. 4.
  T. ii. ff. 33, 42, Henry of Hessia, Consilium pacis, v. 49 nn. 2-4, 50 n.; ff. 132, 142, 146, 155, Council of Pisa, 83 n. 2, 84 n., 87 n., 88 n. 1; f. 180 et seq., council of Constance, discourse of Gentianus, 110 n. 2; f. 194, D'Ailly, 104 n. 3; f. 228, 104 n. 1; f. 230, 103 n.; f. 234, abdication of John XXIII., 105 n. 2; ff. 272, 278, Gerson's orat., 107 n. 2, 108 n. 1; f. 297, John of Antioch, 108 n. 2; f. 348, Theodore of Niem, de fatis Joh. XXIII., 89 n., 91 n. 2.
  T. iii. ff. 69-71, Jerome of Prague, ep. of Poggio to Aretino, v. 378 n. 2, 377 nn.
  T. iv. i. f. 23 et seq., v. 104 n. 2; ff. 26, 28, J. of Chlum on the imprisonment of Huss, 328 nn.; f. 32, 329 n. 2; f. 41, John XXIII., 105 n. 1; f. 69, 108 n. 2; ff. 87, 88, Zabarella, 109 n. 2; f. 180, discourse of Gentianus, 110 n. 2; f. 213, 326 nn. 2, 3; f. 281, sentence of John XXII., 111 n. 4; f. 307, second hearing of Huss, 344 n. 1; ff. 311, 312, the schism in Prague, 256 n. 1; f. 317, preaching of Huss, 257 n. 2; f. 327, Huss and the martyrs of Prague, 288 n. 2, 290 nn. 1, 2; f. 325, the Oxford documents, 244 n. 2; f. 393, the blush of the emperor, 369 n. 2; ff. 432, 433, resolution provided in case of Huss' recantation, 357 n.; f. 447, his farewell to his jailors, 371 n. 1; f. 495, complaint of the knights of Bohemia and Moravia, 376 n.; f. 638, Jerome of Prague, 372 nn. 3, 4, 373 n. 1; f. 643, 374 n. 1; ff. 672 and 753, burning of the bulls, 286 n. 1; ff. 680, 681, trial of Jerome, 372 n. 1; f. 683, 372 n. 3; ff. 752, 753, 285 n. 2; f. 757, 377 n.; f. 758, 254 n.; f. 1307, Dacher on the Conc. Const., 118 n. 2; ff. 1419-1424, the protest of the Germans, 122-124 nn.; f. 1452, agreements of the council, 126 n. 1.

Vandals, the Arian, persecute the Catholics, ii. 238, 473, 600, 709 (iii. 5 n. 2; v. 312). Take Africa and besiege Hippo, 695. The Manicheans among them, 770.
Varanes (Behram), king of Persia, i. 488.
Varanes V., king of Persia, ii. 134, 135 n. 4, 136.
Varro, threefold theology, i. 7, 86 n. 1. World soul, images of the gods, Jews, 9. Sibylline books, 177 n. 3. Pag. 15, 86 n. 1. See Dionys. Halicarnass.
Vassal, vassalage, influence of Christianity on, iii. 98. Maximus on, 171 n. 2. Priests as vassals, 402.
Vater.
  Kirchenhistorischen Archiv., J. 1823. Heft 2, Neander on the paschal supper, i. 298 n. 1.
Vatican. See Libraries.
Vaughan.
  Life of Wycliffe (Lond., 1831), vol. i., pp. 270, 278 et seq., the tribute to the pope, v. 136 nn. 1, 2, p. 284, 136 n. 3; pp. 312, 314, his short rule of life, 138 n., 139 n. 1; p. 319, Expos. decalog., 139 n. 2; pp. 320, 326, 329, 140 nn.; Vol. ii. pp. 5, 6, on the schism, 104 nn. 1, 2; pp. 12, 13, 14, his sermons, 142 nn. 1, 3, 4; f. 14 et seq., Contra fratres, 142 n. 5; pp. 14,

18, 19, 23, on preaching, 142 n. 5, 143 nn. 1–3; pp. 130, 273, 274, against the necessity of the papacy, orders of clergy, 173 nn.; p. 279, the church, 172 nn. 8, 4; p. 342, Wicklif compared with Luther, 172 n. 2.

Veil, before the sanctuary, ii. 321. Worn by the competentes, 358.

Veletri, iii. 387.

Vendome. See Gottfried of.

Venetians, iv. 56; v. 73, 84.

Veni creator spiritus, v 91, 113.

Venice, ii. 250 n. 1. Peace concluded at, iv. 168.

Venus, temple at Aphaca destroyed, ii. 26. Urania, 84.

Veracity, with the Essenes, i. 46. The Alexandrian Jews, i. 58. The Gnostics, Irenæus, i. 388, 389. Oriental views of, ii. 557 n. 7, 572 n. 6. Origenists, ii. 597. Jerome, ii. 744. The Priscillianists, ii. 778. Augustin, ii. 779. Gregory the Great on, iii 150. Isidore, iii. 151. The Paulicians, iii. 266, 267. Theodore Studita, mental reservation, iii. 541 n. 5. Catharists, iv. 610. Waldenses, iv. 614, 615. See Accommodation, Insincerity, Mendacium.

Vercelli, ii. 184, 312; ii. 379 n. 1; iv. 629 nn. 2, 3. See Atto.

Verden, iv. 33.

Verdun. See Dieteric.

Verinus, vicar, ii. 227.

Vermandois, iii. 42.

Vernacular. See Language.

Verona, Peter of, iv. 585 n. 1. See Notting, Ratherius, Zeno.

Veronica, St., iii. 201.

Versions of the Bible. See Bible translation.

Verus. See Lucius.

Vespronius Candidus, i. 102 n. 4.

Vestals, ii. 35.

Vestments, sacred, adorned with images, iii. 232. See Pallium.

Vettius, Epagatus, the martyr, i. 112.

Vicar of Christ, v. 350.

Vicarii, iv. 212. Vicars, 287.

Vicarious suffering, Basilides on, i. 412. Tertullian on, i. 523. Peter Lombard, Innocent III., iv. 505, 506. See Atonement, Satisfaction.

Vicarius apostolicus, ii. 204; iii. 119 n. 2.

Vice domini, iii. 101 n. 4.

Vicelin, converter of the Slavonians, iv. 33–36, 303. Life of, see Heinrich.

Vicennalia, ii. 32 nn. 1, 2.

Vicenza, iii. 443.

Victor I., bp. of Rome, arrogant claims denied, i. 214, 215. Dispute about the passover, 299, 300, 680. Montanists, 513 n. 3, 525 n. 1, 583. Theodotus, 580. Blastus, 680. In the Decretals, iii. 347.

Victor, bp. of Tununum, ii. 604 n. 3, 605 n. 4. See Canisius.

Victor, bp. of Vita, ii. 473.

Hist. persecutor. Vandal., l. ii. init., Manichæans, ii. 770 n. 3.

Victor I., pope. See Victor I., bp. of Rome.

Victor II. (Gebhardt), pope, iii. 307, 384 n. 4, 387.

Victor III. (Desiderius), pope, iii. 375 n. 4; iv. 121, 124, 349.

Victor IV., pope, iv. 167, 168, 218.

Victoria, the martyr, i. 152.

Victorines. See St. Victor.

Victorinus, bp. of Petabio (in Pannonia), i. 296 n. 5; ii. 376.

Hist. Creationis (ed. Cave, hist. ap. Galland. bibl. patr. t. iv.; Rouh rel. sacr., vol. iii., p. 273, Oxon., 1815), fasting on the Sabbath, i. 296 n. 5.

Victorinus, Fabius Marius, ii. 76.

Victory, altar of, ii. 92.

Vienna (Faviana?), iii. 26 n. 2. Imperial library at, iii. 425 n. 3. Conrad at, v. 183, 192. Jerome of Prague at, v. 246, 372.

Vienne, spread of Christianity thither, i. 84. Persecution of Christians, i. 84, 112–114. Ep. to Victor of Rome, i. 300. Julian at, Epiphany, iii. 45, 343. Metropolitan power of the bps. of, ii. 207. Desiderius, bp. of, iii. 150. Piety in the diocese of, iv. 294. Nicholas of Basle burnt at, v. 392. See Councils, an. 1311. See Avitus.

Vigilantius, ii. 181 n. 2, 182, 313, 314, 373–376, 746; v. 16.

Vigilius, bp. of Rome, ii. 594, 595, 601–608.

Letter to the Monophysite bishops, ii. 594, 595 n. 1. Ep. ad Rusticum et Sebastianum, 603 n. 2. Ad universum populum dei, 606 n. 2.

Vigils, ii. 341, 374, 375; iv. 91, 262.

Vignier, Nicole. See Nicole.

Vilgard (Bilgard), heretic, iii. 602, 603.

Villani, Giovanni, death of Boniface VIII., v. 13. On Clement V., 23.

Hist., l. viii. cc. 6, 8, 63, 64, Bonifaco VIII., v. 2 n., 13 n. 1; c. 23, Colonnas, 5 n.; c. 80. Benedict XI, 19 n.; c. 101, l. ix. c. 58, Clement V., 22 n., 23 nn. l. x. cc. 68, 70, 71, l. xi. c. 20, deposition of John XXII. and election of Nicholas V., 36 nn., 37 n. 1.

Villargi, cardinal, v. 260. See Alexander V.

Villas, i. 79.

Vincennes, assemblies at the castle of, v. 37, 48, 49. See Councils, an. 1333, an. 1378.

Vincentius, Donatist, ii. 251 nn. 2, 3.

Vincentius a Thibari, on the baptism of heretics, i. 310 n. 1.

Vincentius de Beauvais.

Speculum historiale, l. xxxi. c. 40, mission to the Mongols, report of St. Quentin, iv. 49 n., 50 n. 1; of Carpini, 50 n. 2.

Vincentius of Lerins, Commonitorium, or Tractatus, etc., ii. 210, 211, 696; iv. 537. Capitula objectionum, ii. 697 n. 1.

Vincentius Victor, against Augustin, ii. 671 n. 2.
Virgil, iii 483 n. 2, 602 and n. 2; iv. 178 n. 3. IV. Eclog., i. 177 n 2.
Virgilius, Bavarian priest, controversy with Boniface, view of the Antipodes, iii. 55 n. 1, 63. He is made bishop of Salzburg, 63.
Virgines, i. 277. See Παρθένοι.
Virtue, Philo on human and divine, i. 60. In Christianity, i. 277. Hilary on human, ii. 619. Doctrine of, in the Pelagian controversy, ii. 637, 676–684. Prosper on, ii. 693. Necessity of, iii. 421. In God and man, iv. 318, 319. Knowledge from, iv. 433. Above knowledge, Bacon, iv. 434. 'Αρετή πολιτική, iv. 523. Ruysbroch on, v. 404. See Moral systems.
Virtues, of the Christians, i. 76–78, 98, 249, 250. Of the heathen, natural, ii. 637, 680–682; iii. 45; iv. 11; (Abelard on, iv. 378, 379, 383, 384). 520–523; v. 16. Love the root of, iii. 148, 149; iv. 308. Bernard on, iv. 257, 262. Lull, iv. 308. Unity of, iv. 319. The scholastics on, iv. 519–528. Cardinal and theological, iv. 520–523. Threefold division, iv. 523. Exemplary, purifying, political, iv. 524. In relation to the order of reason, iv. 521, 522, 524. Reality of, iv. 561, 562. False exaltation above the, v. 398–401. Right will in the, v. 404. False dependence on the, v. 408. See Morality.
Vis conservativa, iv. 482.
Visigoths. See West Goths.
Visions, as a means of conversion, i. 75. With Cyprian, 236. Among the Montanists, 520. See Montanism, Tertullian.
Second Period. Of Constantine, ii. 9–13; of his victorious army, 20. Augustin on visions, 120, 240. Of Pachomius, 271. Valens, 275. Theodore of Mopsuestia on, 390. Of Jerome, 743.
Third and Fourth Periods. Laurence, iii. 18, 19. Edwin, 19, 20. Boniface, 47. Charlemagne on, 240. Anschar, 274, 283, 286. Priest at Upsala, 293. Severus of Prague, 323. Peswil, 521 n. 2. Lenthard, 603.
Fifth Period. Gaudentius, iv. 42. Raymund Lull, 61, 62. As witnesses of the truth, 80, 332. Gregory II., 86 n. 3. Peter of Amiens, 124. Hildegard, 217. Elizabeth of Schönau, 217. The young nun, 239 n. 2. Bernard of Clairvaux, 252 n. 3. Berthold, 266. Francis of Assisi, 271, 276. Innocent III., 272. As assurance of salvation, 305, 514. Rainer, 326 n. 2. Corpus Christi, 341. Aquinas on, 514. The Greek monks, 529. Militz, v. 178, 179. Margaret Ebnerin, v. 383 n. 2. Merswin. v. 388.
Visitation, church visitors, i. 232, 233; ii. 193, 221; iii. 42, 82, 107, 108, 123; iv. 16, 34, 36, 211, 213; v. 81, 174.
Vita, Victor, bp. of, ii. 473.
Vitæ pontificum, iii. 122 n. 2.
Vitalian, commander, ii. 591, 592, 710.
Vitalian, pope, iii. 25, 193.
Viterbo, iv. 214, 421; v. 74. See Gottfried.
Vladimir, Grand duke of Russia, iii. 329.
Vladimir, Wassily, Russian prince, iii. 329, 330.
Vocations, in the church, v. 214.
Vogt.
   On the Pseudo Dionysian writings, iii. 351 n. 2 On John Scotus, 406 n. 2.
Void, in Gnosticism, i. 374.
Voigt.
   Geschichte von Preussen, Bd. i. s. 267, iv. 41 n 6.
Volga, the river, iii. 329.
Volusian, emperor, i. 136, 711 n. 3.
Votum, with the Catharists, iv. 578.
Votum stabilitatis, ii. 298 n. 2.
Vow, monastic, ii. 288.
Vows, iii. 333; iv. 237, 238, 306, 307. Wicklif on, v. 171. Tauler, v. 407.
Vulgate, the, iv. 369, 425, 568 n. 3; v. 197 n. 2, 269. Emendation of the, iv. 426. Wicklif, v. 149. See Bible revision, translation.

W.

Wadding.
   Annals of the Franciscan order, t. iv. an. 1256, Gerhard, iv. 618 n. 2; an. 1272, Berthold, 318 n. 1; an. 1275, § 4, R. Lull, 61 n. 1; an. 1282, N. 2, Oliva, 620 n. 4; an. 1283, N. 7, his recantation, 621 n. 1; an. 1289, N. 28, 29, 620 nn. 1, 2; an. 1297, N. 34, Oliva on discussion of doctrine, 621 n. 2; N. 35, his writings, 626 n. 2; N. 37, on the death of Christ, 620 n. 5. T. vi., report of Monte Corvino, iv. 57 n. 3.
Wafers, miraculous, at Wilsnack, v. 237, 238.
Waitz, Prof.
   Bruchstücke, neber das leben und die lehre des Ulphilas, ii. 150 n. 4, 151 n. 2. See Maximin.
Wala, abbot of Corvey, iii. 275, 351, 352. Life of, 352 nn. 1, 3. See Acta S. (O. B.), S. iv. p. i.
Walafrid Strabo, iii. 440 and n. 4, 457. De exordiis et incrementis rer. ecclesiasticarum, use of images, 440. Glossa ordinaria, 458. Gottschalk, 472, 474 n. 2.
   De rebus eccles., c. 7, version of Ulphilas, iii. 281 n. 1. Life of Gallus, 36 n. 2. Poem addressed to Gottschalk, 472 n., 474 n. 2. See Canisius.
Walch.
   Geschichte der Ketzereien und Spaltungen, Bd. 8, s. 286, u. d. f., ii. 765 n. T. x. s. 516, iii. 228 n. 1. T. xi. s. 122, iii. 652 n. 7.
Walch, F.
   Dissertations, in the Novis Comm. Reg. Soc. Gotting., t. i. chronology of Easter, ii. 338

n. 5; vol. iv., 1774, Dsunovas, iii. 145. T. iv., Part. philol., De Sabæis comment., i. 370 n. 3.

Walcher.
  Scholasticus, iii. 515 n. 6.
Waldemar, king of Denmark, iv. 31.
Waldenses, origin, history, iv. 229, 303, 592, 605–616; v. 138. Innocent III. and the, iv. 272, 321, 608, 609. Influence in the societies at Metz, iv. 321, 324. John of Paris on the, v. 16. Peter of Dresden, v. 338. Waldensian friends of God, v. 390, 391. See Maitland, Moneta, Philip of Limborch, Rainerio.
Waldhausen, Conrad of, v. 183–192, 258. At Rome, 184. Preacher at Prague, 184, 192. The Jews, 185. Against the mendicants, 186–191. Death, 192.
  Citations from his defence (unpublished), v. 183 n. 4, 184–192 nn.
Waldrade, iii. 353, 354, 357.
Wales, ii. 149. Church in, iii. 468. See British church.
Wallachia, iii. 334.
Wallenrod, John of, v. 368.
Wallia (Wales), ii. 149.
Walsingham.
  Hist. Angl., etc. (Francof., 1603), f. 191, Lollards, v. 143 n. 4; ff. 191, 208, excitement against the clergy, through Wicklif, 148 n. 1; f. 205, Wicklif before the court at Lambeth, 148 nn. 2, 4; f. 275, John Balle, 159 nn. 1–3, 5; f 283, Wicklif, 161 n. 2; f. 286, Wicklif and Univ. Oxford, 163 n. 1. Loc. laud., f. 201, the same, 147 n. 2.
Walter á St. Victore. See Walter of Mauritania.
Walter, abbot of Melrose, life of, iv. 328 n.
Walter, abbot of St. Martin (of Pontoise), life of, iv. 97 n. 8.
Walter Mapes, Franciscan, iv. 608.
  De nugis curialium (see Usher), Waldenses, iv. 608 nn.
Walter of Mauritania (á St. Victore), antagonist of Abelard, iv. 380–382, 410, 450.
  Citations: —
  Letters against Abelard (see D'Achery, t. iii.), iv. 380 nn. 2, 3, 381 nn. 1–3, 5, 382 . 1; f. 525, 450 n. 4. Contra quatuor Galliæ Labyrinthos (Boulæus Hist. Univ., t. ii. ff 200, 402), 393 n. 1, 410 and n. 4.
Walter von der Vogelweide.
  (Ed. Lachmann) f. 25, legend of the gift of Constantine, iv. 216 n.; p. 9, f. 35, Innocent III., 173 n. 1.
Waltram, bp. of Naumberg, on Gregory VII. and Henry IV., iv. 110, 116, 117.
  Apolog., l. ii. f. 170 (see Goldast.), the monks, iv. 98 n. 1; c. 36, Mathilda, 113 n. 1; l. iii. c. 3, Gregory on the validity of sacraments, 100 n. 3. De unitat. eccles. et imperii. . i. c. 6, 115 n., 116 nn. 1–3; f. 17, 111 n. 2; f. 66, 111 n. 1.
War, Julian on, ii. 53. Persian view of, ii. 129. Means of extending Christianity, ii. 149; iii. 40. Hindrance, iv. 46,

47, 83. Clergy take part in warlike expeditions, iii. 53, 55, 56; forbidden, iii. 56, 66, 102. Honor attached to military service, iii. 102. Religious war avoided, iii. 304, 305. Religious observances in time of, iii. 311. Nicholas I. on, iii. 311, 312. Influence of the church on private war, iii. 407. Christian influence against, iv. 24, 26. With pagans and infidels, iv. 26, 31 n. 2, 153, 258. The Jews on the prevalence of, Gislebert's reply, iv. 78. The papacy and, iv. 83 and n. 2. Popes accused of instigating, iv. 151, 214, 215. German bishops in, iv. 214 and n. 2. Catharists on, iv. 574. Huss on, v. 281. See Crusades.
Waragians, Norman tribe, Waragian empire in Russia, iii. 327, 328.
Waraskians, heresies among the, iii. 38 n. 2.
Warin, abbot of Corbic (Placidius), iii. 495 n. 1.
Warnefrid. See Paulus Diaconus.
Warner, F.
  Hist. Ireland, ii. 148 n. 2
Wartislav, Pomeranian duke, iv. 1, 7, 9, 16, 18, 24.
Washing the feet of the poor, iv. 295.
Water, used in the Lord's Supper by the Eucratites, i. 458 n. 2. Manichean elect? i. 505. Object of worship with the Persians, ii. 128. Consecrated, iii. 15, 347 n. 5; iv. 15, 317. Trial by, iii. 130.
Wax tapers before images of martyrs, ii. 374. Before tombs, iii. 7. Wax images, iii. 201.
Wazo, bp. of Liege, iii. 605. His conduct towards heretics, 605, 606.
Weak, care of the, ii. 135.
Wealth, Christian use of, i. 271, 274, 277, 279, 280, 282; ii. 314; i i. 166 n. 5. Accumulation of, ii. 129. Voluntary surrender of, i. 274, 277, 279; ii. 265, 314. Of the church, iv. 139, 180, 634; v. 50. Dangers from, iv. 215, 216. Pursuit of, iv. 219, 529. Joachim on, iv. 224. Of monasteries misused, iv. 234, 251. See Jews, Mendicants, Property.
Wearmouth, monastery, Bede at, iii. 152.
Weavers, mystical tendencies among, iii. 599; iv. 565. Cluniacensians, iv. 603.
Wedding feast, with the Gnostics, i. 399 and n. 2, 434. Baptism as a, 477.
Wednesday, observance of, i. 296; ii. 333, 365, 379.
Weck, the great, ii. 341.
Wegesack, iii. 82.
Wegner.
  Theodori quæ supersunt omnia, ii. 390 nn. 1–4, 393 nn.
Wegner, A. F. W. von.
  De Manichæorum indulgentiis, Lips, 1827, p. 69 et seq., i. 503 n. 4.

Weichsel, river, iv. 43.
Weissenburg, abbey, iii. 325, 425, 457.
Welenao (Welna), iii. 272. Monastery at, 277.
Welenowitz, Nicholas of (Abraham), v. 250, 251.
Wenceslaus (Wenzel), king of Bohemia, v. 241. His relations with Rome, and with the reform party in Bohemia, 252–256, 260. Burning of Wicklif's books, 261, 262. Letters to the pope and cardinals in favor of Huss, 271 and n. 2. Espouses his cause, 272. The committee of ten, 273, 275. Albic, 276. Bull of John XXIII., 277, 286 n. 1, 287, 291. Edict concerning this, 287. Edict against the forty-five articles, 292. Efforts for the restoration of peace, 295, 297–299. Alters the constitution of the senate, 299. Sigismund, 317, 348. John of Reinstein, 328. Huss on, 335. Life of, see Pelzel. Letter to John XXIII. see Palacky, iii. 1, f. 258. To the cardinals, see Pelzel. See Palacky.
Wenceslaus, martyr, v. 290.
Wends, spread of Christianity among them, iii. 323–327; iv. 31, 32–36 (see Pomerania). Empire of the, iv. 32.
Wenilo, abp. of Sens, iii. 489.
Wenzel of Duba, Bohemian knight, friend of Huss, v. 320, 321, 342, 343, 348, 358, 367, 368.
Wenzel of Janow, v. 192.
Wenzel Tiem, v. 321.
Wenzeslav of Bohemia, iii. 322. Life of, 322 n. 1. See Balbinus.
Werden, monastery, iii. 79.
Weser, river, iii. 82, 273; iv. 33.
West Gothland, iii. 292.
West Goths, ii. 160; iii. 4 nn. 1, 5, 9, 129 n. 2, 164 n. 6. Relation of church and state among them, iii. 96 (105). Relation to the Roman church, iii. 117, 118, 152. Compare Goths.
Western church, Epiphany in the, i. 301 n. 2. Doctrine of the Trinity in the, 585, 605–608, 610.
In the Second Period. Character of the, ii. 466. Celibacy, 181. Ordination, 185. Transfer of clergy, 187. Duties of bishops, 188. Ordination of deaconesses, 190. Widows, 191 and n. 2. Church unity, 200. Theocracy, 202–208. Contrasted with the Eastern, 204–206, 214, 383–387, 617, 618, 624, 678. Archdeacons, 217. Idea of the church, 240. Monasticism, 263, 294–300. Images, 329. Observance of the Sabbath, 334. Passover, 337. Quadragesima, 339. Epiphany, 343. Christmas, 344. Pagan festivals, 349, 350. Position in the great doctrinal controversies, 383, 384, 386, 471. In the Arian controversy, 433–435, 440, 452–454, 469–473. In the Meletian schism, 458. In the Eutychian controversy, 573–582. Doctrine of the Holy Spirit, 469–471. Origen, 387, 595. Edict of the Three Chapters, 600–608. Anthropology, 616–712.
In the Third and Fourth Periods. Theocracy in the, iii. 92. Interstitia, 93. History of doctrinal development, 141–168, 456–530. Scientific life in the, 156. Image worship, 233–243. Compared with the Greek church, 530. Participation in the controversies of the Greek church, 551–553. Relations with the Greek church, 553–586. Apostolic decrees, 557 and n. 6. Unleavened bread in the Lord's Supper, 581. Treatment of heretics, 604–606.
Relation to the Eastern, *in the Fifth Period*, iv. 104, 215, 458, 528–531. See Eastern.
Western empire, iv. 172. At Constantinople, 539.
Western sects, iii. 592–606; iv. 565, 592–644.
Westminster. See Gilbert.
Westphalia, iii. 44; iv. 71, 80.
Wetstein.
On the Dialogue of J. Martyr, i. 668 n. 3.
Wezel, ep. to Fred. I., iv. 161 n. 2.
Wheat and tares. See Parables.
Whitby, synod at (Pharensis), iii. 24 n. 1.
White robes in baptism, ii. 341, 342, 360
Whitsuntide, iv. 18, 19, 53, 54. See Pentecost.
Wibald, envoy, iv. 161 n. 3.
Wibald of Stavelo.
Ep. 147, appearance of Bernard, iv. 144 n. 1.
Wibert, archdeacon at Toul.
Life of Leo IX. (Acta S. April 19), iii. 378 n. 5, 379 n., 381 n. 2, 385 nn. 1, 2.
Wibold, abp. of Cambray, iii. 410 n. 3.
Wichin, bp. of Neitra, iii. 318, 319 and n 3, 320 and nn. 2, 3.
Wicklif, John, v. 48. Life and character, 135–173. On the secular power of the pope, 93, 146. Realism, 135, 165–167, 261. On the last times, 135. Appointed tutor of Canterbury Hall, 135. Displaced, opposes payment of tribute to the pope, 136. Doctor evangelicus, 136. Chaplain to the king, 136. Doctor of theology, 137. Ambassador to Gregory XI., 137. Against the mendicants, 138, 140, 142, 161, 171. Curate at Lutterworth, sermons, 142. On preaching, 142, 143. The Lollards, 143–145. Attacked by the mendicants, 145. Condemned by Gregory XI., 146. Tried at Lambeth, 148. Sickness, 148, 149. Translation of the Bible, 149–151. On transubstantiation, 151–153, 337. Doctrine of the Lord's Supper, 153–157. Insurrectionary movements in England, 158–160, 161. On the authority of prelates, 160. Outward reform, 160, 161. Property of the church, 160, 161, 170. Earthquake council,

162. On predestination, 167, 168. Salvation by Christ alone, 168. Saint worship, 168, 169. Number of sacraments, 169, 170. Thesaurus meritorum, 171. Prophecy of the reformation, 171. Justification, 172. On the church, the papacy, 172, 173.
Wicklif's influence on Huss, and the Wickliffite movements in Bohemia, v. 240-242. His writings, at Prague university, 241. Forged document under seal of Oxford, testifying his orthodoxy, 243, 244. Jerome of Prague, 245, 246, 371-373 n. 2, 376, 377. The forty-five articles, 246-248, 264, 265, 278, 291, 296, 316, 335, 345, 352. Bull of Innocent VII., synod at Prague, an. 1406, 247. Right of lecturing on his writings restricted, 248. Dola, 251. Zbynek's declaration, 252, 260. Complaint against Huss, 258, 259. Bull of Alexander V., 259. Wicklif's writings burned, 260-262, 286. Huss and Wicklif, 268, 269, 287, 302, 331, 337, 343-347, 356, 357, 363, 368. Wenzel, 271. John of Leitomysl, 341. See Lewis, Walsingham, Vaughan.

Citations from his writings: —
A short rule of life, v. 138, 139. Contra fratres, 142 n. 5, 143.
Dialog. lib. quat. (ed. Wirth. Francof et Lips. 1753), ff. 8, 10, 14, 25, ideas in God, v. 166 nn. 4-8 ; f. 16, faith and nature, 166 n. 2 ; f. 23, the Scriptures, 151 n. 3 ; f. 26, the possible, actual, 167 n. 1 ; f. 28, omnipotence, 167 n. 2 ; f. 41, general conceptions, 165 n. 2, 166 n. 1 ; ff. 74, 101, predestination, 167 nn. 3, 4 ; f. 105, 168 n. 1 : f. 126, martyrdom 145 n. 2 ; f. 130, vicar of Christ, 173 n 2; f. 131, on preaching, 142 n. 2 ; f. 144, 171 n. 5: ff. 148, 154, 164, 166, necessity, 168 n. 1 ; f. 171, 172, Christ and the saints, 168 nn. 6, 7 ; f. 174, canonization, 169 n. 1 ; ff. 180, 181, 215, sacraments, 169 n. 2, 170 nn. 1, 2; f. 189, 145 n. 3 ; ff. 190-204, transubstantiation, 152-154 nn.; f. 196, 145 n. 4 ; f. 225, orders of clergy, 170 n. 3 ; ff. 232, 234, 237, secular goods of clergy, 170 nn. 4-6 ; f. 251, confession, 171 n. 1 ; f. 271, prophecy of the reformation, 172 n. 1 ; f. 278, indulgences, 171 n. 2 ; ff. 280, 284, 171 nn. 3, 4 ; f. 294, the earthquake council, 162 n. 5 ; f. 296, 163 n. 3.
Exposition of the decalogue, v. 139, 140, 142. Feigned contemplative life, 139, 142 and n. 6, 143. Letter to simple priests, 142. Letter of excuse to Urban VI., 165 n. 1. Of prelates, 172 n. 4. On the schism, 164. On the church and its government, 164. On the truth of holy Scripture, 242. Tria ogue, 155, 156 ; l. iv. f. 198, 157 n.; f. 201, transubstantiation, 156 n. 2 ; f. 202, adoration of the host, 156 n. 3. Wicket, 155.

Widows, care of, i. 253 ; iv. 299. Bishops protectors of, ii. 176, 177 n. 1, 755; iii. 105. Deaconesses, ii. 191. Distinguished from, ii. 190 n. 2.
Wietow, castle of, v. 372.
Wigbert, abbot, iii. 74.
Wigbert, monk, among the Frieslanders, iii. 43.
Wigmodia, iii. 81.
Wild beasts, Christians thrown to, i. 100 n. 4, 111, 113, 114. Gallus, iii. 35.

Wild cucumber, iv. 582 and n. 2.
Wilderness reclaimed by the labors of monks, iii. 29, 37, 53, 55, 74, 75.
Wilderod, abp. of Strassburg, iii. 369 n. 1, 372.
Wilfrid, abp. of York, banished, labors in Sussex, iii. 22.
Wilfrid, presbyter, iii. 24.
Wilhelm, abbot, life of, iii. 403 n. 2.
Wilhelmina, iv. 638.
Wilkens.
Geschichte der Kreuzzüge, Bd. 3, Abth. 1, Beilage 1, Chronicle of Jehoschua Ben Meir, iv. 74 n. 1. Bd. 6, s. 186, Francis at Damietta, 59 n. 2.
Wilkins.
Conc. Magn. Brit., Deynoch's reply to Augustin, iii. 17 n. 1. T. i. f. 2, Irish synod (an. 456), 53 n. 6 ; f. 41, synod of Hertford, 25 n. 2 ; f. 59, law of Ina, on asylums, 105 n. 1 ; f. 202, treaty with the Danes (an. 905), 288 n. ; f. 298, Canute, 290 n. 2, 291 n. 1. T. ii. f. 172, council of Chichester, iv. 628 n. 1. T. iv. f. 156 (Lond. 1737), law of Richard against Wickliffite teachers, v. 163 n. 2.

Will, of God, Origen on, i. 570, 589. In the gift of grace, Augustin, ii. 631, 686, Cassian, ii. 688. Prosper, ii, 698, 699. De vocatio gentinm. ii. 702. Conditioned and unconditioned, ii. 698 n. 2, 699. One with knowledge, iii. 474. Anselm, Abelard, Hugo, iv. 453-456. Wicklif, v. 168. Absorption in the (iv. 367) ; v. 402, 403, 406.
Will, of man, in the act of faith, Basilides, i. 425. Hermogenes, i. 617. Aquinas, iv. 511, 512. Power of the, i. 415, 416. Self-will, i. 612, 615 ; v. 402 (denial of), iv. 523. Mutability, i. 618, 619, 627, 638, 656 ; ii. 406. Freedom of (see Freedom). Bent of, i. 627, 636, 637 ; ii. 700. Surrender to God, iv. 366, 367, 498 ; v. 402, 403. Ruysbroch on a good will, v. 404-406. Will in Christ, Origen on, i 636-639. Apollinaris, ii. 486, 487, 490. See Freedom.
Willehad, among the Frieslanders and Saxons, iii. 80. In Wigmodia, Rome and Afternach, 81. Is made bishop of Bremen, 81. His death, 82. Life of, 81 n. 2. See Pertz.
William, abbot.
Life of St. Bernard, iv. 252 n. 3, 253 nn. 2, 4.
William, abbot of Cluny, iv. 263.
William, abbot of Hirschau, life of, iv. 86 n. 4.
William, abbot of Melrose, iv. 328 n. 1.
William, abp. of Bourges, life of (Acta S. Jan.), iv. 213 n. 2 ; c. 8, § 29, 336 n. 2.
William, bp. of Alby, iv. 377 n. 5.
William, bp. of Modena, legate, iv. 41.
William, count of Aquitaine, iv. 145.
William II., king of England, iv. 364.
William II., king of Sicily, iv. 530.
William Camden.
Scripta Anglica, etc. (Franzof 1603), life of Alfred, f. 17, iii. 408 n. 1.

William Courtney, bp. of London, v. 148, 161.
William de Champeaux, iv. 373.
William Occam. See Occam.
William of Aria, iv. 448.
William of Auvergne, bp. of Paris (Gulielmus Alvernus), iv. 423. On pilgrimages, 307. The dead sacrifice, 308. On doubts, 326, 327, 336 n. 3. Life in Paris, 413 n. 7. On religious conviction, 432-434. The atonement, 506, 507. Ethics, 519, 522, 523. On persecution, 589. Division of the Bible into chapters, 616 n. 7. His works, 423 n. 4.

Citations: —
De causis, cur Deus homo, c. 5, iv. 506 nn. 3, 4. De fide et legibus, 423 n. 4. De legibus, c. 1, f. 26, on persecution of heretics, 589 nn. 3, 4. De moribus, 423 n. 4; c. 8, t. i., the lectures at Paris, 413 n. 7; c. 219, Parisian teachers, 413 n. 7. De virtutibus, 423 n. 4, 519; f. 137 *et seq.*, natural virtue and that bestowed by grace, 523 n. 1.

William of Auxerre (Antissiodorensis), on indulgences, iv. 350 and nn. 3, 4.
William of Dijon, abbot, iii. 403, 419, 580. See Acta S. Jan.
William of Malmsbury.
Life of Aldhelm (Acta S. Bolland. May, t. vi. f. 82), c. 3, Bibles imported into England, iii. 152 n. 3.

William of Nogaret, v. 12, 13.
William of Paris. See William of Auvergne.
William of Puy Lorent. See Chronicle of Puy Lorent.
William of Rubruquis, Franciscan, visit to the Mongols, iv. 51-56.
William of St. Amour, against the mendicant orders, iv. 282 n. 4, 283-286, 288, 316, 618 n. 3; (v. 150). Louis IX., 285 and n. 5, 300, 301 n. 1. His banishment, 289 and n. 2. Beghards, etc., 303. Eternal gospel, Joachim, 619 and n. 3, 620.

De periculis novissimorum temporum, iv. 283; cc. 12-14, 284 nn. 1, 4; f. 38, 619 nn. 2, 3; ff. 91, 97, 286 nn. 1, 4; f. 92, 285 n. 3; ff. 208, 209, 310, 391, 395, 413, arts of the mendicants, schism foretold, 284 nn. 3, 5-9; f. 419, 285 n. 1; f. 440, 286 n. 5. Respons. ad objecta, f. 92, 303 n. 4. Sermon (opp. f. 500), 618 n. 3, 619 n. 4.

William of St. Thierry, writings against Abelard, iv. 393 and n. 2, 394 nn. 1, 2. See Bibl. Cisterc., t. iv. f. 112.
William of Thoco.
Life of Thomas Aquinas, iv. 422 n., 423 nn. 1, 2.

William of Tyre.
On the crusades, iv. 125 n. 3, 126 n. 3. See Bongars, f. 641.

William of Utrecht, iv. 109.
William Roskild, life of, iv. 206 n. 5.
William the Conqueror, king of England, iii. 529 n. 3; iv. 83 n. 3, 87 n. 3, 88 n. 1.

Willibald.
Life of Boniface, iii. 46 n. 2, 50 n. 2; § 23, 49 n. 1, 50 n. 1, 53 n. 2, 69 n. 1.

Willibrord, presbyter, among the Frieslanders and Saxons, iii. 43, 44. Archbishop of Utrecht, 44, 47. In Denmark and Heligoland, 45, 79. His death, 45, 65. Convent founded by, 81. Life of, 43 n. 4.
Willimar, priest, friend of Gallus, iii. 34-37.
Williram, abbot, translates Solomon's Song, iii. 471.
Wills, ii. 78. Law of Constantine concerning, ii. 167. Right of making, forbidden to heretics, ii. 285. Drawing up of, iv. 290. Of Louis IX., iv. 282 n. 1, 302. See Testament.
Wilsnack, v. 237, 239.
Wilteburg, iii. 44.
Wimbert, abbot, iii. 52.
Winchester, bps. of, iii. 47, 52, 408 n. 1; v. 125.
Wine, with Marcion, i. 503. Use of by monks, ii. 289, 299. In the Lord's Supper, ii. 365, 366; iii. 282, 571 n. 2. Mingled with water, iii. 498, 581 n. 1. Paint from images mingled with, iii. 546. Waldenses, iv. 614 n. 5. Abstinence from, iv. 594. Withdrawal of the cup from the laity, see Lord's Supper.
Winfrid. See Boniface.
Wintar, physician, iii. 75 n. 2.
Winterthur, iv. 318 n. 1.
Winterthur, John of, on the interdict, v. 42, 43. Expectation of the return of Fred. II., 44.

Chronicle. (Thesaur. hist. helvet., Tiguri, 1735), f. 6, an. 1340, Berthold, iv. 318 n. 1; f. 29, interdict against Louis IV., v. 24 n.; f. 39, Benedict XII., v. 41 n. 1; f. 60, an. 1343, interdict in Constance, v. 42 n. 1; f. 69, gift of Constantine, v. 42 nn. 2, 3; f. 78, an. 1345, 43 n. 1.

Wippendorf, iv. 34 n.
Wisdom, in Gnosticism, i. 389, 411, 420, 443 (see Sophia). Origen on, i. 588. Bernard, iv. 255. Christian, iv. 625. Of God, ii. 400; iv. 241, 456, 457, 459, 460, 482, 502, 623, 625. Of Satan, iv. 573.
Wise man, the ideal, with the Stoics, i. 16, 106.
Wise men from the East, The, ii. 344; iv. 553.
Wismar, iii. 326.
Witches, witchcraft, iii. 56, 429, 443 n. 1, 591 n. 4; iv. 90, 91 and n. 1. Agobard on, iii. 429.
Witepsk, v. 373.
Witiza, king of Spain, iii. 118.
Witmar, monk, iii. 276.
Witold of Lithuania, v. 373.
Witstack, Stettiner, iv. 26-29, 26 n. 2.
Wittekind, iii. 79. Consequences of his rebellion, 81.

Wittekind, monk of Corvey.
Annales, I. iii., conversion of Harald, iii. 289 n. 1. See Meibom.
Wives, Christian, i. 78, 280-283; ii. 7, 83, 84 and n. 6, 85, 261, 262; iii. 12; iv. 294, 297, 302. Of priests, iii. 53 n. 6. See Mothers, Women.
Wizards, iii. 429, 448 n. 1, 591 n. 4.
Wladimir of Plozk, Russian prince, iv. 36.
Wladislav, Hermann, Polish duke, iv. 4, 6.
Wladislaw of Poland, v. 373.
Woksa of Waldstein, v. 286 n. 1.
Wolf.
Anecdota græca. (Hamb. 1722), t. i. et ii., Photius contra Manichæos, iii. 244 n. 1. T. iii. f. 17, Euchites, ii. 280 n. 3; f. 182, ii. 279 n. 1.
Wolfgang, monk, iii. 382. See A. S. (O. B.), S. v.
Wolfgang Lazius.
Fragmenta quædam Caroli Mag., etc. (Antverp. 1560), Rabanus Maurus, de virtutibus et vitiis, iii. 457 n. 5.
Wolga, river, iii. 329.
Wolgast, history of its conversion, iv. 19-21.
Wollin, history of its conversion, iv. 3, 9-11, 16.
Woman, creation of, i. 56 n. 1.
Women, in the early church, influence in the diffusion of Christianity, i. 78, 128, 172, 716, 721 (iv. 283). Persecuted, 98, 138, 155, 664. In public assemblies, 181, 182, 303 n. 4, 329 n. 1, 678, 679 (ii. 190 n. 1). Place in the church, 188, 255, 281-283. Teachers of their own sex, 188 n. 1. Dignity, 280, 281. Dress of, 281, 282. Study of Scripture, 721. See Deaconesses Marriage, Montanists, Persecution, Persecution at Carthage, Virgins, Blandina, Felicitas, Perpetua, Victoria.
Second Period. Influence of Christian, ii. 7, 74, 83 and n. 6, 84 and n. 6, 85, 138, 139, 261, 262, 396. Pagan, 81. Law of Licinius regarding, 19. Deaconesses, 189-191. Study of the Bible, 262 and n. 4, 316, 317. And the monks, 286. Sect of, 376. Predestinatians, 705. In monastic life, 744. Works of benevolence, 752. 756. See Anthusa, Constantia, Læta, Marcella, Monica, Nonna, Nunia, Pulcheria, Theodora, etc.
Third Period. In the image controversies, iii. 213, 219 and n. 3, 542 n. 1 (see Irene, Theodora). In church assemblies, Charlemagne on, 242. Paulicians, 252. Good works, 282. Influence in extending Christianity (see Individuals, Bertha, Clotilda, Frideburg, Nuns, Olga, Sarelta).
Fourth Period. Influence in Rome, 367 n. 1. Pilgrims, 367 n. 2, Schools for girls, 427 n. 2.

Fifth Period. In Pomerania, iv. 8, 12. Pious mothers, promote monasticism (12), 233, 234, 249, 250, 252, 422. Extend the gospel, 13. Protect missionaries, 20. Mongol, 53. Influence at court, 141 n. 1. Fallen women reclaimed, 210, 299, 312 and n. 4, 318, 600. Care of sick and poor women, 299. Influence of Robert of Arbrissel, 246, 247, 249. Female benevolent societies, 267. Order of St. Clara, 276. In the begging orders, 286. Waldenses, 321, 611. Education of, 584 and n. 4. Bond women, 601. Henricians, 600, 603. Dolcino, 632. See Beguines, Elizabeth of Hessia, Hildegard, Matilda.
Bible read by, v. 150. Militz, 175, 176. Dress of, 175, 185, 192, 223. Conrad, 185, 190. Janow, frequent communion, 220, 221; piety of, 221, 222. German, 381. Margaret Ebnerin, 383 n. 2. See Mothers, Widows, Wives.
Wonderful, rage for the, i. 62. See Supernatural.
Wood.
Hist. et antiq. univ. Oxon., f. 203, misuse of the seal of Oxford univ., v. 244 n. 1.
Woodhall, v. 135.
Word, the, i. 251. And the church, i. 512, 645. The creative word, i. 372, 565, ii. 475. With the Ordibarii, iv. 571. With Alexandrian Jews, i. 66. Gnostics, i. 440, 441 and n. 2. With the apostle John, i. 575. Anselm, iv. 457, 458, Abelard, iv. 459. Aquinas, iv. 464. Oliva, iv. 625. Janow, v. 208, 209 (see Logos). Made flesh, i. 302; iv. 258, 259, 505. Power of man's, iii. 396; iv. 474. Words of Christ, iv. 576, 595. Huss on the, v. 239, 264, 267, 324, 334. See Logos.
Words, disputes about, i. 382, 506 n. 1.
Works, in Pharisaism, i. 64. Good, Justin Martyr on, i. 76. Meritoriousness, i. 395, 647. Gnostics, i. 436. Legal system of, i. 645, 647. Simplicius on, ii. 107, 108, 109, 110. Jovinian on rightconsness by, ii. 307, 308. Chrysostom, ii. 319. Hilary, ii. 620. Augustin, ii. 627, 630, 638. Pelagius, ii. 636-638. Aidan, iii. 21, 23. Amandus, iii. 42. False reliance on external, iii. 101, 130-132, 138, 139, 146, 169, 432, 433, 452; iv. 302, 304, 348, 387; opposition to, iii. 131, 132, 138, 139, 148, 149, 171, 433, 442, 593; iv. 217, 304-312, 365, 387, 510, 514, 561, 562. In the sects, iv. 448, 572 n. 2, 579. Charlemagne on, iii. 131. Joachim on, iv. 224, 225. Francis, iv. 274. Abelard, iv. 387. Wicklif, v. 140, 141. Janow, v. 212. Tauler, v. 384, 385, 408. Eckhart, v. 394. Ruysbroch, v. 385, 386, 398, 399, 400, 403-405. See Opus operatum, Outward.

Works of God, iv. 456. See Creation.
Works of supererogation. See Supererogatory.
World, relation of Christianity to the, i. 1-69, 70, 92, 180, 181, 217, 218, 252, 273, 276, 277-279, 650; iii. 1. With Celsus, i. 163. Oriental contempt of the, i. 379. Intelligible and corporeal, with Origen, i. 624-626, 634, 638. In Gnosticism, i. 384, 387, 393, 455; spiritual and sensible, i. 373, 375, 426, 432, 433; of light, i. 444; corporeal, i. 449, 458 n. 3 (iv. 578). In Parsism, Manicheism, and Buddhism, i. 479, 482, 483, 503. Montanism, i. 513. Struggle of Christianity with the spirit of the ancient, ii. 1, 161. Period of appropriation and assimilation of the, ii. 161, 262, 263. Scriptural meaning of the word, ii. 242. The created, ii. 476 (see Creation). Renunciation of the, ii. 635; and appropriation, iv. 623 (see Monasticism). Confounding of Christianity with the, iii. 251 (see Spiritual and Secular). Of sense and spirit, iii. 257, 258, 263. Lower and higher, iv. 567. Destruction of the, iii. 164 n. 3, 470 and n. 2; iv. 575; v. 93.
World-former in Gnosticism, i. 380, 397 n. 1. See Demiurge.
World to come, i. 546. Of spirits, 621.
Worldliness in the church, v. 1, 324. See Secularization.
Worldly spirit among the Jews, i. 62. Employments forbidden to the clergy, i. 198, 199, 604. Worldly influences in the church, iv. 152 (see Secularization). In Monasticism, iv. 529, 530 n. 1. Worldly possessions of the church, see Church property.
Worms, bps. of, iii. 40; iv. 203. Diets at, iii. 378, 380 n., 381. Crusades from, iv. 74. Assembly at (an. 1076); iv. 106-109. Concordat of (an. 1122), iv. 143 and n. 5.
Worship, Neo-Platonic conception of, i. 25, 26. Alexandrian Jews, 58. Christian, 288-335. Pliny's report to Trajan, 98. Commodian on, 686. Place, 289-291; (iii. 311). Symbols and images, 292, 293. Seasons, 293-302. In the *Second Period*, ii. 314-379. Freedom of, 14 n. 1, 18, 21, 25. Of one God, 25, 28. Forms of, 259. Of Christ, 56, 425, 489. Seasons, 331-352. *Third Period*, iii. 123-140, 142. *Fourth Period*, iii. 425-455. *Fifth Period*, iv. 393-354. Wicklif on, v. 140. Worship of the creature destroyed by the atonement, iv. 506. Worship of the Gnosis, i. 476-478. Manichean, i. 502-505. See Image worship, Saints, see Sects.
Worship, pagan, i. 672; ii. 4, 8, 9, 17, 35, 74. See Paganism.
Worth, subjective relation to civil or ecclesiastical dignity, v. 351-353.

Wrath of God, ii. 62.
Wratislav, duke of Bohemia, iii. 322.
Wulf. See Wulflach.
Wulflach, Stylite, iii. 28.
Wulfram, bp. of Sens, among the Frieslanders, iii. 44.
Wulfred, English ecclesiastic, iii. 292.
Würdtweln.

Ep. 83, Boniface and the bp. of Cologne, iii 71 n. 2; f. 142, ordinance of Boniface, 137 n. 1.

Wursing (Ado), iii. 45, 79.
Würzburg, Cilian at, iii. 38. Bishopric there, 55. Schwartzach, iv. 103. Bp. of, iv. 107.
Wysehrad, v. 298.

X.

Xantes, iv. 244.
Xenayas, bp. of Hierapolis (Philoxenos), on symbolic representations, ii. 331. Syriac version of New Testament, 589. In the Nestorian controversy, 589. Monophysite, 608, 613 n. 2, 615. Ep. to Abraham and Orestes, 615 n. 3. See Steph. Evod. Asseman., t. ii.
Ξενῶνες, Xenodochia, ii. 169 and n. 1.
Xerophagiæ, i. 521 n. 1.

Y.

Yarl Hakon, governor of Harald, iii. 296.
Ydros, Bernard, Waldensian translator of the Bible, iv. 606 and n. 4.
Yemen, ii. 142.
Yeres, iv. 281.
Yoke of Christ, iv. 156.
York, archbishopric, iii. 16, 19. Archbishops of, 19, 22, 154. Synod near, 24 n. 1. Egbert and Alcuin at, 79, 153, 154 (see Eboracum). Wicklif, v. 135.
Young, Christianity and the, i. 78, 99 n. 3. See Children.
Young men in the spiritual orders, iv. 280, 281, 284, 286.
Ypres, iv. 400.
Yule (Jol), festival, iii. 294, 295.
Yves of Chartres. See Ivo.
Yves of Narbonne.

Ep. to Gerald of Bordeaux concerning the Catharists, iv. 583 n. 2, 584 n. 2.

Yxküll, in Liefland, iv. 36-38.

Z.

Zabarella, Francis, cardinal, bp. of Florence, v. 109, 110, 272, 344, 345 and n. 1, 346, 355, 360, 368, 379.
Zabians. See Sabæans.
Zacagni.

Monumenta vet. Test., Greg. Nyss. Antirrhet., f. 130, ii. 485 n. 1.

Zaccheus, ii. 306, 364, 689, 690.
Zacharia.
- Bibl. Pistoriensis, t. i. f. 64. Comm. on IV. Kings, by Claudius of Turin: ep. of Claudius to Theodemir, iii. 434 n. 3.

Zacharias, ii. 642 n. 4; iv. 396.
Zacharias, abp. of Chalcedon, iii. 570, 573 n. 3.
Zacharias, bp. of Anagni, iii. 562, 565 n. 5, 569.
Zacharias, bp. of Chrysopolis (Scutari).
- Comm. on the four gospels, l. iv. c. 156, Berengar, iv. 337 nn. 4, 5.

Zacharias, head of the Paulicians, iii. 250.
Zacharias, pope, report of Boniface to, iii. 53 n. 7. Bestows full power on Boniface, 56. His conduct towards Adelbert and Clement, 62. His conduct towards Virgilius, 63. Censured by Boniface, 64. Metropolitans, 65 and nn. 1, 2. His decision on the petition of Boniface that Lull might be made archbishop of Mentz, 67. On Boniface's second proposal to resign his office, 67, 68. Supply of vacant bishoprics, 401 n. 4. Deposition of Childeric III., iv. 110, 111; v. 15.
- Epp. ad Bonifac., 59, 60, the pall, iii. 64 n. 1, 65 nn. 1, 2.

Zacharias of Urie, priest, v. 107.
Zähringen, duke of, iv. 177.
Zaphar, in Arabia Felix, ii. 142.
Zbynek, archbishop of Prague, v. 237-240, 247, 248. Change of relations with Huss, 250-252, 255, 259, 300. Wenceslaus, 255. Cited to Rome, bull against Wickliflitism, burning of Wicklif's writings, 259-263. Proceedings against Huss, 260, 263, 271-275. Compromise, 273-275, 296. Death, 275. Jerome of Prague, 373. Ep. to John XXIII., 273 n. 2.
Zdenek of Labaun, v. 298.
Zeal without knowledge, iv. 73. Of the latter times, Militz, v. 200. Univ. of Paris on, v. 353.
Zealots, Jewish, i. 38. Among the Jewish Christians, i. 342. In the Alexandrian church, i. 529. Among the monks, ii. 289. See Fanatics.
Zebrak, v. 293.
Zechariah, ch. 3, i. 609 n. 1.
Zechariah and Elizabeth, ii. 642 n. 4

Zeitz, bishopric, iii. 32-.
Zelautes, iv. 291, 617.
כלי, i. 613.
Zendavesta, i. 491 n. 4.
Zeno, bp. of Verona, ii. 90, 320.
- Works (ed. Ballerin, f. 129), ii. 91 n. 1.

Zeno, the Stoic, i. 18 n. 1; ii. 62.
Zenobia, i. 142, 603-605.
Zephyrinus, Roman b., i. 581. Ep. 2, in the Decretals, iii. 347 n. 3.
Zervan Acarene, in Parsism, i. 488, 489 and n. 3; ii. 127.
Zeus, in Stoicism, i. 16, 18, 19, 20. Porphyry, i. 173. Julian ii. 8 n. 3, 58, 85. Redeeming, ii. 115.
Zigabenus, Euthymius, iv. 530.
Znaim, Peter of, v. 244, 245.
Znaim, Stanislaus of, teacher of Huss, v. 235, 244-246. His position in relation to Huss, 277-279, 295, 299. Huss on, 279, 309, 310.
Zodiac, the, i. 383 n.; ii. 777, 778.
Zoërard, Polish monk, iii. 334 n. 2.
Zokotara, i. 82, 83.
Ζῶν πνεῦμα, i. 492 n. 1.
Zonaras.
- Annales, deposition of Photius, iii. 568 n. 3. L. xvii., Paulicians transported to Philippopolis, 587 n. 1.

Zoroaster, i. 369, 402 and n. 3, 408, 416, 452, 479, 480, 482, 486, 488, 493; ii. 125, 137, 268 n. 4; iii. 587, 590. In Pharisaism, i. 40. See Parsism.
Zosimus, bp. of Rome, ii. 208. In the Pelagian controversy, 547-651, 657.
Zosimus, pagan historian, his works, ii. 114.
- Citations: —
- History, l. ii. c. 16, Maxentius, his superstition, ii. 12 n. 1; c. 29, Constantine, 23 n. 2; and Hosius, 31 n. 4. L. iii. c. 9, Salust, 45 n. 3. L. iv. c. 3, law of Valentinian against Paganism, 90 n. 4; c. 36, Gratian declines the robe of supreme pontiff, 92 n. 1; c. 37, Theodosius, closing of the temples, 97 n. 1; c. 59, Theodosius in Rome, 90 n. 5. L. v. c. 46, Honorius, repeal of edict excluding pagans from offices of trust, 102 n. 5.

Zurich, Arnold of Brescia at, iv. 150.
Zuyder Zee, iii. 72.
Zwentibold (Swatopluk), Moravian prince, iii. 317, 318, 320 and n. 2.
Zwentipolk, son of Henry the converter of the Wends, iv. 32.
Zwingli, iii. 602.

www.ingramcontent.com/pod-product-compliance
Lightning Source LLC
Chambersburg PA
CBHW031741230426
43669CB00007B/432